LITTLE DID I KNOW

Cultural Memory
in
the
Present

Mieke Bal and Hent de Vries, Editors

LITTLE DID I KNOW

Excerpts from Memory

Stanley Cavell

STANFORD UNIVERSITY PRESS
STANFORD, CALIFORNIA

For Cathleen, Rachel, Benjamin, David, Alex, Liza, and Sasha

Stanford University Press
Stanford, California

Printed in the United States of America on acid-free, archival-quality paper

Library of Congress Cataloging-in-Publication Data

Cavell, Stanley, 1926–
    Little did I know : excerpts from memory / Stanley Cavell.
        p.   cm. — (Cultural memory in the present)
    ISBN 978-0-8047-7014-9 (cloth : alk. paper)
        1. Cavell, Stanley, 1926–   2. Philosophers—United States—Biography.
    I. Title.   II. Series: Cultural memory in the present.
    B945.C273L58   2010
    191—dc22
    [B]
                                                    2009037156

Contents

attends Passover seder at my grandfather's house. (I feel I
should repeat that sentence slowly.)—The man the family
called Thomas seems my grandfather's black twin. (This
sentence too.)

LITTLE DID I KNOW

Part 1

July 2, 2003

The catheterization of my heart will no longer be postponed. My cardiologist announces that he has lost confidence in his understanding of my condition so far based on reports of what I surmise as symptoms of angina and of the noninvasive monitoring allowed by X-rays and by the angiograms produced in stress tests. We must actually look at what is going on inside the heart.

Even if I had not eight years ago officially retired from teaching, summer months for teachers are not ones in which routine obligations can serve to shape the days in which life is suspended until the hospital date for the procedure is settled and the time comes to pack a bag for an overnight stay. Apart from learning of the risks in the procedure's actual performance, there are the frightening statistics (frightening even when reasonably favorable) that doctors are obliged to convey to you, not alone of problems incurred in or by the procedure itself, but those of its possible outcomes. In the instance of catheterization the possible outcomes are mainly three: one, that no further surgical intervention is necessary, so that either a change of diagnosis or of medication is in order; two, that instruments roughly of the sort involved in catheterization can be (re)inserted to open and to repair where necessary arterial blockage; three, that the blockage is severe enough, or located in such a way, that bypass surgery is required. (The possibility that nothing can be done was not voiced.) In a previous such period of awaiting surgery, a dozen years ago, I controlled or harnessed my anxiety by reading. I had found that I resisted the efforts of a novel to attract me from my world; I needed the absorption of labor rather than that of narrative. I discovered that reading a book by Vladimir Jankelevitch on the music of Debussy that I had discovered in Paris and brought back a few months earlier, meaning to read it at once (I was planning a set of three lectures, in the last of which the Debussy-Maeterlinck *Pelléas and Mélisande* would play a pivotal role), effectively concentrated my attention, partly because of the beauty of the musical illustrations along with the very effort it required for my rusty musicianship to imagine the sounds of the illustrations unfamiliar to me that Jankelevitch includes in his text, partly because of the specificity and fascination of his words, and partly also because I was kept busy consulting a French dictionary for the evidently endless words in French that name, for example, the effects of sunlight and of clouds on moving water.

This time I am not inclined to house my anxiety as a secondary gain of reading, but rather by a departure in my writing, to begin learning whether I can write my way into and through the anxiety by telling the story of my life. (Or is it the other way around—that I am using the mortal threat of the procedure, and of what it may reveal, to justify my right to tell my story, in the way in which I wish to tell it? What could this mean—my story is surely mine to tell or not to tell according to my desire? But of course the story is not mine alone but eventually includes the lives of all who have been incorporated in mine.) I have formed such an intention many times in recent years, and there have been autobiographical moments in my writing from the beginning of the first essays I still use, and from the time of the book I called *A Pitch of Philosophy* I have sought explicitly to consider why philosophy, of a certain ambition, tends perpetually to intersect the autobiographical.

But I have until now been unwilling, or uninterested, to tell a story that begins with my birth on the south side of Atlanta, Georgia— where most of the Jews in the city lived who derived from the Eastern European migrations at the end of the nineteenth and the beginning of the twentieth century (I believe I never learned where the German Jewish immigrants assumed the aristocrats of the Jewish population had recollected themselves in Atlanta, having brought with them to these

shores on the whole some wealth and more in the way of secular educations than their Eastern European counterparts and, critically, having
arrived in America and apparently made themselves at home a couple
of generations earlier)—three years before the stock market crash that
began the Great Depression; the only child of a mother who was next
to the oldest of six children, all but one of them musicians, two of them
professional, and of a father, a decade older than my mother, among the
youngest of seven children, so that when I was born my father's oldest
sibling was over fifty years old and that sibling's second-oldest child was
the same age as my mother. The artistic temperament of my mother's
family, the Segals, left them on the whole, with the exception of my
mother and her baby brother, Mendel, doubtfully suited to an orderly,
successful existence in the new world; the orthodox, religious sensibility
of my father's family, the Goldsteins, produced a second generation—
some twenty-two first cousins of mine—whose solidarity and severity of
expectation produced successful dentists, lawyers, and doctors, pillars
of the Jewish community, and almost without exception attaining local,
some of them national, some even a certain international, prominence.
The house I lived in for my first seven years was also home, in addition
to my mother and father, to my mother's invalid mother, and to two of
my mother's brothers. When my minimal family of three moved away
to the north side of the city, a feeling of bereftness and bewilderment
came over me that lasted for the better, or the worst, part of the ensuing
ten years, which involved moving between Atlanta and Sacramento,
California, a total of five times across the country, as my father's efforts
to maintain small shops, starting with jewelry stores, successively failed.
We were in California at the last of those transcontinental train rides
(the first, in 1935, when I was nine years old, whose memory dwarfs the
later ones, took what was described as four days and three nights, on
seats covered in green velour that did not recline, stretching out [as it
were] on which to sleep at night meant looking up through my window
toward a sky where the moon would repeatedly and unpredictably vanish and reappear; soon realizing that the effect was due to the train's
[that is, to my] trajectory did not negate its magic) when in January
1943 I graduated high school and a year later entered the University of
California at Berkeley, where studying music and writing music for the
student theater and the companionship of fellow students and teach-

ers devoted to the life of the mind and of the arts, even if sometimes incoherently, showed me possibilities I seemed always to have known existed but had not had continuously attested for me since the days of music at that first house in Atlanta. By the end of college I had come to realize that music was not my life. How that crisis eventually produced the conviction that a life of study and writing growing out of philosophy was for me to discover, and how that was affected by being rejected for military service in the Second World War because of an ear damaged when at age six I was struck by an automobile (a trauma inextricable from the trauma of leaving music), and how that rejection was an essential element in my motivation to spend two weeks of the Freedom Summer of 1964 lecturing at Tougaloo College, a black school outside Jackson, Mississippi, and why I changed my name in the months before I left for Berkeley, having just turned seventeen years old, and what it meant to me finally to leave teaching at Berkeley to teach at Harvard, and to have encountered the work and presence of such figures as Ernest Bloch and J. L. Austin, and to have known deeply gifted friends, some renowned, and eminent colleagues who modified my life, and to have worked over decades on doctoral dissertations with students of the most superb promise, some about to be, or who deserve to be, famous, others still struggling to write as well as they think and as they imagine, and from the beginning of my professional life having lived with children whose inescapable, if not always convenient, expectations of me were an essential protection of me against less loving expectations that might have destroyed my hopes, are registers of the rest of the story.

Such a narrative strikes me as leading fairly directly to death, without clearly enough implying the singularity of this life, in distinction from the singularity of all others, all headed in that direction. So the sound of such a narrative would I believe amount to too little help, to me or others. What interests me is to see how what Freud calls the detours on the human path to death—accidents avoided or embraced, strangers taken to heart or neglected, talents imposed or transfigured, malice insufficiently rebuked, love inadequately acknowledged—mark out for me recognizable efforts to achieve my own death. That, then, is what I have wanted authorization to speak of, which includes the right to assume that something has been achieved on the paths I have taken, obscure to me as that achievement, as I begin this story, may be.

I seem now to glimpse a possible cause of my impulse in invoking so early in the story the work of Jankelevitch. It was not alone because he is one of the rare figures for whom writing about music has been a significant part of a significant philosophical body of work, but because of learning that with the ascendancy of Hitler, Jankelevitch forswore forever reading and mentioning German philosophy and listening to German music. My recurrent, never really avid, interest in this experiment has been not so much in fathoming its hatred but in trying to imagine the practice of the renunciation. It might seem like imagining Faulkner's three-legged racehorse. (The effort occasionally reminded me of times, surely familiar to others, in my childhood when, safely indoors, I would see how long I could keep my eyes closed and move through familiar rooms, perhaps change my shirt or my socks, or find and eat a piece of bread, in order to imagine what it would be like to be blind.) And surely an interest lingers in attempting to grasp why for so long philosophy seemed to be taught to me as a process of renunciation, and lingers past that in the thought that to refuse some balance between forgetting and remembering the suffering of injustice, the monstrousness of tyranny, is to court monstrousness.

July 4, 2003

Trying to fall asleep last night I realized that if I had wished to construct an autobiography in which to disperse the bulk of the terrible things I know about myself, and the shameful things I have seen in others, I would have tried writing novels in which to disguise them.—But how about a philosopher's or writer's autobiography, which, like Wordsworth's *Prelude* (quality aside), tells the writer's story of the life out of which he came to be a (his kind of) writer?—But Wordsworth showed that that story had to be told in poetry—or rather showed that the telling of that story was the making of poetry (Emerson calls something of the sort a meter-making argument), keeping the promise of poetry. To do something analogous to that work I would have to show that telling the accidental, anonymous, in a sense posthumous, days of my life is the making of philosophy, however minor or marginal or impure, which means to show that those days can be written, in some

sense are called to be written, philosophically. Something this means
is that, like poetry, philosophy as I care about it most, exists only in its
acceptance, in taking it out of the writer's hands, becoming translated
one can say, finding a further life. Acceptance does not mean that it
is agreed with, only that disagreement with it must claim for itself the
standing of philosophy.

I might say that I am halfway there already, since Wittgenstein,
more to my mind than any other philosopher of the century just past,
has shown that, or shown how it happens that, a certain strain of philosophy inescapably takes on autobiography, or perhaps I should say
an abstraction of autobiography, and this is how I have understood
Wittgenstein's *Philosophical Investigations* and J. L. Austin's procedures,
in their appeals to the language of everyday, or ordinary language,
namely, that I speak philosophically for others when they recognize
what I say as what they would say, recognize that their language is
mine, or put otherwise, that language is ours, that we are speakers.
Here is why Wittgenstein emphasizes—something habitually thought
false on the face of it—that he does not advance theses in philosophy.
What he says is obvious (come to think about it) or it is useless. (Then
what is its use?) As in Emerson, and in Thoreau, this turns out to mean
that the philosopher entrusts himself or herself to write, however limit-
edly, the autobiography of a species; if not of humanity as a whole, then
representative of anyone who finds himself or herself in it. Philosophy
for such spirits is written, as Nietzsche put the matter in the subtitle of
Thus Spoke Zarathustra, "for everyone and no one." (Nietzsche would, I
surmise, have picked that up from Emerson's sense of speaking to "all
and sundry," or failing to.)

A trouble with this idea from the beginning is not that it is pretentious. It is a specific attitude one takes to what happens to the soul,
no more pretentious than sitting on a horse, or sitting at the piano,
properly, although there might be reasons for modifying or contesting
propriety. A trouble is that I am not sure that those who write out of
a sense of a history of oppression would be glad to adopt this posture.
I believe that certain women I know who write philosophically would
not at all be glad to adopt this posture, or feel spoken for by one who
does. Nor do I know that men or women who sense philosophical roots
beyond American culture will be moved to test my representativeness.

So I might say that testing it is all I am doing. As a Jew I am bound from time to time to wonder in what sense the anti-Semitism punctuating European philosophical thought speaks for me, while I do not know what it would mean for me to claim that I speak for Jews, or essentially for Jews.—Such reflections are not said looking over my shoulder. I mean to be speaking not by assuming cultural identities or purities, but from the posture in which I may discern the identities compacted in my existence, a matter of attaching significance to insignificance, and insignificance to significance.

Freud is our most famous exemplar in this form of discrimination. But Emerson and Thoreau and Nietzsche and Marx and Kierkegaard and Wittgenstein are good at it, most of them famously so. Better than Jane Austen or George Eliot or Anna Akhmatova or Willa Cather, or than several women early in my life, not alone my mother, that few beyond their circle of friends have heard of? Who is asking? From what posture? (A note on posture. When my mother would pass by the piano as I was practicing she might say: "You're playing from the fingers. The strength has to come all the way from the thing you're sitting on; and you are slumping.")

But won't these scruples about identity be interfered with by my sense that I am writing as an emissary from another time? What time would that be? If what I have in mind is the time in which I grew up with, and with stories of, immigrants preserving their lives in the stark freedom of America, of persisting fears and of savage ambitions and of forced marriages, and of desperately preserved or rejected or redis-covered observances, how do I know but that what I say will better, more helpfully, be received by a young Cuban poet teaching Span-ish in a community center in Buckhead, or a middle-aged Vietnamese high school teacher, with a taste for philosophy, keeping the books for her older brother's restaurant in Allston, than by a native, distracted Harvard sophomore from a broken Jewish home in Fresno for whom, for example, black-and-white films are still, as a group, old movies. Do I need to know?

Having begun by speaking of postponing, or overcoming post-poning, the subjection of myself to one of the more recent, now quite common worldwide, fantastic advances in medical interventions, performed in a darkened room with so many planes and volumes of stands and screens and masked persons moving among them, somehow unified by interspersed isolated concentrations of light, that it struck me, prepared doubtless by my sedation, that we might be headed for interplanetary travel (I would be told that if I had required this intervention as recently as ten years ago it would have required open-heart surgery—so postponement is not always an evasion); and then going on to speak of postponing, or lacking, a way or a right to begin writing a consecutive memoir, I can hardly ignore the fact that I have not yet found a sure start, but instead that speculation about telling my story seems to want to take over the telling.

The delay of, or by, philosophy is I suppose humanly unavoidable in the long run, so long, that is to say, as philosophical reflection remains available as a companion to a human existence. If it does then there must remain conditions for calling upon philosophical reflection, for example, the willingness to find yourself lost, a necessity attested explicitly since at least the opening of Dante's *Inferno* ("In the middle of life's journey . . . I found that I had lost the way") and all but explicitly, as I read it, as late as Wittgenstein's *Philosophical Investigations* ("A philosophical problem has the form: I do not know my way about"); and I would include here Thoreau's report at the opening of *Walden* of finding himself disoriented, perceiving his townsmen as crazed, uncommunicating fanatics. This is, in turn, understandable as a vision realizing Emerson's having remarked, "Every word they [his conforming countrymen] say chagrins us," hence brings out the fantastic confession in Emerson's apparently casual observation, namely, that every word he shares with others (which is essentially to say, his every word) is ready to cause him chagrin.

In my case the experiment of calling upon a steady companionship of philosophy in telling my life involved a decision, or it was coming accidentally upon the simple thought, to begin entries of memories by dating myself on each day of writing (not however on consciously doubling back for the purposes of editing or elaborating an entry), allowing me to follow a double time scheme, so that I can accept an invitation in any present from or to any past, as memory serves and demands to be served, that seems to have freed me to press onward with my necessity to find an account of myself without denying that I may be at a loss as to who it is that at any time, varying no doubt with varying times, to whom or for whom I am writing. What is thus further left explicitly open is precisely what counts as the time of philosophy. This precompositional agreement with myself to compose by means of dated entries (with an underlying expectation of maintaining an overall temporal directedness in the material depicted, however unsynchronized as it were with the times of depiction) brings attention back regularly to the fact that the most I can expect to provide will be excerpts from a life—so that I can finesse the question of beginnings by repeatedly bringing a day's or an hour's writing to a close without anticipating when a further time for beginning, of inspiration or of opportunity, will present itself.

But isn't the question of imagining the recipient of what news I can bring really settled by my earlier recognition that I count on attracting or reattracting the ear of someone already interested in parts of my published work, since this should imply someone who will be interested in what I write here, which after all comes out of what Edgar Allan Poe might call the same pen? In case that seems rather too obvious to mention, I might observe that I have had to learn the hard way of my unsteadiness as a judge either of what is obvious or of what may interest others in what I write. (Coming back here from what is appearing to be the end of this project, some two years after beginning it, I report that much of it strikes me as intellectual autobiography well before I get to detailed accounts of what has been largely an American academic life, emphasizing questions of intellectual influences in my professional life less than, or not in independence from, questions of how it has happened that my openness to just those influences and inspirations had to come by way of the precise events of just this childhood and adolescence, whose telling has seemed to me to alternate between the unnoticeably common and the incommunicably singular. I cannot say that I am particularly surprised by this impression given that my emphasis on philosophy as the education of grown-ups entails an interest in the intellectual lives of children and of adolescents.)

July 5, 2003

When my father was given a Jewish name in English by the immigration officer at Ellis Island, and asked for his birth date, he replied with a big smile, "It is today!" (The family's Polish name, Kavelieruskii, which I have also seen on some document spelled Kavelieriskii, was like so many others in these circumstances judged unintelligible. I have been told that Jews arriving in America who had a little money could buy nice names, meaning ones with rose or silver or gold in them.) This story was reported by my father, who was well known in our circles, a considerably larger circle in Atlanta than in Sacramento, for his talent as a teller of Yiddish stories. If he invented this tale of giving the date of his birth, that is as interesting in its way as if it actually happened. I knew the story as early as I knew that he and his siblings did not know the exact dates, even years, of their births. I hang on to this talent of his for improvisation as an antidote to the causes I have had for hating him. I do not mean only that I use it to remember that I also care about him and grieve for him. I mean that to destroy the value of that talent in my eyes would be to destroy something I treasure as a plausible inheritance from him. I mean also that it reminds me of the causes he had for hating me, for example, that my English was unaccented. Is that really a credible cause of hatred? Consider that it meant that my future, unlike his, was open. Of course exactly this difference was also something he wanted. He was, for example, more ferocious in insisting on my practicing the piano every day than my pianist mother was.

July 6, 2003

I saw things I should not have seen. (So much of my adolescence was spent—perhaps much of adolescence means—hiding [because harboring?] knowledge of my elders. Like Hamlet.) When I was fourteen or fifteen years old I saw a toothless, unshaven old man, in a threadbare overcoat in summer, cheat at pinball in the corner cigar store a few doors down the street from my father's pawnshop in Sacramento. The man was something of a familiar figure in a tradition of lunchtime gatherings of pinball players around that machine, and while I had not recalled seeing him actually play the game before now, he turned out to be a skilled player, reaching a score on the machine that automatically won him a free game. He, however, pretended not to know this, ostentatiously took out a nickel from his overcoat pocket, and seemed to put it in the slot as he hastily pushed in the slide for a fresh game, having in fact concealed the coin in his left hand and put that hand briefly back into his pocket. Several onlookers had called out to him not to insert the nickel and, having failed to alert him in time, demanded that the cigar store owner refund a nickel to him to award him with the free game he had won, or rather lost. Dishonor comes cheap; or perhaps this was rather a chance for extracting some small vengeance for the assumption of dishonor.

We see our fathers naked, we men. In 1961, returning from Berkeley to Harvard to defend my belated Ph.D. dissertation, I took my four-year-old daughter, Rachel, with me to have her spend a few days with her grandparents in Atlanta while I was in Cambridge. I had brought the latest issue of the reconceived *Commentary* magazine for reading on the plane between Atlanta and Cambridge. In the early 1960s, *Commentary* had become rather more than equal competition with that era just past the reliably great years of *Partisan Review*, emphasizing a Jewish perspective but maintaining an independently high level of intellectual seriousness by publishing, for example, installments of Paul Goodman's *Growing Up Absurd*. (Names. If Paul Goodman had been born in Paris his name, so I thought it comprehensible to say on reading him further a decade later, specifically some of his fiction and the belatedly published theory of literature he had presented as his doctoral dissertation, would be as famous as Foucault's. Unless, of course, he had not managed to survive long enough to escape on the last boat from France to New York in 1940. Comprehensible maybe, but sensible? What is the point of saying it? Wittgenstein's perpetual, terrifying question.) When the Travises came for dinner the night of the day I arrived back in Atlanta and saw the magazine I had dropped on my parents' coffee table, they expressed astonishment and asked how it came to be there. My father said he had brought it home. While they were impressed by how much more Yiddish my father knew than they, and may also have recognized that he had a better way with people (well, with strangers) than they had, they prided themselves on their intellectuality—having enough knowledge about Judaism and Palestine to know that they were not themselves seriously learned. But they were on various Zionist committees and were abreast of current topics and events. I cringed from my implication in my father's lie about the magazine, or rather I despised his pretense, or rather I absorbed the stain of his mortification (perhaps compounded with the mortification at being mortified) in not having known the significance of the magazine on his coffee table, made grotesque by his willingness to humiliate himself in front of his only child. Still, with what right did the Travises assert their intellectual superiority over my father (let alone question his honesty), whose sensibility of suffering and humor so far outstripped their comparatively studied, second-generation, literalism? (It is easy, indeed agreeable, to imagine having reveled in helping along my father's chance to baffle these old friends by claiming a connection with a strain of contemporary Jewish intellectual culture that matched theirs. But that would have required him to acknowledge the pretense to me, allowing me to join in a conspiracy that implicitly told them to go to hell, rather than implicitly telling me to go there, where after all he was a familiar. What would it have required for me to have been the one able to offer him that interpretation, and congratulate him on his coup? Merely some sign that the gesture would not have been taken to have heaped further coals on his head.)

The Travises were just younger enough than my father to have been born in America, so their English was unaccented, even practiced, and they could give public speeches without fear of being shamed because of a mispronunciation or grammatical mistake, and so they could hold offices in national, even international, Zionist organizations. In immigrant centers in, say, New York, arguments could perhaps be held in Yiddish. But was my father's Yiddish, though as good as anyone else's (that I had come across) of his generation in Atlanta, up to the level of extended argument? It was decreasingly practiced, except in certain conventional conversations, principally with his father, after he arrived in America at age sixteen (approximately), in 1905, twenty-one years before I was born. Before his mother died, she might well have demanded that he speak English to her, since she had, after settling the family, continued in night school longer than my father, because she was intent on learning to write as well as to speak with reasonable propriety the language of their new country. She was regarded in the family as its genius. In Zabludova, their shtetl in the region of Bialystok, her ability to speak and to write in Yiddish and in Russian and Polish suited her to be a public scribe of this community, sitting at a table in whatever served as the post office, reading or composing letters for others, missives of love, of proposals of marriage, of bereavement, of news about work in America, and of the prospects of sending for the rest of a family awaiting word from afar. I have only a single memory of her, being taken to see her once, evidently just before her death, in a bedroom in the large house I grew up thinking of as my father's father's house (so large that I never entered all the rooms on its second floor, nor penetrated to the end of the dark stone-walled, dirt-floored basement in which my grandfather was, mysteriously, said to make wine).

Since my father had gone to night school on these shores only long enough to pass the language test for naturalization, he was as ashamed of his written English as of his accent in it, and I assumed it was for that reason that he never wrote a letter to me. Is it only now, heaping together these ornaments of chagrin, not knowing whether it is to treasure them in isolation or to disperse them to the winds, that I realize I would have been flattered to have received letters from him in the relatively uncomplicated Yiddish in which I could follow his jokes?

The following anecdote stands for many. Early in our stays in Sacramento, I would have been no more than ten years old, at a restaurant having supper after a Sunday afternoon at the movies, a rather loud, good-hearted waitress and my father carried on some banter on first meeting; then after she brought our orders and things had calmed, she asked my father where he came from. He ignored her, but she persisted. "I mean, I can't place your accent."—"Do you think I have an accent?" He asked for the check without taking another bite of food and we left. What would I have had to know, or imagine, to decide whether to love him for suffering so terribly or to despise him for sacrificing us to his self-contempt?

At the end of World War II it was my father who was the first in Sacramento to form a Zionist organization there and in neighboring small towns as far away as Placerville, in Gold Country, with the immediate purpose of collecting money to send to Palestine. Some years later, in recognition of his role in leading a number of younger couples to discover some pride in their Jewish roots, he was elected President (or Honorary President) of the original chapter he had been responsible for forming, which meant that he would have to give an acceptance speech at a dinner at which this honor was to be announced. He telephoned me, then in my second undergraduate year at Berkeley, to ask me to write the speech for him. I tried several drafts, but he found what I sent unusable because it was too complicated. I knew he was right and that my failure to provide suitable words for him to say in public showed a fool's rigidity of moral imagination, of the capacity to put oneself in the other's shoes (let alone his socks), which even then was a virtue I particularly treasured. (I feel sure that early criticisms of the writing in the first books I published, to the effect that I cultivated too much complexity, or too much something ["self-indulgent" was a repeated charge], hurt more than they might have otherwise—I had after all waited to publish books until I felt I had a fair judgment for what was too much, though I suppose a fairer judgment for what was not enough—because of the failure of my talent a quarter of a century earlier to meet my father's need of it.)

To explore this virtue of imagination was the lasting part of my motivation, after I began writing music for the student theater at Berkeley, in taking an acting class in which the required reading was Stanislavski's *An Actor Prepares*. It will be a mysterious connection I assumed with Ernest Bloch when my second summer in Berkeley he mentioned to his class that he was reading Stanislavski. A balancing absence of mystery and connection years later will be the thought that my philosophy teachers would not have accepted Stanislavskian exercises as bearing rigorously on the issues of what we were calling the problem of the existence of other minds. (But then those teachers did not need me to write speeches for them.) Of what extenuation were the facts that my father did not want to sound like himself and certainly not like me? The truth was that I could not help him be what I wanted him to be or what he wanted to seem to be. An additional truth is that I was too raw a prig to find a further alternative.

July 7, 2003

I believe I can date the moment at which I realized that my father hated me, or perhaps I can more accurately say, wished I did not ex-

ist. (And, I do not deny, came to respect me, if you include in this attitude the mixed satisfactions in knowing that others respected me. But
one thing at a time.) My mother will eventually explain one segment
of his response to me as that of jealousy, without going on to suggest
what grounds he may have had, that she may have given him, for this
specific condition. I knew he was envious of people with more money than he, or with grander stores, or with insignia of small fame. He
seemed free of this self-punishment in relation to people he believed to
be genuinely possessed of learning and cultivation, which he regarded
as simply beyond competition or accident or envy. (He and my mother and I listened together to the principal comedy programs marking
the heyday of nighttime radio, those of Jack Benny and Fred Allen and
Jack Haley. My father and I never missed *Information Please*, where the
host Clifton Fadiman set to a panel of raconteurs and scholars featuring Oscar Levant such multipart tasks as—I seem to recall—"I'll read
you a line from a play of Shakespeare's and you identify the play and
the character who says it and quote the next line." This task was meat
for John Kieran, a sports writer for the *New York Times* who declared
himself as reading through the collected works of Shakespeare every
year. After the display of one such triumph my father fervently pointed
to the radio, saying: "They are the aristocracy." To whom, out of what
vision, was he speaking? Was it to me, to whom he once or twice had
said, "You must have a trade," and not infrequently asked me, "Are
you headed to be a chair man [that is, not the leader of the band], like
Meyer?") On my brief return to Atlanta the day after the defense of my
tardy dissertation at Harvard, I accepted, I am glad, and still somewhat
startled, to say, his proposal to accompany him to the warehouse of a
manufacturer of academic robes and be fitted at his expense for a Ph.D.
robe in Harvard crimson. (How he learned of the existence of such an
establishment I never determined.) It was a private ceremony in a process of forgiving each other, to whatever extent colored by insincerity,
yet clear and not without immediate effectiveness. Ceremony in human existence is no more measurable by its utility, though philosophers
sometimes seem to argue otherwise, than the possession of language is,
or living in common; you might as well argue the utility of possessing
a human body.

But if I allow myself to speculate about the role of ceremony in the lives of creatures vulnerable to tragedy and madness (shown in *King Lear* as the consequences of the perversion or negation of ceremony) I may never get to the date of revelation of paternal hatred I was coming to. Some wish to delay it is understandable; to postpone it indefinitely has, I can see, become dangerous, its silence blocking something irreplaceably valuable.—But why does it always fall to me to be the one asked to understand? It took me a long time to get to that question, one I would hate to have bequeathed uncontested to the young I care for.

The moment came as my mother and father and I had just been driven, in a couple of cars, with whatever last belongings we could carry, to our new apartment on the north side of Atlanta, a world away from the house I had lived in from birth, where my mother's ailing mother could get out of bed every day long enough to maintain the narrow bed of marigolds that lined our driveway there, and to teach me how to make the letters of the alphabet and how to play solitaire, and then double solitaire, which occupied precious moments of our mornings and afternoons, and where two of my mother's younger brothers also lived, whom I idolized for their laughter and their roughhousing with me and teasing me and for liking to read the Sunday comics with me, and for their beauty and glamour when they dressed on weekends in their striped dress trousers and tuxedo jackets and left the house with their violins to play for people in some land where the people danced all night. This house was visited every day by my mother's youngest sister, who by my calculations, four or five years older than the youngest brother, was seventeen when she married a rich man, and who would pull up to the house, making an event of the repetition each morning, honking the commanding horn of her bright yellow Buick coupé, with the rumble seat in which to ride was to be heaven-bent.

What conceivable or sane reason could there be for moving away from this paradise? I think I may have felt a glimmer of madness, with no concept for the feeling. Perhaps the glimmer was of the first condition of childhood in a culture of isolated families, that whatever your fate it was not your own and was not commensurable with the fate of other children you might encounter. Tragedies of childhood do not illustrate the wisdom in identifying character as fate. I had finished first grade (well actually it was second grade, because I had been "skipped" a grade in the middle of that year), so, born in September, I was about to celebrate my seventh birthday. That would make the year 1933, a black year of the Western world's depression.

Walking up the stairs to the top floor of the boxlike three-story brick apartment building—stairs with a runner of ribbed dark rubber covering most of the width of the treads and risers of the stairways, a path for perpetual strangers—the catastrophe of the move broke over me in waves that I have periodically felt have never entirely stopped breaking. Entering the strange apartment, I found the living room oddly to be less illuminated than the room beyond it on the right, separated from it by an arch. That further room would have been, in my familiar house, the dining room, but it turned out here, on giving it some attention, to be made up as a bedroom, with my parents' bedroom furniture positioned in it. A number of women friends of my mother's, most of them familiar to me, were with her in that room saying something about wanting to surprise her by having set all this up ahead of time. I somehow knew at once that this meant, something I had I suppose been told, but that would have meant nothing to me, that my mother and father and I were going to live here alone. How then would I know where my beautiful uncles and my grandmother were going to live and how we would keep in touch with them? I could not picture them anywhere else than in our old house on Atlanta Avenue. I evidently kept my feelings to myself, and wandered around trying to take an interest in the combination of familiar and of strange objects in the living room. I recognized an ornamental object on a table at the side of the sofa, a purple glass bowl, somewhat wider but less deep than a drinking tumbler, set into a molded dull silver stand and covered with a dome top of matching silver inset with purple glass panels. I lifted the silver dome off the bowl to discover that it was filled with small chocolate-covered mint wafers whose tops were sprinkled with tiny white dots of hard candy, a treat I loved to sample when these used to fill this container in anticipation of company coming to the old house.

I noticed that I was not alone in the room. My father was standing silently in the semidark at the other end of the sofa, apparently looking out of a window. I do not know if it would have crossed my mind before then that I had almost never been in a room alone with him, indeed that I knew him much less well than I knew everyone else who had lived in the house I grew up in. (If I had thought to seek an explanation for this it would doubtless have been that he worked all day and then waited at the Fox Theater, where my mother played the organ during intermissions and played the piano in the pit orchestra for the vaude-ville shows between the movie screenings, to accompany her home af-ter the last show, and on Sundays he was at what was called "the Club," more formally, the Jewish Progressive Club). The last show ended well past my bedtime, and I used to try to stay awake to hear their car return home, sounding as if it gasped for breath as it headed down the steep driveway to the back of the house, down from my bedroom window, and then hear the motor stop and two car doors slam shut. I imagined them getting out of the car, my mother from the left since my father did not drive, then walking up the driveway and across the front porch into the house, measuring my accuracy of imagination by how closely the distant sound of opening of the front door coincided with my imagina-tion of their having reached it. On the times I managed to keep awake, I would pretend to be asleep when my mother, soon after entering the house, came into the back bedroom to kiss me, as if my unawareness proved the freedom of the gift, and the depth of my possession of it. (Her skin would be cool from the night air, and the wind was caught in her hair.)

As I took one of the speckled wafers from the purple bowl, I said aimlessly, but somehow to break the silence with my father, "I didn't know we had these here." He lurched at me, wrenched the dome top and the wafer out of my hands, and said in a violent, growling whisper, "And you still don't know it!"

July 8, 2003

This is the moment I described as dating my knowledge that my father wanted me dead, or rather wanted me not to exist. Can it not equally be described, and less melodramatically, as a familiar case of displaced affect—here from his own sense of disruption and who knows what anxiety in leaving the old house and feeling useless in the new one, onto a handy object for venting? But then why was I such an object, in-stead of a source, for example, of solace, or of one needing solace? Be-sides, the explanation invoking displacement would fit better the possibility that he had been moved, without my intervention, to take a murderous dislike to the purple bowl on the dull silver stand; I was then merely an innocent bystander who had intercepted his rage. Now that I tell the incident it seems just as clearly to date my knowledge that— whatever else I felt for him or wanted from him—I feared and hated my father, and conceived the idea that our passions were linked. From as early as I can recall, it seemed less that my hatred was caused by his famous "temper" (famous to those he lived with, especially to my mother, who was also afraid of it, and, something obvious to me, punished him for it by remaining essentially, dismayingly silent for days after one of his deeper outbursts), than that my sense of distance from him or ignorance of him was the cause of his rage at me. If this was merely the temper of his temperament, why did I take it personally? Why did my mother? This is not as idle a question as it sounds—implying that a seven-year-old has some choice over how to take an assault by a parent. When later in my bedroom at the back of the new apartment I found a time and place to release my state of numbness and to cry uncontrollably, I seemed to find I was crying for my father as much as for myself, crying over whatever it was that had left this man bereft and incoherent. He is as alone as I am. And my mother?

It is as if I knew then that I would one day find a way out of the devastation he could make of his island, and knew that such a day would never come for him. (Don't tell me no man is an island.) Not of course that I escaped it entirely, but I have made headway in keeping, as it were, my knack of adopting his powers of devastation separate from my own causes for despair. I think of the clearer time, some seven or eight years later, when, in another rage, he picked up my empty clarinet case from the dining room table, tried to tear it apart, and took it to the back of the kitchen to throw it in the garbage. This was one of only two times in the sixteen years I lived with him that I recall his attempting to show remorse. He returned with the case to the dining room, laid it on the table, saying, "Maybe it can be fixed." Did I actually reply out loud, "Something in me will not be fixed"? That would not have meant, in feeling the injustice of this treatment, that I could not at the same time see his despair of finding justice for himself. It is common to observe that life is unfair. It would be less common, or less easy, to say if it were said more plainly: It's a mad world, my masters.

Yet I know that without a certain caution I could take on at this moment a version of his murderous melancholy, not fully sure whether it would be in response to him or in identification with him. How could I have failed to be suspicious, no matter how many years later, when I found philosophers asking such questions as, "Do I know your pain the way you do?" My principal problem was not that of doubting my knowledge of the feelings of others but rather of standing apart from them, or failing to. Not to know them would require exorcism.

I have wondered whether it would have been easier for me to break the spell of my father's rages if they hadn't unforgettably struck me sometimes (when, as it were, I didn't take them personally, say, in memory) as bound up with his talent for humor and for his sense of the moral pertinence of humor. Arriving unexpectedly to visit my parents overnight in Sacramento some months after I entered the university at Berkeley, I said to my mother (she alone doing the driving) that I wanted to use their car to see friends the next morning, and she agreed. My father intervened to say that she had promised our neighbor the use of the car at that time. My mother replied: "But then I hadn't known that Stanley would be here." I believe I can still reasonably approximate the rhetoric of his responding moral satire: "Oh I see. Stanley is here. Therefore all obligations, all friendships, all right and wrong are to be suspended for the duration. Stanley is here. If only the reasonable request had been for any other time other than just this time, then you would keep your promise. Too bad for the world and its needs. Yet the world must understand that *Stanley is here!* But if I am alive tomorrow morning that promise will be kept." Once when I asked my mother why she married my father, she replied, "He is a serious man."

If I say that to keep a mother's unconditional love within the realm of rational society a father's intervention is necessary to convey what a promise is, I would not want this to prejudge how deep a man's tenderness may reach nor a woman's expectation. With what is sometimes referred to as the fragmentation of families, the division of so-called social roles is bound to exist under experimentation. Here is a reason for the emergence in literary theory of the idea of understanding texts or scenes from within particular "subject positions." It is also, consequently, a reason I have increasingly found myself emphasizing that no set of subject positions in principle exhausts my subjectivity. To justify this insistence will have to await a time of more patient philosophical occupation.

Something is already happening here that takes me particularly by surprise. It was an important, relatively late moment in my recurrence to passages in Wittgenstein's *Philosophical Investigations* that produced the recognition in it of what I might call Wittgensteinian irony. In a passage I have in mind, Wittgenstein recognizes that "our investigation" "seems only to destroy everything . . . important" but insists that he is "destroying nothing but houses of cards" (§ 118). Read more persistently, however, the moment conveys a recognition of inner devastation, expressed explicitly in a phantasm of the rubble of a destroyed city ("leaving behind only bits of stone and rubble"). (I recall that Thoreau shows himself to have acquired wood for his new cabin by demolishing an old shack.) I do not leap to the conclusion that my attraction to philosophy was as to an intellectual region from which I might avert or provide reparation for scenes of inner devastation. I do, however, now intend to bear in mind the thought that this has been a cause of my particular attention to the words of *Philosophical Investigations*.

Something else here is especially obscure, or unintuitive. If asked whether the moods of men or of women are more likely to control my own, I would at once answer that I was more attuned to the moods of women. But while I have been disappointed and interested and perplexed and saddened and made happy and been frightened, even maddened, by the moods of women, I do not recall this particular sense of devastation through them—a sense that not I, or that within me, was broken, but the world. The very problem is that the world remains as it is, but pointlessly. What counts as a defense against another's moods?

July 9, 2003

I knew the details of my mother's work at the Fox Theater (the most patently fabulous movie palace I have experienced, domes and minarets arising on its outside made of white bricks, while its inside viewing space suggested a Middle Eastern courtyard overarched by a night sky with visible stars and, I think this is right, moving clouds) from my having been picked to appear there, during the late summer that I would turn seven, to be the youngest to perform in what its program called "The Fox Kiddie Review," as part of a special stage show featuring the talents of children of whom the oldest and tallest was a girl of crushing beauty whom in retrospect I would guess to have been thirteen or fourteen years old, old enough to have developed a woman's shape but not enough to be living without surveillance. On what must have been the day of the dress rehearsal of the program my mother took me backstage before she was to join the orchestra in the pit, to help me get into my Indian chief costume (my piano piece for the occasion was an offering entitled "Indian Drums," which I can still play flawlessly on demand), into a room not far from where a man was standing by a board of switches and levers, which marked the place I had been shown from which to enter the stage between interminably high and heavy curtains. My mother explained that we need not bother to go downstairs to the men's dressing room (meaning, I now realize, that she could not go with me into the men's dressing room).

The room she led me to instead featured a row of tables with square mirrors, each mirror outlined on its four sides with unshaded perfectly round light bulbs, the tables lining the length of one wall. My mother was evidently running late for her own rehearsal because, having helped me slip the tight upper part of my costume over my head and then firmly adjust my headdress, whose feathers reached almost to the floor, she left me to get on my trousers by myself and slip into my moccasins. That is how I happened to be alone in that room when the girl of crushing powers entered, and without so far as I could tell glancing at me there struggling with the belt of my trousers in the middle of the room, walked to the wall of mirrors, took off her clothes, sat at one of the tables, opened a leather case from which she removed and spread out before her a series of bottles and jars and brushes and combs and began to brush what I now recognize to have been dark pancake makeup down one of her arms, starting from the shoulder. I think that is what I saw, although it took some time for me to understand that she had taken off really all of her clothes, upon which recognition I was propelled from the room by an invisible force of nature, something like a consuming wave of aromatic mist. I remember various forms in which Greek gods appeared to mortal women they desired and sought to attract, but at the moment not comparable forms assumed by goddesses.

Of course this deity had no cause to consider, or notice, her appearance to me. The appearance she chose for her audience—as I learned after completing my opening part of the rehearsal when I managed to find my way to the empty house seats to watch the rest of the misnamed, or incompletely named, "kiddies"—involved a skimpy costume of shining white cloth and a headdress indicating an American Indian princess, her mesmerizing long arms and legs all the color of the makeup I had witnessed her begin brushing on herself. Her singing of "The Indian Love Call," climaxed by her shooting an arrow the width of the large stage, concluded the "Kiddie Review."

I tried once or twice during the ensuing week of two shows a day to interest this mythical being in the cosmic fact that we were both Indian royalty, by leaving my costume on and stationing myself by the stairs down to the men's dressing room until she walked off the stage and had a chance to remark the closeness of our connection. Evidently I had failed to place myself in clear enough view for that. But I knew what I knew, and it was satisfactory. Another time that week, awaiting a delayed moment at which I would meet my mother to drive home, I found a place at the back of the theater from which to watch the cartoon whose stirring music I would hear backstage after our performances. It had already begun, and what I saw turned out not to be humorous. There were a frightened crowd of people in a street shown running from a huge black bird who swept down and covered them with a black cloth on which the word DEPRESSION was printed in huge blurry white letters. Then a drawing filled the screen of the face of a man I recognized from a picture in our house identified with admiration as that of President Roosevelt, and the audience broke into applause. On other days I walked out of the stage entrance and on the outside of the long side of the theater climbed up a couple of flights of stairs to an open plaza where kids from the review were playing and where I would see a further long flight of stairs over the entrance to which a sign stated "Colored Entrance." The British empiricists had a theory that held every idea in our heads to be derived from the effect of elements that left impressions upon us. They were dead right about the lasting impression made in such a case as this sign.

July 10, 2003

My father's rages sometimes brought on what my mother called his "attacks," which she also sometimes described as acute indigestion, from which he more than once was reported to have fainted, and once reported almost to have died as he was being rushed to the hospital. From the time I knew of these events, I took the onset of his reddening face and his gritting teeth and his shouted words as signs of death at the door, and of course believed I might sometime be the cause of its walking in. My most direct, or full, experience of one of these events can be dated as from the last year I lived with my parents, at age sixteen, which meant that I was in possession of a driver's license. We had for the third time moved from Atlanta to Sacramento (the last of the sequence of continental crossings), when my father's brother proposed to establish my father in a pawnshop of his own, an offshoot of my uncle's much larger and, it seemed, effortlessly remunerative pawnshop. My father felt ashamed of his store, but less ashamed than he had been of working for his brother, and grateful to have found some way to get out of debt after the failure of his respectable jewelry store in Atlanta, the one of his failures most directly caused by the Depression. And he took some pride in several facts about his pawnshop—that it was run honestly, nothing in it, for example, called a diamond or said to be of gold unless it was a diamond and of gold; and it was the one in a line of several blocks that housed pawnshops that was closest to the beginning of the respectable, upper part of K Street, the main street of that Sacramento then, between 6th and 7th Streets, one block nearer to that respectable part than his brother's pawnshop, which was between 5th and 6th Streets, and just one block before the beginning of a sequence of proper ("credit") jewelry stores, beginning at 8th. (Beginning at [or near] the Sacramento River was 1st Street, and the streetcar ran from there on a straight path until [I believe] 24th Street, when it turned right and in something like another two or three miles would have reached the stop nearest our apartment. The main part of downtown, the principal region for shopping, ran from 6th Street, where the only serious department store was catty-corner to [my memory is that in the South the phrase was "kitty-cornered from"] my uncle's pawnshop, and generally increased in degree of fashion and prominence of office space to

11th or 12th, where it began to thin out of the realm of exchange to become lines of dwellings [whether by now on the whole becoming boardinghouses I would not have known]). My uncle's and my father's were the only pawnshops above 5th Street; only those lower lent money on clothes, and my father, unlike his brother, even refused to take in guns and musical instruments. His business was strictly with diamonds, with gold and silver, and with good watches, whose value he knew.

My mother had given up her music career in Atlanta to find herself eventually working regularly in my father's store in Sacramento, and I came to work there every afternoon after high school, and every weekend, and every day throughout two summers. I had, on the occasion on my mind at the moment, just entered the pawnshop after school when my mother approached me to say that my father had fainted but that he was now revived, sitting out of sight behind the safe in the back of the store, and asked me to get my car and drive him home so that he could get himself cleaned up.

As I pulled up to the front of the store, my mother helped my father walk across the sidewalk and get into the car. His skin was white and moist, his mouth slack. The drive to the neighborhood of our house took scarcely ten minutes. After moving through the few downtown streets I had time and attention to notice that my father was holding a wet handkerchief out of the window to let it dry against the wind. He turned his head to the window, leaned out as well as he could, and vomited briefly. The smell was strong, and I realized at the same time that he had soiled himself. I do not remember what help I was in getting him up the flight of stairs to our apartment. My next memory is of sitting alone on the sofa backed against the windows of the living room of this place that was charmless for me and that I knew I was spending my last year in, when my father reappeared at the arch separating this room from the dining room, and, looking somewhat recovered after a shower and in fresh clothes, drawn but not as pale, stretched out one hand for support on the side of the arch straight across the room from where I was getting up from the sofa, and said: "Mensh iz gornisht" (Mankind is nothing). He was a serious man.

My car I called it, not to distinguish mine from theirs, since they had not acquired one after the first move to Sacramento. It was in the trunk of my wonderful, brave 1935 apple green Oldsmobile coupe (unlike Aunt Bess's yellow Buick, this car could not bear an accent over the name of its model) that I transported the music stands and their lights and the library of arrangements for my band. When I became old enough for a driver's license, the owner of the luggage store next to my father's store offered to sell me the car for 250 dollars. He and I would from time to time discuss, or mention, music. Sometimes he would ask me about my band, and how much money we were paid, and whether as leader I got more money, apparently interested that according to the musicians' union the leader was to be paid twice the scale for other members (their scale for our usual engagement, a four-hour dance ending no later than 1 a.m., was nine dollars) but that the history of the band did not seem to me to warrant that distinction in pay; sometimes he would walk into the store with a new album of records he had just bought with some pride of cultivation. (In fact these displays were the first time I had seen albums of classical music. My experience with records was with the ten-inch jazz singles that played for about three minutes a side. I would have known, had the possibility crossed my mind, that symphonies and concertos and operas would not fit on a single record, not of course even a twelve-inch record, even on both sides. So what caused my surprise in encountering these albums? I seem to need some concept of accelerating ignorance, an increasing quantity measuring per day the connections not made and implications not drawn by me. I early concluded that if I were to amount to any-thing, it would derive from finding the fruitfulness of trancelike states of mine in which everything is news to me, as if everything real has to be born in me. It is not an ingratiating quality. Yet Abraham's Sarah laughed at improbable pregnancy.—Then why not ingratiating? That there is some early narcissistic investment in play here I do not doubt. Early narcissism may be thought of as a kind of necessary, if dangerous, postponement, say, a suspended recognition of separation, of a world apart from me, a wish to show oneself, to make oneself, hence one's work, worthy of love. I think it may be a perception of some such ambi-tion that helps shape the disapproval aimed my way in the accusation of my writing as self-indulgent.)

By late 1942, almost a year into the war, with several greatly ex-panded air bases close to Sacramento pouring money into the local economy, my father's store began doing well enough to start paying off its debts, as well as older debts my parents would sometimes allude to. I proposed to my father that, after two years of afternoons and weekends and summers working in the store, I felt it would be an appropriate token of appreciation for him to produce the 250 dollars for the purchase of the green Oldsmobile. (The only money that came my way from the store, drawn daily from the till, was for lunch. One summer this characteristically consisted of fifty cents each day, twenty-five cents for a hot roast beef sandwich, ten cents for a thick vanilla milk shake, ten cents for a comic book or perhaps *Time Magazine*, and a nickel tip. Not six days a week for ten weeks at the same lunch counter wore out for me the genuine pleasures of this routine.) Alternatively, he could advance the money for the car, and, since the band was playing fairly regularly, I could pay it back at perhaps five dollars a week, most weeks, in about a year. Evidently the picture this proposal, or pair of proposals, presented to him prompted my father to buy the car, and nothing more was said about a loan in this house of loans, nor any question raised about whose car it was. (Although my father never drove, there was a photograph of him, among the box of photographs my mother collected in a shirt box, sitting behind the steering wheel of a car. For years I simply took this, falsely, to mean that he had once driven.)

The car was indeed appropriate, to the pitch of mythic accuracy. From the constriction and surveillance and pummeling repetitions of the pawnshop, this faithful companion meant expansion and privacy and improvisation—commodities otherwise to be found only in great cities.

July 11, 2003

A sense that my very existence and its desires and possibilities might of themselves bring on my father's death was in contest with the sense that he was indifferent to me, which I interpreted as my being strange to him. An expression of this sense manifested itself at a signal moment in my sixth year, learning some hours after the fact that I had been struck and knocked unconscious by an automobile as I ran out into the street, just up and across the street from my old house on Atlanta Avenue. I seem to have the sensation as well as an image of running down the Jacobs's driveway into the street, without a glance in any direction but straight ahead, along with an image that I associate with the impression of a car bearing down on me as I was picking up the ball I had chased into the street. Whether or not that image can be accurate, the first thing I remember about what I would soon learn was a hospital, was opening my eyes to see a large number of people standing around me, my mother and father at the foot of what was perhaps a bed. I clearly remember asking, "What happened?" Then I no longer saw my mother. (In the retellings I heard of this episode in the weeks to follow it would emerge that as soon as my mother heard me speak she fainted.) It surprised me that my father looked terribly worried, even frightened. I knew that something had happened to me, but I could not understand why he was so concerned about it. Immediately, whatever I was lying on was racing with me down a corridor with men and women running at its sides, arriving in a room with fantastic lights shining in my face and people doing things to me, especially painting my face with stinging medicine. I was screaming at them, "Blow! Blow!" wanting them to blow on my wounds as my mother would when she painted them with iodine, but I was at the same time vaguely aware that the sting of the treatment was not as terrible as I was imagining.

Awakening after being knocked into unconsciousness for what I would learn was three hours must bear some relation to awakening after analogous times of being asleep and of being under anesthetic. Proust's narrator describes his repeated awakenings, or stages of awakening, in the opening paragraphs of his great novel, as containing moments of not knowing who he was (an experience I am unsure that I recognize), something that presents itself to him further as not knowing where to find himself (an experience quite familiar to me, as when, becoming conscious of awakening before opening my eyes, I try to remember what room I am in, perhaps preparing myself for still being away, or perhaps back home). But my question, "What happened?" does not directly express disorientation—I knew immediately who I was, and I recognized familiar faces—but expresses rather some sense of interruption that has changed everything, like a jump cut in a film, as though one might move from reality to reality as one moves from dream to reality or from reality to dream.

I do not know that I ever asked myself whether any register of

experience can be associated with unconsciousness caused by a blow
to the head (or for that matter from fainting, which I have experienced
twice in my life—once as sunstroke, once from the pain of the medical
treatment of my ear injured when the car hit me), or whether I should
at least have managed to bring back news from the world of the dead. If
I ask—thinking that such an extravagance of events should not go for
nothing—what I learned from the interruption of the automobile accident, I might respond by saying that I have retained a certain intermittent and generalized fear of the accidental, of consequences disproportionate to their casual cause (Emerson's liking to associate casualty with
the casual struck me early and hard in my delayed discoveries of his
accuracies), of irrecoverable disruptions, a thread forever lost. Sometimes this takes the form of giving what has seemed to my impatiently
observant children to be unnecessarily elaborate directions, say, to a
visitor about how not to get lost finding our house, across the river from
Harvard Square, or where to meet up with a friend in a large and unfamiliar train station. Perhaps in a time of cell phones this habit should
vanish, anyway become vestigial. But what if the cell phone melts, or
a goat eats it? I am avoiding both obvious and hidden features of my
memory of the car accident. Remembering my chasing the ball into
the street as exuberant, my off-handedly speaking of an intermittent
and generalized fear of accidents should at least be specified further as
a certain fear of the consequences of exuberance. (A sense of the non-
transparent variety of ways in which human action can go wrong seems
likely to underlie my long fascination with Austin's exploration of the
realm of Excuses. I note in passing here that "I was exuberant" would
hardly, for many sensibilities, constitute an excuse for a contretemps,
but is itself in need of excuse, rather like "I wasn't thinking.")

The specification of exuberance also fits the three other of my
childhood accidents that have warranted family retelling, one from tipping upside down in a sedate porch swing trying to make it go higher
than it was meant to, causing a cut on the back of my head that required stitches; a second from leaping out of a swing meant to go high,
but catching my arm on one of the ropes as I left the seat, causing a
fall resulting in a twisted knee that prevented my walking, even with
a crutch (I don't recall why this was so) for some weeks; a third from
showing off to girls that I could ride a bicycle no hands down a hill,

without observing, or understanding, the fact that this particular hill was not only too steep for one of my skill and age (perhaps six) but that it was unpaved, so that heavy gravel turned the front wheel as soon as I lifted my hands from the handlebar and, as I pitched forward onto the ground, opened a gash on the side of my chest, a much reduced scar of which is still visible. Whether these signs of supernatural stupidity come from above or from below remains undecided.

July 12, 2003

I was asking for some learning, or moral, I might have derived from this concatenation of not particularly unusual mishaps, beyond, as it were, a kind of phobia of accidents. I was responding to a recurrent surmise of mine that whatever happens—whatever is eventful enough for speech—is from the beginning accidental, as if a human life is inherently interrupted, things chronically occurring at unripe times, in the wrong tempo, comically or poignantly. This is not incompatible with Freud's view that there are no accidents. What that now means to me is that we chronically interrupt ourselves—say, we fail to give the right quality or quantity of time to our thoughts or deeds, say, let them climax. But how else? The history of a life is no more a matter of one action following another (Austin mocks this idea, which he attributes to philosophers, but he proposes, perhaps properly, no alternative picture) than the history of a culture is. But chronic interruption means the perpetual incompleteness of human expression—unless some manifestation of perpetual human disappointment is taken as sufficient expression. (This thought already arrives at a nerve of the way I read Wittgenstein's *Investigations*, and also at an element of Thoreau's perception of his countrymen as living in "quiet desperation," a transcription of Emerson's having spoken of their "secret melancholy." Here is a way to grasp the need for Emerson's sometimes grating joyfulness and for Thoreau's allegorical bragging. Wittgenstein is perhaps too aware of his destructiveness to allow himself Emerson's "infantine joy," but he may be granted the repeated satisfaction in securing the world, such as it is, for a child.)

Since I have contrasted awakening from a trauma with successive awakenings from sleep, I want to leave a mark here, to find my way back to Proust's speaking of awakening as finding oneself. It was, so to speak, always an accident, vowing two years ago to read Proust's novel through, beginning to end, this time without skipping, when I would want on occasion to check the revised revision of the Moncrieff translation against the French. The translation at this spot does not register Proust's sense of learning who I am as a matter of my finding myself but settles generally for my not knowing myself. Unaware of the discrepancy I would have missed a chance to ponder this crossroads with Emerson's first question in his great essay "Experience": "Where do we find ourselves?"—a text also about the essential difficulty of human awakening ("Sleep hovers about our eyes all day long, as night in the boughs of the fir tree"), one I have previously taken as prompting Nietzsche's first question in *The Genealogy of Morals*, "How should we find ourselves since we have never sought ourselves?" Proust's early admiration for Emerson is not exactly announced in the one mention of Emerson I recall in *À la recherche du temps perdu*, but it is explicit in Proust's notes to his early translations of Ruskin. (Evidently I am not quite beyond the defensiveness of authorizing my gratitude for Emerson's achievement by appealing to the grandeur of earlier readers of his who have sensed something of the sort.)

My memory—following the rough treatment in the painfully bright examination room after awakening from the automobile accident—was waking up in an enormous space filled with pleasant light from opposing walls with vast windows, to see lines of unmistakable beds apparently like mine stretching with no evident end in every direction I could turn my head to, and a ceiling as high as the lobby of the Ansley Hotel (long since extinct) that boasted green marble-looking pillars larger around than a very large person, where the traveling jewelry salesmen who supplied my father with watches and rings used to stay on their route through Atlanta before he had to sell the store, and that had a kind of balcony—polished rails running along what seemed to be brass vines—across the four sides of the lobby, punctuated by lines of arches, almost too high to see up to the people walking behind them. (I had been rushed by the terrified driver of the car that hit me, not knowing where I appeared from or thinking how to find out, to

the anonymity of the emergency room of the Atlanta City Hospital.)
An older boy lying on his back in the bed next to mine was encased
in a cast from the waist down and along each leg, with a wooden bar
strapped by layers of overlapping gauze to each ankle, holding his legs
somewhat spread apart, hence in a mainly fixed position while free to
move his arms and turn his head. It was an unprecedented sight for me,
as if I had seen nothing worse in my life, and surely never imagined
what could happen to someone to require a cast over half his body.
Seeing me awaken, the boy informed me that the morning visiting
hours were about to begin. I felt grateful to him and asked him how
long he had been here; I heard him say months. I found whatever he
had said ungraspable, and when his family arrived and my mother had
not, I began to sob. Had someone not told her where I was? The boy
responded to my tears by introducing me to his family and telling me
that visiting hours had barely begun. When heaven knows how many
deserts of seconds later my mother appeared she explained that she had
been in the hospital all night and was just now trying to convince the
doctors that the family could take care of me at home. The implication
that I might have to remain here—perhaps for months?—brought me
to something with which I still might measure despair. She said she
had to go back to learn what they had decided. I must have blanked
out again, doubtless because of the remnant of whatever sedative had
put me to sleep, since the next thing I remember is getting into our car
on a bright day, into the back where I was to lie down on the seat. My
mother brushed away a blood-stained shirt from the seat as I climbed
onto it. I do not remember whether it seemed remarkable to me that no
one else was there to help my mother manage these things.

July 13, 2003

It was impressed upon me that the price of allowing me to return
home so soon was that I obey strict instructions about getting plenty of
rest, which included taking a nap every afternoon, a ritual I particularly objected to. I recall no particular pain associated with my bruis-
es. Nothing visible was broken, and for some reason, the gravity of the
damage to my left ear was not yet something that I remember manifest-

ing itself at once. Given that this consequence of the accident was fundamentally to affect the course of my life, it is hard to believe that I did
not become aware of it until sometime after I returned to school, and
indeed not until a while after we moved to the north side and I began to
undergo excruciating treatments designed, so far as I was told, to keep
the misshapen ear canal from narrowing further than it already had
done. (The suggestion I took was that the canal might collapse upon itself, an idea that was particularly frightening to me.) This was, as was
explained to me a year or two after Pearl Harbor, before the discovery
of sulfa drugs, precursors of antibiotics. This explanation suggests that
infection and narrowing were connected, something I left as mysterious. What in any case was blank to me was why the only available alternative treatment was to use heavy tweezers with elongated jaws to
clamp upon increasing sizes of hard rubber tubes, or tight rolls of cot-
ton, and force them into my ear canal.

These treatments blur somewhat and join in imagination with the
procedure for removing so bizarre a visitation as warts on my toes the
next year (still within the period of the two years in which we lived in
that northside apartment before our first move to Sacramento). The
new treatment consisted in simply burning off the growths, on the
first day with a flashlight-sized object with a small head that emitted a
small, buzzing flame, and on a second day by pressing a red-hot wire
coil against the skin, experiences that became merged with images
and suggestions of torture when newsreels and narrative films began
to take up the progress of Hitlerism. These experiences echoed in my
memory even in so distant a mode, some half a dozen years later, as
when the Fat Man in *The Maltese Falcon* suggests to Humphrey Bogart
that there are ways of making people talk. It took four adults holding
me down, one grasping each limb—a nurse, my mother, a secretary,
and Dr. Alison himself—to administer the treatment of the warts. I am
told that males characteristically ask themselves whether they could
bear up under torture, and I have heard several women declare that
they know they could not. At the age of eight I was not prepared to
think about the difference between torture and mild or conventional
sadism, nor consciously about the difference between humiliation and
the disintegration of character as these presented themselves differently
to men and to women. But it was nice to know that the treatment for

warts would stop when the perceived good of it, however misguided the perception, was reached.

I could not wear shoes for some days after each of the two treatments, nor walk after the first except tentatively from one room to another. Since the night after the second treatment I was alone in the apartment—I suppose my mother was still playing two (or more?) shows a day at the Fox Theater and the maid who also served for baby sitting was not available—my mother had arranged for my dazzling aunt Bess to come by for me to take me, along with her daughter, to the movies. The flying yellow Buick had now become a sleek black sedan, and to enter it, sensing that I could not put my full weight on one foot for so high a step, without thinking, as if it was the way I habitually entered sleek sedans, I placed one knee onto the notably thick carpet of the car's floor, then the other knee, and then put one foot under me and, using the armrest of the back seat and the back of the near front seat as in effect crutches, slid into a sitting position in one satisfying gesture onto the back seat. The theater was the Rialto, less impressive than the Paramount, both of which names were glamorous to me from stories my mother and her brother Meyer had told of their playing in these places for vaudeville and for silent films.

I am surprised to find that I am vague about what film we saw the night of the aftermath of the warts, but perfectly clear that my younger cousin and I were laughing wildly throughout the whole thing. I have images now of W. C. Fields speeding down a twisting country road in an open car chasing a criminal or perhaps himself chased by police, as involved with keeping his straw hat in place on his head as keeping the car on the road, then all at once discovering that the steering wheel has come off into his wildly flailing hands as he turns to speak to his passenger in the back seat. Walking out after the film I noticed that my feet were not hurting.—So, after all, the postponement in following the aftermath of ear treatments by interposing a roughly contemporaneous siege of painful medical practice has not proved unproductive, marking an early date at which I knew, or from which I can derive the knowledge, that the depth of film's hypnotic or hallucinatory properties is not accounted for by mentioning its usefulness as a pastime.

July 14, 2003

My resistance to the afternoon nap was gloriously overcome by
the one of my mother's three brothers whom I knew least well, namely, the Atlanta (opposed to the Sacramento) Uncle Morris. I must fill in
some history to say how. As the best musician in the family, my mother
was her father's favorite child, something everyone in the family recognized—in fact I recall Uncle Mendel once remarking the obvious fact
wryly. (My mother was, by the age of sixteen I remember being told,
already regularly playing in a theater pit orchestra, for silent movies
and for vaudeville, and making, as she put it, "a man's salary.") Meyer,
the next oldest, was next best, good enough for a career as an orchestra
player, and sometime conductor of theater orchestras, but too readily
discouraged by hard times and the philistinism of those in the hierar-
chy of commercial music—I recall his explicitly mentioning orchestra contractors and theater owners—to survive in that version of the
world of art. Mendel, the baby of the siblings, twelve or thirteen years
older than I, held a scholarship from Emory University tied to his being concert master of the Emory University Symphony. After his third
year at Emory, the funds for the scholarship had vanished with the
Depression (this would have been 1933 or 1934) and he could not afford to enroll for his final year of college. After a couple of stints selling
shoes he began working in his sister Bess's husband's printing plant, of
which he would eventually be the managing partner. He will become
a rich and admired businessman, twice national president of the Printers Association of America, invited with other prominent business ex-
ecutives to the White House, handsome, articulate, married for a long
lifetime to his high school sweetheart, Mynette, who had captured my
seven-year-old heart with each of her gestures or words, as she seemed
to do in the case of all the men who shared our company, for example,
at the Lakewood swimming pool on certain imperishable Saturday afternoons. Despite Mendel's authority and talent, and his capacity to
paint the day with fun, I felt about him an air, or skin, of privacy, a
perpetual reticence even in his grand laughter, registering a perception
that the world held less of value than it promised. I adored him. (Mendel never, I believe, fully regained confidence in the stock market, relying for decades instead on his company, on property interests, and on

depositing savings accounts in each of many different banks just up to the amount federally insured. I have heard similar stories from others of his generation. His laughter was not brought on by jokes but by his perception of the folly of the world. He once said to me: "Don't concern yourself with what you hear about anti-Semitism. Just be three times better than your competition and you'll be all right." That laugh was a long time ago.) Bess, the next youngest of the Segal siblings after Mendel, played both the violin and the piano proficiently enough to keep up with the latest hits represented in the piles of sheet music, with their often excited, even chic, covering pages, on and around her piano, and, what is glamorously more, tap-danced well enough to teach occasionally in a dance studio, accomplishments that, together with a flapper's compact and athletic body, and a vivacity and high laugh that she kept unfailingly at her command, seemed to shuffle the population of any room she entered. Men, many of morose mien, as I realized more clearly from the perspective of our return the first time from Sacramento to Atlanta, unrelentingly attempted to capture her attention, whose span was invariably short. Her musical siblings sometimes expressed impatience with her flightiness. Perhaps they had not recognized in it her own version of their disdain for the ways of the world.

This disdain did not, I think, shadow the temperaments of the remaining two siblings, deprived of the full elevation of music, namely, the oldest, Mary, and the middle brother, Morris. I gathered that Mary was, particularly in my father's eyes, something of a black sheep, having long ago eloped with a policeman, a profession from which it virtually followed then and there that he was not Jewish. Mary's son Joe, large and handsome, was nine years older than I and familiarly visited the house on Atlanta Avenue. His policeman father either died young or disappeared; I think I never met him (though I have an image of him that may have come from a photograph in Aunt Mary's house, where I lived happily for two weeks when I was eight years old, an episode I must not forget to relate). The story I have come away with concerning the scandal of the elopement with a gentile was that the pneumonia from which the Segal father, Samuel, died, three years before I was born, was somehow related to the illness he contracted the night Mary ran away and he went searching for the pair through neighboring towns all night in an open car, in pouring rain. Whatever the medical facts, the melodramatic story expresses the family consensus that the father never recovered from the event. My mother spoke adoringly of her father. I am named for him.

There is on our living room mantel a photograph of a Segal musical group with my mother sitting at an upright piano, her back to the camera, her head turned left in profile looking at Meyer, standing beside her holding a violin and bow in his left hand, while Morris is sitting behind her, at the opposite edge of the piano bench, with a snare drum in front of him. If that isolated drum betokens the basis of Morris's musical expressiveness and ambition, it would not have been of much service in the chamber music (frequently salon music) that my mother and her two other brothers played for pleasure and for profit. Since Morris at an early stage moved away from Atlanta to a small town in South Carolina, I encountered him least often of any of the Segal family. I know that he died in middle age, and the last time I saw him was on the occasion, during one of our returns to Atlanta, in which I lined up, along with some number of his siblings and their children, as part of a considerable crowd on downtown Peachtree Street to watch a Shriners' parade, when eventually there came Morris, proud and hearty in a red fez, marching at the back of the Shriners' band, banging the cadence on a bass drum. His family caught his attention, and his smile brightened as he gave a heightened whirl to each stroke of his cushioned mallet against the drum skin.

It was, however, this Uncle Morris who had had the means to settle the crisis of afternoon nap-taking during my convalescent weeks at home. His brothers Meyer and Mendel devised the bargain with me that if I napped without making a fuss about it, Morris would drive his delivery truck by the house afterward and I could choose any drink I wanted from it. This was the first I had heard of any such truck or occupation. But the next afternoon Morris, dressed in a white shirt and an apparently leather black bow tie and white trousers and a white cap, showing the full Segal smile, appeared in front of the Atlanta Avenue house driving, it emerged, an open truck on which were stacked, higher than the truck's cabin, in mounting, neat rows of shelves, like a pair of a giant's bookcases tilted toward each other back to back, running the length of the truck on each side, continuous cases of bottles of soft drinks, tipped so as to display the full array of their bottles, a tidy jungle of molded colored liquids, orange, lemon, green, purple, faint beige, red-brown, near black. There may already have been, in the 1930s, trucks roaming Atlanta delivering just one soft drink—since Coca-Cola was an Atlanta invention, that is not unlikely. But Morris's wondrous truck would in any case have held every other soda in the whole world, cloud-high cliffs of delights. I feel sure I am right in remembering the true extent of these uncle-magicians' tact, which was not to hurry me in my choice, as if for me there were not something decisive at stake each afternoon, but to urge me to take my time and survey the possibilities, accompanying me as I walked out to the sidewalk in my pajamas and bathrobe. Some days I made my choice by color, other days by the shape of the bottle, or by a certain mild roughness of its texture, or out of the memory of a specific craving, or because I wanted a strange bottle cap for the collection of bottle caps I was beginning.

What happened to my various collections of objects is a set of sore subjects, which may reappear unexpectedly, but which to go into now would ruin the mood of courtesy, of the acknowledgment of the importance of pleasure, hence surely of pain, that had shown itself at my door. I will just note that no collection—clear clutter to my mother's eyes—survived the change of dwellings that began with the move to the north side of town and that continued, moving between Atlanta and Sacramento, roughly every twelve to eighteen months (the second return to Atlanta lasted two years) from the time I was nine years old until I turned fourteen at the beginning of the last return to Sacramento.

July 15, 2003

If I tell with some puzzlement the tale of my Segal grandfather in frantic search of his vanished daughter, it is because, while he and his wife, my grandmother Becky, like the Goldstein grandfather and his wife, were immigrants, the Segals arrived in the United States a couple of decades earlier than the Goldsteins; it always mattered to both strains that the Goldsteins were orthodox Jews while the Segals were, within the bounds of seemliness, virtually secular. My Segal uncles, Mendel and Meyer, would have been hard-pressed, let me just say unable, to say Kaddish in mourning for their parents.

There was another Segal tradition carried by their father that his children failed to inherit, one that by the time I heard of it was conveyed with a certain air of amused embarrassment; I mean his socialism. The uncles would very occasionally speak of something called, so far as I could tell, the Furaine, which seemed to have reference to this part of their father's life. It would come up when the story of The Mountain would be told, never very consecutively.

In my mother's version the story went this way. When she was ten or eleven years old, the family still where so far as I knew they started life in America, in Brooklyn, her father and five or six of his friends were given (my mother did not know by whom or on what conditions) a mountain in Tennessee. Each of this group of friends had a family and a practical trade, one a carpenter, one a mason, one a plumber, one of the wives was a schoolteacher, and so on, and they made their way to Tennessee to set up an independent, self-sustaining community on their mountain. I am unsure what my grandfather's trade was; I seem to recall that he knew something about raising chickens, and had tried his hand at cabinetmaking; by the time the stories get more detailed he owned a grocery store near the house on Atlanta Avenue.

These idealists were, to other members of the Segal grandfather's family at least, figures of mild fun. This grandfather had relatives in Chattanooga. (Whether they had remained behind after the small band left the mountain, or whether they had settled there earlier and were somehow involved in acquiring the mountain, I do not know.) A cousin of my mother's from the Chattanooga branch of the family had run off to San Francisco with a gambling man. We would visit them in San Francisco once or twice on each of our sojourns in Sacramento; this was called "going to the City." The pair had no children, and the cousin, a woman I described to myself as fancy, ran the front part of her husband's cigar store. That space was slim, just wide enough, with a customer standing at the counter, for one more person at a time to pass by into the back of the store, where, pushing aside a thick curtain covering a doorway, a closed door was visible that opened into a back room where, not very rigorously concealed, a card game was in progress. Sometimes the cousin's job in front would be taken over by another woman, but generally, when we visited, her husband would emerge from the back room and take over the front so the cousin could go to lunch with my mother and me. Waiting in the store with my mother, I noticed that the cousin would from time to time, after placing a customer's purchase on the counter (a few cigars, a carton of cigarettes, a lighter, perhaps candies, and I seem to recall nondescript knickknacks also for sale), cast a set of dice out of a leather cup onto a board covered with green felt, then with one hand sweep up the dice and drop them back into the cup for the customer to cast them out. After his cast (it was in my experience always a man), the customer would then at once either put down money and take his purchases, or else take the purchases without paying. Once when I was invited to join the husband—Cousin Abe I called him—behind the counter and make change for simple purchases while my mother and her cousin went shopping not far away at I. Magnin's, the sort of San Francisco store featuring high fashion that Sacramento in those years could hardly compete with, I took the opportunity to look closely at those dice, each of which turned out to have on its six faces replicas of playing cards, predominantly face cards and aces. It still interests me that these players knew at a glance who had won, as rapidly as if they were comparing not sets of small replicas but single cards.

It was at dinner (perhaps in a nearby nightclub owned by a friend of Cousin Abe's) that family reminiscences of days in Tennessee came up. Having regaled the small company with stories of large bets won and lost, and vaguely bawdy tales of his courtship of our cousin in Chattanooga as he was trying to convince her to run away with him to California (tales at which the cousin gave little shouts of disapproval, though I felt distinctly that she was as proud of the implied daring in the tales as she may have been shy of hearing them aired in public), Abe seemed suddenly tickled by a thought, took the omnipresent cigar out of his mouth (it is in connection with that gesture that I recall noticing that his fingernails were bitten almost to invisibility), dropped his head with a virtually silent laugh, his chin almost to his chest, and said, "That was after they had come down from the barg." I might conceivably have asked then what a barg was, but I did not want to give any indication beyond my sheer presence that I had been listening with understanding to these imperfectly censored stories. Children get expert at playing dumb, perhaps out of a sense not merely that they do not want to be held responsible for learning what others do not want them to know, but that they themselves do not know how much more they are learning than they know. This seems to fit Prince Hal's experience as well, however differently, as Prince Hamlet's. This sense of feeling unseen, and willing or needing to be unseen, by one's elders, or to keep one's knowledge hidden from them, is a feeling that starts early (surely earlier than was widely realized in my childhood) and has prompted the way I have sometimes insisted upon reading, for example, the quotation from Saint Augustine with which Wittgenstein opens his *Philosophical Investigations*, describing his reconstruction of his learning to speak, as if with one's first words one learns that knowledge is forbidden, that one lacks the right to it.

I do not remember when I learned that *Berg* was German for "mountain," but I seem then to have been struck at once with the knowledge that "barg" was the gambler's pronunciation of a word borrowed in Yiddish. (The way I heard Yiddish described seemed sometimes to suggest that all its words were borrowed, nothing in it original. Sometimes it was explicitly said, not just by my mother, who spoke it some, not to be a language at all, but a set of sayings, or a slang. And this was the woman who played the piano for Jewish theater troupes as they traveled through Atlanta, and knew and surely understood [though I never remember her conversing in Yiddish, she responded briefly to assertions or questions in Yiddish from my father and his siblings], the words of their sad and their funny songs. She used one or two especially sad ones among these songs as my lullabies.) I generally felt I knew, in a small gathering of Jews with my father present, whether the others knew Yiddish. His not telling a Yiddish joke in the course of a dinner's conversation was proof to me (unless I otherwise detected in him the hesitant signs of a sudden melancholy) that he had surmised that they would not understand; perhaps he had ways of testing the surmise. The gambler's laughter colored the word "barg," or I might say quoted the word, as an overheard term of slang, and this expressed to my mind, along with his contempt for the language (for which language not?), amused contempt for the idealists on the mountain.

That small band of families was sufficiently punished for its lack of practicality when it was unable to contain a fire that burned its little settlement to the ground. My mother recalled with feeling her looking back as they walked with whatever they could carry back down the mountain road. She could tell me nothing further about the fire, and seemed to have very little she wanted to tell about what life was like while the little community was intact. Her father must have managed to get their piano up the road to their land (there would have been men enough to help load it on a truck, if that is how they transported their collective belongings from Brooklyn), since it does not seem imaginable that my mother would not have described what it would have been for her to have lived for a period of a year or more without one. She did note that, as Meyer would have turned five or six while they were there, and since buying a beginner's violin and bow was out of the question because they all lived with next to no money, and since the father's mandolin was not the instrument he had in mind for his oldest son, this father crafted from scraps of wood and string facsimiles of a small fiddle and a bow to scale, and worked each day with little Meyer, showing him, along with reading notes (but I have the idea that my mother taught him to read notes, as she had taught me), the correct posture for supporting and bowing the instrument and the positions on the simulacrum of a fingerboard. This was all the detail of the process my mother gave, but I would sometimes fill it out by picturing the father demonstrating by plucking on his mandolin (whose open double strings have the same tuning as a violin, with the initial pedagogical advantage of frets on its fingerboard) the pitches the boy's fingers were producing, as if the strings he was pressing had been something more than so much twine, as he taught Meyer the tuning of the strings, and where the notes are on the strings, different notes on the same string, the same note on different strings. Each of the four children who took to music became quickly more expert on their instruments than the father was on his. What they at the same time learned from him was that music is a religion, outlasting Judaism and socialism, even if, except for my mother, they would mostly lose their absolute faith in music. (How these possibilities join in a constellation with the religion of Eros, one seed of which was planted, for example, by my Indian princess, is something I owe an account of, I mean of my faith in it. We will I suppose have to reach first the religion of philosophy.)

July 16, 2003

It was four decades later that I perceived what my uncles meant by "Furaine." In the large Jewish cemetery in Atlanta, Greenlawn Cemetery—anyway the cemetery in which every Jewish burial I ever attended in Atlanta took place—at my father's graveside funeral, in 1977, it occurred to me to ask Mendel where his father was buried. (I knew perfectly well where the Goldstein grandparents' graves were, having traveled a number of times to attend graveside ceremonies on that larger side of the family.) He led me up an incline to a further section in the corner of the cemetery marked off by an iron arch in which iron letters spelled out (as I recall or reconstruct it) JUDISCHE ARBEITERS-VEREIN. I said to Mendel, "The Jewish Working Man's <u>Furaine</u>." He replied unhesitatingly, "Sure. I haven't been here in a long time." It was a cemetery for the association as well as for its members.

Visiting Atlanta this past year, on the occasion of Mendel's ninetieth birthday, making him the sole survivor of my parents' combined generation of thirteen siblings, Cathleen and I took along our son Benjamin and his fiancée, Emily, to meet, or meet again, this greatly important figure of my childhood (our younger son, David, had a couple of months earlier while on a summer driving tour of the South paid a call on Mendel at his so-called assisted living apartment on the outskirts of Atlanta), and one of our destinations on the day and a half we had for revisiting recognizable scenes of my youth and taking in glimpses of frightening futures, such as a fully inhabited earth and gated neighborhoods, we drove to Greenlawn Cemetery to put flowers on my parents' graves. From that point I unhesitatingly guided our little group up the hill to the corner of the cemetery with the densest parallel lines of gravestones bearing Hebrew inscriptions, and while various signposts indicated numbers of associations, there was no large iron arch with iron letters. Was it removed? Did I not press forward far enough? Can I have dreamt it? Surely the moment of asking Mendel and receiving his affirmation is too vivid for me to have dreamt it in 1977 and remembered it as real. It would if unreal have had to be a hallucination, something unprecedented so far as I know in my adult life. If I dreamt—or hallucinated somehow—the iron gate, then when I asked Mendel about his father's grave I had figured out in a sudden inspiration of reading that "Furaine" was overheard Yiddish for the German *Verein* (like "barg" for *Berg*). (Out of this epistemological anxiety, sufficiently strong to chance my inexperienced hand at the Internet, I found information of a recently established Association of Georgia Jewish Cemeteries, headquartered in Atlanta, whose unastonished administrator, answering my phone call, took my question concerning the existence of an iron gate of the description I supplied to be a reasonable one and, asking for time to make inquiries, phoned me back an hour later to say that she had spoken to a man who had seen the Greenlawn iron arch within the past year. However, she went on pleasantly to tell me that the exact words of the arch are JUDISCHSE ARBEITERS<u>RING</u>. I thought to pursue matters one further step. "But mightn't its members simply have spoken of the Ring as the Furaine?" "The Furaine. Yes, certainly.")

This path of memory was to throw light on why I was perplexed at the degree of my grandfather's distress over his daughter's elopement with a gentile policeman. And now I find that I have not resolved the issue. Perhaps it has to do with my early romantic sense that socialists were committed to equality, unless it was an even less realistic inference from the fact that my mother was her father's favorite that therefore he had staked less than his happiness on each of his other children.

A few years later, in the late stage of preparing for my Bar Mitzvah, I asked my father more pointedly than in the past why he went to shul if he did not believe in what was being done there, and now it was virtually explicit that I was asking why I had to go, since any training I was being given, with Hebrew lessons, and sitting through services with my father, left me depressingly ignorant of so much of the significance of the events in a synagogue. He replied, "I go for my father." I swallowed my reply along with my contempt, and did not say, "Your father believes. You do not believe. Why should I go for you?" It is a relief to my mind that I did swallow it—preferably adding it to the mad, endless task of absorbing it along with its horizons of companion explanations. How could I claim to know why a son does something for his father, and moreover to know the conditions under which it is worthy of being done? And how did I know what his father did or did not believe? More important perhaps, how did my father know this? I am surprised (if perhaps less than one might expect) to find now that I have no memory of ever seeing my father and his father in conversation together. If they were seated together in the same place it was either on the High Holidays in synagogue or it was in a crowd of family. It would be a long time before I could locate the hollowness in my father's claim of piety toward his father. Hypocrisy was not the issue. Hypocrisy can make people act better as well as worse than they are. There was something he could not say, something stuck behind the tongue, behind tongues. There is no reason his father goes, but his father needs no reason. It is what he does. Without a reason, this son, my father, was bereft and incoherent.

A further note about names. "America" used as meaning "United States" is a chauvinism about which one now seeks to be careful. But for me this use of the word *America* remains important as an immigrant's designation, or destination.

July 17, 2003

The memory of the weeks of convalescence after being hit by the car is filled with scenes of games of solitaire and double solitaire, and of a strange new deck of cards with pictures of various automobiles, each repeated several times, on the individual card faces. I have no memory of the game played with these new strange cards, but I remember it was called Touring and that my favorite pictured car, or favorite new word for a kind of car, or both together, was that of a Phaeton. (I do not re-   member whether I tried to divine, among these echoing images, the vehicle causing my recent imitation of death.) And some time was given day after day to piecing together, with help from Uncles Mendel and Meyer when they arrived home after work, a jigsaw puzzle that must actually have been made by a jigsaw, since it was of wood that I can recall having distinct layers, at least five, of thickness, and it filled the full square of a folding bridge table. When we had at last finished the puzzle, and I expressed satisfaction but some disappointment, the uncles reminded me that we could take our handiwork apart and solve the puzzle again with the picture on the reverse side of the pieces (unlike the sunny view on the side we had solved—I have forgotten whether it really was of a landscape with animals and perhaps some small human figures in the distance, or whether I recall this from a different puzzle and a different period of restful restlessness), which proved to be a night scene with a beautiful sad woman outside a large house and a moon bright enough to cast shadows. We left the finished sunny view intact and on display for several days to be sure that everybody that came to the house had a chance to be impressed.

It was still that very puzzle I had in mind in the hours I spent some decades later speculating whether a picture puzzle was a useful image of (an attractive, mistaken view of) the working of language, in which the interlocking of the pieces represents syntax and the resulting picture, or pictures, represents semantics. This parable lost interest for me on considering that the solution to the puzzle was from the beginning fixed, its only power of surprise frozen; which negates the essence of human speech. Is the parable then more aptly applied to the way people in fact mostly conform to speech, treat their mother tongue as itself a kind of slang of fixed sayings, as my mother thought true specifically of Yiddish? This makes speech not an invitation to conversation but a substitute for it, as if words are essentially passwords to satisfy challenges. I am sometimes still taken by surprise to hear older strangers speak English fluently and without a slight Eastern European accent. There were even in my mother's speech, for all her love of finesse, certain stretches of hardness and carelessness that were inconceivable in her shaping of a musical phrase. But her silences were, where not terrifying, often golden.

Besides a thick brown metallic-tasting tonic that my mother insisted on my taking every day during the months following the automobile accident, along with a spoonful of cod liver oil, which looked or smelled harder to swallow than it proved to be, the new element in my diet, meant to contribute to my getting my strength back, was a broth of what I felt to be of supernatural intensity, as if taste itself could be transformed into energy. Somewhat more than two decades later, visiting my parents in Atlanta from near the end of my graduate studies at Harvard (they had returned finally to Atlanta in the 1950s after my father sold the pawnshop) to tell them that I was going to marry, I awoke unable to disguise symptoms that felt like a flu (the diagnosis turned out to be mononucleosis), and when I appeared later in the day, after having gone back to bed to try to recover from a spell of dizziness, and discovering that I had slept through the afternoon, I found my mother in the kitchen preparing that ancient, intense brew. She was cutting a slab of steak into small chunks and dropping the chunks into a thick bottle (I believe such bottles are used for making fruit preserves) that closed with a heavy wire clip that pressed the cap tight against a rubber seal. I continued to watch as she placed this bottle into a large pot of boiling water until steaming juices inside the bottle cooked the meat so thoroughly as to drain all the liquid from it. On opening the bottle she poured the liquid into a cup for me to drink and dished out the drained pieces of meat for what proved to be my father's dinner. As he tasted the meat, he said with a puzzled frown (normally he loved my mother's cooking) that the meat had no taste and was impossible to chew. Was this awful favoritism an expression of the primitiveness of mother love, or merely a brutal allegory of marital disdain? Even if my father did not notice and interpret this particularly ugly division of nourishment, the act seemed to me to speak aloud of an ancient derangement always uncorrectable by me.

It is not enough to say that my father loved my mother's cooking. I had understood consciously well before the time we moved back to Sacramento for the third time, the September I turned fourteen and started the second year of high school, that it was the only food he ate with gusto, apart from Jewish specialties he could buy in certain shops, bottles of pickled herring packed in sour cream, large kosher salamis imported from Chicago or New York that would be hung by a thick brown string from a hook in a wall of the tiny screened porch off the kitchen (initial slices from which were moist, but hardened as the days past; I imagine a large salami took a matter of weeks to disappear), jars of borscht or, in summer, of schav (a chilled soup made with sorrel and spices), and halvah for dessert. (I was uncertain about the ingredients of the schav, or the version of it he found, having never gotten myself past the muddy look of it to taste it properly. It wouldn't surprise me to learn that I missed something there, since I developed a distinct taste for the rest of this menu.) After a meal at other people's houses my father would return home hungry, saying the food had smelled rotten and was inedible. If there were no leftovers from a meal of my mother's making, he would take one or another of his store-bought delicacies from the refrigerator, or the screened-porch wall, and have them with one or another of the serious breads that were always in the house—a challah or rye or poppy-seed Kaiser roll. The distinctness, the familiar pungency of these dishes, was all the more inviting because their satisfactions were immediate, requiring no preparation, but unlike what most people would call snacks (crackers and cheese, potato chips, half a peanut butter sandwich, cereal, a piece of fruit), these were sumptuous. (They were at the period and the place I am speaking of also exotic, whereas now almost all of them seem available in any ambitious supermarket.) The stretches of fall and winter in New York after graduating from Berkeley, preparing for, and later avoiding, Juilliard, were the first time I had to prepare meals for myself, away from student cafeterias and hangouts. I finessed the issue of cooking, when I didn't want to go out for a meal (a good meal was still quite cheap in New York if you knew where to go), by stopping at a small neighborhood convenience store on the way back from the conservatory, to replenish where necessary the salami and herring and black bread and sour cream that needed no preparation. Evidently I did not want to cook for myself but to be cared for.

My mother liked to deny that she was a cook. She managed everyday meals that so to speak cooked themselves, or needed a minimum of assistance in order to look like prepared meals (typically a broiled steak, or lamb chops, or calves' liver, with boiled or baked potatoes, a sliced tomato, and canned peas or boiled string beans—fresh vegetables generally were boiled). For Sundays and holidays she had a small repertory of special dishes, laborious to make (this was before the days of electric mixers, or anyway before my mother had one, an object that might have suggested she was serious about cooking) and so delicious that whoever partook of them spent much of the time consuming them in praising them and their maker, as if each mouthful bore comment increasingly beyond words. Along with a boiled brisket there might be a potato kugel; sometimes, in winter, the mixture of grated potatoes and onions, together with an egg or two, which were the substance of the potato kugel, would be molded into small balls and cooked in a heavy lentil soup. Some variant of this mixture was also used to stuff a baked breast of veal. Her gefilte fish, one somehow knew, took forever to grind by hand to the right texture, and the ingredients of a lavish fish stew were evidently hard to collect and get to the house at the right time to prepare it very often. I cannot forget the one dessert she sometimes presented, a lemon pie. Nor do I recall that this was made for special occasions. Just conceivably she sometimes made it simply because she herself enjoyed it. All but the pie were versions of Jewish cooking, variations of Eastern European country cooking. When asked for the recipe for one of the dishes, she professed not to be able to say what it was, especially not to know the measurements of seasonings she used (measuring was something she expressed impatience with, outside music, perhaps truly not recognizing that the amount of salt, for instance, that she threw into a boiling pot she had first poured into her precisely cupped hand).

There must have been something my mother would have called a "secret" to getting lentils to the texture they had in that soup; I have never recognized that taste in any later instance of a recipe with lentils, which turn out, to my taste, even when good enough to eat gladly, to be either somewhat hard or somewhat pasty. When I asked my mother to teach me to cook a dish or two, she said it was not worth my time, that she had to do these things, I did not. This worked hard against me, not only when I found myself alone, but when I was a divorced father with a three-year-old daughter. Still, while I remained unable to cook for myself, Rachel and I in effect taught ourselves to do some cooking together—to cook for someone you care about is quite compatible with not wanting to take care of yourself—messy sometimes, but excellent ingredients and the best of intentions getting through.

"The secret" to doing something was an expression my mother employed to acknowledge, and partly explain, anything that she felt was done exactly right. Some few things were in her eyes worth doing right, either for their own sakes, as in playing music, or because doing them wrong made an unpleasant but necessary task more prolonged or unpleasant, as in plucking and cleaning a chicken or dusting under a rug.

The chicken is the only animal along whose path from being slaughtered to being eaten I have witnessed every step. The rabbi who gave me Hebrew lessons in Sacramento was also a shochet, a qualified slaughterer (in his case, so far as I saw, only of chickens), required if an animal is to be declared kosher. Familiarly during the four afternoons a week I took classes with him, particularly on Thursdays and Fridays, in view of the Friday night Sabbath meal, he would be called away to walk from the second story down the back wooden stairs of the former wooden schoolhouse that served for a synagogue and Hebrew school, into a small dirt court, where two or three of us from the small class would follow down half the flight of stairs for an unobstructed view of the rabbi as he removed a leather case from his coat pocket, take from the case a dull-handled razor, whose shining blade he would open out and examine (any imperfection in the cutting edge would cause the chicken suffering and accordingly invalidate the ceremony), then receive the chicken from the butcher's delivery boy, and holding between his left arm and hip the bird's wings quiet against its body, bend back its neck and with the blade in his right hand slit its throat with a single swift gesture, allowing an opening from which a severed end of the windpipe (so I called it to myself) would pop out of the neck, then throw the vanishing creature into a corrugated metal washtub, free to thrash its wings again briefly and to suffocate. It was such a recently killed chicken that would be delivered to my mother for plucking and cleaning, which meant, most impressively (having spread newspapers over the tiled counters at the sides of the sink), removing from the generalized scene of bloody insides the edible inner organs, principally the liver and the gizzard; the neck was saved as a delicacy, and the feet were held over the flame of one of the stove's gas burners for a reason I never grasped, causing the distinct odor that I have assumed people mean in speaking of burning flesh. I imagine that one secret of her cooking was the use, instead of butter, of the schmaltz she rendered from chicken fat. These events took place, so far as I knew, only when we lived in Sacramento—and then only in certain sequences of Friday afternoons. It is a memorable way to welcome the Sabbath, but the chief feature I take from the set of events is the sense of power and competence in my mother's bloody hands and wrists, bringing a slain carcass through every turn to a productive afterlife.

It is with this power that she also could, by herself, lift each of the three apexes (as it were) of her baby grand piano (which has for a quarter of a century stood in the room below the room I am writing in and which I still irregularly play), so that she could dislodge the coaster under the roller of each leg, then roll the piano to the opposite side of the room, and replace the coasters. There is also the rug to consider. The first time I remember walking into an apartment of ours and seeing the rearranged room it would have been obvious that the cause had been the need to clean the room with particular thoroughness, especially under the rug. When I thought to ask who had helped her, I received in return one of her repertory of disdainful glances: "Who do you think?" And when I went on to ask how she could have managed this alone, she replied: "You have to know how. You don't lift the piano, and you don't use your back. Otherwise you can hurt yourself." I took an occasion when I was alone to try this myself. I got far enough to see how it was possible, translating "not lifting the piano" to mean "with a concentration of energy, raising up a third of the piano a fraction of an inch," and taking "not using the back" to mean "keeping the back straight and using the strength of the legs." To have actually experimented nudging out the coaster with one foot and nudging it back again after the move was also barely imaginable, but what I was left thinking about was where the motivation came from to want so fiercely to prove this independence from the world. (Unless that is already a way to describe the motivation. When, rarely, I was present as this process was undertaken, and insisted on kneeling on the floor to remove and replace the coasters as rapidly as possible as she lifted each piano leg, I was pleased that she allowed this, even though it seemed a trivial assistance.) The piano was bought with the "man's salary" she was earning in theater orchestras sometime after World War I, as was her Chevrolet a decade later. The piano was the only physical object I ever knew her to take pride in owning (not, however, to show pride—since who in her world would have genuinely understood its value?), except perhaps decades later for an emerald-cut diamond ring that had not been redeemed from the pawnshop—one more implied tale of private misfortune that inhabited the shadows even of a clean well-lighted pawnshop—and represented the achievement of my father's financial independence, for which they had sought in first moving to Sacramento. It is significant that the piano was a Mason and Hamlin, the only serious American competitor of the Steinway and the one my mother preferred for a private space, outside a concert hall. I would learn from (I believe) a prominent teacher in the piano department at the Cleveland Conservatory visiting his daughter, who was a friend at Harvard while I was a graduate student there, that with the coming of the Depression the Mason and Hamlin factory laid off most of its craftsmen, who moved to Steinway, which thereupon became an unrivaled label in this country.

I knew my mother took pride in beating men at their own game. In identifying with her in an effort to learn her secrets of technique and of strength, was I playing the game she would win or was I learning how to hold my own in it? I also knew that she admired men in the world whom she could not beat (they did not seem to live in Atlanta, perhaps not in the southeastern United States then), men of talent who had practiced longer and more single-mindedly than she. But then her judgment was severe. Horowitz was a genius but too mechanical and careless (this was early in his career). Josef Hoffmann was unassailably great.

And pride in beating men at their game cannot explain the intensity and understanding she would have had to bring to her regime of practicing the piano throughout her growing up. A critical image for me is her description of being awakened for practice by her father every morning something more than two hours before she had to leave for school, after, in winter, he had lit a coal fire in the basement furnace and closed off the heating vents except the one to the living room where the piano was, and made a small warm breakfast for her and sometime later for her brother Meyer, whom he would establish in the kitchen with his violin and a music stand near a wood fire in the well of the stove. This example of a father's admiration for and encouragement of his children, and the expression of my mother's love in recounting her father's attentiveness and responsiveness, lines the memories of my own love of all the spaces of that first house and serves (although this grandfather died three years before I was born, it was he for whom I was named) as a fundamental idea from which, with whatever failures in fact, I derived and harbored the sense of what a father also might be.

I associated the strength in my mother's hands and arms with her ability to play rapid repeated octaves delicately, as in the Liszt Sixth Hungarian Rhapsody. I think I have never heard another pianist do this as well as she. Once on my asking her how she did it she replied, "The secret is to relax." I tried following the secret, which produced mud music. She added: "But your fingers must be like iron." Relaxed iron. I loved exchanges like this, and regarded such descriptions as pedagogically astute and accurate. The secret lay in knowing how to translate them into the motions of one's body. It is no secret that the last step is up to the pupil; but coaches vary in their ability to prompt that step. My mother was sometimes approached to give lessons, but invariably refused on the ground that she hadn't the patience for it. I seemed always to know that this meant she was not interested in it.

Then what interests a talented and fascinating woman? In her case I might have figured out a piece of this sooner than I did, but it was perhaps not altogether late. She wanted to be the one taught, shown new things, and taken to new places of comfort and elegance, to become amazed—ways of course of having informed attention paid to her.

The great secrets, those I knew I craved to have, were ones she seemed to divine when, for instance, taking me on an unprecedented occasion from Sacramento to San Francisco when I was ten or eleven years old to attend a recital of Fritz Kreisler's, she would from time to time during the performance suddenly produce (a gesture I knew well and would glory in when directed to something I had done) an all but inaudible high cry and silently snap the fingers of her hand nearer me and thrust it toward her face, which was turned as if to ward off a blow. This happened as often as not at the end of each of Kreisler's encores, which consisted of several of his short pieces, perfectly familiar to me. These were minor favorites of hers; she played them with Meyer on various occasions, sometimes for friends at the Atlanta Avenue house, sometimes on the radio. I believe I took away a confidence or two to ponder from watching and listening to Kreisler play that day. There was a way he stood listening when the piano was playing a solo passage, especially I suppose in a slow movement, his head and body absolutely still, which I retain as an image of total concentration, ending in a single unhurried gesture that brought the violin back beneath the chin and the bow back to the strings at the instant of the violin's next entrance—as if music had been induced to utter itself.

Part 2

July 20, 2003

Evidently I recall my early convalescence at home with uncles and jigsaw puzzles and playing cards and music and soft drinks with such pleasure, or with such fear of what follows it, that I become distracted from having to end it. I want to follow myself back to first grade in the fall after I had turned six. What I am avoiding is the move at the end of that school year to the north side of Atlanta. Until my first recourse to psychoanalytic therapy, some twenty-five years in the future, I had characteristically taken it as an unquestionable fact of my life that from the time of that first move until I left Sacramento for Berkeley ten years later I did not draw a happy breath. I wondered whether something of the same might be said of my mother. In neither case could it have been exactly true. What is true is that for long periods I spent so much time by myself that a therapist friend of mine will describe something I said alluding to days of that period as expressing a state of sensory deprivation, as if I had been confined in a cave. (I still notice in myself, from time to time, not infrequently in driving through a tunnel, a slight tendency to claustrophobia. Might anybody?) But the years were too riddled with rage and, as precocious adolescence approached, with instances of ecstasy, for despair to have found an unobstructed path.

The return to first grade after recovering from the automobile accident soon turned ominous. My teacher, Miss Somerville, whom I en-

joyed being around, kept moving me to different seats in her classroom
to mitigate the amount of disturbance I caused the other members of
the class with my inability to prevent myself, no matter how many vows
I made, from humming while I wrote and read. Eventually she asked
my mother to come to school and discuss skipping me up to second
grade. Miss Somerville protested that she liked to have me in her classroom but that she seemed unable to give me enough work to interest
me and keep me busy. (How does humming while working indicate
lack of interest? Periodic lack of interest in others, doubtless. But does
this deserve banishment?) This crisis must be marked by the time I was
taken to another room in the school and given some tests (that is what
I say now, but I cannot capture what I thought was happening then,
except that it was not at all unpleasant, and it was a change from the
classroom) by a woman and a man, with, oddly I thought, my mother
present. The tests involved answering a string of questions and doing
things with blocks, like fitting different shapes into their appropriate
spaces on a board, perhaps reading and drawing things. I said to the
two strangers afterward, "You have asked me a lot of questions. Now I
am going to ask you a question. What is the difference between a hill
and a pill?" They seemed surprised, and as I expected, they did not
know the answer, so I told them. "A hill goes up and a pill goes down."
I will hear my mother tell this story of my adventurousness more than
once. She always, so far as I recall, omitted the part after we left and
were walking home, when I told her that I did not think my question
was very good, since a hill goes both up and down. Was I being philosophical, or an intellectual prig?

I understood my mother to recur to that event when a few years
later, in Sacramento, a year or two before high school, I confessed helpless loneliness and asked her why the other kids didn't like me: "Is it
because I am younger than they are [by that time I had also skipped
fourth grade], or is it because I am Jewish?" Unfortunately, and no
doubt distressed, she accepted the question and gave it an answer. "It
is because you are younger." I don't mean that she gave the wrong
answer. "It is because you are Jewish" would have been equally mor-
tifying. Any answer would have accepted the implied assumption that
the other kids, as a body, in fact did not like me; I mean accepted the assumption that there was an uncorrectable, metaphysical mark upon me

that was unlikable. It was clear to me that she was deliberately avoiding the explanation that took the way of being Jewish. Evidently in her mind being young was something I would recover from in time. (Ah, but timing, Mother, as you knew in your bones, is everything.) And besides, isn't being young something I should be proud of, as she was proud of her precociousness as a professional musician? I knew she was proud of the fact that I was as it were ahead of myself in school—that desperately misguided source of pride and perpetual misery—whereas Jewishness was at best, in her eyes, nothing as such to cherish, except, critically, as the source of depth of soul within the rigor of many of the musical artists she most admired. But in my eyes either of these immovable explanations, youth or indelible religion, was a sentence of exile. It was true even of a perfectly decent American public high school of that period that one's fellow students constituted the totality of the world of the present and of the foreseeable future—nothing will change; no hierarchy of acceptance will be overturned.

My mother's guilt in response to my convulsive tears at her recourse to my relative youth was, on the occasion I recall, to say something close to "They told me you didn't belong in a regular school. But what could we do? We knew nothing. Atlanta had nothing. They talked about schools in the North, in New York, where you would find company and feel appreciated. But how were we supposed to send you to New York?" The moral was that I did not belong where I was and that while there was a place I did belong I could not get there. There was some strange consolation in the conjunction of these two pieces of bad news, but the logic of consolation, I knew with my mother's milk, is that you have always lost what you really wanted, or must imagine you wanted.

Yet in fact my mother's choice of explanation may have shown some discrimination. If anti-Semitism is a form of racism, there will be those whom nothing will soften. Whereas a difference in age may not only be outgrown (a promise of no interest to an eleven-year-old, for whom the idea of the year after next is of something a lifetime away) but be neutralized in the present by, let's say, talent. Not, of course, athletic talent, since a boy not yet twelve years old is not athletic competition for young men of fourteen (except perhaps with training in swimming, which was in any case out of the realm of possibility for me because of the early injury to my ear), a fact I had cause to be impressed by any and every day for years. (There would be certain comparatively exotic exceptions, like certain skills I acquired in table tennis and in bowling, but their compensatory roles, or consolatory measures, were as specialized as was the aggression they were able to stylize.) Late in my second year of high school, my musical confidence will intervene, as it were from outside the world, to alter the frozen architecture of esteem.

July 21, 2003

The intervention was some three years in preparation.

It happened this way. Louis Suskind was both my father's best friend and (apart from my father and me) my mother's greatest admirer. She would almost never play the piano at home for the entertainment of visitors. But when Louis Suskind visited Atlanta it was simply accepted that she would be playing for him and that the evening would begin with my playing whatever I happened to be working on. I think particularly of a time early in the second of our moves back to Atlanta. For me it was the year of my Bar Mitzvah and attending Boys High School (now, I learn, having merged with its adjacent Tech High School, it constitutes part of Henry Grady High); for my father it was a chance to keep us solvent by managing a liquor store in silent partnership with Bess's husband, who was using the advantage of a new law by the Georgia legislature legalizing the public sale of liquor to begin a large liquor distribution company. Louis Suskind was pleased on this visit by my progress and wanted me to name a present he could give me. He had, for example, given me the only bicycle I ever had growing up. (An irony of having received it early, still on Atlanta Avenue, when I was somewhat too small for it, is that I was still riding it seven years later when I was too big for it, that is, when it was two sizes smaller than the bicycles of my classmates, so that to keep up with them riding to and away from junior high school was no small feat.) I told him that I wanted to learn an instrument that provided me with company rather than locked me into the isolation of playing only the piano, and that I had set my heart on having a clarinet. Without hesitation he told me pick out an instrument to my liking and have the bill sent to him.

Largesse was his custom. Later on that visit, after my mother had played the Shultz-Evler recital expansion of the Blue Danube Waltz for him, he turned to me and said, "When you play the Shultz-Evler for me, I'll buy you a Buick." I did not for an instant doubt it. The clarinet, and its consequences, however, waylaid any further plans of mine for concentrating on the piano. Uncle Louis, as I called him, was richer than the other traveling salesmen—I gathered that he owned the company that he represented, which may explain why he came through town less often than the others. Also unlike them, he was not a card player and not a storyteller and he was from Providence, not New York. Only years after moving back to Cambridge would I learn that Providence, before and until some years after World War II, was a center for the manufacturing of sterling silverware. So it must have been platters and candelabra, perhaps brooches, bracelets, and necklaces that had first brought him to my father's door.

His build was slighter than that of the others, and his clothes fit him with a perfection the others did not affect, although he seemed more casual in them than the others did in theirs. His shirts were of a fabric I did not associate with men's shirts; I suppose they were silk; they were dark, not white or striped, and his ties might share the color of the shirts rather than contrast with them, whose cuffs were closed not with buttons but with thin oval silver cuff links. When his visits coincided with those of one or both of the Epstein brothers, there were still jokes, but the language was more careful and the jokes were not about women. Uncle Louis was the only one among the visiting salesmen invited to our house for dinner who had remained unmarried. (I might have divined this for myself since the others would from time to time mention their wives and children. But I am sure that my mother at some stage made this explicit for me.) Gifts for my mother also arrived after his visits, interpretable as expressions of gratitude for her hospitality. His giving gifts had the feel, as I interpret my memory of them, of paying his debts as he went along, and I constructed the idea of his life as one in which he craved an independence from the world that brought him what limited satisfactions the world offered. He was a serious man. But the gifts were too lavish, and too pertinent, to be understood simply as conventional gestures, as if they contained meaning that others were left to understand or free to miss. It seems increasingly clear to me now, in this recounting, weighing again my sense of the expectations aroused by Louis's visits and the preparations of particular dishes he appreciated from my mother's hands in addition to the musical evenings, that he and my mother, perhaps one can say, had an understanding, one whose hopelessness was part of its force.

There had been some talk of my father opening a new jewelry store backed by Louis Suskind, featuring his company's silverware. I had pieced together over the years the story of their having been partners in a large and successful such store in Miami in the 1920s, in the years before I was born, the only successful venture I knew of in which my father had ever taken part. That store had been destroyed in the Great Miami Hurricane of 1926. (The day it hit was September 17, as my son David has just found out for me on Google. So that is where my father was the day I was sixteen days old in Atlanta.) My father's description of the event, from the times I heard it (it was not often referred to), ended with his rushing from the store, through swirling water up to his waist, trying to catch up with showcases of watches and rings being carried into the sea. The angry gods of this ruin—I gather there was no insurance then against hurricanes in Florida—were succeeded by their brother gods of the Depression three years later, and the partnership was not revived. I do not remember whether there was a basis for my imagining that the thought, some twelve years later, of a new partnership, was designed to take us to Miami.

Plans along such lines of desire came to an end with a fresh calamity. Returning home one afternoon toward the end of the school year before high school, I entered, instead of an empty apartment, a crowded room containing several friends of my parents' and a number of men whom I only distantly recognized, if at all, standing around the so-called living room, which, in contrast to its aspect of conversation, was silent, except for the sound of a man sobbing, which on taking a further step I saw to be my father, rocking back and forth in an overstuffed chair, holding with both hands a wet handkerchief over his face. My mother quickly appeared to say to me, in agitation but under her breath, "Louis Suskind passed away." As I was unable to respond, she added: "He walked out at night in a cold rain after a steam bath and caught pneumonia." This was not the first time I had heard of such a death to a man still in his forties, or barely out of them. Without the implied elegance of a steam bath, it was how my mother's beloved father was said to have been permanently weakened.

The contemporary progress of this autobiographical adventure has reached some months beyond the date of this entry. (Today's date is December 18, 2003.) I return for the moment to this point in order to plot the immediate trail of coming into possession of a clarinet from its obscure consequences in Atlanta to its clarity in Sacramento on our return there the next year. This may take more than one day of writing. The bargain I made with myself in beginning these autobiographical reflections was that I would write always beginning with specific memories, starting with the earliest, however indecisive or inchoate an instance may seem, and continue a segment only so far as that initial impulse to expression persisted. Without my attempting to measure how closely I have actually been adhering to this bargain, it is what got me started after many failures to enter into the phantasmagoria of presentations of my past. Noting the date of the present antichronological entry is meant not only to give me freedom to explore various degrees of preparation in allowing the story or stories to continue, but is also meant, as my overall progress in my depicted age is consistently reaching that of high school, to register that the ratio of memory to expression, or its economy, is changing. Memories, having on the whole reached my twelfth year, are becoming less mysterious in their presentation, and the impulse is less to decipher the surroundings of their isolated occurrences than to follow links between events that I feel I can in principle tell infinitely, perhaps to the point of extinction.

The obvious point in dating the times of writing was to keep separate the two necessary temporal registers in a narrative, the time of a depicted sequence of events and the time (or place/time) of depicting them. Formally this portrays the fundamental importance granted to the time and context of utterance in the work of Austin and of the later Wittgenstein that has meant so much to me. My stress on the time, or time and place, of depiction is meant to capture what Austin means in tirelessly demanding the context (he would often call this the story) of an utterance and what Wittgenstein means by repeatedly asking to whom an utterance is made. When Wittgenstein asks, "How is *telling* done?" he is in effect asking how it is that saying something, speaking, is done; how it is that someone is in a position to *be* told something. This turns out to be a good question. At what time and place?

As in dating the entries in recording a dream—if Freud is right that dreams link to the residual psychic material of the day before the sleep of that dream, to permit that sleep—the point of dating entries of conscious thought, of marking the separation of registering thoughts, is its provision of a way to refuse the already formed significance that more unified narratives, so many of which I have told or heard in my life, would have me accept. Put otherwise, only in defeating such significance is my interest in telling my story graspable, alive for me. Put still otherwise, so much of what has formed me has been not events but precisely the uneventful, the nothing, the unnoted, that is happening, the coloration or camouflage of the everyday. The extraordinariness of what we accept as ordinary does not manifest its power over us until we are conscious at the same time of the ordinariness of the extraordinary. A stone on which this coupling breaks we might call a miracle or a holocaust, a departure from and within the ordinary that is not merely extraordinary, but irreversibly traumatic. (There may then be such a phenomenon as a retrospective trauma.)

Heidegger's linking the takeover, as it were, of the ordinary by what he perceives as the technological does not seem to me to capture the experience of this break. Nor does it prove possible for me to quell consistently the surmise that the link is designed precisely to miss this, specifically to absorb Nazism, as Heidegger is reliably reported to have done, by casting it as an event to be comprehended along with the modern technology of the food industry and Stalin's starvation of the Hungarian kulaks. Say that we have in some way to miss the particular experience of Nazism in order to go on with our lives. Then the question, in all soberness, is how we can go on. Or isn't it rather how it happens that we do go on. Since "going on" is fundamental in both Wittgenstein's and Heidegger's sense of the human, it is no wonder that I had to write, as if to test whether I might publish a first book, a response to Beckett's *Endgame*, with its questions: Do we go on? Who is to play? Whose turn is it? One of the most gifted students of philosophy and theology I have encountered, a young German woman, said essentially the following words to me early in our conversations: "I love my grandparents. I know that my grandparents loved Hitler, and I cannot think of them as monsters. Does this make me a monster?" Is moral philosophy responsible for responding to such a question?

Another economy of exposition is also beginning to change, namely, between the various pasts that arise and the continuity of the process of composing these pasts in relation to other pasts and to this and other presents. To register this economy was, I soon came to see, a further reason for dating the time of writing, apart from simply wanting separate entries of any resultant lengths. But now that the full draft of this manuscript, as of the date of returning to this segment, has in its historical current reached the point at which I am about to enter the university at Berkeley, I have felt the need to go back over the material, both to remember its successions and to find where clarifications and more background and points of reference will help an interested reader continue with it; it will not be possible to note and date each of even the substantial elaborations I enter. The supplementary bargain I am making with myself is that no change will be entered that is not motivated by, and can become continuous with, an entry already in place. To link entries with the time of writing is so to speak a formal consequence, beyond let us say, the allegorical occasion of opening my text with the procedure of catheterization. (The point of confessing that I was as conscious of the allegorical turn as well as the reader will have been is to remind us both that, whatever ineptness I have to put up with in myself, one of them is not the writing of an inept novel.)

During the period in Atlanta that will contain Louis Suskind's death, my mother had returned to her career (perhaps she would simply have described it as returning to playing the piano commercially), this time as part of the orchestra of the dominant radio station in town. (Sacramento was not a large enough city for one of its radio stations ever to have supported a resident orchestra.) From the clarinet player in the orchestra she found the name of a teacher for me, who accompanied me to pick out an instrument at the large music store a few blocks uptown from my father's liquor store. I had known the music store from my trips there to buy a new piece I would have graduated to in my piano lessons, each time passing from the gaudy displays of sheet music for recent hits through the arrays of drums and the shining saxophones and trumpets and trombones along the reaches of the store. The clarinet I ended up with was, if not the best, one that came with

a case whose plush lining conveyed an array of glistening shades between dark orange and purple that in my excitement rivaled—though
I lacked the resources to know it then—my sense of Proust's notations
of the horizon of a late summer sky against the sea in conjunction with
the glistening contents of a child's bedpan.

There is a reason I would not have asked my parents for the instrument. My father was in the habit not of giving me presents but of
withholding presents others had brought or sent me until I had done
something he regarded as deserving a present. My mother was, I assumed out of fear or confusion rather than agreement, unable to contest
this behavior.

The clarinet teacher showed me how to form the mouth in order
to produce intelligible sounds out of the instrument, but he and I generally failed to hit it off, and I largely taught myself to play the instrument
by working through an illustrated handbook that evidently came with
it. The fingering was for the most part rational; I mean that for the most
part lower and higher pitches translated consistently into a direction in
which more or fewer fingers came into play. It was clear at once that the
clarinet was going to do for me what the piano would, so far as I could
see, never do. I would be able to read the single notes of clarinet parts
as fluently as my mother could read music at the piano (something I
despaired of ever learning to do, something I felt indeed was a mystery
that could not be learned), and it would thereby provide companionship. By the end of the summer, as I entered Boys High, I was good
enough at the instrument to merge my playing within the large clarinet
section of the marching band, one of whose regular obligations was to
appear at the Friday night high school football games, one of the two
pleasurable or at least communal activities I found for myself in those
months of my life. The other such activity was bowling duck pins on
Sunday afternoons, sometimes with two or three boys with whom I had
coincided in the preparations for our Bar Mitzvahs. I had a knack for
the game, and I added some practice to improve my skill by bowling a
line or two alone on Saturday afternoons after my piano lesson. These
practices took place at the (surprisingly to me) large set of bowling alleys
on one of the upper stories in the same building as the studio of my then
piano teacher, who proved to be my last, a location that was (as I reconstruct the architecture) also either the same building, or the one flush

with it, that housed the plush but comparatively small Loew's Grand Theater (which nevertheless would host that year the extravagant world premiere in Atlanta of *Gone with the Wind*, its facade transformed into a remote but clear facsimile of the facade of Scarlett's plantation Tara)— all this field for activity on Peachtree Street halfway between the music store and my father's liquor store.

After some weeks of this routine an older boy I recognized as from Boys High came over to my lane and asked to join me. He appeared to me somehow too old for high school, perhaps because of his heavy upper body and his dark rough face with indistinct, collapsed features, reinforced by the conviction I developed that he lived alone, a conviction that started with his offering to drive me home when our games together had run somewhat late, and surmising that the large, not new, convertible car he was driving was evidently his own—the disarray of possessions on the back seat and floor were not the effluvia of a family car. It turned out that he was on the school's bowling team, an organization until then unknown to me, and he asked me to try out for it, since the team was being reorganized for the spring semester.

The high school bowling teams around the city competed against each other every Monday afternoon after school, which provided not only an admirable alternative once a week to my returning home to an empty apartment but also something for which I was oddly rewarded. The high school bowling matchups and team scores were reported in the *Atlanta Journal* on Tuesdays, amid the blizzard of numbers covering spread pages containing the latest scores in all sports, national and local, that the paper deemed worthy of noting. The winning teams and the highest scores of the day, for each of the high school bowling sets played on Monday, were reported in small but bold type along with the name of the high scorers. This proved to include my name often enough so that I became rather accustomed to open the paper to the sports results to check that the name was there when it was due. The members of our team received medals at the end of the season. It was perhaps not the final evidence of fame that I envisioned for myself, but for that spring it served as an unanticipated, and however peculiar, continuous link to a shared reality. Something in my behavior proved to cast a shadow others could perceive.

There came to be a further, somewhat illicit tinge to my bowling

adventure. The older boy and I, after some weeks of our Saturday afternoon practices together, were invited by some older men to join their
open game played for money. Each player put up a quarter (a coin that
I could still use then to purchase a sandwich at a café counter but is now
used mostly to purchase twenty minutes on a downtown Boston parking meter), and there were generally six players in the game, on adjoining alleys, so the winner of a game was ahead a dollar and a quarter.
(I've forgotten who paid for the use of the pair of alleys, but even if that
came out of the betting pool, the fee could not have been more then
twenty or thirty cents a game for the pair.) After six or seven Saturdays
I had amassed twelve dollars in winnings, more cash that unarguably
belonged to me, in 1939, than I had ever held in my hand or had any
rational private use for—as if I could only conceive of spending it all
at once or not at all. I felt it was not really mine, and, having no bank
account of my own (at least none I had the use of), I had nothing to
do with it but hide it. I stopped going to the Saturday bowling games
and after some further weeks showed the money to my mother. She
was reassuring about my confusion, but unhelpful about why I felt so
guilty (whether anticipating consequences from the police or from rival
criminals was unclear), and there was no instruction forthcoming about
whether to open a bank account for it or to make myself a budget or to
translate the ill-gotten gains into presents for others or for myself.

Something I did not tell my mother concerned that piano teacher
and the reason I stopped practicing for my lessons. His studio was comfortable, with a number of glamorous black-and-white publicity photographs, of former students of his it emerged, in frames on a long table,
with inscriptions some of which were written in white ink, which I had
never seen before. He was slight and very short and walked with two
crutches of the kind that ended not at the armpit but above the elbow,
the kind you knew were not going to become souvenirs after a period of
healing. It must have been a month or so into my lessons with him that
I felt enough at home there to remark on the comfort of the room. He
asked if I would like to see the rest of his apartment. Moving through a
room that was a kitchen, but with the sink and counters lowered so as
almost to suggest part of a child's playhouse, we entered a smallish room
with apparently nothing in it but walls of drawers of different sizes fitted

with large white porcelain knobs. After using some of these to pull open
a number of drawers that contained neatly arranged sweaters or shirts
or socks or underclothes, he pulled open what proved to be a door disguised as the surface of four or five large drawers to reveal a bathroom,
and another opening onto a closet with racks again lowered, and, for
a finale, at the farthest wall, pulled down most of the lower part of the
wall which became a fully made-up bed, the outer edge supported by
two short wooden legs that had somehow been concealed within the
structure. "I have everything I need here. A man comes in to clean and
to bring me supplies. I rarely go out." Marveling at what this life must
be, I followed him back to the piano to start my lesson. He sat beside me
on the bench. I had got well into my piece (the Mozart D Minor Piano
Concerto) when he reached under my arms and unerringly, through my
pants, squeezed my penis, whose nervous erection (which I think I was
until then not conscious of) evidently made itself obvious despite my
clothes. He asked: "What have I got?" I neither answered nor moved.
My memory is that we actually finished the lesson. I may have gone
back two or three times, or pretended to my parents to continue going,
not being willing to tell them about this incident, or to think what it
was I might tell them to warrant never going back to the lessons. But,
even ignoring my general lack of interest in what this teacher had to say
about music, my new alarm and amazement at this man's mysterious
life and intentions froze the situation. Whenever images of that episode
have occurred to me, I have asked myself what an appropriate response
to his advances might have been. What I remember feeling was not
exactly fear, not exactly anger, not exactly guilt, not exactly pity. That
there was a right to outrage did not occur to me. Perhaps this is an instance that prompts one to ask whether English lacks a word here. But
where exactly is here? Is that the same question? Or have I answered
that question?

When, as I expected, the teacher phoned my mother, and told her
that I had not been appearing and anyway that he had been going to
suggest that I was not interested in further improving my piano skills,
I merely pretended that I couldn't concentrate on the piano for the
moment and wanted to spend my time working at the clarinet. I was
relieved, but perplexed, that this ended the matter. It seems that I was
more mysterious than ever to my parents.

July 24, 2003

The catheterization of my heart was performed on July 22 with a result that was neither the most frightening nor the least. Open-heart surgery was not required, but repairs were considered necessary to several partially blocked arteries, in the form of three so-called stents, or mesh metal tubes, which were put in place to keep open, even I gathered to rejoin, the newly opened vessels. Some twenty-four hours after this experience, during which I was shown X-rays of the arterial pattern of my heart and asked, while drugged but awake on the operating table, to approve the process of repairing its damage—an experience, I judged, hardly less strange than traveling to Mars—I walked out of the hospital quite confidently under my own powers.

Not the least bizarre moment of the brief hours in the darkened space capsule disguised as an operating room was provided by the narration of results by the surgeon (spoken of by a series of nurses and assistants of various kinds as a favorite virtuoso of this procedure) immediately at the conclusion of the procedure, while pointing to an X-ray of my heart taken at the outset. I do not remember how I was propped or how the transparency was lowered and lighted so that I could examine it. "As you remember there are three breaks or blockages in the arteries that needed, and could receive, repair. The first and the second posed no special problems. When we turned to the third, however, the first stent we tried was too small. The second we tried was still too small. But we found that we had one of the still larger size left in stock. It worked. You're lucky this is Tuesday. By the end of the week we sometimes run out of these large sizes, especially the new medicated ones." I was being told that from the normal management or the conventional economies of a famous hospital, in a city famous for its hospitals, it followed that a recurrent, predictable emergency, unrelated to medical competence (not perhaps unrelated to community health plans), might have resulted either in my not having the principal third of my indicated treatment completed, or else having it completed with inferior materials. The concept of luck does not quite seem to grasp the situation.

I see that a few days before describing this experience I had undertaken to explain my claim that the intervention of a new form taken by my musical talent served to rescue me from an intolerable social impasse, a conviction held in place by various sources of confirmation that I belonged in no place that I had so far conceived as some place in which for me to exist. Fantasies of relief were woven, as around a mesh tube, around the event of coming into possession of my clarinet. When I was not practicing the instrument, I was listening obsessively to recordings of the Benny Goodman and the Artie Shaw bands, memorizing and copying down what solos of theirs I felt I could best negotiate, and drawing various configurations of the kind of decorated music stands, with my initials on them indicating the band's leader, used by all the big bands visible in movies of the period, extending to larger and larger imaginary bands on variously deployed platforms. When I would first read Freud's answer to what men want of their lives—the admiration of men and the love of women, or you might say, rescue from a life of unshareable orgasm—I might well have recalled, I hope with some tenderness, my bursting hopes for wings with which to express myself in the showy form they took of privilege in a perfectly expressive society of artistry.

The fantasies in fact came as close as most of this caliber to proving practical. But the scope for this realization was not visible from my thirteen-year-old experience in Atlanta. At the end of a second year at the liquor store, an experience that had evidently soured, my father received an offer from his Sacramento brother to set him up in his own pawnshop—a promising location was opening and Uncle Morris had more stock in his own store than he could handle. We arrived back there, for the fifth, and what would prove to be the last leg, of these continental crossings, at the end of the summer of 1940, just after my fourteenth birthday.

Soon after entering the McClatchey High School, I found that the fairy godmother responsible for the well-being of the school's extracurricular activities presented me (not exactly with a formal ball to attend, but) with something I thought immeasurably better than attending a ball, namely, with the dance band essential to the existence of the ball. But an invitation to join the high school dance band, superbly named the McClatchey Melodiers, was still two large steps away. First, I had to take my clarinet playing to another level; second, I would have to become equally accomplished playing the saxophone. My ability to sight-read on the clarinet with confidence got me an invitation into the school orchestra to play second clarinet. It was clear that the older boy playing first clarinet—Jack Litch, who would become a friend—produced a tone patently more convincing and more subtle than mine, and I asked him to introduce me to his teacher.

What I learned from that teacher within a matter of a month, about producing the classical tone of clarinet playing, and more generally about breathing in woodwind playing, and about how to choose more appropriate reeds, enabled me to play consistently the range of the instrument with an approximation of the sound familiar to me from what little I had then listened to attentively of symphonic music, which mostly meant to me to learn how to get a certain richness of tone without using the vibrato that, in the uses of Goodman and Shaw, had seemed to me essential to the glamour of the instrument. But the fluency I wanted was not going to be much furthered, I felt, from this teacher both because he was not an accomplished player of the instrument and because I felt more in command of the theory and life of music than he had reached and become able to communicate, stuck in his studio above the music store in Sacramento as other grown-ups of my acquaintance were stuck in other stores. My ability to learn from myself proved to be enough to support my visions then.

Acquiring comparable facility playing saxophone should not, I figured, on the basis of half an hour's experience of the instrument in consultation with a member of the high school marching band, require much more accomplishment than coming into possession of the instrument, since the embouchure of the clarinet was, initially if not ultimately, transferable to the mouthpiece and single reed of the saxophone (not the other way around—the more precise and firmer control demanded by the clarinet was not prepared for by the laxer sufficiencies of the saxophone; and the fingering, up to a point, was in several ways simpler). I asked my uncle Morris to borrow the C-melody saxophone—an already fully outmoded member of the family of saxophones, though I was as yet only vaguely aware of this—that was the only saxophone unredeemed by its pawner, and was hence for sale in his pawnshop. (How either of us knew this identification of the saxophone completely escapes me; I suppose it was identified as such by its pawner and duly entered on the pawn ticket.) I had been offered several dollars by members of the high school dance band to play dinner and dance music the next night for some gathering organized by the parents of one of them, and no one in the band beyond the pianist and the drummer and one trumpet player were, for some reason, free or willing to accept the engagement, and that felt skimpy to them. I was quite irrationally confident that one day's familiarization with the saxophone would stand me in good enough stead to participate. It happened that I was right, or right enough, and moreover the C-melody instrument was by fool chance the only saxophone that would have served, since the music the ones responsible for this musical date brought along had no specific saxophone parts. With a C-melody saxophone I could play a violin part, or read from the piano part over the pianist's shoulder. All the modern saxophones were "tuned" in either E-flat (the alto and the baritone) or in B-flat (the tenor and the soprano). (This means that the length and continuous expansion of the slender cone formed into the various sizes and shapes of saxophones are measured so that the stopping of the holes yielding what is named C on every saxophone yields the sound not of the so-called concert pitch of C—as the piano and [other] stringed instruments do, and, it happens, flutes and oboes do but English horns do not—but instead sounds B-flat on a B-flat instrument and E-flat on an E-flat instrument. A very experienced player can compensate for this by "transposing" what he or she is playing into, one can say, a different key from the one there in the writing before his or her eyes. I was far from that ability then, but there would come a time when having acquired that ability had a decisive effect on my life.) The good angel who had provided me with that C-melody saxophone that night—yielding the sound of C when I fingered C, and D when I fingered D, and so forth, hence enabled me to join in an evening of profitable music making—if he or she had loved music, would have prayed to high heaven to be struck deaf through those unearthly hours.

But joining the band more particularly meant choosing whether to buy and improve my tone and learn the modern idiom either of an alto or of a tenor saxophone. Without entering into the prudence of finding out which of these the school dance band needed more urgently, I chose the alto on completely independent grounds—I might say artistic grounds, but they were also in a clear sense deeply prudential. I already knew enough to be fascinated by comparing the undeniable geniuses of tenor saxophone playing of the years around 1940 (Lester

Young, Ben Webster, and Coleman Hawkins) and not to be outclassed,
even in fantasy, before drawing a serious breath to play, I chose so as
to avoid them. (Charlie Parker's alto saxophone was several years in
the future.) Moreover, I had divined that playing lead alto in a swing
band, which I had no doubt I would do, required general musicianship
more than the ability to improvise, in which I was all but completely
untested.

I am surprised to find that I have forgotten the details of the route
by which I acquired an alto saxophone. Recalling the initial look of it
in its case, on its side, in a golden sleep, takes over the moment. I know
that it appeared after a few months of that last recoil to Sacramento,
soon after the episode with the C-melody relic, since by the beginning
of the spring semester early in 1941 I had joined the school dance band
playing lead alto. This was too soon for my parents to have come into
enough money, after the expenses of another long journey and before
the new store had begun establishing itself, to have produced such a
thing. But it was just past Christmas, and my memory is that I had
not received a present from my parents for my Bar Mitzvah (but the
question of giving or the absence of giving presents in our basic family,
and the companion question of where necessaries should be bought,
are their own subjects) and, I have to speculate, my spending every
night in my room imitating and transcribing for hours the clarinet improvisations from Goodman and Shaw recordings worked to convince
my father of my seriousness about this new enterprise, or anyway to
soften him. (It occurs to me now that the death of Louis Suskind may
somehow have helped prepare moments of softening toward me. If I do
not consider that my mother had a hand in this it is because I find that I
am not confident about imagining discussions between my mother and
father, especially ones that would be initiated by her. Exchanges between them in my hearing, namely, when my mother was not silent and
my father not enraged, took the form characteristically of judgments
about friends or family members of theirs.) But there it was, opened on
the dining room table as my father came home one winter night from
the store, saying something about Uncle Morris wanting to help. (I had
worked during the previous summer in Morris's pawnshop, during the
only time my father had employed a salesman in his store, a former
employee of Uncle Morris's. My services were necessary but primitive,

mostly sweeping the floors, cleaning the glass showcases, polishing the gold and silver objects for sale that seemed so easily to lose their glitter; and, a task of a certain interest if not much skill, fitting new plastic crystals, replacing the dull or scratched ones, over the face of the railroad watches that were so common among unredeemed pawned things put out for sale, in a store four or five blocks from Sacramento's active railroad station.) If this gleaming saxophone had been another pawn pledge, it was to my eye indistinguishable from a pure deliverance from the mint. I must have said around our apartment—but without supposing that it would have meant anything very specific to my father, and perhaps not perfectly specific even to my mother—that I needed (not simply wanted, nor desired, nor craved, which were irrelevant) an alto. But how did he, or Morris, know that *this* was an alto?

The band was the foundation of our high school institution known as the Wednesday Noon Dance, held each week on the basketball floor of the school's gymnasium, heavily attended throughout the ranks and clusters of the student body, though dominated by the senior athletes, and attended as well by a number of men and women teachers, who I suppose were the chaperons or sponsors of the institution. Two or three of the football or basketball players achieved a mythical aura by asking a young woman teacher to dance, and certain girls would know that their abilities on the dance floor served to level the playing field in the competitions with girls who were prettier or classier but squarer. The band was also the anchor of the theatrical extravaganza of song, dance, and skit that marked the end of the school year. The institution of the student dance band, as of any other organized extracurricular activity, had to be sponsored by a faculty member, in our case Mr. Guidera, called Joe by the members of the band, whose subject was mathematics. (Since his classes were my favorites, and I was especially good at algebra and geometry, he and I were on the best of terms.) I had turned fifteen at the beginning of my second year in that school, and just after Pearl Harbor a few months later, Joe Guidera was drafted into the army. Among the consequences of the official beginning of America's entry into World War II, the swinging McClatchey Melodiers were scheduled to be disbanded—no more Noon Dances, no more year-end theatrical.

We learned about this only when the band had assembled for a scheduled practice session as school resumed after Christmas vacation, in January, and Joe did not appear. He had evidently had too much on his mind to allow him to take explicit leave of us, and I do not remember who informed us officially that day that we did not exist. What I remember is saying to the members of the band that we did exist, that we had another year together before any of us would be drafted. I proposed to take over the role of rehearsing the band and become its leader and, if possible, book dates for us. The proposal was immediately agreed to, as if it was the obvious course to take, and we went forward with the rehearsal. The school administration, given the general air of emergency, saw fit to allow the rules about faculty sponsorship to lapse in this instance, and the band's life was continued on its regular course, including the weekly dances and the year-end theatrical. Beyond this normal schedule, we were hired to play for the Junior Prom and the Senior Ball and, as word spread, almost every weekend we were profitably engaged by some social group originating in the high school, or by a group with which individuals among our schoolmates were connected.

I was a made man. No student had ever been the leader of the band. The social, or say, secondary, gains were incalculable. The losses were no less significant, but somewhat less obvious. One way to figure the losses is to admit that the band, while enjoyably enthusiastic, was not wonderful. There was at least one weakness in each section, so a full, swinging sound was never really sustainable. I and one other player (who went on to play saxophone professionally) could have found work in a much better band (had we been free and there had been such a band left functioning in that small town then). This meant that the band played consistently beneath or against my aspirations, or else I strained to imagine that we sounded better than we did.

But among its extraordinary powers it led, directly if accidentally, to the greatest source of musical inspiration opened to me by my sojourn as a saxophonist. The high school band's bass player, John Hebert, was one of the few black students in the school (not perhaps as few as there were Jewish students). In late 1941, Hebert told me that a large band was being formed to play the music of a composer and arranger who had moved to Sacramento to work as a technician at one of the new air force bases. His recommendation had been accepted to ask me to sit in at their next rehearsal on Sunday morning as lead alto, since the player they began with in that role had not worked out. It would turn out that almost all of this band's members—there would prove to be only one other white person besides myself—were drawn from that migrant population, attracted by the possibility of high pay and a job classified to make them exempt from military conscription. The address of the house we were to rehearse in was close to the downtown district, but in a section of town, not notably different in aspect from many others I knew, that I did not remember encountering previously. The rooms of the wooden house were small, and the sound of instruments warming up led me immediately to it. What were evidently the living room and dining room were filled with music stands and adult black men assembling and tuning their instruments, or setting up music stands and arranging chairs, all well into their twenties, a generation, it seemed, except for Hebert, older than I. Harrel Wiley, the composer and leader, a tall man with a short beard, greeted me, introduced me to his wife, and pointed out his two small children in the next room.

Most professional swing bands then contained four saxophones—this one was scored for five; most contained three trumpets and two trombones—this one was scored for four each. We had almost to huddle together to fit into the house. Wiley handed out parts to each of us of a piece he had just finished, copied out in pencil. When he counted off the tempo for a downbeat the ensuing force of sound was so strong that I feared the house could not withstand it, and I was so thrilled by it that I felt I could barely continue playing. After a minute or two, Wiley, playing tenor saxophone next to me, stopped us to give us tips about the music. The other players were laughing and muttering with pleasure. The saxophone section of a swing band, playing as a group, sets the general continuity or basis of the sound; the brass section dominates the tuttis for climactic passages, and provides—apart from solos—contrasts and punctuations of color and rhythm. So the lead alto in such a band is perpetually responsible for maintaining the drive of the music. Everything we played that morning (a substantial sample of everything we would ever play) was an original composition of Wiley's, not simply an arrangement; and the ideas were more advanced than any I had heard outside of the Ellington band. One of our tunes, and riffs from others, to this day from time to time goes through my head. After the rehearsal, Wiley asked me if I wanted to join the band. My artistic universe shifted.

Essentially all we did was rehearse, which is to say, play for our pleasure. Being an integrated band (the guitar player was also white, but he was often absent), no auditorium we knew of in Sacramento would agree to rent their space to us. The craziness of the fact that this was a national condition, that a large segment of the musical genius of the country, some of it among the most famous, found nonmusical obstacles in the way of reaching a large segment of those who craved to hear it, had not, at my age of fifteen, yet broken over me. Late in the spring the Scottish Rite organization rented their auditorium (anyway a large room with a stage and no fixed rows of seats) to us. There were so many people, largely black, who attended our evening of music, that even if they had wanted to dance there was eventually little room in which to move freely. People on the whole stood and listened. I did not know how word of what had become a concert had circulated.

The experience of belonging to that group remains an image for me, even a realization, of a world adjacent (in Thoreau's apparently simpler term, it was next) to the world I mostly converse with, one that provides an essential value to me of the world I am known to inhabit. That next world does, I think it is true to say, sometimes fail me; but oftener I fail it, when through depression or distraction I reject it; then it vanishes, like a metaphysical object.

After the concert the basket of donations made at the door was counted. Subtracting the heavy rent for the auditorium, enough was left for each member of the band to take away a token sum to signal participation in the event. We did this once more later in the spring, but it was not a basis on which to keep the band together.

July 25, 2003

My high school band averted the perplexity it would present for me to invite a young woman roughly a generation older than I (more specifically, a bit more than two years older) to the annual dances, a perplexity compounded, especially in the American West, by lacking a car, or a friend with a car, to take her in; or the humiliation of not at- tending, or of attending the dance alone (I don't know if that was done), if indeed these were humiliations—a state of unknowing as painful as the facts it did not grasp. I also felt the exasperated, enforced silence in not wanting it known that I preferred not to participate in voluntary social events, that to attend was to be defeated. Leading the band annulled this painful dilemma at the first downbeat. I did not attend the dance; I was the dance. I was present because I belonged there before anyone was in attendance; my existence was lucid, justified. The profound, logical cost of leading the band was that I did not dance. The dance will not happen without me, but I was not invited to it; I was not among those for whose honor and pleasure it is held. The music was not played for me—except in those instances when, in my disdain, I knew that I was playing better than anyone else present would know, hence in a sense playing for myself, perhaps in a way that made no contribution to the communal effort. What, then, would it be like if the best I could propose came to be recognized as essential to some such effort?

Coming back to this place in my text now twenty-five months after its being written, to do some late editing, I report a delicious cautionary tale printed in a recent letter to the *London Review of Books*. (I omit the dialect in which it was finely told.) A young miner in the north of England became enamored of classical music and would whistle snatches of it as he went to work. An older miner provided him with a further education: "You ought not to whistle Beethoven when you go into the mine. You hear the whole orchestra when you whistle. What the rest of us hear is only you whistling."

I adduce an unlovely, and not perfectly precise, version of such a fable manifested in an incident from the year before leaving for Sacramento and coming to lead the band at McClatchey High, at the site of my Atlanta high school athletic field. The Travises had invited a nephew of theirs from New York to spend Christmas vacation with them in Atlanta, a young man a couple of years older than I (that would at the time make him sixteen or seventeen, about the age of my older cousin Ted, Aunt Ida's older son), billed as what he proved himself to think of himself as being, namely, omniprecocious. He certainly spoke faster than anyone else I had ever met, and persistently strewed his conversation, or monologues, with names (I gathered of writers and sports figures) most of which meant nothing to me. He also struck me as physically more developed—he walked faster than others roughly his age that I knew, and rose higher on his toes than others as he walked.

Ted had evidently invited this young man to a party held by Ted's Jewish fraternity, and the young man in the course of the party offered to distinguish New York Jews from Southern Jews by betting that he could score a touchdown against any eleven of these fraternity brothers by himself using only a center and one blocker. Ted invited me to witness the event, on a field at the high school across the park from my house. Two things were obvious on seeing the sides line up, so to speak. The visitor from New York appeared bigger and stronger and faster than any one of the opposition; any two of them would have a hard time stopping him if he got into the open. Conceivably he could ran fast enough to one side to spread the line and find an opening. I felt sympathy enough with one deranged enough to make such a bet on his private powers that I fleetingly hoped he might succeed. A professional player could do this against children; a grown-up movie character could do it against grown-up movie characters. The visitor was uninterestingly brought down at or behind the line of scrimmage four times. What I learned from this antispectacle was that nothing should be learned from it, a moral all too familiar in my life.

The former tale reveals the beauty and the limitation of whistling. The latter exhibits the folly of supposing that no one else knows what whistling can be. I can readily imagine that someone will think my story remembering our sound in Wiley's arrangements for his black band, as it were invoking comparison with the Basie band of that era, belongs on the side of the delusional. I have to say that on somber reflection I do not really or fully believe that. I place it among those experiences of my life about which I am moved to say: I know what I know.

July 26, 2003

A sequence of musical accomplishments that kept my head above water—meaning ones that allowed a respite from a society in which I had no expected, and so far as I could tell, no definably desired place of existence (without confirming me in a fixed view of the fault to be assigned for this misfit)—does not account for the intensity of the need I felt for such a respite. To gauge that need a little I have to go back yet again to the early move to the north side of Atlanta. That will give me further bearings from which to assess my attempts to imagine leaving the house on Atlanta Avenue. I have said we left it, but to imagine leaving it, forgoing it, is something else. The number of times I continue to think of it convinces me that I have no more expected to recover from its loss than I have expected the misshapen canal of my left ear to recover itself.

I haven't talked about the other children on Atlanta Avenue: about Ragolda Jacobs, from whose driveway, showing off mostly to her perhaps, I ran after the ball in the street; or about Jake, whose epileptic "fits" the rest of us children all knew how to protect him from, never shouting at him to wake up when the center of his eyes rolled up under their lids, even when one came over him as he was walking along the top of a fence, upon which we simply silently followed him on both sides to catch him if he fell; nor about Herman, who laced his talk with exclamations of "fucks," about which he knew pretty much what I knew, that it had to do with our behinds, but impossibly, since nothing could fit there, except, unhappily, enema nozzles. My mother didn't seem to know what he meant either, any more than she knew why babies were born only to people who were married. When I asked her this puzzler she replied, "Nature takes care of that."

There are three events I think of as going together from my experience of first and second grade, before moving across to the north side of town, occurring, as if within the same days, outside the school building, not within its chambers of scholarship, but also not beyond its powers of instruction.

First, there was my coming upon a small group of older children during recess period gathered around the back entrance of the school, where a light fixture over the door had been removed and open electrical wires were hanging down from an irregular opening in the brick facade. A thin but forceful boy standing on the balustrade of the stone stairs was holding on to the wires with one hand and with the other reached down to me. As I took his hand, I felt muffled, repeated jolts of electricity pound into my body and it took some seconds before I came to myself sufficiently to let go of his hand—unless, as I now sense the possibility, or likelihood, he had held on to my hand too tightly for me to choose an end to the electrical transmission. My speechlessness was greeted with laughter by the small circle of onlookers.

A second event was prepared when Miss Somerville announced to the class that Stanley—who would be leaving us for the second grade—was the only one whose mother had become a new member of the PTA, when she attended its meeting yesterday afternoon. So, as promised, Stanley will now be rewarded with the promised prize of being given a free recess. I fought with my mind to put together this consequence with my having mentioned to my mother, at some dim time since I returned to school after my convalescence from being struck by the automobile, this prize of a free recess, knowing essentially nothing about what the PTA was or did and having no reason to believe that my mother could be free to join it or attend its meeting, or would have any formable interest in joining or attending, if indeed she herself might know what the PTA was. At this distance I recognize that playing two stage shows (was it—and three on Saturdays?) a day could leave periods of perhaps as much as two hours free between shows, when the movie and the cartoons and the newsreels were running. Whimsically, or conceivably guilt-stricken at the very irrelevance of my implied plea to take an interest in my bewilderment at what was happening at school, my mother had found herself at this particular Parent-Teacher Association meeting.

No doubt the rest of the class was as surprised as I was, observing my departure to enjoy my prize of a free, and as it turned out, solitary, hence profoundly irrelevant, recess. It was a gray, rather cold day, and I wandered toward the formidable set of swings, made (anyway most of them seemed to be made) to accommodate children twice my age and size. At one end of the set there was a ladder leading up to a slide at the top, the foot of the slide resting on its support in a sand box. This time, however, slightly shivering, contemplating doubtless how to make the most of my chance for unmonitored adventure, I decided after climbing to the top of the ladder not to continue onto the slide but, moving in the opposite direction, to try getting down from this considerable height by sliding one hand along the top of the high metal crossbeam of the swings and then the other to meet it, and now hanging free, inch my way to the vertical metal pole anchoring this end of the structure straight down into the ground. It took me numbers of false terrified starts after getting both hands onto the high beam, which was too large for me to close my fingers around so that I would have to hang essentially by my fingertips, to find the will to let my feet hang clear of the ladder and start the sliding of hands toward the vertical pole. After several slides of each hand, first away then toward each other, my feet touched the far vertical pole, and as I managed to clasp it and lock my legs around it, I flung the top of my body against the pole, hugging it to myself, and slid swiftly to earth. I was shivering more than ever although I felt more than warm. I had aroused myself to a pitch that anyone within a sizeable circle could discern from the bulge at the front of my short pants.

The third event I take away from that first grade of grammar school is one whose shame is perhaps even clearer to me now than the memories are of the electrical jolts and the sexual arousal of the events of the high swings at the far edge of the playground. I had been fasci- nated by the skill and efficiency with which a large black custodian of that school would periodically go over the school yard picking up bits of trash, sometimes quite small scraps of paper or cardboard, by plunging a nail lodged in the tip of a pole into the center of these targets and in a single gesture deposit them into a burlap bag slung over the shoulder and onto the hip opposite to the arm throwing his pole-spear by tipping the weapon into the bag and scraping whatever was captured on its tip against the side of the bag as he withdrew it to aim it again. The pole was about as tall as I was, and noticing also the carved line snaking around its length, I asked the man where he had got it. "I made it." "Can you make me one?" "Uh-huh."

On the last day of school I looked for him to ask him for my spear. He was nowhere I looked, and as I walked away I noticed the object, or one like it, standing inside a shed against the wall near where I had spoken to him about it, and, as it seems to me, without hesitating, I took it for mine and walked away with it, with mounting guilt, comically unable to conceal such a thing, the several blocks to my house, and con- tinued straight down the driveway and into the garage, where I stood the pole up in a back corner, and never looked for or touched it again. I was not, inexplicably, questioned about the object by my uncles, the only ones who visited the garage. And the custodian never, I gather, put together my request with his loss. Little boys marking themselves with the guilt of stealing things is not unheard of, as we know from the tes- timony of Saint Augustine and from Rousseau; and stealing a pointed pole, in its banal symbolism, merely adds comedy to the guilt, the guilty comedy in which mere existence seeks justification.

My philosophical insistence, decades later, that childhood, or let us say, innocence, is, with the reception of language, urged by experience, the desire for experience, into guilt, or let us say, has—I do not doubt—roots here. They are roots with three visible, mutually modifying, branches—the electricity of others, the eroticism of risk, the theft of origination.

July 27, 2003

I cannot at the moment remember the name of the school I had moved to on the north side of town, nor can I but vaguely picture any but one of the teachers there—the one who agreed with me that I had no talent for drawing. It was her practice to order pupils who misbehaved to stand in the corner of the room. One declared form of misbehavior turned out to be thumb-sucking, and the student who was most often, perhaps uniquely, ordered into the corner for that crime I will call (modifying the name out of an evidently imperishable memory of hatred and fear) Joseph Shopman. Joseph was older than the other members of the class, heavier though hardly taller than the others, and seemed a different generation from mine, hence distinctly a paradoxical figure in being punished for the childish gesture of sucking his thumb. (That digit had on it a notable callus just above the knuckle and was a lighter color than its companion fingers.) He always wore a dark, striped, double-breasted suit jacket, and had black eyes and oily black hair that stood out from his head and smelled bad, and wanted to hug me when we were in the playground. When I shrank from these attentions he threatened to beat me up, which he could easily have done, unless I had picked up one of the bricks lying around the school yard and killed him by hitting him on the head with it, which it occurred to me on various occasions to do. But my ability to sprint and dodge stood me in good enough stead.

Little more comes to my mind about the year and a half or so I spent there, as if I had gone into a coma. Is this the period that the pretty term "latency" is supposed to begin to cover? The inaccuracy of that term in my case at that time is that it implies something present but kept back, some possibility that has yet found the ground in which, or amassed the energy with which, or developed a medium through which, to flourish. No glimpse of such a thing presents itself when I try to picture that schoolroom. This would have been the era in which I remember the teacher's handing me a pack of photographs taken of each of the members of the class and asking me to distribute them to their respective subjects. Most of the way through this task I came upon a rather attractive but somehow exotic photograph that I could not match with anyone in the class. I showed it to the teacher and asked her who this is. She glanced at it and replied, "It's you." She seemed to me less surprised by this exchange than I think, and I believe thought then, she should have been.

The tallest member of the class was a girl, who was also the fastest runner among us and by far the best dodgeball player. This may mean that I am confusing this third or fourth grade with sixth grade, which I had in the same school. (This thought has jostled the name of the school into my consciousness; ludicrously, its name was the Smiley School.) It was on my entering fifth grade that we first traveled to Sacramento. My evidence for this is recalling my helpful announcement to a group of my new schoolmates, "A'm nahn yez old and a'm inni fith grade" (in whatever fairness I might be to myself here, it could have been that I was seeking some directions around the Sierra School—the three sides of its sunny central square court were lined with a covered walkway, and each looked liked the others). It would have quickly followed this announcement that as I sat down in my assigned seat, the buttons on the fly of my velvet short pants, in which it was thought I should be ceremonially dressed up for the occasion of the opening of the school year, revealed themselves not to have been fastened. Now it happened that no boy, as I recall the scene, within this room of this Western school was wearing anything over the bottom half of himself but a pair of blue jeans. I had never seen such garments before (except possibly in a cowboy movie at a matinee, but I would not have associated those men's pants, worn as part of slinging guns and mounting horses, with anything to do with child's wear). In addition to my other observations that day, and my accomplishment in winning the contest as the fastest in the group in doing series of additions, I learned that upon leaving school for the day one said "Good Night" to the teacher, even though the sun was high and the sky clear, and also that one did not address the teacher by adding Ma'am to a simple Yes or No, which seemed to me abrupt to the point of rudeness. (To this day, "Yes ma'am," said in all seriousness, might leap from my mouth ahead of my attention, especially in addressing a mature black woman. I might have imagined that this would, over the past quarter of a century or so, be taken amiss, but on the whole I have found that it is taken kindly, perhaps with a certain amused pleasure. I must still be saying it right.)

Lessons in appropriate dress and conduct were meant to be taught me after school that first afternoon when several of the boys, awaiting me in the courtyard, offered to remove my short pants for me on the spot; but my shorter yet faster legs, together with flailing arms, again stood me in good stead, aided by vivid motivation, and I proved to be able to thwart their satisfaction on that occasion. By the next day I owned a pair of jeans—it turned out that this exotic item was easily purchasable in a neighborhood store. It seems to me that I remember hardly being able to walk in them. I wondered how other boys' jeans ever got to be old, worn with wear, hence to conform to their bodies, that is, to move with instead of against their motion. In fact I never have learned to wear them. After some weeks of painful chafing it turned out that yellow corduroy trousers were an acceptable substitute.

Since roughly thirty years after that 1935 fall afternoon in the American West racing for my life to acquire jeans, so large a segment of the youth of the world seemed to have learned how to live in them, or substitute corduroys for them, this recent narrative might seem quaint. But the relation of sensing my clothes to be wrong went with, as both cause and effect, sensing my body to be wrong—not as if it were not mine, but as if I were wrong for it. Would it help to say, not of the wrong gender but of the wrong species? The resonance of this question is sounded explicitly some half century after that afternoon's pedagogical demonstration, when I was writing about Bette Davis's performance in *Now, Voyager*, in my book on Hollywood melodrama, in considering what the film understands her sense of herself to be, in the light of her mother's declaration of her as "My ugly duckling." (This daughter has not, when we meet her, been able to contest the false, I suppose customary, implication that an ugly duckling is an unfortunate duck, whereas in the Hans Christian Andersen fairy tale the superb point is that she is not a duck at all.) In the film this banal but profound image of being out of place, adrift in the wrong circles, suggests, in my reading, a homosexual slant of the character played by Bette Davis, expressed or coded explicitly in the concept of her self-declared morbidity, her having an explicitly undefined illness. In my own case the sense of being exceptional, and both desperately not wanting, and hence wanting, to be so, took different forms in each phase of my life—sometimes as the thought of being too young, sometimes too old, sometimes too Jewish, sometimes too American, for some too philosophical or serious, for others too literary or excitable, say, exuberant. Older cousins of mine, showing each other letters from me written as I conceived the plan after graduating college to move to New York (with one of whom I lived on Long Island for my first six weeks before finding an apartment in Manhattan) and apply for admission to Juilliard, called me a dreamer. Names.

July 28, 2003

In the back and forth of Atlanta and Sacramento, I attended in each place a grammar school and a junior high school and a high school. I leave, at least for the moment, not without a certain relief, the years of grammar school. In my first year at the California junior high school, turning eleven at the beginning of seventh grade, my mother had left my father and me alone together for three months while she went back to Atlanta to play in an orchestra that her brother Meyer was made conductor of, an attempt in 1937 or 1938 to revive vaudeville at one of the movie theaters that a few years before had found it financially more sensible to turn itself exclusively to showing movies. Though she was a more accomplished player than Meyer was, he was her favorite conductor. And of course she would be his favorite pianist in anchoring a pit orchestra. It was the first chance in years (it would prove to be the last) for Meyer to find a position in the world of music commensurate with his talent. No doubt that helped my mother withstand the crime of abandoning my father and me to each other's mercies. She, in retrospect, understandably had her own irresistible motives for going, both to resume her career as a musician and to escape the moods of my father. Whether this was in fact some trial separation is perhaps unclear. I was in any case hostage to her returning. And I know that divorce had more than once crossed her mind, as explicitly it had his. Twice I recall his going to sleep for the night in the unused twin bed in my room, saying it is too late for a divorce. As Cary Grant says about a doubtless related matter in *The Philadelphia Story*: "That's no good. That's not even conversation."

One of the most illuminating range of musical stories I loved hearing from my mother was of how Meyer, in distinction from this and that other hack conductor in her history of orchestra playing, unfailingly alerted the orchestra for a new departure, of tempo or texture, that was not simply a matter of cues for the individual entrances of sections and solos, but of gestures of preparation, as action developed on the stage, to each pertinent player well ahead of cues. "You couldn't get lost when he conducted." I thought of the Meyer stories a decade later, during my second year as a music student at Berkeley, in the class Ernest Bloch came down from the coast of Oregon to give each summer. Bloch, as much as any teacher I have experienced, altered the contour of my life, altered what I was reading, how I was reading, what I hoped for from intellectuality as well as from artistry. The course lasted two hours every weekday for six weeks. It was quite characteristic of Bloch to interrupt a train of thought, not infrequently involving a story about some famous musician he had encountered over his long life, stopping himself with a question and demonstration, such as: "Do you know what conducting is? It is only this. Clap when I give you the cue." He stared at us, at each of us it seemed. It was a theatrical gesture of pedagogy well suited to his temperament. Suddenly and in one motion he flung his arms outward and plunged them straight down. There was a smattering of tentative claps. "Try again." He held his arms out before him, waited for our combined attention, then simply let them drop to his side. There were further tentative claps, some perhaps sounding together. "Once more," he said. He held out his arms; took us in again at a glance around; then with an open-mouthed intake of breath, sprung his arms high in a tremendous upbeat, and after a matching pause, the fingers outstretched except for the index fingers of each hand touching the thumbs, drove his arms down hard to his waist. The sound of the consequent unison crack was shocking, and produced spontaneous laughter and applause. "The rest you can learn for yourself."

My memory is that my mother left Sacramento for Atlanta some days after the Kreisler recital. My father and I accompanied her to the train station to see her off on the new "streamliner" train, named the City of San Francisco, destined for Chicago, where she would change to the Southern Pacific line for Atlanta. That the City of San Francisco made a stop in Sacramento seemed to me to lend a certain glamour, or anyway mystery, to our smallish capital, helped along somehow by the indirectly lit train car of unprecedentedly plush seats onto one of which my father and I placed my mother's suitcases.

My mother left on a Sunday. This is vivid to me since the next morning, getting ready for school, I found that I could barely manage to fit into either of the two pairs of yellow corduroy trousers that my mother had left washed and folded for me; they seemed to have shrunk. As I repeatedly tried unsuccessfully to get the brass top button completely through its slot, I fell into a comprehensive fit of sobbing. (I have had a number of occasions in a long life to cry with grief over the losses of friends and lovers, but the only other time I remember being convulsed so helplessly with grief was on awakening from a morning nap after having spent the night in my father's hospital room and been told that he had survived the operation for uremia, somehow a consequence of the previous day's operation for colon cancer, the second procedure undertaken as a result of my insistence that a second opinion be solicited to judge the decision that my father would not survive a kidney operation. The second operation saved his life, but it was obvious to all that he would never really recover himself, which proved to be true, although he lived another fifteen years.) The morning after my mother left for Atlanta my father, hearing something or sensing something out of rhythm, came into my room looking puzzled. I was trying to gasp out that I wasn't crying because Mother had left, but just because I'm crying. I suppose it didn't seem reasonable to me to explain that it was because I couldn't button my trousers.

Yet, at this distance, it does not seem so far-fetched an explanation, and surely not one that is entirely false. If this is difficult for me to have come to surmise, it is part, it is even expressive, of the difficulties I perpetually encounter in this recent compulsion to tell my story. To tell some of the story of my relation to clothes seems trivial compared with telling, for example, about the events in the playground in Atlanta receiving electric shocks from an older schoolmate's hand or excitedly risking a dangerous fall in sliding along a high beam, let alone anticipating entries in a list of temptations and humiliations and bouts of vanity to ensue. But at each step I seem to run up against a crowd of related matters that demand their turn at expression but that, if I am to keep in the draw of narration, have to be, at least for the moment, passed by, as if traversing a sensible, or anyway communicable, path of life requires learning, as in the passages where the amusement park tunnel darkens, not to gasp at every skeleton that dances into view. (I note for further reference that it is to be considered whether learning not to gasp at every clear cause for gasping, as the price of participation in civilized life, is a matter of learning to control the body or beyond this of mastering an oblivion of the causes of losing control.)

The week before my mother left for Atlanta, as I was standing in line for the cafeteria at the junior high school, wearing as usual one of those pairs of corduroys, a student I only vaguely recognized turned around to me and asked, "Are you swaybacked?" It occurred to me that others had overheard his question, that perhaps it was for their benefit that he had asked it. In that case the stage was set for me to have parried the question with some such gesture as, "I haven't looked lately. Are you actually a jackass?" But such exchanges were as far then beyond my repertory or my imagination of aggressive male intimacies as was the one-sided exchange fifteen autumns later, halfway through my second year of graduate school at Harvard, as I was standing in line in the Eliot House dining hall with a friend, a fellow graduate student in my year in the philosophy program, together with a chum of his from their undergraduate years at a still all-male New England college, visiting for lunch from a neighboring law school, when an acquaintance of theirs from, it turned out, their recent college past came walking eagerly over to the line with his arm outstretched and an unguarded hello for them. My friend's visiting chum responded to this greeting by saying, "I see you still don't know how to polish your shoes." The acquaintance froze, actually looked at his shoes, stared back, and these three offspring of the same alma mater had a comprehending, say, even fostering, laugh together. Later experience has not I think appreciably deepened my understanding of the workings of that defensively chic camaraderie. I assumed then, as now, that against their shared past an opposite outcome of the aggressive questioning of the shoes would have been just as satisfactory, one in which the newly arrived acquaintance would have seen the trap and instead of falling into it kept his head steady and replied to his old friend along some such lines as, "I was saving them for you to shine." In that case all three might have survived.

Of course I am inclined to speculate how primary a gain one might seek from rehearsing the past, anyway from certain rehearsals of the past. Nietzsche spotted our wish to take revenge on time's "It was." I could wish to counter this fate by speaking occasionally of the task of redeeming the past, impressed by the inevitable lapse of time between an event, perhaps one can say a trauma, of pain or as it were of pleasure, and the discovery of words for expressing it, or of a satisfying stretch of responsive wordlessness. It is the lapse I sometimes recur to by recording it using Emerson's distinction between an Intuition and its Tuition, call this the education of desire, or perhaps by desire. Isn't this what writing a memoir might at best come to? Then how different is this from what we might call an extended recourse to an "esprit d'escalier," as it were a perpetual sense of one's expression as being always unprompt, the appropriate thought always somewhat late, or perhaps dropped, as a slipper on the staircase. I learn, I think, only yesterday of the expression "une langue de bois," a tongue wooden in its inability to utter or alter its expressions as occasion demands, but doomed to repeat itself. Here is a candidate for Emerson's perception that "Every word they say chagrins us." As if being tone deaf is a function of being time deaf. If such are the terrors of writing a life, then how are they not the terrors of speech as such?

I was speaking of the trapping speech of young male intimacy, call it enforced sparring (a fight club?). An avoided trap, in my experience, generally exposes a trap beneath—not exactly what Emerson meant by saying that under every sea there is a deeper sea, but perhaps not exactly not. The apparently preferable, if still imperfect, outcome of the later encounter concerning unshined shoes over the outcome of the questioned and pathetically silenced swaybacked Stanley, rests I guess on the fact that in the later outcome a community had been comprehensibly tested and had held conventionally firm whereas in the earlier case a lost boy was merely thrown for a further loss, explained or unexplained, in either case unprofitably. But what environment was it whose ordinary creatures lived off the emissions of the casts of emotional dice, taught as obligatory, maintained as obsessional, so that, unless you lived in a glory of achievement, or kept yourself mainly in isolation, you had at the end of each day to check your pockets for the stake to play the next day? For what future was this evolutionary selection a strait gate?

A well-known trap of being human is the thought that you can be reparative toward yourself. This is no better, if no worse, than the idea of making a promise to yourself. Even if you keep this promise it leaves you with the sense that you deserve a reward, so what have you won? If you could thank yourself, be as it were obliged to yourself (owe yourself a promise in return for your favor) then you would be predictably thankful. If you can keep a promise to yourself then you can keep a promise you have not made. (I do not understand revenge as obeying this logic.)

If I were doing my best to fictionalize my life stories rather than doing my damnedest to factualize them (with occasional light disguises of identity) I might hold back here the information that the visiting chum from college, whom I came to know better, and who my friend in line would soon tell me was marked, despite his lack of brilliance, with his wealth and connections and his good heart and his masterful and natural friendliness, to become a successful politician from his home district, had attracted and held the attention of a poor, beautiful, brilliant, slightly younger woman whom he was engaged to marry at the close of that academic year, a week after she would graduate from her college. I imagined, in the course of the next year, which the pair spent in Cambridge for his last year at law school and they continued an ongoing argument, not infrequently including the kibitzing of friends, about whether she would now begin the process of taking a Ph.D. in French or whether they would at once start a family, that I was not alone in fantasizing the scandal of doing what I could to tempt her to run away from that marriage into one more romantic than that of the dutiful wife of an aspiring politician. But I had heard it announced as a pair of axioms from the generation preceding mine (or I constructed the remarks into a pair) that gifted men with an uneasy ambition to write marry social workers, whereas gifted women with equally difficult ambitions marry lawyers. A quarter of a century later, after periodic news of this promising lawyer's battles with depression and drinking, I learned that he was found one late night lying in the street dying of a heart attack.

Might I use this knowledge as a judgment on a civilization of obsessive jousting, of a deplorable combination of public heartiness and private bewilderment? That would amount to taking private revenge on a demonic conspiracy between the irrationalities of opaque private torment and the irrationalities of repetitive public demonstrativeness that endanger us all. Whereas I am at the moment amazed, as I am chronically, by the mystery of individual survival, of what has allowed it (the chance growth of a slightly longer beak to reach deeper into a new growth of flowers) and what may prevent it (accidents of weather or of mood or of timing or necessities as understood by a wooden head and tongue).

The only earlier time I had heard the term "swayback" used was in my mother's description of how to make the sign warding off the bad luck of seeing a swayback white horse. You make the sign by touching the ball of your right index finger to your tongue, then touching the implied saliva to the center of the palm of your left hand, and then, holding that palm steady, seal that spot by stamping it with the bottom of a fist made by your right hand. I had actually in my childhood seen a swayback horse alone in a field during a drive in the country (unless I dreamt this), the back with an exaggerated curve in it and the belly comparably hung sadly low. But what would it mean for a human being to be swayback? When I had a chance, I looked in a mirror to determine whether my back seemed to curve in exaggeratedly toward my behind, but the comparison merely left me puzzled, or rather produced a heightened feeling of the tightness at the waist of my trousers, which I somehow imagined might be producing the look of my disfigurement, unless of course they were so tight just because of that disfigurement. I don't know when I first formed the idea that clothes were simply manufactured for sizes and proportions different from mine, call them normal. I imagined that clothes manufacturers had models, like the faces on charts in barber shops, and made clothes to fit them, and that the boys in my worlds of school were born to fit those models exactly, except for the few other Jewish kids in my classes, especially those in California, and one or two fat boys, like Butter, whom the athletes adopted as a kind of mascot—they liked to put coins in the pinball game at the drive-in restaurant nearest the high school and laugh at his inability to synchronize his nudges of the glass-top table display when he would try to amplify the ball's bounce off the springs without causing the machine to tilt. They were going to give him a birthday party in which the present would be to take him to a whorehouse. A present for whom?

Even when I happened to put on a piece of clothing I liked looking at—I think of a sweater of alternating blue and green wide stripes—I couldn't decide whether it was right to wear the shirt collar in or out of the round neck of the sweater. What did people do? How did what was done weigh against the way each looked in my estimation? My father was thought by my mother to be a good judge of jackets. That judgment came into play once a year, buying a new suit for me to wear to synagogue for the High Holidays. Besides, my trust in his judgment was compromised by the unfaded memory of his once looking at my feet—I remember this as from the years still on Atlanta Avenue—and saying that I wore out a pair of shoes every three weeks, whereas he wore the same shoes for ten years, longer than I had existed. He could not have made himself more incomprehensible to me if he had told me that he had not removed the shoes now on his feet, day or night, for ten years. I gathered that our differences were not only measureless, but somehow meaningless. The offer of the message was not so much that I was wrong, as if mistaken in my conduct, but that I was destructive and strange.

And these capacities for self-evaluation in good time found circumstances in which to fuse themselves with my—with what child's not?—readiness to assume guilt. Some years later in Sacramento, a day or so after my purchase of a new jacket, as I walked into my father's store, he announced out of the blue (or the gray, or the black) that I had said I also needed a shirt and some underclothes and socks. He went on to say that he had a friend who had opened a clothing store a few blocks further downtown (down being the direction of the less respectable pawnshops and in general of something interestingly called skid row, but culminating suddenly in the train station, which at that time was still grand). We walked down several unfamiliar streets into an establishment that, rather than the indirect lighting (a favorite of

my mother's among new concepts and effects of design) featured by
the shop with its fashionable jackets and with stacks of shirts and of
soft sweaters and socks neatly arranged within glass cases or on open
shelves along the walls, their very array of colors often unnamable by
me, between blue and green or between red and brown, creating their
own ornamentation of the space, we discovered ourselves in a surprisingly large store with several unshaded and unfrosted lit bulbs singly
suspended from the ceiling, illuminating lines of tables placed against
the walls and one line bisecting the length of the painted wooden floor,
each table featuring several open cardboard boxes of menswear, here
boxes of thick blue or khaki shirts, there heavy shoes, and there underclothes and white socks and, stacked without boxes, overalls and lumber
jackets. One might not know whether the scene was one of unpacking
to stay or of packing up to leave. My father introduced me to his friend
and said to me something like, "You need shirts and undershirts and
socks, don't you? Go ahead, pick them out."

The curse of the jest is, as elsewhere, that no curse was necessary.
If my father had been able to dissociate his pity or terror of this store
from his wish to magnify his stature with a stranger by punishing me,
there is no reason to suppose I could not, taken into his confidence,
have sympathized with the wish to spend money there, even looked for
something I would actually wear. But I am still not sure how I might
have understood or seriously imagined the possibility of his taking me
into his confidence. This would have required his having confidence in,
or respect for, his own desires. And I surmised attacks in him of disappointment in and contempt for himself beyond human solace, beyond
mine surely, since I seemed to serve only to exacerbate these attacks.

If that was in 1943, the year before I left for college at Berkeley,
then it was thirteen or so years later, having returned to Berkeley to
teach, that I one day found I needed a brass collar button for a shirt
with tabs to fasten underneath the knot of a tie and, turning back from
the door of the fashionable men's clothing store that was sure to stock
such an object, I remembered a new very modest store that I had passed
recently around the corner, strangely showing stacks of work clothes laid
out in cardboard boxes on a central long table but also offering dressier
shirts and suits and ties. The lone person I saw at a distance inside was
dressed in dark baggy trousers and a jacket that almost matched and,

because he was wearing a hat as he came my way, I thought he was leaving. When he stopped near me and said something like "Yes?" I asked whether the store had brass collar buttons, accompanying what in the circumstances suddenly seemed to me a strange request with gestures indicating difficulty with my collar and tie. He shrugged and replied, "Who's got them?"

What lunatic error had I committed out of the quick memory of guilt and pity? The store of work clothes years before in Sacramento was meant to be a stable enterprise in a location appropriate for a recognizable clientele. The location in Berkeley, on the contrary, was on Telegraph Avenue, the main thoroughfare beginning or ending at the busiest entrance to the University of California and continuing into Oakland. Its space was, evidently, due to be remodeled and brought into harmony with the respectable shops surrounding it, and during its vacancy was rented out for transactions with discounted goods to be disposed of rapidly. The store proved to be under renovation within a few weeks.

I retraced my steps to the more comfortable locale where my request to an inquiring salesman produced at once from a drawer in the wall behind him several large cards each with a distinct field of golden collar buttons protruding in neat rows. I would ask why I bother to relate such an incident of pathetic effort to reduce pathos, except that what I really need to know is why I am meant forever to remember it.

I wondered early whether the sense of my body, or my relation to my body, as unlike that of others, could be explained by the early losing battle against what the older fraternity boys in high school called abusing yourself, the very words my father had used to me, adding the wisdom that the practice made you crazy, an offer of belief counteracted in the halls of the high schools I knew that teemed with jokes on the subject. The day I was told that it was a sure sign of the practice if you grew hair in the palm of your hand, and I fell for the trap, all afternoon it seemed boys were gathered in circles that, when someone looked at his hand, broke up with laughter. Then, still in the junior high school that produced the question about being swaybacked, there was Floyd, whose eyes were slightly crossed (a circumstance somehow mixed up with this subject), taller of course than I but thinner, with pale skin marked with a few flaming pimples, who from time to time in the locker room before he pulled on gym shorts stroked his penis briefly to reaffirm to the gathering of those that shared his aisle, and occasional visitors from other aisles, that it grew in erection unarguably beyond the size of any other boy's in the school. He once mounted one of the long benches bolted to the concrete floor the length of the spaces between facing rows of individual lockers and announced, beginning with a woman's name having no previous significance at least for me, and continuing " . . . is going to buy this when it gets to eight inches."

My sense of difference was increased, or confirmed, by my having to protect my hands from injury because of my piano lessons. After the crisis in which I jammed both of my thumbs catching a basketball the day before a recital and tried ineffectively to disguise my pain as I performed my piece, my mother's dismay at my poor performance assured that I never made the mistake again of playing ball within weeks before a recital. Not that it mattered much, since games with the boys I knew were essentially out of my league. Their fourteen- or fifteen-year-old bodies jumped higher and reached farther than my twelve-year-old body could match or plausibly respond to. It had no bearing that they were older. They were who I was to be compared with.

The immediate issue of the propriety of clothes was put to rest at the beginning of my last twelve months of high school, when our dance band bought itself matching jackets (which settled things for weekend nights generally—the jackets were usable for nonperforming occasions as well). There was a style for a few years then in which a modified jacket was not fitted but hung down squarely, keeping its shape somehow by its wool back and wool sleeves keeping in shape the loosely fit front linen panels joined with woven leather buttons. No one looked wonderful in them, but no one looked bad, and joined together on a bandstand they signaled a serious intention. For weekdays the matter was settled when I became an officer in the (required) high school ROTC (Reserve Officers' Training Corps) unit, promoted early and largely, I thought, because I could give commands in close-order drill and in the manual of arms that made more intricate and interesting patterns, without mishap, than any other in competition with me. (The secret, so to speak, was that I gave the commands themselves rhythmically, in a way that prepared the movements, like a conductor as it were.) The wool uniform was too heavy for comfort in the California late spring and early fall, the ending and beginning months of the school year, a complete irrelevance to me given that, with the officer's leather shoulder strap crossing diagonally to the belt at the waist to support a sheath and saber, the uniform's jacket draped my body as if made for it. Of course to achieve neutrality in clothes is a fine reason for school uniforms. I quite recognized that the neutrality I found was not perfect—some of the boys were even more resplendent in their officers' uniforms, others still quite sunken. My costumes worked because they both, the military and the musical, on weekdays and weekends, became sufficiently accommodating conditions to allow for the unclouded perception and reception of talent, something like the way a black robe on a judge becomes a condition for delivering a nonsubjective verdict.

It should not require Hegel to make one aware that every intellectual advance brings with it, until the end of intellect, a new register of problems. I had arrived at an unprecedented comfort of circumstances in my existence by making the roles that I had adopted or to which I had been assigned take precedence over my person. Or did these roles select and exercise the talents that I was put on earth to realize? May they produce survival despite misfitness? Can one become the prisoner of one's talents?

I am wandering, making serious questions unanswerable. While it is true and important that early adolescent crushes and crashes were still part of the life I would pack and then unpack in moving to Harvard in 1951 on a fellowship to continue studying philosophy, it is no truer or more important than that immeasurable steps had indeed been taken out of that early locker room—different steps, I trust, or taken differently, by each of the boys gathered there those mornings. I have lost touch for the moment with my young consciousness, or unconsciousness, of those steps, quite as though I am responding to a wish, whether one then or one now is not clear, at once to remember everything and to remember nothing.

Part 3

July 29, 2003

I do not wish to skimp on these miserable and tender tales, but
with the sense of the posthumous in what I have been telling—a sense
no doubt magnified by the fact that I am returning to this search for
ways to tell what should count as adding up to some of my life story after the hospital stay in which my heart, sometimes lax in measuring my
days with its beat, was probed for its reticencies or discontinuities and
that now, just one week after the procedure was done I seem to have
experienced a mild recurrence of the kind of lightheaded episode that
was a symptom indicating the reasonableness of having the catheterization, and that the consequent placement of stents was supposed, it was
thought, to correct—it comes over me this brilliant early morning that
I might not have high-minded time enough to complete telling what I
want to tell. (I repeat that the extent of writing to this point is the result
also of some later return bouts of fiddling and supplementing.)

How in the world would I at this stage know what "complete telling" means here? Much more interesting is the felt need to tell, and the
picture of completion that the need invokes. And haven't I repeatedly
discovered that the writing I care about most can be understood as letting death into the room?—in other words, letting each sentence bear
what finitude can bring to it then and there, and await developments;
not, that is, defer developments, as if all that writing required was the

power of unfolding implication rather than that of inviting surprises, and not ones prepared by a future but ones creating the future.

Most particularly at this moment I do not want to leave things with a collection of naked boys in a seventh-grade locker room staring together at a naked schoolmate's uncanny member, with no further wisdom from the future of that scene to bring back to it other than laughably, or tearfully, inappropriate or ill-fitting trousers, virtuosic close-order drill, leading a band, creating the excitement of danger at the top of a high set of swings on an otherwise abandoned playground, remembered fantasies of rescuing a marvelous woman from a marriage that happened to take a lethal turn, and others of a move on turning seven years old from a house of continuous interest and talk and music to a set of moves and apartments in which I was largely abandoned to silence and to occasional strangers. Is it from such things that an aspiration to philosophy or art or religion has sometimes to be made, if they are to be made at all? Will I understand how the heaven that I know—which contains the Chopin Fourth Ballade and Kreisler encores and the Bach D Minor double violin concerto that my mother and her brothers played when we lived together as a lullaby reward for my going to bed without complaint, and the Mendelssohn Rondo Capriccioso with which my mother in those days would sometimes begin her practicing, perhaps starting it much too slow, and then starting it again several times before entering into its flights of fancy and its pretense at being hard to get—enters and departs from that locked locker room?

I think of the surprise, living just across the street from the grass-covered playing field—nearly the size, I judge in memory, of a professional football field—of the Sierra School the year I was enrolled there during the first of our three stretches in Sacramento, begun within days of passing my ninth birthday, up one day as early as dawn in my bathrobe, evidently down with a flu that from then on characteristically kept me out of school two weeks of every year (could this have to do with our moving every year across the country, so that I never developed or sustained local immunities?), looking out at the school from the double window of our living room and feeling through its sills the unwarmed wind that was shaking the trees at the far end of the field, I gradually recognized a figure who was running past those trees as the large boy who lived two houses down from our house whom I knew mostly from seeing him in late afternoons alone in the Sierra field after it was otherwise empty and the school buildings dark throw a javelin a startlingly long arc along the length of the field, then retrieve it and throw it back again. Now, however, he was running along the dirt track that circled the playing field, in my direction, that is, in the direction of our houses, dressed not in sweat clothes, but in short pants and a matching tank top (something I would not have distinguished from an undershirt), and instead of continuing on the track as it turned along the near edge of field, continued on to the sidewalk and across the street to turn and pass within a few feet of where I was kneeling on the sofa looking out, and continued on, evidently, to his house. He was heavily sweating despite the cold air, and his face (frozen perhaps in pain or perhaps in attention to another world) and his body (molded or sculpted in a way I had never known a man's body to be) had both turned bright red, whether with cold or with heat I did not know. It crossed my mind, treated to this apparition, that nobody will suggest to him that he was not properly dressed, but at the same time my astonishment told me that his way was no way out for me, since no Jew would, or could, run through the winter air at dawn until he turned red.

After we had been in Sacramento for some weeks, the service station at the end of our street was laying in new gasoline tanks underground and refurbishing its modest station house. The two men who ran it were friendly, and several of us students from the Sierra School who lived close by found ourselves on the weekend interested in the progress of the digging and asked to help. The men let us try a couple of idle shovels and after a while gave us each a soft drink. Wandering alone one afternoon after the digging and renovation were done, in a large vacant lot some distance behind the station, bordered on its far side by a dense clump of trees like those on the Sierra grounds, I found almost buried in dirt and leaves at the bottom of a shallow ditch a large heavy glass jar with a metal cap screwed on it, empty except for the untidy residues of disuse. The cap had been inexpertly punched with several holes, I imagined to hold insects without suffocating them, conceivably fireflies, which were a common summer fascination on Atlanta Avenue although I do not recall having ever seen one in Sacramento; any such project had, in any case, evidently been long abandoned since the edges of the holes in the metal cap were rusted. I unscrewed the cap and filled the jar with one of each different thing or creature I came across in the field, a twig, crumbling leaves, assorted bugs, various kinds of stones, perhaps a marble, a gum or candy wrapper, a soda bottle cap, a piece of torn tennis ball, to which I added a penny and a duplicate stamp from my collection, enclosed in a folded envelope, which I found in my pocket. Then I filled the remaining space of the bottle with dirt and grass, closed it tightly and contemplated it, feeling that I had accomplished something important, even solemn. Something will be discovered to grow from this, if it is well preserved, and we wait long enough. I borrowed a shovel from the service station, dug a kind of small cave in a rise at the edge of the neighboring clump of trees and stored my work deep. I merely report the memory that as I was sitting on the mound engrossed in this unaccustomed mood that seemed to enclose and press upon my body, I heard a faint low hum as if produced by the ground, which I explicitly said to myself others could not hear. The memory is so explicit that I might well look for something to read on the subject of hallucinations caused by sensory deprivation.

But what keeps the memory of this small, isolated set of events coming back, perhaps every other year? If I say now that I was burying my life, perhaps to preserve it for some time in which it might be lived, or chosen, I need not imply that these are thoughts I could have formulated then. Nor does the moment strike me as what might be thought of as a promise to myself, but rather as a message cast into time, for a future self I was to become or unpredictably to receive, perhaps to rue or to mock or to abandon or to embrace.

Something else asks for expression here. Two events from roughly these years, or just before, among the earliest I remember hearing announced over the radio, were the killing of the most famous gangster during the years of famous gangsters, John Dillinger, and the execution of Bruno Hauptmann, convicted of kidnapping the Lindbergh baby. As the announcer spoke of execution in the electric chair, the radio gave out a hum that I understood as the sound of electrical execution. It may have been an imperfection in the radio transmission, or the station's attempt at a reenactment of the moment. Either way it was a comment upon a world of retribution. I was, as I recall, for the moment alone in the house, and it seemed to help control my fear to go outside, if just to see live people walking somewhere.

Is to speak of something as "asking for expression" to imply that anyone other than myself has, or might take, an interest in this memory of an impression (or two) of a hum? The impression lacks even the practical interest that Locke and Hume, for example, expect us to invest in experiences they name impressions, moments that may, if anything may (in isolation), suggest or reveal a world. Six decades later I will find myself, teaching a course on opera and film, describing the Overture of *The Marriage of Figaro* as expressing the hum of the world, specifically the restlessness of the people of the world. Perhaps that would not have the interest it has for me without my associating the impression of restlessness (not, I believe, an item within Locke's and Hume's inventory of experiences) with what I call the portrait of the modern subject sketched in Wittgenstein's *Philosophical Investigations*, the subject perpetually seeking peace, therefore endlessly homeless. What justifies me in asking that my impression be shared? I suppose the fact that we are modern subjects. Then evidently I would distinguish this experience (or mood or mode of experience) from the restlessness that Saint Augustine invokes early in his *Confessions*, close to the section of it with which Wittgenstein opens his *Investigations*. Or is this distinction quite evident?

July 30, 2003

I think of a morning, twenty years after burying that bottle, on which Marcia and I were in the last stages of closing up the house we had been living in for some weeks, watching over it for Morton and Lucia White, preparing to drive to New York to depart for a year in Europe. Part of what we were watching over was a large white male cat whom upon our leaving was to be put in his cage and taken to a neighbor's house to spend the last few days until our friends' return. When I went to fetch the cage from the garage and opened the back door of the house, the cat leapt past me and disappeared. He was normally allowed to roam outside at will, returning when he was hungry or lonely, and I knew that a favorite perch of his was on the roof, which at one point came very low to the wall of a path beside the house. He was indeed there and when I called to him he went to the other side of the roof. I had kept him in the house all the previous night specifically wanting to avoid this possibility on leaving, knowing that there would be no time on this morning to let nature, in the form of hunger and loneliness, take its course. We called in the next-door neighbors for support (they were in any case to look after the cat for another day or two), and after a considerable and unruly time of coaxing and the four of us lining ourselves along the side of the roof the cat could jump from, I just managed to grab him as he, for some reason, decided to jump and make a run for it. He evidently did not realize that time was on his side. His cage did not seem large enough for an animal his size to turn around in, but the back of the cage was open, that is, closed only with a sort of heavy wire grate. As the neighbors carried him away in the cage the cat was looking at me through that grate. I had expected that after his considerable harassment he would find a way to express anger or displeasure. Instead he was resting peacefully, as if nothing had happened, or because there was nothing to do under these circumstances. When he turned his head away slightly and rested it in his paws, I had the distinct feeling that he was already saving himself, storing his hopes, waiting. I have a number of times thought of this posture of apparent resignation, perhaps when I have wondered how good I am at grasping circumstances.

For Kant the complete set of conditions under which we can know objects is essentially given and stored in being human, in having a mind (Kant's inheritance of rationalism). An object to be known to exist reveals to us only its appearances (Kant's inheritance of empiricism), and in each case appears to us with all the necessary conditions of its appearance (as caused, as in space and time, etc.). But taking the human body into account and its responsibilities in making something happen, what the circumstances are in which an action may successfully enter the world are open to discovery, found to be favorable or unfavorable, practical or quixotic. Nothing that happens, with the human hand in it, has had to happen; but everything that happens happens along with all its necessary conditions. There is not only time; there is the moment—the moment of judgment, shaped differently in the respective necessities of cognitive, of moral, and of aesthetic judgment.

July 31, 2003

My father found he could not tolerate working for his brother, and after a year in Sacramento we moved back to Atlanta for my sixth year of grammar school, again at Smiley. Joseph Shopman the bully was still there (this time his double-breasted suit jacket was black), as was the nice tall athletic girl, thin and rather shapeless. Entering my home-room I saw a boy I remembered as somewhat aloof and, while not par-ticularly adept at anything boys were rewarded for being good at, good at drawing. I walked over to the table at which he was alone, sketching something. Walking closer to it, I found it to be a beautiful sketch un-mistakably of one of the boys in our class. When he was aware of my interest he folded the sketch and put it in his notebook. I felt a miracu-lousness in this ability and an immediate conviction that such artistry meant that this boy already knew his future of clarity and happiness.

The year was 1936, and the promise of better times had evidently taken my father back to Atlanta to try his luck at another jewelry store. (Who was backing this, and whether my father had preserved some of the stock from his failed store in the event of better times, to be supple-mented by loans from his traveling salesmen friends, I did not and do not know. My mother mentioned several times how awful it was to be in debt, but nothing about to whom they were in debt.) This store also failed, I graduated grammar school, we moved back to Sacramento, my father again to his brother's pawnshop, I to the California junior high school, with its instructive locker room in my future together with the cafeteria with lines out to a terrace on which I will be questioned about the shape of my back. Most of the kids from the Sierra fifth grade seemed to have moved there. Alan and Hollis still ruled the hierar-chy of my acquaintance, a function of their being the main figures for whom all the clothing manufacturers in the world were designing their garments and all the barbers perfecting the one correct cut. Sufficiently sure now in following the basics of the dress code, I banked on my new status as returned stranger to comment to Barbara about the relation between Dorothy and a boy whose name I have forgotten. She simply replied, "You're behind the times." God in heaven knows that was true.

August 1, 2003

I am forgetting that before settling into that junior high (or middle) school, I had initially on our return to Sacramento been enrolled in another, in a different part of Sacramento, nearer downtown. Evidently we had upon this return to Sacramento moved into an apartment temporarily, until my mother could find a permanent (as it were) home for us. Two events stand out for me over the weeks in which I would have been enrolled there. I had missed the opening week or two of the school year, and in the first class I recall, blank outline maps of some part of the world were handed out and we were directed to fill in a number of geographical locations, this information to be found in a book in the drawer of our desks. For some reason the very mechanical nature of the assignment was reassuring to me—I needed no knowledge of what had gone on in earlier days, and maybe I could get off on the right foot here. I finished the assignment and took it up to the teacher, who was writing something at her desk. She glanced at my work and said, "You did it too fast." She did not mean that I had done it incorrectly, since she just asked me to take my seat. So I had after all again not known something, that there was a given or normal time it took to do things properly, or acceptably.

The location of the second event was the school playground, an area about the size of a basketball court (this was downtown, where ample fields of play were not in question), outlined with benches and covered with a kind of rough sand, containing small sharp pebbles that you would not wish to fall on. Students could spend whatever time was left, between finishing lunch and the beginning of afternoon classes, on the playground. (I don't remember a cafeteria; I suppose we were to bring our own lunches.) At the opposite side of the area there was a building considerably smaller than the one containing my classroom. The three or four long steps leading to the entrance to its basement were shaded by the building along the half-dozen yards you could get from the crowded playground and still remain within the school grounds. I found that it was peaceful to sit at the top of those steps and read my book. Through the open windows of the school's wood shop located in that basement, the sound of lathes turning was comforting company, the neutral consequence of productive work with no implication of rebuke. (The students working the lathes were somewhat older than the students I had encountered in my building, but why had they not stopped for lunch?)

Over the door to that basement entrance was a large, round, iron-covered bell, one of several whose shattering ringing signaled the change of school periods. There would be no danger, even though I had my back to the crowded playground, of missing the end of lunch period and making my way back to class. I was immersed in *Les Misérables*. (When I had finished *The Count of Monte Cristo* the previous year, I told my mother earnestly that it was the greatest book ever written. I had started *Les Misérables* some halfway through the train journey from Atlanta, and I had to confess to my mother that I had been mistaken because *Les Misérables* was proving to be really the greatest. While the green velour seats—they were actually cushioned, nonreclining benches with room for two people, but my mother and I each had one to ourselves—were our living quarters for those days and nights, times in the dining car, whose stiff linen table cloths and napkins and whose heavy silverware, produced and changed by black men who swayed through the car like dancers, with full trays balanced on one hand raised over their heads at mysteriously determined separate heights when they passed one another, and others, were magnified in fascination by the changing landscape outside the windows, expanding my imagination of human capacities and necessities.) Something called my attention from my reading. It was not the terrific sound of the iron school bell but rather a sustained silence. The wood lathes were shut down; I looked around to discover that the playground was empty. I had read through the bell and had no idea how long ago classes had begun. I do not remember what scene I came in upon, entering the full classroom, beyond the disapproval of the teacher. This happened again the next day, and I was told to leave my book at home.

A cause for the vanishing of more consecutive memories of that interlude at the start of the return to Sacramento for the second time is linked to the fact that after meeting us at the train station and taking us to an explicitly temporary apartment, my father guided my mother into a back room and shut the door, leaving me with the unpacked suitcases and packages in the so-called living room. I couldn't move from where I had sat down on the sofa, as though all of space was dangerous to move through, trying to understand the feeling that someone wished me dead. I see no reason to forgive flaunting the power of rejection upon an already disoriented eleven-year-old child. Unless it counts as a reason that the consequence of withholding forgiveness may be that one becomes forever unforgiving. One takes, in Nietzsche's idea, vengeance against time. But then that is a way I have understood what my father was doing. Is that why I escaped it? Can I have escaped it?

August 2, 2003

After another year the fraternal business arrangement in Sacramento had yet again become impossible, and moreover the time was approaching for me to begin preparing for my Bar Mitzvah, partly providing an excuse for returning to Atlanta, partly, I imagine, satisfying a genuine wish on my parents' part to reestablish their lives with their familial past in some more recognizable way. The enabling cause was that the Georgia legislature had passed a law legalizing liquor and wine stores, and Bess's husband, ever on the alert for ways to make his money prosper and multiply, had offered to be my father's silent partner in opening such a store, prelude I gathered to his establishing early a large distribution company. Whether my father was less ashamed of managing a liquor store than of working in his brother's pawnshop was not obvious.

Our lives back in Atlanta, in any case, improved in their physical circumstances, a function of the fact that my mother took up again her career as a commercial pianist, primarily in the orchestra of radio station WSB. She was clearly more buoyant, and her playing meant that we had enough money to rent a more comfortable apartment than we had ever lived in before, in a small building set next to Piedmont Park, the most prominent park in central Atlanta.

My isolation, however, became yet more extreme. Now approaching thirteen, I was thought no longer in need of companionship at home, and my parents were, with an important exception, gone weekdays from before the time I came home from school until after my bedtime—my father stayed in the liquor store until it closed near midnight, and my mother's last program at the radio station ended at

11 p.m. The important exception to this isolation was that for a while my mother tried to make it home to have dinner with me—the orchestra's break (probably demanded by the musicians' union) lasted long enough between the afternoon and the evening rehearsals to allow her to spend most of an hour with me, so that if I started preparing the meal before she arrived to complete it she could share it with me before rushing back to the radio station. I would rather this happen than not, even though the additional hello in my day did not in itself balance the additional good-bye. While I cannot regard these arrangements, in the larger scheme of sad things, as inherently tragic, the fact that they were never discussed, so treated as if inevitable, as part of the nature of things, in which I had no more grain of authority than over ice storms, when nevertheless I could not but feel their oddity, colored much of this pair of years in Atlanta with its own air of eccentricity and mystery. I never doubted the depth of my mother's love for me, nor her appreciation of my dreams, or rather of the fact that I dreamt, which made it all the stranger that I knew myself to be essentially abandoned to myself.

It was vaguely supposed that I was to get to bed by 10:00 on school nights, but I regularly tuned into the beginning of my mother's program at 10:30 to listen to the theme, in which the piano was prominent, and generally to hear the orchestra's principal contribution to the show's events. The title of the program, *Welcome South Brother*, signified in its initials, as the announcer made explicit each night in his closing words, the station's call letters, WSB (all Eastern stations evidently began with *W*, as I surmised when I found that several California stations all began with *K*). I have never had much taste for looking upon my life with simple irony, but this nightly greeting, or farewell, persisted in losing its welcoming intention on its way to me whenever I stayed up long enough to hear it.

On lucky nights, between 7:00 and 7:30, the sound of a neighboring table tennis game came through our back windows from the back of a house that faced our nearest cross street. I left the apartment at once to circle around the corner and down a steep driveway to the back of that house where outside its basement door, under the overhang of an enclosed deck, a Ping-Pong table stood beneath the glamour of two overhead lights positioned and shaded exactly for that table in that place, as though pleasure could reliably be planned for. One other neighborhood boy was already there, and our asking to be allowed to watch a middle-aged couple play a more expert, or anyway more graceful, such game than I had ever experienced, was hardly more than a shamelessly transparent request to be allowed to play, and specifically, at least in my case, to be taught to play correctly, the way they played, with form and assurance. The couple of the house, it emerged, were brother and sister, a form of household new in my experience. After no more than two games that night (and, it turned out, many nights to follow), the woman said goodnight and left, but the man stayed and after watching the boy and me play a game offered to give us some tips, if we liked. Given the structure of my days and nights, I appeared more often than the other boy, indeed essentially every time I heard through the back windows the irresistible rhythm of the syncopated serve and the delayed downbeat of the return. After some weeks, having found myself better, steadier, at defense than at offense, I emphasized that side of my game most persistently, and when after a month or so I was able to beat my teacher he seemed to take a certain pride in having designed his own defeat. This modest development of skill in a marginal sport will have small but directly helpful consequences in later crossroads.

To recognize the end of the day and get to bed, I developed the ritual of eating a box of Oreo cookies together with a can of applesauce. But really the ritual is equally describable as an effort to stop myself from eating the entire box of cookies, a sequence of five (was it?) pairs, each pair stacked in a pleated pliable plastic cup, and from finishing the accompanying applesauce, having conceived the idea that this was not a sensible diet. I slowed the eating by inventing new ways of going through the cookies. One way was to nibble around the circumference of a cookie before finishing off the remaining rough-edged center; another was to twist apart the two wafers of each Oreo, eat off the sugary middle spread from whichever of the wafers it largely adhered to, intending to eat only that one of that double cookie. But each night I lost the battle to stop eating before the package and the can were emptied. I recognize that to this day I unfailingly at the end of a meal leave some portion of food, if sometimes quite small, on my dish—as if to reassure myself that I am free.

I said in passing just now that I had reached an age at which I was evidently thought not to need companionship, say, some amal-

gam of steady, even somewhat redundant human comfort. This assertion rather compromises my claim not to look upon my life with irony.
Once I had glimpsed the significance of Wittgenstein's observation in
the *Investigations*, "Our investigation is to be turned around the fixed
point of our real need"—with its implications that our real need, to
be discovered, requires investigation, and that our need pits itself also
against what Emerson calls our conformities, what Wittgenstein sometimes calls conventions—I became alert to the depth, if invoked self-
servingly, of King Lear's early rebuke to Goneril, who had questioned
whether he needed the many, or any, royal retainers over which he
wished to retain command ("Reason not the need. If only to go warm
were gorgeous, why nature needs not what thou gorgeous wearest,
which scarcely keeps thee warm") as well as moved by the fantasy of
Marx's call or promise to use each one's talent and to meet each one's
(real?) need. It is to turn us toward the unending political evaluation of
the confrontation between need and rule (or history) and to compare
this with Emerson's recurrence to the collisions of power and form,
that I have urged noticing the key ambiguity in Wittgenstein's concept
of a form of life. The concept projects simultaneously, as I take it, an
irreducibly horizontal ethnological or conventional axis crossed by an
irreducibly vertical or biological axis, which is in effect to picture human existence as that life-form that eternally criticizes itself—as it were
from below and from beyond—or incessantly declines to.

August 3, 2003

On two occasions I have entered psychoanalytic therapy, both
times with a lingering, more or less implicit, idea that I might seek a
path into practicing clinical work myself. The first time was in Berkeley, when my first marriage was failing and I was discovering that I
was unable to complete my doctoral dissertation, hence threatening
my teaching position. (How it was that I acquired that position without
completing a dissertation is its own story, an essential part of my graduate student story at Harvard.) The second time was in Boston, some
twenty years later, my job not threatened, and divorce not in question.
Cathleen and I, married then for nine of our now thirty-six years, had

just had a son, and I was about to turn fifty, frighteningly unsure of what I would at such an age be able to offer a child. My father was in his late thirties when I was born, and I always thought of him as an old man, beyond the reach of contemporary response or joyfulness—except, notably, for his reliable enjoyment of virtually any movies that came to the principal movie houses. And yet again I had become unable to complete a manuscript that had grown out of the material of my dissertation into an insatiable organism twice the size of the initial, already sizeable, manuscript. I had decided that the material was, after so many attempts, unconquerable by me, and I had entered into a state in which I entertained elaborate fantasies of vanishing from known society. Something analogous had happened in beginning analysis in Berkeley, but then the idea of disappearing (in all banality, into a monastery in Japan, or a psychiatric clinic in Switzerland, or most longingly an anonymous bar in the China Sea) was rather to give those around me a chance to live their own lives free of my confusions and needs and bad timing, whereas in Boston the emphasis was, with no less transparently hostile banality, on leaving behind a legacy of promise unfulfilled.

The age of fifty is well known to be an apt time to experience depressively time's irreversibility or irreparability. And there were factors other than those I have mentioned that I am unwilling, now at least, to pursue to the extent that making sense of them would demand. The analyst I worked with in Boston had lost his faith in orthodox psychoanalytic practice but not otherwise in analytical methods—of uncensored reporting and association, of dream and symptom interpretation, of attention to transference. Eventually I was sometimes on the couch, still sometimes not, particularly when I felt I needed some simple assurance in order to get through the expectations of the day. One symptomatic response of mine was to feel a pain in my back as of an enormous weight that caused me to bend over slightly as I walked. Some kind of inner duel was in progress between my wishing to find help in removing the penitential weight and wanting to present myself as an old man, incapable of further usefulness.

Freud says somewhere that the age of fifty is probably too late for analytic intervention. His reason seemed to be that one has by then become too inflexible for painful change. My own suspicion was that too much had happened to me to be able to recount it within a finite period of time. I felt this particularly when my opening associations to a dream could not nearly be contained within an hour. But then again an assaulting richness of response may be as clear a sign of resistance to saying something particular as a notable meagerness of response may be. This enters into my suspicion of certain current ideas of meaning as always deferred. Perpetual deferral suggests that the meaning of what we say and do is perpetually open to the future. This is crucial, but it slights the equally obvious fact that meaning is at the same time perpetually encircled by the present. Here we need Austin's remarkable insight, at the opening of his essay "Excuses," that our speech is chronically unfair, unjust, unpostponably conveying more and less than we mean, or desire, or owe. The future might or might not offer us relief. (How do we and our moral or political or aesthetic or religious or intellectual or erotic longings put up with each other? Can it have been Hume who in thinking about religion first offered the speculation that the world we inhabit is a world botched and discarded by an inept and disappointed god?)

This second analyst and I eventually spent some time analyzing more or less informally my own writings. The simultaneous fear of inexpressiveness and of overexpressiveness is a recurrent topic in the material I had just decided to put aside as eluding completion by me, in its thesis form called *The Claim to Rationality*, in its revised and doubled form published as *The Claim of Reason*. We sometimes used this uncompleted work as promptings for discussing the relation of philosophy and psychoanalysis, especially of the role of therapy in philosophy, if any, and the role of philosophy in therapy, if that is different—to consider my early life in relation to ideas of childhood abuse and abandonment and neglect, in other words, in relation to isolation and despair and to inexplicable bouts of ecstasy, including intellectual ecstasy. It helped me find a kind of perspective on myself as a specific case, a study of a more or less definite complex of puzzles, with continuing, partial solutions, interesting to me.

August 4, 2003

If I again protest my awareness that the worst things that happen

in the world to masses of children had not happened to me, I do not
want to slight the calamitous waste in my inability to respond with discernible flexibility or imaginativeness to being left alone to deal with
friendlessness, and with unappeasable desires whose intensity seems to
me (now as then) to border on madness, and with an incomprehension
of what was expected in school that I had no one to clarify. When my
history teacher at Boys High School handed me back my report card
he observed, "I really do not know why I did not fail you." Surely I did
not know why. Any more than I knew what he meant when in the classroom he talked repeatedly about the papacy, certainly no inkling that it
may have to do with a pope, whatever that was. (And I would not imagine that my parents would have known.) If we were assigned a textbook
for the course it was unknown to me. It would describe my condition
to say that I did not know where to begin to look up answers to what
I did not know were questions, thoughts recognizable as reasonable to
others. I got through my biology course, which essentially required out-
lining chapters of a book that was left in the desk at school, by a rather
nice method of cheating. (I had done next to nothing in the course for
months, and then in the concluding five or six weeks of the term I for no
reason started to read and to find interest in the book we were to outline and began receiving excellent grades; but since these were merely
weekly grades, they were to be mechanically amassed with my earlier,
rotten grades, not assessed for progress. The teacher at the end of term
read out to the class a list of the numbered grades each student had acquired on the outlines over the term, and directed us to add up the total of our points and circle that number, warning us that he was going
to check to see whether we had done our math correctly. My method,
which went undetected, was, after the first couple of numbers, sometimes to add a few points to a week's number as I wrote it down, then
add correctly to get the total, which I obediently circled.)

No doubt not all single children of parents whose exchanges so
often ended in silence or rage—let's recognize this pair as self-preoc-
cupied with competitions of melancholy—prove to be as unresourceful
as I was in responding to this condition. It did not, I think, occur to me
explicitly that their avoidance of me was a function, essentially on my
mother's part, of an avoidance of each other. My lack of resourcefulness
required some lethal combination of circumstances. I assume, prepared

by the destruction of the life of the house on Atlanta Avenue and the consequent unconcealed eruption of my father's violent temperament, that the resultant paralysis of spirit (something I come back to thinking of sometimes as a multiyear period of coma) was continued, or unchallenged, by the isolation in being at once an only child and being the wrong age to have my classmates as a source of friends, all working with my parents' prolonged absences and their ignorance of what happens in an American high school. My father's final schooling had been a secondary level Hebrew school in Zabludova (his shtetl a few miles south of Bialystok), and while my mother said that she had graduated high school, she also said, more credibly given various circumstances, such as the clarity and rarity of her talent and the family's need of money, that she was playing in a pit orchestra for vaudeville and silent films at the age of sixteen. She was particularly proud to describe the return on her commercial work as "making a man's salary."

August 6, 2003

Life took a distinct turn for the better during the summer after that first year of high school. We were to move back to Sacramento at the beginning of the fall, pushed and pulled. Pulled, as noted, because my father's brother there was offering to back him in a store of his own. Pushed, because the radio station announced that it could no longer afford a resident orchestra. The declared cause was that the musicians' union was reevaluating the rating of the city's major venues for hired performance, and the revised minimum number of musicians required for a resident radio orchestra was larger than the station could support, so the station discontinued the orchestra. The musicians at the station were, I gathered, divided between blaming the musicians' union and blaming the station—my mother seemed to blame both. A further reason must have been that greater reliance on national broadcasting hookups were inevitable for the principal stations of substantial but not major cities, so there became more ways of filling airtime. One of the tasks my mother had occasionally to be prepared for, as the station's studio pianist, was to fill gaps of a few minutes when the less systematized programming routines of what was still early radio required extending the length of some segment for unpredicted minutes. The announcer would on such an occasion invite the listening audience to a "musical interlude." Even in those years a radio station was not allowed to remain silent for more than a maximum number of minutes. I was told this was a matter of law. The only reason I could divine for such a law was to avoid the eerie silence, or broken silence, of a radio tuned to nothing. A thought to ponder. In the days when stations (as later, television stations in their first decades will do) signed off the air between 11 p.m. and midnight, what was left was not sheer silence. Sometimes, with our local stations silenced, indecipherable sounds seemed to tell of distant stations inaccessible while local stations were functioning, but too distant under our local preparation to make themselves clear; and sometimes a large Chicago station, still on the air from a local time an hour earlier than our Eastern zone, would, with some adjustment of tuning, become audible in Atlanta with perhaps strains from a famous dance band from "high atop" (as I recall the announcement) the exotically and rhythmically named Edgewater Beach Hotel. (It was not without a certain lingering thrill that I saw in fact that actually dramatic structure the first time, easily four decades later, when I was being driven from the University of Chicago along North Shore Drive into Evanston to lecture at Northwestern University.)

Glad as I was not to face my Atlanta high school again, I had no particular reason to be glad to be returning to Sacramento, but also no good reason against it, since attending high school would be a new experience there, and while the same group of Western classmates would probably still be mostly intact, there was a distinct tug of curiosity in wondering what differences a two-year interval (there had been no exchange of letters between me and any one of this group) would make in the unyielding circumstances I had left and to see what the passage of time had brought to each of those people who had been so much of the unlikely, unlovely, world to me. It would be a chance to, as it were, observe the world, receive a new impression of it, if not awakening to it perhaps taking some useful interest in it.

My mother's feelings were, as usual, mostly kept in their secret places. While the work at the radio station had become at best routine, there was, there still is, a kind of agreeable salon music, most of it drastically familiar, whose pieces no one would seem to have taken the trouble to compose since they appear to have existed forever, that formed the basis of the WSB orchestra's repertory. Liszt's Liebestraum (featuring my mother's virtuosity in its two cadenzas), Cécile Chaminade's Scarf Dance, the Meditation from *Thais*, Grieg's *Peer Gynt*, sections of Tchaikovsky's *Nutcracker Suite* are among the most famous, and among the best, examples of them. Certain of their cousins, on the whole more ambitious offerings (arias from *Carmen* and from Gounod's *Faust*, Chopin's Funeral March, parts of Mendelssohn's *Midsummer Night's Dream*) were staples of the sound tracks of classical movie cartoons. My children, Rachel, Benjamin, and David, without growing up in total immersion in the world of classical music, would very early sing along with classical themes coming from the FM concert music stations to be found I suppose in any university town, that they would not often, if ever, have heard in concert, or heard me play, and I had to be told from which cartoon this piece of their musical education had been acquired. I have an undying intermittent taste, even sometimes a modest craving for this indestructible music, in certain respects an increasing admiration for it. For years after this enterprise was in her past, my mother and I, hearing such a piece over the air, would glance at each other and say together, not with unmitigated nor unaffectionate condescension, "WSB."

As for my father's feelings about the move, they were also held more lightly than I had known him in the past able to sustain. The liquor store was a dead end with no inherent interest for him. Working in a well-kept pawnshop was no more shameful, and he would for the first time not be working in direct subordination to his brother's capricious wishes and decisions. Moreover it required experience and an expertise in diamonds and watches that he could take some pride in, and it rewarded vigorous haggling, a form of extended conversation that he could relish with strangers, about whose places of origin he regularly inquired and, astonishingly to me, seemed to know or surmise some fact.

Although Cathleen's and my sons were born in different seasons, the older, Benjamin, in early summer, the younger, David, seven late winters later, their Bar Mitzvahs were, for different reasons, scheduled in their respective years on the same date in our reform synagogue's calendar, which fell roughly at the return to school at the end of summer. Accordingly, and uncannily, the portion of the Torah they both read was from Chapter 24 of Deuteronomy, in which laws of usury are promulgated, requiring respect for those who have borrowed from you and left you a pledge (in short pawned something with you), along with the law against gleaning, that is, an ordinance to leave something to undiscerned need, to confess the knowledge that you were once enslaved. And in each of the obligatory speeches Benjamin and David wrote for their occasions, they alluded to the fact of their grandfather's owning a pawnshop, emphasizing perfectly true stories I had told them of his (and for that matter, his brother's) extreme care in giving every chance to those who had pawned things with them to have time to redeem them. California law required at the time I worked in their stores that pledges be held for six months, plus a one-month period of grace, before they could be offered for sale. Grace amazingly is what the law actually called the additional period, and what the police called it. One of my responsibilities in my father's store was to fill out a form with details of each of the day's pledges and walk the page, or pages, over to the police station to be filed. Another of my responsibilities was to go through and remove old, that is expired, pledges to prepare them for sale, making room in the storage safe for the new, and I was directed not to remove any pledge from storage until it had been kept, not merely for the legal span of seven months, but for something approaching a year. If it was a wedding ring, it would be kept for another six months after that.

August 7, 2003

The concepts of grace and of redeeming are only beginning suggestions of the poetry of pawnbroking. Counting, especially counting up the monthly interest owed, upon redemption (I mean upon the pawner's returning with his ticket to redeem his pledge), was another of my responsibilities. Here we encounter certain opening suggestions of the philosophy of the concepts of pawnbroking. The concept of what we count, especially count as of interest or importance to us, is a matter fundamental to how I think of a motive to philosophy, fundamental to what I want philosophy to be responsive to and to illuminate. Something like the poetry and philosophy caught intermittently in the ideas of redemption and grace and interest and importance (or mattering or counting) was of explicit fascination to me before I stopped working in the pawnshop, the year I graduated high school. The first stories I tried writing were stabs at elaborations of such connections. They almost always included what we called the cage, the space at the back of the store not open to customers, separated off by a thin but firm wooden screen from the front of the store and its showcases and shelves of merchandise for sale. The cage was entered through a door opening from one of the store's fixed walls, opened either with a key or by a handle from inside, and while it had horizontal windows across most of its length, making the front of the store visible from the cage, its only fixed, hence limited, open access was through a barred cashier's vertical window marked at its bottom edge with a waist-high shallow shelf, spanned at the top by an arch shaping the order of the bars, through which purchases were paid for and receipts written, and on the shelf of which the pawn ledger would be set, on which the article to be pawned was described (by me or by my mother when we were present) and then signed by clients and the matching ticket torn from its perforated connection and given along with the amount of the loan, eventually to be signed by the customer's matching signature at the time of redemption. While my attentive description of the cage is meant to express my sense that my mother and I were successively, occasionally simultaneously, effectively cooped there, the geography of our store was essentially that of every pawnshop I ever entered (there were over the years probably four of them, all in Sacramento).

My written, or half-written, stories came to nothing, partly because they would prove to become ambitious beyond my experience and my intellectual means, partly because I kept wanting to include in them the occasional but impressive prostitutes and perhaps their clients who wandered the one block over to the store from J to K Street to pawn something, impressive not because they were gaudy, but rather because it did not seem obvious what marked their difference—for some time I imagined that prostitutes, like nurses, wore uniforms—yet I sometimes knew, or thought I knew, from the reactions of another customer, perhaps from my mother's heightened disdain, such a theoretical fact about just this person here and now, of course knowing not a scrap of how she might be living.

If the address on the pawn ticket had been a small hotel on J Street, that would have been a giveaway. My father would habitually take visitors from out of town, coming to meet him in his store, down the one block and point out the almost continuous rows of neon signs with the names of such hotels on them along the far side of the street marking adjacent four- or five-story buildings one or two rooms wide running between perhaps 5th (or below) and 7th Streets. Some of the signs were horizontal, dim and small, running along the edges of a door-wide canopy at the entrance; some of the signs were brighter and tall and thin, running vertically from the entrance up several stories. I never heard clearly enough to understand the excited speech my father delivered walking ahead with his visitor or visitors as he pointed to these signs, but I figured it out soon enough after I began working in the store regularly, and had no need then to keep our visitors company by attending these tours. It did occur to me, on my way coming back from lunch one summer early afternoon—a break that I often began by depositing the preceding day's cash receipts in the bank—to return to the store by a detour along J Street and pay attention to the tiny painted words at the bottom of those signs. The ones I remember read "Transient Rooms." I do not know why these words had failed to attract my interest before, nor why on reading them they seemed disappointing. Had I expected to see something exciting, like "Whorehouse"? And were, or when and where were, whorehouses actually houses? And "transient" was so dull and imprecise a modifier. Did it just mean temporary or passing? But why would a hotel need to specify transience? As opposed to what? Did people live permanently in hotels? Or did the very fact that they specified it mean that it was a code signaling that you could take a room for a fraction of a day?

It would be pointless for me to insist upon specific or fanciful connections between my pawnbroking assignments and the work I would eventually find for myself in writing. Various orders of connections will become undeniable as part of the fruit of these autobiographical reflections, or they count for nothing. I might make two anticipatory observations at this stage. First, the connection between philosophy and the major terms of economic exchange (interest, inheriting, borrowing, owing, terms, conditions, account, utility, obligation, responsibility, etc.) was first made inescapably plain to me a quarter of a century after my last year working in my father's store in coming to begin writing in the late 1960s my little book about Thoreau's inestimably wonderful *Walden*, which is so explicitly and intensely and incessantly about the economic dimensions of a human existence and which precisely— might this now go without saying?—is at the same time a philosophical study of the life of the I who is writing and thinking through a year or two in the perpetually strange and familiar woods in which, if it will, it finds itself. (It seems to me in all seriousness worth considering what Thoreau knew about the origin of German idealism, whether in particular he had got hold of a text, or a description of a text, by Fichte, pointing Kant toward Hegel, whose emphasis on the analysis of the role of the I in deriving the unity and objectivity of the world is announced in the opening paragraphs of *Walden*.) Second, the fact that my sons were able to take pride publicly in my descriptions of my father's honest dealings in the conduct of his pawnbroking business proved to be for me a further gesture toward redeeming my experiences of shame and desperation lodged in, or forming an aura circling, as it were doubling, every diamond and watch and showcase and ticket ledger and brown storage envelope and the ink-stained blotter-lined shelf inside the cage and the broken pens that were circumstances of my life in that store. I do not doubt that their residues play a direct part in making feasible my present writing of this segment of that life, hence in finding usable perspectives upon untold further stretches of it. I believe there may have been a time in my life so low that I would have been prepared to refuse instead of to cultivate this gesture of redemption precisely because of the redemption it must extend to my father's desperate life. Curing, or curbing, this vindictiveness, this recurring, self-destructive longing to consign one's father to hell, is also something for which I owe my children an unending debt of gratitude.

August 8, 2003

In fairness to myself, I had come some distance back from that low rung by a timely distaste for myself and out of experiences with friends. I seem to have realized that the experiences of the pawnshop need not have been without leavening even as they were collecting. I mean to be rendering some sense of my interest in what was happening, or indicating some plausible drift of eventuality to be drawn from it. (An expression among my high school acquaintances to express a worthless task or effort was to ask, "What's the future in that?") I was not as young a child working in the pawnshop as Dickens was in the blacking factory that caused him permanent grief.

At the ages of fourteen and fifteen I was, and could have been more, able to take a certain pleasure in learning from my father the meaning of the written letters and numbers on the tickets attached to each object for sale in the store. If there was a number there, of from three to five digits, this signified that the object had been drawn from the expired pledges taken in pawn and it expressed in code the amount lent. It might also signify that it had been bought outright, which would mean that more money had been paid out for it—in general an object pawned was worth many times what it was pawned for, but produced just the five dollars or ten dollars needed for a weekend, or after the banks had closed for the weekend, and were redeemed days later with a fifty-cent or (if the amount were larger) seventy-five cent or dollar interest charge. Interest was assessed by the month, calculated from the day of the month the object was left and the ticket written. (I have forgotten how it was figured when, for example, an item pawned on March 31 was redeemed on May 1. There is no April 31, which would have concluded a first month, but at the same time only thirty-one days had elapsed, still arguably one month's worth of days. My strong guess is that my father would for a number of reasons not argue the point and figure interest for just one month.) On the last days of the calendar month, just before payday for many of our regular customers, so many pledges piled up that it seemed hardly worth the trouble to mark separate envelopes for most of them before they would be redeemed; but of course the items had scrupulously to be identified and kept separate. That piling up could signal the most venial of human frailties on the part of the pawners it represented—perhaps the price of a savor of human magnanimity, from showing off in a bar by buying drinks for strangers, to lending a friend money you did not have. Yet sometimes even these pledges were not redeemed. If they were not, I might be reminded of the fact in straightening out the pledges or segregating them when they became legally and practicably sellable. Then I would

perhaps imagine the story it happened to speak of. It would not, I believe, have been past me then to wonder who would have the right to
tell its story.

The number code on an object's ticket was cracked by dropping
the number's first and last digits, and understanding the remaining
digit or digits as twice the price lent or paid. This was then the basis on
which a price was named for the customer and bargaining could begin.
I said that there may be on an object's ticket, instead of numbers, two or
three letters written in capital letters. This signified that the object had
not been pawned, but was among merchandise bought wholesale, for
sale new, in competition with the so-called credit jewelry stores beginning to emerge a block further uptown. Objects so ticketed would range
from costume jewelry (mostly too inexpensive or too readily subject to
showing wear to be worth accepting in pawn) to expensive watches,
kept in stock for shoppers wandering downtown in search of special
bargains, and who could get one if they paid cash, or make a down
payment on a "layaway plan." The solution of the code, still meant to
show disguised what the object had cost the store, is pretty. The two or
three letters each represented one of the ten single digits in order from 1
through 9 plus 0, determined by coordination with the order of the letters in the word WANDERLUST, so W = 1, A = 2, . . . T = 0. I was, if
something in the business of running a pawnshop can be called charming to a fifteen-year-old male of my stripe, charmed by these pieces of
knowledge. I am prepared to propose WANDERLUST as part of the
poetry of pawnbroking (unless it is, or was, part of the poetry of the
jewelry business generally). With the advent of computers doubtless all
this handiwork of coding has become pointless.

This information was strictly what I needed to make out tickets
for objects on sale. No further instruction was forthcoming, about, for
example, how my father would arrive at an initial asking price, what
told him that a sale might be lost, how he judged the taste of a stranger
looking for a watch, whether it was merely by expense or sometimes
also by aspiration, whether bringing out a new object would offer a real
temptation or merely dampen interest in the object already in question.
I did not aspire to master these matters myself and to be entrusted to
make sales. It was clear to my father that I had no such inclination,
indeed that to talk people into buying something they might or might

not want was a repellent idea to me. By the way, this can be taken as a prejudicial, you might even say a repellent, idea of what selling and buying are. Mendel will eventually tell me that I had an old-fashioned idea of the institution of salesmanship; he wrote books on the subject. But then his idea was, throughout the long successful years of his life—though he would not have phrased the matter so—that selling is the essential motive of human encounter and speech. A simple difference here from Wittgenstein's vision of speech as the revelation of desire and need is that in Mendel's world we are persistently persuading others that their desires are what we desire them to be. It is I trust not difficult to imagine, from here, the creepiness I felt hardly more than half a dozen years later, beginning the study of philosophy, to find the latest cry in moral philosophy—most notably in two volumes ubiquitous in philosophy departments at the time, A. J. Ayer's *Language, Truth and Logic* and Charles Stevenson's *Ethics and Language*—to be the claim that moral judgment at its best, or most, was irreducibly an expression of emotion meant to move and perhaps persuade. As Cary Grant says in another context over the phone to his managing editor Duffy in the concluding sequence of *His Girl Friday*, as he is instructing Duffy in re-casting his newspaper's front page to expose an imminent unjust execu-tion, certain stories should be left in a prominent place simply because they convey human interest, like reporting a lost or found dog.

A more common mode of the instruction I received in the pawn-shop was exemplified the day my father, sending a customer back to the cage, where the cash drawer was located, for me to accept the money for a purchase, called out an unintelligible syllable to me that I took as meant to catch my attention, as he sometimes called out "Front," mean-ing, as derivable still from hotel jargon, for me to come out into the store from the cage to attend to a customer, engage him or her in conversa-tion, perhaps show the customer around the store, until my father had completed his business with someone else. But since this customer was walking back to the cage, I thought I must have misunderstood. After he handed me the bill on which my father had written the amount and gave me cash that either did or did not require change, I described the object purchased on the bill and marked it paid, handed the receipt to the man, thanked him, exchanged good-byes with him, and as the cus-tomer left the store my father walked back to the outside of the window of the cage and asked if I had been sure to add excise tax. (During the Second World War a 10 percent surcharge was added to certain purchases, amounting to a kind of luxury tax. The American population was in that war together.) My impression was that sometimes my father included this tax in his asking price, sometimes not. I would hear him say sometimes, "With tax that comes to . . . ," and sometimes, "I'll pay the tax myself," as part of the bargaining process. I replied to him that I had not added the tax. He began to go into one of his outbursts of rage, grabbing and shaking the bars of the cage, shouting, "I told you specifically!" I was dumbfounded. When did he tell me? How had he told me? He went on: "I called out to you 'Dus'!" "Dus," Yiddish for "That," was evidently used by my father as code for the word "Tax," or more strictly for the sentence, "Calculate the price by adding the excise tax, and if the customer objects, I'll take over." He must have used the term to instruct my mother; maybe it had been Yiddish slang for a hundred years, or maybe only since shortly after the high tide of Jewish emigration from Eastern Europe and then only among jewelers. But there has to be a first time one picks up the word in this usage, or is expected to understand it. Should I say that my father was a bad teacher, or say that he was no teacher at all? Neither captures the amount I learned in his presence. (If the careful irony in which I cast such an observation was part of my adolescent repertory of response, what to my mind was there in such a creature to deserve a father's love?)

I can become impressed to the point of prophecy by the fact that we are incessantly teachers and learners and ignorers, that others are perpetually informing us about themselves, sharing their deepest secrets with us. This is one way to read the opening of Wittgenstein's *Philosophical Investigations*, something I have over the years proposed reading in various ways. Wittgenstein quotes Saint Augustine's reconstruction of his coming into the possession of language not by anyone's teaching him words (that will happen too, but it will come later) but by watching his elders and learning what sounds of theirs go with what it is they desire. (From whom then do we learn the ciphering of desire?) You can say that this is meant to suggest that learning outruns teaching (as every teacher knows, or trusts) or that since the time of learning is unpredictable, and yet that since almost everyone gets the idea of talking in roughly the same remarkably early interval in his or her life, every act of speaking is a demonstration, hence each the work of a teacher. I would like to mean this as a sublime thought, but at the moment I am reminded of times in which I have felt I may lose the point of speaking altogether, simply never again wish to, or be moved to, open my mouth.

August 9, 2003

Floating, with the onset of the Atlanta summer after my first year of high school, between taking again my inner leave of Atlanta and my unfruitful fantasies of what Sacramento might now have in store, it had not occurred to me that my mother would eventually work regularly in the pawnshop, nor that I would be there afternoons, and weekends, and holidays, especially at Christmas, including some Sunday mornings to help mop the floor and perhaps accept a promising stray customer, and all summer.

I began a routine that last summer in Atlanta of going every day to the new Jewish Progressive Club swimming pool to have a sandwich for lunch at the pool snack bar, if not with company nevertheless not alone, and to pretend to swim while really intent on keeping my left ear from getting wet. This was the same social club, but now established in a rather fashionable setting on the far side of town, that my father spent his Sunday mornings in when we lived on Atlanta Avenue. It was founded, as our synagogue was founded a couple of decades earlier, by the Eastern European Jews on the south side of Atlanta, around the end of the First World War. One of my favorite things to do out of the house in those early years was for my mother and me to go on a Sunday night to meet my father at the Progressive Club and to have supper sitting on a balcony that overlooked the gymnasium where often a basketball game would be in progress. My father said he had been the manager of the club team, something I for some time puzzlingly confused with being its coach; in any case I never experienced any benefit from his position further than this piece of knowledge. He also said he had been chair of the entertainment committee, which hired acts for occasional evenings of vaudeville the club offered its members. He would attribute some of his jokes to those acts, more specifically to staged conversations initiated by what he called "the end man in a minstrel show." For instance: "Mr. Bones, do you see that fine-looking woman walking down the street wearing that beautiful dress?" ["Beautiful" was pronounced as having four syllables and said with a certain accent I could not place]. "I do." "Uh-huh; I give her that. And do you see that marvelous [also prolonged] bracelet she's got on her wrist"? "I do." "Uh-huh; I give her that, too. And do you also see that very lovely child holding her hand just below that bracelet?" "Oh yes I do." "Why that's her sister's child." My father made no faces reciting such a narration, but his timing was such that he never failed to draw sharp, grateful laughter, in which he then joined—and I knew as early as I could make the distinction that he knew the gag was corny and got the laugh using the knowledge of the corniness as part of the fun, a knack certain comedians particularly cultivate. Over my three years as an undergraduate at Berkeley I composed, in addition for that of other productions, increasing amounts of music for the annual revue written and performed by members of the theater students' honor society. My last year, when I wrote the bulk of the music, I also contributed ideas for various of the skits, and we used that old story of my father's for one of our punctual blackouts. It proved to be perfect material for a new member of the theater society who had shown a notable talent for producing a raucous vaudeville delivery. (I might again invoke here the cunning of history, but it is hard to imagine history's bestirring itself for such small change.)

I have remarked that my father was well known in his circles for the stories he told in Yiddish, the most impressive of which were as long as short short stories and whose punch lines were less important than the telling of the stories, making epics out of events of unnoticeably everyday characters (everyday mostly perhaps in Bialystok eleven decades ago). These were mostly reserved for dinner table conversation when his traveling salesmen friends were visiting from New York, with their own sets of stories, and tales of what I took to be their own adventures. I did not understand certain of their tales during the years on Atlanta Avenue, and as my understanding of Yiddish improved I understood why that was and accordingly hid my understanding. But I loved the stories for the attention they held, for the mounting pleasure they constructed, and for the burst of excellent feeling they released, all depending upon the talent displayed in the telling. It was, as I learned it, the strict decorum of telling Yiddish stories that they had to be ap-

propriate to an occasion (as least an initial story had to be; others could
follow their lead if they at least equaled, in some direction, that appropriateness). Fewer of these stories were told when we moved away
from Atlanta, not simply because of the less protected melancholy that
took up residence with us, but because the audience for telling them
dwindled; such an audience was, so far as I knew, virtually nonexistent
in Sacramento (except possibly for my uncle Morris, who however was
humorless, and occasionally for me, happily).

It is, I believe, part of the well-established sociology of Atlanta
(how representative this is of other Southern American capital cities I
do not know) that until the late 1960s, whatever degree of integration
the weekday world of business achieved (among white groups), social
life at night and on weekends took place not only in racially but in
religiously segregated clubs. The Jewish community of Atlanta, at any
rate by the time I experienced it, had segregated itself further between
a club for German, or German-speaking Jews (the "Deitchen" they
were called by their coreligionists), and Jews from Eastern Europe and
Russia (the latter peopling our Progressive Club). There were in 1850, I
am informed by a rare and primitive search of the Internet, twenty-six
Jews living in Atlanta, a town then of something over two thousand
souls, rising to six hundred Jews by 1880, just as the Eastern European
wave of immigrants was beginning. (My paternal grandparents with
their seven children left Zabludova for America, I surmise, as a result
of the pogroms at the turn into the twentieth century. There is a family
story that a sister of that grandfather had been bayoneted by a Cos-
sack.) By the time I recall hearing a figure myself, Jews in Atlanta in
the early 1930s were said to number roughly one thousand families in
a general population of something over one hundred thousand souls.
(That proportion seems high to me, but Atlanta, then as now, was not
a typical Southern city. Another remarkable feature of its population,
which I often heard repeated to visitors in town, was that it contained
a distinctly large class of well-to-do black people. I often wondered
where they lived.) The German Jewish reformed house of prayer was
called the Temple, and its distinction from our orthodox synagogue
was still significant enough in 1940 that I would sometimes hear my
quite enlightened aunt Ida question the suitability of a marital alliance
for certain of the comparatively extensive field of the young among her

relations and her acquaintance, by noting that an intended (or supposed) object of their desire came from a family that "go to Temple."

The Progressive Club came into my life again in the summer of
1940, because, as would happen a few years later to the synagogue,
younger Jewish families with growing affluence and expectations,
raising American children free of accent and of ancient manners,
wanted not only a club in a more prosperous region of Atlanta, but
one boasting the luxuriousness and display of a golf course, which is
I suppose the essential criterion for making the transition to a proper
country club. It would have been my uncle Mendel's idea to get me
visitor's privileges to the club's swimming pool facility for the summer
in question. My father was no longer a member (I do not know when
that stopped, having heard nothing more about it from the time we
moved from the south side of town), partly because he and my mother
worked all the time, and partly perhaps because they never really
knew whether we would be in town long enough to warrant investing
a year's dues, and partly because, while Mendel had been too young
for the old Progressive Club, my father was now too old, or felt he
was, for its new incarnation, having lost connection with its inevitable changes as events changed Atlanta. This is what I understood
his public reasons to be for his withdrawal. I gathered that some old
acquaintances of his had suggested to him that he should be the manager of the new club, remembering his prominence in the Progressive
Club's original formation; but his accent, even though not exaggerated, would have ruled him out as a representative of the modern
club to the wider community. So joining it under these circumstances
would have been for him to have accepted a form of rejection. As for
my understanding then of his reasons for choosing isolation, I seem
to have put aside the thought that there was something—something I
could affect—that might make him happy. The fact that the English
word *mad* means both angry and insane has repeatedly seemed to me
wonderfully perceptive of it.

Besides, his traveling salesmen friends, especially the Epstein
brothers, offered a better bridge game than was likely at the club, and
they knew endless stories about, for example, even better bridge players
around New York. I watched the bridge games in our apartment with
my parents and these friends sometimes just to hear these stories. One

featured their younger brother and sister who had beaten renowned players in a pickup game at a bridge club in New York. Again, naturally, the interest lay in the telling. First there was a description of the playing of the hand in question, emphasizing perhaps an evidently daring but rational finesse on the part of the sister during the endgame, and the punch line of the story came after everything had been played out. The sister, as they left the club, asked the younger brother: "Who are these palookas?" And now Milton Epstein, telling the story, finished by saying: "Sitting to her left had been Jacoby [I think that was the name] and to her right had been Culbertson." The tone of it made life in New York sound as adventurous as if he had said: "To her left was The Shadow and to her right was Batman." And golf would have interested my father about as much, to adapt a Yiddish saying of his, as Sunday would have interested a cow.

While I had no friends at the club swimming pool, I was essentially not out of place there; my presence was authorized by an established member of it. And after all, since those at play there were all Jews, nobody would try to hug me or otherwise harass me without warrant. And there were kids of all ages present. The girls my age or a little older were wonderful to look at, and I could listen with pleasure to them talk and laugh all afternoon. It was worth risking having to spend part of the fall in visits to the ear doctor to jump into the water and accidentally brush against them.

A memory slips in here that has to be earlier than the car accident, yet already containing interlocking concepts of accident and exuberance and the loss of consciousness, in a context of jumping into water. A group of several mothers together with their children had gathered at the small indoor pool, presumably for a children's swimming lesson, in the basement of the old Progressive Club. Designed only for members, hence for grown men, the pool was deeper than a child's height even at its shallow end. But there was a grown-up, perhaps two, presumably the intended teachers, already standing chest high, so I was assured that it was safe just to plunge in feet first. Persuaded by my mother to take off my clothes even in the presence of these other women (I assume at this distance that swimsuits were not allowed in the inside pool; I do not remember whether any of the other children were girls, but two girls on Atlanta Avenue had already visibly swapped the basic secrets with me), I ran quickly away from their eyes and, with a pause at the edge, leapt down an exhilarating distance into the pool. After the shock of the water my next memory is of lying on my stomach on a soft table (evidently some kind of massage table covered with a mat and a towel) with people hovering around it. Apparently my mother, never exact in her descriptions beyond matters of music, had neglected to tell me that I was not to plunge into the water until directed to do so. (But one cannot say everything, anticipate in advance every possible misunderstanding, plausible or idiotic. This is perhaps the originating nightmare of philosophy. For example, you can hardly warn an adventurous, otherworldly child—call him Moses—against picking up an attractively glowing hot coal and putting it in his mouth. So we seem forced to adapt to some version of mumbling. For all my recurrences to the sense of speech as chronically incomplete or inopportune or interrupted or unfair, say, psychically essentially unsynchronized, I think I would not have in this context of urgency spoken of living with mumbling apart from exchanges with Marc Shell about his book *Stuttering*.)

My mother once greeted me as I entered our Sacramento pawnshop, with the message, "Your friend Jack Litch [my companion clarinet player in high school] dropped by to say hello on his way through town. He is a corporal, or a colonel, or something." In a later era when I told her on the phone from Cambridge that I was being rewarded for my performance on the Ph.D. qualifying examinations by being sent to Austria for half of the coming summer, she replied with surprise, "Australia?" Yet in later years when she visited me in Cambridge and, after Cathleen and I married, in Brookline, and, Cathleen having left for work and I having to disappear upstairs in my study for an hour or so to finish preparing a lecture, I would habitually take from a shelf, for example, a quite handsome, generously illustrated edition of Burckhardt's *Civilization of the Renaissance in Italy* and open it before her on the dining room table, where she was finishing a morning cup of tea. I would return to find her still in that place, the pages of the Burckhardt in a fairly distant place. She would look up dreamily, as sometimes when she had been listening to music, saying, "It is so beautiful." I recognized the mood as a power of absorption that sometimes exasperated me and sometimes inspired me. From some historical account of life in an Eastern European Jewish shtetl (diminutive of *Shtut*, Yiddish for the German *Stadt*), I had learned that Jewish women of that place and time never sat down in the daytime. Except, I understood, for religious observance, or out of obligation or fame, as in becoming a scribe, or a concert pianist.

The new club's location was fair enough for cushioning, or keeping inarticulate, my loneliness. It was in the general region of the junior high I had transferred to from California before entering Boys High in Atlanta, so the roughly fifteen-minute bus ride from our apartment was routine. What is distinctly more, two or three streets away stood the still prominent Biltmore Hotel from the roof of which a transmission tower marked the building as the home of the broadcast studios of WSB. So that at the end of each afternoon that I was at the swimming pool I could walk over to meet my mother for dinner in the coffee shop of the Biltmore, wait outside (sometimes inside) the studio at the top of the Biltmore building while the orchestra rehearsed for their 10:30 broadcast, and after the show accompany her home.

In those daily weekday summer bus rides to the Progressive Club, having been early and well accustomed to sitting in the back of the bus with one or another black maid responsible for me, I was at my ease on the bus only when I was standing, holding on to the vertical metal pole at the rear door, unless there were so few passengers that it seemed as if everyone had chosen where to sit. To have sat farther back than any white person (instead, for example, of sitting next to a white person even if it meant climbing past him or her into a window seat, when it was obvious that someone's taking an outside seat meant that he or she wished to be alone) would have meant creating a segregation line of my own, since where black people sat depended on where the farthest-back white person sat. (Reporting this at this distance seems something out of mythology. Yet I do not doubt that it is a true account.) Still, I recall a bus ride on that route at night in which a number of boys from the Progressive Club sprawled all across the long back seat of the bus, and it is not likely that no black person was seated on the bus. Maybe children were exempted from having to participate in this godforsaken segregation ritual (if not from witnessing it). Then it is worth knowing when childhood ends and seeing begins face-to-face.

August 12, 2003

It would have been early in those daily summer excursions, while I was still uncertain which way to walk in the red clay paths in the woods being cleared for the part of the new club still under construction that, as I was hesitating on the sidewalk, having descended from the rear exit of the bus and wondering whether to follow the surprisingly large clump of white grown-ups and children who had descended from both exits at this otherwise rather barren bus stop, a man's cultivated and Northern voice behind me asked, "Are you doubtful about the direction to the Progressive Club?" I turned to discover a youngish, trim man neither white nor black, with heavy, slightly waved, shining black hair combed straight back, dressed in a tuxedo, without a tie, the collar of his gleaming white dress shirt unbuttoned and looking as if it belonged that way. He continued, as I recall it: "The paths change as the construction work progresses. You may accompany me if you wish." I do not know whether, in my amazement, I thought to thank him, but I accompanied him, and whether oblivious to my somewhat stunned silence, or tactfully responsive to it, he observed: "Thursday is domestics' day off." And he added something explicit about the pertinence of this fact, that it meant that attendance at the pool on summer Thursdays is markedly increased with an influx of children accompanied by their parents (mostly mothers of course, or older siblings, though I seem to recall noting that a father or two had arranged to stay away from work on a summer Thursday afternoon). I had seen films in which figures such as this young man appeared whose names I would have known even approaching the age of fourteen, such as Cab Calloway or the Nicholas Brothers. But was this man a band leader or an entertainer, and if so why was he headed alone through what seemed a private path through the trees for the Progressive Club approaching noon as if this was part of his everyday life? And what, if anything, was his relation to those he called domestics, a term I would have bet was unknown, or unused, by any other human being within a thousand miles of where we were walking together? He waved me onto the path to the swimming pool area as he headed away to the now visible main building of the club. I do not know whether I asked or whether I eventually saw for myself, but I feel certain that he turned out to be the headwaiter of the club's formal dining room.

The two domestics, so to speak, that had been part of my life were present at different times during the years on Atlanta Avenue. These women were affordable as maids not despite but because of the Depression, when the difference between having no money and having some money is absolute. Being the most versatile pianist in Atlanta meant that if one musician in town had a job, my mother had it, even if it meant during one brief period playing burlesque, which it was clear, from the one time, or perhaps it was twice, that she mentioned it, was something she despised, marking it as the lowest point of her life. One of our maids was tall and quite inexpressive and played no role in my life that has left an impression; I suppose she mostly took care of my grandmother, who spent most of her time in bed. The other, who would have come during the last year or two of our lives there, was shorter and somewhat chubby and easy to talk with and seemed to know lots of people, especially ones who knocked at the back door, at the back of the small porch off the kitchen. Once or twice I saw her, as I had seen my mother do, invite a sad-looking, sick-looking, silent man into the kitchen and, sitting him at the kitchen table, give him a plate of food to eat. I was glad they did this, but it hurt me to see that the plate was not as full as I knew mine, or anyway my uncles' plates, would be that night. And nobody was sitting with him. I think it was this early that I first heard the bewildering formula, and intimidating admonition, when I had not cleaned my plate, "There are children starving in India." How was my fortune in having food related to their terrible misfortune in not having food? I would love to send them this food right now that I could no longer possibly eat. If in the future I eat less, will they have more? Why speak to me about this when it is too late to do anything about it? Why has this food just here just now become a rebuke to me? Are there not other grown-ups—and why not all grown-ups—who care about this? Am I ungrateful for having food? Is any contentment of mine a sign of my ignorance and of my badness? I am in no doubt that the seeds of such thoughts, as I stared at the unfinished food on my plate, became an inextinguishable part of my sense or emblem of the world's wrong. This is as clear to me as the memory seems to me to be of the smell and feel of the checkered oil cloth, with several small cracks in it, that covered the kitchen table where the family ate supper together. It is almost enough to make one crave philosophy.

Several times a younger black man came to the back door to whom this maid gave a coin or two, whereupon the man wrote something in a small notebook. She explained to me that she was making bets on numbers and that the number she chose on a given day was one she derived from the previous night's dream, that is, from looking up in her dream book what number to assign to her dream. If she showed me her dream book I have forgotten it, to my sharp regret. I think I never heard of dream books again until I read, with startled recognition, Freud's *Interpretation of Dreams*, in which (looking it up again) he compares what he calls "our popular dream books" unfavorably with those of the Graeco-Roman world and those of the ancient civilizations of the East. Then was this "domestic" of my early world closer in spirit to those earlier worlds, including that of Freud's Vienna, than my relatives and friends have been? She also used snuff, something that again came back to my consciousness only years later, this time prompted by portrayals of foppish aristocrats in certain Hollywood costume dramas. And she told me she liked to fish. These expressions of her pleasures alerted me, if not quite awakened me, to the fact that she had a life beyond this house, one with its own desires. Where did she live and where could she fish?

That small back porch contained a metal-lined, lightwood ice box, small by comparison with a moderately sized refrigerator, of which the ice box is the precursor, yet large enough to block partially the entrance to the back porch. I have thought more often about that object than I can account for, with its large block of ice, when it was newly delivered, taking up so prominent a portion of the space it cooled. (I know that the various adults in the house were careful to see that the smaller door at the top of the ice box, covering the space housing the block of ice, was kept securely closed; perhaps because I was casual about that.) I enjoyed watching the ice delivered, especially as the man went to the back of his truck, took up a huge pair of iron tongs, each curved arm ending in a point, surround a block with the open tongs, then close them hard so that the points penetrated into the block far enough in to lift it. I liked even more watching the coal delivered, which was differently dramatic. The delivery truck would drive halfway down the driveway to an opened basement window of the house into which a metal chute attached to the side of the truck would be turned to fit and to rest on its sill, through which a shower of coal was released onto the basement's dirt floor, making a surprisingly neat mound, a few steps from the furnace.

August 14, 2003

I have recounted the story of my mother's father rising on winter mornings well before the rest of the family to shovel coal into the furnace and light a fire so that the house, or certain of its spaces, would be getting warm as he waked his two oldest children, my mother Fannie and my uncle Meyer, while it was still night outside, to practice their instruments for two hours before leaving for school. His pet names for them were Faygele and Meyerle, as my mother was pleased to tell and to remind me. (Meyer would occasionally, even in his ruin, use this pet name for my mother.) It was a treat for me sometimes to be allowed to help one of my uncles shovel coal into the furnace. There were large ducts leading from the furnace to various grated vents in the floor of rooms above the basement, as from a stationary, uncomplaining beast who tirelessly supported the house with its limbs and breath. Fifty years later, when I lived, and where I continue living to this day, in another brick house, in Brookline, one street from the Boston city limits, a house built, at a guess, half a century before the brick house on Atlanta Avenue—namely, in 1870, when Atlanta would have still been occupied in reconstituting itself after the Civil War—this tale of a worthy father still occasionally would whisper to me, in the years when our sons were still in grade school, in my rising and going downstairs before anyone else to the first floor, while in winter it is still dark, turning on the heat (which now is simply a matter of moving a thermostat a fraction of an inch to ignite a fire in the basement oil burner) and after waking the boys, and after Cathleen or I had prepared breakfast for them, driving them to the school bus, grateful for these simple manifestations of my admiration and encouragement of our two sons, manifestations while in themselves trivial labors were at the same time acts that have helped irreplaceably in the work of repairing broken arteries of my childhood.

There is a reason for my having detailed the fact of my going downstairs to the first floor and not to the basement of our house in

Brookline, having merely to signal the point of a pilot light in the basement. That first house of my affection, in Atlanta, was a gabled-fronted one-story structure with a porch along its entire front, its roof extending from the house supported on its outer side by two columns of brick rising from each end of a brick balustrade to the underside of each outer corner. Most of the other houses of the one or two blocks of Atlanta Avenue that were my and my friends' territory, houses and yards and trees and driveways I recognized as well as I recognized my shoes, roughly followed that pattern, sometimes with the front porch screened in. The significance to me of living in a house of more than one story, namely, one in which you go down a flight of stairs to have breakfast, came to seem to me, initially from the early movies I was taken to, a sure image of luxury. One does not really need this mode of expansiveness. But people who had the pleasure of descending a flight every morning, if my early selection of Hollywood images is reliable evidence, seemed to be glad every morning to see one another. This has proved in my experience to be, even if our town house is comparatively narrow, true enough.

A particular image from that Atlanta basement has traveled a long way in my consciousness. After the event of a coal delivery, I would sometimes go down to the basement to look at the new mound of this substance of mysterious origin some of whose black pieces would shine with particular brilliance just then before shoveling had dislodged some of them onto the dirt floor and thrown even more recent dust onto them. If, as generally was the case, near the foot of the mound a few isolated large pieces would have tumbled free as the coal was being delivered, I would take the ax standing next to the shovel against a short wooden wall, perhaps part of a small tool shed, and with the blunt end of the ax head, tap the side of one of these pieces at first too lightly to affect it, but then strike with increasing force, to determine the point at which, if I hit it just right, it would, instead of chipping or crumbling, split apart cleanly into two intact pieces. Evidently I had first seen this effect happen inadvertently. The satisfaction of the sound of the ax tapping the coal, rather as if to test its soundness, and then on lucky occasions the sight of the lump splitting open, perhaps one or both of the halves falling over under its own newly discovered imbalance to rest on a new facet of itself, produced in me a primitive equivalent of the almost silent shout of appreciation with which my mother would greet a perfectly managed musical ornament or cadence, as during the Kreisler recital. In rehearsing the high school dance band I would quite often come up against the ingrained conviction of some of its members that to swing meant never to hit notes exactly on the beat but something like to syncopate perpetually and to bend notes at unpredictable moments, so that I might feel I had to say to them, I trust not insufferably, something like, "Don't anticipate the beat here, and don't be tempted to play louder when the notes increase in speed. Just split the notes cleanly and let them fall." But I never confided in them about the ax and the larger pieces of coal.

Nor did I yet confide to myself the knowledge that I was still at the beginning of learning how to be tapped so that the hardness in my feelings and the fixations in my mind would, if I could become ready, split open as of their own desire, the better to be consumed. Opening up blocked arteries through catheterization is a reasonable continuation of something in this more ancient image of a task of my life, but it speaks of something others have done to me, not in the same way of my instinct to respond.

A "domestic" perhaps more properly so called, whom I knew quite well, was the distinctly pretty and vivacious maid at the house of a rich cousin of my father's, a man who had made a fortune in the tire business, an outgrowth of a car repair and road service enterprise, whose wreckers had become a familiar sight around Atlanta. The basis of the fortune, according to my father, was actually not tires but snow chains for tires. This cousin and his partner had, perhaps on a hunch, cornered the snow chain market in the Atlanta region. After a couple of mild winters the chains were a drag on the business's resources and the partner wanted to dump the chains at a loss. The cousin bought out the partner and the next winter was rewarded with one of the severest snow and ice storms in memory. The leaden chains had turned to gold.

This cousin had a son my age, one of a number of my second cousins (who will produce many more cousins once removed than I have met), whom I enjoyed visiting when, for example, my mother and I were to spend a Saturday afternoon in his neighborhood visiting Aunt Bess in her new house. (Some seven or eight years into her marriage,

Bess and her husband became convinced that they could not conceive and they adopted a daughter. Within the following year they became pregnant. I have heard of a number of similar cases. I believe I know more people, anyway professionally, who would prefer to regard this as coincidental rather than to sense it as crying out for psychoanalytical illumination.)

Part of the enjoyment of my second cousin's house was its general air as of a place in which people still liked to live, and part of it was the banter in which the pretty light-skinned maid, always dressed in a neat white uniform, teased the cousin by comparing his gifts unfavorably with mine in matters of appearance and manners and appetite and talent (she always encouraged me to play something on the piano). I had no serious illusion that I meant more to her than my cousin did, but the game and her laughter were warmhearted, even exciting. When, not often, I think of those visits, there is unfailingly an image of a Sunday noon in which the soiled dishes from a party the night before were still mostly stacked on the available counter space and on the rolling white metal tray table in the center of the large kitchen. There were plates of uneaten, somewhat collapsed yet stiff miniature sandwiches and partially filled glasses. The maid responded to my curiosity: "Try the ham sandwiches if you like. The highball glasses are what's left of scotch and sodas." At the age of twelve or thirteen I had not tasted ham (bacon was familiar to me, fried almost black with eggs for a late weekend breakfast, but ham, inconsistently, remained as if forbidden), and whiskey I knew only from a time years earlier when a relative stranger among the traveling salesmen at a largish gathering at the Ansley Hotel gave me something to drink poured straight from a bottle and, to his hearty amusement, on my trustingly swallowing the drink my eyes filled with tears as my throat burned and I tried to catch my breath. But forbidden stacks of ham sandwiches and the scotch mixed with flat soda that I now tried from a glass virtually still full, were so surprisingly, deliriously luscious that they became a touchstone of moments in which one wonders how well words convey the deliverances of the senses, or how it is that we can know something and be unable to say it—Austin speaks in this regard of the smell of tar, Wittgenstein of the sound of a clarinet. But I know what it would be to take people to freshly laid, still steaming, tar or to present them with the sound of a clarinet. Whereas if I offered another a somewhat stale ham sandwich and a jigger of scotch mixed with flat soda I might well remain uncertain whether I had supplied the conditions of intense pleasure I experienced in that former hour, which after all was a product not only of these tastes and that context but of the history that led to my astonishment by them.

Shall I surmise an irreducible mystery between the experiences of one human being and those of another? This seems hasty. I am sure that my cousin and the warmhearted maid of his house did not share my experience then. But then it was not important to me to try to communicate it. So is my question whether, if it becomes important to me that a particular person know a particular experience, I might lack the resources to communicate it? Must we become artists in order to express experience so unmistakably that we not become isolated, desolated, by ecstasy, or by confusion?

I recall wondering at my mother's ability to play rapid repeated octaves at the piano and receiving from her the baffling advice in effect to construe my hands as stretches of relaxed iron. If the world of music sometimes seems to me too complacent in its trust of such communications, the world of philosophy often seems to me too distrustful of them. So I keep on the move.

August 15, 2003

I have remarked that when we gave up the communal house and moved to the north side of Atlanta I lost track of where my uncles and my grandmother had moved. Mendel kept in touch with us, anyway with me. On Saturdays he would sometimes phone to say that he was leaving work early enough to take his girlfriend Mynette to Lakewood Park where they would have hot dogs for lunch and then ride in the boats and that they would pick me up and take me along if I would like. He might as well have asked if I would care to visit Paradise. I knew from earlier such arrangements that the pair would probably not arrive until somewhat after noon, but I went outside about eleven in the morning and sat on the top of the three or four concrete steps leading from the sidewalk up to the path to the apartment building to await their arrival. It would not have been reasonable to suppose that I might otherwise have missed them, that perhaps they would have left without me if I had not been visible outside when they drove up. What apparently seemed to be reasonable to me was to imagine that the passing cars and trucks and wagons and bicycles on the considerable thoroughfare outside our building were elements of a parade, harbingers of the arrival of this impeccable pair, of concern to an entire city. (The street was actually simply called Boulevard, as if nothing else in the city would be named, or count as, a boulevard.) The arrival at the lake was each time not merely not disappointing; I would say it was undisappointable. The hot dogs and the rowboats were indeed self-evidently those served and in service also in arcadia.

Bits of news of Uncle Meyer's travels and travails would reach me, mostly from remarks about him made by my father, whose attitude toward him, or his absence, was one normally reserved for promising artists who have died leaving a palpable sense of work just begun. Meyer had once upon a time been promoted from the position of concert master to being the youngest conductor of the Howard Theater orchestra, the most prominent theater orchestra in Atlanta. (The Howard Theater is the name my mother and Meyer used for it; the rest of the world knew it in its reincarnation as the Paramount.) One of his first acts was to move to fire several members of the orchestra who were not up to his plans for the orchestra's future. It happened that one of these members, the flutist I believe, was the girlfriend of the owner of the theater, who blocked the firing. Meyer protested that it was now his orchestra; the owner of the theater observed that the theater was and would remain his.

Meyer quit the position, or was fired from it, went to New York and, whatever else might have presented itself, auditioned to play in a hotel and radio orchestra led by Ben Bernie, a name of some renown in that era of radio's expansion. The story becomes hazier to me at this point. Either Meyer wasn't offered the job he wanted, as first violin, or he was encouraged to wait for some little period until the orchestra would be adding members. Whatever the circumstances, he returned to Atlanta and refused to look further for work as a musician. He will have another chance as a conductor five or six years later when a smaller theater tried the experiment of bringing back vaudeville in a prominent way, the time my mother left my father and me alone in

Sacramento for three months. A year or two past that unsustainable experiment, Meyer surfaced as a violinist in the small radio orchestra along with my mother at WSB, for what proved to be its final year. He could still produce the smile he shared with his brother Mendel and it still warmed my soul, but he had fully become what my father accurately called a "chair man," not a conductor, not a soloist, not one in whom an idea originated and produced an effect. It went without saying, though there were sometimes pertinent syllables dropped, that my mother found it grotesque that an affable banjo player should be the conductor of an orchestra in which Meyer was one of those to whom he gave directions. But whether she blamed Meyer or the world or some other agency was never clear to me, nor, I am equally certain, to her. When my father observed that my wandering from the piano to the clarinet to the saxophone was perfect preparation for my becoming a chair man, I believed the fear was actually as much for me as for himself, and while I believed myself to have other plans, I had none I could spell out, for him or for myself. And did it really make no difference to his imagination what group of chairs my chair might eventually be placed among? (Perhaps this texture of fear and constricted knowledge, with its anticipatory echo of the endowed Chair of Aesthetics and the General Theory of Value I occupied at Harvard during my last decades of teaching amounts only to some private joke certain lesser gods are reduced to telling one another.)

The last job Meyer ever had he got through my father's intervention; it was as assistant manager of the beer and wine store that was in effect a small adjunct to the liquor store my father was managing for successful nephews on his side of our family, who owned the hotel of which the liquor store was an adjunct. (Georgia law did not, anyway then, allow wine and beer to be sold within the same doors as hard liquor.) I learned this almost, it seemed, by chance, in the mid-1960s, just thirty years after the move away from Atlanta Avenue and Meyer's sojourn in New York. I date this new knowledge as two or three years after my father had been operated on for colon cancer, in the winter of 1962–63. It was the operation that, while in a sense successful, had left him permanently weakened, and I continued visiting him from Princeton every three or four weeks in its aftermath, where I was spending that year at the Institute for Advanced Study, a circumstance that itself

warrants some account, a circumstance that meant that I was also flying from Princeton to Berkeley every month to spend time with Rachel.

This, in effect, transitional year, departing Berkeley permanently
for Cambridge and Harvard, was the first time Rachel and I were living in locales remote from one another. I amassed no advice, and little
understanding, of how to manage the distress of such a fact. Rather
than suggesting that one must learn to become a connoisseur of degrees
of distress, I might say that pain associated with some specific, finite
possibility ought to be bearable in a way that, associated with mere
lingering helplessness, it is not.

The academic year 1962–63 is a candidate for having conjoined
the most demonstrably successful and the most inwardly incoherent
stretch of my life. I had the year earlier completed my Ph.D. dissertation, just in time to be eligible for promotion to a tenured professorship
at Berkeley where for five years I had been teaching without the Ph.D.
Not every senior member of the Berkeley department was enamored
of my writing and my teaching, in each register struggling for breath-
able intellectual air, seeking specifically and I suppose insistently, even
somewhat boisterously, an inheritance out of history into the present,
by way of the work of Austin and of Wittgenstein. My senior colleagues,
perhaps with certain dissenting voices, voted to postpone their decision
on my case for tenure until the following year in order to see what more
I would put into publishable shape to add to my two published papers,
certainly not an impressive quantity. (Two publications from the early
years of graduate school in UCLA I literally had no further use for; the
two recent efforts will eventually become the opening essays of my first
book, *Must We Mean What We Say?*) I had no plans for publishing further
work within the next year. The suggestion from several of my younger
colleagues that I might, as the expression goes, carve out two or three
papers from my dissertation was something I had no thought whatever
of pursuing. From the beginning of the conception that got me well
started on the dissertation, it was going to be all or nothing. I do not
recommend the attitude; I merely report it.

Before I had a chance to respond to the department's decision
to postpone considering my further appointment (I had in any case
no alternative to propose), I received an invitation to a tenured position at Harvard, where my tardily submitted dissertation had evidently

made a more consistently or definitively favorable impression. Given this change of circumstance, the Berkeley department allowed itself to skip the postponement and to match my invitation to tenure. I have throughout my life in the academy been protected from disastrous intersections of the operations of favor and of money and of the mind. I had not even applied for my initial appointment at Berkeley. I was officially offered that initial position a few weeks after a conversation with the chair of the Berkeley department during his visit to Harvard among other philosophy departments on the East Coast on a search for prospective candidates for an unannounced position opening at Berkeley. In that conversation I said that I felt unready to begin to teach, that I had become dissatisfied with the dissertation I was working on, and that I was about to go off for a year to Europe, intent, especially in view of the fact that something I would surely be asked to teach is aesthetics, on continuing a belated education in the visual arts that I had recently begun making serious progress with. I added that I would welcome the candidacy for the position if it were agreed that I could be given an initial year's leave of absence and allowed to begin teaching without the Ph.D., in effect offering my having been awarded the previous year a Junior Fellowship at Harvard as a promise, if not an equivalent, of the doctorate. (In fact it was an originating motive for establishing Junior Fellowships that they form this equivalence, a motive that had largely vanished by the time of my selection.) From the perspective of today's management of universities, what must now appear as a comically languid species of bargaining was, in the ancient hierarchies of universities fifty years ago, apparently accepted as within the bounds of the reasonable. By the time my ship sailed for Cherbourg in the late summer of 1955, I had accepted an invitation to join the philosophy department at Berkeley on my return a year later.

    I had hoped that spending the year 1962–63 at the Princeton Institute would allow me a neutral space as it were to try to comprehend my life and make a sensible choice between the new, matching offers from Harvard and Berkeley. More important than the choice of universities—Berkeley and Cambridge were in any case the places I knew best and loved most, and a choice between them merely meant to me that I was saying a difficult good-bye to one or the other—was the fact that I was at the same time saying a painful, permanent good-bye to my marriage, and my primary consideration was accordingly whether living in Cambridge or in Berkeley would maximize the chances of my remaining close to the child of that marriage. If Marcia moved with Rachel to New York, which I knew she was considering, then Harvard was the obvious choice. But what if the very fact of my remaining on the East Coast would prompt her to remain at the distance of Berkeley?

I recognize that this rush of thoughts about matters that will eventually demand more careful attention is an effort to delay approaching my late encounter with Meyer. It was the last time, it turned out—and indeed it felt at the time unmistakably so—that I would see him.

The colon operation had left my father consigned to wearing a colostomy bag, which he did with admirable public humor and a capacity for adaptability that I would not have thought him capable of. He was already quite accustomed to living with the device at the time of the overnight visit to Atlanta and to this final liquor store that I am seeking to recount now. As I was about to leave for the airport and the flight back to Boston, my father asked, "Aren't you going to speak to your uncle Meyer? He's in the back store." Although I hadn't seen Meyer in years, and while this particular turn of events was news to me, it rapidly made obvious and awful sense to me, having from time to time heard of Meyer's further adventures in hard luck, that my father had installed Meyer in the small beer and wine store behind the large liquor store so that he did not have to live on handouts. It was no surprise that my mother had not informed me—that is, would not speak—of Meyer's return before she and I said good-byes at my parents' apartment and I got into a taxi to stop at my father's store before leaving town.

Meyer looked at me with what I read as puzzlement as I entered. He would have been roughly sixty years old, and he looked twenty bad years older than that. In case he couldn't place me I said my name the way my older relatives in Atlanta mostly still say it: "It's your nephew Stan." He smiled as well as he could; something was the matter with his teeth or his jaw, and in a soft, hoarse voice he said, "Hey, Stan." After an awkward hug and exchanges of how long it had been, I was at a loss. It was clear that he had been drinking. I asked aimlessly whether many people had been in his store, adding that my father's in front had been pretty quiet while I was there. Meyer replied: "Just niggers." In all my years of living in and of visiting Atlanta, I recalled no other time at which any relation or friend or acquaintance of mine had spoken that way, in such terms, to me. I had often wondered where Meyer was living, imagining for years, when I would hear about women he had run off with, one or two of whom he had married (that all were gentiles was implicit in the hush and rush of the narratives), that they were glamorous seductresses, irresistibly attracted to him because of his beauty and his talent and the world's lack of appreciation of him. What degradation can have reduced this possessor, like my mother, of perfect pitch, this refined performer of Bach as well as of Sarasate, and knowing interpreter of Kreisler (one of my most significant introductions to the judgment of art, when we were still living together, was hearing Meyer express his love of Kreisler as a violinist, contrasting this with his being merely dazzled by Heifetz's technique), to speaking like white trash? Did he even know what he was saying? My shame for him, of him, made me feel like a child, as if I wished I had never grown up.

Did my father know this about him? Or know something further? It happens that in recent days, returning for late editing two summers after the date of this entry, I learned in an unprecedented telephone call from Sarah Browne that her husband, Aunt Mary's son Joe, had died suddenly of a heart attack. We had been together several years earlier at Mendel's ninetieth birthday dinner where I discovered that Joe, who was unforgettably well over six feet tall as I was growing up (inevitably inspiring from strangers and relatives such original reactions to his imposing presence as "How's the weather up there?"), although he was still handsome and vivid, had become a couple of inches shorter than I. He said he was eighty-five, still on call as a municipal judge, and planned to live to be one hundred. Sarah and I, after her announcement of Joe's death, stayed on the phone for most of an hour, she alternately weeping and reminiscing about her life, spent living with Joe for sixty-five years, having married him when she was seventeen. Sarah was therefore already Joe's girlfriend at the time of the weeks I lived in Aunt Mary's house. I remember Joe then talking on the phone with her in a voice so low that it could not be deciphered across the space of the small living room. This was a talent motivated by the days of the Depression when houses were crowded with family members trying to get by and in which there would have been at most one fixed telephone. In the course of her reminiscences, told, when she was not weeping, in a strong voice and in clear and pertinent detail, Sarah invoked the fact that Meyer's alcoholism had become so pronounced in his last years that he spent most of his waking life in a daze. (I am unsure whether this description, which could have been plain and pure, was meant as an excuse.) And Sarah is the woman who, it emerged, had made herself available to my mother after she had moved into an assisted living complex, to drive her on errands for shopping or perhaps for a dental appointment. Sarah put this, charmingly to an ancient Southern ear, as having "carried her" to and from these destinations. Sarah also dropped the remark that my mother's father, always painted as a loving man by my mother, was a tyrant to his wife and family and had, as she put it, arranged the marriage of my mother with my father, who had won her father's favor.

When my mother would speak unforgivingly of Meyer for turning away from his talent, my father's characteristic response would be to reply, with jaw-clenching fervor, as if he were barely withholding rage or despair, "Meyer was great." While I could never get past the most obvious speculations about what caused this solidarity with Meyer (he and Meyer were both subject to my mother's disapproval, and both were intimidated by the velocity of the success and acclaim in the world of business achieved by Meyer's younger brother Mendel, who as it were had freed himself for worldly competition by giving up, or somehow sublimating, his relation to music), the knowledge this afforded me of my father's understanding and admiration of a talent in search of a world in which to find itself recognized, had come to my aid in my defying him by continuing to study music at the university (a project associated in his mind with tragedy, anyway where men were concerned) and again in defying him by abandoning a life of music just when it seemed I might make a success of it. My trust in a kind of general human judgment on my father's part was based, or ratified (I do not know how; I merely so far report the fact), by overhearing his telling a story to visitors in Sacramento of his experience in Atlanta sitting with a white man (I seem to recall the scene as that of riding on a bus, but it might have been that of sitting on one of the swings ubiquitous on the porches of the southside gabled houses I have described) who, on being introduced to a black man, greeted him by standing up to shake his hand. My father's admiration seemed beyond expression, as if his audience could not appreciate the magnitude and elegant bravado of this gesture. "He actually stood up!" he repeated, as if the white man he was sitting with had with that gesture taken his life in his hands, maybe not his alone. My father admired serious men.

Part 4

August 16, 2003

It was the year after we moved from Atlanta Avenue in 1933 that I was sent to stay for two weeks with my mother's sister Mary, the runaway, back on the south side of town (it must have been either summer or during Christmas vacation, since there would have been no way to get me back and forth to school from there), while my mother went to New York at the invitation of an old musical associate of hers. It turned out, astonishingly, that Mendel was at that time living at Aunt Mary's house (I don't know what I thought had happened to our old house, nor do I recall hearing the term "Depression" spoken), and Mary's amazingly tall and handsome son Joe was still living at home, so the house contained a person I loved and it was in general full of movement and lively voices. Above all, to my wonder and delight, there was again someone in the house apart from myself all day long. Aunt Mary was, while quite understandable as family, virtually a stranger to me, but she was welcoming, or rather treated me with the same friendly, laconic distance and occasional laugh, sometimes followed by a mild cough, that she seemed to treat everyone else. She was so much thinner than her younger sisters, in her body and in her sunken cheeks, that I was not sure I saw the family resemblance. I attributed what I perceived as a strangeness in her walk to this thinness; she seemed to be jarred with each step she took, as though there was no cushioning between her and the floor. (Floor is right; I think I never saw her leave the house.) But everything was slightly strange about Mary and her house—her accent, her cooking, painted wooden surfaces where you would have expected wallpaper or tile or a rug. She favored breaded and pan-fried steak, which I found delicious but do not remember having had before, and grits with butter, which I knew well and relished. I thought this variation must come from the way gentiles live. Perhaps it is the influence of this utterly uninformed thought, or irrelevantly informed, that I would now attribute the overall difference of Mary's cooking from my mother's to the basis of its preparation in lard rather than in schmaltz. After dinner one night I found Aunt Mary sitting alone at the now clean oil cloth covering the kitchen table, smoking her usual cigarette, sipping between puffs from a small glass of dark liquid. She gestured for me to sit down and visit. She said she was taking her cascara, a word I happened to know to name a laxative. I do not recall hearing the word since. She added, "I drink it like wine." The concept of anorexia would not enter my vocabulary for another fifteen years, taking psychology courses at UCLA, where the exotic diagnostic category "anorexia nervosa" seems hard to identify with today's illusory familiarity with the issue. (Going over my perception with Cathleen I find that the feature of the laxative perhaps suggests bulimia rather than anorexia, but since I am only giving my impression I allow myself to lay decisive emphasis on binge eating and furtive attempts to hide or disguise this as essential criteria of the concept of bulimia, and these features were so far as I ever saw or heard absent in Mary's calm and self-satisfied routines of eating little and of drinking cascara like wine.)

Whether because, in her late thirties, Mary was already turning gray, or for some other reason, her hair was dry and seemed blacker than any hair I had ever seen (I would now say it was obviously dyed black), and that, or some other fact, made it look brittle and feel unyielding when I kissed her goodnight. There was a photograph of an adolescent girl in a white dress with flowing hair down almost to her waist among the box of family photographs and mementoes Mary took out to show me. I felt I ought to recognize this young girl since so many of the faces in the box were the ones my mother had also put in an album, but I could not place her. As I held it up to her and before I could ask who it was she said quickly, "Yes, that's your aunt Mary,"

followed by the abbreviated laugh and cough. I hope I did not actually
say out loud, "But you were more beautiful than your sisters!" I imagine
it would hardly have mattered whether I actually said it since it must
have been written on my expression, and in her mind long before that.

August 17, 2003

I had brought a new red mesh bag of several dozen marbles with
me to Mary's house, and I was playing with them in the open smoothed
dirt (or clay?) space at the bottom of the back stairs when a tall thin boy
in overalls from one of the row of small houses extending back from
the other side of the space walked over, along with two boys about my
age. The tall boy said: "Want to play for keeps?" I must have nodded.
He went back to his house and returned with a large musty glass jar almost filled with marbles, almost none, at a glance, new. He set down the
jar, picked up a twig, and with it drew in four or five sweeping strokes
a large, well-formed circle on the ground. He set up five or six of his
marbles an inch or so apart at the center and along a diameter of the
circle: "Now you put in." I extended his line with a matching number
of my new marbles. He motioned for me to go first. I was not going to
show my innocence by asking what the rules were, so, kneeling outside
the edge of the circle, I took a large marble from my bag as my shooter
and bending forward flicked it with my thumb as hard as I could at the
surprisingly great distance of the centered line of marbles at risk. My
shooter rolled toward the line and made a notable break in it, but neither my shooter nor the marble or marbles I hit managed to reach and
cross the perimeter of the circle. "My turn," the boy said. He picked
up my shooter and handed it to me. He then knelt down on one knee
at the edge of the circle, the opposite leg stretched out straight to the
side, lowered his head, and instantly, without his seeming to move, his
shooter flung itself, without touching the ground between, upon one of
my new marbles. Both my marble and his shooter flew out of the circle.
I could not with a windup have thrown the marble with the velocity his
mere thumb achieved. He walked over to pick up both of the marbles
involved, mine he tossed into his jar of marbles, his shooter he lined up
again outside the place where roughly it had exited the circle. He then

repeated this routine, without missing, until the line of marbles he and I had staked were all in his jar. He then without a word picked up the jar and walked back to his house. The two younger boys with him had started to giggle, and they ran off after him.

I figure the nest of lessons to be derived from this display were cheap at the price of a half-dozen marbles, indeed of a medium-sized bag of new marbles, since I threw the rest away. I understand these lessons not particularly to warn about confidence games, but rather on the contrary to suggest the range and distribution and guises and histories of genuine virtuosity.

The day I met the virtuosic Bernard Williams, visiting from Oxford at the Princeton University philosophy department for the spring semester of 1963, both of us without our families (it was the second half of my year at the Princeton Institute for Advanced Studies; Bernard's then wife and their daughter were to join him in six weeks), we arranged to have dinner together that night, and we talked until dawn. He had read both of the papers I had published, in the second of which, "The Availability of Wittgenstein's Later Philosophy," I refer to a piece of his, one of his earliest, that had appeared in the cultural journal *Encounter*. Bernard seemed pleased and surprised by this and asked about it. I mentioned that Austin, whom I had known at Harvard in 1955 and again at Berkeley in 1958, had singled him out for praise among the young Oxford philosophers. This admiration was not reciprocated, Bernard finding Austin cold and insufferably dogmatic, in contrast, he added, to the tone of my first essay, "Must We Mean What We Say?" in effect an homage to, anyway an extended and grateful study of, Austin's work. Bernard did not disguise a quizzical air in reporting that Austin had annoyingly pushed to have graduate students and the younger dons at Oxford read that early essay of mine—I was unsure whether the report was quizzical because my piece was neither cold nor dogmatic or because graduate students bristled at being asked to read the work of another graduate student (an American student present in Austin's seminar then will, soon after I moved to Harvard to teach, report that reaction to me), or because Austin was pushing an homage to his own work.

I said to Bernard that the two friends I talked philosophy most with at Berkeley, each arriving there from Harvard within a year of my own return, were also not unequivocally pleased with my labors over Austin. Thompson Clarke, who had spent some time at Oxford, expressed distrust at Austin's philosophical manner (his air of, say, dismissive humor in replying to the unconvinced), although Clarke was more indebted to Austin than he admitted to himself, as was, in my view, Bernard; and Thomas Kuhn, for reasons not clear to me, was suspicious of what he felt was my undue fascination with the details of Austin's work.

I was moved to add to Bernard that both Clarke and Kuhn were doing work that would change things in philosophy. He had heard of each of them, not just from the fact that I express my indebtedness to each of them in my early papers, and he replied: "I get the alarming sense that American academic life is dotted with land mines." I understood this to mean that from the vantage of a life spent at Oxford you readily imagine that it is in effect your birthright to know everyone whose work might impinge upon your own. Since no such idea is apt to occur to anyone working in North America, I came to rely on my judgment of talent as firmly as on that of accomplishment. My sense of Kuhn and Clarke early was that their talents in relation to their projects were such that land mines were irrelevant to them. Their efforts in the world may not succeed, for the endless reasons that efforts may not succeed in the world (and I already felt that there are more such reasons in America than elsewhere, more promises more visibly thwarted here), but they will not be outstripped, or if they will be, only by means of their own contributions.

In our last conversation before the Williamses were to return to England I allowed myself to say to Bernard that I thought his writing did not do justice to his thoughts and interests as I was coming to know them. I may actually have said that I thought he was better than he wrote. A risky plunge, but I had invested in our friendship and evidently needed to test it. His response was to reply, as it were standing apart for a moment from his brilliance and charm, that he recognized this and did not accept it as final. Something I did not risk saying to him, then or ever, was that I also thought one must perpetually write better than one is. So although I felt he tolerated a considerable amount of nonsense from me, I did not learn whether he would have swallowed that one quite whole.

August 18, 2003

The invitation for my mother's New York trip during the vacation weeks I was eight years old staying at Aunt Mary's house came
from Harry Salter, a name I vaguely recognized from my mother's rare
stories of her past, stories I loved to hear, as the violinist who had organized and led the quintet of musicians—a string quartet together
with my mother—that played dinner music at the Coral Gables country club, neighboring Miami, during the year before my mother left the
group to give birth in Atlanta to what would prove to be her only child.
When she recurred to memories of that engagement, the luxury of its
setting encouraged her capacity to endow descriptions of her memories
with a glamour and an immediacy that could excite me in their telling quite to breathlessness. (I thought to ask my son David, while he
was searching the Internet at my behest for the date of the Miami hurricane, to find out, if that were possible, whether the storm had affected Coral Gables. The answer was that 75 percent of this new Florida
development had been destroyed by that event. For my mother, at any
rate, my birth would have been a solace for catastrophe, not an expression of it.) I anticipated during her absence in New York that she would
bring back fresh such descriptions. Nor was I in the least disappointed, being treated to narratives of neon signs so fantastic that they told
whole stories and of concerts held on rafts in a body of water strewn
with lights. The name of Harry Salter was about to achieve a certain
fame since he had been named to succeed Erno Rapee as the leader
of the Radio City Music Hall's orchestra, the most famous, I guess the
only really famous, among all theater orchestras in the country. Every
Sunday morning our radio was tuned to the half-hour national hookup
of Erno Rapee conducting that orchestra in what would now (perhaps
would already then) be called a pops concert. Her visit was to discuss
whether she would be interested in becoming the pianist of the Radio
City orchestra. I do not remember that I knew this before she left. Perhaps she kept it from me because there was no point in saying it unless
it was going to happen.

When she told me she had turned it down, and my momentary
thoughts of unknown glamour were caged, I wanted to know why. She
replied at once that my father would have nothing to do in New York.

I could not say, even if by then I would have had the means, and increasingly the motive, to say, that the Count of Monte Cristo would
not have asked himself what he would do if he succeeded in escaping
prison (but of course he did have plans based on that success). It would
have meant, that is, breaking up the family. I tried then, and more than
once in subsequent years, imagining life with my mother alone in what
I imagined was a New York apartment (the only room I formed an
image of resembled a large space I may have seen Fred Astaire dance
in or Irene Dunne walk through in an evening gown, lit to throw shadows, sparsely furnished with sleek white chairs and couches on a tiled
black-and-white floor). I could not imagine how my mother would find
a school for me or manage to get me there regularly. I rather figured
she could not imagine these things either, and the conviction pretty
well settled in me that she was afraid to face the initial isolation and
the unlimited competition of the New York world of talent. She craved
the adoration, whatever the failures, and I suppose fears, of my father
(together with the decisive fact that he had known, and been picked
for her, by her father) and the position of being the self-evident best in
whatever group she joined in Atlanta—which was and is not New York,
but was far from nothing in the South. And a singularly significant gain
was that it left intact her world-encompassing disdain. To be in various
ways insufficiently appreciated is I suppose better than to be sufficiently
appreciated, as, according to Friedrich Schlegel (and Emerson), to be
misunderstood is better than to be understood. The following year we
moved to Sacramento for the first time. There she will find something
I cannot imagine she had clearly imagined, a world wholly bereft of
theater or radio orchestras, not to mention friends or familiar family.

So an early trip to New York marked her life as such a trip had
marked Meyer's. Did it occur to her to ask herself whether she too had
(not thrown away her talent exactly, but) not set her talent free?

She told me part of Meyer's story that my father never mentioned,
namely, that Meyer had early fallen in love with a Jewish girl (in my
mother's lingo she would have been a beautiful girl, because something
bad had happened to her) whom his parents persuaded him against because she was poor and would interfere with his prospects. My mother
was convinced that Meyer never wished to recover from acceding to
this tyranny. The reverse had happened to my mother, persuaded into

rather than away from a marriage. But my mother was not an adven-
turess. Leaving her marriage would have been a scandal whose isolation was not the isolation she had chosen for herself.

Yet these comparisons are not the heart of the matter as I count it.
The heart has to do with my certainty that my mother's saying she did
not want to break up the family meant she wanted me to understand
that she gave up this chance for my sake. So now both of my parents
have staked their claim to reparation from me for the fact of my existence. The reparation out of what my mother named my father's jealousy of me, I think I understood not necessarily, or solely, as my having
stolen a love that was justly his (that is something he had to take up with
my mother, in their mysterious and frightening quarrels, something his
rages doubtless regularly took up with my mother, so that I am in some
part grateful for those rages, insisting upon his existence), but understood as my obviously becoming prepared for a life he was denied every
day. The other claim for reparation came out of my mother's certainty
that I would accomplish a life of recognition for her, not instead of her
but on her behalf, wearing her colors. My father actually reported to
me—I do not remember when, whether at a time at which I may have
seemed to him to have lost all sense of my way, or when I had received
an award or an appointment whose achievement was a mystery to
him—that she had announced to him that she would rather have been
my mother than the mother of an emperor. I suppose in his astonishment at her extravagance (for whom, beyond the memory of her father,
did she play the piano?) he took this as some kind of acceptance of him,
since to have been the mother of an emperor would have required a
king, or the makings of one, for her husband.

August 20, 2003

The last move to Sacramento, after the Progressive Club summer in 1940, happened in time for us to get settled (an apartment had
been rented for us; as it happens it was the upstairs of the duplex we had
moved out of for our last return to Atlanta) in time for me to enter high
school on the first day of the school year. After my experience of the
previous year at Boys High in Atlanta, the academic part of what I have

spoken of as my coma years was still intact. I do not know what documents, if any, the Sacramento high school had to go on in assessing the credit due my first year of high school in Atlanta, but I was directed as a new arrival, or perhaps specifically as a transfer from outside the California school system, to speak to advisors sitting at one or another table set up in the school cafeteria, each of whom treated me as unexpected. I was asked how much algebra I had had and I answered that I wasn't sure, which seemed to satisfy them. Then I was asked whether I was to be on the x, y, or z track, where, they were obliged to explain to a stranger, x meant the academic track and z the vocational track and y meant neither, somehow in between. These distinctions turned out not to determine (anyway in general) which courses you must or might take, but simply what weight or meaning would be attached to the grades you received. Every grade received was accompanied by a marker indicating one of the three tracks. An A(x) was the highest possible grade, F(z) the lowest, the former unattainable by anyone on a y or z track, the latter unreachable by anyone on an x or y track. An A(y) was equivalent to a B(x), higher grades than any grade attainable on the z track, where an A(z) was equivalent in value to a B(y) and to a C(x). (Since—but I did not know this then—admission to the California university system required, and was guaranteed by, a B[x] average in high school, admission could be achieved by an A[y] average, and was a priori unachievable on the z, or vocational, track.) I replied that I supposed I belonged in the middle, since I had plans neither for a university education nor for vocational training. I go into these arcana in order to be clear about an event, preceding my social awakening in my joining and then leading the dance band, that specifically prepared for my academic rescue.

My first semester at McClatchey High School was uneventful, where mathematics continued to interest me and provide me with a measure of praise; the rest of my course work was desultory but not punishing. At the start of the second semester, our English teacher became ill and the class was taken over, for the rest of the year it turned out, by a young substitute teacher, a woman, on first impression somewhat awkward and rather too thin, with an air of intensity and undisguised intellectuality that we were not accustomed to, something like twenty-five years old as I picture her now, a different generation and temperament from the man she was replacing. She was evidently new to California, from New York I believe I heard, so the signals of the various social hierarchies in this school meant nothing to her, and contrariwise her somewhat alien manner seemed to make most of my classmates wary. I was immediately attracted to her obvious interest in the unusual things she was saying and impressed by her impatience with members of the class who were used to being praised but who volunteered answers that this teacher said "settled for too little." She wasn't courteous, and was even sometimes abrupt, not I thought out of ill will but out of a general nervousness; she was distinctly smarter and quicker than we were used to, and her desire to communicate was clear and objective and gained the group's respect. After some weeks she remarkably gave as our writing assignment the reviewing of a film playing that week in Sacramento. I seem to recall that it was *Hold Back the Dawn*, with Charles Boyer and Olivia de Havilland, which I discovered not long ago still plays on cable television. To my astonishment, and I suppose that of the rest of the company, before handing back these papers with her written comments, she read my review aloud to the class, followed by a clipped "Good, isn't it?"

The custom of the school on the day on which report cards were filled out was for each student, when called, to take her or his card to the teacher's desk at the close of each class and have the teacher enter the grade on the card and sign on the appropriate course line. As I got to the door leaving this classroom I noticed that our substitute teacher had entered an A(x) on her course line on the card. I returned to her desk and said to her that I understood the system to be such that I should not get a grade marked on the x track. She replied in that brisk and unencumbered tone: "I gave you the grade your work deserved. I can't help what the system is." This encounter has naturally entered into my idea of what a teacher can be, but more generally informed my imagination of the permanent effects an act of acknowledgment and a sense of justice, independently inserted into the course of the world, may have.

August 21, 2003

The next year and a half I was preoccupied with the band, in fact with two bands, or really four bands, on their different trajectories. I graduated high school in January 1943, as did many of the other members of the McClatchy Melodiers. As a number of its members had turned, or were about to turn, eighteen they were eligible for the draft and were deciding whether to enlist and exercise some choice over their service or whether to wait to be called up. I had turned sixteen the previous September and was trying to enter a navy program that accepted recruits at the age of sixteen and a half and subsidized (and monitored) eight semesters of college (compressed into two and two-thirds years) in return for a somewhat extended commitment to national service. For the moment we tried to keep the band together. The bass player had already been drafted, but I hoped we would at least be able to keep the half-dozen dates we had on our schedule over the next month or so. By then we had as a group joined the musicians' union and were entitled to sign up to use its hall on certain nights for rehearsing. (I had been handed a letter on the bandstand one night a few months previously, by a man who then immediately departed and who had been standing in front of us for a while, as if listening to the music, as certain people had begun to do as our playing improved. The letter informed me that because some members of the band were under eighteen years old, working after 10 p.m. was in violation of the California Child Labor Law. It was from another among the people standing there, in a friendlier mood, that I learned that this was code for "Join the musicians' union or we'll get the law enforced." When I replied that I knew that you had to be eighteen to join the union, the reply was to lie about my age, which will not be contested. All this proved to be quite accurate.) The union hall happened to be on J Street, at roughly the same latitude as my father's store on parallel K Street. I had bought several new stock arrangements and scheduled a rehearsal to go through them before the approaching two weekend engagements. Just before we assembled for the rehearsal I learned that our pianist had been ordered to report for induction into the army. This was crippling, particularly since I was not familiar with the professional musicians in town and had no idea where to get a congenial substitute. We began the rehearsal anyway, I guess on the chance that some solution would materialize. Perhaps I imagined I might take over the piano and go with three saxophones. Or we might just leave the position empty. (It had not occurred to me to ask my mother to fill in for us. Nor can I seriously imagine it now. Just where is the transgression?)

I had noticed that a stranger, a man perhaps in his early twenties, had appeared at the top of the stairs to the entrance of the hall, evidently attracted as he passed in the street below by the sound of the rehearsal, and was leaning against the doorjamb, listening to us play, dressed, although it was a springlike evening, in a camel's hair overcoat. After I handed out parts to one of the new arrangements, I saw that he had slid onto the piano bench, which was near the door, and as I counted us off he began playing—playing, indeed, in a different world from that of our former pianist, knowing how to fill a moment of silence with a flourish of response and using an ear for harmony that went altogether beyond what was called for on stock arrangements. I somehow knew to say nothing until the rehearsal was over, which the stranger had joined in until the end. Then I walked quickly over to him to delay his leaving and asked him to join the band for the rest of our engagements. His reply was almost inaudible but seemed to be, "I don't know, man." "But you're the answer to a prayer; I love the way you play; the piano was empty because our guy was drafted. Help us, if only just this weekend." He objected, still just audibly: "I don't have clothes." I said that I had an extra tuxedo. (Quite true, but I've forgotten why or how; perhaps a friend had left it with me when he was drafted.) "Come a little early to the date and you can change into it. You know where the Eastern Star Temple is?" He did. "Friday and Saturday nights," I continued, "beginning at eight." Before he could answer I walked away, packed my clarinet and saxophone, and collected the music. When I eventually took a chance to look over at the piano, he was not there. I was certain that he would show up Friday night. And indeed he arrived early enough to change, reluctantly, into the tuxedo. But he maintained his pride by having no shoes to wear other than the scuffed brown pair he had entered in.

August 22, 2003

This man, Bob Thompson, remains the only person, outside of family, from that era of my life, my life before beginning it over again in college at Berkeley, with whom I have remained more or less reliably in some kind of regular, even close, touch. The day before he appeared at our rehearsal he had returned to California, having been drafted into the army just after completing high school and discharged after nine months when an attack of asthma incapacitated him. After a month or more in a hospital in North Carolina, he was soon discharged from the army and returned to civilian life by way of a first visit to New York, a place that occupied a permanent locale in his imagination. He represented my first experience of an encounter that I will one day learn Aristotle could have counted as a serious friendship, one, namely, with whom conversation eventually became endless and concerned getting to some depth with everything of mutual and expansive concern. With him these concerns began with music and musicians and took in the remaining arts, so far as these were measured principally by, let's say, the *New Yorker* of the period, not so bad a measure of discovery in those years for two American male late adolescents from unlettered families. The magazine's humor was, and attracted, I suppose uncontroversially, the best in a certain register of drawings and in samples of educated, intellectually unstrenuous but deliberate and stylish prose, that America had to offer on a moneymaking basis. While I confidently say now that its seriousness was flawed, to characterize the particular nature of its embarrassment by intellectuality would require characterizing America's own intellectual suspiciousness, or more accurately, its public distrust of original intellectuality (in the land of Jefferson, Melville, Emerson, Gertrude Stein). I will come to see this as bound up with this culture's chronic skittishness about philosophy.

Just sixty years after the evening of the band rehearsal in the Sacramento musicians' union hall that set off this recent path of association, there appeared a couple of weeks ago in the *New Yorker* a substantial and obscurely motivated review of texts celebrating the two hundredth anniversary of the birth of Emerson, by the celebrated John Updike, who is able to, and willing to, string out a list of banal and careless criticisms of Emerson's pretensions, unwilling or unable to paraphrase subtly and accurately any of the Emersonian sentences he disparagingly cites. Whom is he protecting? What public service is he thereby performing? I recall that among the best, and most admired, of *New Yorker* writers, as well as a sometime actor, in its high Algon-

quin Table period, was Robert Benchley. One of Benchley's signature
routines—memorialized in what movie theaters used to call short subjects—was a spoof of a professor of hopeless pedantry trying helplessly
to coordinate his notes with the placards of diagrams he was displaying
on, and knocking off of, an easel. I imagine that any culture, in possession of writing developed sufficiently to relate stories, has been moved
to get laughs, or tears, from pretension and distraction and pedantry. A
difference between Benchley's routines and Updike's routine criticisms
of Emerson is that Benchley told it funny. Whom am I protecting? A
fear of the lack of sophistication and depth can produce as shallow results as the lack of sophistication and depth.

The great virtue of the *New Yorker*'s specific level of genuine sophistication was that it was more widely shared than any other comparably ambitious American cultural dispensation before or since (I
offer that as an impression open to correction), its documentary prose
suitable, for example, for reviews of Broadway theater still in something
of its prime, as well as for reportage on boxing and on horse racing, and
for touching upon the intellectual scene in Greenwich Village, as well
as, for a need, recording the debates between émigré defenders of De
Gaulle and of Pétain on saving the honor of France in 1940. I know that
one of my sources of loyalty to Hollywood film of roughly this period
is its connection with that dispensation of sophistication, even though
I know that what I have come to say about film, or the way in which
I say it, would not have been, and is not, welcome to the intellectual
taste expressed in those gleaming pages (shuffled, famously, with their
prominently glamorous advertisements), which lets itself appear to fear
above all things intellectual difficulty, for example, prose that suggests
it might, even sometimes must, be read twice. It is good to know and
to claim your own taste in things; it is bad to be incapable of letting
your taste be challenged. Snobbery readily presents itself as a form of
tastelessness manifested by those with some real taste.

The music Bob Thompson and I talked about and listened to by
the hour or the afternoon or the day and night was mostly current jazz,
and here our taste was uncompromised. The Ellington and Basie and
Lunceford bands, and Art Tatum and Teddy Wilson and Billie Holiday, were obvious gauges of our horizons, extended into, for example,
the Eddie Sauter arrangements for Benny Goodman. Bob was the first

person I went with to a film looking forward as much to the conversation afterward as to the film. Our reconstructions of a film (often in the larger Hart's cafeteria in Sacramento, where musicians would often around midnight begin wandering in after playing a date) invariably began, and usually ended, by remembering, and judging, all we could of the music, or the film's sounds more generally, working up considerable enthusiasm over such details as that the pitch of the doorbell that initiates the opening sequence of the film echoes the pitch on which the title music ended.

We soon discovered that we had also shared a musically passionate past. In the year my parents and I had moved back for the last time to Sacramento, fifteen months before Pearl Harbor (after which national mobilization and the military draft would mean the breakup of the major swing bands), a name band came through Sacramento something like every other Saturday night to play for dancing at the Sacramento Memorial Auditorium. (I don't recall the Ellington band, or surely any other black band, being booked into that venue.) By 6 p.m. on those Saturdays, two hours before the beginning of the music, various people—of various ages I seem to recall, but my attention was not on them—would begin assembling at the front of the stage, in numbers that eventually made a loose file along much of its width, primarily to establish a place where we would remain standing until midnight, since to dance was not our object there (any more than it would have been at any serious concert), but also for the pleasure of watching the band get set up and the players put their instruments together and hear how they warmed themselves to the evening before them. Thompson and I discovered that we both had been faithful members of that fantasy-struck line of listeners. We would accordingly have as a shared memory the night that Tommy Dorsey's orchestra arrived, providing in my case, as it happened, a permanent, if fragmentary, image to my construction of the good city. As the players had about settled themselves behind their individual music stands, a black man entered from the wings who, without my looking carefully, I knew to occupy a different realm from, say, the black band boy who had been unloading instruments and assembling the music stands and adjusting their lights and laying out the books of pertinent parts on each stand. This new man came straight to the front of the band, dressed not uniformly with the others but in obviously elegant, casual clothes, handed out some sheets of music to each player, gestured for quiet, and signaled to the pianist to strike a note as reference for the others to tune their instruments. (Would it have been an A when at most two stringed instruments were in question [bass violin and guitar], whose players might easily have taken their A's before settling in their positions? Perhaps it was B-flat. I had never played in a dance band nor was aware of one in which the players were asked to tune their instruments, ahead of playing together, in common reference to the current piano. This was instruction in serious business to be undertaken; artistry is artistry.) After listening for a few moments, the man called for quiet again, then said some words and counted off for the band to play from the new sheets he had handed out. I assume my astonishment, more than my ignorance, was too great for me to have recognized or to remember what they were playing. It wasn't long before this man waved them to silence, and then directed their attention briefly to another passage. After that he held up both hands to signal satisfaction, waved and walked off. The name "Sy Oliver" reached my ears from among those lining the front of the stage, a name I could place as the (or a principal) arranger for the Tommy Dorsey band. Since Bob and I constantly discussed arrangements and arrangers—Bob Thompson will become one of the most successful arrangers in Los Angeles during the 1960s and 1970s—Oliver's name would not have been hard for us to care about knowing.

August 24, 2003

And we talked about women, and about music and women, and about writing and music. In my comparatively brief exchanges with my male high school classmates I remember either that they did not talk about the girls they were known to be linked with and whom they would be taking to the dances my band played for, or else there were references to a whorehouse in Roseville. But these were mostly fraternity boys, closer friends with several of the other members of the band, who were their fraternity brothers, than with me. Their high school fraternity was the locus of a contretemps with the several band members who belonged to it. They had asked me to present myself for membership in it, and when I replied that they knew I did not live that kind of life—I could hardly say it was because I was Jewish and too young, since these facts were well known to them, and indeed they seemed to want to make it a point of honor to show that they could get me elected, Jew and all—my argument collapsed and I agreed. This meant going to one of their family houses to meet the rest of the members. My father warned me not to go. "It only takes one blackball to keep you out. And that is inevitable, no matter how many friends you think you have." I wanted to prove to him that what was inevitable was only his fear of such rejection. But I was blackballed. I handled the situation badly. The truth was that that group, apart from the players in the band, and maybe an actor or two, meant essentially nothing to me, so that I would have felt fully as awkward to be accepted as to be rejected. But I could not say this to the ones who had tried to make the thing happen. So I could not find a way to assure them that they need not be embarrassed on my account, that such a rejection was part of our world, and so try to keep our better than respectfully polite relationship from souring. Something else was true of our world, or of my part in it, that I could not say, namely, that I knew I would leave Sacramento within a year and with no idea of returning.

In Bob Thompson's life, women at that moment were either objects of romance or else distant "exotic dancers" in the Club Rendezvous where he was hired to play the piano by a trumpet player (who had been left by some ostentatiously playful god with the three central fingers on his right hand and blind in one eye, no more intact than he strictly needed to be in order, within reason, to ply his trade), the two of them joined by a drummer, without whose accents a strip tease would have been a poorer thing. As part of pursuing the romantic strand of things, initially concerned with Bob's high school sweetheart, he and I on one occasion traveled to San Francisco just, it proved, to stand outside her house for better than an hour and then to return on a late train back to Sacramento.

There was a piece of our shared past that surprisingly did not come up until years after we met. Some time before the period of the Saturday night dances at the Sacramento Auditorium we had both been present at the Benny Goodman band's concerts as part of the 1939 San Francisco World's Fair. Some two years older than I, Thompson had apparently learned of these Goodman appearances as far away as his hometown of Auburn, California, in the hills of Gold Country, north of Sacramento, and traveled to them, alone, in San Francisco. My mother and father and I were about to return to Atlanta (for what would be the final time we moved there together), and a visit to the World's Fair, in the company of my father's brother and his sister-in-law, was evidently something of a recognition of our leaving (again). My fascination with Goodman's playing, especially with his small groups, including Lionel Hampton and Teddy Wilson, was the background of my mounting craving to learn the clarinet. (Artie Shaw seemed to me, by comparison, somewhat studied, and no black player to my knowledge had mastered the depth of technique demanded by the clarinet comparable to the unfathomable achievements of black musicians in the cases of the tenor saxophone and the trumpet and the piano.) So when soon after we had passed through the entrance of the fairgrounds I heard the Benny Goodman band playing its opening theme song, I was not shocked but merely pleased that the fair was playing over its loudspeakers Goodman recordings so familiar to me. Then within a minute or two I found that I was on a path at the back of a crowd of people seated outdoors in rows sweeping back from a shell bandstand on which the actual Benny Goodman band was playing what we were hearing over the loudspeaker, and as Goodman raised his clarinet for a new entrance, it was not a perfect repetition but a slight variation of something that had become a part of my brain. An ecstasy enclosed me (as if what had only existed for me as sound had of itself materialized on the instant) that made essentially incomprehensible my mother's repeated questions to me whether I was coming along with them to the exhibitions of the fair. I saw a seat open near where we were standing and motioned to my mother that I was staying there. After an hour another intermission and a further show were announced, and when my mother returned I asked her to join me, saying that when the crowd dispersed I would get seats close to the front and save one for her for the next performance. What excuses my mother made to the others I did not imagine. To consider leaving the music of the spheres for a glimpse of earthly innovations seemed unthinkable to me. To hear the familiar arrangements played live, with inevitable and enlivening alterations in the improvisations, confirmed for me as it were the knowledge of existence, in the form of, or a prophecy of, the reality of happiness. Whatever unanticipated forms the prophecy will recognize, and however many awakenings may be necessary from my coma, I had received proof of a world beyond me.

August 26, 2003

By the date of my thirteenth birthday—September 1, 1939, the day Hitler invaded Poland, the official date of the beginning of World War II—we were back in Atlanta and I was about to celebrate my Bar Mitzvah. The first time I remember hearing the war discussed my mother and I were sitting at lunch, with a number of others, on her sister's (Aunt Bess's) screened-in terrace, in the house we called the Mansion—it featured such luxuries as a clay tennis court, a professional pool table, and a steam room, and one end of the long living room resolved into a semicircular alcove enclosed by floor-to-ceiling windows, its rounded floor raised two broad steps from the rest of the room, so that the piano installed there was protected, as by the sacredness of a stage, from attentions that were not serious. (In that respect, the steps' worth of protection proved to be inadequate.) It had just been announced that England and France had declared war on Germany, and I offered the opinion—if a free-floating set of grammatical sounds may even loosely be called an opinion—that the war would be over in a matter of weeks. Bess's husband, Jack, laughed heartily as he replied to that prophecy, "If you are sure of that you can make a lot of money." I could not imagine what he meant nor why that was a response to my utterance. I felt certain, however, that it was not merely a rebuke of my nonsense but expressed a view of human folly more cynical than any other I had been faced with.

At some stage I excused myself from the luncheon table, I suppose to find a bathroom on the second floor, and as I reached the top of the stairs, and walked a few steps, on my right side an open door to a bedroom revealed, extending from the bedroom's far side, exactly above the screened terrace I had left, an enclosed sun porch on which an extravagantly beautiful woman was standing in profile naked beside a cot over which was draped a large beach towel, staring at herself in an ample round hand mirror, her free hand smoothing her long dark hair. I managed after a moment to continue past the door before she could glance in my direction. I do not remember how or when I got back downstairs. Presumably there was a back stairway.

What this experience consciously added to my knowledge, or intimations, of ecstasy was the pain within joy, not alone the pain of delay, or say, detour, but the pain within the sheer extremity of experience. It was the opposite twin of the experience of the world's insufficiency in meeting humankind's desires, as in the experience, for example, of Shakespearean romance. Here the experience was of the body's insufficiency to house the materialization of its desire. (The concept of sublimity was not then in my repertory.)

This was evident in my response to the Goodman band and familiarly present in my responses to great jazz. But it would be some years before I recognized the fact—testimony of the fact of finitude—to be under examination among the works, in the other realm of music, that I at the same time loved extravagantly, to the point of pain, in, for random examples, Chopin's études and ballades, or Bach's unaccompanied violin sonatas. I knew that no composer could exhaust this fact of music from the time I realized that even Chopin could not approach by means of a simple diatonic melody (as in the counter-theme of the G Major Nocturne, whose excited opening theme is running thirds and sixths) the intensity of expression in, for example, the simplicity of the variation theme in Beethoven's last piano sonata. The limitation of actuality, for example, of sustaining reliable closure with it, seems openly announced in the desperation of the dozens of repetitions hanging on as if for dear life to the concluding C Major triad of the Beethoven Fifth.

Within a month or so after that lunch at the Mansion, Aunt Bess introduced us to two young German Jewish refugees, boys two or three years older than I, whom she had volunteered to sponsor in a safe life in America. However one was to understand the contrast between the frozen expressions and monosyllabic English words of these strangers and Aunt Bess's cheerfulness as she directed them into and out of the back seat of her car, her familiar episodes of cynicism or anger or impatience were at such times quite out of the picture.

August 27, 2003

It would be most of a year after meeting Bob Thompson and the breakup of the high school dance band before I entered the University of California at Berkeley. Nothing certain had yet happened to cause me to imagine that my sixteen years of the experience of life called for, or were subject to, systematic intellectual continuation. As for earning a living, I supposed that that could be done by playing in bands that actually used and developed my talents. But such matters were overshadowed, or put into suspension, by the fact of the war. I have mentioned my learning of a navy program that accepted boys of sixteen and a half into an officers' training program combined with a college undergraduate education. And I have related elsewhere my resourcefulness—after passing with sufficiently high marks the intelligence test for that program when it was administered later that spring in Sacramento, and I was accordingly directed immediately to take a physical examination at the Navy Yard in San Francisco—when arriving at the eye and ear station of the physical examination and the doctor on looking, or trying to look, into my ear simply said, "Go home, son," I had the inspired thought of asking the navy doctor if I brought back a letter within an hour or so from my family physician, who had followed the progress of my narrowed and misshapen ear canal since a childhood injury, attesting to the fact that its condition would not substantially worsen, whether he might change his decision. (The background of the inspiration was my having somewhere heard that a concern of doctors at induction physicals is that a prior medical problem could after demobilization be declared "service-incurred," hence its treatment charged in perpetuity to the government.) The doctor said to bring him the letter and he would consider it. Then the realization of my inspiration required phoning Cousin Abe (the shady gambler from Chattanooga with whom my mother's cousin had run away to San Francisco) to ask if he could give me the name and address of a doctor who would be prepared to write a letter for me making up a story, one that would satisfy navy induction doctors, to the effect that my damaged ear was not as serious as it looked. (In fact I had had no major flare-up for a couple of years.) He said he would phone me back, and I gave him the number of the public phone box I was calling from outside the Navy Yard. I do not remember whether as I waited for his return call I sensed that my existence had remained roughly on course or whether it had veered all at once into the fantastic. Cousin Abe phoned back minutes later with a name and number, and the doctor was expecting me when his receptionist showed me into his office a reasonable taxi ride later. He wished me luck as he handed me the letter. I have no memory that he actually looked into my ear, but my name was spelled correctly. The letter worked, and I concluded with a kind of solemn exultance that I had been accepted.

What nevertheless served, or helped serve, to reject me was my being surprised to be told immediately upon my return to the Navy Yard to report at once for an interview, in which I proved (still sweaty and disheveled from having anxiously rushed through traffic from the Navy Yard to the doctor's office to pick up the doctored letter and back again, and finding myself seated in the center of a room lined along three walls with a dozen or so men, most of them in officers' uniforms) to have become essentially speechless. My inspiration had run out. With any time for thought, or given a moment with any person of experience that I might have discussed my plan with before getting on the train to San Francisco, I could have found the wit, when I was asked why I wanted to join the navy, simply to reply, quite truthfully, "To serve my country." But the single thought occupying my mind was that I must conceal my wish to be a musician. That was in early 1943. The war was going badly; it was still time for my bad ear to be overlooked. I replied, amazingly, that I wanted to be a lawyer (I had heard of a family acquaintance, a lawyer, who had been drafted). "The navy doesn't train lawyers, son." There is no clearer moment in my life at which a radically chance throw, or halt, of the spirit closed off one detour in the quest for my death. I was later told that the navy was at that period still in various regions subject to anti-Semitism; but I had another cousin by marriage who had been inducted as a lieutenant junior grade, but then again he had a master's degree in psychology. By the time I turned eighteen in the fall of 1944, the outcome of the war had become clarified, and when I was called in for the army physical and heard from the doctor the exact words of the navy doctor upon looking, or trying to look, into my left ear—"Go home, son"—and again tried the question, "Suppose I brought you a letter from my family doctor . . . ," the army doctor simply tonelessly repeated "Go home, son," and turned away.

August 30, 2003

The circumstances of taking the navy's written intelligence test brings out, too clearly for me to pass it by, a certain superficial, not to say farcical, yet somehow signature texture of my adolescent life. The background is that I had lately heard of yet a new way to get rid of facial pimples—my case was not as severe as those of a number of my male classmates, but to me a cause of sufficient chagrin. The new way was not, as in previous months, to use faithfully a further brand of recommended soap or to submit to X-ray bombardment that caused the skin to peel, but required establishing a regime of drinking a quart of tepid water before breakfast. When this was told me I at first took it as a satiric comment on my former desperate and ineffective measures. But there was just the possibility that some form of inner cleansing was to the point; at least it was harmless. The point of the water's being tepid seemed to me unnecessarily punishing until I actually tried drinking four glasses of cold tap water straight down one after the other. The interval before having to urinate was generally no longer than the time it took to get on some clothes and drive to the California Junior College (now Sacramento State College), a mile or so further from our apartment than McClatchey High School, where I and a couple of other members of the band had, more or less aimlessly, signed up for some music courses we rarely attended. On the morning of the navy examination, which happened to be scheduled at the junior college, my mother had failed to wake me up (doubtless expressing her view of my plan) and I slept until some ten or fifteen minutes past the time the examination was scheduled to begin. I dressed frantically, thoughtlessly downed the four glasses of water, drove to the designated building (there were open parking spaces, so this must have been a Saturday), and upon entering it I was gloriously excited to see a sign for the men's restroom at the end of the hall. Then follows a comic routine surely older than Roman theater. As I hurried toward the restroom, a door halfway down the corridor opened and a man intercepted me, asking whether I was there for the navy examination. I said yes but that I had to use the bathroom first. "You're more than half an hour late already; if I close this door now you won't be allowed in to take the examination." The extent of the forces the body can mobilize in an emergency is a subject I know little about, but I can here lend my testimony to my having been constrained to take, and made capable of taking successfully, a two-hour examination in less than an hour, the last to enter, the first to leave, not unaware of having made a spectacle of myself, with my tensely whispered apologies.

August 31, 2003

The summer of 1943 was approaching, and I was without a formulable goal. The Harrel Wiley band still met from time to time, but the continued lack of places to play eventually dampened our spirits. Several of us from that band did, however, play for War Bond Rallies (the most august of these in Sacramento was built around the personal appearances of Ronald Coleman and of Lynn Barrie). Roughly the same few of us played Saturday nights, I less often than the others, at a black bar in a region near K Street but in the direction opposite to that of J Street. I vaguely remember published addresses on L and M and P Streets—these would have been the location, a few blocks further uptown, of state office buildings near the Capitol, and its notable gardens meant to prove that anything can grow in California, with sufficiently elaborate sprinkling systems. It occurred to me that the black bar was not far from the house the Wiley black band practiced in, but I was unable to draw the monumentally obvious conclusion that we were playing in a black neighborhood. (A favorite English expression of my father's was "Ignorance is a blister." I am an old and faithful exemplar of that wisdom.) My mother asked me not to go to that bar, saying she had heard that there had been a killing there and that drugs had been involved. Just possibly she actually had heard this; the radio at the store was often on, and at home the late news summary was habitually tuned into, though she often gave the impression of continuing to be lost in thought at such times. But she also just possibly understood my feeling of heightened, conscious safety in these dangerous surroundings. What could happen to a young white boy in the company of half a dozen indomitable black fathers, even if they were scarcely ten years older than I, to protect him? What they expected of me was a decorum in the bar that it was an honor to obey, specifically that I dress in a suit and tie, as they did, and that I stay within the band area even during our breaks. I was sometimes teased by the deeply impressive women whose eyes and voices and gaits enhanced the interest of the world I knew and that spoke of further worlds unknown, from which I could only wish they would not settle for teasing me. The idea of being indomitable was not deflected by Harrel Wiley's himself obviously suffering from some debilitating illness. In the bar he would play his tenor saxophone holding a lit cigarette between the third and fourth fingers of his right hand (I had not then known this as a signature gesture of Lester Young's), never taking off his hat, and sometimes turn his chair with its back to the room and crowd himself with seeming discomfort into a corner, pulling his horn as close as feasible to his body, evidently because the consequent isolation, perhaps magnification, of his sound against the walls increased his capacity for concentration and meditation, stopping playing only when overcome with a prolonged fit of coughing.

September 2, 2003

A further chapter of my ignorance about where and how black people lived, perhaps especially my ignorance that this continued to be a problem in the North, was put in evidence the year I lived in New York after graduating from Berkeley, supposedly continuing my music studies. Among the acquaintances from the Berkeley contingent of musicians who had moved to New York recently and whom I would see from time to time that year were Henrietta Harris and our common friend Bill Schauer. Bill had enrolled for a master's degree in musicology at Columbia, with the thought of teaching in high school. He was a strong man, devoted to his Catholicism, intent on becoming a good man, a decent singer at ease with his knowledge that he could not survive in the competitive world of performance with the various stars among the Berkeley performers and composers. We felt sympathetic to

one another without exactly being personal, and from the way he spoke
of Henrietta, I became convinced that he was irrecoverably in love with
her. Had it not been hopeless, I mean unrequited (she was in her turn,
Bill told me, hopelessly in love with a composer of our acquaintance),
he would have been fully prepared to face the difficulties in those years
of a racially mixed marriage. It was not, however, for that reason alone,
as I saw it, that he became a priest, or not that reason that precipitated
this decision. He had been failed on his qualifying examination for the
degree by a professor whom he felt had behaved treacherously to him.
(My memory is that the professor had set questions on the examination, on subjects or periods, that he had said would not be required.) Bill
regularly ran for some miles every day as a way of controlling his passions, and discovered that he had come intuitively close in his rage at
this professor to choking him to death in his office. I believed him when
he ended one of his walks by stopping at my apartment to tell me of the
incident, as I believed him when he said he didn't know how he could
live with what his impulse had revealed to him about himself.

Henrietta had come to New York to discover what the chances
were for a professional career for a black woman who was generally
thought to be the most promising singer in Berkeley in the years I knew
it. She had been the principal singer in a production there of Purcell's
Dido and Aeneas and sang the part of Electra in a concert version of
Mozart's *Idomeneo*. For a concert of new music late in the fall of that
year in New York, she looked me up to ask me to accompany her in a
performance she had agreed to give of two of Leon Kirschner's songs
in a concert of new music. Kirschner had been one of three stars of incontestable magnitude in Roger Sessions's composition seminar my last
year at Berkeley (the others were Earl Kim and Andrew Imbrie). Preparing the performance of the songs brought Henrietta and me closer
together and allowed for more random conversation than the total of
our encounters during the years we had both lived in Berkeley.

Some weeks after the performance we met again at a New Year's
Eve party in the Village given by two gay and somewhat older members of the Berkeley theater community who had moved to New York
several years earlier and so far found rather bleak fortunes on Broadway. As Henrietta, sometime after midnight, but before the party was
breaking up, got up to leave, I offered to see her home. She accepted,

acquiesced I might say, since I felt she was somewhat hesitant. Could I not have failed to understand where taking the A train uptown took you to? Others seem to be born with such wisdom. (The train to my so-called studio apartment off upper Central Park West was the similar and the altogether different AA.) The explanation kindest to myself was that there were many stops on the A train between the Village and Central Park West, and Henrietta raised no question of Harlem in my mind. The train was crowded, and she and I found a seat together riding backward facing two black men who began engaging me in ostentatiously loud and flippant conversation, asking me among other things who my friend was. Henrietta ignored them. But when we got out at 125th Street and began walking further up Broadway, I saw to my surprise that the only people on the nearly empty streets were black people, as if I had never heard of Harlem. Before I could formulate my surprise, or form the thought, that the magnificent Henrietta Harris, renowned in our circle of acquaintances, had been living, far from her friends that I knew, in Harlem, she stopped walking and turned to me. "Don't you see that you are in far greater danger here than I am? Please go back." It had evidently never occurred to me that a black person would not know by looking at me what my life with music had been and therewith comprehend that that life of mine exempted me from participation in the tragedy of racial injustice. She stopped the lone taxi headed our way, opened the door, and said to the black driver that I needed to be taken home, which in fact was roughly twenty short blocks away, at that hour a drive of a few minutes.

September 3, 2003

Remembering the shame of my impotent gallantry that night, I am moved now to fill in a somewhat further promise of my glimpsed history with the black world by saying who I remember, or fantasized, the men involved to be when my father expressed himself as having been transfixed with admiration by the spectacle of a white man in Atlanta rising from his seat in public to shake hands with a black man. I imagine the white man (quite realistically, as will come out) to have been Eugene Debs, who served time in Federal Prison in Atlanta from 1919 to

1921, having been arrested after giving a speech in wartime against the Espionage Act. There is a family narrative among my Goldstein relatives according to which Debs, accompanied by the warden of Federal Prison, attended a Passover seder at my grandfather's house. The truth of this phantasmic tale is to my mind wholly verified by a combination of considerations. For example, a recent biography of Debs reports that Debs and the warden became friends.

No one in the prison took Eugene Debs, who while serving his sentence received close to a million votes as the Socialist Party candidate for President of the United States in the election of 1920, to be an ordinary prisoner. Accounts of his incarceration emphasize his friendly relations with all the social strata and positions represented in the prison. Further, one of my father's older brothers, my uncle Joe, was at that time chaplain to the Jewish prisoners in Federal Prison. (I remember, on first learning of this occupation, my shock at the thought that there were Jews who were criminals.) This uncle, older than both my father and the Sacramento uncle, had unlike them received rabbinical training before the family emigrated from Poland. In Bialystok he had been in the same Yeshiva class as Harry Wolfson, who would still be Professor of Jewish Philosophy at Harvard when I entered the graduate program in philosophy there. Wolfson attended my first wedding, in Boston. My father's sister Ida was my source for the information that their brother Joe was first in his Yeshiva class, and Wolfson second. I never thought, or had the chance, to verify this with either Joe or with Harry Wolfson.

Joe was my father's intellectual idol, famous in family circles for having what was called a photographic memory, allowing him (anyway something allowed him) to recite by heart seemingly endless passages from the Talmud. Wolfson was also well known for his powers of recall. (Sometimes it seems that the Jews have bred themselves for this capacity. Will it not occur to them that it may be a curse to be unable to forget anything?) It was Joe who came to say to my father, "We're no longer Jews from an old country; we are Americans. America has saved our lives." He may have had other reasons for his decision to distance himself from Judaism, or let's say, to forget the "old country." I had little chance to test any such possibility since by the time I was born and was consciously functioning at family events, Uncle Joe had moved from

Atlanta and rarely visited the city. Joe ritually phoned my grandfather's house at every Passover seder that I attended there, when so many of his family were present. I never thought to ask why it was that they were willing to answer and to take turns speaking on the phone on a Jewish holiday. Perhaps there is a prescient Talmudic distinction between placing a phone call (that is, initiating a ring and paying for it) and receiving one, or being handed the phone, which places no responsibility for new work, prohibited on the Sabbath and on most Jewish holidays.

But there is more evidence for the veracity of the Debs Passover story. Aunt Ida, intelligent and forceful—not infrequently bullying to the point of reminding her extended relatives of their neglect of familial duty, from visiting a hospitalized cousin to attending that cousin's son's Bar Mitzvah or engagement party, but no one could match her own schedule of such observances—gave time to those same Jewish prisoners in her capacity as a social worker. Part of the family story is that Debs had taken a fancy to Ida during her visits to the prison. Joe or Ida would have been the source of the further story, one my father loved to relate, of the occasion on which when Debs walked into the prison cafeteria, on the first day of his incarceration there, all the other prisoners stood up. Clearly it would have been through Joe and Ida that the invitation to a seder would have been broached.

(Within the past year—I am writing this on a late run-through of editing in September 2006—anticipating a visit to Duke University to give a lecture, I phoned a grandson of Aunt Ida's, my cousin Ted Levitas's son Steven, a prominent lawyer living in Raleigh, North Carolina, to arrange for him and his wife, Betsy, to have dinner with Cathleen and me during our stay in Raleigh. Before I rang off, knowing of Steven's interest in our family history as well as in Southern history generally, I mentioned that I was eager to confirm the story that his grandmother had encountered Eugene Debs during his imprisonment in Atlanta and indeed had known him well enough to have invited him to seder at her father's house. He said he did know something about that encounter and would like to talk about it at dinner. When the following week he and Betsy and Cathleen and I were seated in the Duke University hotel dinning room having drinks and getting reacquainted before ordering a meal, Steven produced an envelope from the inner pocket of his jacket and carefully took out an obviously ancient folded sheet of paper that he carefully spread open and handed to me. The neatly typed but by now slightly blurred words were addressed to Aunt Ida and signed by Eugene Debs, dated in the early 1920s, warmly congratulating her on her forthcoming wedding and expressing regret that his schedule did not allow him to come to Atlanta to help celebrate the occasion, and continuing several sentences longer to indicate that this was not merely a formal response.)

The black man I envision as the object of Debs's overt and public respect was called Thomas—I never heard any further part of his name—whom I expected to see whenever I was visiting my grandfather's house and so knew as a regular companion of my grandfather's. By the time I knew him, he had a beard as full and as gray as my grandfather's, always wore a black hat and black suit, as my grandfather did, and spoke with him in Yiddish.

Thomas was said by Aunt Ida, who among our family knew him and his circumstances best (since after her mother's untimely death it was she who managed her father's household), to be a lawyer "in the negro community" and to have been born in slavery, which suggests that he was a child when the Emancipation Proclamation was passed in 1863, seventy years before the year we moved from the south to the north side of Atlanta when I was a child. Thomas would accordingly have turned eighty during the years my mother and father and I were attending Passover seder in my grandfather's house through most of the 1930s until 1942, when we so to speak settled in California. My grandfather was, I gathered, a few years older than Thomas, but both of their ages were for me something mythical, like my age now. My grandfather died in 1951 at an age, according to the family, reaching nearly one hundred years. Thomas was treated as something of a sage by members of the family, but I was told that before he died he announced to that Roosevelt-intoxicated New Deal Democratic clan that he was advising those who listened to him to vote Republican. His idea seemed to be, according to my dismayed father, that America will never give up the idea of the segregation of the races, so whoever within the black community can attain respectability for themselves should do it. What had brought on this declaration, and whether it was at the end meant as some rebuke constructed out of memories of the members of our family, or rather as a gesture of exception for some of them, I do not guess.

But while Debs and Thomas could have met at my grandfather's house, it is not certain that that would have provided the kind of public occasion that seems essential to my father's awe in telling the story of respect—unless, as is in fact not at all unlikely, Debs had also attended synagogue with the family before the seder and afterward walked along the crowded sidewalks after services with the family the three short blocks to my grandfather's house and was seated on the porch swing with my grandfather when Thomas had strolled over to the house to wish the family a "gut yontif." (*Yontif* is Yiddish for Hebrew *Yom Tov*, meaning "holiday," literally "good day" backward; so "gut yontif" might be taken to say "good day good." No cause for complaint here; it is not hard to make sense of it. Any complaint on my part would amount to regretting that I know too few with whom to share the amusement.) It does me a certain good to flesh out this moment with Debs and Thomas in a factualizing document the way it does me some good from time to time to imagine what ordinary thing might have been said or done at a given moment to have changed the drift of the world.

Part 5

September 4, 2003

Entering the University at Berkeley was still, after graduating high school, most of a year away, and I have described that interim year, after the navy disappointment, as, at least for the ensuing months, goalless. Playing in dance bands for money, and for ennoblement in one genuine swing band, exempted me from working in the pawnshop, so I was glad to accept one offer that took me through the spring and another that ran through the summer, though neither was artistically engrossing. The former was to play tenor saxophone in what was known then as a three-tenor band (to which were added two trumpets and one trombone, along with piano, bass violin, and drums), I imagine the minimum number of players that would add up to what was then called a dance band, in this case the house band of the El Rancho Motel, playing through dinner and for dancing an hour or two after that. Everything about the music was seamlessly uninteresting. I got the idea that that was the point. Since it provided more or less unobtrusive but pervasive veils of sound, guests at dinner would be less aware of their inability to keep conversation going, and the favorite brightish tempo of the music was a cover for the inability to dance, since there was nothing you could actually think to do that would be governed by that tempo—you could no more actually dance to it than you could march to it. It was rumored that the motel, done in hacienda style, and plausibly

respectable looking with a garden in the central courtyard, was a favorite place for state legislators when they were in town to take female
company for an evening, or perhaps for the off-hours of an entire law-
making season. That made sense to me of the enterprise of nondancing.
The motel was just over the Sacramento River beyond the city limits,
across a bridge that formed an extension of the street (M Street?) that
lined one edge of the Capitol grounds. I cannot think where I got hold
of a tenor saxophone for those ten or twelve weeks; perhaps Uncle Morris's pledges came through again; perhaps someone among the musicians from the junior college going off to the army had left an instrument in my safekeeping.

     The origin of the summer band, in contrast, or my part in it, was,
and remained, mysterious. An offer came my way from a reputed Latin
American band leader filling out a band in Sacramento to go on the
road for the summer, to join the group as its pianist. The permanent
core group consisted of the leader and two fellow Latin Americans,
a thin drummer who walked with a limp and a strikingly attractive
female vocalist, and further included a North American bass player
who had done the bulk of the band's musical arrangements. The idea
of playing on the road was sufficiently interesting for me, evidently, that
I was never interested to learn, or I have forgotten, how this unlikely
combination of circumstances had come about, to begin with, how the
leader had learned that I was a pianist. Like the arranger, this man was
also a bass player, but he might as well have played a different instrument, or learned its possibilities on a different planet, having little to
do with being part of an ordinary rhythm section. He was a classically
trained virtuoso, as he proved at our first rehearsal by suddenly walking
to the back of the band and taking over the instrument to demonstrate
the feel of a Latin American beat, ornamenting the straightforward
writing of the arrangements with glissandos and a velocity of plucked
scales that I had not before conceived as producible on the instrument.
Since the point of the demonstration was also to establish his musical
credentials with us, I report that it succeeded. Indeed it explained to me
why he could not possibly subordinate his own playing to the needs of
these arrangements. But then how had he come to subordinate his life
to such an organization as this summer pickup band? He was well into
his thirties, handsome, and wore, morning as well as evening, a jacket

with a handkerchief in its breast pocket and a carefully tied necktie or kerchief. His dark skin always seem covered with the thinnest layer of white powder, which I associated with the evocative aroma he brought into the room.

October 6, 2003

It is Yom Kippur, and more than a month since I have been able to continue these autobiographical reflections, or better, this doubly (at least) chronological diary. Principally the month was a time of preparing, and delivering, responses to nine papers on my work read at a conference at Uppsala University. Cathleen and I are just back from that exhilarating and encouraging week in Sweden, after which we stopped for four days in Paris, where I gave an interview to *Libération* in anticipation of the publication of six uncollected film essays of mine in a small book in a new series initiated at the Bayard press under the title "Le cinema nous rende-il meilleurs?" a translation, or rather allusion to, the title of an essay of mine, "The Good of Film."—What does an "encouraging week" mean here, or leave unsaid, since I have never learned to travel well? Travel suggests for me a screen of memories and decisions of its own, oriented around questions of my life marked by the shifts of what I have variously called home, and of course by the inevitable wondering, beginning the second day in a new place, of what it would have been to have been born just here, where the lives are uncannily similar and different from mine, evidently tied to the familiar wonder of having had different parents, hence the sense of oneself as an unfound foundling. I leave these wonders here for the moment as suggesting the issue of the contemporary academic's nomadism, remembering and seeking nourishing conversation, often within the shelter and inspiration of former students, dispersed to the winds it sometimes seems, after the intensities of years of extended companionable labors, or encountering a familiar unfamiliar stranger who has fastened upon a thought in a text of mine whose interest I had believed I had failed to make perceptible.

Nor can I venture a proper continuation now. It is time again for letters of recommendation to go out, and while I had composed several of these before leaving for Sweden (two on behalf of tenure promotions, another for an initial teaching appointment in England), more await me, and two lectures involving further travel are approaching. The principal lecture, four weeks away, is unwritten, though I have been reading in preparation for it on and off for much of a year. It is a celebration to be held at Mount Holyoke College in Massachusetts, less than a two-hour drive roughly west of Boston, to mark the occasion, sixty years ago, of a conference held there intended as an exiled continuation of annual conferences that had been mounted at a twelfth-century abbey in Pontigny, in Normandy, spanning the period from before the First World War to the beginning of the Second, by such figures as Gide and Claudel and Maritain and comparably prominent French intellectuals and artists and their guests, including during one year an appearance by Walter Benjamin. The idea of the conference six decades ago at Mount Holyoke was to invite as participants a number of the French writers and academics who had made their way to America ahead of, or despite, the Nazi occupation of France (an idea inspired, and made feasible, by Jean Wahl's having been appointed in 1942 to a professorship at Mount Holyoke), to be joined by distinguished American writers, philosophers, and artists to present papers and to join in discussions with invited guests, in surroundings that Mount Holyoke's illustrious alumna, Emily Dickinson, could perhaps not, by her lone historical presence, or absence, commemorate or consecrate, as evidently the presence of a twelfth-century abbey has sometimes done elsewhere in time and place, at least not before an assured public. In America we are free, or forced, perpetually to fight personal battles for our memories of our country. Since neither my parents, nor other relations of mine, were present on these shores when Emily Dickinson illuminated her segment of it, it is always a question how I am to, or was to, participate in the pride the Pilgrims are said, and sung, to have taken in this land.

It is an astounding promise that each new wave of immigrants to these shores may find a way to this participation, and an astounding grief when the pride is abused or debased by, after all, earlier immigrants, and then again an astonishing exhilaration to find, for example, that the magnanimous writer produced in the family of the Thoreau immigrants in Concord claimed sufficient independence in describing his construction of himself—in a work begun ten decades before our present Mount Holyoke colloquium, some seventeen miles down the road from where I am sitting now in Boston, namely, at Walden Pond in Concord (Thoreau walked it once from Concord to Boston to hear Emerson give a lecture)—to perceive that patriotism had become a "maggot" in his nation's consciousness. Yet my father died and is buried here, my mother beside him. ("Here"? Yes, if the Jewish portion of Greenlawn Cemetery in Atlanta, Georgia, is part of the land of more recent pilgrims' pride. Abraham Lincoln, at any rate, took such pride in the Union that he would not, in the words of Shakespeare's Henry V, part with a village of it.)

This particular intervention from, or depiction of, the present moment of this writing out of the overall chronology of its depictions of past moments is meant to emphasize that the moment to be celebrated at Mount Holyoke in four weeks, embedded in the summer of 1943, is the very summer I had become, to all appearances, becalmed in Sacramento, about which this autobiographical writing began mimetically feeling itself to have run aground. A plainer justification for the intervention is that the originator of the idea of the oncoming, proud commemoration at Mount Holyoke of the rather defiant commemoration there sixty years earlier, specifically asked me to allow whatever autobiographical impressions seem pertinent to fixing that time to enter into my contribution to the event.

So just as I have arrived in the overall or underlying chronological drift of this autobiographical writing at the summer of 1943 with whatever consecutiveness, or illusions of it, the intention to recount aspects of my life has produced, and found the impulse stalled at a stalled summer, not perceiving what I might wish to call a further chapter of my story, or a motive, or motif, in my memories of it—the sense of a direction of events overtaken publicly by world war and privately by the need or the chance to leave what was called home—a way is offered me not to go forward into that summer and its imagined beyonds, but backward into it from the beyond that actually came from it, the way not of self-justification (which was precisely what approaching that summer consecutively, from before it, seemed to me to deprive me of) but the way of commitment or assignment, namely, to present the keynote address of a colloquium commemorating that summer, an invitation offered to me because of a certain standing my writing and teaching have found in spots of the academic world those six decades after that summer, a standing that provides who can tell what tests and measures of self-justifications.—And what do I imagine "because of a certain standing" to betoken? My "standing" has, from the first writing I published that was meant to establish it, been in question professionally. From the first essay of mine I still use, "Must We Mean What We Say?" the writing expresses restiveness with philosophical professionalism. Of course I felt I was managing to express this very restiveness philosophically—importantly by not denying that the philosophical was precisely what was in question.

Since philosophy's irreducible demand of itself chronically to bring itself into question remains an essential theme for me, where may the standing come from to express participation in the theme, as it were before there is any ground to stand on? And how indeed do I know that such invitations to give keynote speeches come from standing more than they come from my questioning of standing—as if after all my sense of the importance of this dialectical impasse may be more widely shared than I have realized? And then again, maybe the invitation came from another meaning the summer of 1943 has for me, one I recorded in an autobiographical moment included in three lectures I will present in Jerusalem half a century later, in 1992, published under the title *A Pitch of Philosophy*. I was sixteen the year of that early Mount Holyoke summer, and I note in the opening one of the three Jerusalem lectures that my father and his family immigrated to New York when he was sixteen (or thereabouts—family dates and ages were inherently vague among this branch of what were to be called Goldsteins), and that my older son, sitting next to his younger brother in my audience in Jerusalem, was then sixteen. The obvious does sometimes manage to catch my attention as I like it to, in the present case the possibility that my writing contains good effects that are beyond my control, or in Emerson's idea, contains forces beyond the writing itself ("character teaches above our will"), so that what I have despaired of communicating is sometimes what a reader finds most unmistakable in it (including the despair).

October 7, 2003

Present at Mount Holyoke in the summer of 1943 was the composer Roger Sessions, whom I would study with at Berkeley two years
later. Possibly Christopher Benfey, who was, as head of the Humanities
Center at Mount Holyoke, the organizer of the commemorative colloquium, whom I had known and talked with when he was writing his
dissertation on Emily Dickinson for the English department at Harvard
ten or fifteen years earlier, was aware of my connection with Sessions
(like Dickinson a sometime resident of South Hadley, Massachusetts) in
inviting me to address the colloquium, and asking me to be freely autobiographical. Partly this latitude must have come from his own sense of
strata of history that are made of the accidents of encounter, and of the
permanent impressions created, early or late, in or by those encounters.
Partly accordingly it would have come from his assurance that I would
not be likely to let an academic idea of decorum prevent me from recounting an anecdote Sessions recounts, in a published set of interviews
he gave in 1985, concerning the premiere of *The Trial of Lucullus*, Sessions's first completed (one-act) opera, an anecdote in which I make an
appearance as the clarinetist in the small orchestra for which that continuously gorgeous, inspired piece is scored. The story is simply that on
our opening night's performance the experienced oboist, sitting next
to me, who was responsible also for playing English horn in the occasional passages calling for it, whispered to me that his English horn
had somehow become unplayable, whereupon, asking him to turn his
music stand so that I could read his part, I produced his ensuing solo
on the clarinet, which contained an essential cue for the singers on the
stage. It is quite impossible to give a just flavor of the moment in question without counting on a perception of anxious strangeness in undertaking to transpose at sight, and in performance, an English horn part
onto a B-flat clarinet, demanding an interval of transposition (down a
perfect fourth) that one would be unlikely ever to have had occasion
to calculate, let alone to execute, all magnified by the difficulty of Sessions's music. I hope to have kept the friendship of that brashly confident younger self I maintained, so I report with late pride that in the
event I made nothing much of the event, evidently assuming that I had
mostly shown a cool head and competent musicianship.

It is not all that Sessions assumed. One of those to whom he told
of the event was the composer Milton Babbitt, whom I met in Salzburg,
Austria, in the summer of 1952, where I had been sent, on the recommendation of the Harvard philosophy department as a reward for my
performance on that year's Ph.D. qualifying examinations, as one of
four graduate student assistants to participate in the Salzburg Seminar
in American Studies. Babbitt charmingly, upon our first being introduced—taking his own amused delight in his friend Roger Sessions's
open-hearted delight in every aspect of the conditions of the life of music—regaled the clump of the young who had gathered around him
with a description of Sessions telling the story of the broken English
horn, an event five years in the past, to every composer at the recent
meetings of the International Society of Contemporary Music. This
was the first I heard of the event's amounting to a story. When the next
year I was nominated for a Junior Fellowship in Harvard's Society of
Fellows, Babbitt, at a gathering in his apartment in New York suggested
that I should ask Sessions for a letter of recommendation, since the idea
then of the Junior Fellowship was still that it gave a graduate student
the freedom and standing to pursue studies not perfectly defined within
a single graduate program. Speaking of acquiring standing, election
to the Society of Fellows produced the most decisive and effective shift
of institutional standing that I had experienced in my life. Standing
begets standing. (Another manifestation of the Saint Matthew Effect.)
The fellowship, as I have indicated, was essential in producing an invitation to an assistant professorship at Berkeley—the position I most
desired in the world—in the absence of a completed Ph.D. dissertation.
This will have to occupy another set of stories, but it should already
serve to alert us, in examining the justice of standing, to look in each
case for a mysteriously broken English horn.

    The most distinguished, or ambitious, text presented at the origi-
nal Mount Holyoke / Pontigny colloquium in 1943, so far as I know,
was Wallace Stevens's reading of his essay "The Figure of the Youth as
Virile Poet." Benfey may possibly have known that I have more than
once used a line or two of Wallace Stevens as accents or guides in texts
of mine, and he may even have specifically imagined that I was pained
by the knowledge that a few years later, what would be Stevens's last essay, "A Collect of Philosophy," variously related to the text Stevens had

read at Mount Holyoke, would be turned down, after having been invited, for publication in a professional philosophical journal, the *Journal of Metaphysics*, edited by Paul Weiss, who also spoke at the 1943 Mount Holyoke / Pontigny celebration. Whatever the rights and wrongs of this invitation and that disinvitation to publish Stevens's piece, I was when I learned of it, while a graduate student at Harvard in the 1950s, left with the feeling that philosophy owed Stevens a decent response to his repeated plea for a response from philosophy's, let's say, self-possession to his all but obsessional efforts to place the connection of poetry with philosophy, or of what he also specified as imagination with reason, in both his poetry and his prose. Whatever the specific intention of the invitation to me to participate in the commemoration of the original Mount Holyoke celebration, I interpreted it as asking from me such a response, however partial, to Wallace Stevens's early, repeated claim upon philosophy.

But to arrive at some perspective on my acceptance, so understood, of such an invitation commemorating an event sixty summers earlier, I will still have to remember my way from that 1943 Sacramento summer playing sprightly yet somnolent tenor saxophone across the river at the El Rancho Motel to the following January and down the road ninety miles to Berkeley. Otherwise I shall not arrive at Juilliard so belatedly and confront there the disintegration of my ambition to compose music, replaced as it were by reading Freud ten to twelve hours a day, successively contracting the symptoms of hysteria and of obsession depicted in the *Introductory Lectures*, staggered that I had graduated college having, it seemed, read essentially nothing and having articulated views for myself of nothing, neither—recalling topics about which I consciously suffered from having no serious understanding—of Stalinism nor of T. S. Eliot's anti-Semitism nor of Santayana's claims to be a philosopher and almost a poet nor of the use of myth in the modern novel nor of why *The Magic Mountain* opens with the question "What is Time?" nor of whether Kafka's writings should have been published against his wishes nor of whether a serious artist had to be modern nor of why D. H. Lawrence was and Virginia Woolf was not repelled by philosophers at Cambridge nor of how Stravinsky could be serious in expressing admiration for Bellini nor of whether Hollywood films were art the way Russian and Italian and French films (of which I had by then seen one or two each) were art. But then why would I have thought of returning to the university to find out such things, and who knows what others, since I had not already found them there? If half a year after abandoning Juilliard I had not returned to California and entered UCLA I would not, two years later on, have met when I did the two people most responsible for making the case for my receiving a fellowship from Harvard to continue graduate studies in philosophy there. And so, indefinitely, on.

So is it completely necessary or completely contingent that I have come to this place to tell the story of how I did not die of many catastrophes? And if it is neither, what, again, is the story of a life? And where is a place and what is a form in which to tell it?

November 27, 2003

I have been home from the Mount Holyoke / Pontigny conference for almost three weeks. I report, continuing my remarks about the standing required to challenge standing, that the question of the right to speak came up for me forcefully within these weeks, during which I have edited my talk about Wallace Stevens and composed a reply to an intervention, during the discussion after my delivery of it, by the literary theorist and historian of French literature Jeffrey Mehlman, a participant in the Mount Holyoke colloquium. I had insisted in my paper on the pertinence of Euripides' *Hippolytus* to Stevens's Mount Holyoke essay on the Virile Youth, locating in that play the significance of Stevens's image of a young poet in the modern period taking as his new muse "a kind of sister of the Minotaur." I claimed that Stevens could not, by that mysterious phrase, mean Phaedra, one of Hippolytus's real, as it were, half-sisters (along with Ariadne), but rather have in mind a counter-Phaedra, a counter, that is, to Phaedra's cursed deprivation of the right to speak. Mehlman asked why I neglected the perhaps more specific pertinence of Racine's *Phèdre*, for which the Euripides play is an explicit source. In supplying a consideration in response to the question, I contrasted Euripides' study of the danger of promising with Racine's more general sense of the treacherousness of speech, or obscurity of the right to speak. Poets have to risk both—accept and claim the

promise of poetry before you have the proof that you can withstand the
consequent prophecy and poverty, and contest with monsters for the
right to assert your own language and its imaginary city. In the background there is Wittgenstein's famous tag at the end of his *Tractatus*:
"Whereof one cannot speak, thereof must one be silent," which I have
taken as a response to Nietzsche's admonition at the beginning of the
second volume of *Human, All Too Human*: "One should speak only where
one must not be silent."

My conscious neglect of, even refusal of Racine and siding with
Euripides was in effect a continuation of my defense (and puzzled rebuke) of my teacher Austin, against Derrida's homage and dismissal in
his reading of Austin's theory of the performative utterance, of what
words do as well as mean, or do in or by meaning something. (This defense emerged, belatedly as so often with me, in the second of my Jerusalem lectures in 1992. But my simply not mentioning Racine as using
Euripides is a symptom of a perverseness or ostentatious tempting of
rebuke that arises from time to time in my writing that I do not understand, a sort of horror of stating the obvious while at the same time my
medium so often and essentially invokes the status of the obvious.) The
intellectual crisis caused for me in receiving the brunt of Austin's work
is still (counting from 1943) a dozen years into the future. In reaching
the crisis of giving up my search for a relation to music that mattered to
me in the way I would come to imagine a life of the mind could matter
to me, I discovered that I had never, as I might say, chosen my life, or
suffered its choosing me, but accepted the tow of a certain talent. The
crisis precipitated by Austin's appearance on the scene, in contrast, left
me with a set of fragments that seemed to have some obscure but essential relation to the expression of my desire for a world. In the former
case (the silencing of meaning in music) I felt I had misplaced the world;
in the latter case (the philosophical questioning of meaning in everyday
speech) I felt disoriented with the discovery of a further world.

November 29, 2003

I said there were two bands that occupied the spring and then
the summer of 1943, providing money enough to justify an existence

outside the pawnshop, the first of which was the resident band at the El Rancho Motel, where in the ten-minute breaks each hour, required by the musicians' union, I either listened to the conversation of the old men in the band (all in their late twenties with some exemption or disability keeping them out of the armed services) talking so far as I made out about union politics or their insurance policies, producing repeated vows to myself that my future would never look like theirs; or I talked with the Latino waiters in the kitchen, who would offer me pieces of pie and coffee. The second band was the one that materialized in the offer from the Latin American bassist who mysteriously had picked Sacramento as the place from which to put together a band to go on the road for the summer playing, it turned out, resorts at the Russian River and in Santa Cruz. Here was my chance to leave home without committing myself to any further life. That I was in this case being hired as the band's pianist had the virtue that I would not have to suffer directly the faults of intonation and ensemble playing from within the belly of the band that a hurriedly formed mostly young group was likely to produce, but that I could instead isolate myself in the relative autonomy of the piano and the relative freedom of supplying introductions and ornamentations tactfully inserted into silences that needed shaping. The problem with this fantasy was that I had never played piano in a band, and my classical piano training had not extended to learning the notation of lead sheets (melodies with the nicknames of accompanying chords). Moreover, I had still not systematically practiced, let alone mastered, the knack of reading piano music at sight.

My mother's ability to sight-read at the piano was legendary in her musical circles—to me it was for so long purely a display of magic— and a benefit to me of learning to play clarinet and saxophone was, as I had predicted, that the sight-reading of the single lines allotted to these instruments was as immediately available to me as piano music was to my mother. I was going to say that this made sight-reading as easy for me as reading words. So just this easy was reading piano music for my mother (no doubt within limits I hadn't yet experienced). But if she was reading words then what was I reading? Letters? Or was she reading phrases and sentences?—as I must have surmised when I turned pages for her, since she always nodded for me to turn well before she had played the last measures on the page. And how was it that some pianists

I knew who did not know music or play the piano as well as I were able to read better than I? That I had decided to understand, nor rather not to understand, sight-reading to constitute a mystery, one revealed to my mother that I was not to attempt to fathom, was not made fully or undeniably conscious to me until some ten years after the sunless late winter afternoon I walked out of my composition lesson at Juilliard six or seven weeks after term began in January 1947, knowing that I would not return.

There is an identifiable occasion on which my defensiveness against penetrating the magic of sight-reading was itself consciously penetrated, as suddenly as, also belatedly, I had that year first smoked and allowed myself deliberately to inhale a cigarette, amazed by its stabbing and total deliciousness. The musical occasion occurred during my second year teaching at Berkeley, on an afternoon at the house, appropriately enough, of Joseph and Vivian Kerman. Joe Kerman was already, as Professor of Music, prominent as the author of *Opera as Drama*, and the Kerman house was spacious and beautiful and it, and its furnishings, was in sufficient disrepair not to require formal attention and was welcoming to a somewhat shifting but stable group of academics from the departments of music and English and history who met there for the easy and spacious conversation it inspired and because some kind of music making was likely to be in the foreground or background. Letting myself into the unlocked house, calling out and receiving an answering call from somewhere to go on in, I found on climbing the half-dozen stone stairs of the entrance hall leading up to the large living or drawing room that the origin of the sounds of desultory fooling around at the piano at the far end was a man about my age, compact, his hair not shaved but cut as close to the scalp as any I had seen, whom I recognized as having heard play in a number of local chamber music or song recitals and as having been described by the Kermans as the busiest pianist in town.

He rose from the piano to shake hands, told me the Kermans had said I was coming over and that I played, and said he was in the mood for Schubert as he picked up a score from the side of the music stand, in the horizontal oblong format of piano music for four hands, made room for me to sit at the lower end of the piano bench, and opened the Rosamunde string quartet. My first wife, Marcia, and I had collected a considerable library of four-hand music from antiquarian music stores while traveling in Austria and Germany the year before coming to Berkeley, and although she and I played four hands regularly, it had never occurred to me to wonder how it was that I was able to read this music comfortably at sight. True, it wasn't like reading the piano parts of Brahms's chamber music, yet it wasn't single lines either. It happened that I had never played this Schubert quartet, but I felt no hesitation in following my new acquaintance as he positioned himself at the keyboard and gave the downbeat. I have never lost my taste for the shocking pleasure of hearing, especially at one's own conjuring, the sounds of the sometimes too-familiar monuments of the standard symphonic and chamber-music literature rendered immediately but with so interesting an alienation by two people sitting together at a piano.

We were into the piece, perhaps as far as getting into the development section of the first movement, when I noticed, vaguely, that my partner on this occasion was somehow restive on the bench. Without stopping playing, he rather shouted at me: "Are you *reading*?" meaning reading this at sight for the first time. I stopped playing. I was flushed with some version of anxiety, as if I had not produced something but only promised something I could not produce. I made up a hurried excuse and left the room; indeed I wound up going for a walk and not returning that day. Some secret had evidently been revealed. Inviting what threat? Was the shout of surprise produced by pleasure or by pain? And suppose, as not infrequently happens to me, I had instead of a connection felt an estrangement from my display of some talent, the keyboard now not an invitation and extension of will but a barrier to it, and had made a fool of myself.

December 1, 2003

I had begun working with a psychoanalyst (once a week was what I could afford), faced with the breakup of my marriage to Marcia. A recurrent topic of my concerns was also my failure to make progress on my doctoral dissertation, the practical consequence of which, if unchecked, was that I would lose my position in the Berkeley philosophy department and have to look for a teaching position in another town, not merely a vastly less agreeable circumstance but one further jeopardizing the normalizing of my relation with our daughter, Rachel, then some three years old. About a year later, as I knew the dissertation was taking shape, and in fact I could sometimes hardly write fast enough to keep up with the flow of ideas, I developed the symptom, when I left the apartment I had taken when Marcia and I separated, and found myself out of sight of it, of having to return to the apartment to make sure I hadn't left the stove on under the coffeepot or a lit cigarette at my desk, whose consequence would be that the building would burn down along with the mounting, unique pages of my handwritten manuscript (this was the late 1950s). (I had heard stories of writers who, for example, put manuscripts inside a cellophane wrapping and then closed them in a refrigerator when they left the house. But I also heard that this was not reliably effective.) When I reported the symptom to Dr. Hilger, bless him, he responded at once: "Are you afraid that the manuscript is too bad or that it is too good to exist?" I thought at once of the fear of showing my ability to read. (I also seem to recall that it was in connection with this question that I first wondered when it was in my early life that I began fearing medical checkups for the reason that I might produce an erection.) It is obvious enough to me that something moving me to think philosophically, more characteristically than in the case of the philosophers I have grown up with, is less an impulse to refute a text that attracts me than it is to read it differently from the way it seems to ask, but asks. This has not seemed to me to be an avoidance of the argument of a text but an alternative way of engaging it, a way of creating a future in which we both, the text and I, learn something about ourselves.

In response to Freud's declaration in *The Interpretation of Dreams* that, in matters of the unconscious, psychoanalysis has hitherto waited in vain for philosophy, I have thought it important to observe that while this seems to say, unambiguously, that psychoanalysis instead of waiting for philosophy must now break with it, the passage can also be said to confess, or claim, that the waiting is no longer in vain exactly because psychoanalysis has transformed and satisfied an expectation of philosophy. And when Wittgenstein observes, in the opening section of *Philosophical Investigations*, "Explanations come to an end somewhere," I urge that this be seen as a kind of philosophical joke, since Wittgenstein has hardly begun anything to be called a serious explanation. It can help to see this by reading the line not (only) as saying, "Explanations come to an *end* somewhere," which is true and important, that is, it emphasizes that explanations are finite; but (also) as saying, "Explanations come to an end *somewhere*," which emphasizes that one should be wary of assuming one knows where in a given case this somewhere will be—in the present case, for some purpose, what Wittgenstein has depicted himself as saying by way of explanation may suffice; in other cases an explanation a hundred times more detailed might not suffice. But such readings, I keep finding, make certain readers impatient. It is important for me to understand why this is so, since it tends to make the reception of my work as a whole grudging, even when its results are not challenged (on the contrary it is the very banality of such truths, the fact that perceiving them requires no expertise, or standing, that seems to cause offense), something that has caused me considerable disquiet over the years.

And recently, in reporting my having cause to read Racine's *Phè-dre* again, I find I am thinking of the dangers of claiming the right to speak, evidently necessary at once to the idea of having a self, however continuing (or failing or refusing to continue) in formation, and of participating in a democratically conceived order, however postponed. And yet, isn't the right to read closer to the right to understand than it is to the right to speak? Yet again, in sight-reading music, there is no such obvious distinction between reading and speaking. There, to read is (in its obvious form) to speak. (As it is, come to think of it, in Wittgenstein's chain of examples of reading in the *Investigations*.) There is of course such a thing as reading a score, say, an orchestral score, silently, but that is not what sight-reading is, and what shows an understanding of the music in that case is open. Presumably one has had, a culture has had, to learn to read silently, an almost unnoticeable accomplishment whose implications seem vast. I seem to recall teachers using the expression "read to yourself" to mean read silently. And I recall along with this direction the pang I sensed in the implication that (unlike reading to another) in silent reading one is not, no one is, really being spoken to, not having that infinite pleasure. (Is reading Braille more like seeing words or like hearing them? Is reading print?) And now I think again of Marc Shell's book *Stuttering*, soon to appear, in which he proposes a link between Hamlet's paralysis in acting and a paralysis in speaking what he knows.

December 3, 2003

In thinking how to prepare myself for joining the traveling band as its pianist, I remembered having introduced myself to a pianist whose playing Thompson and I had been impressed by in a bar when we went there to listen to a friend auditioning for a job playing on the days this pianist was off. I found her a wonderful-looking woman, large and with too much blond hair and eyes too insistently blue for some tastes, and her smile, which was rarely conferred, featured rows of very white teeth that seemed to be all the same size. She was fairly obviously a bit old for me, so my being moved to compliment her on her fluency might have produced disinterested praise. And perhaps I managed to express my sense that she was too casual in her ideas and, with her ear and facility, should push herself to take more chances. On the chance that my cheeky little effort to make an impression had succeeded, I looked her up again at the bar and asked if she ever gave lessons, telling her what I needed to learn within the next two or perhaps three weeks if I was not to make an immediate fool of myself as a band pianist. She said she had taught but not any longer. However, she offered to show me what I needed to know, if I already knew as much as I seemed to know. And so she did, over the course of two or three weeks of excitedly chaste afternoons, which included providing me with her fake book (I think that's what she called it) from which I copied out dozens of tunes and the accompanying chord symbols she taught me how to read.

The two resorts at which the band played, for four weeks each (I vaguely recall that there was a third, scheduled for a shorter time, but images of it escape me now, or have become unrecognizable to me), lent themselves to the same routine. Afternoons were reserved for rehearsals—and here I acquired my first full taste for being places in their off-hours, as in a restaurant/bar before customers were admitted, the chairs still hung upside down from the tabletops, leaving the floor clear to be washed and waxed. My idea of off-hours is of time behind the scenes; rehearsals rather than performances; possibilities rather than actualities; uniforms laid out, not yet donned; anticipation uncompromised; members only, not mere observers; knowledge and reality, not rumor and appearance. Mornings free, with passes provided to band members to use the resort facilities—at the Russian River the main attraction was canoeing, which I did for much of each morning; at Santa Cruz the attraction was an amusement park, in which I had my first experience of a serious roller coaster—in which to meet the girls who will hover around the bandstand during the dancing and with whom I would make tentative, tempestuous plans to drift away with after midnight, the era in which I came to know, to inhabit, the distinctiveness of morning at its earliest, most adorned with time and eternity.

In my keynote address to the Mount Holyoke / Pontigny remembrance, I seem to detect something of the knowledge I acquired then of that interval of night giving over to day, first light, the moments in which sunrise initiates its oncoming contention for illumination, the time that Wallace Stevens marks for poetry, and that both Thoreau and Heidegger describe (Thoreau with greater clarity and, well, conceptual thoroughness) as keeping alive the power of true awakening. Arriving at the Russian River, I had not yet acquired the concept of groupies.

December 4, 2003

Not long after the band moved to Santa Cruz, the band's dashing singer asked if I would as a personal favor make an arrangement for the band of a song written by a young friend of hers from Latin America who had just died. I had on various occasions sketched arrangements, but never copied out the parts and heard them played. After rehearsals I lingered on the bandstand to use the piano in working on the arrangement while the waiters came and went preparing the place for the late afternoon and evening crowds. In a week the score was in effect done—but the transpositions for the saxophones and trumpets would have to be made at the time of copying the individual parts. Enough people, including the singer, helped with the copying so that this was done within another week. Taking up the piece in rehearsal was a fiasco. The song itself was sweet and straightforward, but having never heard the realization of anything I had written, I had tried anything that occurred to me. For example, when I called for the four brass players to use mutes, I specified that each should use a different mute from the others, just to hear what that sounded like. (I remember clearly only the names of two of the mutes, the straight mute and the cup mute. A third lent a kind of buzzing to the sound, due to a plunger in its center [this may be what is now called a Harmon mute]; a fourth looked like one straight mute stuck inside another, giving a soft sweet sound—perhaps this was what was called a Mellotone mute.) The result was quite uninteresting, except that I was interested in that fact. Again, I distributed chords in an ensemble passage for the saxophones so that the tenor saxophones sometimes played higher than the alto saxophones, which meant that each instrument was playing in a somewhat unnatural register. And so on. It was clear, at least for this collection of musicians, that the writing was unusable. But for me the experience was superb.

December 5, 2003

What I knew of serious roller coasters came from the convincing drama my mother drew in my imagination of her thrill as a girl in taking the legendary ride at Coney Island while her family still lived in Brooklyn. At Santa Cruz, approaching the ride, I heard the girls in the roller coaster screaming before I looked up and saw them in near free-fall, and when the little train of cars dragged to a halt at the platform of the exit and entrance to change passengers, I was too alarmed to get on board. A cycle of laborious ascents followed by screaming freefalls repeated itself several times. Shall I therefore never share one clear source of my mother's youthful thrills? Without deciding, I found myself sitting on a bench in the front car as a guard swung down a steel bar and locked it across my waist. At the top of the first drop I shut my eyes; at the bottom I abjectly promised God that if he let me live I would never do anything so mad again. When the train pulled to its stop I was immobile. When the guard unlocked the steel bar and I stumbled out of the car and went through the exit, I felt my book of free tickets in the pocket of my trousers, took one out and without thinking walked back through the entrance; this time I lowered and locked the steel bar myself. The next time we stopped I simply handed the guard a new ticket.

I did this until the tickets were gone, perhaps some half dozen in all. As I stood up, my mind was so distant from my body that it was all I could do to make my way down the walkway to the exit. I wondered whether this is what drunkenness feels like and whether it is a pleasure. And I thought: Never, henceforth, will I have to say that I am afraid to take someone on a roller coaster. Say to whom? And was this achievement worth breaking my vow to God?

Of such repetitions was the fabric of those weeks woven, time lapsing before the lunging of the eye to the sea's horizon, time electric enveloping the contours of the summer's bodies. In public hours only two developments count as distinguished events marking the progress of that summer. First, as the weeks passed, my newfound dance band piano playing was improving. I became able to start improvising at the piano with sufficient point and originality to, from time to time, make the lead saxophone player shout out with approval (this was Matt Utal, the only player in my high school band who shared my ambition to spend life as a musician); I found that I came to count on finding new inventions of phrasing or harmony to create that companionable response. (Reaching this point in a late round of editing, I was moved, in a sentimental mood, to determine whether I could learn the current whereabouts of Matt Utal, if he too had survived to this moment. Even my primitive skills with Google produced the information that he had for decades played in the reed section of the Les Brown band, familiarly known as "The Les Brown Band of Renown," which I find some still recall, a highly successful so-called big band in and beyond the era of the major fame of such organizations. Out of an impulse not unfamiliar to me but almost never acted on by me, I actually phoned the number given for him, or someone of that odd name, on the Oregon coast (not far from where Ernest Bloch had lived), and actually had a piece of archaic but well-remembered judgment, happily, with perhaps no less gratification than for myself, ratified.) Second, our band played one afternoon each week for the patients at a servicemen's convalescent ward at a hospital in the center of Santa Cruz. Hearing our indelicate sounds there unshielded by the bustling crowd of night dancers all washed, as were all other visible objects in view, including walls and ceiling and floor, by the untraceable speckles of colored lights reflected from the revolving multifaceted mirrored globe hung from the ceiling of the otherwise dimly lit ballroom, I wondered how clearly our intention of sympathy and solidarity could transport itself across this small town and make itself felt to whatever attention could be spared and granted by men silently recovering from their wounds in their sunlit recreation rooms. On one of these afternoons a local singer asked if I could accompany her in a couple of arias after the band had played. None of the work I had done with my bar pianist in Sacramento had improved my ability to sight-read proper piano scores. In my desperate humiliation I said that I had broken my glasses and could not read accurately without them.

Forty-five summers later a seminar for teachers sponsored by the National Endowment for the Humanities would be held at the Santa Cruz branch of the University of California, an expansion of that university unforeseeable from that war month of my playing in that locale, and my accepting the invitation to join the faculty of that seminar was consciously tinged with the pleasure of imagining returning for the first time to look for traces of those distant weeks. The roller coaster was gone, but the building was still standing whose first floor had held various amusements such as pinball games and whose second floor, now closed off, constituted the ballroom with the turning mirrored globe where the band had played every night. I remembered accurately where the restrooms in the building were, but on approaching them I found the stench so strong, and the filth covering the floor so comprehensive, as to overpower competing needs. I had not, I think, anticipated much in the way of a tender moment with that scene of my past, but I felt deprived of having some choice over how much of the memory to let go.

I find myself remembering the concluding sequence of Orson Welles's *The Magnificent Ambersons*, in which a long tracking shot moves backward through a house now empty whose rooms in the course of the life of the film we have seen opulently filled. I have not, I believe, viewed the film since first seeing it when it was released, so I do not remember the film concretely enough to judge how satisfying an end this achieves for the film, but the drastic shift of feeling remembered in this passage brings to mind, oddly, Wittgenstein's remark roughly halfway through the *Investigations*' meditations on "seeing-as": "I should like to say that what dawns here lasts only so long as I am occupied with the object in a particular way." I say this association is "odd" since in the case of the altered house it is not alone my way of occupation that is gone but the house itself that is, as it were, irretrievable. I would like to say of this remembered shift of feeling not that it is in particular *my* occupation with a thing that has past, but that history has passed it by.

A little more than a year after the summer of playing resorts I was called for the expected army physical and I again heard late in the process the doctor say precisely, on looking into, or trying to look into, my left ear, "Go home, son," this time immovably uninterested in my offer to get an explanatory letter from my family doctor. Walking out I was surprised by the strength of a sudden access of melancholy since I had not really expected a different outcome. (By September 1944, a year and a half since the experience of my navy physical, the tide of war had shifted and there was not sufficient reason for the army to take a chance on sick ears.) Before receiving that confirmation, I had, with a group of several dozen other men, been taken to a room and directed to sit around a long table on which there was a scattering of medical history forms and a few pencils. But instead of telling us to fill out the forms, a young soldier began reciting from memory a list of dozens of diseases, ordering us to raise a hand if we had ever had any of them. I do not recall whether many, or any, hands went up. We were then moved to a large empty room and, lined up in several rows, told to strip naked for the usual taking of vital signs and hernia coughs and prostate probings. After dressing and lining up to enter areas marked by signs taped to the walls for psychological testing and for eye and ear tests, I saw that a number of men in our group each now had a slim board across his chest, about the size of a modest lawyer's shingle, or a country road sign, hung by a leather thong around the neck, neatly stenciled with the single word ILLITERATE. (So that was why the soldier recited the list of diseases to the group.) It occurred to me to wonder whether these men realized what the signs meant that they were wearing. Then I stared in order to know what illiteracy looked like, and stared again to know what others thought of this mode of identification. I thought I was successfully furtive in my curiosity, but I retain an image of a good-looking tan-skinned man together with the thought that surely all this sign meant in his case was that he did not read English. Without advancing claims for myself as a connoisseur of humiliations, I note that my interest in what analytical philosophy calls the skeptical problem of other minds seems to be affected by such an experience, as in Part Four of *The Claim of Reason*, where I interpret philosophy's habitual doubt concerning the existence of a human other not as an expression of ignorance, but as a denial, of the humanity of that other, a capacity I will eventually come to call "dealing the little deaths of everyday life."

December 6, 2003

The importance of the summer of travel and music lay alone neither in its particular events, nor in its spell of repetitions, but also in the very fact of its lack of horizon, nothing bearing down immediately from ahead, nothing looming from behind. I would turn seventeen on returning to Sacramento, neither an adult nor not an adult. I might even say that to be without a horizon became the point of this moment, a rite of nonpassage, searching for a point of origin, to be zero, to look back at the world, but without exactly dying. (The classical empiricists pictured the newly born mind as a tabula rasa, a blank slate thereupon to be filled with impressions. If you think further of the mind as perpetually yet incompletely being erased or as shedding or shunning impressions, say, as becoming modified by what it is you are impressed by or unimpressed by, you may picture it not as the latest in a succession of states expanding upon following the one you are born with but as one you may be reborn into, a set not of facts but of acts.) I perhaps thought of my horizonless moment as my having become anonymous, since the mode in which I achieved it, or some equivalent of it, was to change my name.

So fateful an event had an almost motionless onset. A week before the engagement ended at Santa Cruz, the band leader asked me to drop by his hotel room after rehearsal. (It wasn't a room but a suite, and the band's singer was present, as various of us had imagined she would be.) The previous night the principal tenor saxophone player had become ill, and the leader had asked me to take over that role since he had found an experienced pianist to take over in turn from me (someone who turned out to be a soldier on furlough). What the leader wanted to talk to me about now was my ability to read at sight through the tenor part of the book of arrangements, and about how much better the ensemble playing sounded with me in that position. He was forming another band to play at the Statler Hotel in Chicago beginning the middle of September and offered me 125 dollars a week to join it. It was more money than any amount I had ever heard my contemporaries to have made. Perhaps this was a solution to my sense of nowhere (whether to escape it or to adopt it would not have been clear to me), and we agreed that I would give him an answer shortly after we returned to Sacramento and I had a chance to talk it over with my parents. But an irreversible step was taken within me before our return home. I will sleep in my parents' apartment again, but I will never live there again. I seem also at once to have decided that if I were going to take on a professional career as an entertainer I would give myself a stage name.

Family names were irrelevant to the neither serious nor nonserious encounters that made up the seascape with girls the world had become. Stan was all that had been called for. But soon after my inward leave-taking from home, one night after the dance was over (our closing theme song was a medley including "Good Night, Sweetheart" and "Nighty-Night") I introduced myself to a young woman as Stan Cavell. The first two syllables of the family's original Russian name Kavelieruskii (changed at Ellis Island not quite forty years earlier) broke away as cleanly as if I had flawlessly cut a diamond. Whether because the young woman to whom I announced it was more impressive to me than others had been, or because I felt more inclined to the world than I had before, I sought her out again and in fact we spent my few remaining days, or nights, in Santa Cruz together. The morning I left she handed me a letter as I got on the bus, and the name was visible on the envelope on my dressing table as I was unpacking my suitcase back in Sacramento. My mother's eye swooped to the envelope, and she asked me who Stan Cavell is. Deep into imagery of escape and glamour, and both embarrassed and frightened by the question, I surprised myself by telling the truth, anyway the part of it concerning the offer of the job playing in Chicago and experimenting with a stage name. I began simply by saying, "It's me." And from nowhere I added, truly, and perhaps out loud, "From now on."

I had had an immediate precedent for this adventure in the case of one of my parents' closest acquaintances. The most glamorous of the jewelry salesmen out of New York with a Southern territory, Milton

Epstein, who made an appearance earlier in my narrative, had a son, Melvin, whom we knew from Milton's stories to have spent much of his time playing the piano in Harlem, an image against which I pondered my experience with the Harrel Wiley band. Milton would also have told us that his son had taken the name Mel Powell, because when my mother and I heard, on one of the fifteen-minute radio broadcasts of big bands around dinnertime that were common in that era, the opening theme of the Benny Goodman band, and after a few minutes of our consequently undivided attention heard the announcer inform the audience that the next piece would feature the Benny Goodman trio, Goodman and the drummer (Gene Krupa then?) now to be joined by a young pianist named Mel Powell, a certain immeasurable expansion of the universe of contingency and significance and aspiration at once commanded the mood of our small apartment. This happened within some months of my leaving to travel for the summer playing piano with the rapidly assembled band.

But for me, the experience of reentering the world unknown to the world, the freedom to perceive without position, as if behind the mask of rebirth, did not perfect an attachment to playing in a band, but on the contrary introduced a decisive degree of reflection into my relation to music; nor did it require the staging of a stage name to validate the wish to name myself. In short, I knew within days of the return home that I would not join the new band in Chicago. For all the bassist leader's virtuosity on his instrument, he was clearly not committed any longer to playing, and while I was too good to continue playing in anything like the band I had just left, I was not ready to attempt to play in what were called name bands. Besides, the players who had created the sounds of the serious big bands were now mostly in the army, and if there were jazz musicians still around Chicago that I could in principle learn from, it was both too soon and too late for that. I was too inexperienced to live their life, and I discovered as suddenly as closing my empty suitcase that I no longer had any intention of finding a life as a performer. The energy I had put into the single arrangement I had written that summer had helped teach me that music now meant to me writing or nothing. The plan to go through with a legal change of my name in preparation for entering university to study music formally, beginning in the spring term, all at once became the task of that autumn.

December 7, 2003

I could not imagine my father agreeing to the plan to change my name, but as things unfolded he never explicitly participated in the decision. Perhaps my mother had unleashed certain of her powers to threaten him into silence on this deep gamble for freedom, and he had for years had some sense, at least according to my mother, of my despair of the world I knew, and perhaps felt some measure of guilt for his role in producing that state. Or he felt so baffled by the plan and repudiated by it, by the extremity and rejection of it, even perhaps so stunned by its sheer possibility—an epitome of our differences, my gesture declaring the search for a life I could want, not merely endure, in America, but at the same time a mark of our sameness, since now, like him, I would bear a name I was not born with—that it left him wordless, as if bewildered by the withdrawal, somehow now pointless with respect to me, of his rage.

The legal process was more impressive and elaborate than I had expected. In a witness box in a large, ornate courtroom, empty except for small, evidently unrelated clusters of people sitting or standing here and there, uninterested in my case, I had to declare that I was moving across the country to live with relatives who had already changed their names. It was true that two branches of the Goldstein family had gone back to the original Russian name, but these cousins had both chosen as its analogue the name Cavalier, using from the Russian the first three, rather than two, syllables. I could not understand myself to want to identify with those family members in opposition, as it were, to my father. What I had not realized until this present writing and its attempt to peel back certain further layers in this decision, is that it forged an unexpected identification of my father with his brother Joe (as well as with the successful Milton Epstein), the brother my father so admired, the rabbi who had wished to put the old country behind them as the hopeless slaughterhouse it so garishly was, since one of the changes to the name Cavalier was made by one of Joe's two sons. It occurs to me now that my father might actually have sought his idol Joe's advice in the matter. The courtroom appearance was the first step of a legal process that required placing a notification of this intended change of name in some newspaper, to run every day for ninety days, in case there were nefarious ulterior causes for this adolescent's way of adopting himself.

I don't know when I came to sense that a reasonably accurate account of such causes would have, or should have, filled the columns and sections of a major Sunday newspaper every day for ninety days, proposing an absolute autobiography. (Is anything other than the whole truth even a partial truth? And is anything the whole truth?) At the same time I would have come to realize that my simple notice was one of scores of such things each day putting ordinary lives at stake, perhaps many meant, like mine, to alter their drifts into new, undivinable futures.

The question, What is news? (as if what news is has itself changed), became the origin of a new film genre (new at least to me) combining documentary and film noir narratives that appeared during World War II, in which the image of the story behind the headlines, and the idea of a night in the city as a web of a thousand stories, entered into film's self-definition. I was already in New York, after Berkeley, when *Naked City* (with Barry Fitzgerald) and *Kiss of Death* (with Victor Mature and Richard Widmark) and *Crossfire* (with Robert Ryan and Robert Young and Robert Mitchum) were released. *Citizen Kane* can be said to be the greatest, almost parodistic, representative of the genre of the story behind the story, of the mystery of the ordinary. (Fritz Lang's *M* is an obvious precursor, or inspirer.)

Most of this past November was spent responding to the copyedited manuscript of the next book of mine scheduled for publication, *Cities of Words*, the transformation into chapters of a book of the course of lectures I developed over my last decade of regular teaching at Harvard, on moral (or Emersonian) perfectionism. I am holding out for calling the twenty-three lectures "Letters," and keeping so far as manageable and sensible the sound of the classroom in my text. A recurrent theme of the course, following the consequences of recognizing that Emersonianism provides the intellectual texture of remarriage comedies, is the perpetually contested relation of public and private; and the image of the newspaper almost never fails to appear significantly in these films. The last time I gave the course I was still trying to articulate this feature of these films with the exactitude and consequence they keep seeming to me to demand. If I say that newspapers are designed to make public what is both private and public business, I might say of novels that they are meant to make private what is public and private business, make them mine. In these terms, film brings an unprecedented, if not unanticipated, medium into play that questions the distinction between public and private. This makes the medium of film inherently philosophical. (Philosophical here contrasts, as explicitly in Wittgenstein's *Philosophical Investigations*, with the scientific, on the ground that philosophy does not seek to tell us anything new but rather to understand what human beings cannot on the whole simply not already know. Yet we are shown repeatedly in the *Investigations* that one cannot *tell* another something unless it is news to that other. It follows that philosophy takes place before or after we tell things to each other, in art or in rumor or in confidence or as information. So what moves philosophy to speak?)

December 8, 2003

I wrote that autumn—sixty years ago perhaps to the day—to the University of California at Berkeley for its Catalogue of Courses. (I am unclear how I learned that universities publish such things. I imagine the fact was contained in the packets of material the navy had sent me.) There, sure enough, under the navy ROTC listing, I found such courses as (so I recall a sequence of them) fire control, which seemed ambiguous as between how best to put out fires and how best to deliver them. Neither seemed to me courses I expected universities to concern themselves with, but I knew enough to recognize that total mobilization involved science, and that in 1941 the United States had been, in a sense to its credit, unprepared for total war. Before pursuing these questions very far, I turned to the listing under the Department of Music, where the very names of the courses were celestial music to my ears—harmony, counterpoint, fugue, orchestration, ear training, composition. Here were the springs from whose drenching I would heal my increasing consciousness of ignorance and lack of training. My interest in turning through the catalogue's pages fed upon itself. I had as if discovered the ultimate book, as suspenseful and revelatory as the best novels I had read. Every page contained mysteries, and, evidently, keys to them, sometimes fields of study whose names, without understanding them, promised me liberation—philosophy, anthropology, topology, historiography. Liberation from what? To what? Is it liberation that wings provide? It was as if I had hitherto not known what a field of study was. Hebrew is taught as a language, like other languages; Victor Hugo is a poet as well as part of the history of the French novel; there is something called non-Euclidean geometry; Peer Gynt is a character in a play of that name; *Faust* was a play before it was an opera; modern novels are retellings of myth; folk tales have a structure. Knowledge is itself a world; there is order to it; it is acquirable. At Berkeley everyone must day and night be talking to everyone about everything.

Nor will I be disappointed by what I came to discover. The music department turned out at that time to be housed in a small two-story shingled structure, roughly of a kind to be found on any street in the Berkeley flats, kin to others on the university campus that were said to have served as barracks in World War I, and removed enough from other structures to keep the sounds of music instruction reasonably discretely to itself. On my first day in Berkeley, walking up the structure's outside wooden stairs to present myself to the department secretary to learn how to identify myself as a music major, a conversation in the reception room between a student and a man whose neatly trimmed gray beard did not make him look particularly old was continuing with the older man saying, "Whenever I hear that piece, I believe in immortality." I had come to the right place.

Part 6

April 8, 2004

Why there is a four-month hiatus between entries indicated at this date is not easy to reconstruct, coming back now in the summer of 2006 to complete the editing and annotating of these accounts. Perhaps the cause, rather than or in addition to so long a hiatus, is that I had shuffled certain entries, or inserted entries at earlier dates, without carefully noting these exceptions. Whatever the mechanisms of forgetfulness involved, I must assume this long lapse signifies, whatever else, an influx of anxiety coloring the years of my late adolescence, marked by the seam across my life figured in my change of name. It has occurred to me to call this change my second chance. But I am not sure what it would mean to think either of the event or of its consequences as happening by chance. Yet in another mood I might think of myself as having been given countless chances, some clearly taken, some obscurely, countless others not. Here I am, unaccountably.

I think again for some reason of my early experience of *The Count of Monte Cristo* and recall the hero escaping prison by throwing himself from a high cliff or parapet into a cold body of water and as he hits the icy surface of liberation letting out a shriek of colliding terror and ecstasy. More than once in my life that image of a leap and the sound of release has crossed my spirit as the very sign of my years falling between the expulsion from home, perhaps from homelessness, and the

trials of discovering or constructing or transfiguring necessarily am-
bivalent analogues of freedom and arrival. Evidently some such challenge was not part of my consciousness at this point in baffled narration
four months ago, when my strategy seems to have been to go on to say
enough about my ensuing undergraduate years in Berkeley to allow me
to reach beyond them, as it were, and then come back to considering
Berkeley as events drive me back. In that case I would also have been
counting on some more usable perspective as my steps after Berkeley
will take me to a year in New York seeking to weigh an unthought life,
then wandering back and down to a vaster and to me unknown part of
California for what turned out to be three years at UCLA learning how
and why I imagined philosophy was mine to discover, followed by four
years at Harvard trying to prove or disprove this to myself and possibly
also to two or three others, then a year of deliberate traveling in Europe
before returning to teach philosophy at Berkeley.

To speak of my initial three and a half years as an undergraduate student at Berkeley as providing me with a college education is
to say too little and too much about those years. Too much, because
the only seriously systematic learning I acquired was an initiation
into the theory and composition of music, and this could in principle
have been acquired at least as well in a music conservatory. Too little,
because what I learned, it seemed, in every exchange overheard or
undertaken, was what there is to be learned, what world there is to
hope for, how to talk and think about my life, that the greatness of the
arts and the achievements of learning were the right and the work of
human beings not essentially different from myself, that there were
paths, known and unknown, toward the heart's desire, that there were
friends, known and unknown, along those paths, that day and night
were not debarred from each other, that one could be free in both,
across both. The places at which one comes to such recognitions (call
it Berkeley, call it this room in this house on this or the other street
in Berkeley, day or night) are apt to become sacred to oneself, and
one learns to protect them from the acid realities of those for whom,
for so many different reasons, these clouds of ideals never produced
rain, nor commanded the patience and luck to wait for or to pray long
enough for drenching. A time will come when I will wish to warn
philosophy of over-intellectualizing its speculations, of courting mere

words. But not before years in which intellect and its swarming words are also the food of love.

I entered the university at Berkeley for the spring term of 1944 (though the calendar would have indicated late January or early February), a time when there was more on the mind of American universities than monitoring the curricular choices of adolescents released into the world who were not immediately being prepared for national service. For my first college year I met the two conditions said to be required by so-called land grant colleges, namely, ones founded with the subsidy of state holdings, first to enroll in ROTC (required only of males) and second to prepare oneself otherwise for some potential national service, which, for reasons not explained to me, was satisfied by taking a course in a foreign language. Besides these givens, I enrolled each semester, beyond perhaps a course in English or American literature, in five or six music courses, some as heavy as counterpoint and harmony and music history, some as useful or congenial but comparatively or even wholly undemanding of time outside of the classroom, as that in ear-training or in piano ensemble (the performance of works, under coaching, for two pianos).

The ensemble class was offered in my second semester, taught by Marjorie Petray, a rumored, mysterious figure whom I had heard about late in the spring of my first semester as having spent time, after graduating from Berkeley in the late 1920s, studying and giving concerts in Europe, mostly Germany. When on an afternoon soon after receiving that description I saw a vivid woman, not old not young, hair cut short framing strong, somewhat dark, features, dressed with an elegance and finish suitable for giving an afternoon recital more than for holding a university class, wearing a scarf of a color perfectly contrasting with that of her darker dress, its ends floating behind her uncertainly, as between heaven and earth, stride from the music building over to a car I could not name (and I could name any American car) parked illegally close to the building, I was sure who this figure was before I heard behind me my music history professor remark, to no one in particular, "The music department can relax now; Marjorie Petray is exiting the campus." Naturally I vowed inwardly to study with her.

On walking into the ensemble class at the beginning of the following semester I learned that admission to the class, and assignment of partners to prepare a two-piano work, was done by audition, to be held then and there. Having quit piano lessons soon after entering high school, concentrating instead on the clarinet and the saxophone, I had no work in my fingers to audition with, and indeed my resistance to the solitude of piano playing (unable to allow it to become the solace and fruit of solitude, which happened to some extent only after I had done what I for a long time called "giving up music") meant that I had never carried with me the capacity for playing for others anything beyond the pieces I was working on for my lessons. The audition proved to require performing no complete pieces, however; evidently because sixty seconds of playing was quite sufficient for Marjorie Petray to take the measure of your talent, indeed to penetrate your soul. This time she was wearing a sports jacket into whose pockets she thrust her hands as she paced around the room of the Music Annex—essentially a large, shingle-covered shack a short path from the music building, and housing, among a store of band instruments, a pair of decent grand pianos, placed end to end so that performers face each other over a clear separation. This woman's immediate and doubtless permanent judgments, briefly but strongly uttered, worked not to intimidate but to inspire (I suppose that was the point), prompting me to recall that I had something to use as a sample for her of my capacity at the piano, something I used sometimes to test the sound and warmth of a piano, or propose a relationship with it, before I worked at it on my harmony and counterpoint assignments, namely, the opening bravura theme of the Liszt D-flat Fantasy Impromptu (featured, I would learn some dozen years later, in Max Ophüls's film *Letter from an Unknown Woman*, made it happens the year of my brief use of this theme of Liszt's in my audition). I stopped playing as the theme was about to elaborate itself, as if I could have gone on to the end were there time and need. As I turned to Marjorie Petray, she held me, I believed, with her eyes briefly before turning to the class to remark, "Isn't it fine to hear a man's touch at the piano?" If I have over the years involuntarily recurred to that moment, I have pondered whether that daring, invidious compliment was one of her fearless objective judgments, as if she trusted herself to utter only undeniable truths, or whether she had allowed some further power to leap out in it.

The adolescent crush it furthered in me was something whose ba-

nality even then was as plain to me as was the superb pain and pointless-
ness of it. It did lead briefly to my proposing that I have some private
lessons with her to work on a few pieces with the idea of bringing my
piano playing a little further into the present than I had left it. After
three or four sessions every two weeks it was obvious that I was not prepared to spend time seriously working at the piano any further and that
using the occasions of the lessons as opportunities to be in the magic
presence of this woman and observe the splendor of her house and the
life it framed for her had no useful purpose. This fact rose fully to the
surface at what proved to be our last lesson, when she disappeared at the
sound of a crying child, and returned with a baby held with her left arm
supporting the child sitting, in effect, against her hip, while conducting
with her right arm as she sang correcting the shape the phrase I had just
mangled. I remarked to her that I had not seen a baby held that way since
my mother—her clear and distinct predecessor in a sequence of accomplished, magic, judgmental women in my life—instructed a niece of hers
in the advantages of that posture (that it is securer than holding the baby
against the shoulder, that it frees the mother's other arm for various tasks,
that it keeps the baby facing in the direction of the mother's activity). (It
is worth thinking whether these advantages are as it were automatically
satisfied by the later familiar invention, late at least in the Western world
that I knew, of the baby carrier/sling. That invention leaves out the question, for example, of the mother's satisfactions by the touch of the baby.)
Taking a step further, I note that the expression of some particular pleasure in hearing a man's touch at the piano took the form in my mother
of her claim, or self-observation, that she played like a man. A young
man may survive the fear of disappointing such women, outfacing the
suspicion that they are unsatisfiable.

My successes at Berkeley, as I came to consider them, can be taken
as modeled on that audition for Marjorie Petray. All were based in some
way on fraudulence. Anyway, as Gertrude Stein likes to say, that is the
way I feel about it. Felt about it already then. For the three and a half
years of my college life I had produced no substantial, finished work,
however youthful—no developed composition, no extended fiction, no
serious essay—yet some clear promise for my future had evidently been
unshakably established among certain of my acquaintances. It felt anything but unshakable in me.

The situation seems to have been this. I had managed to produce work over the years by keeping it closely tied to my classes in music and in literature, or to various performances playing the clarinet or the piano, or to the music I had written for the university theater, where I had in each case done something, or a series of somethings, quite small (incidental music, and songs, for productions, an essay with a burst or two of passion in it), each fit for, sustained by, particular occasions. While these efforts, or some quality in them, struck others as promising, for me they did not add up as a direction or invitation to originality. This discrepancy between my lack of conviction in what I could show and the conviction it seemed to create in others is what I am calling fraudulence. It is true that I had really done whatever I said or shown that I had done, but I could not go on, or reliably promise, to produce worthy continuations. More than half a century later I am prepared now to see in this discrepancy the seed of a curse I associate with the figure of Tannhäuser, in whom an aspiration to artistry initially and repeatedly produces an effect in excess of (anyway, other than) anything he understands himself to have created, whether an effect of love or of hatred. In each case his singing succeeds in attracting the passion of a woman, and in each case he comes to sing the wrong song to each of them, or to sing wrongly to each. One of the women successfully intercedes for him, once for his life, once for his redemption.

I speak only of the seed of a Tannhäuserian curse, one no larger than my efforts themselves then. If I have, in the ensuing years, warded off its flowering this must be understood as intercessions on my behalf having on the whole been apt and timely. To what extent I am responsible for this—either for the unanticipated excesses of effect or for the intercessions—it is, I suppose, part of the motive of this present writing to discover and assess.

In Boston in the mid-1970s, three decades after these Berkeley student days, I will hear at the dinner table of musician friends from the years in Berkeley when I had returned there to teach philosophy, and who had themselves recently moved to the Boston region, that Marjorie Petray had long ago committed suicide, leaving two children and a rich husband. How had her curse, whatever it was, failed to be deflected?

I have sometimes in conversation characterized my exhilaration in moving from Sacramento to the university at Berkeley as so strong and so constant that for my initial months there it distracted me from the wish for sleep, anyway from the knack of preserving sleep. That cannot of course completely be true, but part of what it captures is a stretch of life in which, along with a varying selection of two or three other music students, I would spend all night, four or five nights a week, in the music building doing theory assignments for classes, playing one of the several pianos inadequately sound-proofed from one another, listening to the library of recordings, and endlessly writing the beginnings and rebeginnings of compositions or orchestrations. When sleep overcame me I might stretch out on one of the tables in the tiny library for an hour or so, and at some stage before the next day's classes were scheduled to begin, have something for breakfast on the way back to my room in one of the boardinghouses that surrounded the Berkeley campus, for a shower and sometimes another nap and a change of clothes. How we had possession of keys to the music building escapes me now. The confiscation of the keys, however, toward the end of the semester, is perfectly memorable, coming in response to a small fire started when one member of the nightly group carelessly disposed of a cigarette in a wastebasket. There was no damage beyond the basket and its worthless contents, but our cleanup afterward had left telltale signs.

By the time I returned to teach in the philosophy department at Berkeley, nine years after graduating in music, part of the old shingled music building was used for supplementary philosophy faculty offices behind the ugly and view-destroying new building housing various humanities departments, the music department itself having been relocated in a grand building designed, after the war and with the consequent national expansion of college and graduate education, in consultation with the music faculty, containing, beyond a flowering of classrooms and offices, a glamorous chamber-music auditorium and dozens of practice rooms.

During the years of World War II, summer classes at Berkeley were displaced by a third full semester of courses, an arrangement that allowed the work of a college education in preparation for military service to be completed in under three years. (Mine took a semester longer than the minimum because I had failed once to register in time to receive credit for the courses I was intermittently attending, and because I had, in my erratic choice of courses, even after seven semesters, failed to enroll in ones satisfying a second natural science and an American history requirement.) By the fall semester of my first undergraduate year, that is to say, after a spring and a summer semester, I had settled into something that looked more or less like a predictable life of study and performance (performance consisting mostly in playing clarinet in the university symphony, and in various chamber-music recitals—there were plenty of pianists around). A fellow student I hadn't known well, but whose work had impressed me in the various music theory courses we had attended together, Gordon Connell, who had always disappeared after class meetings and never participated in the endless conversations and rehearsals in the communal atmosphere of the music department, early in the fall asked me to have lunch with him and a friend. (He and Jane Bennett will marry and move to New York about the time I enter graduate school at Harvard in 1951. They were the only members of the group of wonderfully talented and dedicated actors in the university theater during my years of contribution to it who will contrive to live the life of professional theater, supporting themselves and eventually two daughters—from time to time aided by a gig for a television commercial—starting out with a joint nightclub act, and moving to a continuous succession of supporting or featured parts on and off Broadway, so that one or other of their names will punctually appear in Playbill programs through all the decades of the second half of the twentieth century.) The friend at lunch, Frances Pepper—the daughter of the professor of philosophy at Berkeley who ten years later in Cambridge will offer me the first of my positions teaching philosophy, back at Berkeley—was also, it immediately emerged, deeply involved in the university theater, and the conversation was dedicated to describing to me an annual production for which the members of the dramatic honors society, called Mask and Dagger, wrote and performed songs and skits (an event called the Mask and Dagger Revue) held each spring term, running for two successive Fridays and Saturdays (including matinees on the Saturdays). (I had remained unaware of this institution during my first semester the previous spring.) Gordon spoke of his taking on again, as he had been the previous two years, the responsibility for writing or for motivating the music of the revue, and he proposed that I might join him this time, primarily or initially working together with him in composing the extended music for the show's most elaborate effort, the climactic "production number," a story told in dance, and to contribute otherwise as occasion and inspiration arose. One member of the honors society whose flair and perpetual energy for theater I would come to know well—she would play Regan when the following year I wrote music for a production of *King Lear*—was a particularly accomplished dancer, marking her university days with multiple blazes of glory. (One of the most famous of what were called production numbers is Richard Rogers's "Slaughter on Tenth Avenue," from *On Your Toes*, of 1939, which was an inevitable model for us, as was Leonard Bernstein's music for the recent *Fancy Free*.)

Writing for musical theater was not one of the ambitions I had imagined for myself in the world of music, but the very proposal of it established the wish to explore the idea. Gordon and I, after developing a loose scenario that included a solo dance, a pas de deux, and an opening and closing ensemble, using the pair of pianos in the fateful music department annex late each night, began to improvise for each other musical ideas for these segments. Our first two sessions in this mode, liking and amplifying the offerings we received from the other, were so enjoyable and fruitful that we continued in this, for both of us, unprecedented process of joint composition until after some two weeks we had the music for the production dance completed. We made a recording of it for rehearsals, and we performed it for the dress rehearsals and for the performances, but never found the time to write it down. The rest of my contributions to the Mask and Dagger Revue of 1945 was a love song and various bits of incidental piano playing and improvisation. All were gratifyingly appreciated, and I was rewarded by the rare honor of being elected to the dramatic honors society after having worked on only one production. I had found a home within the celestial city of learning and art.

I had found at the same time, working with Gordon, an unforgettably lucid and inspiring standard of sophistication and wit together with a lyrical gift in writing songs and words for theater music. I liked, and was convinced by, most of Gordon's work better than I liked and respected my own at that stage. If these registers of affection did not alter (Gordon had after all had some years of experience before we met) then this realm of musical work, at least, would no longer form part of any future I might imagine for myself in music. When I have sometimes wondered why Gordon's work never became more widely known than I am aware of, I have stumbled over the question whether this outcome has been a function of some mysterious mismatch between his taste with that of the world's, or whether he was one of the two or three men I have known whose powers of self-criticism persistently outran their sense of accomplishment and helped depress their productiveness. Stumbled over the question, because in these cases I could never decide whether this was a function of too little ambition or too much.

In addition to two subsequent annual Mask and Dagger Revues, I would compose incidental music for a number of university productions, roughly one each semester. Socially the most impressive of these efforts was orchestrating and conducting the music for the Kurt Weill / Moss Hart musical *Lady in the Dark*. (I invited Bob Thompson to leave Sacramento, take a chance on a semester in college, and join me in orchestrating the score. This invasive invitation in effect asked him to change his life, and he accepted.) Intellectually and artistically, the most lasting of these efforts was writing music for the production of *King Lear* (running, it will emerge, just over four hours, with two intermissions). It was here, playing music cues at the piano for scene rehearsals, and for run-throughs, and, assembling and rehearsing a small orchestra, conducting dress rehearsals and eight performances, that I came, not without considerable anxiety, to the first clear inklings, consciously and unforgettably, that I was more interested in the actions and ideas and language of the play, and in learning and understanding what might be said about them and what I felt I had to say about them, than I was in the music in which I expressed what I could of my sense of those actions and ideas and words (though doubtless writing music in response to the play had led me further into its world than, at that stage, I would or could have otherwise found myself). It is to this production, intermittently still on my mind twenty years later, that I refer in the course of writing my essay on *Lear*, the first and longest of my published essays on plays of Shakespeare, that closes *Must We Mean What We Say?*

I might, in principle, have come to a comparable realization about my interest in my music after my success with Gordon and the first revue. Whatever the intensity and range of enjoyments I derived from that experience, I had had little steady sense that what I was writing came from the heart of my talents, whatever they were. Unlike

Gordon, while I knew a smattering of "show tunes," especially those
that had become "standards" for swing bands and for jazz interpretation, I could not confidently place them, as Gordon could, in order in
the history of American musical theater, nor associate them with their
original casts; and however fascinated I was to learn—from Gordon or
from Mary Jane, another immensely gifted and celebrated member of
the student theater, or former member, now after graduating keeping
close to her theatrical comrades by teaching theater in a neighboring
private school—that this or that bit player in a Hollywood movie was
an accomplished actor in Broadway theater, I was not moved to make
independent efforts to know the detailed extent of this history and these
borrowings. What I had contributed to our exhilarating enterprises,
and will go on at Berkeley to contribute to, had a certain originality,
but I felt it to be a part of nothing further I could see that would take me
with it to astonishing places. I surmised this then, but it was nothing I
could then formulate for myself.

My perpetually deprived senses and intelligence were now slaking
themselves in various aspects of working on theater productions, including trying my hand at painting and lashing flats for a set, and once,
in addition to supplying incidental music for Saroyan's *The Time of Your
Life*, I made recordings at the local radio station of segments of the
music I composed, which were then played as various characters in the
play, according to its stage directions, would put money in the juke box
of the bar in which the play was set. Saroyan's stage directions named
the popular tunes that he wanted to be heard as from the juke box at
those junctures, but I took the occasion to motivate my own music and
to set my own ideas of mood and character individuation, so that music
from the juke box became part of the fiction of the drama on the stage,
not simply background for it, an innovation of which I evidently remain
proud. And I once provided a play's sound effects. This was for Philip
Barry's *Holiday*, whose trickiest sound effect requires, in the act that is
set in a room on the third or fourth floor of the central family's Fifth
Avenue mansion (in the film, it is Katharine Hepburn's favorite room,
or refuge, to which she invites among others Cary Grant), that whenever the door to the room is opened, sounds of an engagement ball, which
the Hepburn character is boycotting, are heard several stories down).

Beyond the general communal pleasures and satisfactions of help-

ing to create, and celebrate, a successful production, quite specific, permanent revelations were gathered into my sensibility from the specific
intellectual ambience of theater, I mean from something beyond the
odd shape of the literary education provided in getting to know an un-
systematic sequence of plays better than almost any of the works of
literature I was reading otherwise. The fruitfulness of theater's intellectual ambience comes not simply because working on a production
of a play creates a sheer familiarity with it that exceeds the knowledge
gleaned in customary exposure to other objects of literary study, but
because the work overtly and continuously demands explicit and systematic exercises of imagination and articulation, from being thrown
into the analysis and interpretation by the initial and fundamental
practicalities of tryouts and the fatefulness and surprises in casting the
various parts of a work for the stage, to the eventual and perpetual
considerations of the possibilities of mood and condition in which each
line can be delivered then and there, and responded to then and there.
These of course are considerations not alone of what each line means
(which comes to imagining the motivation and setting for its utterance)
but of how to achieve, to materialize, the expression of what you may
say it means. These fragments of expression are not items buried in a
bottle, but at their best are open lines of discovery. And such tasks are
in force even when the work in question has been made by William
Saroyan or Philip Barry or S. N. Behrman or Thornton Wilder and
not by Chekhov or Synge or Brecht or Shakespeare or Sophocles, all
of whom were represented by university theater productions during my
undergraduate years in Berkeley.

I must assume it to be obvious that I regard my quite continuous undergraduate immersion in theater as early, specific preparation
for my eventual conviction in the interest and importance of Austin's
practice of philosophizing out of a perpetual imagination of, as Austin
put the matter, "what is said when," why a thing is said, hence how, in
what context. I note that my first extended readings of literary works
that I felt warranted publication are devoted to two dramas, *Endgame*
and *King Lear*, both included in, and in a sense provide a structure for
my *Must We Mean What We Say?* and in that sense served to convince me
that this collection of texts added up to a book. Most generally it was in
the process of contributing to the realization of works in the university

theater that I began the irreversible awareness of the intimacies and intricacies called upon in the discoveries of the intersecting worlds of art and of thought; said otherwise, of the erotic and the intellectual registers in human encounter.

Our production of *King Lear* proved to be memorably, extravagantly successful. Indeed it may be that no experience of theater I have been exposed to in my life has made a greater lasting impression upon me. Partly of course that is because it is the only play of Shakespeare's that, from working with it and hearing it repeated over two months, I came to know not only from memory but from having worked, it seems, to weigh with others every word in it. And partly also, beyond the extremity of achievement in that instance of the Shakespeare corpus, because this production featured in the parts of its many warriors, students who had entered, or returned to, the university on the G. I. Bill upon their demobilization from active service at the end of the war the year before. The entire company of actors seemed inspired by the presence of these somewhat older, experienced young men; every audience felt the energy released in the hours of those performances; no part, however small, seemed uninformed by it. These experiences created in me a renewed revelation of the fact of theater, led me to ponder forever what it betokens that in that production of *Lear* the dancer in the earlier Mask and Dagger Revue played, as noted earlier, a viciously seductive Regan, and that Frances Pepper, so apt for laughter, played an icily unmoved, unmovable Goneril, and that the Cordelia was played by a sorority girl who during extended stretches of freedom during rehearsals played poker with the boys, punctuating its events with high giggles, but who onstage seemed to reduce her ample size into that of a bewildered but brave and innocent young woman with a ravishingly gentle voice. (So memorable was this Cordelia that one might well forever wonder, as Lear's Fool had similar cause to wonder, which was the frame of reality and which was theater, the sorority or Lear's daughters. One might? Might she? Which one?)

It was in Jan and Jon Caffrey's living room that conversations involving more than two or three people concerning productions—past, present, or to come—indeed concerning any matters related to theater (what was not related to theater?), unfolded. The Caffreys were the first, of the generation of friends forming the core of the university theater in that era, who had married, and hence naturally constituted a focus around which their comrades would impose themselves out of their need of home. Having moved away several years earlier (I believe so that Jon could take a job teaching) they had just returned to Berkeley as the place they would try to make a life, no longer perhaps to participate in directly, but surely to be next to, a familiar and thriving university theater.

Berkeley then was one of the two places I have known (Cambridge will become the other, putting Manhattan aside in which I was a mere visitor) about which considerable numbers of people have felt that life much beyond its borders was not seriously to be considered as a permanent possibility. This continued into the years in which I returned to Berkeley to teach in 1956, still before Berkeley stamped itself on the national consciousness with its prescient student movement beginning in 1964, two years after I had returned, with a year's detour to the Princeton Institute, permanently to teach at Harvard. It was not uncommon to hear—perhaps the rumors exaggerated the extent of the numbers—that graduate students would keep completed Ph.D. dissertations undisclosed and unsubmitted to their departments rather than conclude their lives as students at Berkeley.

I shared this sense of the preciousness of Berkeley. Both times I migrated from the place it was with terrible, lingering pain. The second time demanded a choice between continuing to teach at Berkeley or accepting the invitation to Harvard. This was, while hard to weigh, easy to figure, given that the one absolute requirement of my life then was continuing, after the breakup of my first marriage, to participate in my five-year-old daughter Rachel's life. (How the move to Harvard decisively improved the chances and quality of that participation will be important for me to explain.) The first time I left Berkeley, having just completed my undergraduate course requirements and about to turn twenty-one years old, I felt I had created a complex of expectations, open and hidden, that I had no way to fulfill, and only confused feelings about whether I would want to fulfill them. The open expectations concerned what I was to do with myself, if not to continue with music or theater or writing. The hidden expectations concerned whom I was to do it in company with. I still felt responsible to make myself comprehensible to my parents as well as to my friends, and again I was unready to declare myself, but craved a new spell of anonymity. It was now too late to make myself exactly anonymous, but there remained an obvious, even classical, locale of anonymity, New York City. The beauty of the move there was that its motive could be covered with the declared intention of applying for admission as a composition major in the extension division of the Juilliard Conservatory (extension here just meaning that the only regular enrollment there was as an undergraduate, a time now passed for me). This would mean that the move would have the appearance of being a natural extension of the life I was most clearly identified with.

April 9, 2004

I do not deny that enrolling at Juilliard was something rather more than a cover for my confusion, anyway more than an external alibi for being elsewhere. I had early in my life formed the thought of attending Juilliard, I suppose around the time I acquired the consciousness that life did not have to be as grim, as without invitation, as it familiarly came to seem to me to be. Sometimes the consciousness was made explicit, especially as late as high school, for example, in my mother's saying to me during the time of the pawnshop, "You don't belong here." The name Juilliard was one that from the beginning was linked in my mind with an imaginary place where people lived who were capable of receiving enjoyment and inspiration from one other, together with the ennoblement of shared practice and beauty, where my devout wish for such things would not of itself exile me. I had viewed, or will soon come to view with a sense of old recognition, more than one film over the years in which, characteristically in a flashback made in montage, the youth of an accomplished performer is placed in a music conservatory, where a cacophonous heaven of the fragmentary sounds of students practicing instruments would fill the floors of a building (perhaps the camera rising outside the height of the building, listening furtively and randomly through its windows) and would propose to me the very image of possibility, of a further world of sense, of comprehensible efforts linked to comprehensible and wonder-working work.

Today is Good Friday. Last Monday night, it happens, was the first seder of Passover. I am reminded that I have recurrently thought of my parents' lives together—and I guess almost without exception of the lives of their generation that I knew—as unleavened. (Music making, until I began playing in bands, was essentially a separate land from which my mother would intermittently bring back news.) One midrash in the new Haggadah I used at our seder this week (seder in our house always includes non-Jews, or Jews with no Hebrew and little or no experience of Judaism from their childhoods, and we distribute among the fourteen or fifteen of us a variety of presentations of the Haggadah, the text read communally, dictating and discussing the order and specifics of the meal, with varying translations and commentaries, the variations themselves inviting discussion) interpreted the separating and removing of leavening as the rejection of vanity, of excess, of every register and crumb of puffery. I like the interpretation, until the idea of rejecting vanity seems to extend to every desire that goes beyond strict need and presides not over a period of eight days but over the days of the year. "Reason not the need. Allow not nature more than nature needs, Man's life is cheap as beast's. If only to go warm were gorgeous, Why, nature needs not what thou gorgeous wear'st, Which scarcely keeps thee warm. But for true need." But King Lear cannot contain himself further to speculate about what true need is, or what nature needs. Can Lear's outburst here not have been produced by a terror of loneliness, a recognition of the need for others, colored by the downfall in being the wrong age, prompting his corruption of an abdication ceremony as if to demonstrate the corruption or folly of all institutions, the emptiness of all social order, hence a vision of humanity as ruled merely by nature, suddenly commanded by nothing human or divine, making nothing happen, absolutely uncreative, since nothing will come of nothing? How has such a state become the stuff of madness? I recall that Nietzsche will ask, in a new introduction to *Human, All Too Human*: Who today knows what loneliness is?

But my invocation of the unleavened is more obviously produced by the familiar idea, as the Hebrew Bible puts the thought, that in preparing to leave Egypt the Jews had to leave in haste, eating the chaste bread of affliction and innocence "with their shoes on and their staff in their hand," ready for departure. I felt of every place I ever moved to with my parents that we existed with bags packed and stuff near our hands, poised for departure.

I would learn of other forms this fragility of Jewish residence will take. A distinguished Harvard colleague roughly my age, growing up in Brussels, recounted to me his being given by his grandmother on her deathbed a velvet case containing three gold coins each worth then about three hundred dollars and told to keep them until they could save his life. On the day, in 1940, that he learned the German army had crossed the border into Belgium, he packed a bag and offered a taxi driver the three coins to drive him to Paris, from which he succeeded in making his way to America.

A staple of my moods was my parents' separate versions of depression. The difference in their quality was, among a thousand other ingredients, their individual senses of what they had been deprived of, or saved from, call it the Egypt of sumptuousness and of oppression. My mother knew beauty, but not how to surround herself sufficiently with it. My father knew my mother, but not how to attract her undivided attention.

April 10, 2004

Berkeley's renowned views of San Francisco Bay and its bridges had duly widened my horizons. I came to be aware of the points at which the setting sun would progress from winter, behind the city, to inch, or to foot, day by day across the twin towers of the Golden Gate Bridge and by summer reach well up into Marin County, then retrace its steps to its version of hibernation. It suggested lines of imagination to a beyond of the given, the stingy givens of immigrant fears, a sense of transcendence away from the pawnshop world of unleavened things. But these experiences were largely still airy nothings with little more than fixated local habitations and a few names. In New York I seemed to find a place less to invest my gains than to assess my losses. I remarked just now that New York was a classical locale of anonymity, meaning that its democratic indifference to masses of strangers was what I felt precisely that I needed, a place in which to have a nervous breakdown, or say, more politely, suffer an identity crisis, without apology.

Just conceivably, Juilliard would prove to provide the environment in which I would complete some of the items in my collection of unfinished music manuscripts. Acceptance there as a composition major required submitting a portfolio of work as part of an application. For the spring semester the deadline for submission was some weeks before Christmas. I did indeed over the next two months of autumn—with no other appointments or assignments to avoid, no set of expectations to combat represented by any of the few people I was in touch with—put together a kind of suite of the incidental music I had composed for *King Lear*, including an opening processional and a concluding dirge, and between them rather extended fanfares, tuckets, and alarums, variously called for by approaching and entering and embattled royalty, and elaborated storm effects, and the ethereal sounds Lear hears upon awakening from his madness and recognizing Cordelia. Beyond this I polished two songs I had written for a Mask and Dagger Revue; and, for the centerpiece, actually finished the first movement of a sonata for clarinet and piano. My application was successful, but I now knew, almost thoroughly, almost face-to-face, almost calmly, that the prospect was irrelevant. I mean that I found the music I had written to be without consequence. It had its moments, but on the whole I did not love it; it said next to nothing I could, or wished to, believe.

How could it have been otherwise? If I could not have completed work to be shown at Berkeley to Ernest Bloch and Roger Sessions, the music of both of whom I unreservedly believed in, as similar in seriousness as they were distant in procedure and sound from each other, why would I be inspired to extend my cunning to strangers at a place called Juilliard, where I mostly sat in its cafeteria on winter mornings reading Freud, nursing cups of coffee, and writing words disconsolately in a journal? Henry Brant was my assigned composition teacher—a piece of his had recently been performed at the school, a concerto for flute accompanied by nine flutes (so it was described to me)—and he was palpably bored by the work I showed him. I essentially shared this feeling, and within a few weeks I stopped showing up for my lessons. Vincent Persichetti taught the class in orchestration, and I knew how to get compliments for my ingenuity there, as I did in my conducting class, taught by a man whose name I recognized from more than one of the programs of Broadway musicals I had attended. The conductor was quite congenial, retiring, even somewhat distracted, in manner, as if he had seen and heard everything that he was prepared to be surprised by—he was in fact rather older than the other teachers I was dealing with and the idea of spending six nights a week, and two afternoons, conducting shows whose music, however marvelous in its way, had no inexhaustible depths to explore, and above all was not mine, presented itself to me without a touch of the glamour that any association with New York performance may still have held for me.

The point I remember as the highest of my successes in that conducting class was reached the day the conductor, emphasizing the necessity and possibilities of score reading, picked me out to accompany him at the piano in playing from the orchestral score of *Petrouschka* while the rest of the some eight or nine members of the class gathered standing behind us to peer over and around us at the music. With the direction, "You take the high parts and I'll take the low," the conductor gave me a moment to orient myself on the opening page, then indicated a downbeat with his body and a grunt, whereupon my fingers flew at once to the opening shimmer in the high instruments. I had had little direct experience of score reading at Berkeley, and, for that reason as well as others I have noted connected with reading, I had no confidence that I would succeed in anything further than making a fool of myself. But in the event some minor deity made it possible for me to get a fair amount of the music assigned to me onto the piano, in notable ensemble with the half of it undertaken by my partner, and after arriving at a stopping point he arose from the bench, shook my hand warmly, and joined the class as it broke into applause. So once more a musical success presented itself to me as accidental. I had little idea how I had arrived at a sense of lucidity as we were playing, of the clarity of individual lines and the various transpositions required by clarinets, trumpets, French horns (steeling myself especially for the alto clef of the violas, which I had never made quite perceptual for myself), hence came away with no confidence that I could, on demand, present myself as capable of repeating the feat. Nor had I met anyone with whom to discuss this condition, neither the feat nor the doubt.

Yet this laborious path to nowhere had, I laboriously came to understand, been essential for me. Music had my whole life been so essentially a part of my days, of what in them I knew was valuable to me, was mine to do, that to forgo it proved to be as mysterious a process of disentanglement as it was to have been awarded it and have nurtured it, eliciting a process of undoing I will come to understand in connection with the work of mourning.

April 11, 2004

An image for the undoing, as I pick up the thread now, is a passage from the opening chapter of *Walden* that I have had occasion to return to more than once since rereading the book in 1968, in which Thoreau declares, "Our moulting season, like that of the fowls, must be a crisis in our lives. The loon retires to solitary ponds to spend it." Thoreau insists on this crisis as humanly imperative; for us it "must be," whereas the loon comes "*as usual* [my emphasis], to moult and bathe in the pond." The seasons of nature do not determine the crises of human nature, which charges itself, rather, with finding and making the time in which to take up responsibility for shedding skins of illusion, for cleansing and assessing interests and responsibilities that are no longer, perhaps never were, necessary to oneself, and for deepening others that only I can assign myself and that I will become lost in losing. Nor do nature's seasons, nor any less predictable changes in weather or place or circumstance, assure me that my stripping of myself has been thorough and my recovery complete. New York and Juilliard were reasonable ponds, even lucky, in this sense, that they provided me with the concentration of solitude and the pertinence of interest to take me back to whatever strands of my existence—inherited, cultivated, enforced— had bound me to the raft of a talent of mine, causing the rest of desire to exist as foreign and terrible song, to live within these familiar bonds again exclusively, either to acknowledge them mine or to let them drift away, mourn their loss, recede from them strand by strand, voice by voice.

And there came a late afternoon, not more than six or seven weeks after beginning classes for the spring semester, an ending of the

Juilliard school day still turning dark by six o'clock, on which I formed the thought—I remember marking the moment by staring upward, as I was standing on a crowded Broadway bus headed downtown after a late afternoon class, at the chipped and scorched plastic cover of one in the two rows of lights extending the length of the sides of the low ceiling of the bus—that I would not be returning to Juilliard.

I asked myself quite explicitly whether I might go to pieces and seemed to decide that I did not know how. (This sounds quite compatible with having gone to pieces.) If you have sat at length by the bedside of a person dying, the death you have awaited should come—should it not?—as no surprise. Nothing has happened; something has stopped happening. (Yet my mother, returning from her mother's bedside during our first sojourn back in Atlanta, said to me, eleven years old: "A natural death is a terrible thing, struggling for breath, the death rattle." A natural death more terrible than a violent death? I had not thought my mother capable of paradox, except sometimes in describing music.) I decided that no one need know of this break in my life until sometime around the end of the spring semester, let's suppose the middle of May, some two months away.

April 12, 2004

The routine I had established in the early fall, rarely broken, in getting some of my compositions in a condition for submission to Juilliard, was to write all day, breaking briefly to forage for leftovers for lunch and most often take myself out for dinner, varying in pleasure depending upon whether my progress with a piece warranted a moment of celebration or a continuation of mere sustenance. Milton Lyon, with whom I shared the apartment, and whom I had met the year he spent in Berkeley, my third year there, was away from the city much of the time, traveling to wherever an agent could book the nightclub act he had developed with a singer, a woman whom he knew from his undergraduate years in theater at Carnegie Tech, while during his days in Manhattan he was in the city looking for more serious work in the world of theater, coaching or directing. At Berkeley he had played Marchbanks in Shaw's *Candida*, creditably, even professionally I thought, though he insisted that he was not much of an actor. Far more worldly than the academic theater community at Berkeley, however talented it was, he rather mocked, but not without reliable affection and admiration on both sides, the superb, not to say religious, Stanislavskian devotion of the young Berkeley aspirants to the majesty of theater. He ended one conversation after a rehearsal of *Candida* by saying roughly, and saying it roughly: "We may talk about my motivation to the end of time, but if we decide that I fall to my knees on this line, then I will fall to my knees on that line, every time." He went on to construct a full life in theater, dying shockingly in his sixties at one of his pleasures, playing tennis.

Milton's and my lives would rarely cross in later years, but two or three years after our eight or nine months living as it were together in New York he phoned me while I was still at UCLA to say that he had more coaching work than he could handle and that if I were by now convinced that I could not leave music, I should come back and become partners with him. The thought that philosophy was in its turn not working out for me was hardly unfamiliar to my mind, and if this invitation had come during one of the worst of these periods of disorientation I might have taken this way out, or back. But really the momentary relief in the thought of giving up my new—unless they were old—aspirations would have been a feeling that I was still at least memorably good at something real. The decision was taken out of my hands on learning that the Harvard philosophy department had offered me a fellowship in its graduate program.

After abandoning the cover of Juilliard, I would read all day and then about around eight or nine at night get cleaned up and take the AA line to Times Square for a meal at a coffee shop and afterward find a late film, often on 42nd Street, where the rows of former so-called legitimate Broadway theaters, running between 6th and 8th Avenues, were around 1948 the sites of reruns of Hollywood talkies. These were chosen and juxtaposed with no discernible ulterior artistic or intellectual aim—I recall Spencer Tracy in *Dr. Jekyll and Mr. Hyde*, Ronald Reagan in *King's Row*, Paul Muni in *I Am a Fugitive from a Chain Gang*, Katharine Hepburn in *Stage Door*, Margaret Sullavan in *Three Comrades*, Ronald Coleman in *Lost Horizon*, Carole Lombard in *To Be or Not to Be*, Margo in *Winterset*, Ann Harding in *Peter Ibbetson*. I would eventually learn from James Agee's collected film writing that he had also conceived an affection for the members of these audiences, some asleep, some intensely alert, when he was writing his vital film reviews for *The Nation*. It is the place and the era, or I guess just before the era, saluted, backhandedly, in an Astaire routine of mythic depth early in *The Bandwagon*, from 1953.

Once a week, occasionally twice (even before Juilliard), I would attend the theater or the opera. For the longer-running productions there was generally an isolated cheap seat available (for example, for Judy Holliday in *Born Yesterday*, or Laurette Taylor in *The Glass Menagerie*), or for the new successes that I could not wait to see (Brando and Jessica Tandy in *Streetcar*); for shows that were probably not going to make it (and for operas), I would take standing room. Standing room for the theater was one dollar, for the opera two dollars. If you managed a place in the standing room area immediately behind the rear partition of the orchestra seats, you could put your overcoat over the railing and lean on it. If you did not, free-standing through an opera was an exhausting proposition, even when at the City Center an evening offered an implausibly late appearance of Maggie Teyte reviving, as it were, her role as Mélisande. The revival was on the whole not a good idea; but not even the implausibility of her obligatorily long wig, of a red unnecessarily bright, could dispel from my imagination the fact that this woman had sung this role for Debussy. My education, call it establishing touchstones of the imperishable, was not entirely being neglected. Some may find that such memories are not those of intoxicating mountain rambles and scanning woodland lakes. I beg to differ.

There is education within education. I had learned of Debussy's connection with the name Maggie Teyte from perhaps the most cultivated of the teachers of theory and composition my first years at Berkeley, Charles Cushing, who had in 1930 won the Prix de Paris (a two-year fellowship to study and compose in Paris, awarded periodically by the Berkeley music department). From his occasional recitals of vignettes from those years—for example, of attending the premiere of Stravinsky's *Symphony of Psalms*, along with every musician in Paris—it was clear to me that this period, in fact as well as in memorialized description, represented for this man some absolute realization of intellectual and artistic radiance, but of such a kind that served not so much to inspire a semblance of continuation as rather to form a perpetual reminder of its own absence everywhere else, from then on.

Mostly I would walk to and from my apartment for afternoon classes at Juilliard. On the evening I felt the integument of my life peeling away—how could it be shrinking?—since I was on the Broadway bus, I must have been headed downtown, perhaps having arranged to meet Mary Jane, whom I had encountered at that same New Year's party in the Village after which I had found myself desperately out of place in Harlem. She had also left Berkeley in time to take a job that year teaching acting and directing plays in a small New England college, and after the new year we began seeing one another when she came to New York. My first glimpse of New England was on the train ride through light snow to Connecticut to see one of her productions. While she had been part of the culture of theater and film that was of the essence to me at Berkeley—hers are among the performances I remember immediately from those years—from a lead in a Broadway comedy to one in the *Oresteia*, staged in the university's remarkable, if inexact, Greek Theater. We had not really become friends during Berkeley days until our final summer, when I did the music for a production she directed. We had lost touch entirely by the time I left Berkeley to say good-bye to Sacramento and to my parents on my way to New York, a pause in plans lengthened a bit by discovering that I needed eyeglasses. Indeed I was told that I had probably needed glasses from the time of the car accident fifteen years earlier, a fact mysteriously undiagnosed, or lost in the complex consequences of my damaged ear. But now when I would see Mary Jane in New York I learned something of the extent of a life truly, I might say metaphysically, absorbed in theater.

A weekend together would start with an afternoon film (for example, *Gentleman's Agreement* had just opened, and of course she would know that Celeste Holm had opened as Ado Annie in *Oklahoma*); then after dinner another film or, preferably, the theater (perhaps Eva Le Gallienne was reviving alternating evenings of *Hedda Gabler* and another Ibsen play; and Katherine Cornell had received poor reviews for *Antony and Cleopatra*, which accordingly we had better not delay seeing), and then after a drink another film would occur to her (*The Search*, which I had not paid attention to, was starring a promising new actor by the name of Montgomery Clift, or a Swedish film had opened, called *Torment*, with a young actress named Mai Zetterling who was said to be interesting, which turned out to be directed by Alf Sjöberg and remarkably well written by a certain Ingmar Bergman). The next day a morning film might be added to the regime, but I was generally not up for that leg of the journey. No doubt Mary Jane's insatiability was deepened by having at her disposal only certain weekends in New York during the school year. Learning by drowning was something I was familiar with when the river of hours was somewhat balanced out by an active contribution of performance and analysis and discussion. Here the drowning felt unprotectedly like gorging, bears filling themselves for a time of unconsciousness, of exhausted expressiveness and impressionableness, except perhaps for the talent of dreaming.

I had already found that there are things to be learned only in this way of random extravagance, of being overwhelmed by the knowledge of what there is to know, of what cannot be mastered, of the necessity of developing an instinct and memory for reserves and hints and fragments of tendency, for trusting something like those glimpses or flashes of light across the mind so dear to Emerson. But allowing the inscape to be populated and colored by the impressions and expressions of countless crossing lights, exacts the wager that when the time comes you will find your directions of attraction and repugnance among and across those that are so far, some perhaps forever, sourceless and nameless.

When the time of my teaching for a living came, this learning, or experience, in living with mounting reserves that have for unpredictable stretches of time found only scattered free spaces for expression, became indispensable to me for making writing a palpable part of the academic year, I might say for a working understanding of the fateful differences between specific postponement and general procrastination. It will allow me to say credibly to my students that there is, and need be, no perfect time and place for writing, and to answer the question, perhaps walking away from class, "When do you write?" sometimes by saying, "I'm writing now." Probably I had then understood writing as having a grammar containing ideas of preparing to write, which includes anticipating or imagining being alone, call this being free to write, wherever I will happen to find myself, for however long, or short. Put otherwise, if I had waited for woodland or lakeside walks or insisted upon midnight crawls I would not have found whatever ways and places I have found.

April 13, 2004

My craving for portions of reading during the months bent on completing my portfolio of compositions was largely guided by my discovery of literary/political quarterlies, primarily the *Partisan Review*, following, as time permitted, beyond its pages the writers of stories and essays it published (Saul Bellow, Isaac Rosenfeld, Bernard Malamud, Robert Warshow) and the writers it reviewed or championed (Kafka, Mann). The legacy, if I may call it that, of anti-Stalinist socialist aspirations living somehow with a commitment to high modernism, is one for which I am permanently grateful. After my consciousness, or I can say the fact, of parting from the imagination of a future for me in the world of music, my reading turned for some time fairly exclusively to reading Freud. Over the weeks in which I was reading through the *Introductory Lectures on Psychoanalysis* I discovered in myself—I might even say, I contracted—every symptom Freud had by then discovered to be expressive of hysteria, and obsession, and psychosis. (I later discovered that I could do something analogously alarming in reading a physician's handbook.)

The only person I knew with whom I could discuss such things was Mary Randall, still in Berkeley, to whom I began writing letters, and receiving replies from her that I awaited painfully almost from the day after posting one of mine. These letters of mine, and their replies, sometimes ran as long as twenty handwritten pages covering both sides of the page. Exchanges with Mary had begun in the fall, with my incoherent, theoretical attempts to justify my having left for New York—the letters often as evasive as the escape itself—breaking an understanding with her that after graduation I would remain in Berkeley and continue our conversations, a certain virtual life together, talking mostly about my sense of bafflement and failure, and of what had happened to her that she had, after a precocious beginning as a writer, put the idea of writing aside, and about whether my admiration of her, and perhaps her gratitude for the admiration, or wonder at it, amounted to love, or

whether the gift of her attention to me seemed to me to demand a return that I felt incapable of, or whether I was too timid or conventional
or unimaginative to overcome the difference in our ages and experience. I was eight years younger than she, eighteen when we met, she
twenty-six, the mother of Belle, a dazzling six-year-old daughter, and
married to Belle's father, George, a man perhaps ten years older than
Mary, a painter she had met in college, who sometimes spoke of taking
up painting again and who came and went in Mary's and Belle's lives.

When I visited my parents after graduation from Berkeley to tell
them of my plans to return to Berkeley (there had been no graduation
ceremony; it was in September that my requirements for the undergraduate degree were completed; I slinked away from college as uncer-
emoniously as I had stumbled into it), their wild opposition was, if possible, increased as it increased the definiteness of my plans beyond any
intention I actually had, agreeing defiantly with their surmise that I
was thinking of marrying Mary. They begged me to take time to think
about the idea and asked what had happened to my plan to enter Juilliard, which they had initially opposed as financially wasteful (which
in some literal sense I knew it surely was) but which they now urged
upon me. I recognize now that the idea originated with them that I
should consider their subsidizing such a year as further back-payment,
between countries it would be called reparation, for my years in the
pawnshop. The experience of those years was beginning to acquire an
interest for me, converting the ignominiousness of them, transfiguring
even the needless starkness of their deprivations into matters of revelation, so that I was willing to take their bribe, perhaps indeed bribing
them to tender it, namely, to allow mysteriously that there might now
be some recompense for what I felt those years had cost me. Forgiveness
was not yet in the picture—something that would require not merely
recovering their own suffering, but in turn forgiving them precisely for
that legacy of dissociation, frozen rage against rage, in myself. There
must be a land beyond bribery.

Mary's letters manifested the gifts of mind and the talent and authority in her experience of writing that I so admired in her (so far beyond, I felt, the accomplishments of my contemporaries who harbored
thoughts and dreams of being writers), and receiving them increased
the guilt in recognizing that I could not return them in kind, enhanced

by the shame of my superficiality in supposing that what I owed her was a show of talent. Here is another woman, counting as an older woman to me then, who saw some promise in me, and was better at something I cared about fundamentally than anyone else I knew, as strong a writer of prose (in stretches of its immediacy and invention, though she claimed to have been able to finish nothing, or quite to understand what, if anything, her subject amounted to) as, I felt, much of what I was reading in print, who yet was stymied at carrying it into the world, at openly declaring its value.

I know something about the cause in Mary's case, in a sense better than I know, or feel I understand, the holding back in my mother's case, but Mary's story is not mine to tell. Yet a fragment of her story is, or was, in a sense public, and was one of the first things I learned about her. While still in high school she won a writing competition by composing an essay on the poetry of Genevieve Taggard, in the 1920s and 1930s a prominent so-called social poet, interested in theory and committed in practice to feminist and socialist causes. I learn just now from Google that none of her books are in print, nor has anyone else mentioned her in my hearing or sight. I learn also that she died the year I was living in New York. Mary's essay was sent to Taggard, who wrote to Mary with an invitation to visit her in New York if that were ever possible, an invitation Mary did not respond to. One of Mary's letters to me in New York included a self-rebuking account of the invitation (perhaps she had heard of Taggard's death) recognizing that a relatively famous person might also be lonely and would welcome a visit or a note from a stranger, adding roughly that she had been incapable of sufficient moral imagination (I don't believe she characterized the idea this way) to recognize that accomplished people also suffer from the common cold.

April 14, 2004

What more precisely was, or is, my sense of debt to women of what I perceive as unrealized promise? Is it fairly straight guilt that I should want, and somehow be preparing, to do something that they have been prohibited from doing, or from taking satisfaction in doing?

Was it a fear that they may withdraw their belief in me upon discovering that it is based on nothing, that is to say, upon learning that I had done nothing? But they knew what I had and had not done. Well then, upon seeing what I came to do and finding it disappointing? But that is more directly a fear I felt before myself, that I will not prove to be better than I am.

I looked forward to each of my sessions of reading Freud's texts as to falling into a kind of trance of absorption and a security of being known, accepted back into the human race. And my participation in Freud's sense of his discoveries as an intellectual and spiritual adventure of fateful importance to Western culture—I wouldn't have known how to begin distinguishing it from what I imagined the work of philosophy to be, something about leading the soul to the light—led me to allow the idea of becoming a psychoanalyst to take hold of my imagination.

Spring was approaching, and a while before dusk I would occasionally begin walking along Central Park West with the idea of winding up at one of the restaurants I knew around 50th Street and Broadway. Generally I would take the AA train for the second half of the distance, at 79th or 72nd Street, but on a time that I ended up walking the full fifty blocks, I had begun paying attention to the discreet brass plaques at the entrances of the familiar but always formidable alignment of apartment buildings I was passing, often with the name of an M.D. presented on their entrances. The thought occurred to me, out of my lack of knowledge, that these were sometimes announcements of the presence of psychoanalysts somewhere in these celestial fortresses. Having until then never thought of any occupation for myself that was not some natural unfolding of talent, the mysteriousness of settled adulthood, together with the impenetrable complexity of New York, seemed to me embodied in the rebuking richness of these looming walls. For what I believe was the first time I tried imagining what the specific conditions were, and how and when and in what order they had had to come into play, necessary to the setting of human beings in command of an orderly existence in such places—not a few people, but thousands, overlooking the lights of Central Park at twilight, presumably with many more thousands of people arranging the world and its lights for their comfort.

Around the turn of the year, out of what particular circumstances

I have forgotten, I was taken by an acquaintance to meet relatives of his who lived in such a building. The elevator remarkably arrived within the foyer of their apartment, from which a door opened upon a forest of furniture that occupied a room at once comforting and of an expansiveness I did not associate with apartments; the chairs and sofas and tables and lamps and rugs (more than one large rug, something I had never before seen in a single private room) struck me as not having been positioned there but having materialized in place. The father of the family knew from his young relative that I had just enrolled at Juilliard and, somehow eliciting from me the further fact that I had played in swing bands, began reminiscing about the time he had invited the Benny Goodman band to be introduced on his radio program. "They turned out to have no opening theme, so I told Benny to make a swing version of *Invitation to the Dance.*" (It occurs to me that that may have been the title of the radio program in question.) "He kept it as his opening theme song from then on."

So this man, appearing here and now in person essentially to be no different from the members of my father's generation whom I would have met at the Jewish Progressive Club, is claiming to have been the origin of sounds that had existed from all eternity. This was not a rational proposition. Nor was the opaque suggestion that the von Weber waltz was the source of Goodman's fox-trot. I remember nothing further about that exchange, but it would have been less than an hour later that, on the ride back down in the apartment elevator, left to my own thoughts, I recalled that the name of Goodman's opening theme was, after all, always announced as "Let's Dance"; and this recognition was itself an explicit invitation for me to go over in my head deliberately the then still famous opening bars of the arrangement that Goodman used of his opening theme song, something I might have done, without deliberation, in a certain mood on any number of unremarkable days. And this time I recognized that I had always heretofore, with evidently willful shallowness, heard the Goodman band's delivery of the tune upside down, persisting dumbly in turning a deaf ear to something I claimed earlier, with reference to playing lead alto in Harrel Wiley's black band in Sacramento, that I had already surmised, something not well formulated about the role of the reed section in swing bands as setting the texture of a piece, the brass section offering variation, or-

namentation, accent, and the celebration of tuttis. When in the past I
had found myself syllabifying the Goodman theme, either for myself or
to jog another's memory, it was uniformly the ornamental, jagged figure for the trumpets I reproduced, glorying particularly when halfway
through the seventh bar Goodman accepts the invitation presented to
his clarinet to enter the excitement of the dance. But underneath that
activity, grounding it, the saxophones, sure enough now in my remembered hearing—having begun on the opening downbeat, half a beat
before the trumpets began their syncopation—are playing, as it were
calmly, the Weber tune, no longer in three-quarter waltz time, and at
about half the velocity of the tempo in which you would expect to hear
the tune.

The particular chagrin in recognizing one's injustices to works, as
to persons, that matter to one's life, or cross its paths, is hardly lessened
by its awful, I suppose, inevitable, commonness. In the present case it
is some bitter solace to record that no musician I have spoken to about
the origin of the theme, since my access of this open piece of knowledge,
has ever claimed to have recognized the fact, not even an academic
expert in the particular history of swing. If it turns out that the Weber
connection had been merely assumed among band players, and is cited
in some Goodman biography, my distant solace for ignorance might
vanish, my initial chagrin stir again in a rueful wince of deprivation,
but the sense of revelation would remain present. The pain so often accompanying an influx of knowledge, exquisitely in the mode of coming
to understand what one cannot simply have failed to know is, I suppose,
a minor curse upon intellectual vanity that God thought to include
in the summary punishment of our common parents for their race to
swallow knowledge whole, or say, in their temptation to transcend the
human. But how could I have known then that this overturning of false
assumption by a reversal of listening was a model of philosophical experience? Exactly.

April 16, 2004

I had learned that certain prominent European analysts close
to Freud were not physicians, but just because the idea of postponing

training in analysis until I had gone through medical school, and before that gone back to college to undertake premedical requirements, seemed quite fanciful, my inner state required that I bring what reality I could to my fancies. I decided to find out what the specific requirements for medical school were and to determine how odd in fact it was for someone to consider this course after already graduating college. My apartment was not very far from Columbia Physicians and Surgeons Hospital (I think that was the name), and the morning I had planned to speak to someone there and to acquire their catalogue I awoke with the feeling of a speck of something in my eye. I tried the obvious remedies I had used successfully in the past—flushing the eye with handfuls of water, pulling the lid by its lashes away from the eye perhaps to discover a fallen lash—to no avail. The eye was watering to such an extent that I had to keep daubing it with a handkerchief, nor did it occur to me to postpone the subway ride uptown (I had made no definite appointment to appear there) until I had resolved the problem. By the time I arrived at the reception desk, I was holding the handkerchief so that it firmly covered most of my face. I seemed unable to make myself intelligible to the receptionist concerning just what catalogue I wanted and with whom I wanted to speak and about what, so in a frenzy of impatience and opacity I turned away and left the building. Once outside the door, standing on the plaza before the building, the discomfort in my eye vanished, and as I took the handkerchief away from my face I realized that I had contrived to appear at this place in effect masked.

I recall laughing out loud at this Freudian masquerade (I persist in the view that New Yorkers do not pay attention to such public displays) and on the spot decided that I was going about my new idea of becoming a practicing clinician backward. I have to continue from where I have found myself, interested but largely ignorant of what Freud is, of what Freudian training is, of what philosophy is that I should dimly think it part of the picture, and of how all this fits with the impulse to write that was coming over me, and of what I wanted to do about my persistent, even increasing, craving to know what there is to know. By the time I had returned home to 102nd Street, I had determined that I would go back to college, which seems to have meant to me, not for perfectly clear reasons, back to California—perhaps the idea was to find a way and a place to begin again. But then back, of course, not to

Berkeley and Mary, but to a further refuge of anonymity, the University of California at Los Angeles. A long-distance phone call revealed that, with my bachelor's degree from Berkeley, I could enroll in the UCLA graduate school as a special student, meaning without declaring a field, and, since I was legally a California resident, take four courses a semester with a registration fee of thirty-four dollars, for an indefinite number of semesters.

Part 7

April 17, 2004

My mother and father seemed almost relieved to support another year of experimentation associated with study—actually it turned
out to be most of two years before I could get paid enough money as
a teaching assistant to support myself for the remainder of the three
years I stayed in Los Angeles. Some of the money it took for me to live
the second year came from accepting the job, during the summer before that year's classes got under way, of rehearsing (and singing in, and
conducting) a quartet of voices to become the chorus for the Jewish
High Holiday services (Rosh Hashanah and Yom Kippur) at a conservative (that is, neither orthodox nor reform) congregation in the Fairfax district, which rented the Fairfax movie theater for those services—
it would, in that district, in its normal theatrical function, have in any
case been largely empty during those holidays—to accommodate the
expanded numbers who predictably would wish to observe for these intervals, perhaps to ponder, conceivably to mend, some of the fabric of
their religious pasts. That is tangentially what I too was doing, however disguised, and perhaps what the cousin of mine was doing who
had recommended me for this work. He had been living in Los Angeles for several years, studying voice and eventually participating in an
amateur opera company at the moment preparing a production of *The
Magic Flute*, in which he was singing the part of Tamino no less, and for

our quartet of High Holiday voices he had recruited his companions Papageno and Sarastro (both gentiles). It would not have occurred to me that we could in effect adequately disguise the lack of training in my voice within the inner parts of this small group, but with my accuracy of pitch and confidence in sight-singing, and some experience in attuning voices within a chorus, along with some ongoing tips in voice placement from my cousin (having to do with relaxing the throat and singing within the mask), we were sufficiently pleased with ourselves.

Six or seven years older than I, this cousin, Harlan Liss, was the youngest of four children of my father's oldest sister, and while I was living in Atlanta he would have visited from Columbus, Ohio, no more than two or three times (Aunt Ida, so far as I could tell, called him Harlem), yet he and I both appear in the most complete family photograph of the combined Goldstein and Segal families in my possession or that I know exists, containing some thirty figures, taken when I was four or five years old, an event I remember clearly, verified by my clear memory of looking away from the camera just as the picture was taken, a gesture immortalized in the photograph. (That the photograph was taken in Atlanta is shown by the appearance in it of my mother's mother, whose frailty never permitted her to travel.) Harlan's father was a cantor, and Harlan was reported by his oldest brother, Burt Liss—who all his life kept in regular touch with the Atlanta basis of the family, always to be expected, with grateful welcome, at family gatherings for Bar Mitzvahs, college graduations, engagement parties, weddings, and funerals—to have a beautiful voice, and was being encouraged to think of a career in opera. It was not always easy to tell the quality of Harlan's voice from our work in the preparation of the High Holiday quartet since he mostly held it in check, both in order to blend with the other voices and because the presiding cantor of the congregation, a decisively less gifted singer, was the only one who was to sing, that is, to pray, individually and representatively. But a few times Harlan unleashed himself, often incited by Sarastro or Papageno, and the brief effect was startlingly exciting. Harlan's gift was a source of pride for Burt, who had made a considerable amount of money in business but the sustenance of whose life was a love of learning (he was a benefactor of the University of Notre Dame, in, or next to, Burt's adopted home of South Bend, and eventually appointed by President Hesburgh to serve on the President's Board of Advisors) and a devotion to the arts (my mother was a figure of adoration for him), neither of which had been parts of his fragmentary education.

Encouragement of Harlan's voice was said to have come from no less considerable a source than Jan Peerce, a prominent opera singer who was himself a cantor (for conducting the High Holiday services at a large Chicago congregation, Peerce was reported to have received a fee of fifteen thousand dollars, which shortly after World War II, when I learned this, was slightly more than twice the annual salary of the assistant professorship at Harvard offered a friend finishing his Ph.D. dissertation in the Department of Psychology at UCLA). Peerce was a good acquaintance of Harlan's and Burt's father, a fellow cantor at whose house Peerce was a visitor on his trips to Chicago. I say that encouragement was "said to have come" from Peerce. I early came to look with suspicion on the familiar claims of immigrant Jews to have a "close personal friend" in some high, or anyway remote, place. It could mean anything from having a tenuous business relationship or being members of the same congregation to having had dinner together, say, at a large Zionist fund-raiser, and perhaps sitting at adjacent tables. If it was truly what we might call a friend who was under discussion, my father, for example, rather than boasting of the friendship, a good sign in him of distant connection, would tell how the friend was faring the last time he saw him, or recite an adventure of their pasts. But I had no cause to doubt Burt's assertion that Peerce, whenever he performed in Chicago, was a guest at his and Harlan's parents' house for dinner. As an observant Jew, Peerce would in any case have had to be particular where he took a meal, and he had on more than one occasion heard Harlan sing.

During the weeks of our preparation for the holiday services at the Fairfax Theater, Harlan received notification that he was selected to compete in the national competition to perform with the Metropolitan Opera Company. Early that fall—that is, within a matter of further weeks after the High Holidays—before the regional stages of the competition were to begin, a distressed Burt phoned me to say that Harlan had been diagnosed with cancer of the pharynx, the operation for which required cutting his vocal cords.

April 18, 2004

My first semester at UCLA, in the summer of 1948, was spent
pushing further my interests in psychology and in literature. The psychology department was dominated by experimentalists, and I found I
had some interest in running rats through mazes, and even took some
pleasure in being a subject of, and thinking about, psychological assessment tests, pressed into service by my growing circle of acquaintances
among the psychology graduate students. Among them was a young
woman in the clinical program whose combination of intelligence and
striking good looks was something about which I imagined she could
have truly said, as Lana Turner roughly says to John Garfield when
they first meet in *The Postman Always Rings Twice*, "Yes. I've looked like
this since I was fifteen years old, and ever since then, men have been
giving me an argument about it." I offered her no such thing, not that
year, for multiple reasons, but primarily because my fearful desperation to give some orientation to my fallow confusions took all my attention. But the general hostility to Freudian thought in the psychology
department seemed to me, in my innocence of the academic world, to
be surprising and arbitrary and stultifying, and the theoretical diet, including the repetitious and abstract discussions of the requirements of
a scientific theory, were obviously intellectually paper-thin. The classes
in literature I happened to wander into irritated me in somewhat similar ways. The theoretical discussions there also seemed to me formless
and uselessly abstract, and the level of literary criticism was irrelevant
to the psychic emergency I was living in and to the aspects of my sensibility that had become attuned to and encouraged by reading such
journals as the *Partisan* and *Hudson* and *Sewanee Reviews*. Eventually in
both the psychology and in the literature classes, names of members of
the philosophy department began to be invoked by students asking the
most interesting questions, especially the names of Hans Reichenbach
and Abraham Kaplan. The next (fall) term I registered for four philosophy courses, and within some weeks of beginning them I began to feel
I had found something like a home, call it a neighborhood, anyway a
place to remove my shoes and lay aside my staff—I mean that I stopped
imagining that there might be some clearer place elsewhere for which,
for me, to search. It was not perfect, primarily no doubt because of my

intellectual inexperience or awkwardness, but it was sufficiently clear to me that any better place must start from here.

Nor was it pleasant. It was painful to realize unprotectedly and repeatedly that I was at least as ignorant of the material assigned to us in these classes as any first-year undergraduate, some four or five years younger than I. It was out of such a feeling—while having my hair cut in the barbershop in Westwood Village (the fashionable region of civilian life adjacent to the UCLA campus), at the edge of which I lived in a kind of commercial dormitory, a two-story rectangular stucco structure consisting of about sixteen evidently identical rooms for rent by the week or month—that I said to myself, looking at myself in the mirrored wall, reflecting the barber holding up behind my head an opposed hand mirror to show me that I was losing my hair, "Then it's over." The nearest, simplest gloss I can provide for the thought was that my youth was over. I was reminded of two remarks from letters of Mary to me in New York a few months earlier: "For you the really serious has become seriously real." The other, which she attributed to Joseph Conrad, ran roughly: "He was submerged in the isolating sea of life, where the possibility of a moral existence begins or ends." (This is a reasonable articulation, or distant memory, of a passage or two in *Lord Jim*.)

My difference from the genuinely young with whom I was now cast together was that I had nothing else I meant to do with my time but repair my ignorance (I almost said, "furnish my vacancy"—but that would have been a mean vibration from the memory of the way that new room of mine struck me). That first term I enrolled in Reichenbach's deductive logic class (using his recently published logic textbook, which would be reviewed savagely by Quine the next year); Kaplan's aesthetics (reading Roger Fry, Clive Bell, Dewey's *Art as Experience*, Percy Lubbock's *The Craft of Fiction*); Robert Yost's continental rationalism (reading Descartes, Spinoza, and Leibniz); and Donald Piatt's pragmatism (reading mostly Dewey, primarily *Human Nature and Conduct* and *Theory of Valuation*, the latter a monograph appearing, oddly to my mind, in a series called the Library of Unified Science, in which, in its original monographic guise, Thomas Kuhn's *Structures of Scientific Revolution* will appear a dozen years later).

In the exhilarating opening weeks of the logic class, it crossed my mind that when I had gone far enough in logic I would be able to translate or transpose the texts, especially the ones I was reading in rationalism, whose thoughts I felt to be important but mostly incomprehensible to me in their motivation and order, into this wonderful symbolism, which I felt I understood perfectly. In that case, it occurred to me to conclude, I should postpone reading the English texts and devote myself to the study of logic until my mastery of it was equal to this task of complete translation. I checked this excited, troubling insight with my teaching assistant in the logic course, who informed me that when logic got really interesting and powerful it left natural language quite behind, which was too hopelessly vague and ambiguous to serve as a medium of serious philosophical analysis. This seemed to produce a vision of pleasure in him rather than, as in my case, a mixture of disappointment and somehow exhilaration at the prospect of eternally recurrent confusion and controversy over unfathomable perplexities. I seemed to be asked to make a permanent choice, in blind ignorance, between what I wanted to understand and what was truly understandable. Would I have to move on from philosophy after all, and so soon?

April 19, 2004

I wanted to believe in what I was reading of Dewey's, but it seemed to me to proceed in a combination of good sense with intractably abstract assertions (e.g., "Habit is will"), with which, for all the texts' emphasis on usefulness, I felt I could do nothing but repeat them. Kaplan's aesthetics course seemed to take me away from philosophy, though I did not trust this reaction. This man obviously represented some kind of future of the field of philosophy. There was a rumor that Rudolf Carnap, Bertrand Russell, and Hans Reichenbach had each said of Kaplan that he was the most promising graduate student they had ever met, and his interest in the arts, and the range of his literary and anecdotal reference, was, particularly in combination with this intellectual authorization, dazzling, and clearly not just to me alone. At a reception for new students in philosophy around the middle of the semester, he added to the mythology of his reputation by confiding to the group of us surrounding him that it was not true that the University of Chicago, where he had been as an undergraduate, frowned on athletics; on the contrary, he himself had been captain of the debating team.

He was decidedly thin, and his encouraging laughter increased the somewhat emaciated impression of his face. The reference to debating stuck with me. Kaplan was the most fluent lecturer I had, or perhaps still have, ever heard, but I kept leaving his lectures feeling that I had heard balanced accounts of the sides one might take on some particular issue; so far so good. But there was a residue of suspicion that something had been withheld from the discussion, or covered over, as if this were dictated by his unshakable imperative to fluency. It wasn't that I wanted him to take sides, exactly. Then what did I want? I was left with the sense that Kaplan viewed philosophy as a matter of looking around a question until you became indifferent to it. I could not accept that that was more or less what he actually believed. It was not the sense he gave in speaking of questions in political and moral philosophy, where in fact he did take sides. (It was distinctly helpful to me in that era and place that he was unencumbered in announcing the desperately obvious [but in my hearing not infrequently contested] fact that Stalin is a dictator; Trotsky was hardly more than a name to me.) How was aesthetics different? Were its issues not matters of living and dying? And was philosophy doomed in these regions to spectatordom?

For Piatt's class I wrote a final paper on Dewey running to more than seventy pages. I wish I could find it now. I liked Piatt's ready, perplexed, and, I gathered, largely unrequited love of philosophy, and I was sophisticated enough with a certain air of dashed hopes among my elders to be touched by the sincerity of his occasional anecdotes about his student days, I suppose in the early 1920s, also at the University of Chicago, where he had taken, by his count, eleven courses with George Herbert Mead and written his dissertation under Mead's supervision. Mead is a figure whose originality some promising graduate student is, I still think, apt to discover in every generation. He published, I believe, next to nothing in his lifetime, but several volumes of his lecture notes were published posthumously. This early in my encounter with professors of philosophy I was alerted to a sense of some professional eccentricity in the relation between a philosopher's thinking and his or her teaching and publishing. I wanted Piatt to have evidence that his course could be inspiring, and I would also have felt that a madly out-sized paper would actually be read by him. And the fact is the course did inspire me, even in its helpless expressions of disappointment and impatience that philosophy had turned away from dealing with some-thing Piatt repeatedly named "human problems." I put into that paper about every suddenly discussable problem, or crisis, human or cosmic, intellectual, moral, aesthetic, or religious, that I had been revolving in myself increasingly over the past year, where "discussable" meant dabbing from a Deweyan palette of terms to lead me on, with end-less appeals to "habit," "experiment," "will," "context," "interpersonal transactions," "value vs. valuation," "instinct vs. intelligence," "means as ends," "this-worldly and otherworldly," filling it with assertions I was impelled to voice, scarcely caring what the best-known defenses of them, or objections to them, might be, amazed by the sense of progres-sion itself, as if the goal would take care of itself, often making an old thought interesting because of the strangeness of its apparel, but orderly enough in stretches, often turning back upon itself as if that itself was integrating, to hearten me to think of myself as producing philosophy. I knew enough not to show this work to anyone else, but the result of completing this outburst of fervent if jagged expression, and Piatt's ex-travagantly favorable response to it, had longer term effects on me that I still range on the side of sanity.

I would not at the time have been able to articulate these ef-fects, but what now strikes me at once is that, without exaggerating the objective or academic accomplishments of my text, I found—with considerable, unexpected relief—that completing it did not serve yet once more to extend my sense of fraudulence. The work did not prom-ise more than it delivered, whatever that was. I did not feel that Piatt had been duped by it, but that he saw its desperation and aspiration for the raw things they were, and could allow its lunges for originality and heightened sense to be justified—at least one time—by its talent and its diligence, or say, by some comprehensible, even, in a disorderly world, necessary, taunting between imagination and ignorance. Mary had written to me in New York: "You want to write a great book with-out having really studied one." (One of the first things I knew about her, from her husband, is that she had read her way half through the list of the hundred Great Books named in Mark Van Doren's *The Lib-*

eral Education. I knew she had dropped out of college after a year or so at the University of Washington. I imagined she had begun reading through these volumes systematically while staying at home with her infant daughter.) The next year Greta will ask: "Are you just one more smart Jewish boy counting on redemption by being a genius?" While I knew enough not to take these mocking descriptions simply meanly, I also did not take their raillery as random. I felt I should be able to distinguish tones in each between the intention to introduce an ironic cleansing of reality into the composition of my inner life, and the warning against banal and unhelpful male fantasies that they had both been called upon in their pasts to ratify for others (others other than me, and other than them). Greta got around to adding, "It's only the work that matters." I took the message from both to be roughly that no one, and no institution, unless you allow it to, can tell you what you are meant to do, nor whether you are doing it. Along with the implied message that people (men, mothers) and institutions had in her case, not hers alone, undertaken, not unsuccessfully, and without the best will in the world, to do precisely that telling, there was also anger, directed if not at me then in my direction, as if asking me whether I was worth imparting this knowledge to, which perhaps only a woman can (or could then, in certain circumstances) impatiently yet effectively impart to a man. There is a Platonic comedy or tragedy of distance and intimacy here that I am not capturing; it has to do with some question of whether it is sexual gratitude or spiritual gratitude that is the trickier to express. In Greta's case the question was permitted to be settled when we agreed that we were not each other's ego-ideals.

April 20, 2004

A couple of years later, halfway through my first term at Harvard, walking with me, after dinner in the Harkness cafeteria, to my room on a slight detour to his own on the floor above mine in one of the new ensemble of spare graduate dormitories at Harvard designed by Gropius, Marshall Cohen will ask me, "What is it you want to do?" Following me into my room he began interestedly, but soon with mounting, comic feverishness, to pull out various famous texts of philosophy (fa-

mous because classical or because currently fashionable) from my bookcase and from the wall-long shelf running above the windows against
which my desk stood, shoving each volume at me in turn, and asking of
each, "Is this enough?" Among the first candidates I specifically recall
was Ryle's recent *The Concept of Mind*; and John Wisdom's *Other Minds*,
among the last, reaching above my desk by standing on my desk chair,
may have been *Thus Spoke Zarathustra* or the *Critique of Pure Reason* or the
Oxford Basic Works of Aristotle. Whereupon, as he climbed down, he
broke into not quite controlled and wonderfully charming giggles. He
collapsed into the armchair next to the desk, took off his glasses to wipe
his delighted tears, and declared, "I gave up supposing I was a genius
my sophomore year at Dartmouth."

Marshall and I were naturally cast as friends and competitors by
our fellow graduate students and by our teachers since we were the ones,
among our contemporaries preparing for Ph.D. qualifying examinations in philosophy, whose devotion to literature and to music rivaled
our attention to philosophy. His confession of self-evaluation drew from
me one clear reaction (I find I do not know whether I said it aloud): "So
that is what gives you your power." It was a power of something like
judgment palpable in him, part moral part aesthetic, exercised in the
first instance upon the intellectual accomplishments and public manners of a wide range of the members of our generation present in the
dormitories, almost regardless of field, and then exercised upon their
teachers, and even extended to a knowledge of the ranking of certain
law students (some of whom were friends of his from Dartmouth) and
to certain Ph.D. candidates in literature and in fields beyond the humanities, assessing their chances of eventual distinction, and sometimes
those of their teachers, intellectual and social. My apparent indifference
to these matters exasperated him, as did my ignorance of the positions
he would inform me were held by powerful fathers of this and the other
Harvard and Radcliffe undergraduate (I could not imagine, to begin
with, how he knew so many undergraduates there, attributing this, I
guess, to some further mystery of communication among those with
Ivy League connections), but he mostly forgave me for these shortcomings because of my talent, musical to begin with, however rough-hewn
some of it would have become around the edges and at the surface. He
was far better read than I, not only because he had had so much bet-

ter an education, especially in literature, than I, but also because my reading was hampered by a desire that everything I was moved to or assigned to read become extensions or conditions of my own thoughts, by negation or by transfiguration. Mere curiosity could not assuage this hunger. So that, for example, studying for the qualifying examinations, which rationally demanded reading through effectively unlimited lists of articles and books with a kind of neutral or collector's or fugitive's interest, was not simply onerous, but excruciating for me. I began to take Benzedrine tablets in order, I thought, to stay up very late studying, sometimes all night, two or three nights a week. That was not false, but I will come to the realization that a more immediate reason for the drug was its counteracting of my growing anxiety and depression.

I think of the time that first year when Marshall had borrowed a pencil from me and as we parted I was prompted to remark: "N'oubliez pas de me rendre mon crayon." He immediately replied, unguardedly, "You *are* smarter than I am." I simply assumed he was responding not to my correct French but to the application I had found for a line said by Mme Chauchat to Hans Castorp in *The Magic Mountain* (invoking that relation as a fanciful, sort of reverse allegory, of Marshall and my sallies). (I had read the novel while an undergraduate and have not read it since. I don't know that I have the courage to look it up now.) And since I was certain that Marshall knew Mann's novel better than I, I felt again that I had accidentally fallen upon one of the few lines I could have quoted from that novel and was fraudulently giving the impression of a command beyond my means. Given my contempt for such behavior, which I priggishly regarded as an aberration of the air and actuality of hard work encouraged and rewarded at Harvard, and having, from my education on the opposite coast of America, acquired no standing defenses against socially ratified pretension, what was I to think of myself? I took the accuracy of Marshall's criticisms of me to be worth the pain of receiving them, and sometimes even to be delivered out of an affectionate concern for my innocence.

For the moment I want to complete my sense of the sanity supervening upon my pouring out my immature philosophical heart in that initial, unbridled philosophical effort of mine for Piatt's pragmatism course. I had demonstrated for myself two aspects of what I thought of as philosophical that have never ceased to elaborate themselves in what

I write. First, the task of description, of some so far undefined species, is more fundamental to philosophy, or constant in it, as I care about it most, than the tasks of explanation or argument. Since philosophy has no knowledge of its own, its power must lie in uncovering obviousness, in a sense becoming undeniable. (This is not the same as one's becoming certain.) This is a thought (or prethought) that prepared the way for Austin and then later Wittgenstein to count so decisively for me, and that blocked a certain way of appealing to Freud's discoveries. (Freudian explanations were everywhere and may or may not prove convincing. What was undeniable were the cases, the description of symptoms and their articulations that my body seemed directly to absorb.) Second, nothing of human interest should be ruled out as beneath philosophical interest, so that when philosophical strictures slight or stylize my experience, the philosophy is no less brought into question than the experience.

The year after I submitted my paper to Piatt, his waning teaching career was visibly threatened. His seminar on naturalism met one night a week at his house, and as often as not he was unable to walk unaided to his armchair, and once there almost incapable of speech, beyond slurring the phrase "human problems." The rumor spread that some terrible event in his life had rekindled his alcoholism. It was one of the glimpses of academic life behind the scenes of which graduate students can acquire a fair repertory. I was proud of our group's handling of the situation, which was on these awkward nights simply to discuss the assigned reading in Piatt's presence but essentially without Piatt's participation. Why this unspoken decision to engage in this theater was not impossibly awkward I cannot reconstruct, but I attribute it to a knowledge of human complexity one might put past the tact of mere graduate students. I can testify at this distance that one who has gone through the emotional and intellectual squalor of a divorce, and at the same time felt the reality that a dissertation may not be followed to completion, and become lost in an affair of the heart, and been faced with one's ineptitude as the single-parent part of each day and week of a three-year-old daughter, is apt some morning or evening, feeling incapable intellectually and physically to put aside an inner chaos and to crawl one's way toward material receding from one's grasp, ought to have no trouble recognizing the impulse to walk into a seminar room some late afternoon and declare that, while the assembled young might not realize this, there are times when muttering "human problems" seems the maximum that a teacher has to offer the world. If there is any meaning in assigning a cause to my never having exactly succumbed to this impulse, I might invoke the times the image of Piatt sitting impassively under a glaring lamp has crossed my mind, together with the thought that if I ever once allowed myself this latitude I might never find a cause to come back from it.

I do not know when Piatt retired, but the next year when I asked for recommendations from the members of the department I had worked with to support my application to Harvard, I got the impression that it was Piatt, invoking the early paper I had written for his class, who in effect arranged that the UCLA department should prepare a full departmental recommendation for me. It was reported to me not long after I arrived at Harvard that the most memorable moment in the department meeting at which applications were finally ranked was the arrival of a telegram from Piatt urging my acceptance in a rhyming couplet. The Harvard department might not have been altogether charmed by this, but evidently they were not irreversibly discouraged.

By the middle of the second year at UCLA I had in effect completed a philosophy undergraduate major (twelve philosophy courses), and I received a teaching assistantship giving me relative financial independence. Among the other courses I took that year was one of Kaplan's in which the comparison of pragmatism and positivism was the guiding thread, especially in moral philosophy. A fellow student in the course, Alexander Sesonske, turned out to have written a paper with a drift similar to mine, a wish to defend pragmatism's sense of the moral life against positivism's. Kaplan liked them both and suggested that we find a way to combine them and submit the result, with his recommendation, as a joint publication to the *Journal of Philosophy*. Sesonske and I had already discovered a sympathetic streak in each other. He was Kaplan's age, roughly a decade older than I, married and the father of an infant, and had at the beginning of the war been drafted into the army from a life in New York as a race track tout; then after seeing battle in the war as an artilleryman, he used the G. I. Bill to fund a university education that he would, I gathered, never otherwise have contemplated. He had somewhere along the line developed a considerable skill as a draftsman (he produced a fair simulacrum of Matisse's *Dancers* as a fresco on the exposed broad side of his stucco garage) and a developed taste in the arts generally. Whatever the actual value of our joint paper (and its successor a year or so later) to the cosmos of philosophy, the sense of participating in a world beyond the classroom was balm to the perpetual reminders of one's sore limitations through the years of graduate study. Beyond expanding the imagined world, Alex and his wife, Sally, provided the rare comfort of occasional family meals with them and their baby daughter in their small apartment (one of a series in a considerable housing project designed for returning veterans) that spoke remarkably of an intact civilization beyond the humiliations of grade grinding.

In part my initial paper for Kaplan's course had been motivated by a conversation overheard, not by me alone, in a corridor of the philosophy department in the first months of my introduction to it, between Hans Meyerhoff, with whom I had not yet taken a course, and a graduate student I recognized from one of my classes. I mentioned in accounting for my months in New York hiding out from Juilliard (I never officially resigned from its rolls, and while I scarcely believed they would send out an alarm for derelict musicians, a cloud of delinquency in its direction sometimes hovered about my existence) that I had begun reading literary journals. A memorable, brief piece in *Partisan Review* was by a certain Hans Meyerhoff, identified as teaching philosophy at UCLA, a mysterious piece of information surely not without relevance to my having found myself in that place the following year, vaguely expecting an understanding environment. Meyerhoff's piece was a lyrical, moving response to his having read a description of the early death of Thomas Wolfe recording a stroke that had overcome Wolfe in the lavatory of a moving train and had rendered him unable to remember how to unlock the door for help that he had a few minutes before locked for privacy.

The conversation I have in mind now was between Meyerhoff and the young teaching assistant I had consulted in the logic course I was taking. A number of other students were already gathered there witnessing the event. As I approached the group the teaching assistant was saying, "We know now that every assertion is either true or false or else neither true nor false; in the former case the assertion is meaningful, in the latter case cognitively meaningless. If you go on saying to me that this line of Rilke's is cognitively meaningful, I smile at you." Meyerhoff was in evident distress. He would of course have heard roughly this positivist refrain before, but for some reason he had been drawn in a weak moment into an aggrieved effort to defend a work important to him on grounds that may or may not have been important to him. And this defense seemed at this moment, as similar moments have so often seemed to others, to demand that he deny what seemed undeniably true, however insufferably asserted, in this assault on his treasured convictions. To discover a different mode of response to such an assault became as if on the spot an essential part of my investment in what I would call philosophy.

Nothing short of my concentrated experience of the work of Austin and later of Wittgenstein will lead me with reasonable conviction toward some productive such response; it is part of my undying indebtedness to their work. Austin's "Other Minds" had been published a few years earlier than the conversation I report, but no one of my acquaintance was then prepared, or moved, to refer to it, in my hearing. And before I left UCLA I discovered a mimeographed copy of Wittgenstein's *Blue Book*, effectively a draft of early material in *Philosophical Investigations*, in the bottom drawer of the filing cabinet in the outer room of the departmental office, where I was told to look for extra reams of typing paper. The existence of *The Blue Book* and *The Brown Book* had also in my world gone unmentioned, and judging by my reaction upon first attempting to read *Philosophical Investigations* on my own some four years later at Harvard, they would have, without further philosophical experience and culture than I had at my disposal, been unlikely to do me good.

Philosophers have periodically offered advice, more or less philosophically justified, concerning the order of learning in which to approach the study of philosophy. While I have never firmly believed in, or rigorously followed, such advice (say, Plato's in *The Republic*—where the very reading of *The Republic* while an undergraduate major in philosophy is a fairly direct contradiction of its views on education—or say, Heidegger's [is it in *Being and Time*?] where he suggests that studying Aristotle for sixteen years is good preparation for reading him [Heidegger]), I am familiar with the thought that there ought to be an orderly course of preparation for what is commonly thought of as a path. I am I think more impressed with the counterthought that there cannot be such a course, for the reason that there is no predicting what text, or conversation, will produce in this or that mind, a conviction, I might say, in the reality or presence of philosophy, without which such a course cannot seriously begin to take effect.

April 21, 2004

Soon after the publication of the joint piece by Sesonske and me at the end of my second year at UCLA, it was attacked at a local philosophical conference by a teacher from the philosophy department at Santa Barbara (where Sesonske would turn out to spend the bulk of his career). I suppose I was no more hurt to learn that our paper was not immune to question than pleased to find that it was thought worth taking to task. I had little impulse to quarrel with the objections; I mean I felt that they came from as recognizable a concern for the material as our paper did, but I had little sense where progress might lie. Hilary Putnam had recently arrived from the University of Pennsylvania, by way of a detour of a year of graduate work at Harvard that for some reason he had found disappointing, to study with Reichenbach. Just my age, the son of a distinguished literary figure, the translator Samuel Putnam, having been immersed in philosophy and linguistics and mathematics throughout college, and doubtless before that, Hilary Putnam possessed accomplishments that seemed to place him in a different generation from my own. (I learned some years later that he had been interested in Kaplan's presence but had found, as I came to find, an unwillingness for exchange in Kaplan, for all his gestures of friendliness, or I might say, found a barrier to discussion in his very fluency that could not be breached. It was a puzzle not easy to put aside.) In the discussions at that small conference, Putnam showed a freedom of speculation, a justified confidence in the pertinence of his interventions, that seemed to me to go essentially beyond anything else being said there, by young or old. I knew from experience of comparably impressive interventions in discussions of music and in certain registers of literature, but in philosophy I saw starkly what my excellent grades helped shield me from, not merely that my education was barely begun, but that I had little sense of what steps to take to acquire a sustenance that I lacked. I had by then taken, and listened to, a number of courses for which I felt due gratitude, yet it was as if from that day I knew that I would have to begin yet again, and somewhere else. How could I tell whether this was a reliable assessment of my condition or simply another iteration of my knack in creating a habitation for myself in which I became isolated and lost?

Habitation is perhaps an exaggeration. It is a fair description of my life in Los Angeles to say that for most of that era I lived nowhere. With the exception of the first semester of my second year, when a bedroom opened in a thoroughly agreeable apartment in a house on the beach in Santa Monica rented by two other graduate students in philosophy (who would finish their degrees and leave Los Angeles at the end of the following summer), I existed for two years essentially following a routine that became established in that initial commercial dormitory I have described. I stored my clothes and few books in my rented room and for the most part slept and bathed there, but I had no visitors and, except occasionally for an hour after midnight in bed before turning off the light, did no reading or writing there. I took all my meals at the student cafeteria or at two or three affordable and good cafés. My essential reading and writing were done in the graduate reading room newly established on the top story of the university library, open every day from 8 a.m. to 10 p.m., where everyone who knew me (and some who did not) knew I could be found most of the time it was open (or where a note could be left for me). At closing time I would more often than not drive along various routes where good movie theaters would be about to begin their final screening of the day, and there were essentially enough within a twenty-minute drive from the campus to fill in the week until the bills changed. If occasionally no new film attracted me, there was a bar in Beverly Hills with a good piano player where I would go for a beer. The only regular disruption of this routine came, the second half of the second term, when every Monday I was taken out to dinner at a good Los Angeles restaurant by a young teacher filling in (I've forgotten the details of how this happened) by taking over an announced introduction to philosophy course that I thought might help me get better organized.

The teacher was a considerably older graduate student just finish-

ing his Ph.D. dissertation, who had already accepted a position for the
following year as Assistant Professor at the University of Missouri. In
fact the course did help me, and I must have made this clear in the
midterm paper the class was assigned, because the teacher, Holmes
Bearden, in his comments on my paper, invited me out to dinner the
following Monday night after class, and it turned out that the invitation
was repeated every subsequent Monday night until the end of term.
The first of these nights out—driving to La Cienega Boulevard, which
in those days was lined with somewhat gaudy restaurants serving delicious, relatively straightforward American dishes (in more than one
such place elegantly attired waiters rolled out directly to the customer's
table, astonishingly to innocent eyes, a steam table, covered by a curved
metal shield half of which opened back into itself, to reveal a roast of
beef from which a portion would be cut to order)—Holmes explained
that he gave himself one night a week off from his dash to finish his dissertation, and the night was Monday because the friend with whom he
shared an apartment, a professor of economics at the university, taught
a Monday night course. In fact both Holmes and his friend William
befriended this pent student, quite strange, quite familiar, terribly perplexed in the course of finding himself in finding philosophy. Their own
friendship was, among their friends and acquaintances, legendary for
its strength and depth. Some thought it included romance. I believed
their assurance that it did not, and accepted their making this explicit
to me as a remarkable show of intimacy to a recent acquaintance, obviously meant to assure me of my safety in their company, a gesture
suggesting that they understood me, surely correctly, as, if not entirely
innocent, fairly inexperienced in the ways of the world. William was
short, fierce, greatly learned in European and American history and in
the history of ideas. A sense in him of iron will and independence—it
was, for example, impossible to interrupt him when he was into one of
his historical disquisitions—was, it seemed, expressed by an intermittent, very slight hesitation of speech, the trace of a bad stammer he suffered until his adolescence when he cured himself of it over a summer
by marching early every morning along a deserted beach in the coastal
Texas town in which he grew up, shouting to the waves the poetry or
speeches he had memorized in English or in Latin. Whether he actually said he had stuffed pebbles into his mouth as part of this therapy,

or whether I include this classical image out of my sense of the mythical depth of the indomitable young, I cannot say.

It occurs to me that I may at that period have been presenting a somewhat forlorn aspect to strangers, and the world I moved in was indeed almost entirely one of strangers. In part Holmes may somewhat have been prompted to single me out by, as I learned before the end of term, his decision to look for an alternative to a life in philosophy. He was careful to assure me that the decision was a judgment upon himself not upon philosophy. New things were happening in philosophy, but they did not seem to call upon him; they made him feel outdated, and I gathered that certain religious preoccupations he brought to the subject intensified the feeling. His story might, and perhaps was meant to, have had a certain cautionary effect on me. He was intense, intelligent, diligent. Was there actually no suitable place for him in the world of philosophy?

The path he found was to arrange an interview with a senior executive of an oil company with headquarters in Los Angeles and list for this man his own understanding of his talents and accomplishments. He then announced that since he had come to feel that there was no longer a professional audience for the kind of philosophy that he most cared about he would use his accomplishments to acquire some genuine power to make things happen and do some good in the world. On Holmes's account, the executive responded first by telling him not to smoke during an interview; then after a comparatively brief continuation he said that they would find a place for him and see what happened. Something in this image was not irrelevant to me when, stuck in a dissertation half a dozen years later at Harvard, and yet once more faced with plausible work of mine that was insufficiently convincing to me to continue with, I entered into what would prove to be my last serious bout of deciding whether to leave the field of professional philosophy. This time the perplexity resolved itself when Austin appeared halfway through that year, the spring term of 1955, to present the William James Lectures at Harvard.

The sheer human kindness Holmes had held out to me was unforgettable. The six or seven Monday nights of enforced rest from work in themselves did me various kinds of good but supplied no clear immediate precedent I found I could use for continuing their good, since in trying to keep up with Holmes's three martinis before dinner and wine with dinner and a highball afterward, it was all I could do, even with my approximations of his capacities, to walk from his car up the stairs to my room, once or twice finding myself fully dressed upon awakening with the light the next morning on top of the covers of my bed.

Holmes and William were essential in talking with me about the wisdom of applying to Harvard, where they had met the year they each held a fellowship there, before driving together to California. They somehow grasped the sense I expressed of needing to begin yet again, and testified to the fact that Harvard was a place to live a life of thinking and working unlike any other they knew about—surely unlike anything I had found at UCLA, which, entering my third year, they and I felt I had explored about as far as my interests allowed—and that it would be valuable to me even if it simply provided a place for me to exist alone without the stress I was evidently now living with. It began to occur to me again that my mild life had become quite deranged.

April 23, 2004

My first copy of my *Cities of Words* arrived from the Harvard Press a week or so ago. There has been a little flurry of interest in the book since two film reviewers have mentioned it in connection with the recently released film *Eternal Sunshine of the Spotless Mind*, written by Charlie Kaufman (the writer also of *Being John Malkovich* and of *Adaptation*, which I have seen, and of *Human Nature*, which I have not). These reviewers describe *Eternal Sunshine* as following the contours I have traced for the genre of remarriage comedy, prompting me and Cathleen and Benjamin and David to see it for ourselves (they all see more new films than I do so they would not have needed much prompting). I don't know that the connection is clearer in this case than in other recent cases, for example, the Brad Pitt / Angelina Jolie *Mr. and Mrs. Smith*, but it is more interesting, since the film itself is more interesting.

This little flurry of interest caused me, given a familiar perverseness I live with in myself, to become irritated yet again by the persistent sense of exoticism my work creates (all but invariably finding that someone moved or assigned to cite it feels this quality must be mentioned, especially but not solely beyond the academy). My *Pursuits of Happiness* is almost a quarter of a century old. Why is it still unclear—surely to me—whether it is well enough known or is essentially unknown? (I know, I know. Why should it be either? Surely very many worthwhile books are neither. But people who refer to the book do not treat *Pursuits of Happiness* on the whole as most would treat generally unknown books.) The not infrequent references to it by critics responsible for regular columns have done something in my relation to that book that no other sources could do, namely, demonstrated the pertinence of this work of three decades ago to new films that can be spoken of as part of the present, perhaps even of the future, of filmmaking. That the book is still alive for me, still productive, is demonstrated in *Cities of Words*, which is the presentation of a course I offered in Harvard's core curriculum over the last decade of my teaching at Harvard, in which the sets of comedies and melodramas I have devoted a book each to are cast systematically in a new light, namely, as embodying a specific register of the moral life, one I relate to moral perfectionism, a register running, if largely unheralded, throughout Western philosophy and literature, from Plato and Aristotle through Dante and Montaigne and Jane Austen and Emerson and George Eliot and Nietzsche and Mill to Heidegger and Wittgenstein.

But I was about to describe how my initial move to Harvard came about. The conference at which the first of the two papers I wrote with Sesonske was discussed closed my second academic year at UCLA. Kaplan invited the two of us to accompany him the following August to a week-long set of meetings of nine or ten philosophers to be held on the California coast in Monterey, at the Pebble Beach Country Club, sponsored by the Rockefeller Foundation, to serve as reporters of the events there. Our responsibilities would be essentially to prepare accounts of the group discussions of the individual papers that each of the participants would be preparing in advance and to submit these accounts to the Foundation within some weeks of the conclusion of the meetings. The idea of the gathering, as I interpreted it, was to assess the state of philosophy now just five years after the end of World War II, which had, along with its world-historical consequences, caused massive changes in the American academic scene. In philosophy, the immigration to the United States of leading philosophical figures from

Central Europe, such as Reichenbach and Carnap and Hempel and Feigl (prepared by Quine's having spent a year in that Europe in the early 1930s attending the lectures, among others, of Carnap, and more distantly prepared by Schlick's visit for a semester to Berkeley in the mid-1930s), had effected a reception of logical positivism's mode of analytical philosophy that rapidly became the avant-garde of a number, I believe most, of the dominant philosophy departments in the country.

In addition to Kaplan, others in attendance at Monterey were Wilfrid Sellars, Charles Stevenson, Morton White—prominent, rising names in the profession—and Max Black, as the senior member and chair of the group. The chance for a private assessment of the state of philosophy in congenial, open, even amusing circumstances—in addition to the two formal discussion sessions each day, we took our meals together in the country club's ritzy dining room, where the group at its large round table at dinner would joke, more nervously than it might realize, about the impression a collection of rumpled, tousled professors must be making on the paying customers—was, for me, of course, immeasurably, lavishly interesting.

A further consequence was the onset of a further turn in the disposition of my life. Late the afternoon of the concluding day of discussions—the group would disperse the next morning—Morton White invited me for a walk before dinner. He asked about my plans, and after the intensity of the week's events together, and in response to his friendly inquiry, I was unguardedly forthcoming about my sense of having reached the end of something, of feeling that I needed to start again, that I was still convinced that philosophy was for me but that I had not found my feet in the subject, and that while I felt at once uninspired by the prospect of a further year resembling the year just past, I had formed no idea of an alternative. I am confident in my memory that he replied in roughly the following terms: "I am not surprised to hear that. Would it help you use the year better if you made plans to transfer to the Harvard Ph.D. program in philosophy the following year? Think it over and if you want to do it I'll support your application in our department with a written recommendation, which will help. Applications are due sooner than you might expect. Let me know what you decide." It was still early in my awareness of what smart and experienced teachers are in a position to know about the young. That they can also sometimes be badly mistaken is hardly remarkable. My own sense of my conduct in these meetings was that it had been essentially uninformative, not to say invisible.

By the time I packed my bag for the return drive down to Los Angeles the following morning, I had assembled in my mind what I knew about the current Harvard philosophy department, which did not include a very definite idea about its location, beyond being some place outside Boston. White's own *Social Thought in America* had been featured in a course taught by Meyerhoff, who had praised the book above most works published by contemporary American philosophers; and I had been put onto C. I. Lewis's *Mind and the World Order* (surely by Kaplan), which greatly impressed me; and an introduction of Henry Aiken's, I believe to a reprinting of Hume's *Dialogues on Natural Religion*, had struck me as urbane in its prose in a way that spoke of a liberality of mind I was finding to be a rare virtue in contemporary philosophical writing. (Quine's "Two Dogmas of Empiricism" would not appear until the turn of the year, when my application had been sent off, but it served by then to intensify my already intense desire for my application to be successful.) But these elements, each of which was of pertinence to me as well as to Harvard's prominence (as opposed to Reichenbach's singular element of prominence at UCLA, which was not of particular pertinence to me, emphatically not since his most prominent book in those years was on the theory of probability), had not added up to the thought of my actually attempting to enter that foreign clime until White's suggestion. Not even when in the background I remembered Benjamin Lehman, a glamorous teacher from the English department in my undergraduate years at Berkeley, telling one of those stories expatriated Harvard graduates like to tell to convey to the less fortunate the unrivaled swank of Harvard. "After dinner, around the fire in an adjacent common room, George Santayana was talking with a few of us carefully but effortlessly well-dressed young men, and asked us: 'Can you read Goethe in German, Dante in Italian, and Lucretius in Latin?' No one claimed to be able to read all three. Santayana replied: 'I too am very ignorant.' And then added, 'Not that ignorant.'"

I would not have known then what a university common room was, nor heard yet of Santayana's *Three Philosophical Poets*, but I had read his *Sense of Beauty* and I knew intellectual yearning as I knew the feeling of difficulty sometimes in catching my breath exposed to beauty. No other university had created a concrete image for me of such a kind. Then why had Harvard not hitherto occurred to me as a possible destination? I could recur to the idea, or fact, that I lacked much practical knowledge of the world; but it equally makes sense to me to say that I did not want to ask for anything (to promise anything? to show ignorance? to display need? to want justification?). Maybe Morton White even knew that about me. He had thought to ask me.

April 24, 2004

The drive back from Monterey to southern California—Sesonske and I again alone with Kaplan for four or five hours, with no convenient distractions—reversed our mood almost as completely as our direction. We were somewhat solemn rather than nervously jocular; ruminative rather than expectant. There were the inevitable forays of postmortem memories and criticisms of the events of the week. Wasn't it nice that Max Black, as chair of the occasion, had, after Kaplan's fluent, extemporaneous presentation on the state of aesthetics, declared that he felt compelled to break the decorum of such a meeting and publicly commend Kaplan for the excellence of his remarks? And how about Stevenson's already feeling so confident about the fame of his *Ethics and Language* (which indeed was one of the most frequently quoted books of English-speaking philosophy in the years after the end of World War II) that he could refer to certain phrases in his book as part of accepted philosophical patois? But mostly we felt that we had been given a fair picture, or say, a representative set of samples, of the current state of new trends in philosophy. Sesonske's and my ability to judge representativeness here was perhaps an excusable illusion created by the week of feeling let in on the backstage workings of the profession. But Kaplan's confirming judgment was something we accepted as authoritative. So it was a marked moment for me—one I knew I would be returning to—when after a stretch of silence Kaplan said: "It was indeed informative. But it is important for you to remember that analytical philosophy is not all there is to philosophy."

Would that not have been something worth voicing during the

week of meetings? Was it news? Saying it in our isolated, departing automobile seemed to make it something of a secret. I suppose I had been
harboring something like this secret in my dissatisfaction with my education. But Kaplan's sense of revelation, or confession, rather suggested
(taught) that I was right to go on keeping my dissatisfaction secret. If he,
having established so thoroughly his analytical credentials, and seemingly possessed of as complete a command of the fields of philosophy
as anyone was likely to have (he once introduced himself as "a former
student of biology, like Aristotle"), was not able to write philosophically
and acceptably out of his deeper convictions, what could open that possibility? Was he expressing a sense of his own sense of stultification, or
vowing privately that he must change his ways? I was about to turn
twenty-four, so I knew that my fellow passengers were accordingly in
their early thirties. Maybe both ages could provide scenes of more or
less expected crisis.

Kaplan gave a response, as it were, to such questions not long
after we returned from Pebble Beach—perhaps it was at the annual
meetings of the Pacific Division of the American Philosophical Association, or perhaps it was simply an occasion on which Kaplan decided
to read a paper to whoever in the department (or beyond it) might be
interested in what he had to say, or the latter was preparation for the
former. My memory of the occasion is of sitting in an uncrowded sunny
room on comfortable chairs—not a venue either of an APA meeting
nor of the UCLA philosophy department—and Kaplan has concluded
his remarks by saying, "To be is not to be the value of a variable. [Thus
explicitly, and by no means merely comically, negating an assertion of
Quine's in 'On What There Is,' published in 1948, that had achieved
instant notoriety.] To be is to be of value." Kaplan's private response to
analytical philosophy had become public. Perhaps the challenge was
implicit in his having begun lecturing on his new fascination with Asian
philosophy. But the mimicking of Quine was a new step of explicit challenge. And I felt baffled by it. To begin with, I did not know whether I
believed that to be is to be of value, or more exactly, did not know under
what conditions it was sensibly uttered. I found it, so to speak, voiceless.
It seemed to come from nowhere in Kaplan's work that I knew, so that it
could have been a cry of despair as readily as an encouraging reminder.
It seemed a more immediate challenge to Raskolnikov than to Quine.

So what? Was the point of this challenge to deny that Quine was producing (valuable) philosophy? This seemed a hopeless task (what would its audience be?), another disheartened, belated stab at wiping off the positivist smile in the philosophy corridor.

The flowering of Kaplan's dismay, indeed its hopelessness, was, to my mind, expressed in his *New World of Philosophy*, published in 1961, as if inaugurating his move from UCLA to the University of Michigan for some ten years (after which he moved permanently as Professor of Philosophy to the University of Haifa). This book had originated as lectures delivered a year or so earlier at UCLA. Reports of these lectures (I was still teaching at Berkeley) included the fact that the largest auditorium on the Los Angeles campus had to turn away roughly the same number of applicants to attend the lectures as the number it was able to accommodate. A ticket for these lectures was said to be as hard to come by as one for the annual Rose Bowl football game. Kaplan's fame as a lecturer was not hard to imagine for one who had been drawn to his classes ten years earlier. The reports included the fact that at least half of the new course of lectures considered various systems of Eastern philosophy. This produced a still further pang of hopelessness in me, deriving from this announcement an implicit despair of continuing philosophy, and not alone Western philosophy. More accurately, I had derived this sense from the course on Asian philosophy Kaplan had given my last year at UCLA. The course consisted of outlines of various systems of Eastern philosophy, nothing, I felt, that competent textbooks on the subject could not do. (Kaplan had, as part of his participation in an organization to advance East/West philosophical exchange, received support, again I believe from the Rockefeller Foundation, for a six-month tour of Asia, meeting with philosophers in a succession of countries.) Perhaps he had found a way to convey his interest in these philosophical expressions, I mean their satisfactions to him, as part of a context in which our philosophical present was alive for him. My disappointed response to the report of a set of public lectures and a distant memory of their pedagogical origins was in part a function of my projecting my own periodic temptation to despair of philosophy, or of a productive future for myself in its academic profession. I was in 1960 in the late stages of writing my dissertation, so much of it concerned with Wittgenstein's search for conviction in philosophy, in the face of its chronic tendency to repudiate itself.

I did not pick up the book that came out of Kaplan's public lectures until the late 1960s, some four or five years after returning to Harvard to teach. I discovered then that, in succeeding chapters, two of the tracks of Western philosophy Kaplan considered were late Wittgenstein's attention to ordinary language (which Kaplan thought empty), and Heideggerian phenomenology and existentialism (which he found obscurantist). So he was announcing his rejection of precisely the two principal orientations in which I had come to find some possibility of continued philosophical life for myself. When in the 1980s I first visited Israel, I asked philosophers what Kaplan's effect had been there, what legacy he had left from his presence in Haifa. All I spoke to had known him, and they mentioned his early book on method in the social sciences as a work still read. When I pressed them further, declaring that a number of people had early in his career expected him to be one of the signal spirits of twentieth-century philosophy, they seemed unmoved by the idea. To jog or supplement my memory of the dates of certain of these reminiscences of Kaplan I searched, uncharacteristically of me, the listing of his work on the Internet (where, by the way, his birth date is given as 1918, not 1916, as I had thought). The accounting in Google of the range of topics on which he published papers and gave public lectures helps recapture for me the rationality of the extreme expectations he inspired early. Is any other field as careless of the intelligence it attracts as philosophy is?

April 25, 2004

There had again come to be women in my life in graduate school, although, in various ways, conditionally. I alluded to Jenny early in my account of existence at UCLA, the incontestably attractive graduate student beginning her dissertation in clinical psychology. Sometime early the second year, she sought me out in the graduate reading room late one afternoon—I had seen her there from time to time; we could be said to have a literally nodding acquaintance—to ask if I were up for a coffee break. As we strolled to the cafeteria I asked how her dissertation was going, to which she replied that that was actually something she wanted to talk about. It emerged that the work was not going well, that she had broken up with a long-standing boyfriend, and that she had wanted for a long time to speak to me because of her fascination by my ability to work so diligently. I seemed never to be away from the library table, reading, writing, taking notes. Is this work assigned by courses, or is there some larger, more personal project in view? She had never expected to get less than A's through her college and graduate career, it had all come easy to her, she knew how to please, there was always time for fun. But now she was having trouble shaping an idea for a dissertation into practical form and increasingly finding herself distracted. When I asked what her idea was for the dissertation, she persisted in wanting to learn what I was working on that could command so much time and attention.

Coffee extended into dinner, and within a couple of weeks we had come to expect to be together part of every day. The basis of the friendship was all but explicitly the project to rescue talented Jenny from her worrisome lack of direction and, not incidentally, from the depredations of men. Our companionship was amusing (causing interesting women to laugh has in it some of the rewards of fairy tales), and I was soon helping get her to her therapy appointments twice a week on time and discussing the design of an experiment she might propose for her dissertation. The possibility of romantic involvement arose in due course, but after a stretch of tentative intentions it gradually lessened on the understanding, so it seemed, that I was different from other men in needing nothing, evidently a paragon of refined sublimation and renunciation. It was, in essentials, a view of myself I had come to understand very well. Why it should be a view I could not only derive reassurance from but accept, under certain circumstances, as obligatory, as if in payment of an infinite debt, was anything but clear to me. But plain living and high thinking were still recognizably the view I maintained of my conscious path. The consequent low-grade emotional squalor of these months—denied jealousies, nursed rejections, fear of being thought emotionally stingy, and anger at the fear, producing a generalized emotional cowardice, or infantilism—was somewhat

held in check by affection for Jenny and by the habits of work that
were keeping me productive, even intellectually adventurous. It was, in
short, as a way of ending this punishing affair that the idea of moving
across the continent to Harvard had an increasing allure, yet another
secondary gain. Well, tertiary.

Greta was older than I, having completed her Ph.D. in philosophy several years earlier, but because of her marriage to a professor in
another field, she was debarred by the nepotism rules of that era from
a position at UCLA, even if her independent cast of mind, let alone her
gender, would have made her a serious candidate. Whether she wanted,
and how seriously, a teaching job I did not guess. I suppose I imagined
that she was working on a book that would announce her claims to
attention. For a while we met every week for lunch, at which our conversations sought deeper explorations of philosophical aspiration than
any others at that period of my life. Her view of what philosophy could
be went beyond any academic portrait I had been offered, and her
taste in intellectual matters, in what must be taken seriously, although
she had studied with Carnap, extended to long discussions she introduced about Hannah Arendt's *Origins of Totalitarianism*, which had just
appeared. ("Arendt is in her forties. But she has done it. This cannot
be taken from her.") Greta had written about Dewey with admiration,
but we agreed that his transfer of the idea of means and ends from
instrumental into aesthetic and into moral contexts, meant to reveal
the rationality of value discourse, was a dead end. She had prepared
a review of Bertrand Russell's recent *History of Western Philosophy* (she
gave me a copy of the obscure journal in which it appeared) in which
she observes, "If there is a wisdom of the ages, Russell does not speak
for it," a remark I particularly admired and that she said had cost her
more than one friendship. She had a considerable knowledge of theology (her background was Lutheran) and was the first person to speak to
me about Kierkegaard.

The erotic contour of passionate, not simply heated, intellectual
exchange was again obvious. I mentioned earlier that Greta and I fore-
stalled complication here by agreeing that the physical and the psychological stars were not aligned in our case. Was the role of ego-ideals
part of the wisdom of the ages? If I successfully kept intact a working

measure of philosophy's beneficence through the ensuing raw years of professional shaping and harping, this fortune was due in my mind to no source more than to these conversations.

My third year at UCLA was a study in the desultory. My spirit was preparing for a move. I do not imagine that I could have remained in Los Angeles if Harvard turned me down. I could not think about that then. Jenny and I thinned out our time together. In addition to grading papers and teaching sections, I tried my hand at poetry, played handball with Joe Handlon, an old acquaintance from music days at Berkeley, an English horn player who had burned his instrument after misplaying a solo passage (from one of the Debussy *Images*) with the San Francisco Symphony at a summer concert, and was now at UCLA finishing a dissertation in experimental psychology, and I sometimes went alone to a movie in the afternoon. I have forgotten how I learned that there was a decent grand piano in a gymnasium at the foot of the hill leading up from Westwood Village, where, between an early dinner and the walk back up to the library, I would occasionally pause for an hour improvising on show tunes, perhaps to keep in touch with the somehow reassuring remnants of an old talent, perhaps for the sheer pleasure of invoking the exuberant and so often perfect, if from a certain perspective limited, American accomplishments in popular words and music, effortlessly including the unfathomable inspiration of its grateful and resourceful immigrants. (About improvisation and the marriage of words and music: Thompson told me of witnessing Ben Webster, tenor saxophonist with the Ellington band—whose playing sometimes outstripped his natural competition with the other two geniuses of the tenor saxophone contemporary with him, Lester Young and Coleman Hawkins—having joined a small group in a club on 52nd Street in New York, once suddenly stop playing in the middle of a chorus, seeming bewildered. Asked why later, Webster replied that he had forgotten the words.)

I spent an inordinate amount of time on my Harvard letter of application, advised by Holmes and William, who also cautioned me to keep my grade record unspotted in the pair of courses I was enrolled in now, in case Harvard wanted my most recent transcript. A month or so before I left in August, Thompson moved to Los Angeles, having abandoned a secure haven writing for the studio orchestra at NBC in

San Francisco, to seek his fortune in the treacherous land of the dream machine. He and Jenny would drive me to the train station for my departure to Sacramento, a brief detour on my way to Boston. Waving good-bye to them I wondered how long they would remain without feeling, I guess being, justified in taking revenge on my escape. I feel sad writing this, sadder now than I remember feeling then, when I had again lost heart in the known.

Part 8

April 29, 2004

I do not remember when I began thinking of myself in my writing as better at endings than at beginnings but in conducting my life as better at beginnings than at endings. At the moment I am trying to capture now, I find I do not know how I adjudged the ratio, in what I felt I was doing, between ending again and beginning again.

By the time I got off the train for the first time in Boston, in early September 1951, I had just turned twenty-five years old, which meant—since I had every intention of beginning graduate work (again)—that I would be three or four years older than most, I imagined, of my classmates, those who were entering graduate school straight, or almost straight, from graduating college. Not only was youth over—that should have been purely a blessing, given what I thought of my youth—but I was distinctly no longer precocious.

The Harvard form assigning me to a room in the graduate dormitory complex, or some document accompanying the form, described the transportation routes from Boston to Cambridge—from South Station, the principal train station of the city, the Red Line of the subway system ran, as it still runs, directly to Harvard Square. Evidently it would not dare do otherwise. Arriving at the recently completed new graduate dormitories (some way would have been found to note that they were designed by Walter Gropius, hence a name one had better attach significance to), I could at once have sensed a further stage in maintaining, or respecting, my anonymity—no longer that of a state of namelessness in a city of indifference, but that of a shared condition in being named to formal privilege. I would at once welcome the spare equality among the rooms in these light yellow brick dormitory structures, implying a common life of ordered study, each room measuring twelve feet by eight feet, providing space—in addition to a desk and a desk lamp and a desk chair and a bookcase, there was a fake-leather armchair, and a sofa-cot—for a sliding-door closet that took over most of the length of the short solid inside wall, stopping only to leave an opening for the door. The short wall opposite the closet and door wall featured windows running across the middle third of its height, looking out onto the large polygon of grass around which the complex of six buildings was angled. The dominant building, forming the main entrance to the complex, contained on its ground floor, in addition to coat racks and restrooms, a large, remarkably comfortable, heavily used, sunken common room next to which a ramp led up to a vaster but equally comfortable cafeteria, whose facilities were shared largely by those assigned a home in one of the five three-story structures making up the graduate residences. I had gratefully signed on to the dormitory meal plan, which served twenty-one meals a week during term time. After for so long living nowhere, I leapt at these comforts of routine as if they would solve the chaos of unproductive false starts and random ignorance and fragmented relations making up my life in which I had had nothing but time and no time to take. Again, since everything necessary for a primitively civilized existence was now assigned and signed from the beginning, nothing had to be privately planned or to be asked for. While the academic routine will prove demanding, even consuming, preparation for any and all of it was in principle predictable and enjoyably surveyable.

April 30, 2004

The aspect of a sanitarium was reasonably disguised by the comparative raucousness, so it seemed to me, of the number of law students who took meals in the graduate commons along with students in academic fields and who possessed clearer—anyway more specific—intellectual goals and standards than the study, for example, of philosophy can mostly provide. What was welcome in the prevailing climate of formality, not to say regimentation, was continued in styles of dress and of lecturing. Harvard was still a male school, although Radcliffe women had begun to share Harvard lectures. (The women were still segregated for examinations, where in contrast to the men they were on the honors system.) To West Coast eyes, dress was more uniform in the graduate common (not, however, as rigid among graduate students as for Harvard undergraduates almost all of whom lived in one of the eight Harvard Houses, where neckties as well as jackets were required at meals) perhaps simply because there were so many more men in the population than women, and because in the land of four seasons, rather than in California's two, winter jackets began to appear as the school year began, and they were characteristically worn to classes. What sense there was of a year's class of graduate students as a coherent group, intellectually engaged with each other as well as with a corps of teachers, was driven not by age nor by participation in the life of a Harvard House, as was the case with most undergraduates, but by field of study, and in particular by the shared specter of sitting for the Ph.D. qualifying examinations, which in philosophy were scheduled over a period of two weeks at the end of the year's lectures—four three-hour written examinations in history, ethics, metaphysics and epistemology, and logic. They were required to be taken at the end of the first year, with one chance, if failing them was not below a certain level, to repeat them at the end of the second year.

I had imagined, starting in a new place, that I would postpone taking the examinations until the following year, fearing that at my age a lack of some distinction, let alone failure, would be fatal. The head of the department, Donald Williams, in the obligatory interview with first-year graduate students during my second month in Cambridge, rather cheerfully, even breezily, disabused me of the possibility of postponement, whereupon I gave up auditing the lectures of Harry Levin and of Talcott Parsons and began systematically attending a full range of philosophy lectures, as my fellow more practical graduate students were doing, by faculty members whose work I did not know and who would that year be involved in the process of setting and grading the Ph.D. qualifying examinations in the spring.

Something like half of the twenty-odd students who took the examinations my year (not all of whom lived in the graduate dormitories; hence not all were well known to me) successfully passed them, which I had no reason to believe was anomalous. The shared ordeal meant that numbers of our fellow students were as significant a part of our education as our teachers were, which in turn created a certain sense of responsibility for one another, hence a certain ground of reparation for the fact that we were inescapably in competition, anyway incessantly compared, with one another. The more sophisticated among us knew how to make others pay (say, with a pinch of humiliation) for a scholarly tip about an article here or a chapter there that should be paid attention to; but we gave, and were given, the tip.

It is not hard to recall, over the din of voices in the graduate cafeteria, or in the grill kept open in a corner of the cafeteria until midnight or so, or at Hayes-Bickford (the favored among three prominent commercial cafeterias open all night in those years in Harvard Square) the distinct voices, in addition to Marshall Cohen's, of Hubert Dreyfus, Gareth Matthews, Samuel Todes, Hugo Bedau, occasionally as the spring approached joined by Ronald Dworkin, a senior philosophy concentrator who would avoid the communal misery of the Ph.D. "prelims" by leaving Harvard after his imminent graduation to continue distinguishing himself at Oxford. The disorientation on moving from the intellectual weather of the American far West to that of Harvard Square (an experience sometimes celebrated, I believe, to this day in the apt phrase "culture shock") was for me less a function of what seemed to be known (no one, for example, knew as much about music in our circles as I did), than a matter of what was, or is to be assumed to be, so well known as to go—to go only—without saying. Not everything was perfectly different from my second year in Sacramento in seventh grade.

Our professors were comparably affected by this organized concentration of fear and determination, however refined. Their lectures— I speak of the classes of C. I. Lewis (two years before his retirement) and of W. V. Quine and of Donald Williams and of the young Morton

White and Henry Aiken—were directed and polished in a way that at UCLA would perhaps have seemed quaint. I do not mean that, for example, Kaplan's lectures had been casual or disorganized, but they were displays of individual accomplishment rather than invitations to participate in professionally working things through. The general air in Emerson Hall—of course there were exceptions—was that the dominant trends of the contemporary profession of philosophy as such were being addressed, responded to, out of these Harvard classrooms. The reigning formality (first names were on the whole not used between faculty and students, even graduate students, on either side, until at least qualifying examinations were successfully out of the way, and in some cases not until the dissertation was signed) had, I think, the apparently paradoxical consequence that graduate students were regarded as participating in a common enterprise with their professors as—what most were destined to be—part of the next generation of the field's professors. The sense of the work in the classroom mattering to the professional work of a field was something verified in the way I had witnessed the Harvard faculty's published work received at the distance of UCLA. This attitude toward one's work is not the only known form of intellectual seriousness, but it is serious.

Here I ought to be able to raise more clearly than I feel I can, the ethos of certain institutions, what it is in those who identify with them that credibly shapes and sustains or crushes aspiration. That Lewis had been one of a generation of graduate students in the Harvard department whose thesis was signed by Josiah Royce, while William James and George Santayana were still members of the philosophy faculty, was part of Lewis's aura. For whom does one write? For whom does (did) one write a dissertation? For whom in philosophy, in American philosophy?

The teaching assistants, older graduate students in the department, were almost as unapproachable as the professors. Thompson Clarke, who will as an intellectual companion become the dedicatee, along with J. L. Austin, of my *Claim of Reason*, was, in this first of my years at Harvard, Lewis's teaching assistant for the last (or next-to-the-last) time Lewis taught epistemology. Clarke's comments on my papers for that course were the most meticulous and provocative of any I ever received in any class. When that spring another graduate student, Burton Dreben, gave a lecture to the department, to give an account of the result in logic he had recently achieved, he was introduced, to a packed classroom, by the chair of the department, Donald Williams, whose announcement that Dreben had just been elected to the Harvard Society of Fellows, whatever that was, made it sound as if he had been beatified. (It was this year at Harvard that I acquired the concept of the famous graduate student. It made a pair with the concept of the famous assistant professor, of which Abe Kaplan was the first instance I knew; later figures would be rumors of Benson Mates at Berkeley and Sidney Morgenbesser at Columbia.) A vice of generally recognized importance is the attraction to self-importance. (I do not, I think, know what people mean when they accuse others, so often and easily, of taking themselves too seriously. Why in the world should one not take oneself with utmost seriousness? Because it would cause me to take others insufficiently seriously? I do not believe that. Then because it would make me consider myself important, or more important than I am? I believe that even less. But if importance, or false importance, is what is feared, then say that. Or is the supposed fault that it would make me humorless, incapable of laughing at myself? God forbid.) I think of various versions of the following piece of wisdom that came my way over my decades at Harvard, meant to explain the compounding decline of an academic department's importance, or perhaps to decry a new appointment to the faculty: "Second-rate people like to be around third-rate people. First-rate people like to be around first-rate people." Do first-rate people speak so—except in their fourth-rate moments?

May 2, 2004

Cafeteria conversation at UCLA as I recalled it could be as intellectually intense as that I found practiced at Harvard in these years, but it was not as continuous or developing in tone and topic over days and months (my attendance was also much less regular at UCLA, where there was a particular pair of reasonably nearby and better inexpensive restaurants than any I discovered then in Cambridge, so my sample of incidents is smaller), and it incorporated the mode of harangue or monologue that would not have been tolerated in the more punitive decorum at Harvard, even in the less severe ambience of the graduate cafeteria as compared with the undergraduate dining halls, whose rigors I would not experience until near the end of my second semester at Harvard. Sometimes the Los Angeles monologues were delivered quietly at a table populated solely by the speaker; sometimes others were seated at the table with him, but whether all, or any, were listening was open to question. The impression of three of the monologues delivered during my first months in Los Angeles I find have remained with me. One concerned a calculation of prevailing winds designed to discover the safest place to move to in order to minimize the effects of fallout from a more or less imminent exchange of atomic bombs. (The calculation picked out a spot on the coast of Peru.) A second monologue, from someone earning the money to stay in school by delivering and installing TV sets—objects still in the optional stage of dispersal—rehearsed his having that morning set up of one of these strange necessities in a house with dirt floors. In this monologist's expression of quite inexpressible irony, it was not clear at whom his combination of anger and amusement was directed, at unjust government or at lax families. A third speaker filled pages of drawings to illustrate ideas that refuted Einstein's General Theory of Relativity; one drawing proved that light traveled way faster than Einstein realized.

May 3, 2004

The difference in my experience between East Coast and West Coast modes of philosophy lecturing manifested itself more fully, and from the opposite side, when I returned after five years to begin a teaching life at Berkeley. The Harvard semester during my graduate years there was twelve weeks long, and a teaching schedule was two courses each term, one lecture course and a graduate seminar that was conducted essentially in discussion, which meant (if you lectured twice a week, which was common, though some instructors added an optional third lecture in some, sometimes in all, weeks) that a new course required preparing a minimum of twenty-four lectures. I have seen gifted, accomplished young scholar-teachers almost break under the strain. It is not the only way to think of lecturing, nor perhaps the most efficient or pleasurable form, but it was common in my experience then and there. In my more than forty years of teaching, that image and mode of lecturing has never quite abandoned me, however modified it became. (For better or worse, explicitly modifying a late course of my lectures soon to appear in print as *Cities of Words* would not otherwise have been for me a feasible project. I mean that I was beginning, in writing successive chapters, from a set of substantial and revised drafts of most of the lectures.)

The Berkeley semester when I arrived there to teach was, instead of twelve weeks, fifteen weeks long, and a teaching schedule (at least for assistant professors) was three courses each term with a graduate seminar in one of the two terms. My first semester I was scheduled to give three lecture courses—a large course (enrolling some four hundred students) in the history of philosophy with full lectures scheduled twice a week supplemented by a weekly discussion section led by a teaching assistant, and two courses (one on *The Critique of Pure Reason* and one on aesthetics) each with three mandatory meetings a week. This committed me to eight lectures a week for fifteen weeks, yielding 120 lectures for the term. Conceived of as formal lectures this is something like the equivalent of writing five or six substantial books the first year of teaching. What conceivably could this mean? Moreover, I had spent the previous year, the first year of my first marriage, traveling in Western Europe, not arriving in Berkeley until just in time to find a place to live before the beginning of the academic year. What is still more, I had come to this first teaching position having discarded what may have proved to be half of a dissertation, as a result of feeling that my work in philosophy had yet again to begin again as a result of J. L. Austin's residence as William James Lecturer my last spring at Harvard. Austin's presence opened lines of thought I recognized almost at once that I had no choice, or wish, but to take essentially into consideration but that, on seriously putting them into practice, left me once again with no body of work of my own to draw on in which I placed confidence.

I know of no less favorable conditions in which to begin a life of teaching. The place was one I was devoted to, and desperately wanted to participate in, yet I had not even the limited expertise of the subject of a completed dissertation to give me a foothold, and no subject on which I any longer had a perspective to guide me through. Humiliation was in store, but so, in good enough time, was an urgency to understand how I had arrived at this impasse, and why, perhaps despite appearances, it might have been worth it.

May 5, 2004

But I lack the mood now in which to try to articulate how this unfolded with reasonable, or anyway survivable, productiveness. In continuing instead with sketches of some of the texture of my belated first year at Harvard, I know I have not done justice to the potentially mortal jousts that underlay the very comforts of formality I have noted. Henry Aiken, out of high motives, and some of questionable height, and out of a genuine capacity for what might be called human sentiment and admiration of the young, offered distinct if limited companionship to several first-year graduate students in his spring seminar, inviting two or three of us on more than one occasion to move from having coffee on a late Thursday after his seminar to dinner at his apartment one street behind Emerson Hall. What dinner at his apartment turned out to mean was to have drinks for a couple of hours, then walk carefully a little before nine o'clock around the corner to the Broadway Market to shop for food before it closed, and, returning to his place with each of us laden with grocery bags, to talk more and listen to favorite recordings of Aiken's, nothing adventurous, but imperishably good things, for example, Schnabel performances of Beethoven sonatas, with incipiently drunken insistences to pay particular attention to a forthcoming passage urged upon us as Aiken would appear momentarily from the kitchen (sometimes he would lift the needle arm and play the passage, more or less, over again, and maybe again) where he was preparing a meal worthy of what we will discover, or rediscover, toward eleven o'clock, to be the talents of a serious and gifted cook.

I would—the most familiar guests took turns in this—keep him company for a while in his small kitchen as he exercised his gifts. He was also one of the best amateur mimics I had encountered, and he would sometimes shock into terrific laughter a small gathering of graduate students with his uncanny hitting off of an imitation of one of his colleague's mannerisms (one of our respected teachers, after all) or perhaps that of a university administrator who had a notable way of suddenly clearing his throat that caused a sound indistinguishable from a minor but distinct shriek. But in his small kitchen, just the two of us present, nothing to call an audience, he wanted to talk philosophy as he cooked (sometimes pausing to demonstrate how to chop quickly while ensuring that you protect your fingers). This really consisted of a monologue of his, delivered earnestly, on which he looked repeatedly for agreement. The fact is I could never be sure that I understood what he had said and wanted agreement about, and I was willing to attribute this either to his or to my having had too much to drink—I surely had had too much, with my lifelong low threshold for feeling its effects—or to both. This always surprised me, remembering my being impressed, even charmed, by the distinct literary flair in the essay of his—and not in that alone—I had encountered at UCLA. So I would be relieved to get back to the living room and to group hilarity, in which Aiken's high spirits were more important than making sense.

I have forgotten how it got started, but Henry began calling Marshall Cohen and me "Kleine," and we returned to him this little gesture of a special intimacy. First names were not avoided with Henry, but there was, however good and close our feelings ran, still something off about using them. Doubtless it had at that stage irreducibly to do, for those of us facing the Ph.D. prelims, with the knowledge that he would in some months be one of the judges of our examination papers, hence to that terrible degree, and even with the precaution of putting numbers on the examination covers to keep them anonymous, he held our fate partially in his hands, or would watch it develop beyond his control. On one of these nights of dinner at Henry's, a law school friend of Marshall's had been having coffee with us when Henry invited the group to his place, and he joined with the rest of the gathering, delightedly, in calling everyone, and being called, "Kleine." Henry's generosity, coming I believed, believe still, however else, from a genuine imagination of loneliness in the life of first-year graduate students, for whom the past accomplishments that elevated them to that stage were now irrelevant, and the future for which they were preparing themselves more or less invisible, is something for which gratitude should not rapidly or readily run out.

He was, with Morton White, of a generation younger than that of the other permanent professors in the department; they were the two teachers with whom graduate students might feel some comparative degree of easy exchange. Aiken was a few years older than White and had been in the department as a graduate student, a favorite of Ralph Barton Perry's (a member of the department remembered mostly for his notable biography of William James, although his main philosophical work, *The General Theory of Value*, is of more interest than one might imagine at this date, as I discovered in an afternoon with it in the departmental library, and had its title commemorated in the title of the academic chair I was given on returning to Harvard to teach), so Aiken knew remote corners of the lore of the department in a way White did not. What Aiken did not know sufficiently usefully were the developments in analytical philosophy that put his devotion to pragmatism, and indeed his entire devotion to ethics and aesthetics, on the defensive. White, on the contrary, having written a published dissertation on Dewey, and followed it with the book on social thought that was making itself known, had gone on to study the technical developments in positivist thought, as represented in Quine's advances, as well as to interest himself in the new wave of philosophy coming out of Oxford after World War II, both developments that were of interest to graduate students and about which Aiken was caught more or less unprepared, anyway imprecisely aware of and unwilling to find out concretely what he found interesting and threatening in these developments. He felt, fairly obviously, not without justice, that his genuine talent was becoming insufficiently recognized. Whether, or to what extent, he also felt it was becoming unavailable to himself, is hard to think about. When White was soon promoted to Full Professor, though Aiken was somewhat senior to him in years of appointment as Associate Professor, Aiken understood this to be a rebuke and could not conceal the hurt it caused him. Ten years later, when I would return to teach in the department, Aiken's drinking had become undisguised alcoholism, and he had, so I was told, been informed by the administration that he would never receive a further raise in rank. Within two years he accepted an offer to move to Brandeis.

An implication of this particular form of administrative humiliation is that, since Aiken was evidently never unable to discharge his academic duties, anyway his teaching duties, he was not open to having his tenure broken for that reason. I was witness to his powers of recuperation early, specifically during my second year as a graduate student at Harvard, when I had become a Teaching Fellow in the course he had developed with Morton White for the General Education program. One night, or rather early morning, a by now, for me, rare dinner at Aiken's apartment ended not earlier than 2 a.m. with Aiken drunk beyond intelligibility. An older graduate student I knew only vaguely stayed behind to get him into bed, and waved off my concern that he would never make it to class in the morning. At nine o'clock Aiken appeared, bathed, shaved, neatly dressed (he always dressed well, even nattily) and engagingly delivered a coherent lecture no different in manner or quality from the one he had delivered two mornings earlier.

But other humiliations were in store. One of the philosophy graduate students had arranged to have Gilbert Ryle, visiting the department from Oxford for a public lecture, speak informally to a group of interested students from various departments in the common room of the Harvard House in which he was being put up. A number of people had crowded into the room for the occasion. The discussion was going well, and was well along, when a commotion at the door of the room turned out to be Henry Aiken, volubly drunk, demanding to be let in—evidently someone had been sitting on the floor leaning back against the door. The student host of the evening went to the door and, taking Henry with him, closed the door behind them. One heard voices in the hallway, and an outer door close. I thought that was well done, until a few minutes later the student came back in alone and took his place again near Ryle. The following day, finding a moment alone with my fellow student, I said that I would have been pleased had he stayed with Aiken rather than leaving him to himself with his disgrace and memorializing his annoying behavior by walking back in alone and across the room. "I wasn't going to let him stop the conversation. And why should I have let him cause me to miss it?" Since I agreed with the first sentiment, and felt about the second that if he didn't understand it nothing could be said to explain it to him, I kept my peace then. But I have had occasion to be reminded chronically of it by a moralism that seems attractive to philosophers even in these days when moral philosophy has reached a level of refinement and prestige entirely beyond its means in my graduate school days.

What I am calling moralism is bound up with a casualness about the question of what I think of as the standing implied, required, in confronting another with moral judgment and about the relation established or modified in leveling the judgment. A talented teacher to whom you owe gratitude for repeated past kindnesses, and whose disgraceful conduct will be underscored by the consciousness of your rebuke, deserves better of you than being deftly turned out of doors, when the only cost to you to help him preserve a tatter of dignity is the mild disappointment of missing the end of a public conversation. Put like this, as a principle, it sounds stuffy (to whom, and when, is it to be announced? what standing does it presume?); as the articulation of a ponderable feeling it seems to me plain enough.

My last exchange with Henry Aiken took place in the grassy corner of Harvard Yard shaped by the side of Emerson Hall roughly facing the back of Sever Hall. I was headed along the path between the buildings, having just entered the Yard through the gate across from the Fogg Museum, when Henry hailed me as he was walking down the side steps from Emerson Hall. It had been a while since his move to Brandeis. I was myself somewhat distracted, and I could not tell at a glance what his condition was. After hellos he began an exchange that developed as follows: "I have to tell you that the *New York Review of Books* has sent me your Walden book to review."—"I'm very glad to hear it."—"But I told them it wouldn't do. I read it twice and—I have to tell you this—the book is not good, it is not up to your best work. It is obscure—I have to tell you this. I sent the book back." I recall replying, truthfully enough, that I was sorry to hear what he had said. I know I felt that I would probably never feel more calmly sure about a piece of work of mine that it was well conceived and well done than I did about that little book on Thoreau's writing. Even discounting passages in it that may have carried some Heideggerian or Wittgensteinian tinge (effects that Aiken would, I believe, have hated), it represented something in philosophy that I knew he cared about and felt had become largely ignored by the profession. I wondered whether he could really stick to his story of my book's failings if the memory of it recurred to him when he was alone. My sense of his isolation is in the moment openly present to me. I did not like the hardness behind which I viewed this spectacle of destruction of a vivid and gifted man. My last vision of him, not long afterward, several months before he died, was in the main dining room of the Harvard Faculty Club. I was eating lunch alone in the small alcove of the room, preoccupied in looking over notes for a seminar that afternoon, when I heard the shout, "Kleine!" In the entranceway across the room Henry, immaculately dressed, had raised both his arms and started to head unsteadily toward me. As I stood up, and gathered together my notes in order to lead Henry back out of the dining room, an older common friend, a colleague of ours from the days in which Henry was still a member of the Harvard department, intercepted him and walked out with him. By the time I looked down to see if I had collected my books and all my papers, and got to the entrance hall, I did not see them. I also did not see them as I walked out of the front door of the Club. I did not go back inside to look for them.

May 7, 2004

I think I do not recognize competitiveness, where it entails a lack of respect, as a characteristic or unchecked vice of mine. Cathleen has explained this as my having been an only child. (Austin once asked me if I had an older brother. When I said no, he replied, "Then how can you know what life is?" an exchange I never have felt I understood, either in its prelude or in its finale.) The relative absence in me of this vice, if I am right about it, call the vice moral stinginess, is probably no credit to me, since competitiveness could much of the time have been made irrelevant out of the greater vice of vanity. I do not mean to deny that I have been wounded by variously caused failures of acknowledgment. But my capacity for admiring the accomplishments of others, being inspired by them, established early in performing music, both in chamber-music groups and in swing bands, has, I believe, never abandoned me. When I would express excitement at someone's musical accomplishment my father would as often as not respond by asking why I was not capable of an equal accomplishment. Had I implied that I was thus unable?

The undoubted and singular favor of one's mother is a well-known source of a sense of being exceptional. In music, competitiveness was in my case mostly irrelevant because performance was never my chief aim, and by the time composition might have been, it was no longer what I had it at heart to do. In matters of the heart, for reasons of isolation I described, and the oddness of my age in all the close companies of which I was part, I had for a long time not known myself to have placed myself in a position to have my heart broken. By the time of high school and the adolescent insatiability of desire, my absorption in musical performance of itself produced its heartfelt satisfactions, what satisfactions I could imagine. At Berkeley I was continuously, or discontinuously, in love with accomplished women—a cellist, a harpist, a bassist, a pianist, two actresses, a writer who taught me the names of flowers—one of whom I never even spoke to in actuality. Then Mary both ended my adolescence and caused me to feel unready for adulthood.

Having staked myself on solving my mysteries by way of the mysteries of philosophy, I found the almost unrelieved competitiveness at Harvard to be something new in my experience. There was no longer any choice in picking what I was interested in and giving that my undivided attention. All the fields of the preliminary examinations had to be taken. Nor was there a way to blur the fact of competition itself—some who take the examinations will fail them, as surely as if there were only so many places allotted for passing. Moreover, given what I considered to be my advanced age then, and given that philosophy was to incorporate and transform the crisis of musical expression in my life, I believed fully that to fail to excel at the examinations would amount to failure as such. I was no longer asking for admittance but for confirmation that I had found what I wanted to become of my life, the basis on which I would be able—as Plato and Aristotle both have ways of saying—to choose my (next) life.

The issue for me was not to prove that this further life was better than another, but to prove that it was mine, that I was born to it, that I was born. Yet the only way I had so far been given to prove some such condition was to win, whether a particular contest was real or imagined. Then the way to make winning pertinent, or rather irrelevant, was to win in such a way as to be beyond or outside evaluation. This is a dangerous frame of mind.

I had been there before. In the class in string quartet writing at Berkeley, the young composer giving the course was strict about our handing in our weekly exercises on time. He announced an unbreakable rule that a late exercise would be dropped a full grade, indicated by the grade's being enclosed in a circle. I was not satisfied until I had submitted a late exercise that received a circled A. (Which, namely, was undefined—what had this grade been *dropped* from? I had achieved the ungradable.) The telltale wrinkle, as I have indicated, is that I was not reliably attached to what I had written, exercise or not. If there is one virtue to be found in these tales of vanity and confusion and sleepwalking, say, my awaiting birth, if not stalling birth, it is that I learned, before I would have thought I had learned anything at all, to treat every word or note I set down with absolute attention and ambition, I mean of course with all that were undeniably at my disposal. ("Oh Stanley, you are so serious." I started hearing this early. How could I deny it? What is wrong with it?) So I could not escape from my work's judgment of me.

The way my competitiveness in approaching the philosophy qualifying examinations expressed itself, seen at this distance of half a century, was sometimes as comic as it was crazy. I use as an instance my Christmas vacation that first semester at Harvard. A number of the graduate students, including myself, who were not making a long trip home (plane travel in 1953 was still a touch exotic), or venturing to join up with an old companion, stayed on in the dormitories for a few days into the Christmas / New Year's break, namely, after the cafeteria had closed for the (perhaps ten days of) holiday. A few days before Christmas the dormitory windows of the graduate center (something like two hundred room windows would have been visible from my room) were dark all night, except for a dozen or so scattered among the buildings. Christmas Eve had no magic for me. I had turned down more than one invitation to spend Christmas in New York. Dinner alone at a cafeteria on Christmas Eve felt as much like an adventure as a deprivation to me. (I would by then have read Freud's definition of neurosis as an inability to feel pleasure as such. But what about an inability to feel psychic pain as such?) Each successive night two or three more window lights failed to go on. By New Year's Eve only one other light, at the far end of the complex, was burning in the late afternoon along with mine. Returning to my room after dinner, I found that my companion's light was extinguished. Some victory. I went to bed before midnight, conceiving indifference to the physical turn into a New Year, if glorying in the isolation of the dormitories, then ruling over an empty kingdom. I thought that I might reward my magnificence with a movie the next day. I have forgotten whether I held on to the thought.

Have I not recaptured among these memories the last Christmas season I worked in my father's pawnshop? The roughly two weeks of Christmas vacation from school naturally overlapped the busiest shopping weeks of the year in the store. And my father expanded the hours he stayed open, as did other stores, but which in his case sometimes meant not closing until around eleven o'clock, as the crowds left the closing of the movie houses and produced some couples walking past our store to their parked cars. I did not always last that long but left when my despair of my life mounted sufficiently to confront my father's disapproval as I departed, if he could not be induced to close for the day, or rather the night. That year Christmas fell on a Sunday, so I imagined that Christmas Eve would be climactically busy with late shoppers still anxiously looking for bargains in notable gifts. When the store was for the moment empty of customers I headed out shortly after nightfall, not yet six o'clock, to have a coffee and something sweet at Hart's Cafeteria, to prepare myself for several further hours behind the cage window. As I reached the sidewalk beyond the store's display windows, I found the sidewalks essentially deserted, on both sides of the street, the lights of Bruener's, the landmark department store across the street, decisively dimmed. Astonished, I called my father out to witness this evacuation. After deciding that this was not an illusion (what was new in this such that my father had not expected it?), and I at any rate interpreting the situation as the population of Sacramento having all at once decided to celebrate Christmas Eve at home, or conceivably at church, we prepared the store for closing, which meant primarily returning and locking numbers of trays of diamonds and tempting watches from the windows and the showcases into the large safe within the cage, turning off all but the night lights, those in the outside windows and those inside the store, front and back, and, I at least remaining in a state of surprised light-heartedness, left to go home and have some supper. If there were an O. Henry among Jewish writers, his Jewish hero would have told this story and summed up its moral roughly with the sentiment: This was my Christmas.

May 8, 2004

As the dates of the Ph.D. examinations approached I began to feel the effects of my regime. I could not sleep when I let myself try to sleep. And I could less and less keep my concentration when I was awake and exhausted. An acquaintance in the dormitories hearing me describe my condition offered me a five-milligram Benzedrine tablet, and it worked so well that I telephoned my mother to say that I must have a prescription for such tablets from a doctor, relative or friend, in Atlanta and have some urgently mailed to me, enough for two a day if necessary until the examinations, a few weeks away, plus the two weeks of examinations themselves. (That would, I imagine, involve breaking more than one law in answering one request; a test of mother love.) I had made it through several years working with musicians who were on various drugs, commonly Benzedrine, whose tablets were affectionately called "bennies" (anyway that was the drug I knew something about, and Thompson followed a recipe whose straightforward directions were to break open a Benzedrine inhaler and soak one of its strips in a shot of whiskey—the condition this potion produced in him was not conducive to study), and I had never been more than mildly tempted to join the experience, or say, to forfeit my innocence. It was philosophy, the pursuit of reason, well into my age of reason, that pushed me over the line.

Years later, preparing lectures for another massive lecture course upon my return to Harvard to teach, I again resorted to these little enabling tablets and this time realized what their help was. Keeping me awake was the least of the matter. They reduced anxiety, and perhaps mild depression, allowing a state of concentration, expressing itself wondrously as freedom from time. The realization made me recognize that I was courting addiction—I was staying up all night unnecessarily in order to justify needing the drug, rather than the other way around. The fear was large enough and the need still confined enough so that I could successfully turn that page when this emergency was past. A few years later, having never smoked until I was past thirty, beginning with the prospect of divorce two years before leaving Berkeley to teach at Harvard, and beginning to write my dissertation in earnest, I was soon smoking three packs of cigarettes a day.

The result of the siege of Ph.D. examinations worked out as I had meant it to, or close enough. Others got high marks but mine were highest. Not the highest conceivable, but distinctly enough that year so that I could use whatever illusion I seemed to need to feel that I had proved something to myself and at the same time left myself with some margin of mystery.

The actual taking of the examinations had skirted catastrophes. A week or ten days before the first exam, on the history of philosophy, I decided to stop reading new material and look over the notes I had been preparing over the months, particularly on material from journal articles. I had not noticed that the pages of my notes had mounted into the hundreds, extending to an ample length of the file drawer I was adding them to, and were not ordered by subject, as if however scrupulously they were made they were filed, or put out of sight, in a stupor. It took me some days to get them in order, and in beginning to read through the history notes I repeatedly found that I could not understand the view my notes described. Further help from a drug was out of the question, and I spent terrible hours fighting with myself over whether I must, or must not, find an excuse for withdrawing from this year's examinations. The unshakable fact gradually prevailed with me that I could not go through this year again.

I was quite convinced after taking that first examination that I had failed it, and only Marshall's and others' hilarious assurances that this conviction was quite common at this stage calmed me sufficiently to prepare for the next. The notes got easier to sort, and the next two ex-aminations were smoother. The logic exam was last, and it was, oddly, the one I was most confident about. Not because I knew much logic but because the requirements for its preparation were clear and the level of technical competence it required was well within the training I had received at UCLA and had continued at Harvard. It was well known that one of its questions would concern Aristotelian logic and another would require doing a proof using the method of so-called natural de-duction. Complete preparation for natural deduction was contained in Quine's *Methods of Logic*, and I spent about an hour of each day over the last month before the ordeal, with relief from the infinite tasks of his-tory and ethics and metaphysics, enjoyably performing all the exercises in Quine's book. The first of the six questions on the logic examination (all were required, all were of equal weight, hence thirty minutes should be reserved for each—already a sign of my frightened logic, since not all were equally exacting) was the one to require natural deduction, as if to say, "If you can't handle this, forget about the rest." I was pleased, until it transpired that, after confidently proceeding, I could not get the proof to work. I had gone through similar proofs countless times, even auditing the last weeks of the first-year logic course to make sure I was abreast of things, so I was making some simple mistake in my proof— unless there was a misprint in the examination. But evidently no one else in the class had drawn this conclusion, and there were people there who knew logic in a way I never will. After a frantic twenty-five minutes or so I decided to move on to the next question and come back to this one. I hurried through the next question and gained five additional minutes to spend back on the first. Again to no avail. I repeated this process, with the same unsatisfactory result, through answering the sixth and final question. The unruly genie of Benzedrine was having his laugh. There were perhaps ten minutes left of the three hours. It was plenty of time—if you can do the procedure you can do it about as fast as you can write. By now the number of crossed-out and erased lines in my attempts illustrated a grizzly story.

So much I am certain of. What I report to have happened next I do not doubt, but I find it hard to believe. When a last effort failed— I said to myself that my mind was grooving its attempts, as baseball pitchers are said to do on repeating a bad pitch several times in a row—I recalled a comment and brief demonstration from the end of a logic lecture that I had meant to but never tried to determine whether I had grasped practically. The comment was that the number of lines in a natural deduction could be shortened by adding a tautology to the premises. I evidently remembered a usable tautology, I suppose it was remembered from that demonstration, because adding it produced, before my bewildered eyes, a proof in four or five, instead of an expected ten or twelve, lines. But I conceived the idea that while adding tautologies was routine proof procedure, it was out of order in natural deduction, that while possible there it missed the spirit of the thing.

And—of course—there remained the question whether I really had produced a proof at all. How could I trust a procedure I did not grasp with anything like the confidence I had in the lengthier, less imaginative process; and I had failed to prove that I had managed even so much as that minimal level the only time my capacity had been openly tested. Yet when the results were announced, the logic examination proved to have received a grade from which it had to follow that the proof was sound.

A variety of consequences led from here. For example, it is a further confirmation of my sense of myself as having at critical times passed a test, or shown some flair, in a way I felt I could not reproduce on demand, so that the event could not be held to my credit, but merely added one more set of false colors to fly or flee under. A specific, equally fateful, consequence was that when the next year the philosophy department nominated me for a Junior Fellowship in the Society of Fellows, it was understood that a departure in its sense of philosophical promise was being asked for. Quine had been one of the original Junior Fellows when the Society was founded in the early 1930s (Alfred North Whitehead was one of the original Senior Fellows), and sometime after his appointment to the Harvard faculty he was appointed a Senior Fellow, namely, one of those who chose the six new Junior Fellows each year. In the opening two decades of the Society's existence every candidate nominated from the philosophy department had been a mathematical logician (those familiar to me, I believe the total number, beyond Quine, were Hao Wang and Burton Dreben, now present in the faculty of the Harvard philosophy department). I was told, indiscreetly, that Quine's acquiescence to my candidacy—namely, letting the range of my interests across fields (a matter in principle of distinct pertinence to the Society's sense of its intellectual mission) speak for itself—was achieved by informing him that I had received an A on the logic prelim (Quine had been on leave at Oxford the previous year, hence had not participated in setting and grading that set of qualifying exams).

But this is a year into the future and requires some time on its own. An immediate reward for my first-year's success in the graduate program, almost immediately after the results of the qualifying examinations were announced, was the department's nomination of me to be one of four Harvard graduate students to serve as teaching assistants at the session of the Salzburg Seminar in American Studies, to meet outside Salzburg, Austria, for six weeks during the coming summer. The idea of the seminar was to invite some ninety to a hundred university students throughout Western Europe, who had experienced the war (still only seven years in the past) on both sides, to live together for these weeks, along with four graduate and four undergraduate students from Harvard serving as informal links to the four American professors who would be offering courses. This imaginative idea was formed by several Harvard students to promote understanding, if not healing, among estranged members of their new generation. And in the event the experience inspired a certain sense of effectiveness in its noble optimism.

Still possessed of elements of the radiating, if now relative, social ignorance of a provincial bumpkin, I had never been to Europe and scarcely knew what steps to take, when it turned out that my nomination to the seminar in Austria had succeeded, to get there. It would be a decisive summer for me. But then just about everything in retrospect seems in my narrative to have been accidentally decisive in my life. Or is this caused by my allowing myself to be unwittingly dictated to by the form or sound of narration, persistently, prematurely seeking sense? From the vantage of old age (some vantage), itself as strange as the past, to which its tendency is to belong, anything in youth can seem decisive. If now I wonder whether I will feel close enough to death to play chess with him, or her, and to have time to consider the endgame, in which the prospect is unforgivingly to close off prospects, I am seeing chess quite as if for the first time in its uncanny lucidity as allegorical of death. Evidently I am still trying to make liberating sense of Freud's idea of life as detours toward death.

Speaking of which—I mean of Beckett's *Endgame*—I believe I never stopped long enough over Hamm's opening line: "Me to play." Who is the opponent, that is, whose turn might it conceivably otherwise be? The case may be that this is itself part of what Hamm has to discover (who is opposed at every turn)—whether it is mainly his interlocutor Clov, or whether it is speech and meaning as such, hence himself in his unrelieved limitations and necessities, or whether it is as it were God. Hemingway, I believe I knew, had said roughly that the opponent of life, hence of writing, is death, who must win, but if you play well, only at the end. This was a fruitful critical hint from him about how to read his work. I think I never gave him sufficient credit for that, I mean for the hint; credit for writing that achieves, near and often enough, the imperishable.

When the results of the qualifying examinations were posted, at the celebratory dinner that those of us who passed had arranged for ourselves, along with a few friends, at the best, recently opened, restaurant in Cambridge (the Henri Quatre), Marshall, out of the blue, toasted me by saying, "Stanley is a great success with the girls. He never says no." Perhaps the humor depends upon some jest well known in our tiny circle at the time, except to me. Or perhaps it was simply a recognition of the mad monkishness of my existence over the past long months, in spite of offers and occasions that I had shied away from in the life I had chosen absolutely, so far as I could tell, beyond the pleasure principle. But that night a woman acquaintance in and from whom, in passing, I had more than once concealed, I thought, my interest, who had joined us for dinner even though she had dropped out of the event of the qualifying examinations for this year, determined that I deserved a more personal reward for my pains. It is quite recently that I learned of the existence of a sociological law called the Saint Matthew Effect, which runs: "To them that hath shall it be given."

May 10, 2004

The summer began with yet a further archaic comedy of ineptitude, now of an innocent preparing to go abroad. Passage on a so-called student ship from New York to Cherbourg, and hence Paris, had been recommended to me by the authorities of the Salzburg Seminar. It evidently was not reasonable for them to imagine that a person old enough to carry money would not know that arranging passage meant arranging at the same time a return passage. Yet such information is not transmitted genetically (and if it were it would not have been transmitted through my parents). Or perhaps what I really wanted was indeed a one-way ticket out of all the towns I had known. Only after settling into a routine at Salzburg would I learn that return passage back to the States at the end of the summer might at this stage be tricky to arrange, but that there was nothing to do about it until I returned to Paris. I had never, so far as I can recall or reconstruct, bought a round-trip ticket on any mode of conveyance, as if each of my journeys was to be the last.

The week before sailing away for the summer I flew to Sacramento to visit my parents (then that, my first plane flight since my mother and I had visited the Atlanta families just after the war, might have been my first purchase of a round-trip ticket; if so it was a piece of learning confined to airplanes), whom I had not seen for most of a year, and to decide what I needed to pack for July and August in Salzburg. I packed two heavy suitcases without ever having been, living so much of my life in California, introduced to the concepts of summer-weight and winter-weight clothes, but on an impulse bought and packed a pair of hiking boots covering the ankles (though I had never gone for a hike over rough ground that perhaps held the danger of snakes), and without knowing how to take into sartorial account that Salzburg was the site of an international summer music festival, nor imagining that ordinary walking within cities of renowned histories for the purpose of knowing them and learning their treasures was something I would be likely to be doing in a way unpracticed in my previous behavior, so that, for example, I might wish to be prepared for sudden rainstorms. My parents had never departed from the United States, and if any of their friends had, no one was talking, or was asked to talk. By the time I arrived at my New York hotel room that June night, during a heat wave, my light wool suit, under the added rigors of lugging my monstrous suitcases through an airport and along hotel corridors (in the days before omnipresent backpacks and before suitcases with wheels and instant handles), was no longer fit company. Did Europe contain dry cleaners in 1952? My directions to the ship's dock informed me that boarding was between 9 a.m. and noon the next morning. Despite my exhaustion, I could not fall asleep, and well after midnight changed my wakeup call from eight to nine o'clock. I failed to hear the call and slept until after ten, still plenty of time, I figured, for a shower. I was, along with the rest of my lack of imagination, not prepared for the traffic along the waterfront, yet on arriving at my assigned dock the place looked deserted. I checked the dock number again, and when I now divulged the departure hours, the driver seemed amazed: "You better take off." The departure hall I entered was mostly empty, except for one or two people going nowhere, and through the side windows I could see several uniformed people walking down the gangway of the only ship now in sight. An official in vaguely naval dress, rushed over to me, took the envelope and its papers from my hand, grabbed one of my bags, and started to run. We got to the gangway with sailors at either side of the bottom stair, and my new friend continued to run up the incline without breaking stride, so that, having deposited my suitcase on the deck, he dashed down past me before I arrived at the top. I was informed that it was too late to deposit my bags in my cabin, but that I had to proceed directly to my assigned station for the lifeboat drill. By the time I found my way to the station, clumps of people there were chatting like old acquaintances. How afterward I found my bags again, and put them and myself together in a now empty male dormitory where perhaps a dozen double-decker cots lined the walls, all but one or two with suitcases on top of them declaring territoriality, is a blur to me. But the passengers on board were, after all, mainly students, and most of them, it would emerge, had in fact little or no more worldly experience of their own than I had, and by dinnertime that first night enough stories had been swapped so that those of us at one of the long tables in the second sitting were introducing friendships of several hours' standing to interesting strangers.

Again music early showed its power to create civilized encounters. Programs announcing events for the five days of the crossing appeared, perhaps at lunch. There was, for example, to be a talent show on the final night, auditions to be held the following morning. A young woman confident of her singing and theatrical skills let it be known (through the network of mind reading and competitiveness that the young seem always to have in play) that she was looking for a pianist to accompany her. Our tastes were not particularly close—the idea I broached of "show tunes" seemed unknown to her—but among her prepared favorites was "Pennies from Heaven," which we agreed upon. She had an interesting manner and a good feel for delivering a song with intelligibility and conviction, so that by the time we had found a suitable key, and I had worked out a stable introduction and a texture of accompaniment that she could feel supported by, we had acquired a small following for our rehearsals in the modestly appointed ballroom that housed the ship's grand piano (I had found a spinet in a smaller, mostly abandoned, sitting room on another deck, which I used to refine my contribution). The event of the show and the events preparing for the show did their work of shaping conviviality, and in general the romance of a sea voyage to Europe, with smooth sailing during the entire passage, while it set the stage for a chaos of something like romance among hundreds of college students recently freed from academic responsibilities, thrown together with the business of life cared for and proximity assured, did not obviously lend a mood of calm or of precise consciousness to private circumstances.

May 11, 2004

The contretemps accompanying the first experiences in Paris of finding an affordable and usable room and source of water and directions and food for most of a week are perhaps not much different from the experiences undergone by hicks among the Hittites. My mind in any case is on the overnight ride on the Arlsberg Express, which I took together with another student from Harvard also on his way to the seminar in Salzburg. The fact of Europe unfolding outside the train windows, the new and changing proportions of tree to pasture, of window to wall, of road and car to horse and plow, and rhythmically the food to be purchased through those opened summer windows at various station stops, hit me harder than my first sights of Paris, which seemed falsely familiar in their pictorial and historical fame. This inarticulate, incipient exhilaration continued on being met the following day at the station in Salzburg and being driven to Schloss Leopoldskron, a distance that will in the course of days and weeks become a familiar walk into the relatively small town. The Harvard contingent had been given an evening of orientation before leaving Cambridge with slides of this eighteenth-century palace, the residence initially of a bishop, in its setting on its own lake, and of its rooms, with rococo walls still intact in two rooms, the large ballroom and the library, after the building had been hit in an air raid during the war. But we cannot have been prepared for the feel of the largely unfurnished outline of magnificence in its spaces, including the covered extension of the structure forming a porte cochère to protect guests in three successive centuries from the weather as they dismounted from their carriages at the entrance steps. This formal entrance was by the summer of 1952 so little used that we set up a Ping-Pong table more or less permanently under its protection.

How the Harvard students who had envisioned these international convocations had discovered and secured such an establishment for their program is something I never learned.

I would later receive a treasured compliment on my participation in the communal Ping-Pong routine. Our group had fallen into the obvious custom of awaiting turns to play the winner, with a given winner retiring after prevailing at most three times. The physicist Abraham Pais, visiting Salzburg, had been invited to spend a couple of days and nights at the Schloss in return for giving an informal lecture there. The second morning he was on line to play, and as I completed a second victory, Pais stepped to the front of the line saying roughly to the one now next to challenge, "I am a guest; I am leaving in an hour, and I want to play *him*" (pointing to me). As he and I after our game walked away together for good-byes, having become interested acquaintances at dinner the night before, I asked why he made a point of playing me: "Was it just another manifestation of a physicist's unrelenting competitiveness?" "Not this time. It was because you play correctly and with consistent style, win or lose. The rest is shit." Our connection would resume a decade later when I spent a year at the Princeton Institute for Advanced Study, where he held a chair in physics.

The first night at the Schloss—before the European students were due to begin arriving the next afternoon—dinner was served to the American teachers and students and staff of the seminar not in its dining room but on its stone terrace reaching almost to the lake. The night was cloudy, so the terrace was quite dark by eight o'clock as these groups of strangers were gathering, the individual tables lit only by a candle each. We were a party of some twenty-five or thirty souls. The faces of the four professors and their families were not clearly visible as we were introduced. The name then becoming famous among these four was not strictly speaking that of a professor, but of the poet Robert Lowell, recently married to the writer Elizabeth Hardwick. They had arrived with a French philosopher whom they had met in Paris, and Lowell at once invited me, the announced philosopher among the students, to come to their room and discuss nominalism with their new friend Claude-Edmund Magny, who had just published a book, or more than one, about the American novel. I had no idea what Lowell meant, or wanted, but I later joined up with the three of them, whereupon an incomprehensible exchange took place that Lowell seemed hugely to enjoy.

A second teacher was the composer and theorist Milton Babbitt whom I had never met but had heard of from more than one musician friend. His stories—he seemed to know every musician in the world and every writer and painter in New York—together with his wife's irresistible laughter, were the immediate heart of our region of the party. A third teacher was a philosophy professor from New Jersey, one whose prominence was more a function, I gathered in my still raw knowledge of the profession of philosophy, of his high administrative rank than of his scholarly accomplishments. The fourth among the teachers was Jerome Bruner, the psychologist from Harvard, accompanied by his wife and two small children, some of whose papers I had read during my term of psychology at UCLA, a set of months that now seemed to me, only four years in the past, virtually lost (although I still seemed to remember a paper of Bruner's describing an experiment on the judgment of the relative sizes, among other things, of coins).

The power and glamour of Lowell's writing and the even imperfect sense of Babbitt's reputation, together with the material they were offering to their groups, forcefully caught my imagination, and I spent concentrated, grateful hours listening to what they read aloud, or played, and discussed. I didn't really need the confirmation I received on returning to the States to recognize that no one in the world could be, from a technical perspective, more knowledgeable, and knowing, about the compositional assumptions of Schoenberg and of Stravinsky than Babbitt showed himself to be, and I was, whatever else, purely elated to be listening again to serious words about music, and more generally about modernism, let alone ones that I found groundbreaking.

Babbitt meant to put me at my ease, or perhaps on my guard, by saying as part of his initial greeting, something like, "I've just come from the annual meeting of the ISCM [is that right? meaning International Society for Contemporary Music]. Roger [Sessions] was there of course and he told your broken English horn story to every composer in Europe." I wouldn't have known the proportions in what I felt of surprise and excitement and embarrassment, nothing unexpected under the circumstances. I stop over this because it is yet another instance of the Saint Matthew Effect, or part of a double instance. When the next year Babbitt heard that I was being put up to the Society of Fellows (I never asked him from whom he heard it; he obviously had communication with the winds) he suggested that I ask Sessions to write for me, since, he added, unimpeachable evidence from another field is just to the Society's taste.

May 12, 2004

This Austrian summer would contain Lowell's first nervous collapse, or the first one widely reported, anyway the one I was exposed to. It is registered in an early entry in Lowell's poetic departure in his subsequent *Life Stories*, about the psychiatric ward in a Munich hospital to which we learned Lowell was suddenly one night transported from the Schloss. Prominent rumors coming to us about its cause were that his mother had died and that he had attempted to run away with a young woman. My personal evidence of some mania came from his having appeared some days earlier in a pent, disheveled state, returning to the Schloss late one afternoon, shouting out my name as he caught sight of me down one of the echoing stone corridors on an upper floor. He had what turned out to be a Bible in his outstretched hands and approached me (he was accompanied by someone, I have forgotten by whom, it was not his wife Elizabeth) saying, "I spent the day in Berchtesgaden. Hitler was a great man, a genius. You are my true Jew. Read this passage and tell us what it means." He was pointing to an early chapter in Romans in which Paul asks what advantage the Jews have, what the profit is of circumcision. My eye fell on the passage asking (I look it up again): "Is God unrighteous who taketh vengeance? (I speak as a man.) God forbid." The strength of Lowell's mood frightened me. What he was saying was awful. But I could not reply in this way to him, nor patronize him by dismissing the moment. I felt that unless I wished to shame him and send him to hell I had to respond to the passage out of my sense of his mood.

"Well," I stalled, but said honestly, "I like Paul's confession or caution in saying that he speaks as a man, that is, in unrighteousness as he speculates about God's unrighteousness. He is talking about the fact that Jews and Christians are all sinners. But what is God to forbid? Is Paul forbidding us to say something that would curse God? Or is he saying that only God can forbid God from unrighteousness? Only God could forbid his own existence. We can only pray that he forbid our speech from cursing God. As Saint Matthew says, our words condemn us." I've probably cleaned this up a little, but I have no doubt about the passage Lowell shoved at me, nor about the budget of words I used (this is not the first time I have gone back to this arresting moment in my life, but the first time in many years), beginning with the confusion about whether the passage is about God's self-absorption or about human fallenness. And the passage from Saint Matthew about our words condemning us had been a touchstone for me of what I wanted philosophy to be able to respond to; it would become an epigraph for the section on moral philosophy in my *Claim of Reason*. Lowell's response was to give a laugh I had heard from him before, hard and brief, as much an expression of pain as pleasure, and, declaring that I was his Jewish genius, he took back his Bible and walked away.

Some fifty-two years later, the year dating this present entry, standing in the entrance hall of our town's (Brookline's) public library, leafing through the published volume of letters produced by the friendship of Hannah Arendt and Mary McCarthy, a volume that had caught my eye on a display table, I came upon Arendt's description of a spookily similar segment of a scene with Lowell at a cocktail party in New York in the early 1970s, declaring to her that Hitler was a great man. She tells the moment as one she had been through with Lowell before, since she writes to McCarthy something like, "I no longer felt I could laugh this off. He needs to stop." Lowell's mood seemed to me, as conveyed by Arendt, to have been tamer by then, as if he suspected he was repeating an old turn.

The first spring after I had returned from Berkeley to teach at Harvard, eleven years after the summer of 1952 in Salzburg, a new Junior Fellow taking meals in Adams House, where I was living again my first years back in Cambridge, told me that Cal Lowell (the name the young man used, implying being in the know if perhaps not exactly in the acquaintance) was teaching at Harvard that term and that he had accepted this young man's invitation to come to the Society of Fellows for dinner, and Lowell requested in response that I be asked to join them. I had seen the Lowells two or three times in the early years back from Salzburg, but not at all recently. I was glad to accept, but because I was still an obsessional preparer of lectures, especially for a new large class, which met on Tuesdays and Thursdays (the Society's dinners were on Monday nights), I said I would skip dinner, which inspired polite and public exchanges, and come over around nine o'clock to join in talking specifically with Lowell and whomever he would be having drinks with in the sitting room after the meal. He was pretty well encircled when I arrived, and a prominent place was courteously made for me. Lowell seemed to be somewhat subdued, anyway not holding the floor. The only topic I recall from that conversation was Lowell's asking me to describe the Institute for Advanced Study where, on being asked for my recent whereabouts, I said I had spent the year between moving from Berkeley and installing myself back at Harvard, and asked me particularly to say what I thought of Robert Oppenheimer, then the Director of the Institute. I remember replying with a vignette of the first of the two occasions on which I had met this legendary, bewilderingly intelligent and self-conscious man. When, as Director, he asked how I was finding the place, and I replied, instead of giving a routine answer to a routine question—out of some cosmically misguided notion of attempting to amuse him, or just get a rise out of him—that I was interested to see during lunch in the Institute's dining hall, even in a superlatively gifted company, that the scientists were on one side of the room, perpetually in raucous conversation, whereas the smaller group of humanists and historians, on the other side of the room, whose business ought to be to further conversation, seemed to be searching desultorily for a topic they had not already been over. While this was not much of an exaggeration, Oppenheimer's only response was to deny that it was typical and to move on, leaving me to deal with the knowledge that the Princeton Institute and I had not fallen in love. After no more than an hour I excused myself to Lowell and his young admirers with whatever self-mockery seemed appropriate for one who had been lecturing for some years and yet took each instance so hard, and departed with a reasonably easy feeling. The next day the young man who had extended the invitation to me on Lowell's behalf came over to me at lunchtime in the Adams House dining hall, at which I had just arrived back from giving the lecture whose preparation I had interrupted to visit with Lowell, and when I inquired how long the conversation had gone on last night, he replied: "A while. When you left, Lowell said about you: 'He's a nice fellow. But I think he's a little crazy.'" I was quite touched by this impression, perhaps by some lingering intimacy of feeling it seemed to me to suggest.

May 13, 2004

A day or two before the seminar was to conclude in Salzburg, the Europeans and the faculty departed the morning after a celebratory dinner while we American students stayed on to help with cleaning up and to share initial impressions of the summer. The American couple who were the directors of the seminar, together with the current so-called European director (an American, having graduated a few years earlier from Harvard) who was resigning his position to return to the States and enter law school, found an occasion to ask me whether I would consider taking over as European director of the seminar, committing myself to at least two years, to begin as soon as I could manage. The current European director (perhaps he was the first, since the seminar could hardly have become well organized much before 1950) had in the past week, at various moments, described to me bits of his unobvious duties, those extending beyond his tending to the business of supervising the staff and accommodating the guests during the weeks the summer program was in session. He had during his tenure lived throughout the year in the Schloss, with a skeleton staff to keep it going and provide meals, making perhaps one or two short visits to the States, overseeing the ongoing work on the building and grounds of the Schloss, but principally participating in selecting the next summer's faculty, and traveling throughout Europe to interview lists of prospective students from whom to select those to be invited for the following summer, and planning programs not only for succeeding summers, but ones that may make further use of the extraordinary facilities of the palace for other portions of the year. He found that, except for a climax of traveling and interviewing during the late winter months, much of each day, beyond the featured summer session, was relatively free, and one's needs were excellently taken care of by the staff remaining in the Schloss.

Here was a choice of a new order for me. It called me on a pair of my related bluffs, or called on me to learn whether I was bluffing, and where. How serious was I about the pain of my lack of cultivation, of awkwardness with languages and too superficial a knowledge of their literatures? And how serious was I about finding a voice in philosophy? The immediate difference is that philosophy cannot be done alone, anyway not arrived at alone, anyway not, having arrived at it, taken to a methodical place alone. I was far from advanced on any discernible such path, but I had devoted four years, the last one a stretch of punishing renunciation and spiritual narrowing, to getting to the foothills of the discipline. If I did not return to Harvard now to use the freedom to follow my philosophical instincts where they led, I most probably would never find them out. If, oppositely, I chose partial metamorphosis into a European cultivation, my contribution to it, I feared, in the absence of a philosophical voice, would remain that of a visitor, not even an ambassador. I had met such visitors to intellectual life stranded at Harvard. But could there be a more perfect circumstance than the position at Salzburg offered from which to sort this out? This circumstance may, put otherwise, present a chance to give more attention to what I was characterizing as superficial knowledge and spiritual narrowing—to turn to the unfinished business I have left whenever I have left some town. But of course there is the possibility that Europe would merely present a new set of towns more perfectly suited as distractions from my distraction. What is the role of the idea that I have more than once formulated as something that requires no examination, namely, that a good plan is one in which I do not have to ask for anything, to place no demands, above all to create no new expectations? What would it mean to have been ruined for love? Or by it?

But by the next day I knew the circumstance was not for me, that I was not interested in the tasks of organization I would be asked to undertake, and that the kind of continuous time I needed to answer the questions on my mind would not in reality be available in the fantasied mornings and twilights on the terrace of a Schloss on a lake near a famous town out of season (but even now I see I have listed the terms so as to express my attraction to them). And by the time my plane arrived in New York ten days later (a return ticket produced, after indications of hopelessness, by a travel agent in Paris, a resourceful young English woman, whom I, having acquired the first stirrings of *savoir vivre*, invited to dinner and the theater—it was a performance of Beckett's *Godot*) I seemed to have understood that my consciousness of my choice not to remain in Europe was sealed by the sense that a new dawn for me had, if ever, to happen in America, as it stood, for all the stiffness and forbiddingness I felt in its philosophical dispensation. That the dispensation was not mine was perhaps itself what there is to make mine. That will mean placing a demand, or as certain Americans had otherwise put the matter a couple of generations before my father arrived hereabouts, staking a claim.

May 14, 2004

Two days ago I received the edited manuscript copy of my contributions to *Contending with Stanley Cavell*, a volume of responses to a range of my work, with replies from me, edited by Russell Goodman. It puts me in mind that it took twenty years from the time I published my first book, *Must We Mean What We Say?* in 1969, for me to begin to learn in print of reactions to its essays, apart from one early, brutal dismissal of the opening two, and of ordinary language philosophy generally, before they had been collected into that volume. It was fascinating, and greatly heartening, to learn in 1989, in the first collection of responses to my work, specifically in an essay by Richard Wheeler, in *The Senses of Stanley Cavell*, edited by Richard Fleming and Michael Payne, that my essay on *King Lear* in that first volume of mine had been discovered almost at once by certain graduate students in English departments, indeed formed a basis for discussion among them in considering certain departures in reading Shakespeare more generally, just the sort of response I had craved and wanted to participate in; but it at the same renewed a pang of disappointment that its words for so long struck its readers as unusable publicly. (No wonder, I think to myself in the mood of that discovery of earlier response, that I could not put aside the motivation to articulate why Austin's theory of the performative utterance struck me as leaving out half the world of responses to the demands, and the presumptions, of one's utterances, those I will lately come to call passionate utterances, in contrast with performative utterances where successes and failures are well defined. You characteristically know clearly, even immediately, whether your declaration of a promise or your warning or your acceptance of an offer of marriage has taken effect, something easy to imagine remaining doubtful about your expressions of love or anger or irony.) I knew that the work I did was better than its (non)reception, and friends permit you to harbor such knowledge rationally.

What precisely friends cannot do is prove that you have made yourself comprehensible to strangers. Is this what I want of writing, that it make friends of strangers and strangers of friends, modifying needless distances and needy intimacies? But how do such presumptions fit with the business of being a professor of philosophy, whose instruction I believe neither to be exactly in that of a science nor in that of an art, however close to either of these one might take philosophy to be? What is the source of philosophy's authority, meant to challenge claims to authority?

I once described the Chopin études as demonstrating that there is no preparation for art that is not already art. Can I say that there is no preparation for philosophy that is not already philosophy? In the case of art, this may be said to a student dealing in fact or imagination with a commitment to one of the great arts. And in that case it is more or less obvious how such a commitment might manifest itself in practice. So a teacher might question its strength in a student. What does a commitment to philosophy look like? With what right, out of what need, might or should a teacher question it?

Now with the passing of another fifteen years and learning of further significant receptions of writing of mine by circles of strangers, it from time to time appears that I have outslept Rip Van Winkle, and, reversing his experience, have awakened to discover that a surprising number recognize me and know where I have been. There are now roughly as many books about my work as there are books of my work. I am glad for this change, and for having lived to see it, but I find I do not know how to take it for granted. I have to resist the temptation to interpret the change rather than to respond to its specific claims. (Returning to this point in editing, in early 2007, I note that the figure of Rip Van Winkle serves to repeat my observation of a lapse of twenty years in learning that something of mine had been read strongly but without inspiring an impulse to make the appreciation public. Several weeks ago at a small conference lasting two days, called to consider the present state and sense of film theory, an Italian film scholar, Francesco Casetti, whose interventions during our discussions I found unfailingly impressive, in an interval before the last of our four sessions remarked to me: "You may not know it but your work is now quite well accepted in Italy. It has taken twenty years for the pertinence of what you do to show itself, to become usable. Now it is needed." I replied that even at my age of eighty I find that I am buoyed to hear this rather than chagrined not to have more time in which to gather inspiration from the fact of it. But I do not understand what the difficulty has been, given the implication that some difficulty has been overcome. If I say that to understand it would mean to understand the causes and paces of intellectual and artistic and political fashion, and to counter fashion intellectually and artistically and perhaps politically, what perspective might I have or claim from which to identify and measure the costs of fashion?

In replying to the essays in the *Contending with Stanley Cavell* volume, I took occasions for insisting on philosophy, of a certain motivation, as tapping the willingness to start again, to go back over one's expressions, leaving nothing standing, or perhaps, as Emerson puts the matter, always just approaching America, these bleak rocks he says, embracing the purity of poverty (with little history of philosophy, and little art of one's own). I have repeatedly spoken in these autobiographical pages of my sense of having to begin again, expressed as the way to an education, to understand what I am meant to do, to find a path, however crooked or unpredicted. This can be a little easy to say. If such things were well said, would they mean that I had already been leading a philosophical life? But that is probably first, or second, among the claims one can never seriously make (like claiming to be morally more competent than another, or closer to the truth). What I can say on my behalf is that I have shown a greater than normal, no doubt sometimes dangerous, willingness to risk the collapse of a project, even of something like a life's work (at least when the life was comparatively or arguably young), when I have known that I have been impressed by a possibility to the point of speechlessness.

It of course cannot be known in advance whether this willingness for change comes in a given instance from self-distrust or from self-trust. (As Emerson, again, puts the matter, more or less: Who in such cases is doing the trusting, and who is the trustee?) I discarded what might have been the first half of a dissertation in the face of Austin's visit to Harvard for the spring term of 1955; from Thompson Clarke's lectures two years later at Berkeley, I knew that I must go beyond Austin's practice by showing that an acceptance of Austin's work provides simultaneously an authentication of the possibility, as well as a rejection of the stability, of skepticism; eventually Wittgenstein's *Philosophical Investigations* will demonstrate, to my mind, that such an idea has to show itself essentially in every sentence of philosophy (even when any given sentence may show no sign of being philosophical); and Heidegger's recasting, or theorization of the ordinary, in *Being and Time*, will emphasize for me how little conceptual attention either Austin or Wittgenstein gives to what each invokes as ordinary or everyday in language or in life. Each such step threatened to drain conviction from whatever I had managed to compose so far, unless it could be found to be implicated already in what I cared about most in what I had done.

Whatever misfortunes entered into my having had to wait until I was just past thirty years old before beginning to complete pieces of philosophical work I was glad to live with (the opening essays, including the title essay, of *Must We Mean What We Say?*), the compensating deliverance of better luck would be that I have not since then felt simply dismissive of any substantial piece of what I have done—not, of course, that I fail to know the travails of false starts, or fail to wish fervently that much of what I have called finished, and published, were not better than it is. But I still find manifest in it, in enough of it, a drift or thread of ambition and patience that (even when I for a while lose the thread) allows me to recall its intention and to keep to my hand material for a truer effort. The standing threat to my conviction in professional philosophy (leaving aside certain works of religious thought) is always the presence of literary works (and philosophy's suspicion of them) that show a grasp of the relation of my life to the lives of others that strikes beyond most of what is called philosophy seems to allow itself to know. I am not willing just to say that Shakespeare, Racine, Dickens, George Eliot, Ibsen, Proust, Kafka, and so on evidently know intuitively what philosophy responds to conceptually. These writers also evidently respond conceptually. Contrariwise, while philosophy too often does not

respond at all, it sometimes registers the intuitive with signature per-
manence, as in Kant: "Human reason has this peculiar fate that in one
species of its knowledge it is burdened by questions which, as prescribed
by the very nature of reason itself, it is not able to ignore, but which,
as transcending all its powers, it is also not able to answer." For me the
ancient contest between philosophy and art, as companions and guides
to the soul, continues, if sometimes only conspicuously to weather.

May 15, 2004

Taking up studies for the second graduate year at Harvard on returning from Salzburg and Paris, I became, along with Marshall and
others in our group who had passed the qualifying exams, a Teaching
Fellow in the department's contribution to Harvard's General Education program, its version of a collegewide core of courses that served
as a sort of distribution requirement over the fields of the humanities
and social sciences and natural sciences. The course was, in Harvard
lingo, Hum 5 (pronounced as it looks), initiated by Aiken and White
with the title "Ideas of Man and the World in Western Thought." Here
I came to sense the possibilities, the potencies, of a course given for
several hundred Harvard students each year over a number of years,
and, in my discussions with students, in and out of our scheduled section meetings, to feel the force of individual and joint ambition in those
whose success has assured, or demanded, further success, often of a
kind in which social and intellectual accomplishments inspire each other. I would learn more about this in coming years, sad things as well as
happy things, but its first brush, for this country cousin, still parched
within sight of the fountain of culture, was absorbing and often painful. I learned from it forcibly that I was not ready to teach philosophy,
but I also learned that, in trying to guide discussions, I would have my
best pedagogical successes when I could combine a response that was
about the internals of an argument together with the externals of a text.
(I speak as a man.) I found myself, for example, wanting to talk about
why Descartes opens his Meditations with a surprisingly long introductory passage describing his mood as he warms to his work. I do not recall that I had anything very interesting to say about this, but it helped

create attention to, and to prepare for surprises in, the specifics of the text. The question of philosophy's beginning, or say, origin, had not yet become for me graspably essential to the question of philosophy itself.

I had learned during my first year at Harvard that there was a study group of graduate students, under the aegis of John Wild, who resigned from the faculty of the Harvard philosophy department a year or two later, working through *Sein und Zeit* mostly by preparing a translation of it, a very reasonable way of studying it. Marilyn—another friend who had decided long before I knew of it, not to attempt the prelims, and indeed left the Harvard philosophy program—showed me some pages of the translation. I thought I felt something of the attraction she felt in it. My response however, or therefore, was to say something like (I compress my feeling over several conversations about the issue): "It is too soon. If this convinces you, you will have skipped over what is unyielding in analytical philosophy, which can actually be learned here and now at Harvard; what you chance, or ensure, is that you will wind up able to use neither." I am not deaf to the stuffy self-protectiveness of this response. And I too had felt the pull as well as the untimeliness in having started recently to read Kierkegaard's *Fear and Trembling*, though here the sense of attraction was not tentative but insistent. Also I felt abandoned by this deep and admirable friend, sharing interests of mine otherwise largely, certainly officially, unshared, who had decided, on grounds not unfamiliar to me, that preparing for the Harvard Ph.D. examinations was destructive, immeasurably so. I hoped my difference was that by immeasurably destructive I could choose not to mean irretrievably so, but just literally unknowably so. Alarming enough.

On returning to Harvard the second year, I moved into one of the two older Harvard graduate dormitories, Conant Hall, across Oxford Street from the set of structures into which I had been safely installed for room and board my penitential first year. My new, or rather my now old, room was easily twice the size of the former one, and equally charmless, or say, unleavened. But by now, and after Salzburg, I began to find these enforced, organizing circumstances of life arbitrary and needless. Yet, as with other early still reasonably youthful scenes of mild discomfort and disorientation, life in that ancient dormitory presents itself with leavening memories. For example, unlike the set of modern dormitories I had begun in, this one actually contained a working telephone, a pay phone box set adjacent to the exact center of Conant Hall's brick box of rooms, at the side of the central stairway on the second of the building's three floors. Whenever that phone rang—not particularly often without some specific expectation, but often enough lasting through perhaps four rings so that some altruistic soul whose room was relatively near the center would answer and then shriek once the name of the desired recipient, await for a canonical few seconds a responding shriek back of thanks, then, depending on the result, leave the receiver hanging free or else apologize and ring off. At this distance the name I remember hearing shrieked most often that year was "Rosovsky," borne by the very man who at Harvard became a greatly influential Dean of the Faculty and whose name is now borne by a distinguished new building at Harvard, providing the Center for Harvard–Radcliffe Hillel. What makes this one sort of Harvard story I am interested to tell is not the simple, historical fact of Harvard's name to attract endowment and confer honor and distinction—those who have spent some time in these precincts have known cases of an undergraduate who has, or could have, lived in a Harvard House bearing his name, because of the name of one of his ancestors. But in this recent case ancestral tradition is not in question and distinction is not exchanged for wealth but earned by incontestably distinguished service. I spent most of my teaching life in Emerson Hall, and while the man himself whose name the building bears never walked those particular corridors his full-bodied brass simulacrum is comfortably seated there, and it has come to matter to me that he and Thoreau had both spent their college years housed two paths from where its doors stand and that among the more personal ironies of history I relish is the imagination of Emerson's capacity to withstand with patience (a critical virtue preached by Emerson) the periods of his name's silence on the inside of this sometimes unthinking, not to say forgetful, memorial.

It was during the fall of the year after returning from my introduction to Europe that I was told I was to be nominated (in Harvard lingo, "to be put up") for a Junior Fellowship in the Society of Fellows. The selection procedure was objectively perhaps no more onerous than applying nowadays for an assistant professorship—soliciting letters of recommendation, submitting work, thinking obsessively about how to present yourself and your plans if you make it far enough through the procedure to be granted an interview. Differences are that here, with respect to the Society of Fellows, you are filled with the consciousness of being still a student, facing eight or nine Senior Fellows whose position as such bespeaks eminence, and at that stage (at mine, at any rate) in the humanities your work and your plans can hardly speak for themselves. Moreover you are asking not for a job, to which you can promise responsibility, but for the moon—put otherwise, for an infinite span of freedom, called three uninterrupted years, in which to prove yourself to be practically promising.

Of the various causes there are for gratitude in being favored by Harvard, none in my experience is more decisive than its effect on a formally uneducated immigrant father. Whatever my father's images of the mysterious life of a university may have been (a favorite characterization my father enjoyed conferring was to note that the son or daughter of a relative or friend of his was a "college graduate," a title whose second word rhymed with "great"), he had some uncontrolled idea of what the name Harvard meant, and from the time Harvard conferred an honor on me so celestial that neither he nor his professionally educated nephews could fathom what election to the Society of Fellows might further betoken, he no longer questioned my decisions for myself. I had moved beyond judgment. My mother's view was, as usual, that there was no cause for surprise, that here was merely one more instance, or sign, of something she had always known I deserved. I say again: It's a mad world, my masters.—I speak as a child.

May 16, 2004

Teaching sections, and desultorily reading with an eye to searching for a dissertation topic, then after two or three months beginning to prepare for the application to the Society of Fellows while at the same time doing what I could to be realistic about it, which principally was to imagine life the next year proceeding without it (something had better be quite manageable, allowing time to push ahead with dissertation work), I recognized that for the first time since my first years as an undergraduate at Berkeley, eight years earlier, I had no standing plans to migrate. I might actually try finding a place to inhabit, one to look forward to being in, to returning to, to inviting people to. This idea was either fulfilled, or displaced, by the award of the Junior Fellowship, which among its luxuries included (for unmarried Fellows) residence for the three years of its running in a suite of rooms in one of the Harvard residential Houses. At a celebratory dinner in the meeting rooms of the Society of Fellows that had been designed for incorporation in the ground floor near the main entrance of Eliot House at the time Harvard received the bequest that enabled it in the early 1930s to build housing for its entire undergraduate body (resulting in a system of six of these brick so-called Houses, later expanded to eight), I had become acquainted with a Junior Fellow in his third and final year who proposed that I look at his suite in Adams House, which he would be vacating at the end of June, and which he had furnished quite comfortably and reasonably. Since his wedding was scheduled to coincide with that move, he was leaving those possessions behind, and if I liked them I could buy them for the hundred dollars they had cost him, hence simply take possession of the place by accepting the key and walking in.

Accordingly, soon to turn twenty-seven, in the summer of 1953, I moved into a set of rooms whose position and whose accoutrements, whose sounds and space, left nothing of its kind for me to desire. I do not mean that I would have chosen it over innumerable other comparable dwellings, but simply that I had chosen it, and the choice made conceivable alternatives irrelevant. My consciousness was, to this extent, now at rest. For the first time since leaving Berkeley six years earlier, the dogs of immigrant depression and compensation, and of the isolation of unexpressed talent, were for the moment stilled, undisturbed even by the guilt of the promise of a life inconceivable to my father, one allowing, even encouraging, the freedom to explore my own thoughts, to live unhounded from outside. Three years of liberation from the gravity of earning money, from appointments and assignments and justifications, was an eternity. The older Junior Fellows would at the beginning of the year, at Monday dinners, joke about such feelings, which they knew to be common, saying that the first year would pass without notice, and that by the beginning of the second you would realize that your tenure was nearly over. What is true is that nothing I did that first year was what I was doing.

What I did was to read almost at random—warhorse novels I

had not been through (of Melville, Dostoevsky, Stendhal, Balzac, etc.), general history, poetry, providing myself with elements of what I imagined to be the normal growing up I had missed. I audited a seminar in Dante taught by Charles Singleton, art history courses taught by Millard Meiss, later of the Princeton Institute (already sensing that I would wish to take the option of spending my third year of the fellowship in Europe), and wrote stories and poetry. I did not avoid philosophy entirely, but the material continuing to come out of Oxford, which dominated much of the discussions among the graduate students whom I felt closest to, while interesting, even indispensable, did not thrill me, and the Wittgenstein study group, prompted by the publication of the English translation of *Philosophical Investigations*, which met for a while in my rooms, excellently led by Paul Ziff, who was recently appointed as Assistant Professor at Harvard, did not convince me that the oscillation of blandness and fascination in Wittgenstein's later work was likely to take me further than the writing of John Dewey had done. These are things I did that year.

What these doings were driving at is difficult to describe. I think of it now as the reverse of the way I described, a month or so ago in these pages, my life in New York after Berkeley, namely, as molting, and more specifically mourning the vanishing of a life of music. In Adams House, on the contrary, I was now less undoing false or halfhearted entanglements than tying my little boat to the world, without particularly considering how it had been set adrift, or preserved me. I had come upon a settlement in which one might walk and explore with some pleasure and purpose.

With the first installment of my fellowship stipend, I bought a sports jacket from J. Press and Co. that, passing the store's windows three times a week on the walk from Emerson Hall or Adams House to Eliot House for a meal at the Society of Fellows, I had picked out as exactly the one I wanted, not the one I thought I could afford, or ask for, but the one that, on further examination of the racks inside, was self-evidently the most beautiful garment in the store, or in any store. It cost fifty dollars, something like twice the price of any single piece of clothing I remembered ever purchasing. I felt daring to the point of wickedness. It was made of a tweed woven of black and brown threads, as soft and subtle as Satan. I was providing myself with, I was authorizing myself to provide, in view of reaching a new season, new, indeed unprecedented feathers, a singing robe. Long after it was no longer patchable and wearable I would never bring myself to throw or to give it away. On some move across the country, accidentally or otherwise, it disappeared.

May 17, 2004

Protected by my institutional ratification, I became interested, rather than oppressed, by the expectations of my extended family. I was the youngest of the generation of my father's family at least one of whose parents bore the unmistakable accents of immigrancy. All the males of this generation I think of, except Harlan, some approaching the age of my mother, were successful dentists, or doctors, or lawyers, or businessmen. They had through my life made an exception of me, associated me with my mother's talent, which was mysterious but palpable to all, and expected that I would make a life of music that would redound to the credit of the family, in fact would (in one of my father's formulas) be a feather in their cap, add an artistic dimension to the family's achievements that the respectability of money and charity and social service could by themselves not fully bring about. But when it turned out that I had left Juilliard and evidently abandoned the idea of the fame and fortune music could win, in favor of the obscure profession of academic philosophy, Marvin and Irving in particular felt (no doubt justifiably) that they had known me, and had cared about me and my parents, long enough to ask how I could throw away what I had—had I not?—worked for all my life, just when I might have come into command of a significant career, in favor, to say the best for it, of a doubtful future. Mendel, whom I saw both the year I was in New York and afterward in Los Angeles, when he was traveling in his capacity as President of the American Association of Printers, was not completely surprised that I had turned aside from a life in music—given his own experience and that of his brother Meyer—but concerned that I was entering a dangerously undefined course of aspiration.

While I was myself confused, and without any real sense of how philosophy and soul-searching was going to lead to making a living—

given that teaching was not yet imaginable—I defended myself privately and quite easily by recognizing their views of music and success
as locked into philistinism. But when I had at Harvard cause to see
something of actual and uncompromised success, tangible proof of its
reality, I took in more fully the magnitude of Irving and Marvin Goldstein's achievements, which were by no means to be calculated merely
in terms of worldly, external gains, extensive as these were—national
presidents of their Jewish Dental Fraternity, and as such founders, layers of the cornerstone, of the Dental Annex of Hadassah Hospital in
Jerusalem. They were before all such things ambitious to have made
themselves into notable practitioners of dental specialties. Marvin's
talent as an orthodontist had produced a sheaf of documents for his
files represented by a recent letter he took out to show me, along with
before-and-after photographs of a patient who had come to him with
a malformed mouth and jaw, during a time I had dropped by at his
invitation to see his new complex of offices on one of my trips to visit
my parents in Atlanta. The letter read roughly as follows, in painfully
drawn handwriting: "Dr. Marvin, you have saved my daughter's life.
You know I have no money. I will send you one dollar every week [perhaps it said specified every month] for the rest of my life. Yours Sincerely, ..." Was it bragging to show me the letter? A Hall of Fame
pitcher, Dizzy Dean, is reported to have said, "If you did it, it ain't
bragging." A questionable analysis, but it is true that if you did it you
have earned recognition for it and it deserves acknowledgment. And
it was obvious that Marvin valued that letter beyond the price of the
thousands of dollars he would have billed a patient of secure means for
the service he had rendered. But bragging was beside the point if I and
my cousins were intimates. In that case they were, even if impurely,
sharing the event. And the Goldstein family allowed itself, certainly
through the presence of my omnipresent aunt Ida, to assume intimacy
with their relations. On that basis, and out of the knowledge that Irving
and Marvin had been of help over the years to my father, I never felt
they were wholly wrong in their assumption of earned intimacy in my
case, even when I felt bullied by it.

My mother was familiarly sometimes bruised by such assumptions, though doubtless also glad for the relief from the burden of preparing, for example, Passover seders, Succoth decorations, the breaking of the Yom Kippur fast. My glad acquiescence to a certain familial surveillance grew with the years as I came to recognize the unyielding determination it took to establish a growing, honorable, prominent immigrant Jewish family within the texture of a Southern city. The Segals had not managed this texture of hardening, although they produced two notable individual successes in Mendel and in my mother. I felt I understood, and shared, a will for recognition based on real achievement, that was meant to redeem, to justify, the suffering and the perseverance of immigrant parents, beginning again and bringing up children in a strange land—redeem and justify them to the land and justify the land to these children's strange parents. If sometimes, even characteristically, the cost of such perseverance was an intrusive familiarity, and if for years I thought of myself as simply shrinking from it, I will eventually think of that remaining sole light on New Year's Eve, across the courtyard of the Harvard graduate dormitories, finally having extinguished itself, and I might then periodically soften, between pride and dismay, prepared to reconsider the transfigured costs and rewards of a family's expectations, whose violence had after all preserved their patched garments in a torn life.

It is true that, in turn, the generation of children born to members of my (second) generation sometimes seemed to bear such later, in a sense lighter, burdens less well than mine did; for some reason they cost them more, anyway differently. Their so-called advantages, and the satisfaction their parents took in providing them, were oppressive in an unfamiliar way. These children took their Americanness for granted, and what did their own parents suffer that required redemption? Their versions of enforced ambition, of substitute suffering, of not being understood by those who had no excuse for not understanding, caused perplexing derailments on unrealistically smooth tracks. It matters, of course, that this third generation came of age during the Vietnam War, when the worth of an American identity was under terrible questioning, of an intensity I suppose not reached since the Civil War and not approached again until the present era in Iraq.

Visiting my ailing father in Atlanta, I watched with him some of the broadcast of the 1968 Democratic National Convention. When the cameras switched from the convention hall and its expected crowds and speeches and interviews, to a scene of police at night chasing young men and women through a park and down dark streets, and beating them with clubs, he asked me what country this was happening in. It crossed my mind that he was half imagining that he was seeing Cossacks remembered from his youth in Zabludova. When I answered that it was happening in America, in Chicago, near the Democratic Convention, he stared further and soon began to weep.

But as I write now I learn that relations of mine who are members of the generation following mine, some with small children of their own, are discovering one another, numerously in California, beginning with Uncle Morris's (the senior pawnbroker) daughter's son and daughter, and with a son of one of Uncle Joe's (the rabbi to the prisoners at Federal Prison) son, and one of Harlan's (the waylaid opera singer) sons, and the two daughters of one of Aunt Ida's sons and a son and daughter of the other of her sons (both friends of my daughter Rachel's, now on the opposite end of the continent from that Western gathering)—this third generation not now setting out with professional credentials duly and dutifully acquired, but following interests in writing, composing, dancing, acting, and in social service for which money is not a substitute or a means, hence producing work inevitably intended for their society's enlightenment and succor, and who knows out of what silent command to compensate for their parents' dutifulness and conventionality?

For a long time I consoled myself for my shortcomings as a father (I am a drastically limited cook, overly protective, unable to swim, prone to self-absorption, and, in the case of my sons, old enough to be my children's grandfather) by telling myself that the demands I have placed upon myself to make my work my own has protected my children at least from the necessity of having to justify my life to me. My adorable older son tells me that I do not know the advanced forms such pressures can take. I reply that he does not recognize the pressures he places on his adorable younger brother.

May 18, 2004

It is my daughter Rachel's forty-seventh birthday. This is pertinent to my having reached, in the underlying chronological drift of this writing the spring of my third year as a graduate student at Harvard, the first of those supported by the Society of Fellows, when Marcia Schmid (eventually Rachel's mother) and I, Marcia having arrived that fall from California to begin graduate study in the Harvard department, were spending most of our time together. By the time summer came we had fairly clearly arrived at an understanding. Driving back an hour or so before dawn from a town along the shore—perhaps it was Revere—where we had heard that there was a roadside diner that still served delicious breakfasts all night, a rumor we could now testify to be perfectly true, Marcia suddenly asked me to pull over and stop the car along a stretch of beach reasonably lighted to the ocean's edge by lamps lining that accompanying stretch of the highway. As I obeyed, without a word she at once opened the door and left the car, ran between intermittent headlights across the road and onto the sand, and, stopping quickly to throw off her shoes and slip out of her dress, so that she was stripped to her underwear—reasonably passing in the dark for a bathing suit—she continued her run over the sand and into the water, plunging into an oncoming wave. I ran after her with no room in my mind for anything but this dazzling display, colored by the anxiety it was causing me. She was invisible for a long minute or two, and then reappeared swimming with another incoming swell, arose and walked toward me, with both hands sweeping her hair back from her face, laughing brilliantly. I am ready to say that it represented in my mind a kind of marriage declaration, both of us asking, both of us accepting it.

That the marriage, so superbly begun, did not last long, deserves a good explanation; I have, I think, nothing of the sort. It was not the case that something in the future replaced it. It fairly soon seemed to fall away of its own weight. It is my view that we were aware of this distancing early, knew that the adventure had somehow stolen from us, even before we left, a year later, for a year together in Europe. Nothing was the matter. We seemed to share everything, friendship, philosophy, music. No one could credibly have been said to know some cause why we should not be given to each other. Yet, if nameless, there was some impediment we could not admit. Our minds were not freely given. We would marry in order to deny that the affair was over. Yet that marriage produced a daughter without whom I cannot imagine what my life would have become. For example, without her I may well not have continued an academic career, and lost the heart for writing. I shall try to explain this when the drift of this narrative takes me back to teach in the philosophy department at Berkeley.

It was later in the summer in Cambridge after the sudden dive before dawn that I was diagnosed with mononucleosis and secondary hepatitis. The two weeks I spent in the Beth Israel Hospital included the arrival of Hurricane Carol, which struck Boston in late August 1954. My doctor assured me that I would fully recover on the condition that I obey his instructions about diet and about being physically cautious, and give myself two months of gradually increasing activity; otherwise I ran dire risks of permanent damage to my liver. Adams House was officially closed for the summer months, but a couple of tutors living in the House besides myself were given keys to the outer doors, and we continued to live in our rooms. As for coming and going, I was forbidden for two further weeks even to walk slowly the single flight of stairs to and from my suite. Learning this during my first days in the hospital, I suggested over the phone to my mother that she not come while I was in good hands in the hospital, but delay her visit so that she could help Marcia with arranging things, meals primarily, for the first weeks after I was released back to Adams House. The three of us mostly had a simply good time, interrupted by occasional spells of weakness and mild dizziness that came over me. Breakfast and lunch were no problem, needing no cooking. Coffee and sweets could be brought in from the café half a block up on Massachusetts Avenue, and almost elegant dinners for the three of us were ordered from Chez Dreyfus, then my favorite restaurant in Cambridge, brought to Adams House each night by Marcia and my mother walking the few blocks to fetch them. That the two women apparently grew reasonably easy and friendly with one another during this odd time of unthreatening emergency secured the sense that we were to become family.

May 19, 2004

As the fall of 1955 opened, I began reading and writing with more orientation toward a dissertation, thinking vaguely to use some new work on the philosophy of mind at Oxford to study the concept of action in Spinoza and in Kant. The opening issue for me was how one determined, in Kant's view, what *the* maxim of an action is—its subjective principle Kant calls it, which the categorical imperative, its attempted objective principle, is to generalize—out of the infinite number of things I can be said to be doing at any moment. The accompanying issue in Spinoza is that human action is not caused, say, not determined, as other physical events are caused. That fall, conversation around the philosophy building was often shaped by collections of papers from what seemed the unremittingly expanding group of accomplished and energetic philosophers teaching at Oxford. Quine had been invited there, and a number of notable Harvard philosophy graduate students had spent, or were planning to spend, a year studying there. Morton White's lectures that became *Toward Reunion in Philosophy*, dealing with much of this material, was the class that all the best and best known of the older graduate students were auditing in those months. They (we) tended to sit in the back row of the seats in the classroom. White referred to them (us) as murderers' row. Clearly enough his amused tone showed that he intended by his description that they were prepared to do away with him, not that they were scheduled to be executed. However amused it was, it accurately registered the civilized violence in philosophical exchange, familiarly alarming to visitors to the subject.

Tom Clarke had returned from a spell at Oxford, where he had gone to visit the English woman he would soon marry. Dreben, just returned from a year at Oxford, an old friend of Clarke's from Harvard undergraduate days and a classmate of his during their qualifying examinations, two or three years before mine, invited Clarke to a Monday night dinner at the Society of Fellows, and the three of us sat, among others, with Noam Chomsky and Marvin Minsky and John Hollander at one end of the semicircular dining table. Someone, for some reason, was prompted to ask Clarke how he had arranged his evidently sudden unofficial overseas visit with his draft board. Clarke replied that he hadn't bothered to ask or tell them, that he was only gone for a month or so. People knew where to find him. This produced a mild outbreak of laughter from the rest of our little group. I have forgotten which of us voiced what each of us felt: "No Jew would have dared."

The Oxford material, Ryle's work prominent in it, distinctly informed and furthered my interest in the concept of a human action, but even as I was writing or sketching numbers of paragraphs and pages that were meant to go into a dissertation, I was building up resistances against the material. It too often began seeming really to be, as a number of my friends thought it to be, just about words, although what dissatisfied me was less that possibility (which I did not predominantly or consistently feel) than a sense that it, or my use of it, was mechanical, that I was repeatedly arriving at conclusions that I already knew. I could not take myself by surprise; and, or therefore, I could not say whether I was losing faith in the pertinence of the ideas or losing interest in what I had to tell about them. Austin was due to spend the coming spring semester at Harvard as William James Lecturer, and while I was fascinated by the talent that had gone into his paper "Other Minds," the philosophical yield seemed to me unimpressive (it crossed my mind that I did not know how to study it), and his "A Plea for Excuses" had not yet been published.

A familiar criticism of Austin's paper "Other Minds" among my acquaintances—voiced as if it represented a fundamental, pervasive error in Austin's way of looking at words and things—was Austin's apparent claim that to say "I know" is to produce a performative (not descriptive) utterance. Hence he apparently implies roughly that, just as when I say "I promise" or "I bet," in appropriate circumstances, then "*eo ipso*" (an intensifier Austin liked using) it follows that I (*ipso facto*) promise or I bet, in the same way if I say "I know" then *eo ipso*, by that fact, it follows that I know. But surely ("surely" was another Oxford intensifier common among philosophers in those years) nothing could be more perfectly absurd as an account of what it is to know. Any theory leading to such a conclusion has repudiated itself. It did me no good to insist that Austin does not say that "I know" is performative, but says only that it is *similar* to "I promise" *in a specific respect*, namely, that just as saying that you promise takes a step, makes a commitment, beyond saying that you fully intend to, so saying that you know takes a step beyond saying that you are, for your part, absolutely sure. This insistence did me no good because I could not give sufficiently serious weight to this idea of a "step beyond," or commitment, in the case of knowing, a step that did not imply that I actually knew whatever I was moved to say I know.

What Austin clearly, to my mind, implies—and something I felt then but could not clearly say—is that the step beyond can be said to be the *same or sufficiently similar* step that is taken in the case of promising, on the ground (something Austin does say), namely, that *you give others your word*. I found *this* connection (this inner connection I might say) between claiming to know and making a promise striking, suggesting a way of looking at language that has become increasingly important to me. (Say that it reveals human speech to be radically, in each uttered word, ethical. Speaking, or failing to speak, to another is as subject to responsibility, say to further response, as touching, or failing to touch, another. To have muttered such a thing then would have seemed, well, literary.)

Reducing Austin's idea to the foolish proposal that "I know" claims, as it were, to bind the shared future as my promise binds part of my individual future, was an early indication that Austin seems fated to be received within the field of philosophy with chronically grudging and superficial regard. For all its supposed illumination, it failed to respond precisely to the ancient question that philosophy famously wants an answer to, namely, what it is to *know* something, to be justified in claiming you know (when "obviously you may 'always' be wrong"), and if in some region of our knowledge, namely, empirical knowledge as opposed to mathematical knowledge, you wish to say that we never know with certainty, never absolutely know, then to go on to say what justifies a lesser claim, say, a claim to believe with a high degree of confidence in the existence of the world. I was for myself convinced that Austin was right in finding something amiss with this ancient philosophical picture of knowing, roughly, as a state at the pinnacle of an increasing gradation of epistemological capacities, ranging from illusion at the bottom, and mounting through degrees of opinion and belief to the metaphysically unshakable at the cognitive top (Plato's picture of the Divided Line in *The Republic*). But I had little idea how to clarify my intuition that Austin's idea of the claim of knowledge as "going beyond" the cognitive accomplishments in being or making sure and certain was not to be *modeled* on the act of promising as going beyond expressing an intention, but was a separate interpretation of excess, say, of my stance toward my accomplishment, my stake in it, expressing authority toward it. Some ten years later I will be able to begin articulating this region "beyond" knowledge by taking into account the concept of acknowledgment. It seems—it was—a small advance, once it is taken.

What the advance required in my case was coming upon a way to make sense of the mysterious and grave events of *King Lear*.

And is it really, even before heavy examination, just foolish to understand the claim to know as binding the future? It binds me to whatever in the future I understand as actualizing or defeating my expectations. Suppose I say (attest) that I know the rope will hold, and then a bolt of lightning severs it. Was I wrong to attest to the rope's soundness, as I would have been wrong in saying so if I had failed to inspect the rope or failed to use the correct knot in securing it? I cannot avoid intellectual embarrassment by refusing ever to claim to know. Good intellectual manners ought equally to cause me equal embarrassment if I have refused the responsibility for authorizing the use of the rope (having inspected it): because of my hesitancy you took the greater risk of ordering the passengers into the other rowboat. Human conduct and thought are inherently vulnerable to embarrassment. I can no more take back the word I have given you and you have acted on than I can take back my touch. Each has entered our history. Apology and reparation may be entered into that history, but they are subject to acceptance, hence to rejection. I would learn how to think further about this from Austin's work on excuses, for which Austin expresses his indebtedness to Aristotle.

Because Austin's visit will have a radical effect on my finding my way to writing the first papers in philosophy that I cared about in a way I had until then awaited in vain, I do not want to say here less than I have said elsewhere about the effect his presence had upon me. So I shall excerpt a few passages, modifying them in a few places, from the brief memoir I composed about Austin at the invitation of the *Yale Review*, which published a collection of memoirs of various figures from various hands in 1987, calling them Encounters.

From the spring of the year 1955 that J. L. Austin spent teaching at Harvard I felt I had derived lines of a life's work ahead of me—at least so far as claims of the ordinary, projecting a mode of philosophical thinking of which Austin was the purest representative, would enter it. The purity was clear enough from his paper "Other Minds," a miniature encyclopedia of ordinary language concerns, and it was testified to by tales from those returning each year from Oxford about the weekly discussions Professor Austin held for the younger philosophy dons there. He was, for example, reported to have given over one discussion (of some two hours) entirely to the distinction between signing "Yours sincerely" and "Yours truly." But it took his presence for me to come to experience his inexhaustible interest in what he called, finely to my ear, the jump of words—an interest arising (I of course supposed) from an inexhaustible faith in the philosophical yield of the details of the language we share and that shares us, and yet a faith that also turned in directions perhaps opposed to his, namely, to help understand why philosophy seems so chronically, even necessarily, to distrust the ordinary. Like linguistics and poetry, Austin's philosophizing, I felt, allowed me—demanded of me I would say—the use of myself as the source of its evidence or the measure of its effect. Whatever philosophy's pertinence to me, I felt for the first time my pertinence to philosophy. I stopped looking for ways to leave the subject.

A year after Austin's semester at Harvard I returned to Berkeley to begin teaching, so it happened that I was present with Austin again during the other semester he spent in America, at Berkeley in 1959, the year before he died, not yet fifty. My memories of him are accordingly solely American.

I have had other teachers, as well as friends and students, with wider learning, or smarter powers of reasoning, or, depending upon how you measure it, greater creative sweep, but I have encountered no one with a clearer and more constant fastidiousness of mind joined with a respect for the vicissitudes of daily life—call it moral imagination. The thinkers I admire most have this joint power. Sometimes, I know, I prefer a manner of thinking that allows more of the darkness of its findings to appear than Austin's does. But I suppose darkness is nothing, or useless, apart from something of the lightness, the freedom of mind, that Austin demanded of himself and expected of his students. After I had "given up" (so I called it) music for philosophy, working in Austin's classes was the time for me in philosophy when the common rigors of exercise acquired the seriousness and playfulness—the continuous mutuality—that I had counted on in musical performance. This may have meant to me that what was happening in Austin's classes was not, as it lay, quite philosophy; but I was at the moment too happy with whatever it was to have cared. That Austin's practice had to do, in its own way, with the possession of an ear, was surely part of its attraction and authority for me.

Others found Austin cold. Of the legends that formed around him, a number had to do with a quality that might strike you as coldness, but perhaps rather as strictness, or perhaps reserve (an idea in need of consideration). Some of these concerned tales of a certain awe he had inspired by his work in army intelligence during the Second World War. But some were quite domestic. A younger colleague of Austin's visiting Harvard told me of a disappointment, even anguish, in recognizing a personal inability to interest Austin in any exchange between them, either concerning Austin's work or apart from it. But when this young colleague confessed her disappointment to a common, rather older, Oxford don, noting that she had been invited to Austin's farm only once, the astonished reply was, "You have actually been to Austin's farm?"

I experienced Austin's relentlessness over the course of falling attendance at his William James Lectures, on the performative utterance, published posthumously under the title *How to Do Things with Words*. How could it have dawned on so few a number—at the end of the twelve lectures there remained not more than one in twenty of the several hundred who had begun the course, or anyway who had come to the initial lecture—that something of decisive significance had been happening here? No doubt stretches of the hours were repetitious and boring, both in the event and sometimes in Austin's justifications of the event. But there are much more harmful forms and causes of reception, or lack of it, than occasional repetition and boredom.

I also experienced a version of the strictness. Already quite rapt with admiration for Austin, and already feeling some credit with him for my knack at producing examples that he found pertinent, I responded impatiently, during a discussion at lunch in Adams House with a circle of students, to a question concerning whether something must be common to things sharing a common name, saying, in effect, "If people want to say there are universals, let them. It doesn't matter as long as they know the facts." I was sitting next to Austin, and he turned toward me as if startled, and said hard, straight between the eyes, "It matters." I felt an utter, quite impersonal, shame—shame, and a kind of terror, as if before the sacred task of philosophy, for having been faithless to its calling. Whatever the values to be assessed in this ex-change, whatever the chances of illusion or romance, personal coldness is hardly the issue. How could mere coldness have lasted, have profited me, to this moment?

Rarely in a lifetime can one know intellectual gratitude of the kind I felt for Austin after his first seminar meeting on the subject of excuses. I left elated, as if I had been shown a route out of the realm of arbitrary, massive demands for consent, as if I were tasting intellec-tual liberty, my own intelligence, for the first time, perhaps the clearest time, or least encumbered with competitiveness or theater (which need not be encumbrances).

Sometimes I disliked Austin's handling of contention. Not even he could unfailingly get beyond the note of the personal, of fear produced from outside, as from mere force, and not from my sense that I am bound to know, that somehow one already knew. But to my mind there were moments in Austin's seminar of perfect spiritual tact, as on the day he deployed his stories to distinguish among excuses such as doing something mistakenly, accidentally, heedlessly, and so forth, when he distinguished among modifiers such as something's being just or simply or purely an accident (one, say, in which nothing further, or nothing more complex, is in play, or mixed in) and a mere or sheer accident (one to which you could be assigning undue significance, or one whose accidental quality is transparent). A student objected, claiming that "sheer" could not go with "transparent" because there is such a thing as sheer wool. Austin was taken by surprise, lifted his pipe from his mouth, and asked intently, "Is there? What is it?" The answer began immediately, but soon continued with a distinct ritardando to the end: "Well, it's a loose weave . . . that you can see . . . through." It was the sort of shocking moment, in the hilarity of its sheer self-imposed self-contradiction, that might cause conversion. Indeed it is my experience that the power of the philosophical appeal to ordinary language is only to be appreciated by an overcoming or overturning of resistance, call it conversion—an appreciation, I mean, at once of the apparent triviality of the appeal and of the radical revelation of its successes. Without now seeking to comprehend the state of the student who as it were could not for a spell let the word *sheer* modify her picture of what wool is, I recall the moment of Austin's response to the description, "Well, you can see through it." His eyes had been fixed wide with attention and were now almost closed, and wrinkled at the corners, the lips were pursed as if to keep from letting forth laughter; and the pipe came back up, the tip not quite to the mouth but to be punched lightly and repeatedly against the chin. Here was serious mirth in progress, and what I read as perfection was the projection of my utter faith, then and now, that the mirth was impersonal, that here a class had witnessed not the private defeat of an individual's experience but the public victory of sweet and shared words—mirth over the happy fact that the world is working out and that we are made for it. I suppose I again romanticize a moment. Then a form my gratitude to Austin takes is the power of such moments, and successors of them, to bear this romance.

Here I add a piece of learning on rehearsing this encounter again. I have wondered why it took Austin's presence, beyond reading his pages, for the essential brunt of his procedures to be taken up by me. Without dismissing such matters as his temperament (which in fact held no force or charm for various others I knew and cared about), I can say now that what I learned from his class was not to believe him but how to study him, and not him alone. It allowed me a sense of freedom that outlasted many false starts at separating what was permanent and what was impatient in his work.

May 20, 2004

Although the philosophy department at Berkeley had allowed me to postpone taking up my appointment there so that I could spend the third year of my Junior Fellowship traveling, I would perhaps, in another world, have found it reckless to leave for a year in Europe, filled with a sense of exhilarated intellectual destruction, knowing that I would return to an obligation to begin teaching philosophy full-time and moreover in the absence of a dissertation. Without even the rationality of considering the compromise of shortening the European tour by half, I evidently considered that I was well more than a year away from discovering a new dissertation, and that even to orient myself with what I had begun to learn, I had a long period of reading and thinking to go through, and that somehow that could be done while I visited every building and painting of significance in Western Europe (apart from which, I told myself, combining ignorance with anxiety, I would not wish to teach aesthetics, something Berkeley had requested of me).

Whether that trip was still on as planned, and even whether there was to be a wedding, was vaguely in doubt since Marcia had contracted a respiratory illness during that spring and moved back to her mother's house on the North Shore of Chicago for perhaps a month of convalescence. She had been there for something like six weeks before it occurred to me that she might not return unless I went there and intervened in whatever mood was being woven at that distance. It was quite clear when I arrived that her mother, who had recently married well (as a minor Jane Austen might still say)—after twenty-five years without a husband, having divorced Marcia's father so early and so thoroughly that Marcia had never met him—was now against Marcia's and my marrying. I had been under the impression that I had established reasonably cordial relations with her. Her charm was strong and available to her, and she was quite devoted to writing poetry, to both of which facts about her I responded with interest and pleasure. She was the daughter of Edgar Lee Masters, the author of *Spoon River Anthology*, a condition of her life that was usable both, but perhaps not always simultaneously, as an inspiration to her writing and as a cause for asserting social standing. The evening after I arrived, she chose the way of the social to demonstrate her displeasure, during a fairly formal dinner at her house, with enough guests to establish securely the formality. Obviously counting on its embarrassing me, she raised her glass and proposed a toast: "To Ike and Dick." Sitting beside me, Marcia's anger flared, protectively I felt, but unprotectedly: "How could you mother? You know I am a Democrat." One felt in the flatness of the rebuke an intimacy and power of feeling between these women, handsome and talented in similar ways, sharing both first and last names, having spent most of a life together unshared by, undiluted with, the presence of a man. I intervened in some hopeless attempt to retrieve the situation: "Dwight Eisenhower is a genuine American hero, and I gladly drink to him. I hope you can allow us to leave Richard Nixon out of this." Marcia senior's husband at once replied that this seemed agreeable and raised his glass. But Marcia junior slammed her napkin on the table and left the room. As I rushed to follow her out, it emerged that we were

headed out of the house. I flew back to Boston the next morning, and
Marcia followed a few days later. It was not clear until the last moment
that her mother would attend the wedding. The bond between mother
and daughter, however, prevailed in the end.

May 21, 2004

After the year driving across Western Europe, periodically stopping for a night or two, occasionally for most of a week, and in the cases
of Vienna and Florence and Rome most of a month each, I had in so-
ber fact seen a high fraction of the paintings and buildings to have received some specific mention in the marvelous Blue Guides of the 1950s
for Paris, and Vienna, and the Netherlands, and Northern Italy and
Rome (supplemented naturally by all the Gibbon that could be read in
a month of evenings), and in Florence (supplemented by Ruskin's *Mornings in Florence*), reading that caused me somehow a deeper tenderness
toward my ignorance through the exhilaration of being chastised by
Ruskin for failing to recognize *the* most beautiful among the sarcophagi
checkering the floor of Santa Maria Novella; and after Palladio in Vi-
cenza, Piero della Francesca in Arezzo, Giotto in Assisi, Mantegna in
Mantua, Venice (with Ruskin again of course), and Lucca (for respects
to Verdi) along the road to Pisa, eventually glad for time to rest, or at
least not travel, back in Milan. There, in addition to so many nights
at the opera or at recitals that the major prima donnas of the period
began repeating their appearances for us (Schwarzkopf, Gueden, St-
reich, Ludwig, Della Casa), we discovered, as an unlooked for bonus,
a small, recently opened museum that had hung enough paintings of
Guardi's and Canaletto's Venice to make forever palpable and interesting their differences. In traveling through Holland and Belgium we
must have slept in a different bed every night for at least ten days, after the succession of altarpieces and spotless museums in daylight. A
number of days had been spent gratefully following tips from Millard
Meiss's course in northern art I had audited the previous fall, namely,
that one should make the time and effort to drive around the circuit of
eighteenth-century pilgrimage churches in southern (Catholic) Germany (Vierzehnheiligen, Die Wies, etc.), which were preserved, dazzlingly

inventive in themselves as well as in contrast to other kindred monuments, precisely because they were meant to be to be walked to, built
outside cities and their factories, hence uninteresting to Allied bombers
a decade earlier. (We happened to coincide with the daughter of that
American art historian in, if memory serves, Vienna. She was spending her junior year in Europe, and we met in a coffee house she knew.
She was perfectly right to assume that she would be the guest, but the
ease with which she assumed that I would pay the bill made me feel
awkwardly old, hopelessly striving to catch up with what any sophomore may be leisurely preparing to know.) We decided to drive to Berlin, partly no doubt to experience for ourselves the monitored highway
we were told, correctly, that we would have almost to ourselves through
Russian-controlled territory, but also hoping at the end to attend the
Brecht theater. Its performances proved to be sold out during all the
time we could give, but we discovered the young Fischer-Dieskau there
appearing in *Don Carlos*. After our return to Munich there was German opera every night, then still staged at the Prinzregenten Theater,
awaiting the completion of the restoration of what bombs had done to
the city's opera house.

In 1955 the meticulous reconstruction of the Vienna Opera
House, bombed near the close (as I recall) of World War II, had opened,
or reopened, its doors with a performance of *Fidelio*, in a production an
instance of which we attended the following January. The year 1956
was the 200th anniversary of the birth of Mozart, who lived until 1791,
the year of old Kant's last major published book, *Religion Within the Limits of Reason Alone*. Looking out at the rows and stacks of glittering box
seats of the reborn opera house, I figured that in 1991 I will be, if I live,
sixty-five years old. What, as Kant asks, may we hope for? And what,
he also almost asked, may hope be crushed by, if reason fails? For the
coming year (I am now revising in 2005) there are, I learn from my
favorite concert music station, preparations under way for the 250th
anniversary next year of Mozart's birth. Is the world aging?—250 years
used to suggest Bach, the span between his death and the twentieth
century. Yet Mozart was born a mere six years after Bach died, which
is as mysterious as conceiving that Beethoven was an advanced twenty-
one years old when Mozart died, but then so, precisely, were Hegel and
Hölderlin and Wordsworth, the last of whom died within three years of

my paternal grandfather's birth near Bialystok (if it is true that in 1950 this one of my grandfathers, the one whom I knew well, and always called with the Yiddish title Zadie, died at the age of ninety-seven, a figure based, as the family has consistently done, on taking him to have been fifty when with his wife and seven children he arrived in America in 1904 or 1905). But the tricks of time, like the relative constancies of space, are increasingly of interest to me mostly as figures of distances from the ones carrying my investments of love, timelessly, presently. I am not sure I remember at the moment exactly how Rilke says that to live a human life is always to be taking leave. Does he note a point at which the waves of arrival and of departure look as alike as joy and grief?

May 22, 2004

The year in Europe was for me a siege of the kind of savage consumption, of intertwining ecstasy and boredom, desire and duty, adjoining my absorption into music as an undergraduate at Berkeley and afterward into theater and film in New York, whose attempt to fill deprivations or depredations of the ten years preceding Berkeley inevitably served at the same time to indicate the endlessness of its extent. A genuine practical purpose it served well, if not sometimes without ruefulness, was to prepare for the ensuing years of writing something like philosophy, which for me demanded long periods of voluntary renunciation of such pleasures. (Why or how did I understand philosophical speculation to "demand" renunciation? Of what? Primarily of pleasure or primarily of knowledge? As if the best that has been thought and known in the world is not to be trusted. At least not when it is repeated. And when it is not repeated?)

Within two weeks of our entering Europe, docking at Cherbourg and driving to Paris for an initial few days, we began the drive to Bad Reichenhall, a small Bavarian resort town where we will locate ourselves for six weeks studying German at the Goethe Institut and where we will learn that salt has been mined from Roman times, evidently the same deposit of salt commemorated in the name Salzburg, a few miles across the Austrian border. On a mild afternoon during our stay, perhaps it was touring on a weekend free of German classes to revisit the scenes of my youth in Salzburg (four years earlier), that we passed a column of U.S. troops heading out of Austria. We were on a two-lane road, and my memory is that we were driving, at significantly reduced speed, past units in the line of these American jeeps and troop trucks for the better part of an hour. We had heard that Occupation Forces were being withdrawn from Austria, and here was an enactment of the epilogue of orders that had been signed and obeyed, reversing the direction of uncountable orders that had been given and obeyed, and deaths exchanged, during a time just over a decade earlier.

On arriving at Bad Reichenhall, a place that seemed to have been hurriedly and completely constructed just weeks before, we had found with little trouble the apartment of a local couple in which we were assigned a room by the Goethe Institut. The only adornment on the white plaster walls of our small room was a photograph of an imposing man, handsome and young in his officer's uniform in, as the photograph informed us, 1936, still perfectly recognizable as a version of the heavier, still handsome, graying, vigorous, middle-aged man of few words who had helped us carry our bags up narrow new stairs to our room in his and his wife's apartment. The words *Legion Condor* were printed neatly at the center of the lower edge of the photograph. The picture was in itself evocative or provocative enough, even apart from the knowledge that I made precise only after our return to the States, that Legion Condor was the name of the German aviation unit Hitler sent to Spain in support of Franco, hence that nineteen years earlier our landlord had participated in the experimental air tactics responsible for the massacre at Guernica.

His sociable, voluble wife, short and rather plump, with whom we mostly dealt, had occasion several weeks later to perform the only cure of a cold I have ever experienced. After turning on the water heater at an unaccustomed time of evening, she drew a bath as hot as I could tolerate it, and when afterward I emerged in my pajamas, wrapped me in a heavy blanket and gave me a full tumbler of mulled wine to drink down. The idea was to sweat the cold out of me, and cautioning me not to put off the blankets all night, she covered with me another as I lay down under the increasing grip—unprecedented for me—of the quantity of wine as I drained the glass. In fact I awoke the next morning clear-headed. Evidently this was a version of what Louis Suskind was seeking when he went for a Turkish bath after a dinner party, still in his tuxedo. But I had been told that that was a way to recover from a hangover, a hard case to compare or compound with a tumbler of wine. That he died of pneumonia days later, according to my understanding of my landlady's theory, shared by my mother's telling me of Uncle Louis's death, came from the fact that no one had given him, or he had not heeded, any warning, or tip of good sense, to avoid walking out after a steam bath without a topcoat into a cool hour past midnight.

On the various occasions on which, over the two months, I would offer my landlady an American cigarette as I was about to take one from a pack I had produced from my pocket, she would invariably accept it, with a polite "Ich bin so frei" (Don't mind if I do) but more often than not, instead of going on to accept a light, she placed the cigarette in a dull silver case large enough to hold three or four cigarettes, saving them for some later time. Once when we had invited the pair for drinks in the neighboring beer hall, I found that, after paying for the drinks, I had run out of sufficient cash to serve for a tip. Seeing me searching my pockets, my landlady calmly advised: "Leave three of your cigarettes."

Part 9

May 25, 2004

Arriving at Berkeley to take up teaching in the fall of 1956, I recognized, not without a sense of foreboding, that something Freud might call a secondary gain in the exhaustively absorbing, diverting year in Europe had been that Marcia and I were not confronted with what the terms of our marriage had become. And the distraction was continued in the general business of settling into a stable existence back, as it were, home. Finding almost immediately an inviting small house near the top of what was aptly called Panoramic Way, I was soon free, or rather forced, to face the reality of preparing my eight lectures a week for my three fall classes.

Experiencing the panorama of San Francisco Bay, facing every day of the year the region of sunset, with a view framing an unobstructed opening to the ocean's horizon, I would easily see the point of two early stories, or cautions, relayed to me by others of my generation who had completed their Ph.D. dissertations on the East Coast the previous two or three years and immediately joined the Berkeley faculty. One story was reported as from the avuncular chair of the English department: "You will have to resist the temptation of disappearing into a golden glow." The other story, from a senior professor of philosophy, was more precise: "There will be a moment a few years down the road when you will suppose you have exhausted the interest of the Bay area and you will have the strength to leave it. When that moment passes it does not return."

Preparation for the two weekly lectures on the history of philosophy came first, given that a group of three hundred to four hundred students was not a beast to toy with. Having taught a section in the humanities course in General Education at Harvard was a help, but the Berkeley group was far more mixed, in talent and preparation. There seemed to be roughly the same number of really apt students in both places, but not nearly the same number of simply well-prepared and interested students at Berkeley, where indeed it was expected that a fair number of students would fail the course (a phenomenon all but unheard of at Harvard, where poor performance was rather treated as a health issue), as if the first year at Berkeley, where admission was based in those years strictly on high school grades, served as a kind of entrance, or continuance, examination. Much of my own preparation in the material came from residues of my regime of studying for the qualifying examinations my first year at Harvard, and I wanted to be free to level with the group, to make explicit the impossibility of mastering all the material we would cover. I explicitly allowed the possibility of a student's dropping the responsibility for reading two of the eight or nine classical texts assigned for the course (with the exception of the Plato and the Aristotle and the Descartes and the Locke texts). My second course, on the first *Critique*, I modeled on C. I. Lewis's Kant course at Harvard (I knew of other former graduate students at Harvard who did the same thing), not anticipating the magnitude of motivating a group of several dozen souls to last through a term in which by its end each of those taking the course for credit would have submitted outlines of Kant's entire text. At something like the pace of forty-five pages a week for each of fifteen weeks (depending on where reasonable breaks came in the Kemp Smith translation), there were some casualties. But the value of being herded through the entire work was not lost on its survivors, including myself, although I have never been moved to repeat the experience.

The work I proposed for my spring term of classes was able to turn to interests closer to my current preoccupations, one course requiring three weekly lectures on contemporary philosophy, where I featured the work of Austin (something I understood not yet to have been introduced to students at Berkeley), which at that stage meant centrally his encyclopedic essay "Other Minds," supplemented by using my notes from Austin's "Excuses" seminar a year and a half earlier at Harvard and from his public lectures "How to Do Things with Words" (on the performative utterance). A foil I adduced for Austin (apart, of course, from his own immediate foils, notably A. J. Ayer's *The Foundations of Empirical Knowledge*), were the chapters on empirical knowledge in C. I. Lewis's *An Analysis of Knowledge and Valuation*, a widely admired book during my years at Harvard, concentrating most particularly on the signal, flat, and consequential disagreement between Lewis and Austin as to whether objective judgments of the world are essentially to be understood as predictions of future experience, a thesis that Lewis held (along with logical positivism, a movement for which Lewis also otherwise expressed contempt in its treatment of moral judgment) and greatly elaborated, and that Austin deplored. Wittgenstein's *Philosophical Investigations* was still essentially a closed book to me.

I ended the term, and the year, without much confidence in my capacities as a teacher, but also without an unrelieved sense of disgrace, since I had spoken throughout the countless hours in the classroom essentially about texts I admired and about what I felt a reasonable human being concerned with the present state of professional philosophy in America might take a healthy interest in. My exhaustion had been such during the Christmas break at the end of the fall term that I petitioned the chair of the department, Stephen Pepper, for relief from one of the three courses scheduled for me for the spring term. I urged that developing six new courses in one year for students in a great university was not compatible with keeping one's self-respect, to say no more; and I am sure I found a way to suggest that since I was only the second appointment as an Assistant Professor to be hired at Berkeley for many years—actually I bore the title of Instructor because I had not received the Ph.D.—the senior professors had perhaps romanticized the memory of what the initial years of teaching were like. In fact whatever it is I thought to say in support of my petition carried sufficiently with the senior members of the department that my immediate plea for relief was granted for the coming spring, and the schedule of courses was the following year officially reduced for assistant professors in the department from six to five a year (not yet to the four allowed to our seniors), with one of them a seminar.

I did not reveal a signal source of fervor in my presentation of the argument for relief beyond my simple inability to imagine beginning again to contemplate 120 lectures for the spring. (It would actually have been somewhat fewer, since one of the three courses for the second semester would have been a graduate seminar, in which I would lecture at most half of the weekly two hours.) I had about the sixth or seventh week of my initial term run into an intractable problem with the lecture for the large course, and instead of around midnight, which would give me time for two or three hours of sleep before preparing the Kant lecture, it had become dawn and I was still not finished with the first lecture. I lay down on my back on the floor of the living room (simultaneously my study) and staring at the ceiling began imagining what would happen if I simply did not appear in the auditorium of Dwinelle Hall at nine o'clock for my big lecture. There would be the conventional period of seven to ten minutes before the lecture was actually to begin, so until then nothing need seem amiss. How long would it take for one of the graduate assistants to take it upon himself to walk down the corridor to the philosophy department and make inquiries about my whereabouts? Would it be six minutes after the expected time of beginning? Nine minutes? Then will they will try to reach me here by phone?—which of course I shall not answer. Someone will be dispatched to my house to investigate. Perhaps an ambulance. I pictured a frustrated knock at my door. I felt reassured by the thought that they cannot *force* me to mount the large stage to give a lecture I did not have. But at that point I drew a blank about what would then happen as I continued, as surely I must, to avoid the campus for the rest of the semester. It must have been this thought, or blankness of thought, that shook me out of my reverie. I got up, organized the pages of the unfinished lecture, and put them aside. Then I tried making notes for the contemporary course, which proved more or less fruitless. A little before nine o'clock I phoned the philosophy office reporting that I was ill and was going to bed, that my classes for the day would have to be called off. And I went to sleep. Later that day the problem with the large lecture solved itself, and I was well on my way into the contemporary lecture. Time and the world stretched before me, mine to play with. But this cure could work only once.

The next term, in addition to the Austin seminar, I continued lectures in aesthetics by asking why it so often seems that philosophical treatments of the fact and of objects of art, as for example in Dewey's *Art as Experience*, which I had lectured on in the fall, were so often less interesting, philosophically and aesthetically, than the objects they were about, or than the significant criticism devoted to those objects, in books such as those of Eric Auerbach, of André Malraux, of Henry James's Prefaces to his novels, of Coleridge and Northrop Frye on Shakespeare. The results were perhaps not measurable, but we had read some wonderful, standard-setting material. Early sessions on Austin in the seminar on contemporary philosophy had created a sufficiently sustained degree of interest that I trusted its genuineness and suggested that we actually try practicing one of Austin's pieces of methodological advice and test for ourselves his claim that it is not prohibitively onerous to go entirely through a moderately sized dictionary with a specific task in mind. We divided up the letters of the alphabet more or less equitably among the members—but I do not remember which of two tasks it was that I proposed. Perhaps it was to check the disparity between Austin's guess, in his William James Lectures (the notes for which were published posthumously as *How to Do Things with Words*), a guess I relayed to the seminar, namely, that there are between 1,000 and 9,999 performative verbs in English, and the fact that in his last lecture he cited, as I gathered from my own notes, fewer than 100 (a figure confirmed in the posthumous publication of his lecture notes). Or perhaps the task was to follow up Austin's dare to get free in aesthetics of an obsession with the beautiful and the sublime and attend to the dainty and the dumpy, namely, to get a list of words, that is, of concepts, that articulate attractive and unattractive qualities of objects, natural and crafted (concepts such as delicate, monumental, stark, gaudy, cluttered, neat, trite, boring, repellent, etc.) and of humans and other animals (cute, frisky, majestic, repulsive), including ones that are not perceptible merely through the plain and healthy exercise of the five senses (as with bright, loud, heavy, tall, smooth). I did not really expect much philosophical illumination from this—the stroke of genius comes in locating what Austin called "a promising site for field work," taking, as it were, an anthropological view of the human as such, and finding promise in surveying terms of excuse and verbs for performative utterances along with ways we encounter (approach, rebuke, seduce, rebuff, embarrass, chastise, puzzle, confuse, baffle, trouble, amuse, etc.) each other. I was more fascinated than resourceful in finding a way to convey my fascination practically, yet since Austin's power with examples had been essential in my forming my conviction in his work, it is not surprising that I would try at first to communicate my experience in the way it had communicated itself to me.

May 26, 2004

Marcia's and my daughter, Rachel, was born in Berkeley (actually over the city line into Oakland where the university health plan principally housed itself) in May. We had not expressed imagining a child to each other, but we had found ourselves enlivened by the reality of the prospect. The summer was free for lavishing attention on this transfiguring presence in our lives. As for collecting summer thoughts about a dissertation, I had learned from some article or other in linguistics that the Russian language contained verb forms that distinguished, among actions, those in process and those successfully completed (or something of the sort), and having got it into my head that a knowledge of this distinction would be beneficial, even decisive, for my work on the concept of an action, I audited a beginning course in Russian for the first six weeks of the summer—instead as it were of putting the time to use by beginning to think back to the place I had got to in my writing before Austin appeared at Harvard, which would mean trying to articulate why his presence drained my interest away from that earlier progress. I knew I was going to have to face this question; I mean I felt there was in store for me a new dissertation beginning with an account of this dissatisfaction. But then why bother now to confess the comparatively evanescent expression of nuttiness in veering off to study Russian, a superficial gesture of the despair of finding a thread to an idea that would bring together the various philosophical impulses in me vying for attention into a coherent work for submission to my former department? What I know is that some four and a half years later I will present some such text to my former teachers as a proposed dissertation. What I still do not know, in a way that satisfies me, is my need then, and with all due differences still now, to trace the education, including its false steps,

that forms the condition of the work I do, that I have found it worthwhile spending a lifetime to do.

Well of course that is the idea drawing on the present writing. I
make it explicit (to myself) to warn myself and any other who may be
present, that the answer cannot appear simply at the end, as a deduction. I feel I have already given ample evidence for an answer, and
indeed perhaps given the answer, or the means for a circle of answers,
could one but take it on.

When did I at any time actually deliberate in such terms? When
did I ask myself, for example, whether I would wish to repeat, or repeal,
the life I have led? At most, day to day, isn't what I have asked myself
no more than whether I was interested to continue what I was doing,
as I was doing it? But in what terms did I describe to myself what I was
doing, or describe what I was doing to myself? I had evidence that I
was capable of following drastic turns in my intellectual or spiritual
life, starting over I typically called it. And I had had more recently the
experience of crisis in which the starting over had to be done not by a
change of place or field, but within a field. But the year of teaching had
not proven to me that the field was mine to explore. There was still no
work I could show to warrant any such assumption.

May 27, 2004

There is a sort of exception to this lack. Helping Austin carry an
assortment of packages to the post office as he was preparing for his return to Oxford at the end of the Harvard spring term of 1955, I told
him I was making notes for a paper I planned to write over the summer, before leaving for my year in Europe, to convey what working in
his classes over the past months had meant to me and asked him, if he
would agree to the imposition of reading it, for an address. By the time
there was no more time that summer I had a text of something over
twenty thousand words, based, beyond Austin's public lectures on the
performative, and his seminar on excuses, also on the Saturday morning faculty discussions on empirical knowledge (to which several of us
privileged seniors among the graduate students were invited), which I

will discover had gone over material not unlike that published in his posthumous *Sense and Sensibilia*. My paper turned out to be about the size of the text I had written for Piatt those years ago at UCLA, and while this time I felt I had composed less a letter to the world than an address to a master, it was still a cry from the heart. I might have wondered whether I would ever get past beginning again. But for the first time I felt I had begun something for myself, I mean something that suggested a tomorrow. The thrill of tender embarrassment is still palpable to me, directed to, or for, that younger self, now after half a century, together with a fresh, frightened recognition of the power the young will invest certain teachers with, scarcely dreaming that those grown-ups are preoccupied with their own headaches and breakups and reputations.

I had given Austin several dates and associated cities along our projected itinerary to which, with an American Express address, he could mail my paper back to me with his comments if he would not have had it in time to return it to the States before our departure in August. The paper turned out to be awaiting me when we had made our way to Vienna half a year after that exchange, the week before Christmas. Austin's comments, or what I made of them, were all that had I hoped for. I called the paper "The Theatricality of Everyday Life" to mark an early strategy I used, with perhaps excessive pleasure, that proposed contrasting the questions "What shall I do . . . ?" and "How shall I act . . . ?" by filling both blanks with a common sequence of descriptions of situations and events and then supplying answers to the resulting questions. For example: " . . . in the event of fire"; " . . . when the vice president arrives"; " . . . if your mother phones." Things you are to do: Phone the emergency number posted in case of fire, and make sure you have arranged for a place to gather outside the house; show the vice president and his party to the ballroom, and explain the delay of the ceremony; tell my mother you expect me within the hour. Ways you are to act: in the first, stay calm; in the second, show him due courtesy, without overdoing it; in the third, express concern over my behavior the last weeks. And so on. Austin wrote in the margin: "Very good and interesting method." Measured by his responses to interventions I had witnessed in discussions with him in seminars and lectures (where I almost entirely kept my counsel, what small counsel I felt I had), this was positively effusive, as even more so were his general comments at the end. A marginal observation along the way that I particularly appreciated was his query, "A bit purple?" I took this kindly. I was used to teachers giving me trouble about my prose, but this was, I thought, the most sympathetic or appreciative worry, anyway the most specific and limited, that I remembered a teacher expressing to me, and no other teacher had proved as decisively important, and practical, for me as this one.

It was not merely the tone of worldly tolerance that I was glad for, but, so I imagined, its worldly recognition that a certain talent and youthful ambition (even one not as youthful as it once was) were, understandably, not always under control, and might be trusted to take care of themselves, or not. I am sure I profited from Austin's having relished his months in America—no English boy could take him by surprise, having himself got highest marks jumping the same hurdles. But he expressed pleasure and wonder at the unfamiliar knowledge and varying accomplishments and unpredictable, even daring, manners of a choice set of American undergraduates. At Eliot House, where he had rooms, he would have had meals with the sons of oil men from Oklahoma and of ranchers from Texas as well as of swells and other immigrants.

May 28, 2004

In these Berkeley years, four new intellectual or artistic influences entered my life, functions of my friendships with Thompson Clarke, with Thomas Kuhn, with Seymour Shifrin (all teachers at Berkeley during my years there), and with Kurt Fischer (who lived in Berkeley and taught in the philosophy department there for a year, but then at the University of California at Davis and afterward at Mills College in Oakland). No one of these figures, I was not always puzzled to discover, was close to any of the others. It would have taken an occasion of some emergency—a concert or theatrical performance or baseball game or departmental meeting or visiting lecturer would not have been sufficient—to bring them all into the same room, even perhaps any two or three of them. How deeply, and differently, each of them shaped my thoughts, it is not easy to specify, exactly because they were so differently important to me; but not as difficult to characterize generally, perhaps, as one might think.

And now, as I recognize that I will go on to epitomize their significance for me, and that I will be remembering and sketching them in isolation from each other, I am impressed by a particular difference in my necessities of narration that have become called upon in these paths or jumps of memory that quite remove them from impulses to count on novelistic effects of interweaving and resolution. I mean primarily that in having to concentrate so strongly on academic nomadism, where figures appear and vanish according to a rejection by one institution and the absorption into another, and where signal events are as apt to be distinct and private as insights, and where a sense of development is largely confined to the life of the narrator, I feel the progression of my stories tending to take on picaresque juxtaposition, but without the interest of physical adventure. (How what has become a lifetime of participation in the modern university allows, if not encourages, a departure from church, political party, club, neighborhood, in their preferred economies of public and private encounters, I should perhaps be able to find occasion to take up.)

Shifrin was greatly respected, loved I would say, as a composer by colleagues and students of his, some of them also performers of his works, and by an increasing circle of listeners. But he seemed to know, born the same year as I was, until his death at the age of fifty-three, in 1979, that his music was not, as yet, accepted as part of late twentieth-century American music to the extent that the music of a number of friends and acquaintances of his had been. This has not changed, I believe. He was, I believe, not unusually prolific, but he wrote young and he wrote steadily, and it is my sense that, with each concert of his work, new and old, his achievements in seriousness and beauty were increasingly felt to rank with the best of his time. And I also knew perfectly well that, while he shunned discussions of reputation, he felt the discrepancy in his own case between achievement and recognition. He and I sometimes discussed this discrepancy, no doubt in part allegorically, in the better-known case of Roger Sessions, whose integrity of purpose over a long lifetime was something that Seymour (not Seymour alone) treasured. The idea of making any accommodation to this situation, even supposing one or the other could have done so, would have been uninteresting to either of them. Sessions was determined to leave the matter of acceptance as a blank mystery; more than once he said, "All I care about is the achievement." But sensibilities as definitive and as different as those of Schoenberg and Stravinsky believed in Sessions and in his musical achievement and showed him as much. It should do. All I remember Seymour ever saying about the situation, commenting on the composers chosen by modern dancers as their collaborators (Copland by Martha Graham, Cage by Merce Cunningham), is "We don't strike the modern dancers as doing the same thing they are doing." Whoever he was including in his first-person plural (Sessions, Babbitt, Berger . . .) his expression struck a heavy chord in me.

Quite as important to me as Seymour's discipline as a composer were his powers as an analyst of music. I attended his musical analysis seminar over several semesters in our first years at Berkeley in the late 1950s. Going through the late Beethoven bagatelles with him, or a piece of Schoenberg's, or the opening movement of the Mozart G Minor symphony, provided experiences I took as exemplary exercises in reading as such, in the unswerving patience it takes to align and account for one's responses to just these crossroads in these present texts, to the ways in which just these specific sounds, in the small and at large, create just these shifting, fecund contexts for one another.

May 29, 2004

I had been introduced to Kurt Fischer on arriving in, or rather returning to, Berkeley late the summer of 1956, after my year of travel in Europe. He left within a matter of days to spend a year at the Philosophisches Institut in Vienna. It will be another twenty years or so before he will return to Vienna permanently, eventually as an Honorat Professor at the Institut. That he lived in his mind simultaneously in Austria and in the United States, speaking of the other incessantly from whichever of the locales he happened to be in, is part of the reason that it was he more than anyone else I knew for years who kept me unmistakably aware that academic philosophy exists, and has existed for more than a century, increasingly and fatefully (with exceptions taken), in two states (at least), in one of them as a continuation of, or contesting of, post-

Kantian philosophy, principally of Hegel and his aftermath in thinkers such as Kierkegaard and Nietzsche as well as Husserl, and in the other as a rejection of this aftermath through the acceptance of the philosophical modes of analysis in Frege and Russell and Moore, themselves preceded by Mill and Hume.

Emerson remarkably, encouragingly I will come to find, anticipated this in his way, as in *Nature*: "Broad noon shall be my England of the senses and the understanding; the night shall be my Germany of mystic philosophy and dreams." But it will be twenty years before I would be able to fashion Emersonian procedures explicitly into my own (in "Thinking of Emerson," from 1978).

What choice can we claim over the writing, or the voice—sometimes it is manifested in a phrase—that carries conviction for us? It is not much help to say: Conviction should not be taken seriously that is not justified by argument. That sounds more like a threat (in my hearing it has typically been more that) than like part of an argument. And then there lingers the feeling that those who recommend the look of argumentation often regard themselves as already knowing the conclusions for which they are inclined to argue. Where is the intellectual adventure, or advance, in that?

The fact that Kurt Fischer and I were both admirers of Nietzsche's work (Fischer's expertise in the corpus of Nietzsche's texts was, is, much greater than mine), and of its anticipations in Schopenhauer and its consequences in Freud, was a standing basis of exchange between us. It was with Fischer that I attended and discussed the material in Andrew Jaszi's graduate seminar on Rilke at Berkeley, and in Carl Schorske's impressive large lecture course at Berkeley on the intellectual history of Western Europe since Locke and Descartes. Schorske's devoting something like a month to a reading of Goethe's *Faust I* was a startling, fruitful act of intellectual conviction.

Kurt's and my lasting friendship was sealed the late afternoon he appeared unprecedentedly at the door of the apartment in Oakland to which I had moved when Marcia and I separated some months earlier. He was on his way back to Berkeley from Kaiser Hospital down the road in Oakland where he had been visiting his wife, recently diagnosed with cancer. He had come to ask for my reaction to the following decision he had just been asked to make. Her doctor had revealed to him that Olga had a matter of months to live, and that if Kurt would not agree to tell her the truth he could not go on managing her care. The doctor's reasons were essentially two, namely, that she will know the truth anyway and her consequent loss of trust in the doctor would be a harmful barrier between them, and that since she and Kurt have a five-year-old son, she should have the maximum period available to her, especially while she is still relatively strong, to prepare the child, and not be confronted with this ultimate task when she would be manifestly weak and with even less time to exist with the boy in whatever feelings, or lack of them, he will find himself having to deal with. It seemed obvious to me that Kurt knew as well as I that he was going to agree to tell her, but he wanted confirmation, or whatever companionship there might be, and I was glad he knew even early in our acquaintance that my feeling for him and his little family was strong enough to want to provide all I could. It turned out by the time he left my apartment and returned to the hospital that it was Olga who told him the truth.

I was asked a couple of years ago to compose a reminiscence of Kurt to be included in a Festschrift for him on the occasion of his eightieth birthday, when he received a medal from the Austrian state. The view of him that that invitation elicited from me strikes me as providing a glimpse of his life from a perspective, different from if not more ample than, the present, private memoir is likely to provide. Neither of them will do justice to Kurt's admiration of human achievement, in various guises and fields, philosophical, literary, medical, athletic; nor to his love of, and desire to understand, women; nor to his attention to the uprooted and the bewildered; nor to his loyalty to friends. But I would be withholding something distinctive of my life if I did not essentially interpolate the earlier attempt here, introducing it by telling a story it omits.

In a sense what my public reminiscence omits, and was in that context otherwise fully covered, is the master story of Kurt's life, at any rate the one easiest to sketch, against which a thousand others have to be placed, the one that precipitated the documentary film about Kurt produced by Austrian television several years ago. In June 1938, in Vienna, when Kurt was sixteen years old, gentile friends picked him up at his high school and took him directly to the train station to join his mother in leaving for Czechoslovakia, ahead of Hitler's army of annexation. A half-Jew (his father was not Jewish), Kurt had not grown up identifying himself with that half of himself; the Nazi Nuremberg laws did that for him. The following year, with the partitioning of Czechoslovakia, he and his mother continued east to become part of the eventual twenty-five thousand Jews in a colony of refugees in Shanghai. There he joined a boxing club, and showing a talent for the sport (he says his talent was essentially as a counterpuncher, a concept that leaves as a silent but stark implication the fact that for this tactic to succeed you have to be able to take a punch), he fared so well in an early succession of bouts that he became the middleweight boxing champion of China. The road to that title required also taking on toughs from the British navy. His ring name, as Kurt let me learn from reading the faded, fragile article he had somehow preserved from an English-language Shanghai newspaper of the period, was Whirlwind Fischer. What he claimed for himself was not that he was particularly talented but that he was well prepared and well conditioned, particularly enjoying roadwork.

The truth of his claim as a runner was brought unmistakably into the present a late morning on the Berkeley campus, some fifteen years after his title bout, by then in no better visible condition than the rest of us, as he and I were sitting, characteristically at that hour of the day, having coffee on the cafeteria terrace adjacent to the philosophy building, and overlooking the large plaza at Sather Gate, the busiest entrance to the university. On the departmental secretary's sudden appearance to us with a message from Kurt's wife that their child had had a minor fall, Kurt bounded down the stone steps to the plaza, and with extraordinarily fluid strides, bobbing and weaving through variously moving clumps of walkers, his arms working close in and gracefully, his suit jacket evidently buttoned since it did not fly back as his necktie did, he disappeared from view through Sather Gate some hundred yards away more quickly than I would have imagined possible.

He was full of information and stories and thoughts, backed with an unusual fund of reading, including medical and psychiatric literature, and wrote elegant English. He did not, I felt, write, or rather publish, nearly enough. I might from time to time have had the poor taste to tell him that instead of writing enough he talked too much, to too many people. (It is like saying of a wonderful horse that he ran past too many horses. It is also not at all like saying that.) The sense that he was blocked from speaking his mind fully philosophically distressed me. I incorporated an implied diagnosis in my various urgings of him to write the way he boxed since in philosophical argumentation counterpunching is heavily rewarded. Perhaps that was already too much on his mind and he was afraid of the effect he might have on those he respected, no longer random toughs from the British navy.

I am prompted to this diagnosis by his introduction of my son Benjamin, when he had reached the age of seven or eight, to boxing. On a visit to our house, Kurt brought us a gift of pairs of matching boxing gloves, one small pair and one large. Having laced the small pair on Ben and accepted help from Cathleen tying the laces on the large pair he had pulled his hands into, he got on his knees in front of Ben and said, "Hit me." Ben was as astonished as I was. Kurt persisted. "I mean it. Hit me as hard as you can. You won't kill me." Ben couldn't do this to Kurt, but he took the event, and the message, away into his future. He eventually boxed as an undergraduate at Harvard (becoming co-President of the Harvard Boxing Club; the other co-President was black, as were most, perhaps all, of the other members) and, four years after he graduated, Ben's elaboration of Kurt's initiation of controlled aggression into civilized exchange appears in the stories in his debut collection of short stories, *Rumble, Young Man, Rumble*, published two years ago. It is good to know that the transmutation of instinct into lyricism is heavily rewarded, is itself a heavy reward.

I gave my memoir of Kurt the title "A Discreet Ambassador." It was printed in English in *Weltanschauungen des Wiener Fin de Siècle*, published from Peter Lang, Frankfurt am Main in 2002, and reads, briefly modified in a few places, as follows.

Except for Shanghai (and nobody but Kurt knows how to count that exception), I have known Kurt Fischer in all the places he has lived—Berkeley, Cambridge, Vienna, New York, Millersville—lived and, except for Shanghai, taught and written as well as conversed. Satisfying a recurrent image of the philosopher from Plato's *Republic* to Wittgenstein's *Philosophical Investigations*, bouts of thinking have always begun for him in conversation, conversation with anybody, young or old, friend or stranger, educated or not. I was aware early that the knack of his presence drew people to talk to him, and his responses, seemingly casual and impersonal, often accompanied by raucous laughter, were evidently unfailing in their ability to show that what they said was real to him, not passing the time of day, but passing with them through a moment of their existence, not calling attention to it, but somehow conveying that it was not lost on him. As though suffering, in its virtuoso capacity for disguising itself, was never a stranger to him. How many who have suffered have, or retain, this blessing, or curse, of perception?

That he always knew more than I about the present population of the university at Berkeley was not surprising; he had been a student there in the years before I arrived to begin my teaching life there in 1956. Besides, refugees had preceded him to Berkeley, a number that was essential to the fame of its faculty, and he knew what courses they taught and, if their fields were anywhere within the humanities or social sciences, and some beyond, what books they had written, as if he were appointed to assess the power of a shattered culture to survive itself, or remember itself within not wholly uncongenial circumstances, perhaps further to alter those circumstances. But within weeks of his arriving as a stranger in Cambridge with his family the year he taught at Harvard, where I had been living again for two or three years, he would instruct me in the scholarly distinction of one of the heads of a department of Harvard's Widener Library, or in the tribulations of the sister of one of the owners of the coffee shop in which he and I would meet for breakfast, or in the difficult circumstances of a younger faculty member I thought I knew reasonably well.

In those days a familiar explanation for Kurt's capacity for eliciting conversation, so often leading to immediate confidences, might have been to appeal to his unjudging air. This would have been a mistaken description of a quality of perception much rarer than the indifference or intellectual timidity that can pass itself off as withholding judgment. The quality is one that begins with his merciless judgments about the savagery and hypocrisy of societies, together with a feeling, combined of varying proportions of pity and amusement, at the folly and the luck, good or bad, in individual responses to social forces so terribly far beyond our powers to control or even very far to perceive them. The quality made him love, but deplore, American "optimism"; it made him detest, but understand, European "realism"—as when after a dinner party in Vienna an older guest confided to him: "I am no anti-Semite; but you must admit that objectively Jews give off a bad odor." The tone in which Kurt related this moment to me, its layers of recognition, humor, contempt, and resignation, would take considerable novelistic skill to capture. Or as when he reported that the middle-aged Viennese couple who owned a modest restaurant in Berkeley—the husband having been a prominent young lawyer in Vienna before the Anschluss—questioned him about how he could think of going back to live in Vienna: "Won't you always be asking yourself, with every new acquaintance, 'Where were you at that time, on that day?'" I seemed to know, without Kurt's supplying an explanation, that he understood the question as years, decades, too late, that he already knew where the ones who stayed had mostly been, namely, getting by, going along, the better among them just wishing to live, the more imaginative hoping they would live without becoming unforgivable. It is knowledge compounded with pity and amusement, a kind of forgiveness in advance at the fate of being alive, and damned. It takes an extreme case of oppression, which tore him from his life in his adolescence, to be posing the question every decently situated human being, after adolescence, either asks himself in an unjust world, or coarsens himself to avoid asking: Where is one now; how is one living with, hence counting upon, injustice?

One evening some years ago, walking with a group to the venue of a lecture I was to present on film comedies of remarriage at the principal hospital in Vienna (invited by a sociologist-therapist codirecting a research project in couple therapy at the hospital), Kurt pointed out to me a set of buildings where Jewish doctors had lived before 1938, a style of architecture in which stone buildings were set flush with the concrete sidewalk and the punctuation of ground-floor windows began waist high and rose, so that with shades lifted you could in passing at such a time have observed the well-off professional families at dinner. After the lecture and discussion, retracing our steps along late streets nearly deserted, I found myself lingering behind, staring at one of these now shade-protected windows, when I realized that Kurt had come back for me and was saying something as he drew close: "You are asking yourself how it could have happened." I had the impression, as I gasped and turned, staring at him, that I had indeed been saying precisely those words to myself. He was smiling companionably. It was one of the times when I felt I knew perfectly one of the edgy registers of experience Kurt found normal. Sometimes one marvels at the ingenuity of our species in learning, more or less, not to go mad.

It is easy to think of Kurt as living between—between his longing for Vienna and his difficult admiration of America; between being a Jew and being a Christian; between or among philosophy, literature, and cultural analysis; a kind and courtly man who became a champion boxer; a man who loves refinement but does not shrink from the crudities of existence, call them the facts of life. I have over the years called on his astounding fund of knowledge for everything from locating an obscure reference in the literature about Nietzsche to advice about a drug to suppress coughing. From no one else's daily intellectual life have I derived so unmistakable an image of a philosophical intellect divided in allegiance between the so-called (superficially so-called) analytical and continental philosophical dispensations, each seeming to reveal the limitations, not to say the impossibility, of the other. And no other image has been so constant a companion of my efforts to refuse to let one half of the modern philosophical mind (after Kant) eclipse the other.

But the image of Kurt as between this and that does not capture another equally palpable quality of his character, a certain aristocratic disdain for tallying up the cost of acting on his desires, whether to treat friends and strangers to an extravagant meal, or to refuse to enter mechanically into philosophical conversation with a new senior colleague who might be, over drinks, in effect interviewing him in anticipation of his review for promotion, a piece of theater to accede to which would perhaps have seemed to Kurt to deny that lives extend beyond their professional definitions. His sympathy was ready for any form of dispossession, but at the same time he could be hard on one's failure to dress properly for the opera.

I am reminded, for some reason, of the time, shortly after we met, of his consulting a physician about a growing ache in his shoulder, who after examining him physically, pressed him further about any unusual strains to which he had recently been subjecting himself, which he continued to deny—unless, he finally thought to relate, that it might have something to do with his infant son's inability, because of severe colic, to fall asleep otherwise than in one of his parent's arms, so that Kurt's nighttime routine began by walking around the apartment with the child until it nodded off and then, so as not to awaken him, sitting on a chair with his infant's head resting on Kurt's shoulder throughout most of the night. I had the feeling that Kurt would do that with the world, if he could find a big enough chair.

The idea of Kurt as an ambassador is meant to record the aristocratic tinge to his temperament, as well, obviously, as the way he has moved incessantly between environments strange, in thought and in manner, to one another. But why, further, the paradoxical idea of him as an indiscreet ambassador? Here I suppose I am thinking of his tendency to bring others together by saying something mildly scandalous, bursting a bubble of pretension—it could be something as mild as declaring that when he goes to a museum he stands with his back to the exhibit and looks instead at the onlookers. Thus to play the clown, to invite the slapstick, forms little alliances between strangers against him, and by the time the joke is out the conversation has found a level more interesting than a catalogue of the day's cultural or otherwise public events.

One mode of his behavior, or talent, reveals, in certain respects more consistently or vividly than any other, his capacity for criticism, for, as Nietzsche put the matter, living in contradiction to today (Emerson had recommended, as Nietzsche would have known better than anyone except Thoreau, living and thinking in aversion to conformity). I am thinking of a certain genius Kurt used to exercise for giving impersonations of his acquaintances, not quite mimetically, but rather abstractly, as a great caricaturist might sketch the famous in a few strokes each. I think I have not seen him do this since he moved permanently back to Europe, and rarely since Berkeley days. After a moment in which he would report a conversation, say, with one of our older colleagues, using very briefly an abstract version of that person's characteristic posture and vocal mannerism (characteristic, but not known as such until this performance), you knew that you had better for the next few hours avoid the presence of that colleague for fear of falling into inappropriate laughter. I heard from students that Kurt would sometimes give an impersonation of the way I lectured. Sitting one day with him in the makeshift coffee shop inside the large, ugly new humanities building at Berkeley, whose construction had destroyed one of the most beautiful panoramic views of San Francisco Bay from the Berkeley campus familiar to me from my undergraduate days there, I asked him to do the impersonation for me. He began to do it, just enough to give me an idea of how it would go. It was at first hard for me to see the points of resemblance, as it is hard to recognize one's own mannerisms, but swiftly the accuracy became brilliantly clear, too clear for my simple enjoyment. It contained, in half a minute, what I took as an appreciative, if surreal glance—it alluded to my Wittgenstein class, which he attended regularly and which I knew he liked—at my tendency to follow unlikely associations to certain extremes, but it ended with what I took as a rebuke to a particular moment in that class in which, in the mirror of Kurt's reproduction, I could discern that I had simply started showing off, a forced, ungenuine moment of vanity. I have no doubt that Kurt's demonstration that day for me, of me, has subsequently saved me from untold false moments I would have had cause to regret.

So for all the withholding of judgment friendship manages, and that I have benefited from in my half century of friendship with Kurt Fischer, call it forbearance, its value has from the beginning been secured by my knowledge of his power to judge, or said otherwise, to exercise his taste.

May 30, 2004

Thomas Kuhn's initial appointment at Berkeley was jointly in the philosophy and the history departments, in both of which he attended departmental meetings and was given voting rights. We were the first members of the philosophy department in, I believe, decades who had been appointed from outside the Berkeley ambience, an ambience still, almost freshly, bearing the mark of original logical positivism left upon it from Moritz Schlick's visit there for a semester in the mid-1930s. A colleague in the department from that period, the possessor of a refined sensibility who retired from teaching three or four years after I arrived, once described Schlick's effect upon him in the following way. "It quickly became obvious that he was more intelligent and learned than any of us, and obvious that I could not defend my religious convictions (which had brought me to the study of philosophy) against the power of his philosophical criticism. I had once upon a time thought of becoming a doctor as my alternative to the ministry, but I was thirty-five years old when Schlick visited, and since my wife and I already had small children, medical school was financially not feasible, so I braved it out in philosophy." This was not the only tale I was to hear over the years of a philosophical calling retracting itself, leaving behind, so far as possible, an unproviding, forbidding, landscape; but this account was lucidly stark in the sense I took from it of chronic American (male) disappointment.

Both Kuhn and I, from our different vantages, brought with us enthusiastic news that, singly and jointly—grating to some, young and old—served to loosen the hold, for a fair number of graduate students, of restrictive doctrines of language and of science, of, let's say, verificationism in both realms; or put otherwise, served to demonstrate modes of intellectual seriousness and fruitfulness that were not intimidated by, nor yet I think unheeding of, positivism's threats of meaninglessness and lack of rigor. Kuhn's invitation to learn how modern science actually developed historically from the revolution(s) of Copernicus and Galileo and Newton and in unexpected ways preserved itself and progressed, or say, leapt, into the future, gave scope for productive and, let's say, revolutionary work, as did Austin's independence and inventiveness that demonstrated its own unflinching, equally impatient and patient, rigor in taking up accepted philosophical views and their pedagogy. ("Let lying dogs sleep" I seem to recall Austin saying, not patiently.) Kuhn was more advanced with his project of recasting the history of science than I was in rethinking what philosophy wanted of itself in the work of Austin and Wittgenstein. And since Kuhn's insistence on certain stretches of intellectual history, in the telling case of the history of science, as constituting revolutionary changes (as opposed to what he called normal science, thus locating and criticizing the received picture of scientific progress as throughout homogeneous and accumulative) seemed to me true of my reading of Austin and my tentative glances at Wittgenstein (and indeed true of what I was coming to call modernism generally), I was glad to attend his courses and to do much of the reading he assigned, especially concerning the New Science in sponsoring most vividly Descartes's intervention in the history of philosophy.

Two initial experiences of Kuhn's perceptions convinced me of the pertinence of what he had to say to the way I felt about the work of the ordinary language philosophers (always meaning, for me, a misleadingly boring title for essentially the work of Austin and eventually for that of Wittgenstein), apart from the interest Kuhn elicited in the sheer fact that science indeed, as I might put it, *has* a history. One experience was his characterizing science by way of its modes of instruction, continuing in its particular ways of summarizing itself and producing textbooks. Another came out in his response to the first informal but extended discussion among professional philosophers that he had in my company attended from beginning to end. As we left the scene Kuhn pressed his fingers to his forehead as if it ached. "I wouldn't have believed it. You people don't behave like academics in any other field. You treat each other as if you are all mad." This seemed right to me, but normal enough, and because normal, suddenly revelatory. The immediate implication I drew was that this somehow manifested the fact that philosophy is not (a) science. Later Kuhn will say that philosophy displays a wider disagreement over measures and standards of what constitutes good and poor professional philosophy than any other academic discipline.

In an early formative conversation between us I told him that his considering instruction in a field as part of the, I might have called it, essence of the field, part of its defining structure (roughly what Wittgenstein called grammar), along with his insistence on the nature of agreement within a field as playing a similarly defining role within it, were ideas to be found in Austin and in Wittgenstein's *Philosophical Investigations*, and this conjunction of his work and theirs helped me see the depth of the ideas on both tracks. (Of course positivism is concerned with education, but not, for example, with the essential role of personal transformation in seeking it. I might have said that it is not concerned with how to study philosophy, taking it as fairly given what diligence and creativity everywhere look like, hence that philosophy worth the name should be taken up as a—branch of—science.) In the conversation I have in mind now Kuhn, perhaps after a department meeting, accompanied me home for a drink, and, talking past midnight Tom was becoming agitated in a way I had not seen. He suddenly lurched forward in his chair with a somewhat tortured look that I had begun to be familiar with. "I know Wittgenstein uses the idea of 'paradigm.' But

I do not see its implications in his work. How do I answer the objection that this destroys the truth of science? I deplore the idea. Yet if instruction and agreement are the essence of the matter, then Hitler could instruct me that a theory is true and get me to agree." My reply I cast as follows, using the words I remember using then. "No he could not; he could not *educate* you in, *convince* you of, *show* you, its truth. Hitler could declare a theory to be true, as an edict. He could effectively threaten to kill you if you refuse to, or fail to, believe it. But all that means is that he is going to kill you; or perhaps kill you if you do not convince him, show him, that you accept and will follow the edict. I don't say this is clear. But it is something I cannot doubt is worth doing whatever work it will take to make clear." Tom's response was startling. He arose almost violently from his chair, began pacing in front of the fireplace, saying something like, "Yah. Yah." What causes conviction? What, perhaps rather, may undo an unnoticed conviction?

After that night we arranged to meet for lunch regularly once a week, whatever other times we might be together, and discuss mostly the material he would develop the following year as *The Structure of Scientific Revolutions*. It was my clear impression that I was learning more from our exchanges, gathering more food for thought, than Tom was, more material about how language is open to the world, or the future, how concepts change, why the openness of concepts to projection into strange contexts is what makes language possible, and in a sense makes necessary, the philosophical attempt to control what it perceives as the laxness or arbitrariness of ordinary language. I sometimes summarize this with the thought that the home of the a priori is not alone mathematical structure but natural language itself. What I know is true is that, given the deep variations in our training and experience, the inspiration Kuhn and I might take from each other underwent sometimes radical changes in finding a place to exist, in however revised a shape, in the other's sensibility. Sometimes the disparity in our manners took a lighter turn. He had a resounding bass voice, not infrequently breaking into an almost raucous laugh. Once, lingering over too much coffee and many too many cigarettes, after a particularly resonant blast of disagreement from him, I replied: "Tom, please do not address me. I am not a convention." He was shocked, put his forehead to the table, and banging it gently several times, he said, in rhythm, and softly: "I know. I know I do that."

He was the product of two distinguished German Jewish families, accustomed to the best of everything in growing up and to being recognized for his intellectual accomplishments. When I told my uneducated father from Eastern Europe that not alone Kuhn but Kuhn's father had gone to Harvard, my father treated the news as something quite beyond comprehension. He repeated the words, as if searching for a history that could make them true. I went on to say that I found Tom's father rather cold and bitter. It allowed me to go on to say: "You are bitter, and angry, and envious, but you are not cold; and I can understand and even respect your suffering. Also you can really enjoy being good at getting people to enjoy your jokes. I'd rather have you for a father than have Tom's father." My father was satisfyingly stunned, and rather stunned me in replying, "You can't mean that."

We were talking in the apartment I had moved to in separating from Marcia. He had flown out to Berkeley—the only time he appeared in my five years of teaching there—whether to try to get me to stay in the marriage or whether to commiserate with me, I never decided. It was then that I said: "Don't feel sorry for the way I live. I like this shabby apartment better than I liked any of the clean and modest apartments I ever lived in with you and mother. I feel less alone here, less trapped. I may yet learn how to put the Goldsteins and the Segals together in myself." Astonished, he recovered himself sufficiently to reply: "It is too much." I felt we had stumbled onto some path or place from which to begin to forgive each other. Whatever else my avowal of spiritual ambition served to accomplish, it was a step in (as I and the psychoanalyst I eventually worked with in Boston put it jointly, as part of our code during the first year of that long analysis) "moving out of Park Drive," namely, out of the last apartment in which my parents and I lived together in Atlanta, a place I incessantly found myself going over in analysis, drawn back to in imagination, as to a place of solitary confinement.

It is against this disparity of Tom's and my childhoods and fathers that I told the following story at the initial, relatively intimate, memorial service after Tom's death. His parents visited Tom just after he had accepted a timely invitation to spend a year free of teaching responsibilities at the Stanford Center for Behavioral Studies, to complete the writing of what Tom always called *Structure*, a task that I firmly believed would make him famous. (Not *that* famous.) The night I joined Tom and his wife, Kay, and Tom's parents for dinner in San Francisco, as we got out of the car in the parking lot and Tom and Kay went ahead to pick up our reservation, Tom's mother and father turned alertly and simultaneously to me, and it was his mother who voiced the question on both their minds: "Why is Tom going to Stanford for the year? Is there some problem at Berkeley with his tenure appointment?" So it must be true, hence conceivable, that even if my parents had themselves attended college and both spoken English without an accent, they might still not have had a generally accurate working knowledge of my life.

May 31, 2004

Toward the end of the summer before my second year teaching at Berkeley, Tom Clarke arrived from the University of Chicago for a visiting year in the department. He had mailed ahead to me, for safekeeping during his packing up for the move westward, a copy of the latest material he was working on, marking especially a manuscript he suggested I might want to read. I read it at once, and at once recognized that it was taking Austin's work further in relation to traditional epistemology than Austin had done in those Saturday sessions at Harvard on empirical knowledge, knowledge based upon deliverances of the senses (essentially the material he presented at Oxford in lectures announced as "Sense and Sensibilia. J. Austin," posthumously published by Oxford, from notes reconstructed by G. J. Warnock). While Clarke was, I believe, C. I. Lewis's last teaching fellow at Harvard—his and my sense of Lewis's philosophical seriousness was an initial bond between us— Clarke's work was not exactly a defense of Lewis so much as it was a demonstration that Austin's criticisms of epistemology, of whom Lewis was a distinctly more formidable, more creative representative than A. J. Ayer (whose writings Austin used as his principal foil in his Oxford lectures, and for which some of his colleagues never forgave him), were misguided, or more accurately, short-winded. Clarke's favorite way of putting this was to say that Austin's considerations "would not be news" to Lewis. This was for me a life-changing observation, no less important for me than Austin's reception had been.

Tom and his wife, Jill, had rented a house on the hillside adjacent to ours on Panoramic Way, a ten-minute walk away, which either
Clarke or I would take at least once most days. Before we got to the
specifics of his manuscript, both of us, I think I can say, excited by the
realization that we were discovering a depth of intellectual companionship in each other that our past acquaintance had not prepared us for,
were interested to learn something about our pasts, about how, to begin
with, we had each shown up at Harvard's, and philosophy's, doorstep.
Very early we compared our experiences of our first year of teaching,
confessing not only that it had been agonizing, but specifically that a
cause of the pain was the discovery that we had no immediate way
of putting our educations into pedagogical service. It was not that the
education was lacking. It was rather that philosophy seemed to have
taken a swerve, as it were, behind our backs and behind the backs of
our teachers. Everyone was aware of the positivist revolution, but there
was yet another turn beyond that, no doubt as a further consequence of
that. Unless one confined oneself to a certain way of doing the philosophy of science and to mathematical logic, positivism, while it had succeeded in putting the history of philosophy on the defensive, had not,
at least for us, stilled interest in the issues the history of philosophy had
defined for Western culture. What the defensiveness undeniably meant
to us is that no traditional question of philosophy could now be taught
traditionally, as though its power were something students could be assumed, or should be asked, to take with the right seriousness. Lewis, at
his age and with his position, could still begin a course in epistemology
by all but taking for granted that his assertions that no empirical judgment is certain and that the only assertions that are certain are those
that describe one's immediate and present sense experience, or necessarily true statements of mathematics and logic, would seem quickly
plausible or be accepted on a kind of faith, anyway on another's authority, by students in a philosophy class, or with no more than an example
or two of how any empirical assertion, any objective judgment about
the world, can fail to receive verification, so come to intellectual grief,
whereupon we are invited down paths of finding substitutes for objective certainty—for example, the immediacy in the senses' relation to
sense-data, or the appeal to degrees of probability. (Dewey's pragmatist
proposal for substituting "warranted assertibility" for "truth" or "cer-

tainty" had already left me cold, for something like the unnerving sense
that I had no wish to retrieve my relation to the world by finding some
warrant conscientiously to *assert* "The world exists" or "She loves me."
I want the world, not some testimony to its existence.)

But for Clarke and me these faiths, or lack of them, had often become rumors, and the paths they projected were to that extent artificial.
What went unaccounted for was at once our ordinary complacency
about assertions (beyond the suggestion that we are ordinarily lazy or
careless or stupid, in contexts in which a sufficiently corrective alertness
or caution or cleverness would seem irrational, not to say psychotic) as
well as our pangs of resistance to the initial idea that certainty must
mean the same as, or essentially imply, invulnerability to the future.
But without articulation here, the philosophical problems now readily
seemed unmotivated, merely academic. (That in fact soon became a
widely shared verdict on the subject of classical epistemology generally.)

Obvious causes of the swerve in philosophy were represented in
Austin's "Other Minds" and in Wittgenstein's *Philosophical Investigations*.
I found Clarke's work profound, and I did not disguise this from him.
But I felt he was doing an injustice to the implications of Austin's work,
to the extent that Austin was at the cause of raising the new problem of
epistemological motivation. I think to this day that Clarke has grudged
Austin his achievements, been less grateful to them for his own work
than he should be. I have myself been guilty of this grudgingness toward Austin; many others have as well. This matters to me and puzzles
me. It is true that Austin is often superficial in his criticisms of traditional philosophy, and this counts, and should count, as a grave limitation in his teaching. But why has this caused *resentment*?

That Austin has not delivered "news" to the likes of Lewis is itself scandalous news, or ought to be. Lewis knew very well—who does
not?—that under ordinary circumstances we do not try, or have the
need, to make our empirical observations invulnerable to every avenue, or possibility, of intellectual grief. Then how *do* we understand
this everyday tolerance of vulnerability, something I will come to call
our exposure to the world? Philosophers tend to cover such a worry
by vaguely supposing that everyday life is understandably philosophically lax. I would like to say that for Clarke and me this attitude on
the part of epistemologists was itself philosophically lax, failing to see

that what is at stake is our relation to our language as such, how we become dissatisfied with its news, such as we glean from it. Such matters eventually became fundamental in Clarke's and my exchanges. Austin was not interested in either direction of laxness—neither in everyday casualness nor in philosophical self-satisfactions—or he distrusted both so unceasingly that he could not see the point of respecting them, much less seeing their human incvitability, that that too revealed powers of language. Yet no intervention in philosophy more clearly than Austin's prompted an awareness of our apparent failures to mean what we say.

I had been invited halfway through my first year of teaching at Berkeley—ordered was more like it—to participate in a panel some eight months later for that year's Christmas meetings of the Pacific Division of the American Philosophical Association, to be held at Stanford University. My insistence on the treasures I was finding Austin to have brought to philosophy was getting on the nerves of some accomplished teachers in and around my senior colleagues in the Berkeley department, and it was their idea, whose point it was not hard for me to appreciate, even agree with, that it was time for me to justify my confidence before a public of professional colleagues. The occasion would require my composing a reply to a paper to be prepared by my Berkeley colleague Benson Mates criticizing, or rather rejecting, the procedures of the new philosophers of ordinary language. I spent a fair portion of the coming summer consolidating thoughts I had assembled about Austin over the first year of teaching, and going more deeply than I had before into the work of Wittgenstein's student Wisdom and of Ryle and reading other colleagues of Austin's such as Grice and Strawson and Pears. In the fall, while awaiting the completion of the paper of Mates's that I was to respond to, I attended Mates's seminar in which he took up critically certain passages in Wittgenstein's *Investigations*.

Mates's paper, when he gave me a copy, two or three weeks before the scheduled meetings, surprised me principally in its concentration on the appeal to ordinary language as such, as opposed to taking on specific passages of philosophers who make the appeal. While I had some ideas for my response, it took a dangerous number of days for me to find a way into the material Mates had broached that matched my convictions in the matter. In the days after the papers were delivered, during the break between semesters, ideas for expanding the thoughts I had arrived at in the paper began coming at a greater pace than I had ever before experienced with any philosophical material. For some days it seemed that I could hardly sit still for ten minutes without beginning to scribble down further hints and implications. Many came to nothing; some found their way into work years later; some went immediately into new or expanded paragraphs of the Christmas talk. Within weeks I had produced a text that had grown to four or five times its initial size.

June 1, 2004

The talk had been well enough received, although Tom Kuhn told me afterward that, while he knew I didn't much care for what Charles Stevenson had to say (during the morning panel that preceded Mates's and mine), I could learn something from his manner of delivering a talk. (I think I never did.) By being well enough received, I mean that those who were pulling for me thought I had answered Mates's objections, and those who were not pulling for me thought I had survived to fight another day. A piece of superb good fortune was that the work in empirical semantics that Mates was relying on in his paper had been done by a group in Norway that was sponsoring a new journal, called *Inquiry* (accepting contributions in English), and they agreed, upon being approached by Mates, to make room in an early issue to include his and my papers, including the whole of my expanded response. (The generosity or forbearance toward my very long text was accomplished by Mates's magnanimity and his influence with the editors at *Inquiry*.) This meant that the first text I published that I still care about (which became the title essay of *Must We Mean What We Say?*) was substantial enough so that I felt for the first time in my life the relief of having something to show for the years that had preceded it.

I declare this relief now. But on a day the week after I mailed off my corrected proof sheets back to Norway, I struggled with myself on and off for many hours over whether it would be more disgraceful to allow the thing to be published or to phone and withdraw it. It now suddenly seemed to me bereft of originality, and even friends must ask themselves why I felt such obvious matters worth putting into print. My frenzy became manageable when at a certain point I realized that it was after midnight in Norway and that no one would be in the journal office to receive my call. By the following day I was merely tolerably conflicted in my judgment of my paper.

What I felt I had shown was to be put to the test soon, in my coming to see further the force of Clarke's work. We had started counting on the continuity of our conversations, and I can describe circumstantially the specific intellectual passage, the time of day (twilight), and the place (pausing during a walk through the Berkeley campus, alongside its landmark campanile), just after Clarke had read the expanded manuscript of "Must We Mean What We Say?" at which the test irreversibly began. As elsewhere, I feel fully certain about the central example here and secure enough in my memory of specific words, to smooth out what the syntax may have been and to present the moment as quotations.

Clarke said: "I accept everything you advance about Austin's positive work. But I still do not share your confidence in its criticism of traditional epistemology. Austin has arrived at the sense that the questions and proposed answers of traditional epistemology are not serious, and perhaps in the work of various epistemologists they are indeed not serious. But is that necessary, and isn't it a question how, if this is true, it can have come about? Philosophers ask, say, 'What do you really see?' in an awkward context. The question itself, however, is anything but awkward. For example, it shares deep affinities, partakes in a similar coherence, with a detective's investigation in which he asks things like 'What did you really hear?' Suppose you have testified that the suspect was in his room all night; but on reflection it is plain that you only heard the sound of typing from the room. Anyone or no one (except someone on a recording) might have been in there. The door was locked; you were unable to look inside to check. So an alibi fails to hold up. You don't know he was there."

I found this to be true but quite trivial, and I replied: "For this to work philosophically, to generalize about the nature of certainty as such, the epistemologist's door is one that could never be opened; it is metaphysically closed." Immediately, and elatedly, I thought, Clarke replied, "Of course you are right." I was astonished, dumbfounded. Clarke seemed to take this as furthering his idea, not as a consideration, in the spirit in which I had offered it, that showed the analogy to fail, or in some way to be inept. How can this be?

A large part of my Ph.D. dissertation, submitted to Harvard some three years later, can be said to be devoted to answering that question (much of which is preserved in bits and pieces of Part One and consecutively in Part Two of *The Claim of Reason*). One path of answer, call it a way of drawing the moral of my astonishment, might be put as follows: Consider that just as I felt the triviality in taking the epistemologist's investigation to be equivalent to that of a detective, so I should see the ineptness in my taking my objection to that discrepancy as final. The discrepancy between an ordinary case of investigation (as revealed in the case of the detective) and the investigation of the epistemologist does not show the latter to be meaningless; the very fact that his question is analogous (showing exactly a discrepancy) with the detective's case, goes to show that it is (to some unmeasured extent) quite meaningful. Indeed if you take the epistemologist's questions seriously, you will feel compelled to answer them, and compelled in a certain way, the way that leads the epistemologist to discover that we do not really or literally or directly *see* objects, hence do not know with certainty that they exist. But then what is contained in the idea of taking the questions "seriously" (nontrivially)? Doesn't that merely beg the question, that is, assume the conclusion that must be argued, namely, that the question *can* be taken seriously? When the epistemologist asks: "Do you really see the back half or the inside of the tomato?" you may reject the question as unrealistic. But then there may persist a feeling that you, for your part, are avoiding the question. You may insist that the question, if meaningful, is just empirical—turn the tomato around and then you'll see whatever you are calling the back half.—Which half would that be? Identify "the back half you cannot see" on a particular occasion by painting it a color contrasting with the half you do see. Then wouldn't you see *that*—unseen—back half if you turned the tomato by just a quarter, or an eighth, or a sixteenth of a complete turn, or if you yourself moved right or left?

The classical epistemologist does not in fact *find* the "part unseen" but virtually *creates* the "part." This is Clarke's discovery. I have regarded it as philosophically fundamental since I first learned it from him. It is presented in his second published paper, "Seeing Surfaces and Physical Objects," part of a collection of papers by relatively young philosophers (in which my "Aesthetic Problems of Modern Philosophy" also appears). Clarke's first contribution was published while he was a graduate student, in the journal *Analysis,* known for limiting itself to very short papers. There was a story circulating around Emerson Hall my first year as a graduate student that Nelson Goodman had suggested to the Harvard philosophy department that they award Clarke a Ph.D. on the strength of this short paper. Goodman was known as something of a lethal philosophical wag, and although this suggestion was meant as a rare salute from him to a young philosopher, it was surely also meant as a jab at the pompous and predictable labors of much of current philosophy departments. In a soberer mood, I still think that a department that could not be so much as tempted to consider the seventeen pages of Clarke's "Seeing Surfaces" as a Ph.D. dissertation ought to be concerned about its mission.

So what is the problem of knowledge? Is it that we cannot keep moving, take in all perspectives, or that we cannot help moving, losing perspectives? It strikes me that an accurate answer to this impossible choice is to answer: "I am I." (No small matter, as I found to my surprise in *The Claim of Reason* [pp. 389 ff.] Now the answer calls to my mind Wittgenstein's apparently trivial response: "This is simply what I do."). Either way of taking the question of how much you see (either seriously and metaphysically or else empirically and realistically) seems a choice, and moreover a forced choice. Suppose you choose to let the realistic observation "You don't know he was there; the door was locked" prompt you to notice that "You don't know the tomato is there because you can't see all of it; the back half is metaphysically closed to you" is not without some sense. If you surmise that you might reassure yourself by putting a mirror in back of the tomato, enabling you to see the front and the back simultaneously, then you're well on the way to metaphysics. Are you prepared to say that in order to know that the things of the world exist, you in all strictness should slip a mirror behind every object, and behind every depth, as it were, of an object that you are prepared to say you see or encounter? Is that a coherent thought? If not, then can the thought that led to it be coherent? It cannot be simply incoherent, because after all it did lead to this picture of perpetual mirrors. Is our only choice one between a question begged or a question avoided? And is this a case of philosophy tying itself into knots needlessly? But how can it happen so swiftly that from trivial questions we

are led into foothills of surrealism—seeming to discover that we do not
see objects (which are not in historical fact hidden) and that we do not
know what simple words mean (when we can ask and answer difficult
questions using them reciprocally with one another and with philosophers) and that we are not well enough acquainted with ourselves to
know when we are speaking with seriousness (which seems to require
little intellectual exertion to agree with—if one is serious).

I add that I have over the years found myself focusing less on the
insight concerning the "creation of the part" than on the consequent,
or simultaneous, creation of the "whole" (I do not recall Clarke following out this aspect of his idea). And since my interests or instincts have
taken me to take the problem of knowledge as derived rather from the
question of the other than from the issue of (simpler?) physical objects,
my attention has been drawn by what we conceive as the moment of
"doubting the existence of the other." I came to understand this not so
much as, or not alone as, the expression of a limitation in myself (call it
a lack of knowledge) as rather my rejection of the other, as of a threat to
my existence. And the question of "knowing all, the whole, the entirety,
of the other" seems to require knowing essentially *more than the whole* of
that other human body, namely, knowing of something "else," something invisible, something related to "who" this is, oscillating between
something endlessly private or else something endlessly public (this particular other is the mother of three, she is a twin, high strung, graceful, a substitute teacher, a truant officer, a trusted friend, divorced, the
recording secretary of her high school class, a mystic, a home owner,
a bowler, a high jumper, a bicyclist, a vegetarian, thin, tall, a college
dropout, her mother converted to Judaism, . . . in short, she has a history, hence conditions that at any time *may* surface). (Compare: "The
most you see is the object's *surface*." The analogous moment for subjects
is something like, "Which of her conditions are, or are near, the surface;
which over the years have proved to be more distant from expression?
Which cannot be unexpressed, like skin color? What is her attitude, if
any is discernible, toward her skin color?") Clearly the sense of endlessness comes into my preoccupation with things requiring interpretation,
centrally with objects of art, but in principle with any work showing
traces of the human, producers and products of language. (Nietzsche:
"The human being has become a work of art.")

Shall we be pragmatic about exactly what, that is to say, how much, we see—shake hands on the fact that we know perfectly well that this tomato is here? Would that make one feel less weird than placing mirrors behind objects for reassurance? The question seems to be how we *can* become in the required sense *un*pragmatic, surrealistically impractical, not to say unhinged, with regard to our most mundane practices.

Clarke and I began attending each other's seminars, and a number of the philosophy students following Kuhn's work also attended these. There was a period of difficult discussions when it felt, to those who had followed my Austin material diligently over the past year, that I was abandoning my commitment to Austin's work. It took a while to show with sufficient clarity—and I was myself stumbling in my attempts to articulate it—what I meant by saying that it only deepened Austin's importance in my eyes to discover that instead of accepting his own sense that he refuted skepticism (or emptied it of seriousness or interest), he showed its possibility, even necessity, that is, demonstrated the persistence of its demonstrably odd, unnatural, yet very specific, questions. In the long run this is bound to mean that skepticism's own self-understanding will undergo change, since it must think of itself as having undercut our ordinary or natural language, which presents itself to a skeptical stance as refuting our common beliefs, and this may be taken as a kind of questioning, or refutation, of these "beliefs" (e.g., that there are others, impenetrable and penetrable by us). But Austin's role in this is not as simple, or say, not as direct, as Austin's initial successes prompted him to imagine. Some students who had been enthusiastic readers of Austin—not most I believe—lost interest.

June 2, 2004

The Clarkes returned to Chicago at the end of the academic year, and within a few months Tom accepted the offer of an assistant professorship in the department at Berkeley. When Tom and Jill moved back the following summer, it was into the house next door to the one Marcia and I had moved to.

Clarke's impact upon me, while it depended upon Austin's having stopped me in my tracks, was as distinct and decisive as Austin's, hardly surprising since Austin's work had also had its effect on Clarke. In some obvious ways Clarke's effect was greater, because friendship was taken up within it. We talked about everything of interest to us, parents, women, children, intellectual pretension or fraudulence, other friends and acquaintances, movies, television, teaching and its impossibilities. And if I indulged him in hearing out revelations about the time it takes to invest rationally in the stock market, and discussions of how to sail the small boat he was thinking of buying, and of the proper conditioning necessary to crew for him (I retain the image of his small, marvelously charming wife, in order to condition her body for the task of redirecting a sail, pulling on a rope tied to the front of their MG and hauling the vehicle a space along a level back road), Tom reciprocated by listening to my doubtless overly elaborate speculations about, or detailed descriptions of instances, for example, of films and Shakespeare and Freud and writing.

But when it was time for philosophy, these other pleasures dropped away. The point of walking as we talked seemed to be a way of putting distance between our thinking and the realm of opinion, of customary or sociable judgment, whether of the value of an idea, or of the value of ourselves. This could take some time, and the time might prove to be fruitless. Anything done well can come to occupy some such air of concentration and freedom. It is as familiar in sports as it is in playing music or (as I once also witnessed) in baking bread. The difference in philosophy is that there is no method of practice that assures progress in the region of this art (although Austin had convinced himself otherwise, and particularly prided himself on this aspect of his achievement). One expects this unpredictability of progress in stretches of composing music or writing poetry. But in philosophizing—perhaps only of a certain kind—there is the odd feature that two can enter unknown territories together. (This is true of playing music but not of composing. One perhaps thinks here of the history of improvisation; let's call it mutual inspiration. But then one has to think whether the point of philosophizing is to create a work.) The sheer unlikelihood of arriving at satisfactory results on any given occasion is I suppose a reason Nietzsche found the idea of lecturing on philosophy at announced times of the week to be ludicrous and retired from his professorship as precociously as he had been awarded it. Something of the sort is true of Wittgenstein. He did lecture, but only when he had something of a ready urgency to present, and only to a group of his invitation. These are not conditions a professor is free to impose upon his or her institution. We are reminded that what we call a professor of philosophy (a figure open to Nietzsche's ridicule) is a relatively recent concept—I mean a concept implying that philosophy is one among the various subjects in which universities offer professional accreditation. (Locke, Berkeley, Hume, Spinoza, Descartes, Leibniz, etc., were not professors.)

But who says that teaching philosophy has at all times to consist of original thoughts? It would be as if performers were required to play nothing but their own music and moreover only music they had not played before. It seemed to me that Clarke found teaching to pose this kind of impossibility, hence to require insincerity, from both teacher and student. At dinner with the Clarkes, on a night well into the period in which Tom's financial investments had enabled him to teach half-time at most, Tom was expressing the kind of agony the pretense of philosophy caused him, even in office hours, going over a student's paper. He described it as an exercise in which much—most—of the time it was obvious to both participants that neither was interested in, or satisfied by, the proceedings. An exercise in emptiness. Jill, who was not hearing anything particularly new, and who had never taught, indeed who saw fewer people in the course of her day than her husband, Tom, did (beyond the university campus), chose for some reason to intervene here. "Just the fact of attention helps the students. All you have to do is feign a little interest for an hour. That's not so bad." Tom shot back with elaborate innocence: "Oh. Do you find it so?" It would have been withering to just about anyone. Evidently not to Jill, I gathered, who, for all her capacity for hospitality, craved solitude as much as Tom did, and knew that she was the only person in the world with whom he could live, and with equal certainty knew that he was the only man she could imagine living with in some state of interest and joyfulness.

What I sometimes figure as his intolerance for pretense or artificiality or superficiality (or on occasion simple courtesy) increased. This is no more a moral judgment on his part than, I might say, a physiological one. I wonder if Thompson Clarke would be amused to hear that it is in this way rather a Nietzschean response to modern humanity. Or

Rousseauian. Or Alcestean. Or Thoreauvian. A certain philosophical call to the moral life risks not only reclusiveness but misanthropy. It is religion's task sometimes to satisfy this call for silence and sometimes to combat it. The idea, I suppose, is not that this is philosophy's libel against humanity, but on the contrary that it is modern humanity's libel against itself.

The three papers Clarke had (has) published, whose intellectual quality is distinct and admired by a small but, however slowly, growing number of young philosophers, moved further and further into the past, and teaching for him became less and less frequent. I sometimes encounter those who have known him who consider that he has given up on publishing the work to which he has devoted his long adult life. If I were given a description of a man otherwise unknown to me who worked essentially alone, eventually not even in discussion with a favorite student or two, who composed philosophy primarily on small squares of paper, and conceivably by now has amassed many thousands of them, I too would doubt that these will be assembled into consecutive prose. But I do otherwise know the man. Only his dying before I do would still my expectation. But his death would do it, because I have no thought that anyone but Tom could manage the work of assembly. (On the off chance that he reads or hears of this moment in my text, I would like to think it might help shock him into composing further whatever consecutive prose he has allowed himself.)

He submitted his dissertation to the Harvard philosophy department in the spring of 1960. It caused a crisis that, so far as anyone knew or said, was unprecedented. The two members of the department who were assigned to read the thesis reported back that they could not evaluate the work; that however strong its originality may be, they found his text more or less incomprehensible. Too many people still in the Harvard department (the venerable C. I. Lewis, a distinct admirer of Clarke's, had retired some years earlier) regarded Clarke too highly to contemplate simply turning down his dissertation. The department formed itself into a committee of the whole, meaning that all members of the department, not merely a normal two-member or three-member dissertation committee, would read the dissertation and all would attend the oral defense. I don't know whether in this form Clarke was asked for face-saving revisions, but he was awarded the Ph.D. Between

Clarke and me—I understood this as assumed—this contretemps was taken as a judgment neither upon Clarke, nor upon the original readers of his dissertation, but on how far he had moved since he had left the department. (He had left longer ago than I, since he had served two years in the army doing psychological experiments, which he found too boring to bring himself to describe. This was after the end of the Korean War.) But I came to believe that the experience of the confusion over his dissertation hurt him more than my admiration of him allowed me to grasp—more specifically, that it shook his confidence in his ability to judge when he had expressed himself with reasonable clarity. Perhaps he had over the years since graduate school taken so many steps of revision and transfiguration of the issues on which he spent every day that he had dropped beyond the shared horizon. When roughly eleven months later I knew that I was in the final weeks of completing a dissertation, central chapters of which were directly indebted to Clarke's work, elaborating and evaluating the kinds of difficulty it made for both ordinary language philosophy and for traditional epistemological skepticism, I became sick at the thought (or, if you like, I became sick, and vulnerable to the thought), not so much that I did not know how to judge the effect of my writing (I do not know where confidence in this matter would have come from) but that it had taken so long to submit this work that it had become my new, conscious letter to the world, and yet it was not at this stage of professional authorization going to be judged by the world but by two or three designated philosophy professors, none with much time on their hands and almost certainly little preparation or sympathy for the extent of Austin and later Wittgenstein that I was putting in play. I was in no position to say to them, as I must to the world, take it or leave it alone. It was an idiotic position to be in, a dangerous one, in this sense a certain repetition of Clarke's.

Leaving Harvard (or staying at Harvard) for a teaching position before completing the dissertation seemed to have become almost a familiar practice among aging graduate students in those years, and the idea of supervision in working on a dissertation, accordingly, was getting lost. This system underwent, as so many institutional matters would undergo, fundamental changes during the early years of my teaching life, beginning five years before submitting my dissertation in 1961. By 1960, federal money was flowing into American universities in order to compete with Russia's technological leap into orbit with Sputnik in 1957. The number of teaching positions to be filled could no longer be managed efficiently with the older gentlemanly whisper of one's teachers into the ears of professional acquaintances who happened to have, or know of, an open teaching position. If only to compete with the other principal departments whose Ph.D.s commanded prestigious appointments at large research universities or at ambitious small colleges that had invested in notable undergraduate philosophy instruction (and in those days, measures of prestige were decisively more rigidly defined and more consequential than they became after the social upheavals of the middle and late 1960s and early 1970s), candidates even from Harvard and its obvious competitors had to apply for positions with dissertations complete, or completed by the time of taking up the appointment. Different as this practice became, its result was not (at the institutions I knew best, Berkeley and Harvard) that dissertations on the whole began being submitted earlier, within the four or five years the department announced as its goal, but that students stayed longer in graduate school, often taking eight or nine years, counting from the time of entering graduate school, for completing the dissertation and receiving the Ph.D. This persists to this day, or anyway to the day I officially retired from teaching, in 1997. I take this as one more sign that philosophy still resists its station as just one more subject within a university curriculum. I say this with no thought that there is any *other* modern institution that better suits philosophy.

It took me ten years after entering the Harvard graduate program to hand in a dissertation. I have described the way the award of a Junior Fellowship allowed me the luxury of feeling I could begin again. The free and variously inspiring atmosphere of Berkeley, in my colleagues within and beyond the philosophy department, and in our students, joining which coincided with my consciousness that I was indeed at liberty to find my beginning, and to follow it out, presented me in effect with the prospect, as I interpreted my situation, of preparing for, and composing, a dissertation in public, that is, in my classes. The thought of writing a primarily scholarly dissertation never again entered my mind from the moment Austin's visit to Harvard dissociated me from my interest in the work I was then doing, or the way in which I was doing it. The dominating, inescapable issue on my mind was to understand the peculiarity of the motivation to philosophy, the source of its conviction—the call for it I will come to say—given that I was not working within mathematical logic, where these questions had satisfying answers (or initial answers), and that I was not writing literature (whatever certain fellow graduates and colleagues might have felt I was doing), yet where conviction was irreducibly a function of everyday words and their orders. What was the power of ordinary or so-called natural language as Austin turned it against established philosophy? This question itself implies that I could never take seriously Austin's repeated suggestions that philosophers were chronically lazy, wily, drunken with false profundity—even if the subject sometimes encouraged and protected something of these qualities.

My classes on Austin's work the first year, however ragged, were essential preparation for anything that would become a dissertation from me. So was, as I have specified, Thomas Kuhn's teaching, which gave substance and detail to the thought of revolutions in thought. If Galileo could outrage an accomplished scientific establishment (and that the opposition he confronted was intellectually accomplished—not, as one was otherwise commonly taught to think historically in those years, merely superstitious and anti-empirical—it was essential to Kuhn's project to show and to understand), then it becomes a question how Austin's work, which often seemed to me sentence by sentence incontestable (or at least as incontestable as any other philosophy I had read), could cause the outrage it produced in my older colleagues. Outrage is what it was. This was evident in my colleague Benson Mates's contempt, echoed in his older friend David Rynin's exasperation (a philosopher whose home was the Berkeley institution named the Speech Department, later renamed and renewed to become the prominent Department of Rhetoric). Rynin, whose course called Semantics was well known among undergraduates of the period, was on the program committee of the Pacific Division of the American Philosophical Association, and it was he who informed me, during my second semester, that a panel had been scheduled for the Christmas meetings at which Mates would present a paper on ordinary language philosophy and I would respond to him. Rynin issued this invitation—summons rather—coming upstairs and down the hall from his to my office in Dwinelle Hall, at the end of a conversation that he began by noting that since I arrived in town I had been saying a lot of extravagant things about this new work on ordinary language. He wanted to warn me that my excitement might be misplaced. "I was around when pragmatism, and then positivism, seemed to be the only futures for philosophy. They have passed their prime, and ordinary language philosophy will pass its prime sooner than they did."—"Maybe if I stick with it until then, I'll be on the ground floor of what comes next."—"Well, let's see how you do come Christmastime."

The impression of anger in such exchanges never left me. I felt certain that this was essential to account for in the call for philosophy, even as philosophy sought relief from dispute and anger. When Socrates distinguishes for Euthyphro the difference between ethics and science by reminding him that in science disagreements are settled by reason (by measuring and counting) whereas in ethics anger and disagreement put reason at stake, why does Socrates not include the question of philosophy, of the correct procedure in philosophy, among the disagreements in which reason is the stake?

June 3, 2004

Yesterday was the reunion of a small group of former Harvard students, and a few others, marking the fortieth anniversary of the "Freedom Summer" in Mississippi, when some nine hundred students from the North traveled to Mississippi to participate in voter registration and in various forms of teaching. About fifteen Harvard students, most of them graduate students, some of them among my closest friends of those first years of mine back at Harvard, spent that summer in Tougaloo, Mississippi, outside Jackson, constituting in effect a summer replacement faculty for the small Tougaloo College. I accepted their invitation to join them there for a couple of weeks to give a public lecture, hold informal seminars and tutorials, and join in presenting a concert together with John and Rose Mary and Helen Harbison. That visit's permanent effects on my life will become explicit in a while. In the documentary film *Freedom on My Mind*, screened as part of our reunion, one of the depicted narrators of the events in Mississippi in 1964 speaks of "reminding" Americans of what America means to be. I felt, in response, something I had never realized so clearly, that I wanted Wittgenstein's speaking of a task of philosophy as "assembling reminders" to participate in some adjacent register of calling attention to something repressed in the present. We need to understand what we know, to take on our education. Can this register of political, public remembering really be illuminated by Wittgenstein's comparatively private, fragmentary philosophical practice?

By the time of Clarke's return to Berkeley in the summer of 1959 I had made little further specific headway with my deepened view of Austin's importance, and Clarke had begun to think seriously of putting together material for his dissertation. I was by then becoming immersed in Wittgenstein's later philosophy. The occasion for this was the invitation I had accepted from the *Philosophical Review* (making an open agreement to do something that I hesitated, on my own as it were, to embark upon) to write a review-essay of Wittgenstein's *Blue and Brown Books*, which had been published in England some months earlier. The two manuscripts comprising that publication are aptly described on Blackwell's title page as "Preliminary Studies for the 'Philosophical Investigations.'" Why or how it turned out that I was ready to go through these preliminary studies with a sustained attention that I had not been able to give *Philosophical Investigations* itself I had no reason, or time, to ask myself. Again I was stunned. Wittgenstein, as it were all at once, seemed to me to have found a way, decades earlier, to think consecutively, anyway fruitfully, anyway with what was now for me continuous interest, out of orientation by what I will come to call the extraordinariness of the ordinary ("A smiling mouth *smiles* only in a human face," *Philosophical Investigations*, § 583), and the ordinariness of the extraordinary ("Does it make sense to say that people generally agree in their judgments of color? What would it be like for them not to?" ibid., p. 226), by their revolving power and impotence, by their sanity and derangement.

Such perceptions might be taken as reasons enough for my absorption in Wittgenstein's achievement. But they do not speak to the condition in which I was courting intellectual absorption. My marriage was explicitly at an end, and little other serious writing seemed to me serious enough, or comprehensible enough, to hold my attention against my sense of failure and of grief at the prospect of separation from my daughter. The air in Wittgenstein's texts of taking on the patience of acquiring language (again) was something I could breathe, as though not simply this or that intellectual problem was in need of clarification, but intellectuality, say, curiosity, itself. The very presence of language and the world themselves had become obscure. My pages of notes on Wittgenstein's texts were becoming more numerous than the pages of those texts themselves. I pestered Clarke with excitements taken out of context, and we arrived at the thought of giving a seminar on the *Investigations* in the coming fall. He had also not yet made himself study that text, having been put off by it more strongly than I.

The seminar in the event was not a success. My material on the "Preliminary Studies" was too inchoate, or private, to broach. The chief secondary sources we had at hand were Norman Malcolm's and Peter Strawson's substantial reviews of *Philosophical Investigations*, both appearing the year after the English translation of the *Investigations* was published in 1953. (I was given David Pole's book on Wittgenstein, the first to appear in English, to review along with Wittgenstein's preliminary texts, but I had not yet read it, wanting first to have some grasp of my own of Wittgenstein's drift.) Success or not, the effort began, in my case a long struggle—brought to an initial head by reading Albritton's paper on Wittgenstein's idea of a criterion that appeared around the middle of the term of Clarke's and my seminar—to say what was right and what was wrong about the sense, more or less shared by these writers, concerning Wittgenstein's ideas of knowledge, the sense, namely, that what Wittgenstein calls criteria are meant to assure our knowledge of the world, Malcolm finding Wittgenstein's case convincing, Strawson and Albritton differently demurring. I had not arrived at a stable view of the matter even by the time I turned to the consecutive writing of my dissertation, beginning in earnest a year later. While Albritton's paper impressed me most in various respects (he and I would not meet for some several years yet), all three were evidently serious and strong expressions of philosophy, and I felt that if I could get to the causes of their differences I would have taken a distinct step toward work that mattered to me.

These initial three writers were in agreement, as I understood them, on the guiding idea that Wittgenstein's aim, or effect, was to refute skepticism—what else was his defense of something like the claim to certainty meant to do? My contrary sense was that Wittgenstein was articulating what human assurance amounts to, that it does not stop short of conviction in the world, but that we ourselves become restive with this assurance, and we have the power to undermine ourselves in the name of an, as it were, unachievable or rather illusory rationality. Human beings cannot, unaided, from a standing position, attempt, hence they cannot in this way fail, to leap forward thirty feet or nine meters (or whatever the precise world record is for the long jump). Nor can they realize such an intention by accident; there is no such intention. But can't they *want* to? And wanting to is internal to intending to, as Anscombe argues. There will be borderline cases here, and various talents and ambitions will come into play. So teachers will always be interested to bring realism and inspiration together into the room.

Here is a place at which it is tempting, all but irresistible, to say that Wittgenstein will recommend a species of pragmatism. What this idea leaves out is an idea of how language allows us—indeed drives us—to be, let's say, unreasonable, impractical, to find that we do not see what we know we see, that we may be shown to have been uncertain of what we thought or imagined we knew we were certain of. To be pragmatic is sometimes a precious attitude to achieve in disputes between nations or neighbors or perhaps between the conscious and the unconscious mind. But when consciousness, or language, attacks itself, pragmatism, or compromise, becomes an attack on consciousness itself. To you it is obvious that statements of fact, which are true or false, hence verifiable, are different from statements or expressions of value, which are neither true nor false, hence not verifiable, hence not strictly speaking meaningful. To me it is obvious that every utterance (statement, evaluation, question, rebuke, curse)—which to be meaningful must have a point, and which is meaningful if it has a clear point—is an expression of value, is something found *worth* uttering. Shall we avoid fruitless argument by agreeing that utterances are partly meaningful and partly not meaningful, or that it doesn't matter which position we take, or that neither of these is a real position, but a matter of what used scornfully to be called semantics, mere words? As Henry James more or less says in a different context, this is fine as long as you can get your mind to accede to it.

I came away from the Wittgenstein seminar with some idea of a moral vision that extends over the range of speech, of the human mind as inherently restless, not to say perverse, of utterance as inherently confrontational. This was no doubt urged along by finding that moral philosophy was recovering somewhat from its desert of repetitive stalling that followed the ascendance of logical positivism in advanced philosophy, a recovery associated with such names as G. E. M. Anscombe, Philippa Foot, Stephen Toulmin, and John Rawls, who write as it were in response to the fact that human beings have aching and comprehensible bones to pick with each other. The idea formed itself for me of composing a dissertation beginning with organizing my thoughts over the previous years by following the ancient idea of assessing the rationality of moral argument by comparing it with epistemological argument; but rather than taking science as the model of rationality for comparison, I would instead focus on those ordinary exchanges that the likes of Austin and Wittgenstein bring to bear in speaking of identifying birds and the signs of bread, and unfolding the grammar of chairs and of colors and of pain, exchanges whose rationality, or failure of it, any of us who can speak can attest to. Then if we can see, or slow down, the progress by which skepticism with respect to knowledge of the world and others can be both caused by and alleviated by appeals to ordinary exchanges, perhaps we will be able to take analogous measures in evaluating the rationality of exchanges in comparably comprehensible moral cases, as for example, ones to be found in Plato's *Crito*, in Euripides' *Antigone*, in E. M. Forster's *Howard's End*, in Dickens's *Great Expectations*, in George Eliot's *The Mill on the Floss*. These are in fact, in order, the sources of the initial list of examples that will eventually appear in my dissertation, unpredicted by me at the time I am describing, and that are preserved in *The Claim of Reason* (pp. 265–67) in the early pages of its four chapters on moral philosophy.

Those chapters will end the dissertation, an end that felt, that was, abrupt, but the manuscript had already passed the official limit of one hundred thousand words. And in a sense I never systematically went further along their path, which I had planned to do, nor drew a conclusion from this work that I could recognize as proportional to my expectations for it. However, I still would not discount the explicit idea of those chapters, to the effect that what makes moral exchange rational is not whether it leads to an agreed upon conclusion but whether the exchange is itself pertinent and clarifies incongruent positions, that is, clarifies the responsibilities for holding respectively these positions. And, moreover, I am prepared to recognize a certain way I found of continuing those chapters that Stanley Bates articulates in his contribution to the volume *Stanley Cavell* in the Cambridge Contemporary Philosophy in Focus series, edited by Richard Eldridge. Bates finds that the chapters in *The Claim of Reason* recognizably prepare my later work on moral perfectionism, a proposal I am impressed by and grateful for, one that required Bates to recapture concretely and convincingly the state of moral philosophy in the Anglo-American dispensation of philosophy bequeathed to its students in the 1950s and 1960s, an astonishing feat I could not imagine myself now attempting to do. And the intuition of human exchange as itself inherently morally derived, or driven, is a way of putting the ensuing, longest, final part of *The Claim of Reason*— that apart from which I do not imagine that I would have published the preceding three parts, which derive, notably Parts Two and Three, sometimes quite unchanged, from the dissertation.

By the spring after the Wittgenstein seminar with Clarke I had, on my and Marcia's separation, moved from Panoramic Way into an apartment at a juncture of small shops on College Avenue, near the border of Berkeley and Oakland, just down the hill from the presiding presence of the Claremont Hotel, where strangers were perhaps enjoying themselves day and night. (The significance of the hotel, as of the fact that next door to my little building was the first bar on this street that led directly to the Berkeley campus, is that I must now live at least, and hardly more, than a mile from the university, required by law of establishments serving or selling liquor.) The philosophy department at Harvard wrote me reminding me that I had left Cambridge without passing the so-called topical examination, and without taking two foreign language examinations, requirements of Ph.D. candidates. The topical was in that era in effect an interview with two faculty members lasting from one to two hours, designed to determine whether a candidate (namely, a graduate student who had passed the department's qualifying examinations) has defined a subject for a dissertation, and a mode of pursuing the subject, that the topical committee (perhaps thus transforming itself into a dissertation committee) is persuaded to approve as both intellectually appropriate and feasible for the candidate. The department voted to waive this requirement in my case provided that I submit a dissertation the following year. My language examinations, however, would have to be taken by the end of the current academic year, to be monitored by the chair of the Berkeley philosophy department.

The plan I conceived for the thesis proved to be practical, by which I mean I found that it translated into sections that could be drafted as lectures for the following year's classes. I scheduled for myself a course on Wittgenstein for the fall and one on moral philosophy for the spring. Over the summer I found what I considered pedagogical means by which I considered that the lectures on Wittgenstein, suitably expanded for the first part of the dissertation (which turned out to be the larger of two main parts), would avoid another fiasco on their submission to the Harvard philosophy department. I would begin the fall course discussing the strangeness of the way the *Investigations* begins its philosophizing, namely, with a quotation (the words of someone else) presenting a portrait of a child learning language as remembered and recounted by that child grown up (Saint Augustine), followed by Wittgenstein's imagined portraits of a primitive language and society. And I would also find a way to justify spending as much time as it took to compare Austin's and Wittgenstein's conceptions of knowledge by comparing each of their views of criteria. (Austin does not use the term "criterion," but he has clear and surprising discussions of the question "How do you know?" [e.g., that this is a goldfinch], and I will say that his discussions amount to providing what I call Austinian criteria [e.g., "By the red head"]). For the spring, the concluding part of the dissertation, namely, what became the four chapters on moral philosophy, took about the first eight weeks of the course to present and elaborate, which effectively used up the time there was to turn them in, as they were completed, to the typist to add to the earlier portions of the dissertation, which, to count as officially submitted to the Harvard department, had to be postmarked by the first of April. In 1961 this date fell on Saturday the day before Easter Sunday, when Rachel and I were scheduled to join in an Easter egg hunt. I was in the event able to take this less as an allegory of my dissertation than as a reward for sending it off.

Some two weeks before this deadline, my professional typist had suggested that we hire another typist to make sure the typing would be completed, since she was well past three hundred pages with no clear end in sight. By the fateful Saturday morning it was plain that we would not make the local post office closing, hence had lost the possibility of getting the manuscript postmarked there with today's (due) date. Kay Kuhn found the one location in our part of the Bay Area that stayed open twenty-four hours a day, hence gave us until midnight. By ten o'clock that night, my efficiency now out of reach, the preceding weeks and months capped at the end stage by not having slept for about forty hours (beyond a nap sitting in a chair), I looked around the typist's small apartment, where half a dozen friends were undertaking to collate the original typed pages and four carbon copies of the dissertation into five integral texts (at well over four hundred pages, this meant that more than two thousand pages were in stacks covering a double bed, and as much of the floor as could be saved after paths to move around and between two small rooms. This presented a hopeless picture, and coincided with my recognition that I could not possibly finish the introduction to the dissertation in time to have it typed and get it to the post office by midnight. It wouldn't happen indeed if I had been finished writing it then and there. I announced to nobody in particular that the dissertation could not be submitted on time. Tom Clarke had about an hour earlier appeared from Panoramic Way to drive me to wherever the open Oakland post office was, and had been dragged into the collating business. His spirit and his good looks were fresh, and he injected some needed energy into the group, who managed a laugh when Clarke suggested that the collating was impossibly boring and that we should simply make five equal piles of typed pages and renumber them. When he heard me say disconsolately that I had missed the deadline he gave a whoop of the laughter I never failed to enjoy from him, reserved for a response when one of his friends said something that struck him as particularly idiotic. "They've been waiting for you to finish your dissertation for about four years, and now that it will be postmarked one day late, and probably get there on Monday anyway, they are not going to read it. That makes real sense!" My spirits revived, the good mood lasted, more or less, with some more food ordered in, and about dawn

Clarke and I headed in his MG into the depths of Oakland. We got back in time for me to shower and get into some clean clothes and pick up Rachel for the Easter egg hunt.

For at least a week, possibly two, it seemed that every time I sat down, day or night, except for a meal, I fell asleep on the spot.

Part 10

June 4, 2004

The writing day to day of the dissertation had taken place as part of a continuing existence in which my ineptitude as a single father was on display, in which a divorce was set in motion and a love affair was begun, and in which five courses had to be taught. In addition to the two I have mentioned, on Wittgenstein and on ethics, designed in the fall term to play directly into the dissertation, I was allowed to give a seminar both terms, taking material of these lectures further in discussion. The fifth course I announced was—out of some impulse and intersection of texts at the time that must have been more specific than I can now piece together—philosophy of religion. The sum total of preparation I could give each lecture of that course (until its final month, after my dissertation will have been sent off) took place by turning over a spate of pages that I could refresh my memory of during an hour in my office before the announced time of the class (pages of Hume's *Dialogues on Natural Religion*, of Kant's *Religion Within the Limits of Reason Alone*, of Wisdom's "Gods," of two or three tracts of Luther, of a paper I had a year or so earlier begun writing on metaphor, etc.) and what thoughts of beginnings and continuations I could collect during the ten-minute walk from my office in Dwinelle Hall to the marble and somehow congenial heaviness of what was agreeably called the Mining Building, awaited there by about a hundred students. I must have figured that if

I survived that experience intact, nothing could kill me, so given the stakes the price was fair.

My ineptitude as the father of a nearly four-year-old daughter was not total. Rachel and I easily amused each other in restaurants, with or without companions, and when we cooked in my apartment the comedy of spills and overcooked vegetables was part of the nourishment. The new rhythm of our lives was not established at once, but we were flexible, and we took our time. On one early Sunday in our world now suddenly become unfamiliar, as I came for Rachel to take her, as planned, and would become a Sunday routine, up in the Berkeley hills to Tilden Park for the superb merry-go-round and the animal farm and the working miniature train ride, she was clearly uneasy as we were walking down the stairs to get into my borrowed car. I said, "I think you're feeling a little mixed up. Are you?" She nodded. We were at the bottom stair, and I sat down on it. "Are you worried about Mommy and whether she'll be all right while we're in Tilden Park?" She nodded and sat down beside me. I went on: "Well, we don't have to go anywhere we don't want to go. We can sit here as long as we like, or we could go for a walk up the hill." When after perhaps a quarter of an hour strolling up and back around to the house, I said: "I didn't bring any books for us to read from my apartment, but you could go get one or two from your room. We could make ourselves comfortable on the Clarkes' patio, or we could take the book with us and go down the hill and get a waffle now" (instead of after the park, at a favorite coffee shop whose name, once so familiar to me, I have forgotten). Clearly my fundamental, not to say desperate, aim was to establish the fact that I could take care of Rachel on my own, which essentially meant establishing new places of our own with something of the familiarity of home. "No. I'm fine. Let's go to Tilden Park." Who was reassuring whom?

A note on familiarity. There came a moment a few years later at which I was perfectly rewarded for such attempts as I am describing now. The summer before I moved to Harvard I taught a summer course at the University of California at Santa Barbara, where Rachel, just turned six, was to join me for the six or eight weeks of the term. Marcia was to spend that time in Europe, and soon before she left she put Rachel on a plane for Santa Barbara. Rachel was reasonably perky getting off the plane, or had become reasonably good at putting on a good face, and when we got to the quite nice house I had rented and after looking over the lay of the land, while we were unpacking her things she suddenly burst into sobs. Throwing her arms around me, and while trying to control her gasps of anguish, she was somehow able to manage to form words that I count among the most treasured ever given to me. "Don't think I am not happy to see you. But Mommy is Mommy. And you are just dear old Dad." To have become as familiar and reliable to her as a pair of old boots, and to have established that it would be my high ambition to be the one to whom she could securely say as much, was a magnificent deed of confidence between us.

The next morning started uncertainly, but together we lifted the mild sadness for the wind to take out of our hands. It is such a moment I would be thinking of in saying, as out of a revelation, silently to Rachel: "Our love for each other does not depend on whether I finish my dissertation." There was no other living soul to whom I could imagine feeling confident, happy, in saying that. It was the best attestation I had that I would get it done, that I would throw off the weight of expectation and do what I had not in recent years been able to do, as if I had never actually formed the intention of doing it, say, making an infinite task finite, hence contrariwise.

I have been speaking in these recent pages awfully easily of my brave plans to combine this and that in my thesis, to spend the summer preparing to give lectures in the fall on this part of the thesis and ones in the spring on the other part, and organize the sequence of shocks I had received from Austin and Clarke and Kuhn and Wittgenstein into a presentable, comprehensible work. There was little concrete evidence that I would manage it. I had written things, but I had avoided the thought of producing a dissertation, in effect a first book, that would determine whether this time starting over was actually starting something. I was thirty-three years old, pushing around, wherever I turned, a barrow of fragments.

Here is perhaps a key to why I ventured a course on religion at so apparently inopportune a moment. Erik Erikson's *Young Man Luther* had appeared a year or two earlier, illustrating Erikson's view of the stages of life. I've forgotten who urged me to read it, but not, evidently, the chord it struck in me. The age of thirty-three was the center of the stage at which a developing human (male?), as I recall the message, finds, beyond the identity crisis, commitment to a life's work. What struck me was that it was precisely a life's work (a concept itself perhaps new to me, anyway new as applied to myself) for which I had been scanning the horizon. But isn't that what I had assigned my dangerously delayed dissertation to discern, to initiate? Was it too late? Was it, even more dismaying to consider, yet again a false start? I seem to have wanted to test the reality of my commitment to what I was writing by learning whether my conviction in it bears up in thinking, in the company of a certain range of modern philosophers, toward the region of gods. This was, in those years of my ambience in professional philosophy, almost forbidden territory, along with the fallowness then of the regions of ethics and aesthetics. Many blessings upon philosophy for learning to distrust experience. Many curses upon it, upon what I knew of it, for so fumbling in finding when and how to trust it.

I spoke a while ago of starting psychoanalytic therapy when divorce explicitly became a possibility. I was taking fantasies into my analytic hour of various ways in which I could vanish from the life I had known and had wrecked, even tasting the relish of becoming a social castaway, of being pointed out to visitors on some distant island as once having been a promising philosophical writer. Certain friends, so-called, had told me that I was keeping too close to Rachel, walking her to school every morning, for example; and too close to Marcia, having dinner with the two of them every week, sometimes more than once; I should back away and let them find their own lives. My guilt almost rose to this occasion. It was surely my analyst Dr. Hilger who said to me: "The unexpected happens to everyone. How many people will Rachel meet in her life whom she knows with certainty would put her safety ahead of their own?"

June 5, 2004

Alexandra, so I will call her, was not my student. We met at a party of philosophy graduate students some weeks after I dropped over the edge of Berkeley into Oakland. She was a teaching assistant in psychology, presumably studying for qualifying examinations. The combination of casually borne good looks, easy and intelligent humor, and a true singing voice, in evidence at various stages through an evening drive, spoke to me again through my rather dulled condition. She danced elegantly, and generally conveyed a sense of freedom in her conversation that I did not associate with graduate student life. It became apparent almost as soon as we started seeing one another regularly, which was soon, that this attractive facade covered an inability to study consecutively for her qualifying exams. "My friends score me at over 140 on IQ tests, but I'm a bust at long-term plans." So while she was teaching me, so to speak, additional portions of whatever I know about the pain and course of desire—preparing me further as it were to complete a reading of Proust, which more than once I had found I was too alarmed by to continue in sequence—I spent some time preparing a rescue operation to move Alexandra toward her Ph.D. I decided, not unfamiliarly, that I could teach what I had not mastered. In fact it succeeded, to a significant point. Her qualifying exams would be given at the end of the term, a couple of months away, and she had been warned that unless she sat for them this time, and passed them, her teaching assistantship would be revoked. I was still reading and taking and expanding notes for my dissertation more than I was writing consecutively, and I proposed that we study together, starting (on days I was not with Rachel) in the late afternoon, breaking for a good late dinner at one or other of the restaurants we liked in the area, and resuming until a conclusion in a late, disreputable hour. By May her preparations had fitted her to sail gracefully through the examinations. We had a cause, a history between us, to weave us together.

An acquaintance of Alexandra's was selling a ten-year-old English sports car that Alexandra coveted. The acquaintance wanted six hundred dollars for it. I proposed a deal to Alexandra that took us both by surprise. My notes and sketches of sections and drafts of chapters for the dissertation now filled several cartons. The items that were fit for an initial consecutive typing had mostly been prepared from my handwriting by Earl, an ex-con recently released from San Quentin who had struck up a continuing conversation with Belle at the café in San Francisco where she was waiting tables. She and Mary had befriended him and formed a road for him back into the rusty rules of civilian life. At Mary's suggestion I taught Earl to read my handwriting, and for a mutually satisfactory fee he had typed out, some months earlier, dozens of sheaves of my pages, mostly elaborated notes, resulting in a battery of odd-looking words (not alone because of the philosophical or academic vocabulary but also because of my incurable insistence on lingering sentences), from which I could fashion more shapely sections. As Earl and I got to know each other some, especially as I heard stories about his own daughter, whom he had visited in the Midwest on his release from prison, but whose life with her mother he could now resume no role in, and occasionally having the opportunity to watch him talk with Rachel, and with Mary's confirmation of his steadiness, I eventually entrusted him sometimes to pick up Rachel after school and bring her to my apartment.

The surprising deal with Alexandra was—since I had decided that I must begin consecutive writing of the dissertation at the beginning of June, namely, at the end of the year's teaching and grading, and since writing still meant for me writing by hand, never having, and indeed not until three or four years ago, been able to compose (other than correspondence) at the computer—that I would borrow the six hundred and give it to her in exchange for her agreeing to type whatever I had written at the end of each day, let's say until we arrived, if ever, at three hundred pages, double spaced, at which point we would if we were not finished, renegotiate. At the time, as I was careful to learn, this more than matched a professional typist's fee. (No favors; pay as you go.) Alexandra felt rewarded whenever she toured around in her exciting car, which, having a standard shift, required that I was, quite gladly, pressed into service to teach her to drive it. In reciprocation, the concrete expectation of having a respectable number of pages to present each day actually served to help me get on with, or bully my way past, rough spots that would otherwise have sent me on one or another detour. Here I could tell myself—in fact it was true as often as not— that I would have a better chance to find solutions when I saw the work emerge from written scratches into typed sentences. And besides—here again comes the inevitable issue of secondary gain, a somewhat misleading expression for a fact of human conduct that is as inevitable as the fact that human speech carries implications and forces beyond our ken—our bargain kept us aware of each other's whereabouts each day, without either of us having to seem to express doubts or to declare rights. By the end of the summer we had driven to more than one beach (none is really convenient from the position of Berkeley), and I had a sheaf of some two hundred typed pages of something that promised to continue.

The submitted thesis six months later was a success; my fears about incomprehensibility proved to be sufficiently unfounded. This was due in essential measure, I believe, to the way it got written, I mean specifically to its pages being so immediately drafted in preparation for, or in consciousness of, the classroom. I did not hesitate to pause over matters that might have seemed unnecessary to go into by colleagues, but I was used from students' reactions to having to recognize what I did as strange, and this very awareness of strangeness, and practice in lessening it, or preparing for it, served me well. Indeed it became an essential topic of the work of writing, irreducibly in considering which kinds of challenges to claims of knowledge are reasonable and which kinds unreasonable, or said otherwise, which more radical doubts are natural, hence not dismissible, and which, or when, are unnatural.

I took Rachel along with me on the trip East for the thesis defense. We flew first to Atlanta, where I left Rachel with my parents while I flew the next day to Cambridge. When I returned to Atlanta two days later Rachel knew more about her grandparents' apartment complex than I would ever know, including lore about how to use the night lights around and within the communal swimming pool behind the second row of apartments, a facility I had never been apprised of on my previous brief visits there.

My first time in Cambridge after five years back in Berkeley was duly shocking. Berkeley's charm—I will never hesitate to call it magic—is obvious. It has qualities that last, but you needn't have felt them to appreciate what greets the senses on first arriving at San Francisco Bay and the views of it from the Berkeley hills. The age of Cambridge and the curve of the Charles River through Cambridge toward Boston, are, in comparison, reticent. Loving parts of the region that are worn with civilization can be something of an acquired taste. Walking with my mother, on one of her visits when I was a graduate student, down Brattle Street out from Harvard Square, many of whose well-positioned houses exhibit a glamour of prestige for natives but to a stranger can appear somewhat shabby, mere things of the past, I pointed out to her a house I happened to know had just been bought by an acquaintance and told her the price I had been told. She stared at it: "For *that*?" Transport that pile to Atlanta, in a neighborhood of houses of comparable age and size, and it was boards and bricks. She knew what comparably aged Southern mansions looked like, often set almost invisibly far back from roads on the western edge of Atlanta, where she had a number of times been invited before the Second World War to play in Sunday afternoon musicales, and where, in the decades of change after the war, several of her richest relatives had bought houses. These in Cambridge, by comparison, were seriously in need of attention. As usual I was caught wandering between worlds. I was readily enough disdainful of those whose acceptance of themselves was a function, among other variables, of their addresses, yet looking out of the windows of the Society of Fellows' rooms in Eliot House, at the greensward running, interrupted by Memorial Drive, down to the river's edge, I would think of what money could once buy that imaginable amounts of money cannot now buy.

By the time I returned to Cambridge for the thesis defense, Marshall was several years into his appointment as Assistant Professor in the Harvard philosophy department and was a tutor living in Eliot House. He was in his element, duly earned by the hard work of his learning, and by the sincerity of his admiration for what money may be necessary for but not sufficient for, say, the manners of the young with famous family names. We were genuinely glad to see each other. He said: "I've become an institution, you know." His good spirits were infectious and I replied: "I'm hardly surprised. I gather I am still an experience." As if in appreciation of my willingness to play the game, he introduced me to several of his favorites at lunch in the House. Afterward several of us went to one of the young men's suites that boasted a piano, where the young man who owned the piano and I read through a four-hand arrangement of the slow movement of the Jupiter Symphony (its trickiest movement from the perspective of ensemble). Marshall was openly proud of both of his friends.

I had not been in Cambridge since Marcia and I had stopped there on our way back from Europe and New York to Berkeley. It turned out that we had arrived a few days before that year's final dinner of the Society of Fellows. On phoning to learn whether there would be room for a farewell appearance of a returning member of the Society, I was assured that there would be, and I was asked to come an hour early to be part of a commemorative photograph to be taken outside the Society's rooms. A print of the resulting photograph is at this moment roughly where it has been for four decades, standing at the front and leaning against a stack of framed certifications at the back of a small mantelpiece in my study some twenty feet from where I am writing this extended e-mail addressed to an undefined future, observed by those figures from a ponderable past. Having passed near this image so many times I can feel, if not quite see individually from this distance, the faces of Marshall Cohen and Henry Rosovsky and John Hollander and Donald Hall and George Kateb and Marvin Minsky and McGeorge Bundy and Harry Levin and Vassily Leontiev and Van Quine, and some fifteen other past and present Senior and Junior Fellows protecting me from evil spirits.—Would this not make them gargoyles? No, there are no longer such gargoyles. But there are still evil spirits.

I remarked to Levin when I arrived at the gathering for the photograph that I had spent a day last week with Paul de Man and his family in Paris (like me, finishing up his third year as a Junior Fellow): "He sends you his regards." Levin cocked his head away, as if to hear the echo of what I had said, and replied in a manner—halting, head turned aside as if still listening rather than speaking, showing his genuinely fine profile—that various of his students have in my presence imitated: "I wish—I could agree—with Paul's taste—in philosophy." Something is awry with each element in that assertion.

Returning to Berkeley after the defense of the dissertation, I was presented by Tom Clarke with two inspired presents. First, he had made plans to take me the following week to my first major league baseball game, San Francisco having not long before our arrival in California acquired the (former New York) Giants. So despite growing up in Atlanta and Sacramento before the major leagues had expanded beyond the northern half of the eastern third of the United States, I was not to be denied the imperishable ecstasy of watching Willie Mays turn around with the sound of the bat hitting a ball (conceivably even before the sound reached him) and, running full tilt toward the right-field fence, make the catch over his shoulder. Second, for the succeeding week Tom had bought tickets for Lenny Bruce at the *hungry i* night club. This was the cause of a thrilling compliment Clarke gave me, or anyway one he knew I would find thrilling. During Lenny Bruce's set,

Tom was sitting behind me with a common friend—I've forgotten who. (Barry Stroud would not join the department until the following fall; perhaps it was a graduate student we were close to; perhaps it was during one of Marshall's visits to Berkeley.) After Bruce's set, Tom and this other were laughing amiably, not hard enough to be rehearsing a Bruce moment. When I turned around to them, Tom said: "We were just agreeing that Bruce reminded us of your two-hour lecture yesterday." Since I did not imagine Tom's comment to have been unfriendly, which would have taken it simply as a simultaneous dig at Lenny Bruce and at me, I heard it rather as a way of acknowledging that one can value the way my mind likes to work, and understand what I am searching for, without an impulse to embrace it for themselves. My wish to keep a number of strata of ideas moving in the same direction, seeming to require perpetual modulations as well as multiple themes, strikes them as an improvisation meant to link insights that, like punch lines, can be reached no other way, but the cost of which is the persistent danger of abusive obscurity. Marshall meant something similar, I believe, when he would say to me years earlier, in various versions: "Bad Cavell is awful." He and Marcia developed a little routine between them in which, after I had come out with one of Stanley's Deep Responses, they glanced at each other, simultaneously clutched their guts, and gasped as if punched.

June 7, 2004

The year before I was putting together the dissertation, Morton White was in residence at the Stanford Center for the Behavioral Sciences. He came over to Berkeley in the fall for a talk to the philosophy department and, with his wife, Lucia, to have dinner with Marcia and me, together with Tom and Jill Clarke. During the spring he asked me to drive down and join him for lunch at the Stanford Center. The principal news of the lunch proved to be to tell me in confidence that Marshall was going to be considered in the coming academic year for tenure by the Harvard department. "I think it probably will be successful, but it is not a sure thing. The administration, and powerful faculty members outside the department, admire Marshall's devotion to the

humanities, but he has published very little. I want to tell you in person
that you have also been on the department's mind, but your failure to
submit a dissertation matters to certain people. It has been suggested to
us in all seriousness that we simply award you the Ph.D. on the basis of
your two published papers. But we really don't do such things. Anyway,
I allow myself also to tell you that Quine is adamant that you should
have spent the last year of your Junior Fellowship completing your dissertation rather than traveling in Europe." I thanked White and told
him that Marcia and I were divorcing, and that while my plans were
definite to begin writing through an idea for a thesis, my mood was one
in which I had no confidence but that my life has irretrievably come
apart, and an appointment to Harvard will not repair that. White liked
Marcia and was visibly saddened to hear this news. I went on to confirm that his concern for Marshall implied that Marshall had not submitted his Lowell Lectures on metaphor for publication. I had read the
lectures at Marshall's request and urged him to publish them pretty
much as they were given. They were not—as Marshall insisted that
they were not—wonderful. But he did not see how to improve them
substantially. I insisted, in turn, that they were better than anything
else I had read in recent years covering the same material, and at the
least provided the most intelligent and comprehensive introduction I
knew of to the subject and to the current literature on the subject. Maybe he could still be persuaded to publish it. "Anyway," I concluded to
White, "Marshall is Marshall. He was made, and has made himself, for
the position at Harvard, representing the humanities to the university
from within the philosophy department. The obviousness of this should
not be clouded by the matter of the amount of publication." White simply replied, "Marshall is Marshall. We'll see."

The following year, in the fall after the spring in which I had
submitted a dissertation and received the Ph.D., White wrote to me
suggesting that I apply (using his name) to the Institute for Advanced
Study at Princeton for a moderately subsidized fellowship there for the
coming year, since he would also be spending the year in residence
there and had some say in bringing in younger people who could, in
addition to profiting their own work, usefully participate in the general
discussion of the population that would be in residence then. A few
weeks later the news arrived that Marshall's tenure nomination had

failed to materialize. Tom Clarke had heard specific rumors about the lines along which the vote had split, but imagining the cost to Marshall was what preoccupied us. We tried proposing to ourselves that maybe getting away from Harvard would do Marshall good, as it incontestably had done good to each of us. But neither of us quite believed this would be true in the same way for Marshall, and the occasions of these exchanges became ones in which we each vented our anger at the sufferings that Harvard and its self-satisfactions seem put on earth to inflict. The inconclusiveness of this perception was that Berkeley had just delivered a comparable blow to Kurt Fischer's hopes of being renewed there.

From this distance it seems to me that not a month then passed before the invitation came offering me tenure in the Harvard department. I phoned White, who congratulated me but offered no explanation of the course events had taken in the department between his and my exchanges at Stanford and the offer to me perhaps eighteen months later. He suggested that I use the Princeton fellowship to postpone my decision, and from Princeton come up to Cambridge once or twice to talk with people and imagine the consequences of the move.

The new chair of the department at Berkeley—I've forgotten whether it was Mates or Karl Aschenbrenner—had informed me some weeks earlier that the department was going to postpone the tenure decision in my case until they had some evidence about how I was going to turn my dissertation into publishable pieces. This was dangerous news for me since I had no intention whatever of publishing pieces of it. It was going to be all or nothing, and, quite apart from the fact that there was not yet a tentative whole there, there was something amiss with the way I had presented the critically important matter of criteria in the *Investigations* and I still could not see my way more clearly through it. Within several weeks of my showing the new chair at Berkeley the letter of invitation from Harvard, the Berkeley department voted my promotion to tenure.

I would not want my feelings here to be misconstrued. There may well have been an unattractive sense of vindication in my attitude toward those at Berkeley who had never particularly wished me well. But primarily I realized then, as I realize now, that these events represent fairly the way academic appointments were, and so far as I know still are, made. Large and ambitious universities are on average probably no less complex, and no subtler, at making decisions about hiring and promotion, and generally no more or less rational in evaluating and balancing talent and productiveness and promise and reputation and loyalty and simple affection, than law firms or insurance companies or sports teams. It is true that the latter have measures of winning and losing apparently more objective (cases handled successfully, policies written, league standings) than universities do. Yet one imagines universities to have the freedom to be better, at once juster and kinder and more imaginative. The tenure system of university appointments is the profound difference to be assessed. Everyone who votes on an appointment has in principle had years to come to know the candidate; and among those already granted tenure, no one in a large department is apt to be in a position to wield the kind of power distributed in the upper reaches of a hierarchy of individuals in an economically or politically driven association.

So the rapid, competitive, turnaround on the vote on my case in the Berkeley department was in particular not to be construed as overcoming ill will toward me on, perhaps, Mates's part, at least not entirely. I think this follows independently from the following evidence. At a meeting of the Berkeley department during my first year there, Mates announced: "There are only two ways of doing anything useful in philosophy. You can learn some logic and use it where you can. Or you can learn some languages and do a little history." (Obviously modest descriptions of his well-known strengths.) At a meeting of the department a couple of years later he announced: "There are only three ways of doing anything useful in philosophy. You can learn some logic, et cetera. Or you can learn some languages, et cetera. Or you can do some literary psychology." I don't know who else but myself would have been a candidate in his mind for this third option. Nor do I take it as mere condescension. Mates, in his disillusion with philosophy, had taken both of the first two options, but the three options have several matters in common—all take a certain diligence and knack, any may, taken far enough, require genuine intelligence, and none can or should claim to be the whole of what is to be called philosophy, or thinking.

What had happened in the case of the humanities appointment at Harvard came out only on my visit months later from Princeton to Cambridge and first meeting Rogers Albritton. It was quite obvious that we were destined to become friends, from my point of view not because of but despite the obviousness of his uncanny knack at achieving virtually immediate intimacy, or immediate virtual intimacy. Both were achieved with me—along, I felt, with genuine friendliness—on his expressing his knowledge that I would want to know how my proposed appointment was related to Marshall's rejection. His account breached whatever decorum it had to in order to assure me that the friends of Marshall's appointment had been faithful in arguing the case. It was the near absence of Marshall's professional publication then, in the early 1960s, together with the absence of a Ph.D. dissertation (the unpublished lectures on metaphor did not for them add up as a substitute for that), which left the department without a sufficient consensus on the appointment. In what I imagine to have been the general air of uncomfortable surprise at the department's negative vote, it was suggested that the appointment should not be construed as tied to Marshall's case, that if the department had needed a philosophical representative of the humanities then it still needs it, and my name came up as the obvious next piece of business. This time the two present readers of my dissertation (the third had been a visiting professor from another university) reminded their colleagues that they had awarded it the exceptional mark of Distinction, and it was decided that it, and my two principal published papers (the two that will become the opening two chapters of *Must We Mean What We Say?*), would be read by the department, after which they would reconvene to consider the appointment. This was to be done essentially at once, as in effect part of the consideration of the same appointment that had preoccupied the department and the administration for some time. At the reconvening of the department Quine was asked where he stood and reported that now that I had submitted a substantial dissertation in time for such a decision, his refusal to consider my case was no longer pertinent. As for the quality of the work, he saw nothing wrong with it, if you like that sort of thing (I think I am reporting Rogers's words accurately, who was perfectly capable of remembering the exact words of an exchange). I found Quine's reported reaction in withdrawing his veto to represent an unanswerable moral justification of his declared materialism. However one understands complex things to think, they do not do the terrible thing of bearing grudges. (So I like to imagine, perhaps contrary to logic.)

June 8, 2004

My last months at Berkeley that year were professionally uneventful. There was nothing more to decide until I moved East for the year in Princeton (even if I decided to return to Harvard, I would spend the ensuing summer in Berkeley to be near Rachel), and I was so exhausted from the enforced dissertation writing that I was content, indeed found it bordering the ecstatic, just to take pleasure from reading whatever I found to my liking and to enter my next major stretch of movie viewing. With the exception of two nights, I had not seen a film from the time I began the routine of writing from June 1, 1960, until ten months later driving the finished product with Tom Clarke to the Oakland post office. Pauline Kael had converted a pair of adjacent small shops three blocks from Sather Gate—being the main pedestrian entrance to the Berkeley campus, the plaza Sather Gate opened onto became the site of the initial massive student demonstrations that will form in the spring of my first year of teaching back at Harvard—in effect into two screening rooms, showing different films and changing films more often than once a week, each room primitive in appointment, each with no more than two or three dozen seats, but each with programs satisfying the advanced taste of the most sophisticated art house audience. It was a glorious span of education. Alexandra and I were regulars that last year.

A secondary register of the decision to take the coming year in Princeton was to have an occasion for ending the connection with Alexandra. It obviously would not survive separation, or say, lack of surveillance. Its freedom and pleasure were intact, but her heart was with those who wanted to keep life in permanent tension and suspension. What better life was there than this of vague study and moving among continuous packs and in shifting pairs? And what better place for this carousel than Berkeley? A particular small cafeteria on Telegraph Avenue was well known for having in its precincts at any time of day a predominance of graduate students rumored to have dissertations done or all but done, but neglecting to submit them because it would mean having no justification for staying in Berkeley, which is to say, postponing the end of youth. After Alexandra passed her qualifying examinations, the idea of a dissertation proved never to remain in consecutive discussion.

But her path, or studied lack of it, being openly hers, was not dishonorable. What was dishonorable was the basis of my constancy with her, that is, the basis of the limitation I put upon it, a permanent distance. Not long after we had established expectations of each other, she veered off on a couple of escapades. I was hurt, in a way that, from my past, might have bound me to a routine of hurts, feeling responsible for an injustice done me. Instead, after an all-night conversation of fancy words I brought us to something that resembled understanding. In fact it was my taking of a moral hostage. There was no serious forgiveness, no mutual recognition, tilted by desire, of frailty or anger or fear, but a stab at a permanent excuse to walk out whenever I wished. I was unwise beyond my years. When I got to Princeton, and continuing into Cambridge, I would find myself missing her sharply and in imagination castigating her and falsely forgiving her by turns, but truly blaming myself for her further escapades. In the end what I said, and found I meant, was that I no longer wanted to be crazy with doubtful and unappeasable desire, that I wanted a commitment, faith in one other, something neither of us could convincingly offer the other.

I think I would not now have phrased things quite this way before living fairly recently with Eric Rohmer's *A Tale of Winter*, a film I kept coming back to sufficiently to write about as a work that not simply refers to, and depicts the concluding scene of, Shakespeare's *The Winter's Tale*, but that forms something like a continuous commentary on the play. The young woman of Rohmer's film (combining elements in Shakespeare's play of Leontes' outbreak of madness and of his child Perdita's exposure and lostness) separates from one of her suitors by saying she cannot live with a man about whom she is not crazy with love. But when the father of her child, with whom she had spent one summer away from Paris, almost miraculously reappears after five years, in which he has not known about the child, the woman seems less crazy— less flighty, less seemingly perverse in her perpetual argumentativeness, cured by faith confirmed.

June 9, 2004

The principal feature I have not entered into my account of my six years of teaching in Berkeley is the discovery that Mary Randall and her daughter, Belle (having changed her name from Wendy), were again living there. In another world they would be heroines of my account as it seeks out the story of my fate. Which means that they are forever heroines in certain of the worlds among the constellation of worlds of my inner, other, lives—well, of this one life, if you know sufficient ways to read it. Our conversations began again, and again with my sense at once of being known by Mary as no one had known me, and at the same time being unable to make myself clear to her. Her independence of judgment was exhilarating and frightening to me; you never knew whether the last would be first in her affection (after Belle), or whether nothing, or next to nothing, was either last or first. The world for her was well lost, except for Belle, who had had some college years and was soon to publish her first poems, and except for the children in the lost world who profited from the special needs education that Mary had become an expert in, and made a modest living from providing. In our conversations in this new era I was never able, for example, to make clear why contemporary advanced philosophy had come largely to avoid serious moral and aesthetic and religious questions and seemed to me so often arid. Mary asked: "Why put up with it? Why not change it, or get out of it?" (She might as well have asked the same—it seemed to feel the same—about my relation to my unlettered parents, stuck in circumstances beyond change.) Which of us was unreasonable or unrealistic—the one who would treat institutions as largely annoyances or the one who might be giving his life to something he deplored? My part of the conversations made what I took as some of my braver insights seem timid, my education still cruelly stunted. I felt that if I could not hold on to that sense of loss, I would be lost entirely.

I do not know whether Berkeley was unusual in the late 1950s for its preoccupation with the dangers of atomic pollution. There was an ongoing concern with the presence of the Lawrence radiation laboratory just over the adjacent hills, and there was a brief public debate over the announced plans for evacuating the Berkeley area in case of an atomic attack, brief in part because the announced plans struck everyone I knew as hopelessly inadequate. But the fears were also attached to more individual matters. X-rays were a recurrent topic of discussion. I was involved with this because my dentist had discovered that I had developed an alarming number of cavities. I seem to recall that he added something about the age of thirty as one in which this is to be expected. What interested me more was his explaining that I did not need to be overly alarmed by the need for the complete set of X-rays his interventions would require. He assured me that his X-ray equipment was efficient and above all that he used the newest, fastest X-ray film, requiring a reduced time of exposure. When I asked what form the danger of exposure took, he replied: "It has a general aging effect." It seemed we were living in a horror movie.

It happens, coming back ten days short of three years after the date of this entry to insert late editing changes into a presentable manifestation of this manuscript, that an appointment for an MRI this morning, new in what I assumed was my considerable experience of diagnostic procedures, scheduled because a sciatic pain in my left leg and buttock has recurred, leaving me unable to walk without discouraging pain, let alone walk for pleasure and for reassuring exercise. The idea, if an inflamed or pinched sciatic nerve is indeed determined to be the cause, is to control the pain with an epidural injection of cortisone. I had, in preparation for the MRI, been questioned about various counterindications for going ahead with it, from issues of recent surgeries or metallic implantations to whether I was claustrophobic. Although I have sometimes noticed, characteristically driving through tunnels, that I am in fact subject to mild claustrophobia, I am sufficiently accustomed to it to have been confident that the tinge of anxiety and of a need for deeper breaths than sometimes I feel I can manage would not interfere with the procedure. This was quite true, even though the noises in the belly of the machine into which I had been encased were more penetrating—cascades of knocks and buzzes and grindings—than any, save one, that I have ever experienced. The exception was a room set aside in the Stein printing plant where Mendel gave me a job during the beginning of the summer before my little family's last move to Sacramento. It was a room in which, because of the noise of metal perpetually slamming against metal, only deaf people worked all day. The noise was that of the shaping of lead type, and the room largely contained the noise by enclosing it with concrete walls with small doubled heavy windows and a wide, thick metal door that slid open and closed. Since a main task of mine was collecting and either discarding or storing used forms of set type, stacking the forms on a wheeled platform that I rolled out of the back of the printing plant and down a ramp in a large garage onto a basement floor, I had to enter and collect metal from that room every day. But I learned something further about claustrophobia today, as it presents itself to me now. I had until now vaguely surmised that it was somehow associated with a memory of being born. But that seemed too fanciful to take with full seriousness.

Yet why just this fancy—suggested, I observe, from my speaking just now of "noises in the belly" of the MRI apparatus? My only rush of fright, I would say terror, during my roughly thirty minutes inside the apparatus, dealt in half a dozen segments of two to four minutes each, announced as such as an introduction to each segment—with one intermission in which I was slid out of the tube in order to receive an injection of dye and immediately slid back in, cautioned not to shift my body—occurred after I was told over the speaker system inside the cylinder that the procedure was complete. Then nothing happened. No voice, no initiating sense of sliding out. Within seconds—that is, after an interval a few seconds longer than those within the procedure that separated the end of one segment and the voice announcing the duration of the next—I began imagining that the attendant had either forgotten me or had dropped into a faint or some catastrophe had visited the world; and left me strapped in place, neither able to move nor make my cries heard from within this hard cocoon. Recapturing traces—fragments I would rather say—of these feelings as I write this, I realize only now that this sense of absolute abandonment by life replicates, calls back, my experience of bereftness when my mother was two or three minutes late (that is, later than my uninformed expectation assigned for her) in coming to my bedside when I awoke, when I was five or six, in the hospital the morning after I had been struck by the automobile. The role of temporal intervals, let's say of rhythm, in ordering the depth and the fragility of human hopes, say, one's conviction in futurity, must be a basis for the profundity of our need for music. So the enclosed space of which claustrophobia speaks, and the sense of breathlessness or suffocation it invites, is further comprehensible as a state in which one's existence has become undetectable.

I was asked by Stephen Pepper to come up to his beautiful and beautifully situated house in the Berkeley hills to talk about my recent offer to move permanently to Harvard. Pepper had retired from the Berkeley philosophy department several years earlier, having for years been its most prominent member, the one whose writing played a recognizable role in and beyond the field of philosophy. His pragmatist views of art were backed in his experience by his notable collection of Japanese silk screens; and his *World Hypotheses*, introducing the idea of root metaphors, is still cited. It was he who had interviewed me at Harvard six years earlier and had made the case at Berkeley for granting me an initial year's leave of absence for travel in Europe before beginning to teach full-time, approving my sense of such a year's importance for me, as well as having welcomed me warmly when we arrived to settle in Berkeley. I knew (it was known, the profession of philosophy was then still quite small) that Pepper had also had an offer some years earlier to move to Harvard, and I told him this as I entered his house for our talk. We agreed at once that it may be as much fun to turn down a Harvard offer as to accept one. I tried to blunt the point of the visit by saying that I really did not want to think about the pluses and minuses of the decision, both because Harvard and Berkeley were the two places that I had ever felt at home and I could not rationally choose between them on their merits, and because the decision would essentially depend on the state of my, let's say, disorganized life, essentially on the fact of my being a divorced father. What I had to consider objectively, as it were, was in which place I stood a better chance of remaining in regular touch with my young daughter, the coming few years being the time in which such a possibility is found or lost. As if he had not heard what I said, or made no sense of it, he poured us glasses of wine and took me out to his balcony, which claimed one of those Berkeley views, real views not just observation posts, but a balcony placed for a reason and trees planted for their orienting and framing powers. "Cambridge is the past; Berkeley"—his long arm and attractive hand holding the glass of wine swept across the horizon, as if toasting the panorama—"is the future." Not quite the same as George Berkeley's having made his

California name by saying, "Westward the course of Empire takes its way," but not without its own plausibility, even if still aimed too high for the concerns occupying my attention. Pepper predicted that his prophecy would be fully manifest in twenty-five years, that I must have felt something of the sort in noting the large number of new Ph.D.s from Harvard and Yale and Princeton who had accepted offers from Berkeley in recent years, in philosophy, in English, in music, in history, in economics. I had noticed, and not I alone. Indeed I had been surprised, and rather disheartened, to find at successive cocktail parties in the huge English department at Berkeley (with a faculty the size of that of an entire substantial private college) shortly after I arrived in town, that a conversation creating fervent participation from a notable segment of the guests concerned recent tenure decisions in the Harvard English and romance languages and history departments. I fumbled for some reply to Pepper, assuring him that I felt sharply how hard it is to imagine leaving Berkeley. (At a quick estimate, at least half of those I knew, who took the westward course in my era, proved to remain.) No one seemed to realize that there was a sad story connected with the sudden emergence of an opening at Harvard for what I do, or seek to do. The impending, extended crises in the humanities, associated with varying importations of philosophy, primarily current French and German philosophy, into literary studies were generally not yet news.

June 10, 2004

My following year at the Princeton Institute was punctuated by plane trips to Berkeley every month to see Rachel (Marcia brought her to Princeton to spend the Christmas vacation with me, wishing herself to spend time in New York), as well as by repeated trips to Atlanta during the fall, when my father's colon surgery went awry. These emergencies, together with the skimpiness of the Institute's stipend, drove me deeper into debt, which in the end my uncle Mendel reduced.

Mendel turns ninety this week. Cathleen and I along with our son Benjamin and his increasingly serious girlfriend, Emily, who has in effect happily become family, leave tomorrow morning for the celebratory party for Mendel in Atlanta. (In the year and some months between writing this and present revisions of it, this ambitious yet clear-eyed young pair have translated themselves explicitly into marriage.) Our younger son, David, this past month, on a week's tour of the South with a friend between the end of the college year and the beginning of his work canvassing for MASSPIRG, a charitable organization, visited Mendel in Atlanta and has warned me that I will find him aged, somewhat stooped but refusing to use a walker, and still quite alert and charming. The twelve or thirteen years between Mendel and me, which for most of my long life seemed vast steps over a fixed distance, have become an easy arm's length. After him—the last of my father's and my mother's siblings—no one I grew up with stands between me and God. The coast is clear, indeed lucid. It is as it should be.

I felt during the Princeton year as never before the sting of being unable to meet the financial obligations of the life I had caused for myself. This was bound to affect the decision I was to come up with whether to leave or to stay in Berkeley. Marcia had said, not for the first time, that she wished to move to New York. That she had in any case to move from the Bay area was settled in recognizing that there was no independent life for her where she and I and our common friends lived within virtual eyeshot of one another. That it would be to New York followed from the general fact that it was after all New York, and in addition from the specific circumstance that a relationship had begun there that she was interested to explore further. My own calculations were as follows, based on the understanding that Rachel would continue to live most of the year with Marcia. In the worst case they would move to New York and I would stay in Berkeley. Worst, since Berkeley's semester was fifteen weeks and Harvard's was roughly twelve and a half, and since Berkeley's salary was lower than Harvard's, commuting to see Rachel would be at its most difficult. In the moderate case, in which on the contrary I moved and they (therefore) remained in Berkeley, my commuting would be rather more manageable. In the best case my move to Harvard would in fact spur Marcia on to make the move to New York, since (especially because she had herself grown up without a father) she strongly felt the good of making it as easy as possible for Rachel and me to have the best chance of remaining a reasonably normal part of one another's lives.

The best found its way to happen. Rachel and I spent much of that first summer back in Cambridge, in 1963, moving into a suite of rooms I again was given at Adams House (in return for participating in House life and events, and where I had lived for two of my years as a Junior Fellow ten years earlier), and she and Marcia moved permanently to New York before the coming Christmas. Rachel and I therefore, beyond summers, could spend every weekend together, alternating Cambridge and New York. She was now six years old, and our beginning routine was for me to fly down to New York and fly back with Rachel on Fridays, and then down with her on Sundays and back alone. Before her seventh birthday the following spring, under the eyes of what were then called stewardesses (a number of whom on the New York / Boston run we had become acquainted with the previous year), Rachel was taking her turn alone every other week. As often as not, Allen Graubard, then a graduate student in the philosophy department, one of a small group among the young who formed the basis of my new social and intellectual life beyond the classroom, would borrow his friend John Mudd's Carmen-Ghia on the alternate Friday afternoons Rachel was due to come to Cambridge and drive me to Logan Airport to gather her up, lending to her and my regular reunions, with his knack for interesting, informative banter, a festive public air that made a context in which Rachel's and my suspended intimacy would have time and space, unlike the foreign air of a taxicab, in which to reorient and reassert itself.

Living in Adams House made such matters distinctly easier, I might even say financially feasible, but at the same time it added, when the academic year began, its measure of fun spending weekends in Cambridge together. In addition to Rachel's acquiring dozens of prospective big brothers who were discovering that they missed their families and any number of whom might invite Rachel on weekend afternoons when she was with me to join them in throwing a Frisbee in the courtyard just outside our Adams House entry, she and I had almost all our meals in the comfortably decent and pleasantly bustling House dining hall, served on trays that were themselves large, segmented heavy round plastic plates (I had not and have not seen their like outside the Harvard dining halls) that we could also choose to fill and bring back to our suite when we wished. My own neediness was accordingly lent all the security an independent, well-functioning institution can provide. It is part of my undying gratitude to Harvard, or, to be more specific, to the unfathomable depth of its wealth and of its power, to make its presence and its wings of protection palpable. And yet.

Since a year ago as I write this, our younger son, David, has transferred from Bard College to become a sophomore at Tufts, and Cathleen and I often drive him back to his dormitory from having had dinner at home with us across the Charles River in Brookline. Driving through Cambridge on the way back, we leave the mostly darkened buildings of the Tufts quad and soon find ourselves weaving through the compounding luxuriousness of the Harvard Law School and Harvard's Peabody Museum of natural history and Harvard's Fogg Museum of Art, across from the philosophy building, Emerson Hall, where William James and Josiah Royce and George Santayana all once upon a time (more precisely, less than half a century before I was admitted to graduate study there, a bit more than half a century ago) taught philosophy, and through the pressing activity in Harvard Square, all declaring the illusory possession of the present as well as of the past and the future, I sometimes find myself struggling against the awful awareness of irreducible arbitrariness and greediness, even where (or especially where) it is inadvertent, in such concentrated (not of course unique) advantage. Such sinful feelings of impotent, if not meaningless, comparison are put to rights in my knowledge of the blissful, irreplaceable luck in having spent my undergraduate years in worlds of music and theater, together with the consequent years of pain in finding that the standards of happiness and accomplishment sketched and promised me then would have in my case to be discovered and elaborated in some other world, among other intimates. (Is it essentially in the trap of being an only child of dissonant parents that I am repeatedly reminded that not all of my friends are of interest to the others?)

The time of my spotty Princeton year had been marked with the initiation of three fateful friendships. I have already described coming to know Bernard Williams, who occupied an odd position in my intellectual conscience. His capacity for friendship and his dialectical force were no more lost on me than on many others. But I counted on something beyond these unmistakable spires. I did not take at face value his grudgingness toward Austin and Wittgenstein, whose influence upon him I felt, as I did in Clarke's case, that he was determined to deny or to play down, encouraged in my suspicion of his philosophical impatience, however illogically, by my belief in the reality of his passion for music, particularly for Wagner. And I went so far as to believe that my holding up to him this portrait of a further and more reticent Bernard, whose capacity for tolerating a greater incidence of obscurity in the expression of sublimity than he (who? which?) was accustomed to claim, was something, was even the particular thing, he wanted from me.

And I have also mentioned that it was when, in the fall of the Princeton year traveling up to Cambridge for a few days, that I first met Rogers Albritton, and so began easing into the imagination of life in a department with such a colleague. But it was with Michael Fried during those days that a first meeting became the persistent emblem of the relationship it initiated.

At a party to which Marshall insisted I accompany him, saying there would be someone there I should meet, a gathering soon understandable to be heavily textured with undergraduates registering names among the peaks of American fashionable society, and including at least one young person destined to succeed a father as the head of a foreign government, Fried and I found ourselves standing in a corner of a typically drab Cambridge apartment of those years, our having been put together by Marshall with something like the words, "You are going to want to know each other." Whenever I have been tempted to write off Marshall's fascination with fame based upon an inheritance of social standing, and the graces lit by taste and money, to a puzzling irruption of snobbery, he would soon do something or judge something that showed unmistakably that he knew as well as anyone how to value these partially aesthetic recommendations against genuine artistic or moral, or for that matter religious, achievement. In another world he just might have been, or become, Swann. (I have one other candidate for this late reincarnation; all in good time.)

From perhaps eight o'clock as the party was still forming until the remaining core of the gathering moved to Boston after midnight to have a late supper in Copley Square, Fried and I stood in our relatively private corner, where at first a radiator was sometimes noticeable as all but unbearably hot, talking about anything and everything that might find a place determined by intersecting axes of art and philosophy and the concept of the modern. What was impressive was not alone the ground covered—as a Princeton undergraduate Fried had studied with R. P. Blackmur, whose essays I had read admiringly in the *Kenyon Review*; and talked with Clement Greenberg, whom I had followed with gratitude in the pages of the *Partisan Review*; and, having taken a year at the University of London after two Rhodes years at Oxford, he had studied philosophy with Richard Wollheim and with Stuart Hampshire, both of whose writings were part of the strain of professional philosophy that I cared about most. In general Fried was distinctly more cultivated (except in the world of music) than I had been at his age, twelve or thirteen years younger than I, and was earlier than I had been at finding a voice of his own to live with, or to live by. But age dropped out permanently that opening night as we found ourselves pushed not merely to new subjects but were led steadily to speak at the limits, and sometimes as it were just the other side, of what we knew and could judge. This was a further species of shared testing, demanding stakes of conviction, of what we each would call knowledge, which were backed, or backable, by nothing more than who we were, or thought we were, and what we could find words for and reject words for. This some-times produced from Fried—rather less from me I think that night, with repeated shocks at my willingness to trust his judgments, or to capture my interest in them, in just the way he voiced them—a long arc of violent assertions, risks of perception, launched with athletic energy that to my mind scored his points across considerable portions of my inner field. This did not strike me as—though others have, on first or second encounter with him, not infrequently taken it for—dogmatism, but instead presented I felt a richly informed and flexible enactment of Wittgenstein's pedagogical warning, or understanding, that at some point in philosophical exchange you are going to have to say, "This is simply what I do," in a way that defines your own sense that you make sense and that offers the other a fair chance to discover the sense. This is a matter irreducibly of philosophical tact, the touch not to distort your life by drawing this line too hastily or crudely, but at the same time not to delay drawing it so late that you miss your life. For two people who are not prone to folly to acquire so swiftly and to maintain the degree of faith we inspired in one another does not happen many times in a lifetime.

June 11, 2004

Back late this morning from Mendel's birthday party in Atlanta. It was held in a private room of an Italian restaurant ("Little Italy" on Peachtree Street, near Buckhead, with "free" valet parking). Mendel's daughter-in law took me aside to ask if I would give a toast to Mendel (she being the spokesperson for her family), or whether I would rather let Cathleen do it. I agreed that Cathleen would do it marvelously but that since Mendel is my uncle I would like to take it on. The party felt to me to be small, or smaller than I had imagined it would be, or should be, four round tables each seating eight persons, few of whom I recognized. In my toast I introduced the visiting four of us as foreigners from Massachusetts. (Returning to my text for editing a bit more than a year later, I have to remember that the Bush/Kerry presidential campaign was then in view, and even in a group of this sort in Atlanta, in which once upon a time one could count on a large swath of Democratic sentiment, I had within the period of aperitifs been asked twice, with concern, whether Bush did not seem to me somewhat tired from having to deal with so much opposition to his plans, opposition especially harsh from my part of the country.) I quickly emphasized to this group mostly of strangers to me that I was born and had spent my first nine years, and three among the following five years, in Atlanta and went on to recount our discovery that afternoon that the house Mendel and I lived in during the opening seven years of my life was still standing, its immediate physical neighborhood more or less intact. (Except for the complete absence of the beautiful, poplarlike trees in my memory that lined both sides of my childhood street—called "shade trees" by the family, though I was always doubtful whether this was the trees' official name or simply a description of their function. I somehow thought it would seem irrelevant to this company for me to mention this question of ancient trees.) The almost unrelieved anonymity of this environment did not deflect me from realizing my intention to celebrate this man who more than any other man had brought happiness into the earliest spaces of my life, even if, apart from the constraints of decorum and disparities of memory, we might now appear to be just two old men capable in this company of little else together than reminiscing in the vein of Justice Shallow and Justice Silence.

A few people present at Mendel's party would have known from my description of the house as on Atlanta Avenue halfway up from Grant Park to Capitol Avenue that it was now a black neighborhood that had once been largely Jewish. (Hardly the only instance one knows of such a transfiguration.) There were no longer stores visible in the neighborhood—such as the grocer's from whom you could buy an apple for two cents—and indeed we had found no other cars moving, and no pedestrians, nor any children playing, as we parked in front of the house. We were accordingly the more surprised—as we had left the car and were observing the house more closely from the space of its nearest sidewalk and I was roughly pointing out the location of its various rooms and noting that the only difference I could see was that the front porch was now enclosed by aluminum-trimmed windows—at the appearance from the front door of the house of a brisk black woman of a certain age with a commanding smile and a movingly welcome manner asking whether she could be of help. Cathleen walked over to her to say that I was showing my family the house I was born in, holding out to her the ancient photograph Cathleen had in her hand of Mendel holding infant me in his arms in that very yard faced by this very house. We had had an enlarged copy of the picture made to be included in an album Mendel's daughter-in-law was putting together to mark the occasion. Cathleen and the woman of the house joined the rest of us, and the woman put her hand on my arm and asked if the "baby boy" would like to come in and show his family where he was born. On entering the darkened living room of the house, we were greeted by a well-built black man in his late thirties who had evidently been watching television and whom our new acquaintance introduced as her son, who put his arms around me and kissed me on the cheek. His short growth of beard was so stiff that it made the embrace almost painful. The woman of the house led us around her tidy domain whose every room seemed to be as I remembered it (except for the large back bedroom, where a wall had evidently been taken down to achieve its present size as a kind of miniature dormitory), including the breakfast nook between the dining room and the kitchen where my grandmother and I played cards, the gaping difference being the absence of a piano in the modest living room. We did not make a full circuit of its only floor, since instead of entering the bedroom that circled back to the living room (once upon a time my parents' bedroom), our host opened its door for us to greet her thirty-year-old daughter, who had Down syndrome—clearly younger than the brother—who was sitting up in a double bed working on an enormous, half-completed jigsaw puzzle, with single pieces, and small combinations of them, scattered over the bed's entire surface. She smiled and waved back at us, and we retraced our steps for an affecting farewell. I am happy to report that although time had begun pressing for us to get to Mendel's birthday celebration we managed, upon Emily's and Cathleen's self-evidently immovable decision, to locate a nearby shopping mall where we found several superb jigsaw puzzles for sale and so were able to leave a satisfying, elaborately wrapped, set of them at the front door of the old house.

The brunt of my toast at the party included showing that photograph of Mendel holding me in his arms outside our old house. Noting it as thirteen- or fourteen-year-old Mendel holding one-year-old Stanley, I calculated as if I were realizing it for the first time that since I remembered being told that the Segal father had died three years before I was born, this meant that Mendel had lost his father at the age of nine or ten; and I knew from my own experience that his mother, living in the house with us, was an invalid and was treated as if this had been her condition forever. I adduced these facts as part of my understanding of Mendel's motivation in having undertaken to become everyone's father, including that of himself, inventing himself. I imagine that it was that idea that prompted Mendel to lean close to me as I took my seat next to his and say that he hoped I would ask Benjamin to write the stories I just told into a book. When Cathleen told Mendel that I had been teaching at Harvard during the spring, so not traveling as much as in recent years, he said to me: "So you've gone back to work. Good. It keeps you busy." I am unsure what he now thinks I do, if he thinks of it. But when his immediate family, his son and his son's wife and their two children, all said they had never seen the Atlanta Avenue house, and seemed indeed never to have heard of it, and that they wanted to, Mendel was notably unresponsive to the idea. I had never continued my imagination of that period of my life, however often images of it pass by on odd days, far enough from Mendel's point of view to recognize that for him it held little if any of the romance I endowed it with, that it was rather a scene for him of death and invalidism and eventually of

bankruptcy, the vanishing of his university scholarship, hence the unnatural or violent end of his university life—that, take it for all in all, a
place I treasured and associated him with represented indissolubly for
him just about everything from which he was determined to free himself. For me not to have recognized this earlier, earlier specifically than
Cathleen's prompting of me, demonstrates again what E. M. Forster
calls, painfully, a lack of moral imagination.

June 12, 2004

Soon after settling in at the Princeton Institute in the fall of 1962
I began what would become a series of trips to Atlanta where my father
underwent the surgery for colon cancer that came up early in this account, and the following week required further surgery to correct the
kidney infection resulting from the evidently botched initial surgery.
(The surgery twenty-nine years later for my inherited colon cancer, evidently accompanied by an inherited capacity for denying the need for
sensible medical checkups, and abetted by the distracted monitoring of
an over-busy primary-care physician at our first health plan—and prepared in advance by having undergone while in my thirties a primitive,
perhaps also botched, excruciating colonoscopy that so terrified me
that I felt I would rather die than undergo another such examination,
wholly unaware that the modern procedure has been perfected to the
point of relative triviality—was still performed early enough [fifteen
years ago], evidently, to cure the situation. I have not kept this news of
medical advance from my sons, and because I have since learned that
heavy smoking is, as in so many other newly discovered instances, a
factor in colon cancer, I attribute part of my good fortune here to Cathleen's having shamed me, at the time of her [our] first pregnancy, into
giving up my sixty cigarettes a day, a labor of love on Cathleen's part
that Hercules could only, from envy, weep at.)

My visit from Princeton to Cambridge that academic year, timed
so that I could attend the annual meetings of the American Society for
Aesthetics (where I read "Aesthetic Problems of Modern Philosophy,"
the third paper in *Must We Mean What We Say?*), turned out to coincide
with the Cuban missile crisis in October 1962. I was in Atlanta as the

terrifying developments were in process, a period in which I was introduced to the unlikely combination of my aunt Bess and old Dr. Morison as a romantic item. My mother disapproved of the combination, to say the least; my father's disapproval of Bess was of long standing. (Bess's infectious social capacities were sometimes accompanied by her more personal histrionics. She is the only person, outside of Hollywood farces, that I have witnessed pick up a full glass of water and shy its contents across a table into a man's face. I wish I knew what her husband— Jack Stein, her only legalized husband, so far as I know—had done or said to prompt this scene. It took place during the period in which I was still consistently pretending not to understand what grown-ups said and did, especially not their innuendoes and their sometimes heightened digressions.) I was moved to remind Dr. Morison, humorlessly, of the time I had been a patient of his and he burned warts off my feet without the use of anesthetic. He replied: "You seem to be doing real good." And he added: "Hasn't Harvard been taken over by communists?" And when I asked why he thought so he replied: "I'm worried about this country." When a couple of years later I remarked to Rogers, during the early stirrings of the student movement against the war in Vietnam as the movement formed itself at Harvard—that in Atlanta people believed that Harvard is full of communists, he replied: "I'm worried about this country." A way of glimpsing the astounding fact of the existence of human language is suddenly to recognize unguardedly that one of the least beautiful minds one may encounter, and one of the most beautiful, must, if they speak the same language, share the core, or cores, of their words. (Shakespeare knows all about this.) Unlike DNA, local abnormalities, as it were, cannot here be repaired, merely addressed.

June 14, 2004

Other factors, or perceptions, would have affected my decision to return to Harvard to teach, even so apparently a transient observation of Tom Kuhn's that history of science was not a West Coast subject. "West Coast" was hardly a well-defined intellectual modifier, yet some years later the expression "West Coast semantics" was for a time in rather general use in my hearing. Kuhn's idea seemed to be that an inherently multidisciplinary field, especially where the field in question crossed sciences and humanities, such as the history of science, required the kind of cultivation that should in principle start early. The idea was that students who fail somewhere along the line to recognize and to be encouraged in a fascination with some aspect of both sides of the brain are unlikely to spend the kind of time exacted by an interaction of some usable exposure to science together with an instinct for interpreting texts, an ideal of education associated institutionally most notably with undergraduate education in private colleges in the eastern part of the United States. My experience in teaching Austin and Wittgenstein, as I wished to explore their effect upon me, had suggested something similar about studying philosophy more generally—unless one was fully satisfied to do work solely within technical analytical philosophy. Austin's and Wittgenstein's differing resistances to philosophy were not expressed, as one might say in the case of logical positivism, by an abandonment of philosophy's history (though they could seem, both to admirers and detractors, to present themselves that way). Their resistances were, to my mind, continuous with philosophy and its original and persistent history of resistances.

Here is a difference in what may be meant by speaking of "therapy" in philosophy, perhaps out of a certain image of philosophizing in Socrates. For positivism something comparable to therapy promises to free you from (traditional, metaphysical) philosophy. For post-positivism, in Austin and Wittgenstein, something like, and very unlike, therapy is the unending, say, interminable, very work of philosophy. (In my view psychoanalysis is a mutation of philosophy.)

I should add that I am not so foolish as to blame positivism for its way of rejecting philosophy. If I were to tap the register of "blame," it would be to consider the effect not of positivism but of the migration of positivism, that is, of the originating positivist figures finding refuge from Hitler's Germany largely in America and in England, where the institutional power of metaphysical thought (epitomized by Heidegger, or by his internal opposition to it), against which positivism ranged itself, was essentially nonexistent. The inherent political resistance implied in the logical positivist's initial vision of reconstructing human existence in the light of reason became, with its migration, narrowly intellectualized as a reconstitution of philosophy under reason as monitored by natural science; put otherwise, as a continuation of the Enlightenment project to conquer prejudice and superstition and fanaticism. Even if that vision, or mission, had continued, it would leave untouched, or leave to others, the existence of mental darkness not illuminated by reason so monitored, say, the existence of chaos and the disheartenment with intellect. Of course it can be said that these are matters philosophy ought not to touch. That is an injunction easily and widely followed.

Then does the post-positivism of ordinary language philosophy suggest that one studies the history of philosophy simply in order to have something for the appeal to ordinary language to refute, or rather resist? But philosophy has rarely been at a loss for something to resist intellectually. (One of the wonders in which philosophy begins is the spectacle of human folly.) As Socrates resisted. Or Descartes. Or Locke. Or Hume. Or Kant. Or Hegel. Or Emerson and Thoreau and Nietzsche. Or Mill. Or Heidegger. Or Wittgenstein. I do not say that such figures resist folly merely (as it were) intellectually. Any more than I say that intellectual resistance in the Western world has been confined to self-declared, hence mostly male, philosophers. An hour or two with the conversation of Jane Austen or George Eliot ought to cure all but the incurable of such an idea.

This is not enough to say. It is in fact pedagogically difficult to know how, or when, to fit J. L. Austin or Wittgenstein into a philosophical curriculum. Too soon, and students, talented and not so talented, may feel they have been given sure correctives to the mistakes of history. They will not treasure and defend insights incessantly lost, nor recognize the incessant force of philosophical "mistakes" in themselves. Too late, and it is, as I have implied, too much to ask to be willing to take yourself apart. If I have a philosophical virtue it lies in that particular willingness—I sometimes think of it as preparation for responsiveness—however clumsy or incomplete the execution. There is a logic of esotericism here, the sense of a need for acknowledgment of the teaching within a teaching, as it were of its moral.

Wittgenstein's advance is to have discovered the everyday and its language themselves to be esoteric, strange to themselves, one could say, to be irreducibly philosophical, prompting us unpredictably to say too much or too little, as if we chronically fail to know what actually interests us. It is with our inheritance of language as Lacan says Freud holds of the Ego, that it continually misrecognizes or (mis)understands itself. Instead of saying we are full of mistakes about what is closest to us, we might say of ourselves that we are filled, as Thoreau might say, with misgiving.

But ill-defined distinctions between West Coast and East Coast intellectual styles were hardly reasons entering into my decision to leave Berkeley for Harvard. I surmised the depth of passion drawn upon in the decision from the weeks in which I could not think of the necessity to resolve the issue without feeling something like fear and rage directed at both institutions. Their standing offers meant that I had to choose between them, not simply think of myself as inhabiting one or other for a time, the only places I had, after turning to the age of seven, relished living in. But since, as said, the decision had been made in view of the literal divorce, such considerations colored the mood in which I would leave Berkeley. Fischer and Kuhn and Clarke naturally entered into reasons for staying. But Fischer and Kuhn, for opposite reasons, were themselves sure to leave. (Fischer, because he would not publish and could not expect to receive a tenure appointment at Berkeley. Kuhn, because he was bound to receive offers from the East Coast, where he was far more at home.) And when I said to Clarke, "Anyway, how can I take a job at Harvard after their treatment of Marshall?" he replied: "Rise above your principles and take the job you know you should take." (What served to negate my principle—let's say it is "Accept no place that has mistreated a friend"—was the questionable way Berkeley had treated Kurt.) Clarke was seeing, more clearly than I, I came to believe, how different, after all, his and my lives must be.

And in the background, I feel sure, was Clarke's not wanting the responsibility of being a significant reason for my remaining at Berkeley. However decisive we were each prepared to say the other had been for him, and however close a friend, Clarke's persistence on his philosophical project, and my persistence in discovering what my course was to be, would not continue to support the hours we had counted on spending in conversation. He needed relief from philosophy, whereas for me philosophy *was* my relief, since it essentially partook of literature and theater and music.

June 15, 2004

After Bernard's then wife, Shirley Williams, and their daughter, a year or so older than Rachel, arrived six weeks into the term at
Princeton, Bernard and I could no longer behave as college chums,
drinking a little too much and seeing too many movies in New York,
just once getting to the opera (*Rosenkavalier* was it? Or did we merely allude to that, and to opera generally, more often than could be justified
to normal people?). Princeton had begun receiving radio stations from
both Philadelphia and from New York, and my bachelor habits profited
from having a choice of classical music stations around the clock. The
Williamses had a television in their apartment, and when New York
announced all-night television that winter, and scheduled *The Maltese
Falcon* the first week at 3:30 a.m., Bernard's response was, "Very high
priority indeed." Like Bernard, Shirley was an admirer of American
culture, especially one could say of its international reach and its declared, if often compromised, democratic ambitions, but she did not
join us for the Bogart offering. After a month or so of expecting to see
one another every day, Bernard, who, in view of the approaching arrival of his family, had rented a car, appeared one evening at my apartment in the Institute complex to pick me up for dinner, and found me
somewhat subdued in my greeting. I was astounded to discover that I
had within seconds revealed my mood sufficiently for him to say: "Yes.
We have become friends. But I am of the view that the best way to handle that is not to tear the thing out of the ground incessantly in order
to examine its roots." I saw the point, both about him and about me.
Of course one of the most charming and intelligent men in the world
would have met many occasions on which to have had to voice that
sentiment.

I felt I understood something about the mystery of energy the cultivated English expend in, let's say, social entertainment, when decades
later in explaining why although he loved many things about teaching
philosophy at Berkeley Bernard found he needed to spend more time
in Oxford, he observed, "I simply missed the social mud." This goes
considerably beyond dishing the dirt, though gossip of an impersonal
kind, about one's own set, is, I gather, thought to be endlessly fascinating. Americans are less likely to regard this practice as a mode of art.

But I speak here simply for myself, as one easily exhausted by the effort, unless for example it takes some level of Freudian perceptions in stride. (One might say: Unless it tears things up, or might wish to, by the roots.) I am otherwise largely deaf to these charms, essentially I suppose because I have nothing I would know to call my own set. Democratic gossip is not impersonal, and it is typically about oneself, generally of no immediate or urgent interest; or about neighbors, of no interest except that of sharing a vicinity; or about shady, or else undeserved, reputations, about which you can do little that is amiable or admirable. The mud that is required to keep socially buoyed, or abreast, and cool, derives, I suppose, in part from the history of conversation at court, where, for example, pregnancies can affect successions, not merely cause squalor, and where standing is almost perfectly knowable, but only by staying in the know; and also in part from those who can hold court in a coffee house. This is how I have understood, from a distance I have always accepted, the etiquette of philosophical publishing at Oxford and Cambridge (except notably for the case of Bertrand Russell, who is exceptional in various ways), I mean the fact that for much of the twentieth century, very much publication would have seemed vulgar there, a sign of not being in the know. To count, one already must know, and be known by, everyone who counts. American improvisation, the ability to find common ground with any passing stranger, is, in such a setting, pointless. (The next step would be to consider the French, who open their set to the rest by means of competing orations. Perhaps this step will become pertinent before I conclude.)

Somewhat delayed that year in Princeton was the encounter, affecting my life one way or another every year since then, of Rose Mary Pederson and John Harbison, who would marry at the end of the year and move to Harvard, where John was to begin his tenure as a Junior Fellow. Conversation with Rose Mary, a prodigious violinist, can get quickly to bedrock. I would not guess whether this depends upon friendship with her taking hold, or whether it establishes the possibility of friendship with her taking hold. Recurring questions for us were, for example: What are the chances of maintaining the standards one knows the art of music deserves and still continue to do what is necessary in order to establish oneself in the contemporary business of performance and recording? What are the necessities of a musician's education? What is new in the new music? Is everything inspired by Schoenberg to be taken with the same seriousness? What is taste? Rose Mary has focused on music almost single-mindedly since her performing talent and her perfect pitch were discovered before she could read words, although having grown up on a farm she also retains all the skills of a farmhand, and the strength of two. John has taken a more complex path, but composers are different in this regard from performers.

They were just establishing themselves in the Princeton musical scene (though since John had grown up in Princeton he had come in his ambitious youth to know Roger Sessions as a generous neighbor). How John had decided upon Harvard for his undergraduate life is not something I have ever thought to ask. I have known him to wonder aloud whether he should, rather than through the university, have gone the route of the conservatory, that one lifetime is already short for the amount of training the ear and brain and hands of a composer have to incorporate. It is true that he is the most widely cultivated prolific composer I have met, his knowledge of literature that of a serious writer. But then he has the knack of an artist at finding and absorbing the food he needs, however eccentric. Last month, on a continuing Sunday radio program to introduce the young to contemporary music, Harbison was the musical guest; as such he was interviewed, and a piece for violin and piano was performed that he had written when he was in high school. It still sounded original, not simply original, but at the same time attractive and generously communicative. Where had the time for it come from?—since he had also made himself into so considerable a jazz pianist as to have imagined that strain as a career.

Rose Mary invited me to practice the Brahms G Major violin sonata with her, and we liked what we were doing so well that we played it in public. This led to our being joined by John's sister Helen, a gifted cellist (also partaking of Harbison cultivation—she had the previous year played the Debussy Cello Sonata as valedictorian of her graduating class at the famously rigorous Smith College), to read through the Beethoven Ghost Trio, and further joined by John (this time playing viola), to read through the Brahms A Major piano quartet. It was the exhilaration of celebrating friendship with the conjuring of great art that went into our reproducing essentially this program at Tougaloo College in Mississippi two years later, as a piece of our participation in the so-called Freedom Summer of 1964, as if to bring shame upon injustice. (I was in fact surprised and greatly moved to discover that the recitals we gave were attended by a sizeable integrated audience largely coming over from Jackson, Mississippi.) That summer roughly nine hundred students from the North migrated to Mississippi to participate in various registers of education, from actually teaching to working on registering black citizens who had never voted, eventually to attempting to integrate public facilities. The Harbisons were part of a group of some fifteen mostly graduate students from Harvard, organized by John Mudd, who were to become the faculty of Tougaloo College throughout that summer. I and two other professors from Harvard, Monroe Engel and William Alfred, joined the group for roughly two weeks each. But I must re-arrive at this transfiguring moment in my experience later, and more slowly.

I had returned from Princeton to Berkeley for part of the previous summer of 1963, to be with Rachel and in order to pack things, essentially books and notes and clothes, for shipping to Cambridge, and to say another good-bye to Alexandra. Rachel and I left early enough to have some weeks of summer in which to begin accustoming ourselves to life in Cambridge, stopping on the way to visit my parents in Atlanta. In Atlanta as well I was to pick out what I wanted from the furniture my mother's sister Bess was getting rid of from the apartment she was vacating, including the offer of a piano she no longer had need or room for. It was arranged that I would meet the moving truck in Cambridge something like a week from the date of their pickup in Atlanta. Rachel and I were to stop over on our way north in order to visit the Kuhns, who had themselves just moved to Princeton. Rachel liked the idea that, for a lark, we might take the overnight sleeper train north rather than fly, so I interestedly reserved a compartment for us. When we awoke the following morning, we discovered that we had both produced lid-crusting cases of conjunctivitis. Rachel let herself be reassured that there was a perfect ointment made to ensure that our eyes would not again be in the least difficult to open after a night's sleep, and that we would buy some as soon as we got to Princeton, a matter of just a few hours now. I was in a misery of embarrassment to have to present the awaiting Kuhns with a famously contagious infection and asked them simply to take us to a pharmacy and then to a hotel.

Kay, with three children, Nathaniel roughly Rachel's age, Sarah and Liza each several years older than Rachel—when Nat and Rachel were some three years old they decided to have a wedding ceremony, and my mother was cheerfully pressed into service playing the Wedding March as the two curiously costumed, charming creatures walked arm in arm ceremoniously from the living room into the dining room of the Kuhn house, where the upright piano stood, to the applause of the small assembly of witnesses—Kay, I was about to say, was unfazed by the pathetic picture we presented disembarking from the train, swept us off to their house and the separate quarters that had already been set aside for us, produced the ointment we needed, left us alone to freshen up with a caution about keeping our towels and sheets in our part of the house, and awaited our presence before serving lunch. This was all a miracle of comfort—but that was its problem. Could I conceivably produce such miracles on my own, on demand, as the single, insufficiently practiced, father of a young daughter?

Part 11

June 16, 2004

Half of my teaching schedule the first year back at Harvard in the fall of 1963 was settled by reasonable, even expected, requests from the department. It was obvious that I was to teach the second semester of the philosophy department's year-long offering in the General Education program, the course initiated by White and Aiken in which Marshall and I and eight or nine others had served as Teaching Fellows a decade earlier, and for which Rogers and Marshall had been in recent years sharing respectively the two-semester course. Its fall semester, taught by Albritton, included the pre-Socratics, Plato, Aristotle, and a Greek tragedy followed by something from Saint Paul and ended with Thomas Aquinas; the reading list for the spring semester when I returned and taught it began with Machiavelli's *The Prince*, Luther's *Preface to the Letter of St. Paul to the Romans*, *The Freedom of a Christian*, and *The Pagan Servitude of the Church*, and Shakespeare's *King Lear* followed by Descartes's *Meditations* and Locke's *Second Treatise of Government* and then after Hume's *Dialogues on Natural Religion* and Kant's *Groundwork of the Metaphysics of Morals* and Mill's *On Liberty* and *Utilitarianism* and Nietzsche's *The Birth of Tragedy*. I tried various ways of broaching the twentieth century. I refused to let the century all of us had been born in and would be in in hearty middle age, in my case in old age, if we survived it—be represented alone by, as might easily have been done in those years, A. J. Ayer's *Language, Truth and Logic* or by Camus's *The Stranger*. I thought of assigning both the first year, but that meant ending with works that were not in the same league of value or influence with those preceding them, and nothing by Wittgenstein or by Heidegger seemed reasonable to get through in a maximum of two weeks. Beckett's *Endgame* seemed to serve well enough for a couple of years, and eventually I would end with a film, which I felt worked pedagogical wonders. The course, however modified by changes in its lecturers and modifications of its assigned reading, bore the same title and number throughout the decades of its existence: Humanities 5, "Ideas of Man and the World in Western Thought." Beyond this, and a course on Wittgenstein's *Investigations* and a seminar of my choice, I was specifically asked if I would give a course in aesthetics.

Each of these efforts in their different ways proved to be transformative pedagogical experiences for me, partly because I was, and felt I was, explicitly beginning again, but this time with some years of experience and experimentation to go on from, and partly because instead of the opening term requiring eight lectures a week for fifteen weeks, as at Berkeley, I was now expected to prepare just four lectures a week for twelve weeks, and partly because the quality of the graduate students in that era of the Harvard philosophy department was in one of its remarkably distinguished phases (several other such phases will form during my four decades there). Present in the crowded Emerson Hall seminar room that first year were, among others, Stanley Bates, Ted Cohen, John Cooper, Allen Graubard, Jack McNees, Mickey Morgan, William Rothman, sometimes audited by Michael Fried and John Harbison, most of whom had just returned from two-year fellowships in England or Germany, rewards for their outstanding undergraduate accomplishments. The fact and the promise of talent in this company are beyond the dreams of avarice. (Not all continued to careers in academic philosophy. Not all had ever contemplated the possibility.) Standards of philosophical conversation, of intellectual conversation more generally, were established whose powers of inspiration remain, I trust, alive for me.

I had found little charm in analytical aesthetics. I had never been convinced by the ways I had managed to bring that strain of contemporary English-speaking philosophy and the individual arts into the classroom together, let alone in my writing. Individual works in the arts never seemed for my taste to talk back sufficiently to philosophy, to find their footing within philosophy, to make philosophy look at its own limitations, its own dependence on literary conditions. What the best or most influential recent literary critics in English (T. S. Eliot, William Empson, I. A. Richards, Kenneth Burke, R. P. Blackmur, Robert Penn Warren, Paul Goodman) had been saying about works of literature remained to my mind incomparably more interesting, and indeed intellectually more accurate, than the competing provisions of analytical philosophy. I wanted philosophy to take on such criticism, perhaps be taken on by it, not, as was mostly the case, to avoid it, or take it by the weaker hand. Art historians (for example, Panofsky, Wölfflin) supplied their own (Hegelian) philosophy that philosophers whom I knew did not improve upon. The analysis of music was, in my experience, and with the obvious exception of Schenker, done best by composers, and in any case assumed a basic knowledge of harmony and classical forms that would have left nonmusicians out of the picture. It was from this sense of pedagogical impasse that I came to the idea of experimenting with what could be said about film, a field in which new work, by directors and writers in France and Italy and Sweden and Japan, had brought new consciousness and interest to the international art of cinema, at a time when American film seemed to shrink before the competition of television.

Film had for me become essential in my relation to the arts generally, as the experience of my extended bouts of moviegoing in New York and Los Angeles and Berkeley proved to me. There was, or I knew, comparatively little intellectual work to start from in the early 1960s, but some of it that I knew was fresh and free in its treatment of film (ranging from Eisenstein or James Agee to André Bazin, a theorist indispensable to the writers/directors of the French New Wave). Philosophers, it seemed, had almost without exception left the field alone. Should this be taken for granted? Or oughtn't the fact of this neglect itself inspire suspicion? Given my restiveness with philosophy's treatment, or avoidance, or stylization, of human experience—a restiveness that is a treasured inheritance from my early reading of John Dewey and of William James—what better way to challenge the avoidance than through the worldwide phenomenon of cinema? And what better time than one that marked, whatever else, whatever sense of festiveness marked my move to a new life and the liberated world of a permanent appointment?

There was, I do not deny, a certain pleasurable indecorousness in the idea of taking film into a philosophy classroom, anyway in the English-speaking dispensation of the subject. Some may have felt that this was part of my intention in pursuing it. But that could only be addressed seriously in the way the idea was pursued, however mixed the motives. I have been pampered throughout my university career, having taught regularly only at the two places I cared about most, and in which I felt most free. Berkeley's democracy was so big that no one not present would know what you were doing in your classroom; and Harvard's aristocratic confidence meant that since you were there what you were doing in your classroom must be correct. The students naturally kept matters reasonable. But the students were also different in the different locales. At Berkeley, you could be the first to tell students that their work showed real talent and have the pleasure of seeing young eyes widening with a somewhat revised vision of themselves and their interests. At Harvard, a student is apt already to have been praised too often, and you might be the first to hold up a cautionary hand, signaling that others were also gifted and that a talent was owed more working attention by its owner than in this case it was being given.

The difference between students in the two places was decisive in the case of the large lecture courses such as Humanities 5, primarily for undergraduates. At Berkeley, in my day, college admission, for residents of the state of California, was based strictly on high school grades, so the first year became in effect an extended admission's examination, resulting in the failing of many students who were not prepared for work at one of the two highest-ranked institutions in the California system of higher education, UC Berkeley and UCLA. (The number of outstanding students seemed to me about the same at Berkeley and at Harvard.) At Harvard, where a student's very presence signified that focused competition had already been successful, and where writing skills had specifically been the object of cultivation, a teacher could, as in my spring semester of the year-long course with Albritton open to first-year students (the four undergraduate years were about equally represented by the students registered in the course), assign the formidable set of texts I listed and expect a large number of well-written examinations and term papers in response to that succession of monstrously famous works, themselves composed after all with human hands out of human need. (It was also a piece of received wisdom, which I do not contest, that at Harvard the difference between students from public high schools and those with preparatory school training was effectively erased within the first two undergraduate years.) What this meant to my teacher's fantasy of audience in lecturing to these groups at Harvard over the years was that I was in each case facing a sample of young fellow citizens of mine to whom anything could be said that I found it worth saying and felt that aspirants to democracy should gladly hear, on the condition that I took pains sufficient to say it, as talent allowed, lucidly and provocatively.

Then there were the undergraduate students I could be said to live with, along with some dozen other tutors, most of whom were graduate students, one or two perhaps assistant professors. While called tutors, the appointment to a Harvard House did not require lecturing or tutoring specifically within that House's population. Although each House was likely to gather a reputation as favoring certain fields, most major fields were represented in each House, and advice from the tutors was freely sought and given. A number of the undergraduates in Adams became good acquaintances and some eventually young friends of mine, based on a sort of abstract license allowing both heated public exchange concerning politics as well as a quasi-hilarious mode of criticism directed to national or local pomposities. Adams House was in those years well known for its musical recitals, as well as for the particularly good quality, real or imagined, of the food in its dining hall, made possible because its location closer to Harvard Square than the other Houses closer to the Charles River, required it in those years to have its own kitchen, separate from the central kitchen joining each of the other House dining halls by underground passageways. The communal ambience that included students and teachers was secured, as I experienced it, by an iron sense of decorum. Among the students interested in philosophy, some I remember whose names I have for the moment forgotten, as, for example, the virtuoso alto saxophonist who practiced remarkably accomplished post-tonal riffs mostly after midnight in a matching sitting room on the floor above mine (sometimes he was called off by neighbors of his who would ultimately bang on that corner of the building's shared radiator pipes—only once do I recall telephoning him myself when, as he immediately agreed, he was being quite sensationally unreasonable); and there was a writer of essays for his classes whose control of a serious, advanced prose style and of intellectual resources would have served well an established writer (I learned a few years ago that when he died he was a leader of a prominent religious community in the far West); and there was the scion of a wealthy Texas family who during the ensuing years of our war in Vietnam dropped out of Harvard and worked with the Black Panthers (he decided in the last days of his final term not to take his examinations, ensuring that he would not graduate, a demonstration I supposed meant to apply particularly exquisite pain to his family).

Those closer to me included Terrence Malick, whose academic major—"concentration" in Harvard patois—was philosophy, and whose expert honors thesis on a text of Heidegger's I would be assigned to advise. Malick had taken a semester in Germany to attend Heidegger's classes, and he knew, and we discussed the facts before he began writing, both that he had read and studied more Heidegger than I had and at the same time that I was the only member of the philosophy faculty at that time who respected and had studied any at all of Heidegger's work, hence that he was likely to receive an unsympathetic judgment from the two readers who would be assigned to examine him, having in effect to be instructing his instructors, something I was hoping his thesis might itself recognizably begin to accomplish. (A familiar story handed down to young students of Hebrew from older Yeshiva students was of a hostile emperor demanding that a rabbi explain the Torah to him while he—the emperor—stood on one leg. The rabbi replied: "Love thy neighbor as thyself." If Malick had happened to know the story it would have been irrelevant. His grades alone assured that he would graduate with highest honors.) Jacob Brackman, a classmate and friend of Malick's who would work on the production of Malick's first two films, *Badlands* and *Days of Heaven*, was possessed of a sharpness of mind and a quick daring of wit that kept him, I sensed, close to danger with official Harvard. More constant and calmer acquaintances from that era, whom I continued, and in friendship continue, to keep up with are Paul Guyer, already as an undergraduate, when not earning his

awarded scholarship by working the steam table in the Adams House
dining hall, making scholarly discoveries that presaged his becoming
a world authority on Kant; and Timothy Gould, a seventeen-year-old
sophomore who had put together usefully so many difficult literary and
philosophical texts that I feared—understandably underestimating his
resolve, not his talent—he might never find time among his excited
intellectual discoveries to place his own voice.

Study breaks toward midnight, for those of us, many of us, who
read and wrote late, were not infrequently shared at one of the all-
night cafeterias that still existed then in Harvard Square—that is, before the abandonment of so many American cities in favor of suburbs
felt to be free of racial strife and to offer better schools and (perhaps
not above all) reliable parking. Those with money who still craved the
cultural amenities of great cities—concert halls, art galleries, lecture
series, old movies—moved close to universities, hence helped to push
local property values beyond the reach of most faculty members of the
staff of those universities. Albiani's was the cavernous one of the three
cafeterias and was the first to disappear (familiar from my graduate
school years, it was gone by the time I returned to Harvard to teach),
its space reconfigured to accommodate several small retail businesses,
any one of which will yield several times the rent of the old cafeteria.
(An educated guess.) The Waldorf was part of a structure that made
way for a new complex that included the Harvard University health
services. (These changes were no doubt for the good, and it is not
news that money talks. I could wish that money at the same time did
not so often bark.) Hayes-Bickford held out for a decent spell longer
(eventually yielding to a Chinese restaurant), and it was there that
in spring, approaching the end of my first year back teaching, having established the routine of writing through the night until the first
sense of light, at which time I walked out and around the corner from
Adams House, knowing that the floors of Hayes-Bickford ("the Bick")
would have been mopped and the tables wiped down and straight-
ened up, and fresh eggs delivered. For a period that first summer I
was often joined by Allen Graubard at these predawns, who would,
because he could not choose between the fields of philosophy and
political science (the latter was, and is, "Government" in Harvard
parlance) arranged to take qualifying examinations in both fields and

LITTLE DID I KNOW

to write a doctoral dissertation that would be acceptable to both, a few years later receiving a double Ph.D.

Although the full domestic shock of the Vietnam War would not for a while yet hit Harvard directly with student demonstrations and demands for change in social and intellectual institutions, horror of the war, and of the forged causes for distending it (by that same President Johnson who signed the sanity-inducing Civil Rights Bill), along with the surrounding traumas of change in and around black communities, were by 1965 causing strife of national scope in relations between races and genders and generations. A locally clear institutional consequence and emblem of change was the increasing velocity of stages in integrating the classes and administration of Harvard and Radcliffe colleges (Radcliffe had, for example, never had a graduate school of its own), including eventually the integration of the Harvard Houses and the Radcliffe dormitories and their satellites. The dress code in the Harvard dining halls was still in effect, but with mounting social and cultural swaying and questioning, a late stage of the code became heralded, if not instantly visible, the day an undergraduate male was emboldened to obey the letter of the code by dutifully wearing a jacket and tie into the dining hall, but now minus a shirt. (Those were the days in which established authority could still be asked to join in recognizing with grace its necessary losses.)

My new confidence of a hearing among Harvard students had a permanent effect on my writing, on my conviction that I could speak from myself and speak comprehensibly. Not so many years later, when I began publishing my thoughts about Thoreau, in 1972, but especially about Emerson a few years later, I was told by prominent Emersonians that my experience of Emerson's and Thoreau's writing could not be the experience that made them figures shared by millions of Americans, since practically no one could understand what I was making them say, at least not without spending all day reading them. But I felt that I had gained conclusive evidence in my Harvard classrooms that that view of matters was false, or say, imaginary, that with company and some reason to trust reading, to trust one's own capacity to read, untold numbers of people (perhaps young people especially) would understand a further range of what these writings were saying to them, for them, that it was not a certainty fixed forever that most will never have the time nor take the opportunity to care about how these former fellow beings have described our lives, that indeed the wager of democracy depends upon wagering otherwise.

June 17, 2004

I had also assigned some Marx in my large humanities course that first year chiefly because the name had taken on satanic overtones in the 1950s and I wanted to recognize his writing as that of a leading nineteenth-century philosopher whose standing as a thinker will outlast his role as providing sacred readings for monstrously tyrannical regimes. I had underestimated, among other matters, the possibility that some students would take this view as sacrilege, like teaching the Bible as literature. After a lecture of mine, a portion of which was devoted to Marx's reading of Hegel's introduction to *The Philosophy of Right*, a student followed me out of class fervently objecting to my light treatment of Marx, saying that it was a distortion to present Marxist thought in the twentieth century without including Lenin as Marx's greatest inheritor, especially in his theory of imperialism. I had read very little Lenin, and this was not the first time I was taught the lesson that in offering a large survey course, in which the range of assignments is apt to, even should, outrun the expertise of most teachers, you had better be more than normally cautious from the outset in making clear your scholarly limitations. I felt differently about a similar fervor expressed to me by an Asian student about my failure to include any non-Western text in the reading assignments for the course. Here I made obvious excuses, pleading time and lack of knowledge, and felt no fault. But in recalling this pair of instances I am struck by their accuracy in presenting an increasingly baffling future, one for whose presence what we knew of education seemed uninformed.

This was the spring of 1964, when halfway into the semester I would first hear of the Student Non-Violent Coordinating Committee (SNCC, "Snick") and of its role in the 1963 March on Washington and in organizing the impending Mississippi Freedom Summer. I had become friends with several of the hugely gifted graduate students I have mentioned. It was Allen Graubard, who had been an undergraduate

roommate of Harbison's, who invited me to attend a meeting at which
the proposal would be advanced for a delegation of (primarily) Harvard
graduate students to join the Freedom Summer project in Mississippi.
The proposal at the meeting was for the group to replace the summer school faculty at Tougaloo College, a small black college outside
Jackson, Mississippi, and to manifest its solidarity with the civil rights
movement by concentrating on education rather than voter registration
(education was one of the explicit charges issued in the call by Robert
Moses for Northern students to participate in that summer), and eventually join the effort to integrate various segregated public facilities in
Jackson. The students were, in addition, inviting several faculty members to join them at Tougaloo for shorter periods, to give public lectures
and hold discussions with students on selected topics. The suggestion
to me was, in addition to involving myself in discussions of philosophy,
that I screen a film and offer a public lecture on it (several students present had attended my film seminar the previous fall). The deep pleasure
and honor of performing at Tougaloo a concert of chamber music with
the three Harbisons is an idea that came up later.

     If there are two kinds of people, those whose instinct of response
to a crisis is primarily political and those whose instinct is psychological, I suppose I belong to the latter kind. Nevertheless, I felt at once that
to refuse the invitation to join this effort would have meant not merely
failing to put politics first, but to declare that I had no marked and
developing political desires at all.

     At a reunion just several weeks ago in Cambridge, some fifteen
(that is, almost all) of us who had participated in the Tougaloo project
marked the fortieth anniversary of that summer. Virtually everyone
present, as we went around the room each taking a moment for a few
words at the end of the concluding evening of the gathering, testified
that the event forty years ago had altered his or her life. In my few
words, I began by recognizing that the experience of the event in my
case, as similarly I imagined in that of the other two Harvard faculty
members who had also participated (Monroe Engel was present at the
reunion; William Alfred, the playwright and legendary teacher, had
died five years earlier) was bound variously to differ from that of the
graduate students who had traveled that time to Mississippi. Speaking
for myself, I went on to testify that my life too has been transfigured

by the experience in unpredictable ways, both in psychological ways, as well as, in some extended sense, in political. I remember the sense of what I wanted to testify to but none of the words I found, which were not to exceed five minutes. The sense would have been touched by some selection of the following thoughts.

That I was thirty-seven years old the summer of 1964 meant that, while past the, let's continue to call it, identity crisis of my early twenties, I was still, I felt, in that stage of life at which irreversible decisions were to be made—in which life was, as formulated in that letter from Mary to me fifteen years earlier in New York, to become seriously real instead of really serious—intellectual, political, sexual, religious, economic decisions (in Thoreau's sense of the economic, learning how you put together the whole of your living, or fail to). The sense of a stand, or stands, untaken went together with a doubt about whether I was coming into some mastery of my own experience. It is a treacherous task. The issue is not to harden experience; on the contrary, that solution, as Emerson and Nietzsche and Freud, for example, forever teach, is an expression of the problem. The issue is to keep experience experimental (as Emerson explicitly says, and some say Dewey means the same), but not with a view either simply to extend experience or to purify it or to make it practical and effective, but to determine whether it is my own, to be acknowledged, or whether it is in a given case derivative of, borrowed from, any of a thousand instances of misidentified rejection or rage or disappointment or sympathy or triumph or longing or love or failure of love. One task still undone in my case was to determine what my age is, and what I imagine it to be.

To be thirty-seven the summer of 1964 also meant having turned eighteen, draft age, in what would prove to be the last months of World War II in Europe, and having been turned down for service because of my bad ear. This meant that I was denied the experience of my generation, the chance to be present to America at a time when America was concentratedly present to itself, at least to those with whom I obviously shared its life.

And yet. Was that my generation? I had, explicitly from my first days in first grade, not known where I belonged, and missing the experience of those with whom I must assume I was sharing life became a theme of my life. But now, exiting the plane in Jackson, Mississippi, in the now strange brunt of this Southern summer heat, and in the accompanying fear that I could not deny had been building in me in anticipation of the sojourn, heightened by the discoveries of the bodies some days earlier of the three murdered young civil rights workers, Chaney, Goodman, and Schwerner, and tightened further by my mother's tearful phone calls the week before, pleading with me not to go, America was for the second time in my conscious life present to itself (the Great Depression was too early, or I was too late, for it to have been mine), and this time, in this unlikely place, or rather perfectly likely, I was present to it. My sense of this meant that I was identifying not (fully, or simply) with the generation closest to me in years, but (as well) identifying with a generation distinctly younger than that, not younger enough than I to contain my children, and not too young to contain, without undue scandal, the woman I would marry three years later.

The sense of identification with a generation, even modified to include partial identification with each of two actual generations, was earnest that there was someone not merely to whom to write, but for whom to write, to speak for, to justify my sometimes unappeasable wish or need to say "we" and know whom I meant, or wanted to mean. At the same time it showed me that this "we" is essentially open to shifts and moreover that the matter of "speaking for" is never an epistemological certainty but something like a moral claim, an arrogation of right, which others may grant or question or refuse. That Austin's and Wittgenstein's ways of appealing to what we say demonstrate the practicality and power of such appeals has been essential to my exhilaration in discovering their modes of philosophizing. The beginnings of this exhilaration are evident even in my first published philosophical paper of continuing significance for me, "Must We Mean What We Say?" And that I have some control over what it is and when it is and how it is that I ask for agreement from others, for acknowledgment that another is spoken for, is something I mean in feeling that in such philosophizing I am coming to a mastery of my experience (not as dominance of it, whatever that would mean, but as opposed to sheer subservience to it, victimization by it). As if in finding the right to speak for others I first find the right to speak for myself. This will be critical in my later recognition of the power of Emerson's writing. ("The deeper [the scholar] dives into his privatest,

secretest presentiment, to his wonder he finds this is the most acceptable, most public, and universally true.")

But then what is the right to speak for oneself? How can such a
thing be necessary, and achieved? Is it a demand to be heard? And
if it is related to a right to one's words, how is this right conferred? I
shall just note here my conviction that had I not spent those weeks in
Tougaloo I would not have claimed the right several years later to speak
for Thoreau's *Walden*. And if I had not recognized *Walden* as a work
of philosophy claiming to speak for me, I would not have felt bound,
or been interested, to claim the right to speak for it. And in that case
there are mazes of other things I would not have found my way to say.
I have been accustomed to think of my right to speak as the capacity to
become responsible for my words, for their being always ahead of me, of
each of us, intentional and at the same time inevitably and perpetually
beyond intention. Here I am thinking of the matter as my right to speak
of my death, of what it is on which my life is staked.

The issue of my generational identifications introduces a structural, or biological, feature in my tendency to be less interested in
where I fit into the institutional scheme of things than in what makes
me restive about the way these things are arranged. It strikes me that
something not entirely dissimilar is true of Emerson and of Thoreau.
They had missed what is called the American Revolution (that is, there
would have been some alive who had not missed it even when Thoreau
entered Harvard in 1837), and they were too old, or in Thoreau's case,
sick, to serve in the Civil War, a crisis that they evidently came to accept
as inevitable. During a dinner party at our apartment the year after
Cathleen and I were married, prompted by the number of friends who
happened to be in Cambridge over the Christmas holidays, including a
number of old friends I hadn't seen in several years, I was surprised by
the difficulty in getting conversation to move. The next day I phoned
Seymour (Shifrin), wanting to know whether he had shared any such
feeling about last night's gathering. "Haven't you heard?" he replied.
I was perplexed. I may have mumbled something back. He went on.
"There is a forty-year-old conspiracy. The message is: 'We're doing
fine. Don't rock the boat.'"

Was this just more of Seymour's endless dissatisfaction with anything but absolute achievement? And will he be as satisfied as Roger

(Sessions) if he lives a long life and has as comparatively few performances as Roger has had? Seymour and I had discussed the fact that
Roger's *The Trial of Lucullus*, a great one-act opera, self-evidently glorious and communicative—on the condition that you hear it several
times over a reasonably short span—had gone, as far as I knew, essentially unperformed after its premiere. And the image of Bloch haunted
me. Bloch had said to the class of his that had meant the world to me,
"When the city of San Francisco, for my seventieth anniversary, dedicated a day to me and gave a large luncheon in my honor, I began my
speech by saying: 'This is the unhappiest day of my life.'" Did he actually say that, or was he telling us, whatever he said, that that is what he
meant? What did he mean? That it was too late for him to savor success? Meaning what? That he had essentially or mostly lived alone with
the knowledge of the genuineness of his achievement? But that would
be libelous against those who showed him that they knew. The next
year the premiere of his Second String Quartet was given at Berkeley.
I thought it the best piece of his I knew, the most advanced, a master-
piece. And the Griller String Quartet, then resident at Berkeley, played
it convincingly and gorgeously. Was this not an acceptable seventieth
birthday present? A proportionate, a happy present? Was not the sheer
gift of having written it present enough? (This may seem overly pious, I
realize. But do we understand why?) Is creativity—anyway of a certain
kind—as apt to be a curse as a blessing? (It can seem in certain cases
that being creative is like being able now to run a mile in four minutes
flat. It is still greatly remarkable, but is no longer world-changing news.
Why, when, should it be?) Can we arrive at the place at which we know,
without rancor or irony, that the relation between achievement and
fame is, especially in the short run, variously and irreducibly arbitrary?
Why should this be different from any other human chance? Fame can
die with you or be born with your death. How many stories are there,
as Milton Babbitt's, told at Salzburg in 1952, of the time he had been
called to turn manuscript pages for Bartók, already critically ill, who
was to perform a piece he had just finished, having had little impact on
the musical life of the country, even just of New York, during his war
years in the States? Babbitt knew at the time that the piece was im-
mortal, and he ended his story by saying: "We always hear, and deplore
it, that Schubert died unappreciated a century and more ago, telling

ourselves that we would have known and shown ourselves better than his contemporaries, forgetting that, in our lifetime, seven years ago, Bartók died the same way."

If, on the road into existence, or, as in Plato's Myth of Er, into rebirth, you could choose either to receive a high gift of creativity that would be insufficiently appreciated in your lifetime, or else receive a still notable but lesser gift that, however, would be more widely and fully appreciated (that is, will reach in your lifetime as high as it ever will), which would you pick? This will hardly serve as a test of immortality, but perhaps as a proof that we live transcendentally.

To Seymour's observation about our generation's wish for comfort, I replied that I did not recognize myself as restlessly wishing to rock the boat, perhaps feeling that there were many boats in many waters and that my craft was mystery enough to me. He said: "You should." Meaning not, I gathered, that I should rock, or wish to rock, a common habitation but that I should recognize the fact of restlessness in my manner.

June 18, 2004

Before considering this perception of my work, and recognizing that the event that prompted this exchange between Seymour and me took place at Cathleen's and my apartment the year after we were married, I am moved to say something now about her and my meeting, at a time when marriage was, for me, so far as I knew, an alien thought.

In the late fall after the Tougaloo summer of 1964, a reporter from the Harvard *Crimson* phoned me to ask about the notice the paper had received that I was to be promoted from the Walter M. Cabot Associate Professor to the Walter M. Cabot Professor of Aesthetics and the General Theory of Value. The young woman doing the inquiring was notably easy to talk with, and we wandered for a good part of an hour well past any matters—of the difference between Associate and Full Professor, and what the general theory of value referred to, and why I had left Berkeley for Harvard, and the fact that I had a young child, and the fact that this reporter was from New York, and that her concentration was English and that, like most of her friends, she had been warned off philosophy although she had heard that my course in General Education was different, and so on—that might fit in a half column in the university newspaper. The following spring, at the annual faculty dinner held by the *Crimson* editors for faculty friends of the paper, I asked to be introduced to an editor named Miss Cohen (I had not been able to recall that the name Cathleen, improbably, was attached to that family name) and was told that she was still a news board candidate and was probably downstairs in the news room. As I left, I found her and introduced myself. Our meeting was in the event amiable but, I thought, inconsequential. I discovered, however, as the new year progressed that I had not lost my curiosity about this presence, now something more than a voice—the companion of I think the first extended conversation bordering on the personal that I had ever had with a New York Jewish Radcliffe undergraduate. I had met some other undergraduates of this description during my graduate school years, and others, perhaps, during my first year back teaching; but this had been a genuine if brief exchange—ground had been covered, for example, concerning what it meant in 1965 to be a New York Jewish Radcliffe undergraduate.

Sometime the following fall, I happened to accompany Albritton to the *Crimson* so that he could place an ad alerting the students in his lecture class to some change of schedule. Just inside the door, as Rogers was nervously looking for some guidance about how to place the ad, I saw Cathleen in the archway ahead, three steps up into the news room, smoking a cigarette and talking with a student I knew who lived in Adams House, an actor and aspiring writer, who had been one of those who had in my first months there habitually tested me with psychologically precocious wisecracks and references and allusions to my motives in living as a permanent professor in a Harvard House, and questions, for example, about whether my taste for film was genuine or whether it was a way to graze off the beautiful, admiring young. Cheeky, but we eventually established a palpably friendly bond.

As I moved within earshot of them he said to her: "How about coming to my room and having a ball?" She smiled wonderfully and answered, "No thanks." I don't know if she had yet seen me, but I was in no doubt that his behavior was for my benefit. The young man smiled back at her wonderfully, introduced us, and left. "So," she said to me.

"So," I replied, inventively. I went on to ask whether we might meet for coffee sometime. She replied that she was free Tuesdays. Her manner was so direct that I had the thought she had been expecting me to show up. The next day was Tuesday.

Before I arrived back at my rooms across the street I knew that something had already happened to me. The good looks, the dark eyes, and the dark hair pulled back tight, the air of fun along with the self-evident quickness of spirit, were all engaging. But something about her posture, half turning her body without moving her feet as I walked up the steps toward her, and the cigarette, and the heavily rimmed glasses, had struck a deeper note. I could not place it at first; I mean that while I pictured myself as something like twelve years old, in Atlanta, in a house I did not, and do not, remember—I seem to have been taken by Mendel to visit a friend of his, the room I recall was somewhat crowded with people Mendel's age, that is, in their mid-twenties, neither chained to the constrictions of the very young, nor incomprehensible with the boredom and fatigue of age, as my father and most of his acquaintances were—I knew that the image had some reference to a place strange to me in which a woman was sitting by a small round table under a bright lamp, wearing glasses with a tortoise-shell frame, sewing something on a child's garment, her legs crossed in a way I had never seen before, the leg crossed over the other did not veer out but clung to the length of the other, the toe of its flat leather slipper reaching down far enough to tap the floor lightly, repeatedly. A conversation was going on around her, and from time to time she would leave the needle in the fabric, pick up her burning cigarette and after a long drag blow out a heavy column of smoke, turn her upper body slightly and say something, traced by the last remnants of smoke, that I was convinced was extremely intelligent, judging from the attention everyone else paid to it.

Nothing immediate seemed to come of this coffee date either, which, unlike our phone conversation, and free of the awkward excitement of our first meeting, was made somewhat inflexible by reality, especially of course by that of the distinctly implausible difference in our ages.(But how many times had I said to myself that the point of being a professor is that you never have to leave school? And doesn't the very fact that the academic year, beginning in autumn and ending with summer, syncopates against the world's year that begins and ends in the dead of winter mean that those who live in both are given every year the opportunity of an extra beginning?) In my imagination at least, we as if silently agreed that we would keep the idea of each other but wait to decide whether to pursue our encounter further.

It again seemed no great surprise to Cathleen when somewhat late the following fall I phoned her during the Northeast blackout of 1965. The electrical failure had ended a Harvard faculty meeting prematurely (which normally ran from 4 to 6 p.m.), since the light in the sky was fading quickly. Because it was late November on the East Coast, this means it was just past 5 p.m. Rogers and I had been sitting together in the meeting and we left together. Once outside it was obvious that the failure went wholly beyond the building we had left, and we headed in the dying light for our respective Harvard Houses, thinking we may be of some use. People were instinctively gathering in the Adams House dining hall, where candles were already in place on each table. Telephone service was not affected, and the news spread that an electrical failure had now covered the entire Northeast of the United States, and that there was speculation about sabotage. I took, or was given, a candle from the dining hall, and learned again, back in my room, how bright candlelight is when it is the only light, and how difficult a city is to navigate on a moonless night with no public lamps. It was a chance to glimpse the meaning of night in a city through most of human history. Reverberations of loneliness, desire, and apprehension produced the call to Cathleen, and the effect of the call was, I believe, comparably magnified. I got the sense that she was still seeing someone else, but we agreed to meet for a drink in New York over Christmas vacation, and she gave me her number there. I was to be in New York for the Christmas meetings of the American Philosophical Association, and when I phoned her then from my hotel she was about to dress for a wedding rehearsal in which she was a bridesmaid and afterward have dinner with the participants. When she named the hotel in which the event was to take place, I noted that I was meeting friends for drinks at the Algonquin Hotel, which was near her destination. She agreed to my suggestion that she step up the tempo and make room to join us for half an hour on her way. It was in obvious respects a pointless plan, but the group of friends I was meeting included Jack Rawls and Rogers Albritton and Ronald Dworkin and Marshall Cohen, and I suppose I wanted a signal opportunity to have the two sides of my life, as it were, or the two imagined sides, meet on an interesting neutral field and test each other.

In the event it was an inspired idea. Cathleen was dazzling in what I supposed was a bridesmaid's gown (it was obviously meant to live for other celebrations as well, not a sweet dress but one of serious and subtle velvet). Her awareness of the group's distinction heightened her charm as well as sharpened her wit, and my friends were indeed charmed and faultlessly gallant. The discussion before she arrived had suddenly concerned, she learned, where to go to hear some jazz, pressed especially by Rawls (my last conversation with whom, some four decades later, was also about music, specifically about romantic string quartets, of which he had a remarkable collection of recordings). It emerged that Cathleen had a couple of suggestions about the Village, and all in all left us sooner than we wished and even happier than she had found us.

June 19, 2004

Back in Cambridge at the beginning of the world's year (the middle of the academic's) she and I began meeting for late coffee or a drink, soon for dinner, and within two or three weeks Cathleen and Rachel and I were together for part of Rachel's weekends in Cambridge. I gathered that Cathleen had made changes in the rest of her life. No more than a few weeks into the spring semester, the last of her undergraduate months at Harvard, walking to dinner, one or the other of us, let's say it was she, came out with sentiments either of us might have expressed by then: "How can we think of marrying? My mother has never had in mind for me a poor professor, almost twice my age, divorced and with a child." The implication, unmistakably understood by each of us, was that we had traveled past the point in our feelings where anything less than marriage would express our imagination of each other. When two or three months later I asked Rachel whether she had imagined that Cathleen and I might marry—Rachel and I were alone in Cathleen's car outside her apartment, the three of us on our way out to dinner, having passed by for Cathleen to get into a change of clothes—Rachel answered immediately, perhaps not impatiently, "It's obvious." What was patent to all who knew us was that the three of us had become accustomed to spending every evening together when Rachel was in Cambridge.

Cathleen and I agreed that I had other things going for me besides poverty and promise, but they were neither clearly evident beyond the precincts of our acquaintances at Harvard, nor paramount, nor perhaps really comprehensible, in this mother's list of virtues. My parents, on the contrary, would be awash with surprise and delight at the prospect, and that fact proved to become a critical part of the bond developing between us. Cathleen's father was not an immigrant, but his self-made energies in putting himself through university and law school educations, and his independence—without starting from, and without intending to or happening to achieve, real wealth—in building a law practice by himself that significantly included immigrant issues, were fundamental to Cathleen's idea of serious participation in the world. It was a basis for her understanding of my past with my father, an understanding no other of the women I had been close to had shown. (Indeed—a fact worth more than a parenthesis—neither of the other two women I had in fact or in effect lived with had grown up with a father.)

Cathleen's respect for, her sense of, the reality of her father's struggles and successes was an essential basis from which to refuse her brilliant mother's contempt for social failure. Yet this woman showed an inexplicable fear of following a profession of her own. Cathleen remembered something about her mother's early thoughts of law school, but nothing about what happened to the thoughts, and it was clear from the way her mother's friends were in terror of her quickness and accuracy in judgments of taste and quality, about clothes and décor, combined with her powers of calculation (she scored highest her year on the mathematics part of the New York State Regents Examination) that she would have thrived, for example, in the powerful position of chief buyer for one of the famous department stores in Manhattan. She worked the *Times* Sunday crossword in ink, sometimes completing it in the kind of time that would be respectable for a national tournament, but never fast enough to win the tournament, which would have taken systematic preparation, something she was willing to give to nothing. So she slept late, read a fair portion of the books on the *Times* best-seller list, and made the lives she touched on the whole less comfortable, if perhaps more interesting, than they might otherwise have been.

My sharpest, or most distinct, success with her was represented not by the books I had written, four or five of which appeared before her death (none on the *Times* best-seller list), but rather by an event one Sunday morning on a visit of ours to Cathleen's parents in New York, not long after our marriage. Cathleen's mother was having unaccustomed trouble continuing, let alone finishing, the Sunday *Times* crossword puzzle. Its title subject was classical music. She consulted me about the blanks she was drawing, and was repeatedly, increasingly, surprised that the answers I kept giving her turned out without fail to fit fruitfully in place and, sharpening the surprise, not infrequently to include names of composers or of pieces and forms of music she recognized, but couldn't put together with each other. But for some reason she was really astonished when she learned that the answer to "Beethoven's Opus 59" was "Razumovsky," a large bird of sound that seemed shot down from the clear sky.

An irony in the devotion to fashion is that other devotions seem more mysterious than they should. This route to sophistication easily leaves one otherwise coarse—not because ignorant of a set of facts, but because unknowing of other ways to live, of what others attach importance to. Putting aside such ignorance is, again, essential to the precious quality I think of as moral imagination. That any serious musician, or informed concertgoer, would know the opus number of Beethoven's three Razumovsky Quartets is not something this woman would have been interested in knowing, or, said otherwise, in fathoming the point of knowing.

I sound miffed. I am miffed. I knew something more at that moment, otherwise quite unremarkable, about what Cathleen had had, through her young life, to contend with.

June 21, 2004

When Seymour spoke to me about my writing, my first book, *Must We Mean What We Say?* had been out in the world for some months. And hereabouts begins the uncompleted map connecting the destinations and origins of the writing I am led or bound to produce. The public response for some twenty years after the appearance of this first book was, to my knowledge, with fond exceptions, either silence or dismay. (This way of putting things already puts matters far more comprehensibly, or definitively, than any stable reaction I would have expressed in those years, anyway before I began to take seriously the likelihood that the way I write—I ask again something I must already have asked here, namely, What choice does one have over the way one writes?—will have to create its own public, which may never be exactly public; and this means that I could never be sure whether what mostly greeted me was indifference or disapproval.) In the months before I showed up to teach in Emerson Hall, the philosophers J. Fodor and J. Katz attacked the two articles I had submitted (in addition to my dissertation) as evidence in the case for my tenure appointment to Harvard, asserting (I believe I recall the exact words) that the articles were "deleterious to the future of philosophy." This looked to be in general a poor welcome back to the East Coast and a difficult introduction to prospective students I would be encountering. When *The World Viewed* appeared two years after *Must We Mean What We Say?* one of the two reviews that came my way declared that the book was sickening; the other granted that my friends might like talking with me about movies but that this should not be grounds for publishing what was said privately. The following year *The Senses of Walden* was treated more kindly, but only among a small circle within the population of those actively devoted to Thoreau. (Good thing I had tenure. What makes tenure a good thing?) This hurt; but I was, so far as I could tell, emotionally agile or labile enough to be almost as interested, in moments even as anxiously tickled, as I was troubled by these extremes, reassured at those moments, even in the absence of very much in the way of counterreaction, that the extremity of these responses could not be rationally motivated. The writing had cost me something, in such a way, perhaps, that it has to, and should, cost the reader something. I did not feel that I wished to *make* my reader pay a price. I still do not see how I could have anticipated this configuration of responses—I mean expected that the books would seem so unpalatable to fellow philosophers and so foreign to those for whom philosophy, or the thought of philosophy, was foreign. Nor do I see what I might have done about it if I had anticipated it.

Apart, that is, from ceasing to trouble the public air. The possibility of ceasing occurred to me. One of the features of my life that kept
me at it was that the public situation went with growing and heartening
responses in my private correspondence. This, however, had its equivo-
cal side. What can do one more good in a moment than a charming
note from a stranger who had found the North Point paperback reissue
of *The Senses of Walden* in an airport bookstore and put the purchase in
his overcoat almost without thinking before leaving for a plane trip, describing his finding that he had the occasion to read the book through
that very night, sitting in a snowbound airport in Salt Lake City? But
then there were those more tortured letters, and more frequent, attesting to the profit that he or she had derived from reading something of
mine, as I will perhaps see from the enclosed reprint of an essay by the
writer of the letter, but that she or he could not find a way in which to
explain the profit (evidently that fact did not itself seem a reasonable
acknowledgment), so I will not find myself mentioned in the essay. The
proposed pleasure in this announcement was rather outweighed by my
sense of being told that what I was publishing was inherently private,
even secret, that this correspondent had in effect accidentally understood something of it, but that this fact was no evidence that I might
count on communicating my thoughts to another other. The danger for
me in such a message was not just this instance of rejected acceptance,
but the claim, which I had little outside evidence to refute, that this
view of my public incomprehensibility, or inexpressiveness, was common, I mean more frequent than any other view (however infrequent
the interest might be in having a view of this matter at all). This was
something that might well stop me in my tracks, since it would deprive
me of what fundamentally motivated the writing, I mean my sheer relation to it, that I had found a place in writing in which I could with a
certain constancy encounter times of lucid happiness, in which a certain sanity held on to the belief that I was, if ineptly, making myself
comprehensible to those of good enough will. (I have found that there
is no more choice over the way one writes than over what makes one
happy. If that is true then what you need to know is what makes you
happy and what you need to do is to write enough to find this state and
keep up with its haunts.)

Yet I felt that what had most intractably discouraged me was not at this stage the lack of public acceptance, but rather the failure in my efforts over some ten years to achieve a final, or stable, version of what I was privately calling *The Claim of Reason*, namely, to complete the revision and rewriting and continuation of my dissertation material that, in addition to finishing the film book and the Thoreau book, I had embarked upon at the Wesleyan Humanities Center during the final stage of my residence there in 1971. By "public acceptance" I do not, I emphasize again, mean a big thing here, merely the confirmation that one's voice has carried in certain instances beyond the circle of familiars, that one writes, in part, irreducibly, also for strangers. Some can play the stranger to themselves. Some friends can play it for friends. It is a burden that has at some time to be lifted. (I won't try to prove it now, but I feel sure that it was Gertrude Stein who said, "I write for friends and strangers"; and equally sure that I owe my preceding several sentences to having read that remark at a younger age than anything I could call philosophy.)

I noted earlier that the idea of the dissertation had from the beginning been to explore the ancient idea that disputes concerning ethical matters are illuminated by contrast or by comparison with disputes concerning knowledge—but that instead of configuring knowledge as it is in scientific discovery, where experiment and quantification, in a word sheaves of information and commitments to paradigms agreed upon, are brought to bear, I would take the concept of knowledge as it is deployed in ordinary challenges to claims to know, ones given so to speak in nothing more than one's conviction in a native language. I had reached the point at which it made sense to say that while in ordinary disputes about knowledge and ignorance rationality depends upon the possibility of overcoming disagreement (the bird is either a goldfinch, as I say, or it is not, as you say), if neither of us knows enough to prove it one way or the other, the world of knowledge has not thereby become cracked, we merely need patience, the extent of the world of our ignorance has for the moment somewhat expanded, and we need to consult beyond the two of us; whereas in ethical disputes (I say your actions amounted to a promise; you say they did not, or anyway that events abrogated the promise), we may lack the talent or the patience to arrive at an agreement, or we may become clear that the issue cannot be settled (between us); and we are unwilling to consult beyond ourselves. Each of us has our reasons. But this does not show that one or other of us is irrational, or that morality is inherently unstable. If we are impatient, we may decide to part company. There is failure here. We can call it the failure to integrate further the moral world. If this does not go too far we can—we do—live with it. The power of the moral world, like that of the philosophical, does not depend upon its being total, achieved, either individually or socially, let alone globally, whatever that would mean. The idea is there for us, is it not?

What has been the case since the birth of philosophy and of the great religions is that while the idea of the moral life has not died, that we recognize that our lives, individual and cultural, are subject to criticism, to being called upon beyond themselves as they stand, this opens our lives at the same time to false claims, to the fanaticisms and prejudices and other darkenings that philosophy has perennially challenged. Kierkegaard says that Christianity does not succeed by force. (I imagine him prominently, along with the logic of the matter, to be criticizing Emperor Constantine's methods, notably ordering the mass baptism of his [pagan] troops, whose leaders would march those under their commands into a shallow body of water, pronounce a requisite formula of conversion over them, and march them out again as Christians. I owe this unforgettable vignette to a class I attended given by the Renaissance and Reformation historian William Bousma, son of the philosopher O. K. Bousma, when the son and I were colleagues at Berkeley. Perhaps it is recorded in pages of Gibbon that I skipped.) Plato had said that the idea of a philosopher-king is paradoxical, I suppose because of its suggestion that the philosophical spirit can be announced and commanded.

Both intentions of exchange, the epistemological and the ethical, are driven by challenging a claim. In making and challenging claims, the disputants put their standing at stake. In disputes about knowledge, your standing is exhausted in the knowledge you can provide. (Standing by itself is not enough to justify expressing your knowledge whenever and to whomever it strikes your fancy to do so. Wittgenstein says concepts are directed by interest. It follows that boredom is a subtler detection of intellectual vice than philosophers have allowed.) In disputes about moral questions, standing is part of the dispute; a successful outcome is not necessarily agreement but a clarifying of positions and receiving respect for them. (This is, I suppose, the chief burden of the four chapters on moral philosophy composing Part Three of *The Claim of Reason*.)

The idea of morality in play here—in which souls are moved to examine one another—is one in which a rational being claims the right to confront (and to have an interest in confronting) another such being, hence to grant that the other is rational, or perhaps to conclude that he or she is irrational. Thoreau, recognizing the likelihood that his words will not convince, namely, that rational beings may disagree, or that not all have achieved a respect for rationality, declares that he would not waste his time reasoning with a stone. But there is already the hint that the time for reasoning in any relationship can run out. Emerson had said, early in "Self-Reliance": "We cannot spend the day in explanation," a remark I persistently hear echoed in Wittgenstein's abrupt declaration, in the very opening section of the *Investigations*: "Explanations come to an end somewhere." Modern (professional) philosophers, with notable exceptions, have on the whole not much interested themselves in describing human life when it is not, or seems not to be, making sense, as in intellectual or moral skepticism. In this, philosophy has suffered from the way it has put distance between itself and theology. Theology is drenched in fallen worlds, the only ones there are, anyway the only ones that contain philosophy (or theology).

June 22, 2004

I would not attempt to settle matters here by insisting that discussion on a moral plane typically takes the form of confrontation whereas on a scientific plane it takes the form of cooperation or competition. Both may partake of any, so one would have to be specific. But whatever the outcome here, something seems—seemed—left out in these ideas, something that runs throughout the opening three parts of *The Claim of Reason*, especially Part One, written at Wesleyan (incorporating bits and pieces of the original dissertation) and which guides the writing of the two little books also completed there, *The Senses of Walden* and *The World Viewed*. What is left out, or left too implicit or guarded, is some step beyond the idea that moral confrontation is in each instance open to, and subject to, rational criticism. What needs articulation is the sense that the root of morality is the fact of acknowledging shared human existence itself, that every utterance of the creature of speech is an exchange (if sometimes one-sided), an act demanding a response, a confrontation that draws blood, or stops or boils or cools or heartens it.

I have noted with admiration Lacan's observation that human beings are made so as to bump into each other. Maurice Blanchot, whom I am reading for the first time, echoes Lacan, charmingly, in the opening pages of *The Step Not Beyond* (*Le pas au-delà*—more literally, or impossibly, both *The Step Beyond* and *The Non-Step Beyond*). Blanchot begins a tale by describing someone who, as he puts it, does not resist the desire to look for people, since he knew that there were people who did not see anyone. (I hope I may be forgiven for thinking this not unlike certain of the little fables in Part Four of *The Claim of Reason* concerning soul-blindness.) Blanchot continues: "How does one go about meeting them?"—"Well, nothing could be more simple: you will stumble upon them." Thoreau says somewhere, roughly, that we have established rules of etiquette (he seems to mean the collection of moral maxims most people live by, or quote) to avoid coming to blows too often, incidents as it were of sheer awkwardness, intensified by overpopulation. (Do unto others . . . ; neither borrower nor lender be; a friend in need . . .)

Thoreau also says, describing his writing, call it his living, that "I thus unblushingly publish my guilt." What he has at that moment just published is an account listing his expenditures on food his first year at Walden. In other words, it is an account of what it cost to keep himself alive (not including keeping warm), which is to say, to persist in existence, the sheer fact of which he understands to establish guilt; we might perhaps say, to establish his lack of justification, as though the food he eats is taken out of the mouths, or bodies, of others. (It is important to learn not to drive oneself mad. It is also important to stress this as something to learn, namely, that the world gives us ample cause for the temptation to derangement.) Emerson had said: "The human is an expensive race. It lives off others." (Is that second sentence actually in Emerson, or is it a memory of mine pressing in from Brecht?) The background for both Emerson and Thoreau will at any time be an access of the realization of slavery, an evil so profound that anyone who is not opposing it is authorizing it, living off of it. (Is this an interpretation of original sin, or a rejection of it?)

For the idea, or vision, of infinite responsibility for the world, the fact of slavery is only the most lurid example. The everyday habitual reigns of injustice are in principle sufficient to motivate the idea. My infinite responsibility for my utterances, perceiving that every thrust of my sense of others and things into the world of things and others is a moral encounter, is how I understand Wittgenstein's and Austin's recognition of the everyday, and philosophy's chronic avoidance of the everyday (philosophy concentrating what human life disseminates at random, hazardously). Knowledge, the product of judgment, is not the ground of morality, but is in its origin moral, the precipitate of perpetual evaluations of the world, assessments of our interests and investments in it, of what counts for us, matters to us, or does not.

But I could not find my way to approaching these recent ideas as a continuation of the chapters on moral philosophy that conclude what I could include from the dissertation. I was no longer there, but not yet elsewhere. A sense of bafflement established itself in me during the last weeks of the year at the Wesleyan Humanities Center that led to my attempt to put aside the hope of bringing the dissertation to a publishable form.

June 23, 2004

In the spring of 1972, the second semester of the year I returned to teaching after the year's burst of productiveness at Wesleyan, I offered a seminar attempting to come to terms with the onslaught of work, received primarily from France, often by way of the comparative literature department at Yale (a couple of hours and a million miles down the road from that era at Harvard) that had begun conquering advanced literature departments as I was completing my initial trio of books. I had first learned of this work the year after *Must We Mean What We Say?* was published, when I was invited, along with several other philosophers, to participate in some days of conversation with a certain Jacques Derrida in Paris in the coming summer of 1970, namely, in the period just before my sojourn in Wesleyan. The invitation came by way of Hubert Dreyfus, a fellow-sufferer through the trial of the Harvard Ph.D. qualifying examinations eighteen springs earlier, then teaching down the Charles River at M.I.T. But having been a Harvard undergraduate concentrator in philosophy, he seemed to take these exams, set by teachers whose tastes he was familiar with, quite in stride, even finding time to continue with his position as photographer for various Harvard student publications and pursuing an interest in continental philosophy that would have then been of at best marginal help writing essays for the qualifying examinations. The invitation from Dreyfus explicitly suggested that I would find Derrida's work congenial to the philosophical preoccupations and style of the essays in my *Must We Mean What We Say?* Eventually I would agree with this in part, taking the congeniality to arise from an alignment of concerns with issues of the question of philosophy, and skepticism, and madness, and writing, and presence, in a style that was academically unexpected and allowed for interpretations of literary works that were to take their place as, or as it were against, philosophical investigations. Whether these are the issues Dreyfus had in mind I do not know.

I have described moments of this meeting in Paris on other occasions. One of the moments was a morning to be given to Derrida's responses to *Must We Mean What We Say?*—especially, I gathered, to my defense of Austin. (It was in the following months that Derrida would present his responses to Austin in a text entitled "Signature Event Context.") But while Derrida indeed showed up with a copy of my book, he and I seemed the only ones who wanted to discuss Austin, since the conversation that morning was preempted by an English philosopher whose name I would have heard but have contrived, as others have, to forget, who, I had been told, believed himself to have produced a refutation of Gödel's incompleteness proof. At the end of those days, Derrida invited Cathleen and me to dinner with his wife in their house outside Paris. These hours were, as the daylight hours between us in the full group had been, unfailingly congenial. As he was about to drive us back to our hotel, he presented me with several small books of his that had just appeared. I was not unprepared for what I found in them, after the past several days in his company, but the alternating attraction and blankness in my responses were here directed to a French prose that was essentially beyond me. It was patent, even from the punning that I did catch, that I was apt to be missing something at every moment. It was equally clear that to improve my responses would require an investment of time and interest that it was unlikely I would give to the task (especially in the absence of some informed tutoring) during the immediately ensuing period at Wesleyan, to which I was bringing unfinished work of my own that had been mounting, with increasing velocity, and no little desperation, over the decade since completing my dissertation.

By the time my seminar began the autumn I returned from Wesleyan to Harvard, Derrida's *Grammatology* had been translated, and Barthes and Foucault and Lacan and de Man were academic news in the humanities, except in professional philosophy, where they continued either unknown or despised, commonly both.

It is bound to be to hard to explain the success of revolutions, for example, not to invoke the existence of a revolutionary situation, which seems precisely the thing to be explained. In the case both of the reigns of logical positivism and later of poststructuralism, one would like to understand what made the state of, especially, the American academic dispensation so often helplessly, not to say abjectly, vulnerable to each of them—or enraged by them. Descartes and others had to overcome Aristotelianism in science, Hume and others had to overcome the rationalism in that overcoming, Kant had to overcome Hume's loss of assurance of the things of the world, Hegel had to overcome Kant's loss of the things beyond the things of the world as they are, Kierkegaard and Nietzsche had to overcome Hegel's postponement, hence anticipation, of the Absolute, and professional philosophy had to overcome Kierkegaard's and Nietzsche's open invitation of the literary back into the philosophical republic. American study of the humanities (and that side of the social sciences) was doubly threatened, to become overwhelmed either by hardening or by softening (by philosophy without philosophy, or by science without science).

Frege's inspiration of Russell's call for analytical philosophy was key in beating back the literary incursion into philosophy and indeed more systematically cast doubt on the source of the literary as such, namely, on the domestic marvels of ordinary language. For those for whom pragmatism's invitation to judge the failings of philosophy seemed arbitrary or helpless against positivism's undermining of the rationality of judgments of value, there was little resistance, however much annoyance, to overcome. And the new criticism (also famously understood to be represented at Yale by W. K. Wimsatt and Cleanth Brooks and Robert Penn Warren) had no fight left in it to match the excitement and intensity of literary and philosophical interpretation of the new thing from Paris. My own self-absorbed understanding was that the American dispensation of humanities, formed in the absence, indeed the shunning, of the study of philosophy, left it incapable of evaluating claims made in the name of philosophy by philosophers from the other side, whereas professional philosophers on this side were on the whole too contemptuous of these claims to study them.

The ensuing, unchecked phantasmagoria of fashion remains, while its intensity, or exclusiveness, has waned, without credible evaluation. I was distressed that Wittgenstein's methodical portraits of the craving for the absolute (of which the philosophical opposition to the quest for "certainty" is one symptom) and of the uncanniness of the ordinary, ideas that could in principle be recognized as common ground with the onslaught from Paris, could get little hearing here on such matters in either region. But my distress was surely to some unmeasured degree a projection of my own sense of failure in being unable to see material of *The Claim of Reason* brought to some conclusion, however impermanent. I spoke a moment ago of my attempt to put the book aside. A less polite way of cloaking the matter is to say that, for the third explicit time in my life I found myself creatively stopped, not understandably challenged and inspired, but at a dead end: the first time in New York, after music at Berkeley; the second time at Harvard, with the appearance of Austin and his work; the third time with hundreds of acceptable pages recognizably my own that I could not lead to a conclusion in the present.

So again it had to do with being defeated by material broached in my dissertation; and again it was accompanied by the impending birth of a child and a sense of incapacity to make a life for a child, and to husband a marriage, in a dreadful world. Cathleen found the best words to say to me, namely, that I did not have to be father and mother and brother and playmate and friend to this child, that being with him and being a loving father was all that was required. But my sense of being unable to provide a living, meaning humanly a justification for living, was undermining. It wasn't a matter, as at Berkeley, during the collapse of my first marriage, of needing the Ph.D. in order to keep my position; it was rather a question of feeling competent to justify my position. The collapse of the manuscript wiped out the sense that I had accomplished anything worth speaking of, specifically anything worth taking into a classroom. After a twenty-year-old identity crisis, and a thirty-five-year-old redemption by absorption in work I believed in, I entered into the banality of a fifty-year-old crisis of misgiving, too little to show, too late altogether for compensation. The experience will eventually and essentially enter into the theme, in the continuation of Part Four of *The Claim of Reason*, of the inescapable human subjection to the terror of inexpressiveness (sometimes expressed, as I have noted, as claustrophobia) and the companion anxiety of exposure. But in the winter of 1976 that realization was unforeseeable. For the second time, in this discouragingly similar impasse, I sought out psychoanalytic orientation.

June 24, 2004

Once a week was what I could afford, and again enough timely progress was made to warrant going on with it. I mean that within several months I could pick up my unfinished manuscript again and feel confident that, with time, it would move. A way of describing what had happened would be to say that this writing had become a pawn in a hidden game I was playing with my life, or to say that there were merely, as it were, neurotic or hysterical issues associated with writing that could be dissociated, or lifted, from deeper matters of what felt to me deformations of character whose discontinuous strata might take forever to map. Would this further journey, as Emerson promised me, come to a comprehensible goal in every step? Conceivably so, if mapping the journey is also journeying, is already the journey. Such thoughts led me and Dr. Smith—that was actually his name, Eugene Smith, bless his memory—periodically to consider psychoanalysis an abstract of religion. But how do you transport the abstract out of this room of magic into the light, or the fog, of actual day? It does not take a Moses to part the waters of comparatively simple self-oppression, merely one who has

walked the night streets with the angel of death and has an ear for de-
tecting imaginary pharaohs.

I must tell something I still recur to with pleasure that signaled in
me the confidence that the writing would be done. Smith was a product
of the Boston Psychoanalytic Institute, but one who over a lifetime of
practice had allowed himself to become as unorthodox as changing
times seemed to him to demand. I did not want at first to use the couch,
and I also did not want at once to analyze why I did not want to. I
wanted to talk and talk, guardedly or unguardedly, and be listened
to and be followed, even when what I was saying was that I saw why
Freud thought a person of fifty years to be too old to begin the work of
psychoanalysis. There was too much to say; too much has happened
that is tied to the too much that is happening now to get to the end
of it or to the beginning of it. If I reported a dream, my associations
were so extensive that the hour would hardly begin to contain them;
perhaps none would. If I began by being unable to talk, and unable to
talk about being unable, then I might at that stratum talk about being
unable to talk about being unable. And then I would be into one or
other continuations of the manuscript, which was so often about talking
too much or too little, and about who starts a conversation, who has the
right to speak, and/or the obligation to respond, and how these were
the same and different in philosophy and in psychoanalysis, and I could
get Smith to laugh at, for example, my tale about producing a phantom
pain in my eye, whose watering provided a public reason for my applying for admission to medical school with a handkerchief over my face,
like a movie bank robber; and I laughed within his laughter generally
at my unconsciousness and belated consciousness of my behavior as
hard as I laughed alone that day in New York. Much harder indeed,
and much longer.

After hearing innumerable continuations about the untouchable
manuscript, Smith offered a suggestion, in roughly these terms: "You
know, a phobic response may not be analyzable. Maybe this is also at
work here. Then you just have to re-create the response and attend to
what happens." He had known for a while that I had packed away the
manuscript and its associated notes in closed boxes, so that I could go
into the study to prepare classroom lectures without facing what I could

not face doing. "It's clear that you have access to many continuations. Why don't you just unpack the manuscript and put it on the desk as you would if you were continuing, but without any intention of actually doing any writing. Just sit there, and let it sit there, for a while."

The following week I began by reporting the results, which went as follows. "I did as you suggested but nothing happened."—"You must have felt something."—"Really nothing. Well—except—I guess for a mild—pervasive—sense—of pleasure." And after a stunned silence, we broke into the grandest of the laughs we had had together. Tragedies are tragedies, but folly can make a tragedy out of what is not tragic, and folly exposed in time may become hilarious. Is it tragic or is it comic that one may forbid oneself a deep source of pleasure simply because it is a source of (unrecognized) pleasure? And can the mere matter of months of more or less aimless talk—what else was it?—actually been what produced a breakthrough here? I did not attempt during term time actually to pick up consecutive writing again, but I left the manuscript in view and I started again my practice of keeping notes of ideas and examples and subgoals to work at or toward.

By the end of the following summer a form or sound had been found for what would be the concluding stretch of Part Four, say, a medium, one that linked it with the opening three parts not by continuing them exactly but by initiating responses to them, discontinuously—discontinuously both with those beginnings and with the discontinuity between the responses themselves. And as the subject more and more became skepticism with respect to the other (differentiating that, as systematically as I could, from skepticism with respect to the external world, namely, skepticism's philosophically favored, all but exclusive, form in Anglo-American philosophizing), I even surmised that the end would be, as in a sense it had been in *Must We Mean What We Say?*, a reading of a Shakespeare play, but now articulating the claim (at best implicit in the earlier book) that Shakespearean tragedy is a working out of a stance toward the world expressed philosophically in a derivative of, or extension of, Cartesian skepticism. I did not, of course, see how to arrive at this ending, but within my expanded confidence I did not doubt that I would find a way. Perhaps. By the close of the next summer the ending made its appearance in time, that is, before fall lectures began.

June 25, 2004

This was September 1977; sixteen years had passed since the original dissertation had been submitted to Harvard; I had just turned fifty-one. I did not, strangely, doubt that I would publish these results, in case they were (still) found publishable (the Oxford Press had accepted the work in its dissertation form shortly after I had submitted the dissertation to Harvard—I have forgotten who advised this—but I had withheld it for revision, thank heaven), even though I had the distinct sense that I was not a judge of the value of these revised pages. Not only had I no perspective on them; I was by then too out of touch with secondary material on Wittgenstein to try to make comparisons there. I was not the only one who testified to having lived for years with insights gathered from early readings of Wittgenstein (Albritton and Kripke were notable others who had said so in my presence). What I took to constitute a kind of external proof of the pages was in the liberation they provided me for other writing.

Within a month of turning over my new manuscript to be typed cleanly for publication, I wrote the most extended piece, and I felt the best, the freest, that I had devoted to a single filmmaker, namely, on the films of Dušan Makavejev. Within little more than a year I went on also to publish "What Becomes of Things on Film?" a further small theoretical text on film that I have used repeatedly since; and a, for me, experimental piece on hypocrisy called "Letter to Alceste"; and my first essay on Emerson, "Thinking of Emerson"; and a reading of *The Lady Eve*, which in effect announces the idea of remarriage comedy. If the amount of work is not overly impressive, the continuity of it and the fact that the last two essays begin essentially new projects that will keep developing within the present is not without its bearing on some new relation I had come to occupy toward writing. In the event, what impressed me most, I think, was the rapidity with which each of these things was done, the sense of my feeling in each case unencumbered by inessentials (further citations perhaps owed or an apology) in turning to a task of expression. It is before all that quality of liberation that I attribute to the completing of *The Claim of Reason*.

I hope I need not assert my consciousness that productiveness does not justify publication. But this new sense of creativeness confirmed my sense that the material of *The Claim of Reason* had roughly realized itself, had assumed what identity I could confer upon it. I could not imagine what I would do to *revise* it any further. It could, I know some felt, be made trimmer. I could pick out passages in it that I felt I would not want to live without. But I could not convince myself that they would have their effect apart from the terrain on which or out of which they were developed. The dangers of self-delusion or self-protection here are plain enough. At some stage I said to myself, in effect, that the work is what it is—on the whole it either will or it will not show that whatever blunders and blemishes remain will prove reasonable costs of doing business with a very long and increasingly eccentric enterprise. As my sons' generation, or I suppose it is now that of my grandchildren—helpfully intone in response to boring explanations: "Whatever!" But at least I said my farewell to the work with pleasure.

I associate the publication of *The Claim of Reason* with the year Sandra Laugier spent at Harvard, attending lectures and seminars and completing her research for her doctoral dissertation on the work of Quine. She will become the principal translator of *The Claim of Reason* into French, nominated for this role by her doctoral supervisor, the philosopher Claude Imbert, Professor at the École Normale in Paris (a relationship beginning in the years just before the women's venue of the École Normale merged with the men's in the rue d'Ulm). Claude Imbert had recommended my book for translation to François Wahl, the editor of the significant philosophy series at Editions du Seuil, and extended an invitation to me to give a set of lectures at the École Normale, beginning and sustaining my increasing relation with European philosophers (largely, and until quite recently, mostly advanced students working at doctoral dissertations and beginning, or thinking about beginning, a life of teaching). Sandra Laugier's and my intellectual friendship expanded quickly and eventually included our families as well as widening circles of continuing and precious friends.

I am sometimes praised for attempting to bridge, or somehow communicate, between the dispensation of Anglo-American and continental philosophy. The most I could claim to have done in this arena is to refuse to choose between them or to dampen a student's enthusiasm for either. I could wish to have suggested that the fact that there is no nonirritating pair of titles for this intermittently palpable intellectual divide, itself declares that we (we who are interested in both "sides," the same we who are distressed both by shallow sallies of contempt, or sometimes of imitation, of the one by the other) have no satisfying description of the principal differences in play. The pair "Anglo-American" vs. "continental" (or "phenomenological") is variously false and/ or misleading. A glaring falsification is that the vague identification of America with analytical philosophy deletes the ponderable historical fact that the ensuing revolution in America (and partly in England) that resulted in the hegemony of "analysis" resulted as directly from G. E. Moore's and Bertrand Russell's early revulsion from British idealism and the event of Russell and Whitehead's *Principia Mathematica* as it did from continental thinkers such as Gödel and Carnap and Reichenbach and Hempel, who preserved their lives by immigrating to the United States where their early motivation to preserve rationality from such obscurantist metaphysicians as Martin Heidegger was to some immeasurable sense pointless (since Heidegger did not yet exist here), and their cultural passion or mission in a foreign land was in any case modified or reduced, and at the same time narrowly intensified by their obvious accomplishments, which mostly and obviously outstripped those of their American philosophical colleagues (not, eventually, and notably, the accomplishments of Quine, who had traveled to Europe in the early thirties to study with Carnap). Their mission was epitomized—for many it was lethally and repetitively confined—to purveying a method and an ideology of sense and non-sense, The Verifiability [or Empiricist] Theory of Meaning, that in its argumentative power and moral criticism and its literary and religious irreverence (or terror), appealed to many, even at a guess most, of the most talented graduate students entering the profession of philosophy. How many persons of talent it discouraged from entering the profession is, I suppose, unknowable.

How it was that American philosophically inclined intellectual life was so vulnerable to this storm of logical positivism remains open to question. It seems almost as though American culture had its own motives for a contempt of the register of established philosophy, as if the terrible tension between philosophy and sophistry, part of the origination, and continued grain, of philosophy, had now been resolved, or rendered formulaic. This vulnerability was successfully resisted for some and for a while by the resurgence of new Christian theology out of Karl Barth and Reinhold Niebuhr and Paul Tillich, soon after the end of World War II. But within philosophy there was no methodical easing until a usable reception of J. L. Austin and the later Wittgenstein was undertaken beginning in the middle to late 1950s. (Early Wittgenstein had been, understood or not, part of the forming of the positivist Vienna Circle before the war.)

But geographical proximity is a poor, let's say vulgar, measure of intellectual intimacy, proven by those discoveries of intimate strangers in one's travels and marked by the enclaves of analytical sympathies in Europe and of continental longings in the States. And yet, having returned several weeks ago from a conference on my work in Potsdam, I wish to record, on this last-minute sweep of editing, interpolating this entry's closing trio of paragraphs exactly twenty-six months after its initial date, my sense in contemporary Europe of ease in crossing and recrossing intellectual borders or gulfs that for almost all of my professional life have caused me grief—as if beyond the States it requires no apology to take it for granted that philosophy is part of intellectual life quite generally. I do not wish to underestimate the possibility that an "ease" of understanding might be encouraged, or mistaken, by the self-selection of my audience and by neglecting what remains irreducibly specific in studying philosophy. Nor do I wish to deny how often I have felt the common distrust of philosophy by American intellectuals is enabled by the lamentably simple and dishearteningly arbitrary fact that philosophy is on the whole not made some definite if small part of the curriculum of American public high schools. First-year students in college are met with a flood of new and fateful decisions and requirements and interests and occasions—not to mention that it becomes much harder to allow yourself, as beginning the study of philosophy has from the beginning demanded of oneself, to resemble, in moments to become, an intellectual fool. Musical performance more famously and strenuously demands an early engagement, but there waiting too long will place simply unanswerable demands upon one's hands and ears and negotiable postures.

Part 12

June 26, 2004

Writing Part Four of *The Claim of Reason*, its concluding and longest part, produced one way out of the sense I had expressed fifteen years earlier in "Aesthetic Problems of Modern Philosophy" (in *Must We Mean What We Say?*) and have lived with ever since, namely, that "philosophy is in one of its periodic crises of method," a sense "heightened by a worry . . . that method dictates to content; that, for example, an intellectual commitment to analytical philosophy trains concern away from the wider, traditional problems of human culture which may have brought one to philosophy in the first place." This observation, at this distance, seems too obvious to say out loud. But actually becoming aware of oneself as caught within such forces is bound sometimes to produce surprised, discreet shrieks. (It was an observation common to American transcendentalists to account for their reaction against current philosophy. A most poignant instance for me.)

Two large or I might say institutional issues were, increasingly in writing Part Four, inescapably on my mind, presenting themselves as if for the first time to be constant and immovable threats to my finding a way toward completing *The Claim of Reason*, I mean the divide between the dispensations of analytical and continental philosophy, and the prohibition of literary obviousness or ambition in writing philosophy. I think I had never imagined that contesting these conditions could be effected by flouting them. Their causes are deep, as deep as philosophical responsibility. To maintain that these conditions have become unnecessarily fixated is empty if a counternecessity is not expressed—expressed *as* counter, with its tensions and ambivalences on its face, not attempting, not wishing, a merely opposite stance. Say it is to maintain a distrust (even a certain praise) of ordinary language not by comparing it with, say, analyzing or where possible replacing it with, mathematical logic but by contesting it with itself, so continuing philosophy's ancient challenge to consider one's life. (I said earlier that rewriting and completing the promises of my dissertation was to be all or nothing. It had become, some two decades later, now or never.)

So I philosophized as continuously as I could, incorporating literary texts when they would insist, and whatever of the literary came into my manner, without embarrassment (lines and images from Wordsworth, Yeats, Blake, Shakespeare, Dickens, Melville, Kafka, Conrad, Mann, Proust, and so forth had impressed me, say, become unforgettable for me, before philosophy had, or rather, before I was taught differences between literature and philosophy), and I periodically offered as a sort of overriding justification of my practices—or rather as a source of coherent tips to reading the results of such efforts—my readings of Wittgenstein's *Investigations* that took its restlessly roving center to demand literary as well as philosophical responses, and moreover philosophical responses for which analytical training in searching out arguments, while not dispensable, was not perfect training. (The idea of a "roving center" was something I first articulated early in reading Emerson, in saying that every sentence of an essay of his could be taken as the topic sentence of its paragraph.) The responses I received to what I was doing were not infrequently colored by falsely positive and falsely negative gestures; I mean the work was liked and disliked not infrequently for the same reasons, for example, for the sheer fact of its encouraging what was called literary interventions. To my dismay (and somehow endlessly to my surprise) I seemed to be dividing readers from one another whom I had imagined I might be opening to each other. But not always, and hearteningly not by readers whose responses I had reason most to trust and to treasure. (I do not understand why it was only after philosophy became identifiable for me that after years of all due respect to them, I fell in love with the writings of Jane Austen and of George Eliot.)

June 27, 2004

I am not unaware that events in my life are becoming intellectual events, nor that this links up with what in my early pages I noted as the tendency of my narration of events to be overtaken by the desire to articulate the event of narration itself, or say, the conditions of the present in which what there is to say can be said in the way it is given to me to say it. That is the region to which the drama of my life may be said largely to have migrated. I had discovered for myself—been knocked off balance by the knowledge—that "the mind, mind has mountains." Said otherwise, with the publication of *The Claim of Reason*, I was content that my life show, if steadiness of attention will manage it, the drama that the pleasures and concerns of family life, together with those of friends and students and the sometimes extended obligations of academic life, exact in return for supporting a life of writing. The bets by now are long placed. But then part of what I have also wanted to show here is that childhood events, early and late, are already irreducibly intellectual, and that those events are already adventures, as Mark Twain and Charles Dickens and Sigmund Freud, credits to the human race, are known to insist.

I have seen such adventures unforgettably in our frighteningly delightful and fascinating sons. I shall not at once claim that the few intellectual forays I have it in mind now to recount from their early years should count as philosophizing, as my old friend Gareth Matthews might wish to do, as in his pathbreaking work on children and philosophy. One reason I see for being wary of asserting too close a connection between childhood bewilderment and adult perplexity is that, explicitly, Socrates invents a world of philosophy by confronting assertions of people who claim to know what the world is, already producing as it were unthoughtful philosophy, so that the philosopher's immediate task is to reveal their bewilderment to them and get them to stop. Whereas thoughtful responses to childhood's reflections are not to lead them to self-repudiation but to help them go on, to further their exploratory responses, as if listening for orienting echoes of their assertions as they wonder what the world is, what its things and persons are to expect of each other.

Blocking adult certainties philosophically is a way of asking that childhood be remembered; drawing out childhood uncertainties is a matter of suggesting that adulthood not be sought too quickly. Another way of identifying the perspective I wish to achieve is to say that for the child the state of bewilderment or wonderment is as natural as the acquisition of language; they are one another's cause and consequence.

A favorite example of mine concerning our older son, Benjamin, essentially includes my mother, specifically Ben's behavior at my mother's funeral, so to tell it I need to fill in some background. In 1981, before Ben's fifth birthday, my mother, soon to celebrate her eighty-first birthday, agreed to move into an assisted living complex in a pleasant suburb of Atlanta. Things went well at first. Others of her generation were living there, and a number of them whom she hadn't seen for half a century remembered her from her days as a prominent musician in town. They made a fuss over her and asked her to play the piano for them, perhaps after a communal meal in the dining hall. She pretended that there was little left in the old girl, but she condescended to accede to the request, with éclat. One evening two or three months later, cooking herself supper in her apartment, her fire alarm went off when she had fallen asleep and something frying in a pan began sending up smoke. Then within a matter of weeks or so after that event she appeared at the dining room in her negligee, and persisted in expressing oppositional amazement at the shocked reactions of her former friends and their guests. The choice she was given was either to move into the adjacent nursing home or to find a way to be cared for privately. It was obvious that she would come to live with us in Brookline.

Things again went well for a while, until a month or so after the move it became clear that my mother needed effectively constant supervision. I had, climactically, left her turning the pages of a magazine in the waiting room of my psychoanalyst's office when I went for a shortened consultation with him, and when I returned she was gone. The office was on the twelfth floor of a modern apartment building, and she was in none of that floor's four corridors. Praying, if my dry mouth could offer a prayer, that she had taken the elevator down to the first floor, I pressed the elevator call button hard and repeatedly and after an interminable wait and ride down I glanced at the empty lobby and asked the attendant behind the undisturbed marble-shelved reception window whether he had seen an eighty-year-old woman walk past

within the last twenty minutes or so. He had not. I hurried back to the
elevators trying to form a clear enough space in my mind in which to
decide whether to start searching each floor and if so whether to begin
low or high when I realized I had better walk back and tell the attendant what I was doing. But what I instead said to him out of a sudden
inspiration was rather, "Have you seen a nice-looking well-dressed six-
ty-five-year-old woman pass through recently?" He answered at once,
"Why yes. She just walked outside." Racing outside I saw my mother
sitting stolidly and staring straight ahead in the front curbside seat of
a taxicab parked in the drop-off space immediately at the entrance of
the building. When the driver saw me walk toward them and call to
my mother, he jumped out of his seat and hurried around to me saying
frantically, "I didn't know what to do. She just kept saying 'Take me
home.'" I thanked him, paid him the fare of a trip to our house, which
he was reluctant to accept, a trip I had made by taxi more than once,
and explained to my mother that I had brought my car there after all
so the taxi was not necessary.

Cathleen was able in a matter of days to find someone to live with
my mother in the apartment we hurriedly had had constructed out of
three remnant rooms used for storage in the basement of our house,
where there were intact fittings from which to anchor and elaborate
a reasonably modern kitchen and bathroom. In 1874, when the string
of five townhouses was built of which ours is at the end nearest the
riverway and trolley tracks, the basement was the location of servants'
quarters, attested by three neat little bells, disconnected but still hung
from curved metal strips over the door down the inside stairs from our
kitchen to the basement apartment. ("Basement" may give the wrong
impression of the design of these townhouses. The first floor, namely,
the floor opened onto by the house's main, or front, door, is entered by
walking up a half flight of stone steps, eight steps in fact, so that with
a mild decline as the plot of land reaches some forty feet to the back
of the house (far enough to cover a descent equivalent to another good
half flight) the back basement door is flush with the ground, and the living room and small bedroom of the downstairs apartment are exactly
aboveground with ample windows while its kitchen and bathroom at
the other end, namely, the front, of the house have higher walls and
smaller, higher windows.)

"Someone" to live with my mother indeed. Cathleen found a service started by a young woman tired of practicing law called the Student Housing Exchange, that discovered matches with local families who would provide housing for students who exchanged various kinds of household work, from child care to gardening. This enterprising woman turned out to suggest at once someone she described as perfect for our needs, someone enrolled at Boston University, half a dozen blocks from our house, in its program in Occupational Therapy.

When later that afternoon, at the time arranged for an interview, the doorbell rang, I had no idea what to expect. Who is it who cares for the old? Probably those with no gift for it, with problems of their own. Instead, standing at the door was an angel still redolent from heaven, a beautiful young woman with a radiant smile to whom my mother was immediately drawn and with whom the young woman seemingly at once established communication. It emerged in fact that Myona's special concern in her training in therapy was with geriatric issues. My mother had on the spot acquired a further, loving child, and for the following eight months she was happiest, indeed to all appearances happy, in Myona's company. This became undisguisable when it developed that my mother had become uncertain who I was. She sometimes referred to me as her brother, but when she recognized that this was somehow mistaken she became nervous and wanted to leave us at once and go back down to her apartment. It eventually became difficult to persuade her even to have a meal with us. Some six or seven weeks before she died, when everything from her ability to walk, to her capacity for continence, were failing her, we felt we should follow the increasingly insistent medical advice to move her into a nursing home. The second or third establishment we visited, in our neighboring town of Newton, was sufficiently convincing, in various ways. A notable advantage was simply its location, which allowed me, with hardly more than a twenty-minute detour, to drive to the nursing home on my way to or from meeting my classes in Cambridge. When the afternoon of our exploratory visit there my mother on her own initiative made her way to an upright piano against a wall in a room off the entrance hall, the sounds she made on the instrument were mostly incomprehensible. I could make out in those fifteen or twenty terrible seconds certain distorted shapes of the Schulz-Evler "Blue Danube," now a destroyed spider's web. She recoiled from her attempt, uncomprehendingly, before I reached her to guide her back out. Her impulse to go to the piano seemed to speak of a measure of her comfort in the place, even of what acceptance she could muster to a surmised necessity. She died there some nine weeks later. The diagnosis was a series of mild strokes.

I note briefly the presence of a wicked, invisible, not to say incomprehensible star guiding these recent daylight memories of my reactions then. I have said that an immediate criterion of assessment in choosing a nursing home for my mother, almost certainly her final home, was to consider the significance of its being convenient for me to travel to and from. This protective inhibition of emotion, parading as practicality, is something I seem to have explained to myself as my having over the preceding months, and increasingly, exhausted the number of felt good-byes a reasonably ordinary human being could withstand. This sense of a heavy emptiness remained with me quite constantly from then through the time of my mother's funeral, after which a mild mania ruled my little world, expressing itself, for example, in my wanting to be with Ben every minute he was not in school, play more games with him than usual, outside and inside the house. For example, using Playmobile figures as our base unit of measure (some two inches tall), we constructed a regulation football field roughly to scale by taping together more than a hundred laundry shirt cardboards, stretching some twelve feet in length, counting the two end zones. Fully unfolded, this magnificent arena made our living room, housing also a grand piano and two large sofas, impassable, but the narrow entrance hall that led past it to the dining room could be used on game days.

I am interested to note that the nine or ten weeks of vacant preoccupation I felt, or did not feel, or cannot now usefully describe, during my mother's residence in the nursing home, were precipitated by my reaction to her demonstration, or discovery, that her musical ear and body had forsaken her. I know that my figuration of the sounds she made on that piano as a destroyed spider's web bears some interpretation—both about what expertly playing virtuosic piano music is, and about what mothers are. What I report here is that this event caused in me the greatest shock of fear, a cold thrill throughout my body and skull, of any of the events of my mother's wretched decline over the preceding twelve months. This was not a simple prefiguring of my inevitable visit by the angel of death, but a garish image of his or her appetite.

My mother's graveside funeral in Atlanta was conducted by the rabbi, long retired, who had joined the congregation the year I was born, and moved with it from the south side to its opulent setting, with plenty of parking, in a new, wooded development within a once distant and exclusive (not to say once restricted) suburb. Rabbi Epstein knew the prominent Goldstein family well and for over half a century had many occasions on which to admire and compliment my mother on her accomplishments. He included in his remarks at her grave his memory of my mother, barely twenty years old, having been called upon, not long after he moved to the Atlanta congregation, to accompany Yoselle Rosenblatt (one of the illustrious names among orthodox cantors in the world of that period) on his visit to Atlanta, and during the same season to accompany Enrico Caruso when, as I seem to have made out, Caruso's own pianist was suddenly taken ill. These have been treasured stories for me most of my life, told to me by various people, family members and strangers, but never by my mother. Of course she would have known that it was unnecessary.

Among my associated thoughts on this summer day of writing about the increasing participation, religious and civic, of the Jewish community in Atlanta's communal life more generally, a participation so notable within it of the extended and growing Goldstein family, I find myself thinking of a certain disadvantage, or deprivation, in the new area of convenient and open parking spaces provided by (nonorthodox) synagogues. In my childhood on the south side, while the congregation was still stricter than it became and many from "the old country" were still alive and maintaining their orthodox, observant, ways, some who had moved across town were also loosening their specifically religious ties and instead of moving back across town into a hotel on Jewish holidays within walking distance of their familiar lifelong synagogue (driving a car on the Sabbath, as on religious holidays generally, indeed turning on any machine, was defined as work, and disallowed) would, primarily the generation born in America, drive back home after services and back again for services the next morning, parking their cars on the streets at discreet distances from the observances.

A secondary gain of this infringement and courteous concealment was, since the Jewish High Holidays—Rosh Hashanah and Yom Kippur—variously fell (as determined by the Jewish lunar-sensitive calendar) at the time of the baseball World Series, that during breaks in the day-long religious services one could join a small group gathered for the moment around an advantageously parked car outfitted with a radio, to check on the score of the game currently in progress. This was especially urgent during the season of 1940, in which Hank Greenberg of the Detroit Tigers, a rare, and the first, Jewish champion player of the national pastime, had been given a dispensation by his rabbi to play in that year's World Series. Of course turning on a radio was forbidden during these days of observance. We knew that exceptions to this rule were made for emergencies, like illness or war; or perhaps we figured that if Greenberg's case could count as an emergency (many other people's careers would be jeopardized by his absence), so could the intensity of our desire to follow the results of his presence.

But the turn to my mother's funeral was intended as preparation for my telling a story or two about five- or six-year-old Benjamin, who had spent many mornings playing cards with my mother after we had settled her in our house, being read to by her, or playing out stories with her (often violent) involving the little humanesque Playmobile figures, and sometimes having lengthy conversations with her overheard by us in the next room that not always but not infrequently went roughly along these lines: "OK Bubbie, I'll take the red-and-white people and you take the black-and-white." "Good. Which are mine?" "Now Bubbie, you take the black-and-white people and I'll take the red-and-white people." "Fine. So which ones are mine?" This eventually subsided when Ben simply divided the people and did the bulk of the talking for both sides.

Now I can tell the principal story this sketchy background has been meant to prepare. When the rabbi at my mother's graveside dismissed the company of several dozen people in attendance (all family, including in-laws, neither of her closest two women friends had survived her), Ben refused to leave as I took his hand. He insisted, "The coffin is still here." I replied that since Rabbi Epstein had dismissed us he must have his reasons. Ben still would not be moved. He and I, and the rabbi, and two workmen standing aside holding shovels, were the only ones left by the grave. I glanced at the rabbi, who motioned to me to remain. "The child is right. The service is not over, but we have fallen into the custom of dispersing those in attendance as we lower the coffin and cover it with earth." This admired and distinguished old man had begun walking around to us on the other side of the open grave, and pulling a shovel from the place it had been stabbed into a neat pile of soil, invited Ben to put his small hands on the shovel's handle between the rabbi's large hands. Thus enabled to assist one another in wielding the large implement, they repeatedly, as the coffin was lowered, together sent small clumpy showers of earth down surprisingly softly tapping upon the coffin's lid in accompaniment to the rabbi's completing the chanting of his canonical prayers. Afterward, as Ben and I held hands to walk over and rejoin the withdrawn gathering of participants, I was, I suppose undisguisedly, pent with uncomplicated yet mysterious elation at witnessing this inspired, lucid linking of generations before and beyond mine.

July 4, 2004

Ben was, I calculate, two months shy of his sixth birthday that late spring, and when David had attained that age, and into his next year, with Ben some twelve or thirteen years old, I was still—perhaps it was a matter of having resumed—from time to time singing lullabies to David. (This was more for my sake than for his; perhaps I shall find occasion to consider why.) I discovered that show tunes made excellent lullabies: favorites of ours were, of course, Gershwin's "Summertime;" which is in its theatrical origin explicitly a lullaby, along with "Our Love Is Here to Stay," "Over the Rainbow," and "I'm Old-Fashioned;" there could also be invocations of "It Had to Be You," "Singin' in the Rain," "Smoke Gets in Your Eyes," "A Foggy Day in London Town," or "Embraceable You." If a song, sung softly, and usually in a free tempo, had failed to set a sufficiently contemplative mood, we might go on talking a little afterward. I was moved by recording these memories to retrieve and to turn the pages, for the first time in years, of the red-velvet-covered journal that we used as David's Baby Book, which Cathleen and I were not unduly obsessive about keeping current, but after the usual statistics of the opening months of lightning changes in weight, length, foods accepted, intentional motions and intelligible noises made, we would from time to time be struck hard enough by a moment in subsequent months and years to remember to inscribe it.

I begin with some moments entered by Cathleen:

[April 15, 1989, just turned five]
Lying on the floor, bored and a bit sleepy waiting for me to keep my promise to play with the Duplo train:
David: "Is this real life?"
Cathleen: "What else could it be—a story?"
David: "And we're in the story."—Then a minute later: "I mean, we *are* the story."

[June 11, 1989]
Jim Conant's dog Thera is staying with us for three weeks while Jim visits Lisa in Oxford—constituting a kind of trial run for our life with a dog from my perspective—and David and I were walking her on Friday in one of the few respites from rain we've had since Tuesday. I suggested that we walk her over to Lily's to meet Lily's dog Ginger and to show her to Lily's family. David said: "But if Ginger is a he then Thera and Ginger will fall in love and we'll have to stay there two days."

[July 15, 1990, an incident from the preceding month]
As I write this Stanley is telling Ben that the television is not a dialysis machine, it can be turned off without doing anyone harm. After I told David no snuffling at breakfast, when he snuffled I said, "That's an illegal snuffle." He replied: "I'm not breaking the law. Maybe in your book I'm breaking the law, but in the world's book, I'm not."

[Later July 15, 1990]
David and I were driving back from depositing Ben at the second week's session at Mike Andrews' Baseball Camp. Scooting down Beacon Street, we were driving alongside a trolley car and decided we were racing with the trolley. After Washington Square, where the trolley had to stop, it was clear that we had far outdistanced it and I turned to David and said, "We beat its . . . (whispered) *ass.*" We both laughed and David beamed at me and said, "Lucky your mother didn't hear you say that!"

Now some of mine, ones that essentially bring the entries to a close:

[Still July 15, 1990]

At bedtime:

Stanley: "You seem a little sad to me."

David: "The world seems an empty place."

S: "That is a very sad feeling. I know the feeling. Why do you have it? Is it because Thera is leaving?"

D: "And also because I can't swim and can't read well enough."

S: "I remember when you were just about ready to walk. You kept standing up and then sitting down in a hurry. You were very frustrated. It's a sign something is going to change."

D: "Mike Andrews' Baseball Camp was a big mistake."

S: "Why?"

D: "Ben throws the ball to me *much* too hard."

[January 10, 1990, on a separate sheet of paper folded and stuck in the back of the album]

At bedtime, on the way up to his room, he collects some possession of his from the floor of Cath's and my bedroom and then leans against the edge of our bed. I sit down beside him.

David: "I have a worry in my life."

Stanley: "What is it?"

D: "I don't want any animals to die."

S: "Which animals are you worried about?"

D: "Whales. Do you realize how much harder a whale's life is than ours?"

S: "What makes it so hard?"

D: "Because there are whale killers. Whales are so big and they have to live in so little water."

S: "Do you know that lots of people feel as you do and are working to convince people to stop killing whales?"

David's eyes were glistening with tears.

[July 28, 1990]

At bedtime, lights out, holding hands then as usual.

Stanley: "David, you seem especially nervous."

David: "I don't know which side of the wall the Hammerheads go on."

S: "You mean your new swimming group?"

D: "Yes. One kid says one thing, one kid says something else."

S: "Why don't you ask a camp counselor? You know some very well."

He is still fidgety—his legs up in the air, pressing the upper bunk of the bunk bed.

"Is there something else on your mind?"

D: "I just don't see things the way you do."

S: "I wish I could see things the way you do. I like the way you see things."

D: "I like the way you see things too.—But I'm worried."

[August 11, 1990]

I was telling Cathleen how David had felt about not having friends at camp and I looked around at him and I said, "If you don't like the way I'm saying this, don't let me. Speak for yourself."

He answered: "I like the way you're saying it." I looked at him again, and he added: "I mean it."

Later that night, at lights out:

Stanley: "You OK?"

David: "My head hurts. My tummy doesn't feel too well. And I myself don't feel too well."

[Undated]

After an installment of a bedtime chapter's reading from one of Andrew Lang's series instanced by *The Blue Fairy Book*, David says: "That princess [the mean ugly one] is over-due with her soul. She should give it back so someone else can use it."

[January 17, 1991]

Sometime during our bedtime talk:

Stanley: "I wish I could tell you how wonderful you are."

David: "What's the matter? Can't use words?"

S: "I'm afraid they won't be good enough."

D: "Daddy Shmaddy has the best answers in the world." ["Daddy Shmaddy" was a favorite invention of David's for a while, obviously affectionate, but with, I thought, a little teasing edge to it suggesting that he knows that I must know that I sometimes like to overdo things.]

I interpose an entry of Cathleen's from a year earlier, in which she lists a number of outbursts from David, among them these two:

"Tell Daddy to get down here as fast as he possibly can."

"I'm so mad at Daddy, I wish I had another Dad. I wish Daddy was thrown away in the garbage by accident. Dad's pathetic!"

[April 1991]

Coming downstairs at dawn to find me still writing in the dining room, David says: "I had a good dream. It was the greatest."

Stanley: "Tell."

D: "I was just coming back, thinking there was something I had to do. Then I opened the door and saw a giant and I knew what I had to do. I killed the giant."

[Sometime earlier in 1991]

Rachel and Alex [her two-year-old son] are here. Rachel is still upstairs; David, Ben, and I stay seated around the dining room in the middle of breakfast as Cathleen has followed a suddenly inconsolable Alex into the kitchen and is trying to comfort the distressed grandchild. Ben asks whether he can help, and starts toward the kitchen. David says sharply: "Ben, leave it alone. She was a mother to us. She can handle it." Ben stopped, sat down next to me, looked at me slyly and happily, and whispered: 'He's so masterful.'"

Images of these brothers' heartening encounters recurrently work to remind me that the deepest and quite conscious wish of my childhood was practical, however unrealizable, I mean the wish, from the time I also turned seven and the first house I knew was taken from me, to have had a brother and companion. The wish has I feel certain entered into various forms of friendship I have found, some brief, almost invisible, some plain and permanent, some continuous, others intermittent, with men and with women, with young and old, apart from whose constellation I do not know what I would have had to say. (I must not deny that my knowledge of enmity or resentment shown me over the years has also motivated my writing. I trust I do not delude myself in imagining that often when I have written in anger it has been meant in protection of friendship.)

July 20, 2004

In the years before *The Claim of Reason* was published I was told a number of times by readers who claimed some sympathy with their sense of my projects, that I could not expect to get a hearing until I explicitly gave an account of the relation between my work and the work of Derrida. This was particularly frequent after talks I would give traveling outside Cambridge. If on occasion I felt the response to be sympathetic I might try to explain why, if that were true, my case was hopeless. Even if I felt moved, or felt remotely competent, to give such an account, who would want it or be able to use it? To understand it a reader would have to be willing to understand me, and for that purpose Wittgenstein and Austin, and moreover some familiarity with American and English academic philosophy and some admiration for American and English literature, are decisively more pertinent than having read Derrida. But of course I saw that I was avoiding the issue, namely, why I seemed to be peculiarly hard to understand. I remain unable to perceive myself as essentially exotic. But by the close of the 1970s I began to feel time was on my side, both because *The Claim of Reason* had found an end, and because my first attempt to respond to Emerson had, to my mind, been distinctly remunerative (an intellectual virtue particularly prized and voiced by Austin). It would be another dozen years before I actually wrote explicitly and consecutively about a text of Derrida's, taking up in his "Signature Event Context" (in the middle and longest chapter of my *Pitch of Philosophy*) his reading of Austin's *How to Do Things with Words*. I am not sorry I did not try it earlier. That chapter of mine was quite excruciating to write, and seemed to me, the last time I tried, quite excruciating to read.

What is certainly true is that, with my tastes in philosophy and in literature and in psychoanalysis, the outburst in the 1970s and 1980s of translations of brilliant writing from France associated with the names Bataille, Blanchot, Levinas, Lacan, Leiris, Deleuze, Derrida, Foucault, Barthes, aware of each other (to say the least) and responding to the Hegelian and Nietzschean and Husserlian and Heideggerian and Freudian aftermaths in German thought, threatened to saturate the academic humanistic air in my parts of the landscape. And that this strain of European writing was largely successful in ignoring not alone Frege and Carnap but as well as later Wittgenstein and Austin could not be ignored. The immediate problem for me was not alone the massiveness and continuity of the French-German outburst, nor its general cultivation of competitive obscurity and paradox and brilliance; the problem was at the same time the incessant issue of what would count (for me) as usefully (remuneratively) understanding any of it. I mean count as understanding it without repeating it, which of course many were willing, say, eager, to do—a sort of identification with the aggressor, it struck me.

The spread of such a condition of repetitiveness was having, to my mind, a harmful effect on what I knew of education throughout the humanities and related social sciences in the United States, a high cost, in some sense needlessly high, for the notable individual achievements it also inspired. The French thinkers were assigned in the absence of an insistence on a working, that is, textual knowledge of, for example, Kant and Hegel and Husserl and Heidegger. The French were often playful, but few on this side of the ocean were in a position to be creatively and usefully playful in return, on the same fields. I have remarked that the first and longer of the two parts of Wittgenstein's *Investigations*, consisting of 693 numbered entries, can be understood (not entirely fancifully) as 693 responses to the words and implications and effects of the single, unremarkable paragraph the book opens by quoting from Augustine's *Confessions*, in that way providing a developing picture of what philosophical understanding appears to Wittgenstein to be. What would it mean to apply this picture of understanding to the reception of the French writers, including their relation to their German host texts? The intelligence shrinks.

The task posed by the new influx of texts, it seemed, was at large something like the reverse of this form of concentration, not one of perpetually probing and returning to portions or slips of a work but, say, one (if not of ignoring it at large) of swallowing it whole and raw. (Derrida is clearly a kind of exception to this.) But how at any time has philosophy suffered change? Influential philosophers have generally been influenced by those they take as their competitors, or say, equals, not by always or even often by refuting them (as taught in the schools), but by altering the terms of argument, say, reconceiving or rederiving the subject. This is sometimes articulated as one massively influential philosopher misunderstanding those he cites, not doing his lessons. It looks like major passages in the history of philosophy.

My idea was that whatever similarities turned out to be real between what I wanted from philosophy and what the principal dispensations of philosophy at my disposal approved of one's saying, would be arrived at, at best, not at the beginning of what I saw myself wanting to do, but as a result of it—say, by the way I was finding to read Wittgenstein and Austin and Thoreau and Emerson and Shakespeare (and others who make decisive cameo appearances in the course of what I write, such as Luther and Montaigne and Pascal and Jane Austen and Poe and Wallace Stevens and George Eliot and Beckett, all teaching me how, and to learn how, to read) and to take film and its evocations to heart as the latest of the great, worldwide arts. This posed no particular risk to my mind. The fact that, for example, Thoreau and Emerson were not on the whole read philosophically by philosophers was not a separate obstacle to my being understood. To provide and encourage their philosophical reading was an instance of the work I saw to do.

So it should be a surprise neither that I have been desultory (which does not exclude certain intensities) in my study of the French outburst nor that from time to time a text from that tidal wave has been cast onto my shore that I have felt drawn to live with for a while. The particular cause has accordingly varied. The most deliberate came out of my long-standing wish to consider Freud's thinking as a competitor, or a kind of successor, of philosophy. I knew that a number of the graduate students whose dissertations I was advising were in some way interested in reading Freud, and I invited them for a late afternoon beer together specifically to discuss an idea I had for my courses for the following year. The idea was to use early Lacan seminars, the first and second having just appeared in English translation (and in view of the Roudinesco biography of Lacan, which provides a sketch of the Parisian ambience in which Lacan functioned, a text that, for example, actually lists those who attended Kojève's lectures on Hegel in the 1930s), with their unapologetic recourse to philosophy and theology and literature in reading Freud's texts, as the basis for a year-long (two-semester) graduate seminar working through thoughts about the relation of psychoanalysis and philosophy. The plan would be to read through Lacan's texts at a self-enforced tempo, so that we actually worked all the way to the end of at least one of them over the months of a semester, reading at the same time the texts of Freud's (as far as was feasible) that Lacan would focus on, along with literary texts explicitly in play (Sade and *Antigone* were prominent cases), of course emphatically taking into account philosophical references (Hegel and Heidegger are the most persistent)—all this against the background of the reading of Wittgenstein in my *Claim of Reason*. I offered as a pervasive suggestion of mutual pertinence between the *Investigations* and the texts of Lacan I had started reading that their respective tripartite registrations of psychic or linguistic functioning—Lacan's symbolic, and imaginary, and real put together with Wittgenstein's grammar, and pictures or images, and the ordinary—must somehow serve to illuminate each other.

The graduate students at this gathering were Steven Affeldt, Nancy Bauer, William Bracken, William Bristow, Paul Franks, Eli Friedlander, and Arata Hamawaki. Along with James Conant, who was the first of this permanently inspiring group to complete his dissertation and leave to take up a teaching position and whose capacity for friendship together with an almost dangerously disruptive capacity for intellectual curiosity made him central to the group's coherence, these young philosophers had attended, and set the tone of, seminars announced by me in preceding years, on Emerson, on Romanticism, on the Ordinary, providing a continuity of intellectual purpose unmatched in my decades of teaching. Earlier undergraduate and graduate students, many friends of each other and eventual friends of mine, are again, in this mood, outstanding in my mind (Stanley Bates, Ted Cohen, Francis Dauer, Timothy Gould, Allen Graubard, Paul Guyer, Barbara Herman, John McNees, William Rothman, and Naomi Scheman, from my first decade back at Harvard; Norton Batkin, Arnold Davidson, Juliet Floyd, Karen Hanson, Marian Keane, Marya Schechtman, from my second decade; and later, Alice Crary, Brent Kalar, Katalin Makkai, and Abraham Stone), but in those earlier years the projects undertaken in the dissertations being produced, for all their individual talent and richness, would not be, or have been, thought to have immediate bearing, however clear certain affinities, each upon the others, throughout the group, as was the sense in the last group of which I was part. Hence my asking for the meeting with them to determine whether they as a group would in principle be interested in continuing, as it were, to be the core of further seminars reading Lacan for a term, and if it proved profitable, to continue for a further term. If the answer had been negative, I would have sailed in safer pedagogical waters.

I pause for a moment, as I might at so many crossroads, to marvel at the depth and sweep of sheer talent and sociability manifested in this swift listing of a score of the graduate students with whom I have worked on dissertations over the decades. Some of the names are by now immediately recognizable by many members of the American Philosophical Association. I again testify that those who have not continued with their formal studies in philosophy or whose publications have been less frequent or more tangential to the field than I might have wished, contributed on a fully equal intellectual basis in our discussions. That almost all of these names have shown up, and will or might any day show up again, on my e-mail Inbox, and their bearers appear in town for a meal or a drink, is a fact apart from which I would not understand the sense of my intellectual life. If I say that I have drawn confidence from these relationships at times when my relations with my own generation have been discouraging, I will be invoking a region of the sublime territory of the morality of teaching. I do not mean merely vulgar dangers such as playing favorites among students but subtler emotional bribes that deny the asymmetry, over their years of their enrollment, between students and teacher, that they are definitively less responsible for my intellectual security (however significantly and permanently they will affect it) than I have been (with others) for theirs.

Calling up the sense of some common purpose, not needing any precise restriction, among the members of these groups of the young, reaching in various instances back to members of overlapping earlier generations of students and teachers, reminds me of a recurrent topic of exchange between Tom Clarke and me in our first years at Berkeley concerning our sense of the lack of community in our experience of studying philosophy, a sense of paradox in this circumstance since philosophy was obviously and irreducibly bound to the possibility of continuous, perhaps interminable, exchange. At this distance the topic seems plainly to express his and my individual senses of isolation. I leave a mark here to remind me to take up an exchange some thirty years later between Hilary Putnam and me during the introductory meeting of a joint seminar we were offering on Wittgenstein's *Investigations* in which Putnam in opening the session expressed his (justified) impatience with certain devotees of this text who leapt to the criticism of so much of philosophical reflection as nonsense. I think I remember correctly his responding to such an attitude by saying: "These philosophers cannot show other philosophers even the degree of respect that anthropologists find owed in their description of the practices of the Azande." I liked the implication that the practices of philosophers should be given detailed description, but I then asked whether philosophers could really be conceived as constituting a community since first of all their business is to question their fellows, and second, but more decisive, they are notorious for questioning whether others really belong to the, as it were, community of philosophers. I realize that those who regard Wittgenstein as what they call politically—one might say communally—conservative habitually cite in their favor Wittgenstein's remark "Philosophy leaves everything as it is" as saying that philosophy does not, and indeed should not, rock the political boat.

Here is a fair instance causing my own recurrent feelings of isolation among the members of my generation of teachers. I understand Wittgenstein's remark, contrarily, not simply as passive but simultaneously as active, as naming a task, in particular as resistant to philosophically violent change, namely, politically or ideologically sponsored change that fails to be responsive to "real need" but instead obeys ill-conceived, power-driven, repetitive shards of philosophy, rocking and sinking boats or life rafts that lie beyond an arbitrarily drawn horizon, swaddled in poor descriptions of the present, let's say the everyday. This requires perpetual attention and surprise, becoming friends with sleeplessness.

(Another intervention from a day of editing in 2007.) Apart from its concluding sentence, the preceding paragraph is so close to a description of what I imagine George W. Bush's violent, indifferently repetitive, mind to be like—yet without including its terrifying, its grotesque, ignorance—that it may miss its mark as epitomizing a more general statement of how I wish philosophical criticism of politics to proceed. There came a time during the Vietnam War when I interrupted myself during a lecture, moved to say that I could no more ignore that morning's news, at least to notice it in common, than I would be able to withhold attention to the cry of a child. At the same time I registered my sense that this very acknowledgment signaled the victory of violence over thinking. Then sometimes thinking must turn to destroy its peace, to observe havoc, in order to attract its own protection. Having spent more than two years furthering this memoir (to give myself more peace than in any way other than exchanges with friends) in this time of what so many of my friends regard as the most unsparingly lugubriously impaired administration in American history, I ask for mercy on my soul.

July 21, 2004

I noted that there were various causes for my awareness, and wariness, of the rush and reception of literary-philosophical publications from France. A rather different cause has occurred in my conversations over the years with Arnold Davidson and his insistence on the decisive importance of the work of Michel Foucault in this reception and eventually, with specific pertinence for me, in stressing the relation of Foucault's late work on the care of the self to what I was calling moral perfectionism. This culminated in Davidson's and my offering a joint seminar on Foucault and Freud at the University of Chicago in 1999, for which Davidson assigned us some of this work of Foucault's. It did indeed fascinate me, but I found it hard to use, mostly I thought because of its attention to Hellenistic philosophy, which was—is—perhaps the most painful blank in my philosophical education; it nevertheless confirmed my interest in texts across Western civilization (and beyond, so far as I could glimpse beyond) contributing to and participating in aspects of moral perfectionism. When it came time for my opening considerations I outlined a project in comparing Freud and Austin and Foucault on the subject of accidents and slips or lapses in human existence. Freud is moved to interpret moments of asynchrony between motivation and behavior as specifically revelatory slips contrasted with an aptly functioning body and mind, whereas Austin and Foucault wish to see the need for excuses and the preparation for the accidental as essential to what possessing a human body and mind makes perpetual and inevitable. But it was not until just this past year that I read Foucault's published lectures at the Collège de France on the hermeneutics of the self to discover for myself a sense that Foucault's program there, whatever the professional success of his scholarship, is to respond to a reading of ancient philosophy as the inspiration of current philosophizing. Its pertinence to what I have described as perfectionism, however different in motivation (for example, I begin from a counterreading of Rawls and from a sense that Emersonian and Thoreauvian perfectionisms take on preoccupations evident throughout Western philosophical and literary culture), crosses paths at alarmingly many points with what Foucault translates and perceives as the care of the self. I am not at an age at which to make promises to follow out desires of learning and of new acquaintance, but I can attest here sharply to the desire inspired by these connections.

But there was an obscurer cause of trepidation in taking on any fraction of this new material. I have elsewhere spoken of my shaping and guiding, during the summers of 1968 and of 1969, one of the two groups constituting the International Seminar at Harvard, invented and directed by Henry Kissinger in his early years at Harvard. The closest friends Cathleen and I made in those summers were the poet Claude Esteban and his wife, Denise, a painter, with both of whom we formed lasting bonds. We visited them during the summers of 1970, 1971, and 1972, spending as much time together as we could in the house Denise designed and supervised the construction of, or reconstruction of, beginning from the shell of a fourteenth-century farmhouse, in the town of Lacoste, in the Vaucluse in Provence. Lacoste is one small town among many others in its region, but like its companion towns it has its story. (Lacoste's story is woven about the presence in it of the castle of the Marquis de Sade.) In August 1972 we spent the first half of twenty days there with Claude and Denise; the second half we stayed on alone, as they left to arrange for a showing of Denise's paintings in Nice. The day before they left us, Claude visited René Char at his house in a neighboring village. I was about to say it was Cavaillon, but that is too big and bustling a place, where market day brought forth melons enough to sweeten the palates of parched multitudes. So is Carpentras too big. The other names that still register with me are Goult, Apt, and Bonnieux. (I have, after a happy search, just turned up the name of the reasonably neighboring village that Char was born in, L'Isle-sur-la-Sorgue.)

The day of the Estebans' departure, Claude gave me a copy of Char's *Les Feuillets d'Hypnos*. Published in 1946, it is marked by Char's participation in the Resistance. Claude told me that he addresses Char as "Capitain," a form of address that acknowledged at once his prominence in the war (or the war within the nonwar) and in French letters. The coherence of French cultural life is, or was, so intact that certain figures can not only confer upon you the right to write, but virtually appoint you to the station of a writer.

Char's French was in obvious ways intermittently out of my reach, and my pocket French-English dictionary was too poor for me to have been able to produce even crude full translations while we were there.

But some things were clear enough. Above all the peculiar voice I imagined in response to Char's early remark, given the context of his presence in the fighting, that he would have to write hastily, because he had to get back to the joint work at hand. I got the sense that he was speaking under his voice, confidentially, but confidently. Such impressions had the effect of prompting me to begin a concerted effort to see what I would have to say in aphoristic-like observations or tiny narratives, which if they materialize at all are composed in haste, each all at once, and for private communication, a series to be returned to, and left, at any hour. Somehow the isolation enforced by the onset of the Mistral, which the Estebans had warned us might happen during our time there, encouraged this practice.

August 1, 2004

I have recently also uncovered the three French school tablets, or rosters (each called a Cahier de Devoirs Mensuels) that I filled with writing during those ten days, and I shall copy out here a selection of the entries that appeared, deliberately favoring some that prefigure in my writing topics or thoughts not only perhaps in the pages of this memoir. It is clear to me now that without that ten days of quite deliberate departure and direction in my writing—the fact of them and the aspiration of them, the concentration of them, each and all, whatever mixed value their results may be found to have reached in the event and in themselves—it seems hard for me to imagine (I mean that it may not have occurred to me) that what became Part Four, the largest and concluding part, of *The Claim of Reason* would have been mine to do.

A Sheaf Transcribed from My Lacoste Journals, Summer 1972

After two days of Mistral, the sun was strong but seemed dead, like a wartime zinc penny. ###

At Oppède we walked across a stretch of flat, arid ground sparsely covered with fragments of slate-tinted tiny stones and came upon a rough outcropping of substantial, rounded, deeply scored stones that looked like brains. ###

They plant stands of trees for windbreaks, but these provide no protection we could divine from the Mistral. The only way we found to alleviate the headache everyone told us was caused by the wind was to get into the car and drive in any direction, reasonably fast, with the windows closed. Whatever the correct physical explanation of this effect, the impulse seems to have been either to race or to attack the wind. ###

Why does just *this* tree fill with birds? Every tree has secrets that it keeps from its leaves. ###

When we wanted citizens of the world what we had in mind was not tourists, especially not ones preoccupied with avoiding tourists. ###

"Did you say something?"

"No. It was the window."

That is the sort of conversation you can have in Provence. ###

"Did you say something?"

"No. It was the horizon."

Where can you have that sort of conversation? ###

If you have looked only in the light of noon, you will be astonished to see, one late afternoon, the length of an ant's shadow moving. ###

The wind has died. ###

In America you can think to take something either by storm or with a grain of salt. As, for example, time. ###

In English you can play dead, not play alive. English has something to learn. ###

Far across the valley, headlights are tracing mountain roads, as if to memorize them. ###

You cannot make an omelet without breaking eggs. No, nor by breaking eggs. ###

Perhaps there is no collective guilt. There is surely collective shame. ###

I am ashamed of America. So perhaps there is hope for us both. ###

My most radical students are not ashamed. Will they know if they have become shameless? ###

If the state is a ship, the citizens are likely to become a sea. ###

There was right on both sides, nevertheless I laid siege to myself. But when the city fell I could not distinguish action from passion and let many escape. ####

If one can learn only what one is ready to learn, doesn't it follow that it is impossible to know whether you are teaching anything? You have to learn how to make yourself worth stealing from. ###

When my father would tell me, "You can learn from anyone," I was mad with rage at his ignorance of my despair of my ignorance. Now, thirty years later, I can perhaps take the observation as a high compliment. ###

On reading a review of my second book, *The World Viewed*, forwarded to me in Lacoste: The reviewer as much as says there is nothing of value in my prose, but he has barely glanced at it, or under its edge. Like a good bluff, his remark was unexpected and alarming. Like a bad bluff, it was too weak, because the deed to my ranch was already on the table. Now his is too. (This is an exaggeration about him, not about me.) ###

If you envy the writing of René Char, won't you, for example, have to envy France the Occupation? ###

The danger with short poems is that they start sounding like aphorisms. The trouble with aphorisms is that they can sound like jokes. The worry about jokes is that nothing is funny. ###

"A joke is a short oral narrative with a punch line."
"That definition assumes that I know what a punch line is."
"My error."
"All right. I admit I know what a punch line is."
"Not unless you know what a joke is."
(The opening line came years ago in conversation with John Hollander. My memory is that it stopped conversation.) ###

A short narrative without a punch line: Snake, sneak, snack, snooze. (Did I pick that up somewhere?) ###

Epic narrative: Sea legs. Glad hand. Slap happy. Sweet tooth. Soft touch. Loose lip. Hard knocks. Tough luck. Fat chance. Slim pickings. Mad money. Last laugh. ###

We are all split. The schizophrenic denies this. ###

You have it backwards, like observing that occasionally women have been given names of certain familiar flowers. When, or for whom, is that backwards? ###

Claude would during the day, perhaps in the kitchen to take up a cup of coffee upstairs to his desk, turn on his portable radio for a few minutes to the music station. On one such occasion the offering was Ravel's Bolero. Claude says: "Well, it's something." He went on to say that he was just repeating what Ravel had himself said about his Bolero. Telling me this Claude's eyes brimmed with tears. He recovered himself by explaining that Ravel was already quoting something, something said first (I believe I remember accurately) about the Arc de Triomphe, something like "It is there; it exists; you have to go around it." ###

I realized I could not at the moment remember how the Bolero ends. Stasis is now desirable in itself. Is this an attempt of music to wrest free of its exploration of time, or say to achieve eternity by circling time? Virtuosity survives in knowing how to end. ###

I myself am better at beginnings than at endings. I mean in my life with others. In writing I am better at endings. ###

A child says the Emperor has no clothes on. Who will tell us there is no Emperor? ###

The eye teaches skepticism; the eyelid teaches faith. ###

Imagine! There are still butterflies.—This thought was my startled response upon seeing a white butterfly in flight. Much later and in another country I find that the thought appears exactly so in Beckett's *Endgame*, which I had read a decade earlier. Naturally I would like to say that the exclamation came as a transcription not of Beckett but of the butterfly. ###

At Lacoste, after a meal outdoors and before completing clearing the table, bees given a chance are attracted to remnants of meat in such densely packed numbers that together they completely and precisely cover their meal from human eyes. This image does not speak of nature's fragility. I was not moved to think: "Imagine! There are still bees." Shall I take reassurance from this? ###

Some write because they are in prison; some because they are not. Some read because they are ill; some because they are well. It is hopeless to envy one another. ###

"If you were me, wouldn't you have done the same thing?"

"Without doubt. On that condition." ###

Prose: The fox of fact; the dogs of words.

Poetry: The dogs of fact, the fox of words. ###

Bite the coin that feeds you. ###

In bad company the face gets wiped off your smile. ###

"A cathedral needs flying buttresses to withstand the thrust of its aspirations."

"A cathedral, my friend, needs buttresses because the outward thrust must be grounded."

"You're right. I said that to annoy you." (And why did I think it?)

"And why did you think it?" ###

Gregorian chant. A single line is reflected against its own reverberation. Hence in walking while singing it, the pace is as determined as that of a tango. ###

Thoreau walked hours every day. He said it was to put Concord behind him. What would he have done if he had lived to see television sets? Learned how to repair them. ###

Harbison tells me that before he can begin composing and find his own notes he has to let last night's television jingles work their way out of him. ###

Advice on being human. Do not stomach what you have no taste for, for you will develop the taste. ###

Nothing human is alien to you? Then you are not human. ###

I drove past your house all night. You telephoned my house all night. So much for modern conveniences. ###

Vampires do not just bite, and not just on the neck. A stake through the heart would have killed you and I knew where you slept all day. But I also knew how you look when you sleep and how you are when you wake, or not quite wake, so your secret is safe with me. ###

To wean me you painted your breast black. Now I am addicted to black. ###

Partly because of you I know the involuntary cry. Perhaps solely because of you I sometimes do not take God's name in vain. ###

Despite what French says, not every foreigner is a stranger. ###

A computer has a memory but no memories. Roughly like a person in a rage. ###

Claws, beaks, tusks, fangs, words. Shells, wings, hues, words. ###

Assume a virtue if you have it not. The first time you give your coat to a poor man you may do it to please the priest. The second time you may do it for yourself. The third time you may do it for the poor man. ###

I see the bruise on my thigh and I wonder that I cannot remember the painful blow that must have caused it. I see the bruise and I wonder what the mind looks like. ###

Go to where reason has fallen and help her. You will be tempted, but do not promise to restore her crown. It is for her to reconsider herself. ###

It would be most convenient if fashion seeks to be the last word. Since nothing in life is really last, that would leave me all the rest. Not me alone, I trust. ###

My immigrant father perpetually suffered from indigestion. No cooked food, unless prepared by my mother, was native for him. It was the physical companion of his reaction to his speech, perpetually aware that no language (Polish, Russian, Yiddish, Hebrew, English) became and remained native to him, but each was abandoned, frozen, or broken. Nevertheless he was able to say: "Man will never reach the moon, because when he arrives there it will no longer be the moon." ###

We knowers, we teachers, we sources of speech, still have to trust the ground of reality to shatter language precisely into our words. ###

There are only twelve notes. There are only seven deadly sins.

There are as many deadly sins as seas, as many notes as disciples. ###

The circle of poetry, the line of physics, the point of religion, the plane of philosophy.

But geometry reconsiders. ###

Paris Match 19 Août 1972. "Au 41e coup, Spassky abandonne et se lève pour applaudir Fischer avec la foule. 'Mozart! C'est Mozart!' crie le vieux maitre argentin Najdorf qui suffoque d'enthousiasme." I seem to know what Najdorf felt. I am not sure what he could have meant if he had cried out, "C'est Mahler!" Perhaps in this case he would not have cried it out, but been more confidential. In any case I suppose I will never know what he saw in Fischer's 41st move to have had the expression called from him, as if struck breathless by an achievement of perfect lucidity, sublime elegance, and effortlessness.

Can I imagine that someone might have called out, being thus struck under such circumstances, "God! It's God!" No more than I imagine that you might look up at the stars and cry, "Mozart! It's Mozart!" ###

The music of the spheres. The air of the earth. ###

Five senses and just one world. The odds were fair enough. ###

I am home. Then why am I homesick?

Part 13

August 9, 2004

From the beginning of these reflections I have welcomed a re-current structural sense in my narratives—consciously taken up gen-erally only with the announcing of some everyday crossroads, famil-iar to me but subtly out of my rhythm or perhaps familiar in story but new in happening to me—that telling my life may all at once take on the texture of philosophizing about my life, quite as if these are not in-dependent journeys. So it is perhaps not entirely surprising, if appar-ently void of intention, during last-minute preparations for leaving on a weekend excursion to Martha's Vineyard to visit the parents of Ben-jamin's girlfriend (to whom, by the time of this editing, he has been married for almost three months), that a text I took up at the last min-ute from some stacks of unread books periodically nagging my con-science to shove into my backpack, together with the active notebook of my journal and late issues of the *TLS* and the *New York Review of Books*, and my shaving kit and a pair of proper sandals in case there is an obligatory cocktail party (items that will not or that I would rath-er not fit in the one small suitcase we are otherwise limiting ourselves to), along with my medications featuring pills for high blood pressure and for controlling cholesterol, was Maurice Blanchot's *The Writing of the Disaster.*

Blanchot is the last of the string of impressive French thinkers who had as if all at once attracted a dominating fascination for the minds of so many of the advanced humanists, or perhaps rather anti-humanists—except on the whole for philosophers—and certain social scientists in the English-speaking academic world for several decades after the 1960s, to have made his way to my table. Why this late, all but accidental encounter of mine happened when it did has an empirical answer, and certain consequences, which I shall indicate; but it had little deliberate intellectual preparation. Its making itself felt over these recent weeks serves to remind me of my growing sense that I am trying to bring this project of remembering and memorializing to some mode of ending at the general drift of time marking the completion of the writing of *The Claim of Reason* in the late 1970s, which is also to say, during the peak of the academic reception of the new generation of French thinkers (after the generation of Sartre, Beauvoir, Merleau-Ponty) on these shores, and that I have said very little about the effect of that reception on my consciousness of my writing, beyond suggesting that I know and admire considerably more of it than colleagues of mine tend to know who deplore it, and far less of it than those who live upon it.

The difficulty of conversation over the Anglo-American / German-French divide of current philosophical temperaments was characterized by me, in lectures I gave at Berkeley in 1983 (printed in *In Quest of the Ordinary*), through identifying what I called the two myths of reading in preparing for philosophical writing. According to one myth the philosopher must have read virtually everything, at least the whole of Western philosophy, broadly conceived; according to the other myth the philosopher will have read virtually nothing. Heidegger is an obvious exemplar of the former myth, Wittgenstein of the latter, whose *Investigations* quotes or alludes to a half-dozen famous philosophical names, but in such a way as to imply that a pertinent passage has just happened to cross his mind, or perhaps been cited to him, an implication that is compatible with his never having read all the way through a whole book; and sometimes there is a quotation from a conversation or discussion, real or imagined, whose source remains anonymous. In the hundreds of entries of *On Certainty*, Wittgenstein repeatedly responds to moments in two papers of G. E. Moore's, and once each, in passing, to Goethe, Lavater, Jesus, Renan, and four times to Napoleon.

These practices are not simply accidental features of different cultural worlds, but are deeply embedded in the competing ideas of philosophy in the two dispensations. Two of the finest philosophers of my generation, the two to whom I have been in clear ways the closest, Thompson Clarke and Rogers Albritton, seemed often quite prohibited from reading much, or systematically, especially much philosophy, rather behaving as if the cost of reading was prohibitively high—so many academic texts being exasperating in their laxness or their irrelevant precisions, or contemptible in their obscurity, and certain others, I suppose mostly classical texts, too demanding to bear under most circumstances, in all cases threatening to stand in the way of the work of their own thinking, often after a moment of having incited it. Left to themselves when they were not working, they preferred, or professed, to read popular magazines (or in Clarke's case to analyze the stock market, or in Albritton's less extreme case to read a novel recommended by an undergraduate at dinner in Quincy House, where he lived) or to watch television. How this relates to the small quantity of the writing they produced—or anyway published—is not clear to me.

What then are the rest of us to do, who profess to have read not nothing and not everything? What in particular are we to take with the seriousness that means that other serious contenders for our attention will go unheard? How much arbitrariness and chance is one to live with in the course of making a living around books and conversations?

Unlike Clarke, who had a family life, Albritton craved conversation and could bring any exchange of some length to philosophical pertinence (he was known to be intellectually tireless in company, keeping concerted conversation going for hours, once that I know of for seven hours, even when he was in pain and in order to get a modicum of relief had to lie flat on his back on the floor). And unlike Clarke, Albritton would read (bits of) anything that a friend or student might urge upon him by means of a question or a puzzle or an irritation or a claim to ecstasy, whether or not, or perhaps especially not, if their expression of their response seemed to keep resisting clear formulation.

At the close of the two-day event in March 2003 memorializing Rogers's death some months earlier, following the sequence of scheduled addresses and symposia various of us participated in, when others in attendance were invited to contribute informal reminiscences, so many marathon conversations with Rogers were reported that one might well conceive of his conversation as having become, whatever else, and along with his classroom lectures, his form of publication. Clarke, on the contrary, became increasingly reclusive. I have imagined that, to the extent that this withdrawal was motivated philosophically, it came from the sense that nothing partial was worth saying, together with the thought that he was on a path to a complete statement of what he once called the legacy of skepticism, and further that to orient another into the details of his excursions over the past decades nothing less than a completed account will now suffice. I could wish that Clarke had been more willing to conduct his education in public, as one might say was Albritton's normal mode (for whom every assertion was of its nature partial and every conversation in principle educative and interrupted). But I also know the cringe, the taste of folly, in permitting oneself that voyage in the company of one's ignorance. Why I myself did not refrain from this folly of making public so much of my writing I attribute to my sense that harboring silence was subject to an even greater vanity.

I remember no conversation, beyond banter, in which Clarke and Albritton both participated. Rogers had moved to UCLA a year or two before Tom visited Harvard for a term in 1974. But their simultaneous presence in my imagination was palpable especially in those recurrent moments when, fully impressed by the sense that we talkers inveterately, all but necessarily, say too little or too much, often mistaking the time for utterance, I would ask myself what makes anything worth saying, or hearing, beyond a sheer need or wish to know, or a reflex of interest, or the imparting of desire.

It is perhaps a mark of the seriousness of philosophizing to be forced to come to some understanding with philosophy's impure craving for purity. Philosophy is not just one intellectual pursuit among others. I once asked Rogers—trading on our young but clear friendship and, I believed, not underestimating what it would cost him—to read the first, recently published, response to the first pair of papers I had put in print and hoped to take into the future (the opening pair of *Must We Mean What We Say?*), an unmitigatedly vicious attack, including the summary evaluation that the work my writing represented was, I believe I still remember the phrase exactly, "deleterious to the future of philosophy." I was unable on my own to put aside the pain of this attack. Rogers took the documents away with him, my papers and the response they had elicited, and, returning with them the following midnight bearing one of his by then familiar frowns of exasperation, but modified with a direct displeasure unfamiliar to my experience of him, he threw the documents on a chair and said with a vehemence I think I will never again see the equal of in him: "Well of course the response doesn't touch you. But it is you I do not understand. How could you possibly have left yourself vulnerable to such ill will?" The gratifying liberation of his challenge produced a certain corresponding challenge in return from me. "I see no alternative. And you of all people cannot expect any assertion to make itself invulnerable. So in my state of perfect gratitude to you I have to warn you of something. If I can find a way to write philosophy that I can believe in day after day I am going to go on doing it. The alternative I can see is to cultivate a private sense of the public world's intellectual vulgarity. However essential that may be it is not enough for me."

Naturally I am alternately attracted to both myths or practices of reading—to have read everything or read nothing—but naturally also most drawn to a view of reading, no doubt illusory, that seeks to capture the wish for breadth in the one myth and for fastidiousness in the other, as for example in Thoreau's determination to test all intellectual importunateness. On the opening page of *Walden* he accuses most authors of displaying an egotism without revealing the state or the stage of the self responsible for it. In the chapter entitled "Reading," his test for whether to read what comes your way is not so much to judge the worth of the text but to judge the quality of your reading. If you know how to read "with valor and magnanimity," then a fragment of newspaper found on the floor of the woods will do you good, expand the world. If you will not know how to read, how to give the best of yourself, Homer will not save you. You might as well, Thoreau clearly enough implies, use Homer's pages for the hygienic purpose for which newsprint may be used after a meal in the woods.

It is not clear what the pedagogical implications are of such advice. In my experience, it was first and most consistently classes in music performance and theory—Ernest Bloch's, Seymour Shifrin's, Marjorie Petray's—that transmitted to me or confirmed for me the wager of life and death in taking up great works of the spirit. Who would advise you to enter the world of music? You can be confirmed in your sense that you have entered it, or be encouraged to abandon the effort. It was related to me by a member of a writing class of Robert Frost's that on the day the first writing assignment was handed in, Frost held up the stack of papers and asked, "How many of you care about what you've written?" When no hand went up, Frost dropped the stack into the wastebasket, said something like, "If you don't care about it, why should I?" and walked out. But then you can use this gesture only once to a given company.

It interests me that the gesture is hard to imagine being well used even once in a philosophy class. Is this because in studying philosophy commitment and seriousness are not necessary, or because it is not a teacher's place then and there to demand or to question them? But isn't it then and there that lack of commitment and seriousness must be exposed? Nietzsche found it impossible—and I suppose roughly hilarious—to demand philosophy of himself at scheduled hours of the week, hence impossible to remain a professor. Kant and Hegel had discovered otherwise, namely, how to make original philosophy academic. It is one measure of what had happened to philosophical life in nineteenth-century Europe between the death of Hegel and the Hegel-inspired or Hegel-irritated writing of Kierkegaard and Marx and Nietzsche in the succeeding two generations, that none of the latter three writers (except Nietzsche very briefly) became a professor. Wittgenstein would also find university lecturing intolerable, even while he sought periodic residence and conversation in a college at Cambridge as essential to his working existence. The figure of a wayward but unusually gifted intellectual presence within but never officially part of a university atmosphere, one who seemed to hold most of what was taught (outside the exact sciences) to be something not only deplorable but to be in need of his or her refutation, is one I have experienced at each of the three universities I attended. In a not entirely different world Wittgenstein might have been one of these, an outside or disreputable figure valuable for raising a doubting tone against avenues of reputability. That Wittgenstein had managed in his early thirties to publish a work widely, in the circles he moved in, recognized as a work of genius (however controversial its sense) deprived him of that option.

My son David just walked into the house to get something from his room to take back to college, and has left a copy of the *Weekly Review* for me (an organ previously unknown to me) in which there is a notice of my *Cities of Words*, recently out. The gist of the notice is that my alternation of assigned books and movies, which formed the subjects of the lectures from which that book is made, obviously does not work, and in any case that I seem more interested in the movies than in the books, the evidence for which is that I sometimes praise the films as masterpieces but approach the philosophical texts spiritlessly. How have I managed to create this impression? It does seem to me on the whole interesting to praise films, and particular passages of films, that is, to show them worthy of serious attention, which the world conventionally supposes to be transient, no matter how permanent the acceptance of the work; and on the whole boring to praise in general terms the works of Plato and Aristotle and Locke and Rousseau and Kant, which I call monsters of fame. But *Cities of Words* is explicitly the presentation of a course I gave during my last years of teaching at Harvard, and it was familiar to me to speak there of these monsters in such a way as to recognize that their fame, perhaps as expressed in the familiar shabbiness of some of the inexpensive editions to be found on the market, could make them seem like fixtures of a known landscape from which nothing new is to be gained, nor, like a ravaged neighborhood, devastated enough to be arresting. A somewhat similar complaint, even from someone who has found earlier work of mine valuable, is that I am just going over the same old films. This negates or refuses the double point I stress, that I never take up a film again that I care about unless I feel that I have something new to convey in considering it, which is part of my claim that the films I have studied, and the limited hundreds of others I imagine they rhyme with, domestic or foreign, are inexhaustible in ways not entirely unlike the great works of the human spirit in philosophy and literature and the comparable great arts; and contrariwise, that the great works need not everywhere be treated with gagged respect, but sometimes rejoice in an introductory tip of the hat.

How these possibilities can so widely—by no means universally— be missed, or refused, is itself of intellectual and aesthetic significance. (I detect perhaps a touch here of long-suffering defensiveness primping itself as well-aimed condescension.) I have perhaps made the mistake of trusting my prose to intensify the intimacy in approaching a single reader sufficiently to form some rough equivalent of the magnification of attention possible in a large and crowded classroom. (It occurs to me that this may enter into what I find to be Austin's virtual avoidance of what he calls the perlocutionary effect of language in his theory of the performative utterance. We possessors of language are pretty well equal in our knowledge of the conventional conditions of—successfully—conveying the force of promising, authorizing, betting, bequeathing, endorsing, etc. [speech acts with what Austin calls illocutionary force], but we vary in our perception and talent in creating and judging the effect of attempts to convince, amuse, appall, excite, astonish, deter, inspire, etc. [acts with what Austin calls perlocutionary effect]. The effects of giving a bad class seem disproportionately large in comparison with the force of a good one, or perhaps they are simply clearer.) But at least now I won't have to learn of the lack of my book's effectiveness all at once.

August 10, 2004

I must return before long to the radical incompleteness of reading, but in having circled around the fact of leading *The Claim of Reason* to an end, I have to loop back to the moment at which I say I was able to leave that book with a certain pleasure. What the caution "a certain" modifies, or evades, is the memory of a bit of symptomatic behavior I was subject to in the weeks following the completion of the full draft of the manuscript, at the end of the summer of 1977 as the academic year was about to begin, namely, a sort of compulsion to laugh out loud, as it were at nothing, or perhaps as if virtually everything that happened struck me as hilarious. If this was indeed a distorted expression of pleasure, the pleasure was quite soon harshly tested.

Two years later at the convention of the American Philosophical Association a panel was scheduled on the book, an event that turned into a painful fiasco. The two commentators were David Hills and Barry Stroud. Hills spoke first, beginning a meticulous account of what was interesting me most, the inventions or improvisations of Part Four, but he went on longer than allowed and, prompted by the chair (Rogers Albritton it turned out), had to cut his remarks short. I was distressed about this because I knew Hills's acumen and erudition at first hand,

and knew by reputation of his long unwillingness to put his thoughts in print, and now I would not learn the rest of his reactions. Stroud dismissed my way of introducing skepticism from the beginning, in a way that seemed to me to miss its spirit entirely, an astonishing development, given his and my discussions, together with Tom Clarke, from whose thoughts on skepticism ours had both begun, over my last year teaching at Berkeley. Something in the delivery of my responses struck much of the audience as abusive of Stroud. I attribute this to my "delivery" because, after the grief dished out to me for my rudeness, I read over my responses and they seemed to me well within the bounds of academic philosophical decorum. I sent my responses to Clarke, who agreed that the remarks themselves were not rude, but that there were misunderstandings on both sides and he blamed himself, repeatedly, for having failed to attend the meetings. It is true that his absence was heavy because of his presence in both Stroud's and my texts, and I was upset enough to suggest my traveling to Berkeley over a weekend so that the three of us could spend a day trying to sort things out. They accepted the idea, but in the event Clarke invited Stroud to his house, where I was staying, and then left us alone. I told Stroud I felt he had not read through my book (something that could not be said without rudeness in public discussion). He conceded at once that he had not read it through, but he added that what he said I said, I did say, even if I went on in the book to say other things. I didn't take it back, did I? I agreed that in a sense I did not. But the whole discussion becomes reframed, in effect begins again, in Part Four; and I had waited years to publish the material for just that reason. Yet to say that publicly would have sounded defensive.

Only then did I realize that I had let my disappointment and dismay trip me up. I should simply at the convention panel have repeated what my book went on to say and let the reframing be judged by the audience, rather than finding new objections to what Stroud had said. But the book was something I had borne silently for too long, and its consequences were too raw, for me to be nimble in handling misunderstandings, especially in the short space between receiving responses and preparing replies. My reaction to the event was to take offense and nurse my wounds. I decided that I must simply accept, what had been obvious enough before now, that my work creates infectious ill will among an imposing body of professional philosophers who know of it (among professional literary theorists ill will is more individual), while at the same time there is no (other?) profession that can simply be asked to welcome it. Even though I had fought this reaction in the cases of hostility against Austin and Wittgenstein, I somehow imagined—perhaps it can be seen as another phase or face of the petulance I am describing in myself—that I would be exempt from such treatment.

August 11, 2004

But then what am I to make of my insistences—isn't that what they were?—on, for example, Thoreau and on film and on Shakespeare and on Heidegger? These enthusiasms seemed to me gifts, particularly in their interactions, that I was helping to bring, in my way, to the (English-speaking) philosophical table. Their interest for philosophy did not seem to me strained. So why were my offerings treated more like thefts, as if these provisions served to deprive philosophy of something ? One obvious answer is that it was not what I was urging but precisely the manner of the urging that caused the disturbance, not the matter but the form. But that would just explain why the case was worse than I imagined. My manner, so far as I could judge it, or even perceive it, did not seem to me arbitrary or imposed, or put positively, it was the ground and guide of my conviction.—But then that is perhaps just the problem, and the reason it is intractable. Shouldn't my philosophical convictions be based on rational argument, not upon personal manner? That seems unarguable.

And yet. Questions, for example, about whether we do or do not know the world as it is do not present themselves to me as resolvable by argument, anyway by what may be recognized as argument in dissociation from tracing a web of assumptions, pictures, myths, prejudices, cravings, presentiments, intimidations, impositions (all elements of the ordinary) that determine the locus of argument and are not ordered by it. Nor do I suppose questions to be resolvable by argument that concerns—to take a fundamental, I hope imperishable, insight of Dewey's and of William James's—the way the classical empiricists distort or stylize experience. Suppose I say that the classical empiricist idea of

LITTLE DID I KNOW

experience as made of impressions creates a stylization of the concept of impression, specifically isolating the picture of making a physical impression, as of a body lying on a stretch of sandy beach, from that of being (psychologically, sensibly, intellectually, spiritually) impressed. Letting the latter idea, that of being impressed, say, struck, by what you find impressive, continue its palpable relation to the concept of an impression (as, for example, Emerson insists upon, notably in "Fate," and at the opening of "Self-Reliance") ties the idea to that of being interested (a critical term of Thoreau's for our relation to the things of the world), of articulating what matters, what counts (as Wittgenstein emphasizes in his use of the term "criterion"). The picture of impressions as an unremitting patter upon consciousness makes mysterious what moves the human to utterance, or keeps it silent.

What would, or does, convince one to choose between these ideas of an impression? In the empiricist case one looks for laws of association; in the opposed case one looks for, let's say, a priori grounds of judgment. (I once interpreted Emerson's thought that "We lie in the lap of immense intelligence" as being his way at a moment of characterizing our relation to our language. It now seems to me appropriate to add that this suggests our relation to our language as one of being asleep in it. But the cradle will rock.)

One can say, in opposition to the suggestion that experience is stylized by empiricists, that the attempt to keep the fullness of the concept of impression makes it unwieldy for scientific purposes. So here philosophizing requires determining what one wants of philosophy. Then how can philosophizing become part of a university curriculum? Can one allow, even encourage, students to determine what it is they want of philosophy? What is the alternative?

The only serious answer to determining the course of philosophizing lies in your relation to the works you care about. And this means to me, in your relation to what allows you to work productively, to think further.

August 12, 2004

In the cases I know best the determination to philosophy has accompanied an intellectual crisis, or resolve. The thing about crises is that, while momentarily creating a spiritual opening, their aftermath may produce an increased hardness protecting the new dispensation (a counterreformation). I am reminded of Thoreau's crack about those who are proud of a second birth, as if consequently there must not come a need for third and fourth births—what you will. They might be small things, easy to miss. Emerson in this connection speaks of introducing a new degree of culture, say, a deflection, as sufficient for a revolution. But here I am invoking an image of thinking as demanding conversion, as though the origination of thinking for oneself is essentially esoteric, as though rationality is not an access to another place but a repeated transfiguration away from the irrationalities of fixation, of psychic paralysis as we stand. "Onward thinking" Heidegger says. And Wittgenstein will essentially appeal to what it is to "go on" with a thought. Such ideas are implicit in Emerson's picture of finding ourselves on a series of stairs. Philosophy is here transfiguring, one could hastily say internalizing, the ancient idea of the self as on a path, concentrating rather on the implicit feature of taking steps, learning to walk away. Such associations are apt, to some, to be distasteful, or at best useless.

In a late conversation with Bernard, I re-raised an old question between us, namely, how he understood his Enlightenment commitments to sort with his love for Nietzsche and for Wagner. The question represents to my mind a paradox of taste not irrelevant in the case of his great friend Isaiah Berlin. I do not regard myself as free of immersion in this paradox. It might even be thought a way of expressing what drives what I have to say philosophically. And it is no good saying that the more obvious paradox is between the love of Wagner and of Verdi, because I find a love of Verdi, perhaps of opera as such, to be quite Wagnerian. This time I related my question to Bernard's review, I think in the *New York Review of Books*, of a text of Heidegger's in which he had suggested that Heidegger may be the only philosopher of worldwide acclaim whom he suspects of being a charlatan. He replied that he was not particularly proud of that piece of his. But this concession does not retract the suggestion.

Something suspicious—perhaps suspiciously apt—about the question is that Heidegger himself characteristically writes as if taking arms again charlatanry. He poses the task of the genuine thinker as

"going to the encounter of the thinker," as if philosophy is the history
of the torch of authentic thinking handed on, in single hands, from one
otherwise impoverished and pretentious generation to another. And
Wittgenstein, and even Austin—two other philosophers held in suspicion by Bernard—also convey such a mood of, let's say, exclusiveness.
It comes out in Wittgenstein when he speaks about the intense difficulty
of thinking (as though few others are up to the challenge, or indeed
have ever encountered the difficulty). I say "even Austin" joins in here,
because while what he preached was his methods, which were to be
open to all, his accusation that other philosophers were questionably
"serious"—a question clustered in the opening pages of his *Sense and
Sensibilia*, an extended attack on A. J. Ayer's book on the foundations
of empirical knowledge—pretty well suggests that they (some among
so-called philosophers? all but him? certainly Wittgenstein some of the
time) were in that case faking philosophy, mimicking it, neither good
nor bad at it, counterfeits. It is, I judge, principally for that bleak cheeki-
ness of criticism that Austin has never been forgiven by certain of his
philosophical colleagues.

Emerson is comparatively sane in his expression or register of perception, charging us in effect with being our own charlatans, our resort-
ing to quoting the sentiments of an unquestionably great name in prefer-
ence to facing our own thoughts. The obligation to combat charlatanry,
false philosophy, is born with philosophy in Plato, in Socrates' combating
of the Sophists. Since philosophy became a profession, monitoring its
own credentials, the issue should in principle not have to arise, I mean
not arise personally, but rather automatically or rather institutionally be
subject to resolution. Otherwise the teaching of philosophy would become merely personal, cultish, a danger to the idea of a university classroom. I believe something of the sort is what Kuhn felt arising in his
astonishment at the angry and wide variation of value philosophers place
on one another's work. To avoid the unattractiveness of these conflicts
is an understandable, even attractive reason for desiring philosophy to
become logic or science. Yet to share the desire would mean giving up
too much of what I care about in philosophy, above all I suppose my
sense that philosophy's self-criticism must remain perpetual, not a thing
for isolated crises. And I have to suppose that a certain admiration for
Nietzsche is one fair test of philosophical desire.

So I wanted some further concession from Bernard here. I take for granted that Heidegger's lectures on Nietzsche in the early 1940s have had a more decisive effect on Nietzsche studies in Europe than any other single work since it appeared. To dismiss it as the work of a charlatan would mean to suppose that half the major writers in Europe over the second half of the twentieth century have been dupes of it, and of course that one is oneself, as one reads and periodically unresistingly admires Heidegger's reading, being duped. But what is to protect one from a surmise that Heidegger was duped, that Nietzsche is himself, in his rage again the fakery of culture, a cultural fake? The most respectable or technical achievement cannot protect itself here. The charge will not in that case be that its claim to rigor is counterfeit, but precisely its claim to philosophy.

August 13, 2004

The claim to represent philosophy is unverifiable not because one lacks knowledge, but because in philosophizing one must not claim to know what others do not know or cannot know by bethinking themselves. (Quite obviously this is not a view of philosophy universally, I suppose not even widely, shared. I declare it as ancient and as still alive.) I offered Bernard the alternative of attributing his exasperation with Heidegger to Heidegger's arrogance and intellectual vulgarity, for example, to his routine disparagement of the assumed (underdescribed) superficiality of others, his repeated claims to profundity, his sometimes facile spirituality, and a coarse, perhaps lethal, inexactness in his treatment of examples.

I emphasize here Bernard's "exasperation," something different, however related, to the sense of dismay that chronically sickens the mind in wishing to understand Heidegger's attraction (however impermanent) to Nazism. This implies that I cannot agree with those who find there is nothing particular to understand here, that the man and the work no more implicate each other than do the lives of physicists or mathematicians and their physics or mathematics. (The idea that there is nothing to understand takes it as irreducibly obvious that the man and the work are separate, like the man and the horse he rides.)

This might be plausible in the case of philosophy if the work explicitly enough meant to ground Nazism were an *aberration* compared with the rest of his work. But it can be taken as *internal* to understanding Heidegger's work to understand its attraction to Nazism. (It is more like the relation between the man and *his way* of choosing and riding a horse; some others might choose and ride roughly that way; some others will not see its point at all.) The terrible fact, one that the picture of simple separation may wish to deny, is that Nazism has its philosophical as well as political attractions. And it may seem that if a thinker of Heidegger's powers succumbed to them—accepted in it a manifestation of his philosophical aspirations, if fully only for less than a year—then perhaps no one is safe. Here is where a perception of Heidegger's vulgarity may be found worth pursuing.

Exasperation is a reaction I have felt at some stage during the three or four times I have offered a seminar in which Heidegger has been featured, and each time the reaction has been overcome by the work's reassertion of its quality. This played out somewhat differently the last time I announced a seminar featuring a Heidegger text, one in which I paired his commentary on Hölderlin's *Ister Hymn* in some detail with Thoreau's *Walden*. I did not disguise my sense that *Walden* is subtler, and more patient, more rigorous, a philosophically more thorough and profound work, than Heidegger's *Hölderlin's Hymn "The Ister"*—both works based upon a tradition that could hardly be less in fashion, something like a romantically inclined reading of nature, in particular, of a body of water. (Nor of course was there any intent to minimize the fact that this text of Heidegger's is one excursion in a vast series of his accomplishments, whereas Thoreau's text is his principal claim as a thinker. Apart, that is, from his vast journals. Whether these will ever become part of his culture's consciousness is an open question, as open, I believe, as it ever was.)

I would like to understand such writing differently, as a contribution to the natural history of the human, invoking the way Wittgenstein ambivalently describes his *Philosophical Investigations*. My exasperation, accordingly, is then a function of my consciousness that the philosophical perception I claim for Thoreau's writing is professionally out of bounds, something merely wayward. The importance to me of not losing my perception of Thoreau's philosophicality, the perception, let's call it, of an American difference in philosophy (something not equivalent to what one would mean, if anything, by "an American philosophy"), is my sense of the ease with which this difference is neglected within the institutions of philosophical education, so that the writing of Emerson and of Thoreau is persistently perceived as philosophically primitive or amateurish. This is painful enough if strangers accept it, but wrenching when it causes us to mistake ourselves, for then we stand to lose the America that is in search of itself. (The circumstance that America is the name of a culture always in search of itself, continuing its originating voyage of discovery, has been attested by its perpetual sense of being in danger of losing itself. The current process of hypnotic deformation in the public discourse of the United States [I speak most obviously of the speeches and interviews of George W. Bush] has struck many of us as taking a new step in its self-stupefaction, in which the terror of terror is used to numb our knowledge of numbness, to disguise the danger of losing ourselves as a state in which we are asked to find ourselves precisely in our exhalations of violence. The greatest of our fears is then realized in finding that almost everyone seems to know this is happening to us and we seem silenced by the very impotence of commonality.)

The circumstances in which I began reading Heidegger, the academic year following the summer weeks at Tougaloo College, having more or less actively avoided this work since my first year in graduate school at Harvard thirteen years earlier, emblematizes an essential fact of my philosophical education since returning from Berkeley to teach for the bulk of my teaching life at Harvard. Shortly after the appearance of the English translation of *Being and Time*, several graduate students (Timothy Gould first among them; I've forgotten who else at the moment) in effect demanded that I offer a graduate seminar on the book, that it was a scandal that such a work was not authorized for discussion in Emerson Hall, refusing to hear obvious arguments from me to the effect that I was not an expert on the subject, asserting instead that if I could with conviction give such a course as Humanities 5, in which no one expected me to be an expert in all the fields crossed by the assigned texts of that course, then Heidegger should indeed seem an obligatory assignment for me. These students must have known that they were shaming me into doing something I was looking for the right to do. It is a way the young authorize the freedom of the old.

And the participation in that early seminar, as it turned out, was, I think it may be said, a local historical event. Not because it was productive (though that was evident enough), and not because it was oversubscribed (the spirit of cooperation was so high that no one wished attendance to be limited), but because for the first time in my experience of the philosophy graduate program at Harvard, first- and second-year graduate students (namely, those studying for the Ph.D. qualifying examinations) enrolled in a course, or audited it faithfully, that was not going to appear on those examinations. This was a risky investment of time for them, but my memory is that basically all of that youngest group attended the seminar, quite as if to show their mates that no competitive advantage would be taken (say in focused preparation for the Ph.D. qualifying work) against this intellectual detour. This was I suppose the first time I had some explicit and undeniable consciousness of the fact that steps or turns in my intellectual adventure were going characteristically to take place primarily in the company of those younger than the members of my own generation.

Particularly before 1972, I mean before my first trio of books had been published, I was concerned that my eccentricities, if that is what they are, or were, would be a liability for those students who were drawn to take tips from them, most fatefully when the time came for them to present themselves for teaching positions. It could have gone without saying—but I was periodically moved to make the circumstance explicit—that I felt free to emphasize my choice of subjects running, in topic or manner, somewhat against the professional grain (the Heidegger was an instance, so was my way of reading Wittgenstein, so will be my seminars, soon enough, on literary theory and modernism, and after a while on Emerson), precisely because I regarded my work as part of the education in philosophy offered by the Harvard philosophy department as a whole, an optional part no doubt, but one, if opted for, that would be seen best in conversation with the present of philosophy spoken for by my renowned colleagues. The graduate students were perfectly aware of this intention, and my concerns about their position fell away upon my learning to trust their assertions that I was behind the times, that association with my work could do as much good as harm, that anyway they were as graduate students as aware practically of such things as they needed to be.

August 14, 2004

Memories of Tougaloo, and of meeting Cathleen, and of the inability to complete *The Claim of Reason*, and the birth of a child, and the beginning of further psychoanalysis, have swamped my attempt to remember the moment in my life of the appearance of my first book, *Must We Mean What We Say?* as the events at Harvard surrounding its appearance in April 1969 swamped the actual event. I began the introduction I wrote to the book's new edition a year ago by referring to those surrounding events as the climax, at Harvard, of the student movement of protest against our war in Vietnam, namely, the occupation, by students, of University Hall, Harvard's principal administration building, and the aftermath of weeks of demonstrations, and strikes, and riot acts, and the pervasive bitterness between and among students and faculty and administrators. Everyone had reasons, and almost everyone, from the other's point of view, was unreasonable. Could the students in general really suppose that being willing to destroy the university was helping to halt the killing in Vietnam, or improve housing for the poor, or put an end to the training of an army officer corps? Could professors who had contempt for the thoughtlessness of students some of whom, over bullhorns, supported extremities that they could not even imagine let alone believe in—for example, urging that no social change was sufficient or valuable until all relations of power were ended—in general suppose that these students were merely making a set of intellectual mistakes? Say that the students were disgusted, outraged, horrified by the incredibility of the causes of the war; by the thought that they will be forced to join in the killing; by the destruction of communality that a government creating that kind of mystery, and exercising that kind of power, can visit upon their society; by the recognition that they, the students, will be blamed for destroying communality because they are unruly whereas those in power over them are privatizing the rules, like tampering with a photograph (as in the Tonkin Gulf incident of 1964, in which a photograph was retouched to make it appear, by a president, Lyndon Johnson, whom I had happily voted for, to record an American vessel under attack). Are disgust, outrage, and horror merely irrationally directed passions under such circumstances? Professors who found the students uneducated in the ways of the world, and who accused their colleagues of having failed to impart education in these ways, might have acknowledged the passions, and might have declared their own, even if all they could presently perceive in themselves was contempt, blunting their own fears of the government's irrationality. This would have been educational.

The concluding essay on *King Lear* in *Must We Mean What We Say?* is in effect a meditation on the failure of politics, on the insufficiency of love and loyalty when government has itself become pointedly irrational. Since it was clear to me that I had assigned myself the role of keeping open what lines of communication I could among and between students and professors, I seemed to exist in these weeks impelled from meeting to meeting. The night before the student occupation of University Hall a meeting was announced to discuss such an action. Attendance overflowed the old Lowell Lecture Hall, where Humanities 5 had met during my first two years of teaching the course. Somewhat more than four hundred students were enrolled in that course, and I estimate accordingly that more than five hundred people were now crowded into the room, some standing, some sitting on stairs, for this moment of political crisis. It remains in my mind the most democratically run, in fact and in spirit, of any large meeting I ever attended. Everyone who raised a hand was permitted time to voice an opinion. The courtesy of the situation was respected by all; I mean that I recall no one taking advantage of the situation, either by heckling or by hogging the microphone. I arrived at the meeting after an early dinner, no later than 6:30, and things were already well under way. Sometime after midnight there were no longer voices asking to be heard, and a vote was called. Those against the proposal to occupy University Hall won the vote, not massively but indubitably.

I do not know who had called the meeting, nor who it was who ran it, nor, apart from a significant number of my friends and familiar faces, the extent and identity of those who attended it. But given the size and seriousness of those present, the sense that the body of those concerned with the unfolding events in the relation of the university and the war in Vietnam had had a fair chance to express itself was, to this witness, as clear as one could hope the knowledge of one's society in distress to be. Yet, despite the vote, the next morning a body of students did occupy University Hall. What I was told, arriving there, was that half the students inside were there to argue the other half out. By night-fall rumors were in the air of a proposed massive police action against the students. I was assured by a housemaster whom I trusted and who had been present at a meeting with the president, that this would not happen. When nevertheless after the mass arrest of students early the next morning the university dissolved into shifting clumps of meetings, I asked at one of them whether the administration had known about the composition of the students inside the building, that they were in argu-ment with themselves. I was told that students had no business taking a vote on whether to perform an illegal action, so all inside debating the issue were equally guilty. Everyone has reasons.

Anyway radicals and conservatives have reasons. Liberals like myself, with jerking knees and bleeding hearts, seem to have no rea-sons; merely, instead, to give interpretations. People will say that a time for talking comes to an end. Of course I would expect to have an inter-pretation of their saying so, since as long as there is time to say so there is time to listen and to think.

The faculty meeting room in University Hall was soon declared physically unsafe for the number of faculty who were now, some evi-dently for the first time in years, or ever, drawn out of their studies and laboratories to attend the special meetings being called; the sup-ports of the floor were in danger of giving way. From an average of somewhat less than a hundred at a regularly scheduled faculty meeting, attendance rose to five and six times that number. We tried moving our meetings to Sanders Theater in Memorial Hall, whose entrance hall is lined with memorial plaques of Harvard men who had fallen on the Union side of the Civil War, and within a week the meetings were moved to the technologically well-equipped Loeb Theater. There a very distinguished professor of art history, who had managed some three and a half decades earlier to escape from Hitler's Germany, rose to declare, in a voice so alarming in its intensity that we feared he was endangering his obviously delicate health: "As I did not lick the boots of the Hitler Youth, so I shall not lick the boots of the followers of Che

Guevara!" Some years later Allan Bloom's best-selling *The Closing of the American Mind* repeated the image of 1960s' protesting students as morally or politically comparable to the Hitler Youth. Why did it not matter in such perceptions that the Hitler Youth were well organized and uniformed and commanded by their government, whereas our students were disorganized, endlessly arguing among themselves, and raising their voices in opposition to the policies of the government? Politics is being invaded by passions suitable for tragedy. Was *King Lear* still pertinent here, in which the need for love (and, let's say, loyalty) and the shame of the need for love, express themselves as the demand for and the refusal of gratitude and political loyalty? (And is it a sign merely of sentimentality, or lack of sophistication, not something of demanding hope, that for years I simply assumed that the facing memorial plaques in Memorial Hall represented Harvard students who died on both sides of the Civil War?)

August 15, 2004

At one of the ensuing emergency meetings of the faculty of the philosophy department, several of my senior colleagues reported to the rest of us their understanding that the third floor of our building, Emerson Hall, one floor above where we were at this moment gathered, was occupied by students who were running the student uprising. (The charge of occupation had been leveled, or perhaps heavily suggested, by the Dean of the Faculty at the most recent faculty meeting, whereupon Morton White, our current department chair, rose and lucidly refuted, indeed rebuked, the charge.) I replied to these alarmed colleagues that my office was on the third floor and that I could testify that while there is a much larger number of students on that floor at more hours of the day and night than you would expect under normal conditions, and that there is a mimeograph machine being heavily used in one of the Teaching Fellow offices, anyone is free to come and go there, and to use their own offices, at any time; nor is anyone being refused admittance to the building. John Cooper, then an Assistant Professor in the department, confirmed this from his experience. He and I offered to walk with our questioning colleagues up the single flight of stairs to the third floor and make the rounds of the corridors, thus verifying that our building, while unusually peopled, was not in any extremer sense "occupied." Our invitation was declined.

I wonder if the visit would have been reassuring to those members of the faculty who were so fiercely contemptuous of the behavior of our distressed students. I had given a key to graduate students to use my office when I was not there, on the understanding that I could have the office, and in tidy condition (as tidy as I left it anyway) whenever I needed it. It would not have surprised me if one of them had been found asleep on my couch. If I had in that case awakened the student and sent him on his way, waving off his apologies, would this have proven my case to my colleagues? They could, on the contrary, have taken this as evidence that something was wrong. Well, yes; something was wrong. We were discussing how those in power might alternatively respond to this wrong.

Shortly after our department meeting had begun, we were waited upon by a delegation of three students from an association of black students. I have forgotten how they produced credentials for the group or for their representation of it, but some of us saw no reason to doubt them. They reported that a delegation from the organization was visiting every department in the university (were other departments also having meetings that night?—how did these students know that the philosophy department was doing so?) in order to ask support for the list of demands they were intending to present to the faculty at its next day's meeting, central among them the demand for the formation of what they called a Department of Afro-American Studies. After a brief set of exchanges most of our colleagues left, taking it (I suppose I mean, deciding angrily) that the faculty meeting had essentially been broken up, an interpretation hard to refute. What remained of the group was John Rawls across the room speaking, as I recall the scene, to one of the black students, leaving me and the other two students at the long table in the center of the room, going over their list of demands. The next hour or so was spent arguing with them over my assertion that if what they meant by "support" was a faculty vote to pass some sort of faculty resolution, their demands would have to be translated into language suitable for faculty debate, and that it would have to be presented to the assembled faculty by a member of the faculty. I said I imagined that the idea of presenting a resolution on behalf of a recognizable group of Harvard students might be done.

Epitomizing the next couple of hours: "Why isn't this translation bullshit the runaround we always hear?"—"I don't know what you always hear. The faculty has its pride and its language, as you have yours. If you want to speak to us, you will have to respect that."—"How do we know your translation will really be what we are asking for?"—"I don't know. We have to try it together, and then see how much trust is going to be required. Look over the drafts we have begun of sentences from your opening paragraphs. If you yourselves believe in them, take them to your group and see if they approve." When the students left, I gave Rawls an account of where things had moved to and asked if he was willing to help. He was, but he was at that moment very late for an appointment he had made with a child of his. We agreed that we would get together before the faculty meeting in the morning and determine who would present what, and agreed further that, since the translation was excruciatingly slow, I might phone him any time to come back to Cambridge and help with that. In fact I phoned him around six o'clock in the morning. The rewriting was not thoroughly completed, and I felt unable to form a further coherent thought. The group had adjourned for an hour.

Upon regrouping we were joined by various others (other members of the black students' association, and a few graduate students—I remember Tracy Strong among them, who I believe had been instrumental in guiding the petitioners to our doors in the first place) who were prepared to do the typing and mimeographing necessary to specify for the large faculty meeting precisely what was being asked of it. The ensuing sequence of events remains almost undecipherable for me. When at the meeting I was called upon by the Dean of the Faculty to read the motion, or petition, I was interrupted, having barely begun, by questions from the floor concerning an ambiguity in the numbering of the paragraphs. Evidently the two documents we had distributed, one of which was referred to by the other, the students' original demands and our parliamentary translation of it, only the second of which was to be read aloud, were, as it turned out in our haste and anxiety, ambiguously numbered in the attempt to correlate them with each other. I felt I might start sobbing, and I remember slumping back down into my seat to confer with Rawls, but virtually nothing further of the ensuing events. Rawls evidently saw that I was too depleted to stand up again, and took the microphone from me to try to clarify what our pages had damnably confused. I heard voices from every quarter of the packed theater, mostly proposals of amendments, but my participation was at an end. Afterward, walking the few blocks from the Loeb Theater back to our apartment on Ash Street, I noticed that in what I recall as an unusually hot day for late April in Cambridge, my whole body was itching; my back, my limbs, and my hands were stinging, an experience I associated with taking qualifying examinations and more particularly with early piano recitals. As I was climbing into bed, sometime after noon (I had not slept for a good thirty hours), the *New York Review of Books* phoned to suggest that I write an account for them of the events at Harvard. I regretted having mindlessly answered the phone and mumbled something about feeling too chaotic to put anything together at the moment. And I thoughtfully adduced my eczema as testimony to my sincerity. This seems to have confirmed permanently these editors' suspicion of me as too scatter-brained ever to do business with.

The students eventually got their department, which, I gather, turned out to require a relatively small step beyond the plans about which Henry Rosovsky (eventually a renowned Dean of the Faculty, in favor of which, years later, he declined an offer of the presidency of Yale) had been in extended conversation with them. I have been told that part of the recorded prehistory of that conclusion is a moment known as the Cavell Resolution (or Amendment). I do not know whether it was essential to the history that went on to unfold.

Whose prehistory records this, or might? Perhaps prehistory is my medium, to give an account of the conditions, call it the context, that have to happen before something happens, so that when the writing itself should seem to come to the point it may well seem absent (the point and the prehistory). This would partly explain why for most of my writing life comparatively few (compared with the growing body of my work) have felt obliged, or if somehow obliged then not prepared, to refer to, that is to acknowledge, something I had written on their subjects. Since its point was in effect apt to be institutionally oblique no one would notice the nonreference. Some exceptions were unfortunate, as when instead of expressing an indebtedness for being led to a surprising topic, a reader cited only a passage of mine broaching an idea with which he, as if for a long time, had found himself in disagreement, thus negating any show of solidarity. (This hurt. But its ground cause was the odd position of philosophy within American academic culture from the time of the importation of analytical philosophy as the avant-garde of the discipline, consolidating itself in the 1940s and 1950s, hardening, disciplining, distrust of natural language and its literatures, so that an invocation of philosophy, of various kinds, could seem not alone abusive but foreign.) Of course there were some whose citations of work of mine were meant as gifts, as if aggrieved for me, and protective. This has dangers of its own, as I have noted. If I have left my students with the idea that it was up to them to make my life make sense, I would unfortunately have perpetuated a misfortune in my teaching.

August 16, 2004

Several years into my old/new crisis in completing *The Claim of Reason*, and my new/old psychoanalytic voyage that will prove to last for some fifteen years, the idea of practicing psychoanalysis again presented itself to me, and this time with the thought that the substance of the wish should be tested. I did not like the thought of letting reality, in the form of increasing age, decide the issue of this recurring idea, its intellectual or spiritual reality. I wanted a useful resolution of the impulse—and why not, with the accomplishment of the finished manuscript of *The Claim of Reason* behind me, fully enter a late equivalent of those mysterious buildings lining my route along Central Park West as I walked my way out of Juilliard and a life of music? The Boston Psychoanalytic Institute was becoming open to the idea of lay analysis, and I was accepted as a candidate for their program of certification. I was more than once warned, by my own analyst and by friends who were analysts, that I would be disappointed in the seminars, insisting that the Institute understood itself as a trade school, in effect imparting paths for what was regarded, properly, as the only serious matter in view, namely, the responsible and effective treatment of patients.

But to be qualified to see patients is precisely what I could not accomplish on my own. After a year of in effect academic seminars, on hysteria and obsession, and on dreams, I expected to be admitted, with other candidates who had begun the program with me, to the clinical seminar in which patient histories would be presented. My application was refused by one of the two analysts in charge of that seminar, on the ground that since I had not begun a training analysis and begun doing clinical work under supervision I would destroy the atmosphere in the seminar room. That seemed to me a mystical explanation, and I responded by saying that this had not been presented to me as a requirement for admission to seminars, but only for eventual accreditation, and I had not yet decided whether to take that step. What the refusal meant is that the two teachers of this clinical seminar (the one in particular whom I had known of through a friend years ago and who I assumed distrusted the idea of lay analysis, and I felt distinctly distrusted me along with philosophy, as I distrusted her reasons) were making a decision that annulled the decision of the Institute to admit me to its program.

At my age, the thought of reintroducing my complexities to a new analyst seemed wasteful, even hopeless. When I was told by friends who were training analysts at the Institute that this would not really be starting again, but merely changing vehicles on the same road, I realized that I did not believe something perhaps essential to the Institute's conviction in its work, namely, that it was the psychoanalytic procedure itself that was totally important, the analyst essentially insignificant. I felt I had plenty of evidence, and experience, that this was not true (or that it begged the enormous question, namely, of whether, and if not why not, the procedure was equally in effect in all cases). Several analysts on the faculty of the Institute who disagreed with their two colleagues' decision, offered to work with me independently, referring the required number of patients to me and supervising my work with them. This was not illegal—I would not go on to claim accreditation by the Institute—but the thought of working outside the walls rubbed me the wrong way, for causes I do not feel I clearly understand.

I had, in any case, begun recognizing a shift of idea in relation to my writing. There were therapeutic registers in the writing of *The Claim of Reason* that I had come to count on following out, one directed to myself and one to my culture at large, or cultures. How these registers differed from attention to a single other (or a single couple, or family) I did not, do not, have to understand in order to sense that whatever psychic satisfaction the thought of clinical work brought me, it was to be a continuation of philosophy's ancient idea of leading the soul up and out of a cave or deeper into a dark wood, in both cases eventually toward light. That this therapeutic impulse in myself might be satisfied only in or by writing, not in talking—however much I thought of myself as loving to talk, needing to, having to talk (hardly itself a recommendation for becoming a psychoanalytic clinician)—somehow increased its allure for me. It meant that the impulse was to result in works, not total, not final, nevertheless certain shareable means of taking arms publicly against the increasing velocity of evanescence.

August 17, 2004

Reverse Rip Van Winkle, I fell into a dream of work, and when I awoke twenty or thirty years and a dozen books later, with the same beautiful trees in mild movement outside my study windows, I found there were a considerable number of strangers who apparently recognized me, or knew what I had been doing.

This discovery coincided with the change of millennium. There are suddenly more books published, or in press, about my work than there are books written by me. Some friends of mine feel that too much of the writing about my work comes from the sense, or let's say the double sense, that it is insufficiently read, either too narrowly or too hastily, and that if it were just explained a little more clearly, its readership would suddenly become fruitful and multiply. I am no judge of this, but I can see, and be grateful for, the impulse to compensate for the work's having been for a long time rather too studiously ignored. I myself chronically refer as I write to earlier passages in my writing, surely out of an impulse to show how the work, early and late, is meant to go together and evolve, but sometimes as well out of a sense, of which I am not proud but not much ashamed, that it has been denied.—What claim on earth is immune to denial? Yet I can see that my incessant perception, or imagination, of the claim for acknowledgment comes from a perception of a world bent on denial, interest in the world withdrawn to the point of chronic boredom, lost in lovelessness.

I would have been glad to be able to ignore whatever I have so far done, that is, to feel that I can simply assume its existence. No doubt in part I resent being confronted with my vanity. But there is something more. If I am ever right about a philosophical idea it is precisely because the idea is not in my possession. The goal of philosophy, as I care about it most, is the obvious, the undeniable—of course, because the adversary of philosophy is self-obscurity. (The more political discourse becomes obscure the more philosophical clarity becomes political.) So I am conscious of trying to write without contention, neither denying nor affirming. (I am also conscious of not being able to make this mood or goal sufficiently clear. Wittgenstein's denial that philosophy advances theses is still taken, I believe, by most philosophers, as a patent, self-deluding falsehood.) This is not the same as saying, or urging, nothing, but it can be taken to be the same, or assumed that others will not understand me to have said a thing, and I will feel denied, unacknowledged. Then I feel lucky to have recommended study of the concept of acknowledgment.

I have also written about skepticism (originally as directed to the human other) not as a discovery of my ignorance but as an act of denial, leaving the other with invitations to, or say, invisible consolations of, madness. Given the dissociations of my growing up, I have been alerted to the circulation of mad touches in everyday life—a disproportionate feint of rage here, a palpable slight there—and craved confirmation that others notice what I notice. Yet how can this be a function of my particular fortunes and misfortunes since the extremity of mood in which Emerson and Thoreau write—"Every word they say chagrins us" from "Self-Reliance," and "I have traveled a good deal in Concord; and everywhere . . . the inhabitants have appeared to me to be doing penance in a thousand remarkable ways," from *Walden*—is a steadying companion to my mind, thankfully not mine alone?

But there is something still more to my tendency to self-reference. I have said of my writing that I habitually fail the first time to get things right, as right as I can. This may or may not be registered in the fact that I am rarely understood the first time through. It struck me as characteristic of reactions to my work when one week my book on the Hollywood comedy of remarriage was reviewed impatiently as an attempt to make something of nothing, and three weeks later the same reviewer explained a new film in relation to the concept of remarriage comedy as if that were a new thought of the reviewer's devising or else a concept well known to the seasoned. But that is still not the real gist of my repetitions. In dealing with obviousness, reformulation is essential groundwork. Two compliments I have felt distinctly heartened by form a pair: In Albuquerque, Gus noted: "You have a way of never repeating yourself" (said about a passage that others might indeed have taken as a pure repetition of myself); some years later in Chicago, Joel remarked: "Students who have been touched by your work are so different from each other."

August 18, 2004

I have no stable sense of whatever reputation has come my way, much less any interesting sense of how this matters. And perhaps others are also genuinely doubtful about whether I need an introduction, or a glance, or an averted glance. Probably the issue arises for me now because I am seeking a way to leave these remarks essentially where they are, so that I have begun looking back at the ground covered. My bargain with myself from the beginning has been to write here of the past essentially from memory, and to articulate memories, however unpromising in appearance, whenever I could, with some idea of how just these events and images have led to, or shaped, a reasonable life nevertheless also devoted to a certain ambition for philosophical writing, or what is meant as such. ("Such"? The writing itself, and what it wishes to invoke as its past and its hopes, is my evidence for it.) Too obviously these events and images might not have led to this outcome, or rather anything recognizable as an event or image might have been otherwise. If I had not run out into the street that morning and accidentally been knocked unconscious by a car, then what? Since that would probably not have prevented World War II, I would have been drafted into the army when I turned eighteen—unless my sense of physical distortion had been lessened and I had been approachable enough to have been alerted to and to have prepared for the final interview after the physical examination for the navy officers' program a year and a half earlier, and been accepted, hence in either case subject directly to the fortunes of war. If we had not moved from the family house when I turned seven, that would perhaps have meant that there had been no Great Depression, and in that case my father would not have lost that store, or if the Great Miami Hurricane had not hit when and as it did he would not have lost *that* store and in neither case would we have moved to Sacramento, and Mendel would have graduated college and not had to become everybody's father. But then no one would have picked me up on Saturdays from an empty apartment on the north side. But that is absurd, if, as I am imagining, we never moved there. These tiny counterfactual links have become impossible before they have hit a stride.

A human life, a human action, human history, at any moment is underdetermined and overdetermined. If things need not have worked out as they have, they have nevertheless forever so far worked out the way they have, including their immeasurable and specific ignorance of that way. If they are to work out well, I have to choose them. Aristotle says I must take my life upon myself; Plato's Myth of Er describes my choosing, after leaving the body of one life, a body in which to live another. For the modern mind this means (mythically) that I am to choose the one body I will ever have. Have I yet begun to choose this one? Or to pity it? Have I become the one who has done all and only what I have done, accepted that what I have done is no better and no worse than it is?

Nothing so out of the way has happened to me quite to explain my recurrent sense of intractable oddness. Without a measure of the oddness of my experience of my abilities, I have wavered between feeling exceptionally stupid and exceptionally bright. If this is normal, it should pass away. But what passes away? Is the sense of being dealt an exceptional hand itself exceptional? Reading Henry James's "The Beast in the Jungle" I felt many must have felt caught by this tricky yet banal sense of one's life as exceptional. Then reading James's later "Jolly Corner" I felt I saw conditions under which the pair in the earlier story might have found a happy ending. When I understood Emerson's "Experience" as another study of the exceptional (yet another man who feels he has missed his principal chance at experience, hence life), it appears to be the human as such that is the exceptional, the locus of the unnatural—so that my case is not singular but representative. I assume that it is for this reason, whatever other, that Emerson speaks of the individual as illustrious.

Part 14

August 19, 2004

I am seeking a way to take my leave now not because I feel I have exhausted effective memory; it would be more accurate to say that memory has discovered itself to be inexhaustible. And I am increasingly aware that memories of my life are so often unforgettably no longer mine, not mine alone, so I have repeatedly to concern myself with considerations of propriety beyond those that are functions merely of my awkward self-revelations. I have in general no trouble keeping secrets; I know many, about myself and others, that I shall take to the grave. What concerns me more is what, after a while, happens to memory, that it becomes as routine as perception, conventional, unquestioned, serving merely to recall, not to reconsider; an instrument of grudges and assuagements, not of liberation. I could say it becomes, as one becomes oneself, externalized, damned to visibility, given to be understood solely in terms of what shows of us, hence inevitably of a stylization even of that. I think here of my various revaluations of Wittgenstein's opening of his *Philosophical Investigations* by his citing Augustine's quasi-memory and description of his learning language, a passage that seems to express a time when memory and dream and hallucination are not yet as dissociated as they will become, and we are as if bearers of invisibility, witnesses of lives we do not understand, or care for, stealing words also with unknown lives of their own. If there is such a task as remembering the present, the task is philosophy's—as if we chronically forget to live.

I spoke of philosophy becoming political when the political becomes mysterious, or openly mad. (In Europe, this might be dated from Rousseau's frenzied perception of the lack of community; in the United States, after the inspiration of the Revolution, from the overthrow of Reconstruction after the Civil War.) A good friend, and a former student of mine, Alice Crary, had scheduled her wedding to be held on Saturday, September 15, 2001, in the garden of a beautiful summer house in western Massachusetts. I had gladly accepted her request that I take on the role of leading what has become called a commitment ceremony. In the immediate aftermath of the destruction of the World Trade Center four days earlier, she and her young man, Nathaniel, were on the telephone with each of the guests they had invited to determine a joint sense of whether to go ahead with the wedding. All, as far as I heard, welcomed the idea of the chance to spend the day together, and away from the imagination of, or the impossibility to imagine, the specific tragedy, and I suppose generally away from the towns we lived in as subjects of aerial photographs.

We arrived, somewhat late the night before the ceremony, at the inn where we were expected, and by the time we awoke and got to the breakfast room the next morning, only one other table was still occupied—by, it quickly emerged, other wedding guests, three women and a man. Cathleen and I had for some twenty or thirty minutes of subdued but not uncordial exchanges with these strangers managed to avoid raising the shared subject on our minds—not the wedding, which was also not mentioned. Then as the other group left, the man, rising, said in what I thought a hearty voice, "We're focused."

He unsettled me. I had heard George W. Bush declare some hours or days earlier that his administration was focused, implicitly declaring that he now knew (the fact and the further threat of terrorist acts had taught him) why he wanted to be president of the United States and that that was all he and his administration needed to know. To keep citizens secure from an imminent attack at any time and any place was not just one among the obvious obligations of the highest office they can vote for (an obligation this president had just failed to meet, a fact he also failed, and will forever fail, to mention), but for him it became the defining, perhaps even, at what public people keep referring to as the end of the day, the *only* obligation, the totality, of that office.

I could not hold back the question: "What are we focused on?" The man smiled, and with added fervor repeated: "We're focused!" The other night on national television news a mother who had had a son killed in Iraq was asked how she felt now about the war. After some hesitation she replied: "Saddam Hussein hated us . . . because we are free . . . he used weapons of mass destruction on his own people . . . he and Al-Qaeda are, they were. . . ." Her voice trailed off. Many people now say (almost three years after this war was crafted, this number has become an overwhelming majority of Americans) that this administration will say anything, and that people will believe what it perpetually says, simply because it takes energy to doubt it, and we have become exhausted, sick at heart. The situation seems to me even worse than that. I do not imagine that people who are repeating, or trying to remember, public words of this sort actually believe what their words say. I think they are fixed or floating in fear and bewilderment and can no more hold opinions or hopes in common, or ones that are in principle open to criticism, than subjects under hypnosis can. Among such subjects the possibility of community, of anything like constitutional democracy, is negated, gutted.

Everyone seemed to agree that the commitment ceremony went well, with satisfactory degrees of seriousness and joyfulness, several close friends saying what only close friends can have the right to say and the pleasure of saying—Alice and Nathaniel saying the vows they had composed, I in addition to calling the occasion to order and calling the order of guests for their words, making explicit at the end my sense of the occasion that since Alice and Nathaniel had no hesitation speaking of the ceremony as a wedding I regarded them as married. But here I confess a sense in myself of letdown, something that I had not anticipated and could not in the moment retrieve. A shoe did not meaningfully drop, a ceremonial glass could not be broken, and of course I could not say "I pronounce you husband and wife." Because of that I somehow felt, out of the absence of experience in participating in this way in such a moment, and, more lethal, my failure of imagination, that I could not in the moment find a way to say, to take upon myself the right to say for those assembled, that *we* regard them as married. Driving back to

Boston at midnight I was berating myself for not having been nimble
enough to provide a closing statement involving all present by offering
something like "Having heard their mutual vows, and believing without reservation in their commitment to one other, I ask you to join me in
affirming their union" and then applauding and congratulating them,
expecting to be joined happily in kind by all present. Then I would
have achieved what Austin calls "up-take" in a performative utterance.
For my having failed here, my excuse will have to be that Austin does
not consider (can that be right?) first-person *plural* performatives (as in
"We, the People . . . do ordain and establish . . . "). And that provides
exactly no solace for me. A closer candidate for an excuse is that this
marriage needed no confirmation; it had been achieved well before
the dawn of the day of commitment. But of course I also knew that it
had been achieved years before that day. And we all knew roughly why
we were gathered here. And we knew further that knowing something
together can still leave something undone.

August 20, 2004

I have said that it was in completing *The Claim of Reason* that I became confident that my writing could go on. That has been the knowledge I wanted to arrive at as a condition of bringing these installments
of autobiography to a close. No one of my first three books—a largish collection of mostly or intermittently recognizable philosophical
essays, a short book on Thoreau, and another on film—and not the
three books together, proposed a clear way to go on. I had the unmistakable sense of having said hello a number of times without anyone
saying hello back, anyone other than friends, who keep one sane but
who necessarily run the risk of affording consolation, as if the worst has
happened. Yet while in addition these published texts of mine did not
at once suggest new directions for my teaching, they seemed to form a
resilient confidence for me that led me through the drastic break represented by Part Four of *The Claim of Reason*.

It had become a matter of taking things far enough. Far enough
for what? To arrive where others are. To achieve, that is, to participate
in, a public. No one else will have arrived there having passed by just

this edge of things in just this broken light. Of course this is no truer of
me than it is of you, stranger. (The friend as stranger; the capacity not
to know, not to have always to remain focused, on guard.)

August 21, 2004

Early in *The Writing of the Disaster*, Blanchot opts etymological-
ly, hence metaphysically (sometimes distrusting this Heideggerian conjunction, but generally admitting its appeal) for the significance of "disaster" as marking our being dissociated or disconnected or disengaged
from the pertinence of the stars rather than, as a dictionary will correctly give its use, to invoke the exclusive inflection of ill-starred. Then for
Blanchot disaster is revealed metaphysically to be, or to have become,
the normal state of human existence, marked by the release from our
ties to the stars, say, from our considered steps beyond, a release that
partakes of an oblivion of the transcendental draw of words, of their
openness to a future, their demand for continuity with past and present. Empirically this aura of disruption is manifested in human-driven,
absolute catastrophes, ones that, perhaps we can say, have strangled
the imagination of God, catastrophes named, let us say, the Gulag, the
Holocaust, Hiroshima/Nagasaki. Then the state of starless action had
evidently not widely become understood in the United States to have
come to pass at the time Charlotte Vale (in *Now Voyager*, played by Bette Davis, in 1942, in the film's once-famous closing words) proposed:
"Let's not ask for the moon. We have the stars." Now that we have lost
the stars, we, some of us, ask for the moon, and since we don't get it, we
will go there again. (Returning to the moon was recently announced,
to I thought considerable scientific and political dismay, as a national
priority.) Anyway, I remember clearly that a young Jimmy Stewart las-
soed the moon and gave it to Donna Reed in *It's a Wonderful Life*. Wasn't
that decently romantic?

I am struck by Blanchot's sense of the fatefulness in relating the
metaphysical and the ordinary—what I once pictured (in "The *Investigations'* Everyday Aesthetics of Itself") as the facing banks guiding
and carved by the river of philosophy. In *Le pas au-delà* the perpetual
facing of the metaphysical and the ordinary is key in Blanchot's inter-

pretation of Nietzsche's Eternal Return, and in his refusal of Hegelian synthesis as the step beyond thesis and antithesis (there are, as it were, only alternating steps between each, and self-transformations of each). Such touchstones of thinking in Nietzsche and in Blanchot bear working relations to ways I find myself reading Wittgenstein's *Investigations*. Ideas of "return" and "turn" and of (the shunning of) "theses" are perpetual and fundamental in the procedures of the *Investigations*: "What we do is return words from their metaphysical to their everyday use" (§ 116); "Our investigations must be turned around the fixed point of our real need" (§ 108). And roughly: "I do not wish to advance theses in philosophy" (compare *Investigations*, § 128). My emphasis on the first two of these well-known Wittgensteinianisms is, I know, often thought excessive. An implication of them is that we are, we live, in exile from our words, turned from them, from the implications of our lives, strangers to ourselves, or rather (since finding ourselves strange might be liberating), shunning ourselves. Starless. A symptom of our being lost to ourselves (philosophy demonstrates that "We do not know our way about") is that we seek a transcendental rescue in, or from, our words. Wittgenstein perceives this as our all but unappeasable yearning to speak "outside language-games," as if this were to work ourselves free of dictation, instead of serving to consign ourselves to it.

The last of my trio of quotations from the *Investigations*, concerning not advancing theses, is still impatiently often found just plainly false. Doesn't Wittgenstein, for example, assert—advance as a thesis—that the meaning is the use? And assert that we need external criteria for internal processes? And assert that there is no (one) internal process that is, for instance, "expecting someone"? And assert that a lot of different things may be called "reading"? Then how about "The human body is the best picture of the human soul"? Is this a thesis, an assertion that is true or false? It can seem that Wittgenstein wants to prevent us from saying or maintaining certain things, especially the very truest things, as for instance, "I know the world exists." Something he undoubtedly asks is that you identify the state of the person to whom you might (seriously?) undertake to *tell* such things, someone whom you imagine needs to be *informed* of them. In my case, reasonably early in starting to attend philosophy courses, I report that I felt imposed upon by being told (or by being asked to accept as true of me) that I believe the world exists, for example, that this piece of chalk, this chair, this hand exists. But of course I also felt that I had no right to take my untutored feeling seriously, combating centuries of sophistication with a limited world littered with ignorance. What was true then, as now, is that the following question demands a serious response: If it is forced, intellectually violent, to say here and now, in the safe haven of, for example, a classroom, that I <u>believe</u> that this hand exists, and also that chair and table—if asserting such things does not express the fact of my relation to things—then what does express the relation? A possible response might be, What indeed? What one thing could (be expected to, used to, really believed to) express such endless things?

Such theses as Wittgenstein renounces (as when G. E. Moore held up and waved his hand and asserted, "I know this hand exists") seeks to inform us of what cannot be news to us, supplies us with something we cannot simply lack, something that is part of the common inventory of those whom you would address, as it is part of yours (you are offering it as common). How can we so easily be distanced from it? What anxiety is stirred that prompts you to test this sample of the common, to insist upon it? Speaking absolutely—or attempting to speak outside language-games—asserts what cannot exactly be meant. In asserting what cannot fail to be known, what have we gained? In denying what cannot be denied to be known, what have we lost?

The translator of *Le pas au-delà* says in her introduction that for Blanchot every step is a false step. I had several days before written (trying out for myself the forced pun on *pas* and *ne . . . pas* ["step" and "not . . . step"]): No step is (just) a false step—thinking not alone of Freud on the significance of "slips" but also of Wittgenstein, for whom the longing to step beyond the ordinary is not fully pacifiable as long as human desire remains recognizable, revealing something essential about the restlessness of the creature of language. But Wittgenstein can equally be summarized as saying that the step to the metaphysical is not an absence but a presence; not a nothing, but rather a step to nothing, a fantasized step, a different opening of the soul, a demand to be deciphered. (Perhaps it is a dream of philosophy's wresting truths from the world—as science may be thought to do—or alternatively learning how to await truth's dawning, as if to know others is a matter of learning their secrets, for example, that they are now in terrible pain.)

But I was asking myself why, after years of rumor, I actually opened a text of Blanchot's, and just this one? Wasn't I just saying why? But there is, as I suggested, another immediate answer. I had been reading a collection of essays on George Eliot by Neil Hertz, a legendary teacher of literature. The notes Hertz supplies for his exquisite readings refer principally to Blanchot. There is also something exquisite in Blanchot's readings and writings, but the intellectual demands that each writer poses invoke rigors about as distant from each other as Matisse is from Lester Young, to mention two faithful favorites of mine who play deadly games with taste. But Hertz clearly wishes to be accessible, companionable, and wishes George Eliot to be understood, whereas Blanchot, not perhaps unlike other theorists who achieved fame as poststructuralists or postmodernists, has what strikes me as a horror of understanding, either of being its subject or of being its object, pinned either way. But perhaps I project this feeling out of a desire to find company (in addition to Nietzsche and Emerson on false understanding, with whom I also associate Wittgenstein on this ground).

August 22, 2004

Reading Hertz on George Eliot prompted me to order Blanchot's *The Writing of the Disaster* through Amazon.com, a rare act for me, since I both still love wandering in remaining reasonably ambitious bookstores and wish to support them. This use of the Internet registers something I hope I may get around to examining, namely, why I am more and more reluctant to leave the house. While I do leave, except for an afternoon walk, I almost always feel it is under duress, not least under pressure from myself, out of a fear that I might freely give in to the increasing impulse to solitude. (I know perfectly well that I am spared dwelling on this choice by the awareness of our children and their children in other towns, and by a present, if limited, knowledge of a number of my former students, however painfully dispersed, in short—beyond Cathleen—by a certain awareness of some for whom I can imagine my presence might still be of some use.) In part I find after forty-one years of steady teaching, with generous sabbatical terms, and for six ensuing years at least one course each year somewhere within manageable commuting distance (at Yale, Chicago, once even at Harvard), through it all knowing on lying down and on rising up what that day of the week was called and what was expected of me in the coming day and days, that I now seem to find myself, not without an odd sense of liberty, looking at the dateline of the morning newspaper's front page to check my alignment with events. I exempt from this impulse to routine unsociability (as if I would be glad to exempt myself from the smallest consciousness that I might be identified with the terrible drifts and mad choices accepted in these years by my native land) my walking Sophie, our family dog, which I do willingly three times a day, quite satisfied that I am accomplishing something both useful and pleasurable at the same time. I have, I think, said that I no longer wish to know for whom I am writing, while I am punctually aware of my imagining that with the formation of particular sentences I will elicit expressions of recognition, perhaps glad surprise, perhaps puzzled disapproval, from specific figures, real or imagined, throughout my life; and I am capable of creating further figures for this purpose. Such constructions help make the disappointments and regrets of publication bearable.

It is, I seem sometimes to have surmised, with writing as it was with Isaac's knowledge of praying. (It may not have been Isaac about whom I heard the story told.) When God, having offered the faithful old man to name for himself a favor from heaven, Isaac asked to know when he would die. God answered that he would only tell him on which day of the week he would be taken, namely, on the Sabbath. So Isaac from sundown Fridays to sundown Saturdays was careful to be in his house studying Torah undistractedly so that the Angel of Death would not dare to interrupt these exchanges with the transcendental. Then one Saturday around midday the Angel of Death entered Isaac's small orchard and began shaking one of his trees, whereupon Isaac, distracted, left off his studying to go out to the orchard and learn the cause of the commotion, and thereupon he encountered his fate. One can hardly expect now any such degree of celestial respect to be produced by faithful reading, but I confess to an inkling that, perhaps out of its show of fellow feeling, writing might give the Angel of Death a moment's turn.

Reading *The Writing of the Disaster* I come across Blanchot's speaking of a horror of knowledge (p. 82); it is a book published the year after

my *Claim of Reason*. So my early registration of Blanchot as manifest-
ing a horror of understanding was a fair anticipation. Such anticipations are quite familiar. Writers of a certain ambition have this knack
of seeming to anticipate one's secrets, as Emerson everywhere insists
they do. What could be more common than a young, ambitious writer
who has not yet had a real say, feeling that he or she has been, or seeing
that he or she has been, anticipated? It is a tender banality. I know the
experience terribly well. I make a point here of claiming my own near
anticipation of a phrase of Blanchot's because, in this memoir generally anticipating the ending of my life, I am becoming freer than ever
from the desire to persuade. ("Belief is not enough" is a way I put my
response to my first fruitful reading of Wittgenstein, in 1962, in "The
Availability of Wittgenstein's Later Philosophy," the second paper collected in *Must We Mean What We Say?*).

It is a related, not identical, point when I question the traditional
epistemologists' idea that in examining the basis of my conviction in the
existence of the world I am examining my "beliefs" about the world. It
is from such a misapprehension (all but impossible to demonstrate, to
turn philosophers from, to have turned myself from) that Austin and
later Wittgenstein, in their faithfulness to the ordinary, are taken to
be writing in support of commonsense beliefs. (Whatever these may
be, one of them is *not* the belief, or opinion, or bet, or shrewd suspicion, or thesis, that there is a world, and I and others in it. It seems to
me conceivable that the idea of the world, or of a stance I might take
toward it, is something Kenneth Burke might call a motive.) My sense
is that Blanchot would encourage me to epitomize this insight (that my
relation to the world is not one of belief) by saying that the existence
of the world is incredible. So when Wittgenstein sets out on the trail of
the distortion (that is, of the violence) in saying, of the tree in front of
me, that I know it is there, namely, that "I know" does not express my
relation to this tree now before me, Blanchot would propose, or give
me the right to say, that the existence of the world is unknown. Perhaps
one could gloss this by saying: It is neither certain nor not certain; it is
beyond, or beneath, or before, the possibility of certitude. The register
is, it may be, what Blanchot means by the neutral. But out of a different
philosophical horizon someone will wish to say, I am both certain and
uncertain; in a sense I am certain and in a sense I am not. But is this a

comprehensible frame of mind, and are these supposed to be unheard
of senses of the word *certain*? I would not, however, wish to rule it out of
all imagination that a certain person, in certain straits, really harbors
the idea that the existence of the world is a very probable surmise, on
a par with the surmise that other human units are very probably the
seats of consciousness.

August 23, 2004

But how did I arrive at the formulation that Blanchot expresses a
horror of understanding? It might have been in response to my interest in finding that, unlike what I know of his peers in the brilliant decades of French thought since the 1960s (Deleuze, Derrida, Foucault,
Lacan, etc.), and their immediate predecessors (Bataille, Levinas, Lévi-
Strauss), Blanchot is impressed by the standing of skepticism, particularly in relation to a remark I have recently found in Levinas: "Language is in itself already skepticism." Skepticism now might conceivably
be thought to be a late response to the horror of knowledge, of being
forced to know what cannot be borne, as if to cage the air. Classically,
or postclassically—I mean from the time of Descartes, when skepticism
is no longer, as it was in the ancient world, a way of life, something to be
achieved through spiritual exercise—skepticism becomes a possible intellectual fate that must be warded off, to be managed by argument or
by distraction, since the world is after all supposed to be abjectly subject
to human knowledge, as modern science is supposed to show. But then
something further happened to the world, something that not simply
challenges the human capacity to know, but, let's say, mocks the desire
to know. It is accordingly a kind of New Fall, or a Second Fall, or a Second Going, of man and woman. Nietzsche called it the death of God.
Blanchot, I suppose, calls it the disaster. (May I think of it as the disaster of understanding, particularly of being called upon to understand
the disaster, rather than to face it?) I have for half a century expressed
what happened to the world to be the advent of skepticism itself, marking a historical departure of the human, inherently at odds with itself,
beyond itself. But in its role in Blanchot, reconsidering, or reconstituting, Nietzsche's Madman's warning against the knowledge he brings,

namely, that it is on its way, hence that he is (that we are) premature, skepticism would be a welcome protection against knowledge for which we are unprepared, for which no one could be prepared, namely, the cost of surviving the disaster, of living in an aftermath, a devastation.

August 24, 2004

I say Blanchot is considering, or reconsidering, this announcement. But if what disaster means is "being separated from the star . . . the decline which characterizes disorientation when the link with fortune from on high is cut" (*Writing of the Disaster*, p. 2), then I suppose it follows as part of the disaster that consideration is no longer a usable mode of thought. Consideration (and reconsideration) speaks of a careful attention to the framework of stars, but Blanchot tells us that the bearing of stars no longer holds for us. There is now no sidereal orientation. There is still the alternation of day and night, hence the dawn that Emerson and Thoreau and Nietzsche propose for our orientation, or renewal. But that first light of life itself requires renewal. (Thoreau: "There is more day to dawn." This is not something to be counted on. Thoreau says it is up to us to anticipate dawning.)

Because Blanchot's recognition of the horror of knowledge does not come up until page 82 of *Writing of the Disaster*, it took me days to arrive at it at the pace I usually walk around pages breaking for me new ground. That very difficulty of going on was I believe paramount in creating the impression of that horror. Unlike the writing of Emerson and of Thoreau, which can seem always to be at, or come to, an end (these writers bring death into their prose, the acceptance of finitude, in each sentence, which accordingly authorizes their ecstasies), Blanchot's writing seems to me rather to be all but paralyzed with the fear that it will not be able to go on, to begin again. I suppose this is a hazard of Blanchot's way of emphasizing the fragment, as challenger of the philosophical system, or (as he also puts it) philosophical order. It is equally part of the later Wittgenstein's achievement to lead thought perpetually to an end, to achieve a peace, however momentary, that acknowledges death. It strikes me as the reverse of Derrida's writing, whose astounding fluency seems not to describe a detour to death but a wager with it, say, a perpetual double or nothing, as if the end, indefinable since it may look awfully like its beginning, may be permanently, or each time, deferred.

Now a whole further line of issues crops up. The mode of thinking I am calling consideration, placing a constellation of ideas within whatever other constellations you divine (reading intertextually, in its various modes, would produce examples), not with the idea of choosing one over the other but of expanding each inflected by the other, combining equations, seems to me something Blanchot means to capture in his idea of the neutral, saying neither yes nor no to a proposal, particularly a proposal of one's own. (I often characterize this as speaking without assertion, said otherwise, without attempting to advance theses.) I think this is the right mode in which to respond to an early question of mine in reading *Walden*, namely, whether Thoreau's notable placements of the word *interest* (stressing the sense of maintaining oneself between an experience and a given interpretation of it, as in "It was easy to see that . . . they would part at the first interesting crisis in their adventures," late in *Walden*'s opening chapter) elucidates the word *unattachment* as in translations of the Bhagavad Gita. I might add to this the question whether Wittgenstein's idea of "returning" (namely, words to their everyday use) is an instance of how Blanchot adapts Nietzsche's idea of Eternal Return, specifically the sense that this does not describe alone a future event, but an event that has already happened, is always happening. (The need for some such idea showed up early in my reading of *Philosophical Investigations*, in my insistence that the return of words is not to a *place*, or if so, then to one in which we have always and never existed—an eventual or virtual ordinary I will say, opposed to any actual ordinary.)

August 25, 2004

I do not know if I shall eventually continue with Blanchot far enough to speculate usefully on whether his idea of the neutral puts into consideration Emerson's account, in "Self-Reliance," of a young boy's capacity to speak out of what Emerson alludes to as his neutrality, a capacity that the step into adulthood deprives us of forever. "The nonchalance of boys who are sure of a dinner, and would disdain as much as a lord to do or say aught to conciliate one, is the healthy attitude of human nature . . . independent, irresponsible, looking out from his corner on such people and facts as pass by, he tries and sentences them on their merits . . . as good, bad, interesting, silly, eloquent, troublesome. You must court him; he does not court you. But the man is as it were clapped into jail by his consciousness . . . watched by the sympathy or the hatred of hundreds, whose affections must now enter into his account. There is no Lethe for this. Ah, that he could pass again into his neutrality!" (Of course I might wish that Emerson had included girls and women in this account. But I suppose he recorded what he saw.)

So something like neutrality appears in Emerson not to be a matter exactly of saying neither yes nor no, if this means withholding or suspending judgment. It is a matter, as in Aristotle's definition of speaking the truth, of saying of what is that it is, refracted in Emerson as speaking neither personally nor impersonally, neither in approval nor in disapproval, neither in accusation nor in exoneration, with neither complicity nor implication, neither for effect nor in abstention. (Austin would say, with neither illocutionary force nor perlocutionary effect, which would for him seem to be humanly impossible, anyway something Austin gives no way of saying; it is, after youth, open only to perfect martyrs to the truth—how many have there been?) It is what Emerson calls speaking with necessity, which for him, as for Kant, is an essential mark of the objective. (One might see this as saying of what is *what* it is.)

The difference here between Emerson and Kant is that the other essential mark of the objective that Kant announces (other than necessity), namely, universality, is never, in Emerson, guaranteed a priori by the conditions of there being a knowable world of things, but proposes a task for each of us in each utterance. Language as such exists, for Emerson, always under the moral law. In Neil Hertz's George Eliot essays, Hertz cites Blanchot's phrase *exigence de dire*. I have not yet found the phrase in Blanchot, so I do not know how it matches up with Nietzsche's saying, "One must speak only where one cannot remain silent," which, not surprisingly, I like thinking of as the source, or stimulus, of Wittgenstein's perhaps currently better-known saying, "Whereof one cannot speak thereof must one remain silent."

These formulations suggest that there are such states as metaphysical cowardice and metaphysical folly.

August 26, 2004

Still, why was a horror of "understanding" the way I wished to articulate an unbearable revelation? If there is avoidance here, it is perhaps attributable to my questionable wish to reduce the issue to a problem I have raised in my various attempts to fathom Emerson's attempts to ground or to reground philosophizing on these American shores. I once called Emerson's too famous essay, or too famously understood, "Self-Reliance" a study of human understanding, meaning to bill it (with its repeated invocations of standing and understanding) as a response to Locke's *Essay Concerning Human Understanding*, and Leibniz's *New Essays Concerning Human Understanding*, and Hume's *Enquiry Concerning Human Understanding*, in which Emerson, like his forebears in assessing the possibility and validity of the human grasp of the world, unlike them does not assume that understanding is everywhere a good thing, in particular not where our desire is to grasp, not alone or in particular the world of objects, but its (other) human inhabitants. The case, or the direction of understanding that Emerson concentrates on is the violent desire of others to grasp oneself, the case in which one knows best that human understanding is not in effect. "Is it so bad then to be misunderstood?"—if, that is, it turns out that recognizing this misunderstanding is the price of maintaining a grasp of oneself, as perhaps it must be: "To be great is to be misunderstood." This may be thought a dangerous sentiment, encouraging what we may call the adolescent fallacy, namely, drawing the conclusion that to be misunderstood is to be great. But in Emerson, to be great can be no more than "to have the courage to become oneself" (as he considers in "Considerations by the Way," a late essay in *The Conduct of Life*), so that all who get the better of themselves—and presumably stand to make salubrious contributions to our lives—are as apt to be misunderstood as others are apt to lack the courage to become themselves. Emerson in effect questions whether we know what it is to understand each other, perhaps to consider, say, take account of, be considerate of, one another.

August 27, 2004

I am not prepared at this late stage of recounting to take much of a further step beyond, but I must pause to record a lovely discovery in the past year or so (like so many I prize in myself it is one that has come to me terribly, I dare say shamefully, belatedly), namely, that Proust, in the preface to his early translation of John Ruskin's *The Bible of Amiens*, cites Emerson from his late essay "Civilization," whose subject is evidently our needing to be reminded of our relation to what in reading Wittgenstein's *Investigations* I have called the farther shore of human existence and its language (in "The *Investigations'* Everyday Aesthetics of Itself"); I have sometimes called it the transcendental shore. "Civilization" is the essay in which Emerson announces the central, focal image of the text in his summary words, "Hitch your wagon to a star." Proust responds to Emerson's point, if not quite his method, accurately and richly: "[In such a cathedral as that at Amiens] men of the thirteenth century came to seek . . . a teaching which, with a useless and bizarre luxury, it continues to offer in a kind of open book, written in a solemn language where each letter is a work of art, a language no longer understood. Giving it meaning less literally religious than during the Middle Ages or even an aesthetic meaning only, you have been able, nevertheless, to relate it to one of those feelings that appear to us as the true reality beyond our lives, to one of 'those stars to which it is well that we hitch our wagon.'" Whether this phrase of Emerson's, perhaps slightly modified, was already famous in 1910, when Proust made his Ruskin translation, or whether Proust spotted its distinction for himself in his reading of Emerson, are to my mind equally credible possibilities. Others have glossed Emerson's phrase to suggest the effort of "aiming high" or "thinking big." Such ideas capture a certain picture of what Emerson may be taken popularly to urge, but in the essay that his star-hitching phrase epitomizes, its direction of action, of passion, is something like the reverse, alerting us to the task of, let's say, receiving high, accepting high, stressing modesty and daily labor (hitching a wagon) as well as magnificence (scanning a clear night sky); the power invoked is not that of leading but of being drawn. Thoreau comparably describes one of his tasks as listening for what is in the wind, and another, this one botched, as having failed to see truly the light in which he hoed his beans.

A recurrent image of mine intrudes again just here, hiding among these high-minded sheaves of thoughts. I have described, soon after I moved back to teach at Harvard in 1963, my appearing at Boston's Logan Airport every Friday and Sunday afternoons either to travel to and back from New York to be with my daughter, Rachel, then six years old, or to meet her plane from New York and one to take her back as she, increasingly, spent weekends with me in Boston. Logan was continually under reconstruction, primarily undergoing expansion in order to accommodate the requirements of the new jumbo jet planes. Walking one late Friday afternoon from the main terminal through the temporary plywood-lined and covered walkways leading to a bank of unfinished new gates—the low ceiling bearing, clamped along its center, a continuous line of narrow pipe from which was suspended a punctuation of heavy wire cages enclosing burning light bulbs—a distinctive, unmistakable aroma all at once attracted my attention, probably not for the first time, which now however came to me as archaically familiar, as from my early childhood, yet one whose source I could not identify. On the late airport afternoon that I recall now, an image crossed my mind of an early evening in Atlanta when I was no more than five years old, sitting in the back seat of my mother's Chevrolet as my mother and I were headed down a long slope ending at a thoroughfare that constituted one of the familiar approaches to our house on Atlanta Avenue. As we slowed for the red light at the bottom of the slope, I was interested in a horse-drawn wagon—neither an unprecedented nor a common sight around 1932—pulled over against the near curb of the thoroughfare perpendicular to our descent, into which we would be turning. At the back of the wagon, featuring what I recognized as a burning brownish yellow kerosene lamp hanging from one of the rear posts securing the unpainted, uneven wooden planks constituting the wagon's side panels, an old man, lit by the lamp, was lifting into his rig a nondescript and evidently quite heavy burlap sack. When the light turned green we eased at arm's length around the man and his wagon for our right turn into the thoroughfare. My back window must have been open, judging from the strength of the aroma given off by the wagon's lamp as we passed. The distinct aroma catching my attention walking in the Boston airport was unmistakenly the same as that of that old man's lamp, unmistakenly therefore that of kerosene. The word came to me together with my remembering having heard that jet airplanes were fueled by kerosene.

So the vehicle of this old man's laborious trade was lit by the same substance that fires our newly accustomed means of unearthly flight. Might we have urged this man, or some equivalent of his now, to consider his wagon to be hitched to these new rising and returning sky objects? For surely Emerson's vision of hitching is also only metaphorical. Only? Then what is the literal or actual truth of these world-historical matters?

August 28, 2004

The possibility and necessity of making oneself understandable is the subject of Friedrich Schlegel's still surprising essay always (so far as I know) translated as "On Incomprehensibility" (Über die Unverstandlichkeit), a smooth translation that disguises the fact that the German root for intelligibility, unlike the Latin, is harped on by Emerson, whose "Self-Reliance," I simply assume, in its harping on (non) understanding, assumes the Schlegel essay. (But I would not really be surprised to learn that Emerson had instead anticipated his reading of Schlegel—for he himself had already had as much cause to know he was not understood, because understood prematurely, let's say as Schlegel had had, as so many readers and listeners are prone to suppose themselves to understand.) In his essay Schlegel attributes lack of understanding to the lack of an ear for ironies of various kinds. I adduce a further irony in noting that Derrida's attack/homage concerning Austin on the performative utterance, "Signature Event Context," in its opening question alludes to, all but repeats, in his accent, the opening sentence of the second paragraph of Schlegel's "On Incomprehensibility." Here is Schlegel: "Of all things that have to do with communicating ideas, what could be more fascinating than the question of whether such communication is actually possible?" And now Derrida: "Is it certain that to the word *communication* corresponds a concept that is unique, univocal, rigorously controllable, and transmittable: in a word, communicable?"

Derrida's sentence is, I trust, meant, not solely but irreducibly, to be comic, to invoke ironically various precisions leading to dead ends. Schlegel is speaking out of the ironic perception that, while called upon to communicate something about his writing (Schlegel says he is writing against the charge that his Athenaeum Fragments are unintelligible), it is he himself who is supplying the writing that is called incomprehensible, or nonunderstandable. But then this is philosophy's undying task, to show that the self-imprisoned human understanding is capable of self-arrest, self-reflection, self-overcoming. Derrida had accepted an invitation to present what is called a communication to an academic assembly, and he knew (as it were, in advance) that what he says will almost certainly not be found to communicate.

But for me Derrida's fun, however much I may appreciate the fluency and the invention, goes philosophically sour. The insinuation in his opening question bullies us into imagining that someone or other, perhaps ourselves, or maybe everyone in general, at least sometimes, or the history of philosophy, or the West, thinks or takes it for certain that the concept (our concept?) of communication, or the concept that "corresponds to" the word *communication*, is indeed, or must be, unique, univocal, controllable, transmittable. And are we then to examine this insinuation or assumption or presumption or prejudice or fantasy or doctrine or hypothesis in all seriousness and then be protected against it, or weaned from it? Why would we wish this distance, or accept it? Because the insinuation is ridiculous? But Austin would think it no more intelligible to be protected against the question than to be asked the question. And Wittgenstein, who in some eerily related sense, does think we harbor, or work ourselves into, such thoughts about our concepts (for example, that every word stands for an object that is its fixed meaning), never spares attention in tracing each beckoning path he finds along which we ooze streaks of madness. He asks us to recognize ourselves to be in a position to question the apparent question of, let's say, absolute understanding. Anything less would not be taking the implicit paranoia of the question with seriousness. (With the very seriousness that Derrida attempts to make Austin appear ridiculous for invoking. The seriousness that really wants an answer. A seriousness that requires real playfulness to express a state like, and not like, hysteria.)

And of course Wittgenstein can be said to write with a continuous recognition that he is not being understood, perpetually directing questions to himself that miss his point or his stance, and that each time we can recognize ourselves as tempted to ask. Perhaps the experiences of Austin and Wittgenstein have left me too often immune to Derrida's brand of play. Yet I am still open to the surprise I expressed nearly twenty years ago in Jerusalem, when Derrida and I both gave talks at a month-long conference there, in asking myself, suddenly (breaking into my essay for the conference that I was preparing on the film *Gaslight*, about a woman being driven mad with self-doubt), who it was I thought I was addressing in the essays in *Must We Mean What We Say?*—written between 1957 and 1968—in writing about writing and voice and skepticism and madness and inheritance and the modern, throughout questioning philosophy's authority and pressing its relation to literature. The cluster of preoccupations are in some obvious sense closer to those in the rough exchanges in 1963 between Derrida and Foucault on reading Descartes than they are to anything my generation of philosophers was concerned with then in the United States, something it took me a decade or two to discover. (In 1962, in "Aesthetic Problems of Modern Philosophy" I say "method is in conflict with content." However different in origin and example this is from Kuhn's idea of the cause of paradigm shifts—where truth about the world has become out of touch with evidence—it would have been part of what I would bring to the table of Kuhn's and my conversations in the preceding years in Berkeley.)

Analytical philosophers do not preoccupy themselves professionally with, for example, my relation to my power of speech, with speech as confrontation, hence with the ineluctably moral fact of assertion, with my declaring my standing in disturbing the world with each of my words; nor with my mortality, my knowledge that I am finite, that my words must, in each prompting to utterance, come to or be brought to an end. This cannot be a matter merely of style, any more than it is a matter of style that analytical philosophy does not habitually veer toward an interest in theology. Carnap would not have to insist, as Heidegger does, that what he is writing is not theology. But the sense remains in everything I write, that philosophy as I care about it most is always discovering its lack of authority, one could even say, its irreducible resistance to establishing itself—beyond what it conceives or reconceives as the field of the a priori, the necessary and universal, namely, the existence of language as such. (Which language?—Each.—So each culture claims truth for itself?—No more than each person does. Hence no more than we limit the degree to which we may become interested in our similarities and our differences, natural and unnatural.) This of course makes the issue of philosophical pedagogy a critical one.

For some, for example, this idea of philosophy will make the history of philosophy at most a hobby of philosophers; for others it makes history all the more essential, or I might say the question of its history.

I say fairly explicitly, in my initial response to Derrida's attack upon / homage to Austin, that Derrida's use (or mention) of metaphysical discourse (for example, that we take the communicability or transmittability of our concepts, of their "determinate content," to be a function of their being unique, univocal, rigorously controllable, etc.) describes an assumption of the institutional establishment of the language of metaphysics that no philosopher working within, if only partially, an Anglo-American tendency of philosophy contemporary with his work is apt to share (knowingly). But Blanchot does something of the kind, so I gather, in *The Step Not Beyond*, where he asks, in effect enacts, what it betokens that we live in the aftermath of the Hegelian dialectic and the Nietzschean Eternal Return. And, however intermittent my initial grasp of his words remains, I find that his ways of exploring the landscape altered by these devastations, paths leading away from them, simultaneously unearth paths toward them, so that I stand to learn the source of my attraction to them as well as the distance I sense from them.

August 29, 2004

I take Emerson in "Self-Reliance" to be characterizing human understanding when he says: "I stand here for humanity;" as well as when he says: "I follow the standard of the true man." To stand for something is to represent it, and I do not doubt that Emerson is simultaneously invoking the idea of standing for something, bearing it. Then the implication is that for me to understand humanity is to bear up under my comprehension and consideration, under the weight of my representation of humanity, under the measure of it, under the way, for example, I am whatever I may be said to be, the way I am a father, a grandfather, a son, an American, a depressed patriot, a Jew, a white man, a professor, knock-kneed, bald, divorced, married, temperamentally inclined to both disappointment and to joy, to solitude and to love, to high and major art and to minor and low, to scorn and to forbearance. To know others is hence to know not the things they are (rich butchers or French bakers or tall candlestick makers) but all the ways in which they are what they simultaneously or successively are, or partially are, or deny they are.

But why is this knowledge something to be borne, something to be *stood*, like pain? Or perhaps like the deepest pleasure? The other is the sign of responsibility, the witness of my integrity or the threat to it, the reminder that I am not, and I am, alone, that, break bread together as we may, we will sleep in our own dreams, and never awake fully. I may have to struggle against the other's understanding of me, or his or her wish or demand to understand me without knowing much about my ways. Which is not to say that I want the other to understand me the way I understand myself—I may not understand myself as well as others may (I them, or they me). Then could I accept their acknowledgment that they are ignorant of me? They may accomplish this readily by not caring about me. No, but I mean accept their acknowledgment that I am a mystery to them. What would show this?

One of the last fragments in Blanchot's *The Writing of the Disaster* is *"Learn to think in pain"* (the italics are Blanchot's). About ten years ago, in my essay "Emerson's Constitutional Amending," I claimed that Emerson's essay "Fate," written in the year of the Fugitive Slave Act (1850), should be read as an essay on freedom and as bearing in each sentence the pain of the knowledge of slavery, not exactly as Walt Whitman bears it, claims in a sense to share it, depicting himself looking at the slave's body in the slave market ("I Sing the Body Electric"), but as a writer and thinker bears it who feels himself or herself at each instant implicating himself in keeping the institution of slavery intact because he is helpless to act specifically to annul it. It is by his silence that he expresses his pain, in a sense holds back the expression, bears the pain. I say there that Emerson has invented the tragic essay.

How, if held back, is the suffering to be known? How is any withheld passion, at any time? Do we consider that we can no longer tell the difference between holding something in and having nothing inside?

More urgently: Why is pain's expression held back? Evidently there is a question about claiming the right to it, to express it. There may be a— let's call it—spiritual vulgarity in expressing pain at the pain of others, here at injustice (take today's global poverty as our version of slavery), without letting it take you over, which unattended to may manifest itself by silencing you or rendering you incoherent. Emerson will come to this, in his violent denunciation of Daniel Webster's support of the Fugitive Slave Act and in his praise of John Brown's murderousness. But here, in "Fate," he speaks as a philosopher thinking, declaring that thinking cannot go on without thinking of slavery (thus perhaps questioning how we understand the conditions of Greek philosophy), which commits him to showing that our conditions—which is to say, all our shared words—are indeed those of slavery, that the air we breathe is pervaded by thoughts of freedom, hence of slavery, that we can no longer put these thoughts aside. And when slavery is past, injustice will take further forms, and when these are past, our separateness, or say, mortality, will remain. Here the spiritual vulgarity of expressing my pain over this condition is not that I lack the right but that everyone has the same right. So it comes to the question, what gives us the right to single ourselves out and open our mouths in all seriousness? And then this is the question of philosophy—the source of the right to speak for what we all know, for what we cannot just not know.

August 30, 2004

One of Blanchot's entries on death speaks of "the awkwardness in dying." Within days of coming across his finding this worth saying, namely, in one of my 3 a.m. searches on television—having faced the fact of insomnia, too wakeful for sleep and too sleepy for work, wary of taking a sleeping pill, having resorted to that the previous couple of nights, and tired of the written word, however light—I have been grateful for our classic movie channel's airings of Charlie Chan or a 1930s gangster film, or Claude Rains in *The Invisible Man*, or something else of James Whale; and just the last half hour of the inferior Hitchcock *Saboteur* on one occasion suited my half mood perfectly. These were all recent off-hour offerings from the Turner Classic Movies channel, but just about any of its trove of movies from my youth would in that mood be fine company, little instances of what I had missed early, or reminders of what I had not missed. On one such memorable predawn excursion I came upon Howard Hawks's *Only Angels Have Wings* as it was beginning, made in 1939 but looking earlier, in I guess the reverse way that Hawks's *Bringing Up Baby*, made in 1938, looks later. (I do not know what the descriptions, or impressions, "looking later and earlier" are based upon. But I have been at this long enough to want to know, and to be fairly good at waiting for a chance to know.) While I recalled having viewed *Only Angels Have Wings* twice, none recently, I had never been moved to ask for its particular contribution to the work of Hawks or of the writer Jules Furthman or of Cary Grant or Jean Arthur or the then little-known Rita Hayworth. It is self-evidently not up to the best work of any of these talents, for example, to Furthman's mythical location for Howard Hawks's *To Have and Have Not* five years later. (To have stepped and have not?)

This later film, so far as I have made myself recall, or check, pays detailed attention to the Hemingway material in his book bearing the title *To Have and Have Not* chiefly, so far as I recall, in the choreography of the early gunfight outside the bar in and around which the action centers, and Hawks could have done that without Furthman's intervention. One or other of them chose to repeat from *Only Angels Have Wings* a perfect Hemingway gesture in which one of a pair of fated intimates suddenly strikes a match to startle the other away from throwing an unwise or unnecessary punch, however richly deserved, at a chiseling newcomer. The gesture elegantly manifests a clear knowledge of, and knowledge of the justice of, the other's perception and passion, and it effects a rational correction without assertion, or rather without denial, without moralism, by participating rather than hindering. In the earlier film Cary Grant strikes a match to deflect Thomas Mitchell; in the later film Lauren Bacall deflects Humphrey Bogart. In the earlier film the piece of business is very fine, but it is only one of a number of ways in which the world of men can show tact in distress, miniature displays of grace under pressure, a form of mutual respect that rational society depends upon. In the later film Bacall's gesture is shockingly, voluptuously pleasurable to ponder, a movement not exactly arising from intimacy so much as establishing intimacy, requiring a leap of understanding that assumes the standing to intervene—acknowledging that standing is the essential in moral confrontation—to intervene in the absence of the standing to *say* anything, a form of silent separation, of mutual respect, that love depends upon.

I had hitherto always passed by the title phrase "to have and have not" with a momentary qualm that I allowed to fade, giving in vaguely to the idea that its sense is fully or satisfactorily given in the idea of society's haves and have-nots and the irony in the image of boats as putting the stupid and craven ritzy together with the honorable and defeated rumrunners. But this time I sat still long enough to attract the original sound of the phrase (especially the slight archness of "and have not"), bearing in mind that Hemingway early liked the titles of his novels to refer to fragments or moments of imperishable writing—*For Whom the Bell Tolls* to John Donne, *The Sun Also Rises* to Ecclesiastes. The fragment for *To Have and Have Not*, come to think of it steadily enough, is right here, in 1 Corinthians 13:2, where Saint Paul declares: "And though I have the gift of prophecy, and understand all mysteries, and all knowledge; and though I have all faith, so that I could remove mountains, and have not charity, I am nothing."

I am again, familiarly, not a little anxious at the thought that this connection is by now common knowledge, so that I have merely spoken the obvious pretentiously, an all but unforgivable tactlessness in Hemingway's code. Or is it actually unforgivable here? It surely would be, if I were repeating something I had heard as though others had not heard it. Otherwise I might require charity. And since for me philosophy is both the study of the obvious and requires the tact, and arrogance, of voicing what cannot just not be known, I am forever running the danger of philosophical tactlessness, or say, spiritual vulgarity. And once an obvious connection is made, the very obviousness that is its only validation makes it appear vividly as something that must already have been observed. What may have kept this particular connection hidden is a predisposition to imagine that such an allusion as that to Corinthians takes Hemingway rather out of his depth, philosophical if not theological.

For how can balancing having and not having bear upon Hemingway's idea of human existence—bear so strongly that not having something reveals you as nothing, not to be counted among humankind?

But isn't it Hemingway's issue that the ability to stake one's existence confers the right to existence, the knowledge that you play your hand for life-and-death stakes without knowing whether you have, or have not, the courage and the wisdom and the perception and the passion and the compassion and the luck to come through well in your own eyes, the readiness to discover that you are something or nothing, and the power to judge a world that make the odds wrong?

This lack of knowledge is not an intellectual lack, something that better intelligence can mend, which means that having or not having charity and perception and courage and compassion and luck are unlike having or not having a thirst or a boat. Sometimes you do not know what you have—even in sense do not have it—until you are faced with claiming it. Philosophers may distinguish between dispositions and manifestations of character. Virtues are not well thought of in these terms. You may manifest courage or compassion with no apparent preparation, or apparent "disposition," for them. The human being, the mortal, as every philosopher and theologian must have ways of testifying, being finite, has limits (as it has, and needs, virtues). "Assume a virtue if you have it not." I take Hamlet's demand of his mother to mean that we necessarily assume virtues since this is precisely the way we have them, a way expressible in saying that we at one and the same time have and do not have them. I suppose this differs from the way we can have ears and hear not or eyes and see not. We may have to discover the possession of a virtue. This seems to me something inciting the power of Hemingway to observe human nature and conduct, and to throw light on the primacy he gives to self-judgment.

This will perhaps manifest itself in relations Hemingway depicts between men and women that some readers find archaic, associated too much with an outdated morality of honor to warrant a full seriousness of attention—to demand a privacy that implies a violence of silence, a contempt for words and for awkwardness that betrays a certain lack of, let's say, humanity, amounting to a kind of romantic misanthropy. Since the ease of this view seems to me incompatible with the aspiration of Hemingway's language, I should say another word, or enter a reminder, about the philosophical depth I understand in what I have described as Hemingway's contempt for the tactlessness of asserting the obvious.

It is the depth that Wittgenstein concentrates in the hundreds of fragments collected in *On Certainty*, where, for example, he works to depict, let me say, the pang of excess in a philosopher's (G. E. Moore's in particular) wish, holding up his hand, to say, waving it, "I know this is a hand," as an instance of demonstrating something one knows, indeed knows best, knows with certainty. Wittgenstein says he believes that in this straight-off way the expression "I know" gets misused (§ 2). Which is as much as to say: We cannot coherently assert "I know," mean it, under these circumstances. But a few fragments later Wittgenstein asserts: "My life shows that I know or am certain that there is a chair over there, or a door, and so on.—I tell a friend, e.g., 'Take that chair over there', 'Shut the door', etc. etc." Put these remarks of Wittgenstein together and they seem to say that I cannot say or mean something that my life shows to be the case, to be true, so that if I did utter the words, or attempt to mean them, I would basically not know what I was talking about in talking about the most basic things my life shows.

This remarkable condition bears directly on the question of philosophical skepticism, on what causes it and why philosophers, why we, you or I, are forced into, and chronically underestimate the difficulty in, attempting to refute skepticism, hence illustrate what Wittgenstein conceives philosophy to be. It bears on why he says that philosophy does not advance theses (which is almost what Newton said about his world-changing natural philosophy), a claim not unfamiliar to me to hear (most recently at a summer conference on Wittgenstein in Kirchberg, Austria) denounced as something like a lurid lie.

When the woman, in Hemingway's story that takes its title from her words, announces that the "hills are like white elephants" (attractively unobvious to say under certain circumstances, poison in others), she expresses and causes the breaking of false intimacy with the man to whom it is addressed. This and her subsequent plea to the man, "Would you please please please please please please please stop talking?" are instances of what philosophers shield themselves from in breaking their intimacy with the world (which something tells them is false), in attempting to explain something, clear themselves of it, when they have no explanation and cannot bear their own silence (as, to take a favorite of Austin's, their conceding that while we might not see the world directly, we see it indirectly). We can say that what they then assert is nothing.

Some philosophers are content to draw this conclusion and seek a way to avoid emptiness in the future. Others, as I find in Wittgenstein, prompt us to consider why being moved to speak in emptiness is a condition that the access of language chronically causes in those whose life-form is determined by language, by the fate of its possession, by the perpetual struggle against the temptation, adapting a phrase with which Nietzsche concludes *The Genealogy of Morals*, to speak in emptiness rather than to suffer being empty of speech.

The Hawks/Furthman *Only Angels Have Wings* came to mind out of Blanchot's writing: "The inexperience of dying. This also means: awkwardness in dying, dying as someone would who has not learned how, or who has missed his classes." Cary Grant is standing over Thomas Mitchell, who has been lifted out of a crashed airplane and been carried inside the pilots' living quarters to be laid on a table, and when Grant tells him that his neck has been broken, Mitchell concludes thoughtfully, objectively, "Then this is the end." He rallies nervously, aware of others present. "Get that bunch out of here." After Grant has ushered them out, Mitchell continues: "It's just that I don't want anyone to watch." (Blanchot recurrently speaks of our exposure, and abjection, in the face of the Other. "Watch," in English, has all the weight philosophy can hope to give to "exposure," as in "Watch with me.") Mitchell continues: "I don't want to pull a boner. [Meaning make a faux pas. I think these are his notable words. I'm surer of the others.] I've never done this before. It's like the first time I flew solo." ("Flying solo" might be the most obvious popular image for what in a few years will become existentialism's motto about human life, that for it, unlike the case of physical objects, individual existence precedes essence.) Blanchot charmingly mocks the interpretation of the inexperience of dying as awkwardness, as if dying were an event to be prepared for, like an exam, or a long trip, or a blind date. I suppose Blanchot wishes to capture something of the infantilization that dying may impose. I am not exactly proposing that adolescent male Americans can learn from quite good movies what philosophically inclined grown-ups may learn from their peers, how to achieve the loss of companionability, to take farewell; I am being impressed by the effort, however awkward, to conceive words that can well be said in the face of the dying. (Blanchot is one who asserts explicitly that living is dying, recognizing I must suppose that all our words are said in the face of the dying. I have forgotten who said: "We pass people everyday who are dying and we fail to say hello.") It is a failure I keep expecting of philosophy to correct.

Grant asks Mitchell, whom he calls the Kid, whether he wants him to leave also, hence to be the last to take leave from him. Seeing that the answer is yes, Grant says: "So long, Kid." "So long," the Kid replies. The camera cuts to Grant pulling the door behind him as he walks out of the flimsy little building. Standing there he seems as expressionless as his final words had been. I think of how often I have wondered at Grant's ability, outside his comic roles, and often inside them, to deliver a line with the flatness of a line in Beckett, and elicit full conviction in his viewer, or watcher. It is a remarkable understanding of the power of film to raise the question of our knowledge of, let's say, the appropriateness of expression to what is expressed—the undying topic of art, an essential of the procedures of philosophizing out of everyday language. We can read nothing in this moment from Grant's extraordinary face. Except the unimpeded demands it imposes upon us, from a time and place always beyond us.

When I phoned my son Ben yesterday, whose voice in the writing of his first book of stories, *Rumble, Young Man, Rumble*, he had found, whatever else, to require his working free of Hemingway's voice, to ask whether he had known, or assumed that there was, a literary source for the title *To Have and Have Not*, and specifically to ask him, as I had his mother the day before, to confirm my conviction about the source in First Corinthians, he gave me responses I was glad to hear, and he went on—after I sketched further my thoughts about Hemingway's insistence upon self-judgment, keeping watch with the self, without looking back, or looking out—to adduce moments of dying in various texts of Hemingway I had forgotten, or perhaps never known.

September 1, 2004

So have I found, speaking of lessons, in this late instance among so many detours of pleasure on the way beyond pleasure, some usable tips from figures who have themselves become easeful shades? Short of that, I have, I find, now closing this writing from memory, been drawn to exemplify, still with some surprise, the condition that telling one's life, the more completely, say incorporating awkwardness, becomes one's life, and becomes a way of leaving it. And now that seems to be as it should be, given that it is a human life under question. The news is that this awkwardness, or say, self-consciousness, or perpetual lack of sophistication, stops asserting itself nowhere short of dying. Maybe this is something my mother was responding to when she reported, after watching her mother die, that a natural death is terrible to see, remembering what she called the death rattle. (Which suggests that, as throughout the progression of human life, human death is not natural, confirming the formulation I have come upon so often in my efforts to describe passages of the human life-form, namely, that the human is the unnatural animal.) I would think of that remarkable idea of death rattling, as impatiently at a door handle, years later in discussing how Edmund's tardy line "I pant for life" might be played, as he, dying, hears the report of Goneril's suicide and thinks to countermand his order, now meaningless, to have Lear and Cordelia murdered in their prison.

Two years before my father died, his failing heart required the placement of a pacemaker. My mother sounded quite exhausted during the phone call from Atlanta telling me of this development. My mother generally telephoned for a reason. My father telephoned when it was Sunday and he realized it. Visiting him the next day in the hospital I was about to make myself comfortable on the one welcoming chair in his room, to read or to nap after the early morning flight, while he was sleeping. A number of nurses and other attendants had been going in and out of his room, checking him, and reading his chart hung at the foot of his bed, and when it became quiet he opened his eyes, looked around the room, and motioned me to come closer to the bed. I wasn't certain he had recognized me since he showed nothing I would call surprise on seeing me, but I quickly decided that he simply assumed I had been present for some time. His voice seemed even weaker than it had been on my last visit, but his expression was intense.

"Do you understand me?"

"You mean can I hear you? Yes."

"No, I mean am I making sense to you right now? I know some-times I get confused."

"You are perfectly clear. Why do you ask?"

"I have to ask you something."

"Ask me."

"Why are these doctors and nurses and the family running in and out of my room as if there is an emergency?"

"You know they had to place a pacemaker for your heart."

"That's what I mean. How old am I?"

"About eighty-three."

"It's enough. It's natural. What is the emergency? If a child is seriously ill, it is an emergency. To run in and out of the room because an eighty-three-year-old man may die is not an emergency. It is ugly to behave this way."

"They are just doing their job. Placing a pacemaker has become a standard medical procedure."

"You mean I don't have a choice?"

"I don't know."

"Tell them to stop."

"That's not my job."

Wondering whether my father would question the philosopher about what a son's responsibility is, or what a wife's is, or what a doc-tor's is, I was about to say that I would tell the doctor about our talk, but my father had fallen asleep. His position appeared awkward to me. I walked out to find my mother.

Index of Names

Acknowledgments

I am indebted for the end stages of editing this memoir to the tact and careful work of my research assistant, Byron Davies, and to Cathleen, who continues to know the words. I am also grateful to the following people who helped in many different ways to complete this enterprise: Norton Batkin, Sarah Browne, Jay Cantor, Hent de Vries, Sandra Laugier, Toril Moi, Susan Neiman, and Bill Rothman.

Cultural Memory | in the Present